AMONG STONE GIANTS

THE LIFE OF KATHERINE ROUTLEDGE
AND HER REMARKABLE EXPEDITION
TO EASTER ISLAND

✦

JO ANNE VAN TILBURG

Foreword by Dr. ANDREW TATHAM
Keeper at the Royal Geographic Society

A LISA DREW BOOK

SCRIBNER

NEW YORK   LONDON   TORONTO   SYDNEY   SINGAPORE

SCRIBNER
1230 Avenue of the Americas
New York, NY 10020

SCRIBNER and design are trademarks of Macmillan Library Reference USA, Inc.,
used under license by Simon & Schuster, the publisher of this work.

For information about special discounts for bulk purchases,
please contact Simon & Schuster Special Sales:
1-800-456-6798 or business@simonandschuster.com

Text set in Iowan Old Style

Manufactured in the United States of America

1   3   5   7   9   10   8   6   4   2

Library of Congress Cataloging-in-Publication Data

Van Tilburg, JoAnne.
Among stone giants: the life of Katherine Routledge and her remarkable expedition
to Easter Island / Jo Anne Van Tilburg; foreword by Andrew Tatham. 1
p. cm.
Includes bibliographical references and index.
1. Routledge, Scoresby, Mrs. b., 1866. 2. Women archaeologists—Easter Island—Biography.
3. Antiquities, Prehistoric—Easter Island. 4. Sculpture, Prehistoric—Easter Island.
5. Easter Island—Antiquities.
I. Title.

GN875.E17 R689 2003
930.1'082'092—dc21
[B]
2002042751

ISBN 0-7432-4480-X

CONTENTS

✦

FOREWORD

✦

No man is an island, entire of it self;
every man is a piece of the continent, a part of the main. . . .

JOHN DONNE'S WELL-KNOWN LINES REMIND US THAT
nothing we do can be done in isolation. Katherine Routledge may well have
thought that while she was on Easter Island the links holding her to the main
were very tenuous. But as Jo Anne Van Tilburg shows, even there Katherine
could escape neither from herself nor from the consequences of her actions.
Furthermore, as the author suggests in the afterword, the phenomenon of
the great stone statues of Rapa Nui arises out of a much wider cultural milieu
than previously thought. It is also rooted in the human response to global climatic change and human profligacy with resources—geographical concepts
that are as important in the twenty-first century as they were in the tenth
when the stones were first carved.

Having worked on Easter Island for twenty years, Jo Anne Van Tilburg is
extremely well qualified to write this book, which is both a life of Katherine
and also a study in the exploration of a civilization. Archaeology, anthropology, geography, history, and psychology all rub shoulders in this biography.
If the author fears that she has become as obsessive as Katherine was in her
research, it is an obsession tempered with an even greater objectivity and
zeal than that found in her subject.

The author considers that "Katherine Routledge's Easter Island work
is . . . flawed and incomplete, but I believe important aspects of it will stand
the test of time." Her own work is thorough and exhaustive. Knowing the
island intimately from many seasons of fieldwork, Jo Anne Van Tilburg
made it her business to research the written sources of Katherine's life and
the island's past just as closely. For several seasons, she was found investi-
gating the English roots and influences of her subject in County Durham,

Hampshire, and London. As the endnotes witness, she ensconced herself in the archives where the record of Katherine's life and work are recorded, conducting her excavations of the documents in England with just as much care as she would use in the field.

As the steward of one of the most important of these holdings of papers, the Royal Geographical Society (with the Institute of British Geographers) is delighted that this work has reached the public. Our aim is to enable as much access to the records—printed, manuscript, photographic, and three-dimensional—in our care as is possible. Our major project, "Unlocking the Archives," seeks to achieve this through on-line catalogues, improved physical access, and the development of educational resources. It is thus both very appropriate and a great honor to have been asked to write this foreword. Jo Anne Van Tilburg has unlocked our archives and those of others in a book that is both truly educational and fascinating; it brings us closer to the worlds of Katherine Routledge and the Rapa Nui.

—DR. ANDREW TATHAM
Keeper
Royal Geographical Society
(with the Institute of British Geographers)
1992–2002

A NOTE ON SPELLING
AND PRONUNCIATION

✦

THE MODERN POLYNESIAN NAME FOR EASTER ISLAND IS composed of the proper noun *Rapa* and the adjective *nui* and is written Rapa Nui. The preferred spelling of the language spoken by the Rapa Nui people is *Rapanui*. All Rapanui words included in quotations are written as encountered in source documents; spelling varies, glottal stops are wrongly noted, hyphens are inconsistent, and the nasal *ng* is written as *g*. In an English sentence, plural Rapanui words are not indicated by adding *s*, but are understood by the sentence context. Rapa Nui place names are spelled and accented inconsistently in all contemporary literature; so, too, are the Polynesian names of many islands. I have not tried to impose consistency, but have used those names that are most widely accepted.

Many English words have variant U.S./U.K. spellings; examples include theater/theatre; organize/organise; traveling/travelling or woolen/woollen; and color/colour. U.S. variants are preferred in the text, although a few U.K. variants widely used in the U.S. (such as *prologue* or *catalogue*) are employed. U.K. variants in quotes or bibliographical entries are retained. My guide in these matters is *Webster's Third New International Dictionary of the English Language, Unabridged.*

British Received Pronunciation (RP) is, by official definition, the standard speech of educated people living in London and southeastern England. According to RP—and in the memories and opinions of present-day Pease and Routledge family members—the name Routledge is correctly pronounced "raut-ledge" not "rut-ledge." Mana Expedition field records were nonmetric, and that is how statue measurements and other archaeological or geographical data are presented here.

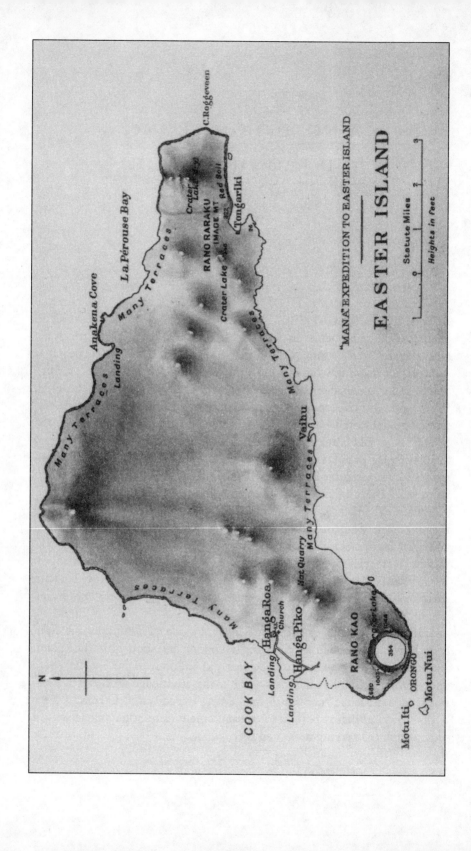

COOK BAY

La Pérouse Bay

Anakena Cove

Landing

Many Terraces

Many Terraces

Many Terraces

Crater Lake

RANO RARAKU
IMAGE MT
Red Soil

Crater Lake

Tongariki

C. Roggeveen

Many Terraces

Many Terraces

Vaihu

Many Terraces

Hanga Roa
Church

Landing

Landing

Many Terraces

Hanga Piko

Mat.Quarry

RANO KAO

Crater Lake

Motu Iti
ORONGO
Motu Nui

"MANA" EXPEDITION TO EASTER ISLAND

EASTER ISLAND

Statute Miles

Heights in feet

PROLOGUE

✦

ONE EARLY MORNING IN 1914—JUST A FEW DAYS AFTER the Mana Expedition had arrived on Easter Island (Rapa Nui)—Katherine Routledge, on horseback, chased fat, white cumulus clouds eastward. The red dirt road stretched before her, the sky was bright and the air cool; the Pacific was blue beyond all imagining. As the clouds tumbled rapidly overhead, deep shadows lifted from the slopes of Katherine's destination: Rano Raraku—the ancient statue (*moai*) quarry.

A collapsed, weathered volcano, Rano Raraku encircles a freshwater lake and is attached, like a barnacle, to the island's flat, southeastern plain. As Katherine drew closer a forest of tall, narrow-bodied, and sharp-featured human figures was gradually revealed to her, each stone image embedded like a lifeless tree in the soft, grassy folds of Rano Raraku's outer slopes. It seemed to Katherine that she was entering a crowded cemetery; the sort of place her Quaker family had once so disapproved of—a place filled with graven images and ostentatious memorials. She pulled hard on the reins and, without turning to look for the two men riding behind her, paused as she always did before entering a sacred place.

The wind dropped, and overhead, a lone seabird screeched. Katherine gazed in awe at the statues—a few figures stood alone but many were clustered in small groups of two or three. They leaned toward each other, or turned away, in silent but suggestive tableaus of familiarity, intimacy, and family communion. Their features were all similar, but their expressions, she recognized right away, were not. Some seemed mildly amused, others patient or thoughtful; a few were filled with scorn or the arrogance of privilege. They appeared, to Katherine's fresh eye, more human than supernatural.

Their enormous size, perfection, and apparent uniformity lent each figure an air of dignified strength. Drawing closer, Katherine realized with a start that every statue was blind. The sun played on the sharply defined, horizontal curves of their protruding foreheads, casting shadows that gave the impression of eyes—but they all lacked eye sockets. In Katherine's unique spirituality such lack of vision meant the failure of prophecy, the absence of the mystical power Polynesians call *mana*.

Dozens of statues were scattered on the ground, and still others lay in two tiers of stepped quarries cut into the cliffs towering over her head. Katherine's searching gaze traced in the rock the vague outlines of heads, faces, and hands. Such recumbent giants, so like the tomb effigies of ancient kings, brought to mind Shelley's words about Egyptian ruins:

> *Half sunk, a shatter'd visage lies, whose frown*
> *And wrinkled lip and sneer of cold command*
> *Tell that its sculptor well those passions read*
> *Which yet survive, stamp'd on these lifeless things.*

Katherine smelled the approaching horses before she heard them. William Scoresby Routledge, his elaborately tooled Argentinean saddle creaking loudly, and their guide, Percy Edmunds, pulled up in the cool shadow of one of the tallest statues. Then all three walked their horses along a path winding through the sculpture forest. Stone picks used to carve the statues were scattered underfoot, and bits of obsidian glinted in the sunlit grass.

Katherine dismounted and followed Edmunds up the gradual rise of Rano Raraku's exterior slope. Turning into the wind near the top of the volcano, her hair in wind-tossed tangles and her khaki duster flapping, she reached into her pocket and pulled out binoculars. The landscape below her was littered with the lumpy stone ruins of hundreds upon hundreds of abandoned prehistoric structures; the entire plain was crisscrossed with modern walls enclosing corrals and pastures. The seacoast was a jagged line of black rock fringed by brilliant white breakers, and beyond that stretched the clean, empty horizon.

Rano Raraku is made of a relatively soft, compressed volcanic ash, or tuff, and looking downslope Katherine saw Scoresby busily pounding away with a geological hammer, taking stone samples. The tuff seemed to be a superb sculptural material, although Katherine could also see that it was fragile. Wind and rain had scoured away each statue's fresh, reddish orange surface color and turned it gray or black, yet the features were still sharp and well defined. This immediately suggested to Katherine that the statues could not have been standing there for eons, and that some of them were probably only a few centuries old. The drama of Rano Raraku and the obvious engineering feat of carving and moving *moai* surpassed anything in her imagination or experience.

Edmunds scrambled along a steep trail that wound higher and higher. The ground leveled out abruptly and he disappeared over the lip of the crater. Almost running behind him to the top, Katherine stopped and caught her breath, raised her eyes, and looked out over a massive, reed-choked lake of dark water shot through with sunbeams and completely surrounded by the collapsing inner slopes of Rano Raraku. Rimmed with bright green reeds and filled with floating clouds, the lake was absolutely still.

Beyond the worn and weathered far edge of the crater, she glimpsed the island's northeastern shoreline and, westward, the rocky expanse of the interior landscape. Katherine descended a vague trail leading through thick grass to her right. The only sound was her ragged breathing and the echoing scrape of Edmunds' footsteps far ahead of her. She wandered along the entire inner base of the crater, passing around and in front of a string of standing statues; most were smaller, darker, and more worn than their compatriots on the volcano's exterior. Also blind, they seemed less congenial and more ancient—cranky, impatient old men uninterested in visitors.

Rano Raraku was, for Katherine, a wondrous spiritual landscape of striking beauty. An audacious, captivating place crowded with eccentric human figures, it contrasted sharply with the island's deserted landscape and made her feel at once at home and at sea, comforted yet challenged. Most important, it energized her forthright and modern intellect and tantalized her sense of discovery. If she could understand Rano Raraku, Katherine reasoned, she could make sense of the island's remarkable prehistory.

The only standing statues anywhere on Rapa Nui in 1914 were those that had been planted, hundreds of years earlier, on the exterior and interior slopes of Rano Raraku. Uncounted others, however, had long ago been extracted from the quarries and transported, somehow, over roads to massive ceremonial platforms, or temples, called image *ahu*. Scattered lavishly around the periphery of the island or dotting the interior, all image *ahu* marked ancestral lands. Statues had once stood erect on the tops of the platforms, but the last one had fallen from its image *ahu* in 1840; only one fractured remnant still remained upright at Ahu Tongariki. By 1914 all traditional lands had been abandoned and Rapa Nui people were clustered in Hanga Roa, the island's only village. Still, as Katherine was about to discover, all image *ahu* held dozens, sometimes hundreds, of human burials. Previous visitors had ransacked some of them, but they were still a mystery—not even their names had been properly recorded.

Today we know that there are 887 statues on Rapa Nui, and 95 percent of them, no matter where they are located on the island, were carved in Rano Raraku. The remaining 5 percent were cut of a rough, bloodred scoria, basalt, or trachyte. There are 397 statues—45 percent of the total—still in Rano Raraku, and about 70 percent of them are between ten feet and twenty-six feet tall. The most gigantic statue on the island is still affixed to the exterior quarry and measures an astonishing sixty-nine feet long.

Rano Raraku statues are male figures, truncated at the waist. Their arms, held tightly to their sides, terminate in magnificently detailed hands with elongated, tapered fingers held flat on the abdomen and indicating the genitals, covered by a loincloth. Only those statues that were successfully raised on image *ahu* have carved eye sockets. A few very interesting statues never erected on image *ahu* are stylistic innovations, and a large, impressive statue in Rano Raraku that Katherine never saw is in a kneeling posture.

While the precontact inhabitants of other Polynesian islands carved portable stone sculpture or larger-than-life wood figures, only Rapa Nui, the Marquesas Islands, the Austral Islands, and Pitcairn possess monolithic stone sculpture. Of these, only the Rapa Nui people carved, moved, and erected stone giants of such extraordinary size and numbers—and with such mysteriously passionate social commitment.

By all accounts the statues represent the ancestral "living faces" of present-day Rapa Nui people. They presided over mortuary ceremonies and were the repositories of spiritual power called *mana*. Rooted in ancient Polynesian beliefs, the statues are unique in design, execution, purpose, and material to Easter Island—a memorable expression, in aesthetic excellence, of spiritual and community life. When Katherine Routledge first laid eyes on them, however, the stone giants of Rapa Nui were the Pacific's greatest enigma.

In the great scheme of the natural world, Katherine thought, Rapa Nui was a lovely island. Its eastern headland rose from the sea in steep and crumbling cliffs; bays were strewn with cobbles and beaches drifted with pink sand. Clouds sometimes shrouded the highest peaks, and sea winds heavy with rain squalled and swirled until, with a rapidity that was astonishing, they disappeared again. Rust-red soils underlay celadon grasses studded with deep green shrubbery. The Pacific, beyond its dazzling white sea-foam edge, was an audible, watery voice that blended, in her memory, with the wind in the trees of her childhood home. In the upside-down world of the Southern Hemisphere it was autumn in April.

The plain surrounding Rano Raraku had been home to thousands of industrious people. For generations they had lived and built here, felling palms to create plantations and then, with daring and perhaps desperation, raising statues as tall as trees. Their story gripped Katherine's imagination; the statues seduced her. She felt a rush of tumbling emotions—an exciting and puzzling mix of isolation, freedom, joy, and fear—and to her complete surprise, she loved the island unreservedly.

✦

BEFORE EASTER ISLAND:

SETTING SAIL

✦

Ancestor Worship:
Southend, 1866

✦

"IT WAS MY MISFORTUNE," KATHERINE SAID ON A BLUSTERY Yorkshire day in 1891, "to be born a woman with the feelings of a man." Calmly she continued, "I'm thinking of going to college." Silence fell over the elaborate family luncheon. Pale winter sun glinted off crystal on the polished mahogany table, and rows of horse-show cups on the sideboard glowed silver. The clock ticked. Wilson Pease, Katherine's younger brother, was home on holiday from Cambridge. He broke the silence to speak up in support of his sister: "I can quite understand," he said, "as English country life is uncongenial for anyone with any brains or taste." Without a word Kate Pease, their mother, simply put down her fork, got up from the table, and left the room.

Katherine was twenty-four years old and miserably unhappy. For the first quarter of her life she had futilely tried to accommodate herself to the expectations of her suffocatingly protective, emotionally withholding widowed mother. At last, she had decided to act. Katherine had the explorer's desire and the scientist's curiosity, qualities considered masculine in the mid-Victorian world of her birth, but also a brilliant mind, a questing spirituality, and sadly, the curse of nascent schizophrenia, a horrific mental illness. Katherine wanted nothing more—or less—than the same opportunity to achieve a place in the world that was so freely given to her brothers, uncles, and male cousins. With determined courage, wry humor, and the honest self-interest her family mistook for selfish willfulness, Katherine metaphorically gathered her skirts around her and made a run for it. Her goal: Oxford University.

Born in 1866 in Darlington, County Durham, England, Katherine was never a great social success in the world of hunting, swarming dogs, and country-house parties. She was athletic enough and could ride and play lawn tennis with skill, but hunting talk bored her to frustration. Katherine was not beautiful, but she was handsome—with clear skin and thick, dark auburn hair with an unruly curl. Her big, expressive blue eyes were Katherine's best feature. The alert intelligence that shone in them made her exceedingly attractive, but sometimes her eyes were shadowed with dark circles, her determined gaze mature beyond her years. Katherine was neither vain nor modest and had a strong commitment to truth that was regarded as tactless. She was not, as a consequence, very popular in the Pease family.

From childhood Katherine had loved the seascapes of Britain. She spent summers at Cliffe House, the Pease family home in Marske-by-the-Sea, near Middlesbrough in Yorkshire, or sailing along the English coastline near the Land's End peninsula in Cornwall, at the southwestern tip of the island. There, when the weather was clear and visibility good, Britain's ancient, haunted Scilly Isles floated on the horizon, "an eternal stone armada of over a hundred ships, aloofly anchored off England." Ancient Celtic inhabitants of the Scillies had raised hundreds of megalithic stone monuments to their ancestors, and Katherine enveloped herself in a childhood fog of seafaring folklore and mythic legend.

Sirens and sea monsters, lapping waves and seagull cries, standing stones and spirits, inspired Katherine's childhood imagination. In her favorite literature islands were metaphors of isolation and death, but they were also seductive and sensual places that offered anonymity and freedom—self-doubt and landlocked fears gave way before wind-filled sails. Katherine was bewitched by the adventures of Robinson Crusoe and, en route to Easter Island in 1914, visited with childlike wonder the Pacific island on which Alexander Selkirk, the real-life model for Crusoe, had been stranded. The sea's romantic promise of freedom, however, was balanced in Katherine's young life by prudence learned through her family's deep devotion to Quakerism, her paternal grandfather's immense wealth, and the magnetic power of his personality over the entire extended family.

It is impossible to overstate the significance of religion in the formation of Katherine's character, the structure of her social life and marriage, her perception of spirituality and mysticism, and her ability to cope with illness. She was born into the Religious Society of Friends (Quakers), founded in 1652 when George Fox, a twenty-eight-year-old shoemaker and "seeker" of religious truth, experienced a visionary revelation that there is "that of God in everyone." Quaker teaching during Katherine's childhood rejected organized clergy, governmental agencies, and dogma (including the Bible), believing that ultimate spiritual authority resided in the conscience of the individual. Friends, as congregants call one another, refused to swear legal oaths and practiced nonviolence, tolerance, respect for differing opinions, and reconciliation. From its inception, Quaker belief in the efficacy of visions—and in receiving the prophetic "Inner Light"—was deep and profound.

At the heart of Quaker life, in Katherine's time and now, is the Meeting for Worship. Unlike other religions, which are based upon solitary meditation, Friends are "gathered" in shared, communal silence that is described, by those who have experienced it, as mystically uniting. A "gathered" meeting empties the mind of all thought, gives release from fear, anxiety, and emotional confusion, makes way for inspiration, and creates wholeness. No priest or pastor officiates, and personal testimony is encouraged. Friends accept the "priesthood of all believers," and those with particularly inspiring gifts of wisdom and communication can be declared ministers.

From the time she was a very young child until she went up to Oxford, Katherine worshiped every Sabbath at Skinnergate Meeting House in Darlington. A modest building that still stands today, Skinnergate's simple interior wood paneling is painted clean white. Tall windows are raised off the floor to prevent the passing outdoor scene from entering and distracting those inside yet allow rich, clear light to fall through numerous panes onto undecorated walls. Rows of simple wood benches with deep blue cushions are arrayed roughly in a square, but there is no altar, chancel, pulpit, or other furnishings typical of Christian churches. Following Quaker teaching and "studying to be quiet," Katherine strove to be united in perfect silence as one of the "gathered" whole, even though she might hear a thousand clamoring internal voices, a private din of questions, prayers, and comments.

Katherine's assigned seat in Meeting was next to her younger sister, Lilian, and directly facing her mother and her father's oldest sister, Jane Pease. Aunt Jane had intense visionary experiences that were to her completely real, and she described what she saw in glorious word pictures that conjured up crystal cities, angel choruses, and heavenly gates. Jane was officially recorded a minister in 1862 and the Quaker community openly regarded her as a "child of God," capable of being spiritually transformed, filled with the literal "Inner Light" of God and speaking eternal truths.

In astonished wonderment Katherine often saw Aunt Jane visibly and sometimes almost violently transformed in body, manner, and voice. Jane chanted—sometimes in fluent German or French—in a peculiar singsong until, rising, she spoke with "all the ecstasy of a prophetess." Jane's powerful and intimate mysticism was impressive but also frightening. Her evident ability to capture and hold supernatural power, then to proclaim God's message, was strongly attractive but wrapped in a palpable element of danger.

In addition to such profound spiritual experiences, Katherine absorbed a lifetime of Quaker history and philosophy. She was taught a sense of self-worth and parity with men, but also vigilance in protecting personal rights that were believed to be constantly endangered or ephemeral. To a certain extent, a rationale for such teaching was embedded within the atmosphere of Quakerism. Early English Quakers, including Katherine's ancestors, were relentlessly persecuted. Meetings were violently broken up, members vilified and attacked, and thousands were imprisoned. Sequestration laws robbed women of property, and some who went into prisons to minister to Quakers were promptly incarcerated in unspeakable conditions. Others were publicly flogged or hanged for teaching Quaker doctrines. In spite of such travails, the first Women's Meetings were held in London in the 1670s.

Quakers of the Victorian era believed in the innate equality of women and men and required no vows of obedience in marriage. This was very much in contrast to how women were regarded—and were forced to behave—in England at the time. Until passage of the Married Women's Property Act in 1870, a landmark in the history of women's rights and basic to the Victorian ideal of a "companionate" marriage, Englishwomen were *chattels corporeal,* or property. "In law husband and wife are one person," declared a great eighteenth-century jurist, "and that one person is the husband." Many Pease women had been required, for both religious and financial reasons, to marry within the Quaker community. Katherine and others of her generation, however, had no financial pressures or practical incentives to marry and frankly avoided doing so. Married or single, they were expected to efficiently manage property, engage in appropriate family business, or fight for social reform.

Katherine's immediate childhood reality, however, contradicted the Quaker model in important ways. Her mother and the aunts she knew best either withdrew from the larger world or conformed to the passive Victorian feminine ideal of conjugal devotion, piety, and grace. Their work in the Darlington community was largely confined to decorous charitable giving during organized fund-raising events. They did not get their hands dirty in the manner of activist Elizabeth (Gurney) Fry (1780–1845), for example, a famous prison reformer who was Katherine's paternal grandmother's first cousin. It was only Katherine (and one or two cousins) who was encouraged by the nonconformist ideals of Quakerism and British feminist intellectualism to look beyond her immediate family for role models and to embrace liberal causes, including the women's suffrage movement.

Some modern English historians refer to the years between 1851 and 1914—encompassing the entire time from Katherine's birth to the Mana Expedition to Easter Island—as the Liberal Age. Charles Darwin published his landmark *On the Origin of Species* in 1859, but mid-Victorian life was already being shaped by strong ideals of individualism and social progress. Tension between rationalism and spiritualism permeated intellectual life, and Katherine, steeped in the oral history and folklore of her family, intuitively grasped that history and myth are not incompatible, discovering one of the basic truths of anthropology. Her mother's formidable storytelling skills became the tools of Katherine's later ethnographic trade, and Quakerism provided the structure within which she intellectualized superstition.

The Quaker practice of meditation proved invaluable to Katherine when she began to suspect, and then to recognize later in life, the gradual onset of paranoid schizophrenia, a disease that manifested itself in auditory hallucinations she called "spooks" or "voices." Turning intently toward the mystical Quaker belief in the ability to channel the Inner Light, Katherine managed and integrated these debilitating experiences, for a time, as a feature of her religion and gained some comfort and control. Intellectual openness—not just to alternative spirituality but also to differing visions of God—was another trait of Quakerism that served Katherine well. The religion, with its messages of tolerance and simplicity, gave Katherine a firm ethical grounding that she sustained until the end of her life, even in the face of severe hardship.

A strong network of devout Quakers surrounded Katherine when she was a child, and their "voices" followed her as an adult. Her paternal grandparents were Joseph Pease and Emma Gurney of Southend, their twenty-seven-acre Darlington estate. The second son of Rachel Whitwell and Edward Pease—bold entrepreneur and the financial "father of English railways"—Joseph was a brilliant businessman, dedicated Liberal, and the strongest male personality in Katherine's childhood. Tall and thin, with white hair and sharply angular features, he lived more lavishly than his wealthy but unpretentious parents, yet clung stubbornly to plain Quaker modes of dress and archaic speech. Joseph Pease dominated his family with an almost biblical presence, and Katherine's father and siblings held him up as a godly example to all Peases of her generation. He, in turn, saw to it that his grandchildren's educations were imbued with his own strongly held religious beliefs, secular ideals, and political philosophies.

Those Quakers who crusaded for special causes were said to have "concerns," and Joseph Pease had many. He worked tirelessly to abolish slavery and the economic exploitation of native peoples in the territories of the East India Company. As president of the Peace Society he was an outspoken advocate of pacifism and abhorred the use of weapons of any kind, no matter what the nature of the conflict. He was a gifted speaker whose deep voice rolled over Katherine's bowed head during family prayers, and whose words of wisdom admonished her in Meeting with certainty, urgency, and command.

For generations all Quakers had been excluded from assuming any role in English government because they refused to pay certain tithes or take oaths of allegiance to king and country. In 1832 Joseph Pease uncharacteristically broke with tradition and became the first Quaker in English history to be elected member of Parliament (MP), representing South Durham for nine years. Despite a deep stir within the Society of Friends and major opposition from many in the Pease family, Joseph Pease entered the House of Commons on February 8, 1833. He was immediately presented with a demand to swear the traditional oath, but he refused on the basis of his Quaker beliefs. After a flutter of angry resentment and a weeklong inquiry by special committee, he won his point and was seated.

Joseph Pease thus reconciled his faith with his Liberal politics, cleverly negotiated a compromise position, carried on a family tradition of passive resistance, and opened the way for Quakers to enter government. Nine men of the Pease family followed him into elected office between 1832 and 1926. In 1906 Katherine was an Oxford graduate and independent woman preparing to marry William Scoresby Routledge, "a very scientific man" about to whisk her off to adventure in British East Africa (Kenya). Nonetheless, she was still so impressed by Pease family accomplishments that she wistfully told her childhood nurse and lifelong confidante, Mrs. Hopper, "I would have liked to marry an M.P. or a barrister."

Joseph Pease amassed an incredible fortune and secured the futures of nine children by shrewd business dealings during the Industrial Revolution. Darlington had a population of about twenty-five thousand in the mid-1800s and was home to all the Peases, whose varied enterprises embraced collieries, limestone quarrying, ironstone mining, brick making, woolen manufacture, banking, and real estate development. Between 1857 and 1902 their firms J. & J. W. Pease and Pease & Partners operated fifteen collieries, seven ironstone mines, and four quarries. They owned brick works that manufactured distinctive yellow "Pease bricks." The smokestacks of their woolen mills in the Priestgate and Leadyard sections of Darlington dominated the skyline until 1984. Strict personal morality, fair dealing, and plain talk were Joseph Pease's ideals, but his massive wealth created a world of profound contradictions and confusing standards in which Katherine and others of her generation tried to find their way.

Workmen who toiled for a pittance in Pease mills and mines were piously lectured on the evils of drink while, at home, their children went without milk. In fairness, however, the Pease family also donated hundreds of thousands of pounds to Quaker charities, schools, and hospitals and provided Darlington with fire engines, parks, the town clock, and a library. In contrast to Joseph Pease's plain Quaker lifestyle, his adult children lavishly displayed the wealth they acquired or inherited from his businesses, yet, at the same time, struggled with varying degrees of guilt. Katherine's attitude toward money veered unpredictably from frugal penny-pinching, even stinginess, to careless or outrageous extravagance.

Joseph Pease taught Katherine and his other grandchildren to appreciate the beauty of the natural world, but all around them smoke and dust billowed from Pease mills, quarries, and mines, polluting the environment and causing health hazards that were obvious even then. Joseph Pease's sons built magnificent mansions set amidst rolling acres of gardens and parks while thousands of their factory workers lived in dreadful slums. Katherine's first cousin, the accomplished author and sportsman Sir Alfred Edward Pease, said that the Pease family "thought they were always doing good work in providing more and more employment" through industry. In fact, however, their "spoiling industrial hand" was turning the lovely countryside of Durham and North Yorkshire into "ash heaps and chimneys and hideous houses under smoking clouds."

Katherine grew into a woman who deeply loved the natural beauty of the northern countryside, but the climate also negatively affected her mood. She had a normal distaste for denuded hillsides, cloudy skies, and the lack of leafy green landscapes, but prolonged winds could also induce bouts of profound melancholy. Katherine was superstitious about dramatic weather phenomena and believed that they foreshadowed human events. Natural disasters, she thought, were omens of personal bad luck.

Joseph Pease's direct and forceful influence on Katherine was a natural outcome of her personality, his all-pervasive moral model, and the dominating role he played in the lives of her parents. The directions of his children's lives, the work they performed within the family businesses, the marriage partners they chose or were chosen for them, and where they made their homes were all determined by Joseph Pease in keeping with their gender, their birth order in the family, and the Quaker faith he espoused. His eldest son, Joseph Whitwell Pease, took a leadership role in the family business and then, after the deaths of his sisters and brothers, including Katherine's father, shouldered the responsibility of advising their children on everything from business to courting. He raised Beatrice Mary, the orphaned daughter of his brother Edward and his wife, Sarah Sturge, and, when his own daughter Emma Josephine died, generously provided a home for her child as well.

Interestingly, though not surprisingly, given the choice between their wealth and striving to live up to Quaker ideals in the prevailing materialism of the Edwardian age, nearly all Peases in Katherine's generation abandoned their faith and joined other Protestant religions that were more tolerant of conspicuous consumption. Katherine, in contrast, considered herself a Quaker her entire life. After her marriage in 1906, however, she was unwilling to sacrifice almost two hours of her time to endure the "uneducated and fervid" in "an ordeal in an airless room" and rarely attended Meeting.

Joseph Pease's wife, Emma Gurney of Lakenham Grove, Norwich, leavened the Pease family's world of business with the intellectual and spiritual traditions of the Gurneys. She was the daughter of Joseph Gurney, a member of the leading Quaker family of the nineteenth century. The Gurneys of Earlham Hall, Norwich, produced noted scholars in such secular fields as art, literature, natural science, social science, and history. Among them were Joseph John Gurney, Quaker theorist and classical scholar; antiquarian Daniel Gurney; Anglo-Saxon scholar Anna Gurney; and Hudson Gurney, archaeologist, Fellow of the Royal Society, and vice president of the Society of Antiquaries. Founding precepts of all Gurney pursuits were a respect for history and a deep interest in making the past a vibrant part of the present.

Others on the Gurney side of Katherine's family blossomed into creative free spirits. A cousin named Richard Gurney was a famous ornithologist and Gerard, his son, a noted eccentric. Gerard turned his mother's kitchen garden at Keswick Hall, Norwich, into a zoological preserve for over forty animals he brought back from safari in British East Africa in 1908. Snakes, tortoises, lemurs, and porcupines had the run of the house, while a boa constrictor and a python lived on the drawing room rug. Occasionally, they would slither up the walls and lie on the cornice. The tolerant Mrs. Gurney usually exiled the snakes to a greenhouse whenever squeamish guests were present, but once, while Katherine and her brother Wilson watched in disbelief, "it took Gerard a quarter of an hour to get the python off his arm!"

Not to be outdone, Sir Alfred Edward Pease's wife, Nellie, kept a pet "bush baby" she had brought back from South Africa. He lived on a bookshelf, hidden behind a row of books, and Nellie liked to take him out concealed in the ample bosom of her gown. One evening during dinner, as the furry creature leaped from the horns of Alfred's hunting trophies to the backs of chairs and tops of pictures, Wilson Pease, who called him the "little rat," was required to chase him down with a butterfly net.

Gurney Pease, Katherine's father, was Joseph and Emma's fourth son and, by any Victorian standard, a "wonderful catch" in marriage. When he proposed to Katherine's mother, Kate Wilson, he was twenty-four years old with thick reddish brown hair parted on the side, a high forehead, a rather prominent nose, and a generous mouth that often smiled. Gurney was deeply devout, and like his father he dressed in Quaker black and addressed others, even close family members, as "thee" and "thou." If he was a mediocre and uninvolved businessman who contributed little to the management of the Pease family fortune, he was also considered by at least one person who knew him well to be "the handsomest and best" of Joseph Pease's boys. It was often said that there was a "rattle" about Gurney, a sense of fun, but he also had a dark side. Severe headaches, profound and unreasonable lethargy, doubts about his spiritual worthiness, and debilitating bouts of deep depression shadowed Gurney Pease's short life.

Kate Wilson, who was a year younger than Gurney, was considered by Joseph Pease to be a perfect match for his son. She was pretty, with thick hair braided in long coils piled high on her head and blue eyes set deep beneath graceful brows. Family journals remember Kate as somewhat vague but with a cheerful outlook, an endearing sense of humor, and a love of poetry. On the eve of her marriage, Kate Wilson was completely ignorant of politics, sex, and the world outside her happy, tightly knit, and well-to-do family. She had a strong sense of self and a light, almost whimsical touch but cared little for the serious, "businessy" world of the Pease family. The Wilson family came from solid and successful bourgeois stock, with aspirations and ambition but without the intellectual accomplishments or desires to make a mark on the world that were inherent to the Gurneys and the Peases. Devout and socially conservative, Wilson family members directed their energies less toward commerce and more toward working within the Quaker faith, and several were dedicated missionaries in Africa and China.

Kate Wilson's Quaker pedigree was well known. Her father, John Jowitt Wilson, was a wealthy wool merchant and community leader in Kendal, Westmorland, who married Hannah Maria Whitwell, his second cousin. She, in turn, energetically carried on a Quaker ministry established by the women of her family four generations earlier and was widely respected and loved. Wilson family members joined the Society of Friends almost from its founding in the mid-1600s, and the public humiliations, beatings, and imprisonments they endured are entered in the *Quaker Book of Sufferings*. By the time Kate Wilson married Gurney Pease the large, affectionate Wilson clan had recovered their economic security and privilege, but a deep sense of fatalism remained.

The Peases were blood relatives of the Wilsons through Gurney Pease's paternal grandmother, and Katherine's Wilson, Pease, and Gurney ancestors had pedigrees that went back three hundred, four hundred, and nine hundred years, respectively. Quaker custom in this era created literal "family circles" because of a prohibition on "marrying out" of the Society of Friends. This tight genealogical barrier against the outside world—and the emotional insularity it created—lasted officially until about 1859, but a Darlington Quaker was disowned for "marrying out" as late as 1865, one year before Katherine was born. An obvious result of such Quaker intermarriage was that the Gurneys, Wilsons, and Peases had a "shared, parallel, or else complementary identity" with dozens of other Quaker families. The negative hereditary consequences of intermarriage were known if not fully understood and partially account for the mental illness that plagued the Gurney Pease family.

Kate Wilson married Gurney Pease in Kendal's large Quaker Meeting

House on the spring morning of April 23, 1863. Kate wore a white satin gown, a white lace shawl, and a white bonnet trimmed with ostrich feathers. Eight bridesmaids wore white gowns with lavender trim, and Gurney sported a new, reddish mustache and chin whiskers. With "hearts and minds prepared," about sixty men and women of the Pease and Wilson families settled into their seats on opposite sides of the room. Kate and Gurney sat on a small, elevated platform as everyone waited in deep, communal silence for the meeting to be "gathered" and the presence of God to be felt. Relatives who felt spiritually moved rose, one by one, to eloquently bless the young couple. In time, Gurney and Kate stood, faced each other, and promised to be loving and faithful but, in the Quaker manner, not to obey. The required witnesses signed the illuminated marriage certificate, and the simple but profoundly personal, intimate, and very happy ceremony ended.

With the support of their united families and the optimism of newlyweds, Kate and Gurney Pease embarked on a honeymoon year of travel and family visits. In the summer of 1863 they sauntered through deep green forests in the lovely Lake District, read poetry to each other while drifting in boats on tranquil waters, and experienced a sexual awakening that Quakers of the era quaintly called a "uniting time." In the late fall of the same year Gurney took Kate to Edinburgh to confirm her first pregnancy.

On August 19, 1864 Kate's first child, Harold Gurney Pease, was born. Harold entered the world, in his mother's words, a "fat and flourishing" baby. Katherine (Katie) Maria Pease was born on August 11, 1866 and named after her mother and grandmother Wilson. Katherine's first cousin, Arthur Francis Pease, was born on the same day and hour, and for a time, a gala party marking their joint birthdays was a Pease family tradition. Wilson (Willie) Pease, Kate and Gurney's second son and Katherine's favorite sibling, was born November 9, 1867, followed by "noisy" Lilian (Lil) on March 21, 1869, and handsome John Henry (Jack) on November 6, 1871.

The Gurney Pease family settled temporarily on an estate called Green Park and then, in March of 1864, moved into Greencroft West, a nine-bedroom mansion still under construction. One of eleven adjoining or neighboring Pease family estates built in Darlington in the 1800s, the house was never completed, although the Gurney Pease family lived there for six years before moving yet again. For the first twelve years of her life Katherine's domestic world was in turmoil, unsettled and temporary. Her adult life followed a similar pattern of restless, changing movement, constantly shifting from town house to country house, from tent camp to shipboard. Katherine was not, however, without touchstones in her life.

Southend, the Darlington estate of family patriarch Joseph Pease, was comparatively more modest than those built by his sons, yet it loomed largest in Katherine's memories of early childhood. Built of dark brick, Southend still has an air of foursquare respectability and northern Quaker solidarity, lightened only by pleasant proportions and a modest entrance portico. Once approached by a carriage drive lined with thick trees that seemed, to Katherine's childhood eyes, to be the entrance to a cemetery, Southend was "gloomy," the walls of every room echoing with the whispers of the many Pease family funerals held there.

Kate and Gurney's family life was carried out with little personal privacy and completely within the Pease extended family circle, dominated by Joseph Pease. If that bothered Kate or prevented her from asserting the independence so necessary, even then, to young married couples, she never said. In the end, Kate and Gurney's journey together lasted only nine short years. Gurney's death at the age of thirty-two had a profound effect on his family, as the death of any loved one does, and it irrevocably changed, and then shaped, Kate Pease's relationship to Katherine and her other children. Guilt, a sense of loss, anger, and an ongoing war of wills became the dominating characteristics of Katherine's relationship with her widowed mother.

Katherine knew she possessed intelligence. "I am," she frankly said, "a very brainy person." Her strong, rational intellect developed in tandem with her spiritual nature in a domestic atmosphere that ranged from patronizing to repressive, and Katherine felt a piercing need to express herself. Her straightforward, bossy ways were shaped by privilege and descent, and preserving her place in the Pease family circle was Katherine's main concern. She was outspoken and routinely challenged the opinions of her uncles, brothers, and male cousins. Such qualities in a male would have been admired and encouraged, but they were regarded as unpleasant in Katherine, and she often rubbed people the wrong way. When she was an unhappy adolescent Katherine asked Wilson, her younger brother and close confidant, "What can I do to make myself more popular in the family?" Wilson replied, "Charm is inate [sic], you are born with it or without it." Katherine's youngest brother, John Henry Pease, thought Katherine showed "outrageous pride."

If the large, extended Pease family gave little opportunity for privacy, one of the advantages it offered was its many points of comparison: whether she was looking for a role model or for someone to pity or criticize, Katherine had a good-sized pool from which to draw. Perhaps the biggest family influence on Katherine's perception of herself came from her unmarried aunts, Jane and Emma Pease. Known in the Gurney Pease family as the "interfering aunts," they were a constant presence in Katherine's life until she was an Oxford woman in her midtwenties. Jane was spiritual and Emma was rational, and their relationship teetered on a line of tension between these two contrary forces. United as one persona, they mirror exactly the conflicting aspects of Katherine's own fully developed personality. Their lives at Southend were models of a dreaded Victorian spinster existence that Katherine feared might become her own fate.

Emma was slender, with lovely skin, big eyes, and chiseled features. Bright and empathetic, like Katherine she was efficient and practical with a quick, impatient manner that many people thought was pushy and sharp. Emma had no close friends but took an intellectual interest in women's issues and Quaker philanthropy, using her fortune to support schools and health and to employ her formidable administrative talents. Emma thought clearly, read widely, wrote well, and had a keen sense of humor. She kept voluminous personal journals but left strict instructions for them to be burned after her death—and Katherine saw that it was done. Emma was devout, but her faith had a strong rational component. Perhaps disappointed at her own narrow prospects, Emma encouraged Katherine to spread her wings for Oxford. Katherine acquired Emma's interest in education and women's rights but also her determination, vigor, self-criticism, stubbornness, and bossy, managing ways.

Jane, on the other hand, sought seclusion and illusion. She spent her withdrawn days lying on a sofa, eating massive plates of teacakes and jam rolls and filling vast numbers of pages in her many journals with flowing script. She was preoccupied with food, filling a great emptiness inside with elaborate meals and teas prepared from heirloom Quaker recipes. Though she glided through the house with the appearance of a duchess, Jane had the heavy "Pease physique" and lethargic temperament later attributed to Katherine. Jane had an aristocratic nose, a prominent beauty spot, a dreamy smile, and a ready laugh. She sought the companionship of young male "protégées" and charmed and flattered them shamelessly.

Jane cherished Katherine and her other nieces and nephews, whom she regarded as "dancing sunbeams," but took little actual interest in their lives. The family thought she was self-involved and self-centered, but realized she was also a romantic who "saw the world through a veil of poetry." Jane had a rich repertoire of humorous and moralistic tales but also knew by heart the North Country's terrifying ghost stories, and Katherine often sat spellbound as Aunt Jane wove tapestries of words and rhyme. Intensely bored by the limitations of her life choices, Jane's brilliant mind turned inward. Her spiritual life grew increasingly rich and charismatic, and she blossomed from a storyteller into a remarkably gifted public speaker and Quaker visionary.

As Aunt Jane grew older and her circle of visitors grew smaller, she led her life at Southend in a world of insular shadows that grew increasingly deeper and darker. She believed she could commune with the dead, especially Joseph

Pease and her brothers (including Katherine's father). She saw their spirits walking on the paths and terraces of Southend, or sometimes lying snug in their graves and, she said, heard their voices. The family ghosts Jane conjured were constantly moving about, day and night, haunting Southend and deeply disturbing Emma. Katherine and her orphaned cousin, Beatrice Mary Pease, were both highly sensitive and impressionable and, under Jane's influence, came to believe that the living could contact the dead and then channel their departed spirits. Though Emma discouraged her in this belief Katherine held it all of her life.

"a terrible blank," 1872

✦

KATHERINE'S MID-VICTORIAN CHILDHOOD WAS ENOR-
mously privileged but shadowed by deep insecurity and even danger. Her
father suffered from a rainbow array of illnesses, and his health and comfort
were Kate Pease's constant concerns, always to the exclusion of her children.
Until Gurney Pease's death in 1872 two major, opposing, but related forces
framed the family dynamic: Gurney's moody and depressive spiritualism and
the unpredictably violent behavior of Harold Gurney Pease, Katherine's older
brother.

Katherine's father was a Sunday-school teacher, a teacher, and then
a superintendent in Darlington's Society of Friends school. He believed he
was called to be a Quaker minister, but his father and brothers assigned him
the unwelcome task of overseeing Hutton Ironstone Mines. A failure at business, Gurney's frustrated self-criticism was fierce and relentless, and a deep
sense of spiritual unworthiness caused him to suffer persistent migraine
headaches. They came on with a "glimmer" and his family believed they
were caused by anxiety. He was also frequently crippled with intense pain in
the joints and muscles of his feet and legs and was sometimes bedridden for
weeks.

For the first six years of Katherine's life the Gurney Pease children were
often left for weeks and even months at a time while their parents restlessly
pursued spa cures or took long holidays abroad to distract Gurney's mind.
Victorians held the unsentimental belief that such absences from family life
were necessary for the parents' mental health and provided emotional discipline for children. Katherine's anchor was her nanny, Mrs. Hopper, who was
with the Gurney Pease family for fifty years, and her closest confidant was
her little brother Wilson. When the family was together under the same
roof Kate Pease was often distracted, and Gurney, at his best, was dreamy
and pious. Even so, the Gurney Pease family enjoyed times of warmth and
affection.

Every August, like clockwork, all Darlington Peases vacationed in Scotland for the "glorious twelfth" opening of the shooting season. They went on expeditions after salmon and trout or took long rambles and picnics amidst fragrant drifts of heather. Kate Pease—with Katherine as her "bright little companion"—would lay out linen, china, crystal, and silver to ceremoniously serve fish, game hens, roast beef, ham, cheeses, rich cakes and custards, and all manner of prepared dishes. Greatly influenced by Queen Victoria's passion for all things Scottish, Kate once took Katherine to see Balmoral Castle. Mother and tiny daughter sat companionably together, sketching the building's facade as Kate taught her to observe architectural detail accurately and to record it precisely. Katherine, her mother said, was "very amusing and very sharp," "sociable, loving and verbal."

Katherine and her siblings jostled wildly for their mother's attention, and Kate played her children off against one another as a means of controlling their behavior. A natural consequence of such childhood competition is jealousy followed by ridicule, and Katherine was the favored target in the Gurney Pease family, probably because she was perceived as the one most able to bear it. She was not, however, and Caroline Joanna Fowler (later Wilson Pease's adored wife "Joan") observed that Katherine suffered from highly developed "family feelings" and was "terribly insecure about her place in the family."

From the time she could walk, Katherine's complicated little dresses and voluminous petticoats were miniature versions of her mother's wardrobe. Dressing Katherine and her other children like tiny adults was just one of Kate's typically Victorian pretensions, all of which imposed adult standards of behavior. Some normal childish displays were tolerated in the Gurney Pease family, but outbursts of emotion were forbidden. Kate reacted to "bad" behavior with tearful disappointment and silent withdrawal of approval, and Katherine and her penitent siblings, in return, prayed and felt guilty. Kate was never openly affectionate with her children, and Wilson was an astonished man of forty-five when his mother gave him the first impulsive kiss he had ever received from her. He had done his elderly mother a favor, and Kate jumped out of her chair and said, "I must give you a kiss, you dear boy!"

Kate Pease and, especially, Aunt Jane spun spooky nursery tales of goblins and sprites. On long carriage rides from Kendal to Darlington or through the Scottish hills, they conjured ghosts with Pease family names who haunted hills and hedgerows. Winged angels and heavenly mansions rose out of silver clouds passing overhead, and as the red sun went down into a gray shroud of mist, Kate's children experienced "stillness and darkness that can be felt." Suddenly, and without warning, terrifying ghosts would appear out of the hedgerows and gallop alongside the carriage, trailing the enveloping scent of death and sending thrills of terror down Katherine's spine.

Such vivid experiences created word patterns and phrases easily tracked in Katherine's adult letters, journals, and published writing. Katherine intuitively grasped, at an early age, the deep structure of family myth and transformed it into a love of history. She could read, write, and recite lengthy Bible passages well before the age of five. Her intellectual gifts created high spirits and "sauciness" that, in Kate's eyes, was willfulness.

Katherine was admonished to hide her intellect and encouraged to take an interest in the trivial or frivolous. Kate read aloud to her from John Ruskin's influential *Sesame and Lilies,* which described the "separate characters" and "true natures" of women. The implicit lesson of virtually everything Katherine was taught in childhood was that females can shape all events, large and small, through discreet, covert manipulation of their husbands, sons, and all males—but never by honest, direct action.

Katherine's older brother, Harold Gurney Pease, was also very bright, but in contrast to his sister, his personality was an unusual mixture of shy, sensitive, rude, and strident behaviors that left his parents at a loss as to how to deal with him. Because Harold had a strange, jumbled speech pattern from the moment he began to talk, the children developed a family language, a secret jabberwocky that they often used in jest as adults. A horse, for example, was a "prancaboo"; train a "puffaboo"; steamer a "pantaboo"; and birthday was "birfleday." Katherine, whose early verbal skills far surpassed her brother's, told her mother, "I love talking good," but was admonished against pride and then teased mercilessly about the way she expressed herself.

Harold found strangers and even other Pease family members terrifying, and they found him unsociable and completely unlikable. He related only to his nurse and his parents and was, in his mother's own words, "cowardly." Gurney encouraged his son's interest in horses and dogs, and Harold became adept at hunting. One of the few things Harold really enjoyed, however, was making maps, and he labored silently for hours to get every detail precisely and painstakingly right. From the time he was a toddler Harold suffered "bilious" attacks and was locked away in his room, screaming unheeded for hours. At such times Katherine and the other children hid or fled, frightened and angry. Nurses came and went, unable to deal with Harold, and by the time he was four years old Kate and Gurney recognized that their eldest son was extremely peculiar.

On warm summer evenings Katherine and Harold were taken on long pony rides, the whole valley of the Tees laid out before them, green with woods and yellow with corn. Too often, however, such childish companionship ended in desperate competitiveness that Harold then escalated into verbal abuse and physical violence. He hit and punched Katherine with no holds barred, pulled her hair and crunched her fingers underneath his boots.

Katherine fought back fiercely and appealed to her mother to punish Harold. Kate Pease unwittingly abandoned her daughter, saying only that a proper response to meanness was prayer and that displays of even righteous anger were not appropriate for little girls. When Katherine resisted this injustice, Kate told her that she had "a serious amount of self-will to contend with" and taught her to memorize and repeat, as a kind of mantra of patience, the words from a favorite hymn:

> Empty my heart of self,
> Of all self-seeking and of all self-will;
> Till as a little child beside Thy feet,
> It loves the sitting still.

Katherine, as a direct result, was caught in a wretched trap that forced her to use all of her intelligence to gain physical safety. Her brother's behavior was unrestrained and unpredictable, and Kate Pease's failure to acknowledge its unfairness—and danger—enraged Katherine. As a result she developed, on the plus side, real physical courage but, as well, a hidden, simmering resentment of her mother that created deep and lasting guilt. She never stopped fighting back but learned to cower more, taking her mother's advice and appealing to Harold's chivalrous instincts by professing feminine weakness. Such dishonesty was not only ineffective but, more important, intuitively unnatural to her. Fortunately for Katherine, she was able to share her feelings with Wilson and he, in turn, could depend upon her. Their closeness gained them mutual protection but also served as a kind of reality check in a situation that made little sense.

The repetitive cycle of Harold's behavior worsened appreciably after his father died in 1872. He might, for example, withdraw from the family circle, retreat to his room, and speak to no one for days, or he might talk obsessively about only one topic in an endless, repetitive cycle that led nowhere yet dominated everything. During an otherwise ordinary discussion Harold might unexpectedly blurt out a totally unrelated string of words related to theology. His humor was completely unconscious, as when he said "it was not nice" for women to become educated and "manly," because "they are much more at home when they are not at school."

Once Harold, who was then a teenager, had been withdrawn for weeks, and Kate Pease staged a carefully planned dinner to bring him back into the family circle. Everyone gathered around the table over an enormous roast turkey, and a halting conversation slowly took shape. Suddenly, Harold blurted out what everyone else had apparently been thinking, which was that the turkey was dry and not very good. His tirade went on and on until Wilson intervened, and an explosion of vile language and flying fists erupted. China and crystal flew in all directions, and as Katherine and the others cowered, servants came running to subdue Harold and drag him forcibly to his room. He was locked in for ten days screaming dire threats, banging his head and throwing himself against walls and furniture.

When Harold finally came downstairs, Wilson refused to speak to him and everyone else walked on eggs for fear of upsetting him. Distant and polite superficiality surpassing even repressed Victorian standards became the Gurney Pease family norm, and the domestic atmosphere veered unpredictably from cautious optimism to nervous anxiety and depression, but the usual feeling was simply all-pervasive gloom. Everyone felt it, but no one acknowledged it. This environment was, in some ways, more profoundly damaging to Katherine's developing personality than was Harold's behavior. Kate Pease's marriage was haunted by Gurney's illnesses, and her eldest son's disruptive behavior was a terrible burden. Sadly, neither Katherine nor her mother ever understood the depth of the other's fear and pain.

The severity of Harold Gurney Pease's disordered thinking and suffocating anxiety was surely recognized by Victorian doctors. Today, his illness would be diagnosed as childhood schizophrenia, a disease in which behavior, brain development, and the environment interplay with heredity—some Peases suspected that the malady ran in their family. Kate received the unstinting support of Joseph Whitwell Pease and, later, his sons in dealing with Harold, but Katherine and Wilson carried the major part of the burden. When Katherine's own mental illness finally defeated her in 1928, Wilson was dead and she faced it alone with teeth-gritting courage.

Kate Pease's health broke for the first time in 1869, the summer after Lilian was born. Just twenty-nine years old, she had delivered four children in six years and now suffered from intense lethargy and loss of appetite punctuated by fits of frustrated and passionate temper. Doctors advised Kate to buck up. They treated her with months of bed rest, separation from her children, freedom from "wifely duties," and a lengthy change of scene, but mood-altering drugs were probably also given. Kate's sister Sarah Wilson came to supervise the distraught Gurney Pease household for an entire year. Harold was in deep distress and three-year-old Katherine was frightened, anxious, and eager to please virtually everyone.

Six months later, on January 8, 1870, Katherine came down with scarlet fever. Harold followed the next day, Wilson and Lilian three days after that. Kate Pease, not yet fully recovered from her own breakdown, faced the terrible possibility of losing four children in one hideous blow. She rose to the occasion and ordered three spacious upstairs rooms converted to a hospital ward, then fired off demands in rapid succession as carpets were hurriedly taken up and all furniture but beds was removed. Doctors were called, two nurses were brought from Liverpool to minister to the children, and Kate Pease and Mrs. Hopper, Katherine's nurse, began round-the-clock prayer vigils.

The onset of Katherine's disease was gradual and began with giddiness, chills, headache, and sore throat. She was restless, fretful, and unable to sleep. Her symptoms rapidly progressed to fever, vomiting, and a vivid scarlet rash that spread over her entire body. Her temperature rose and her pulse raced. She suffered severe pain in the ears, muscle twitching, and delirium. Her throat swelled, causing frequent choking sensations. The normal course of the disease takes four to five days and rarely, if ever, lasts beyond seven days. Katherine was confined to her bed for an interminable five weeks.

She was given tepid baths to bring down the fever and doses of quinine and belladonna every three days. She was unable to keep food down and could eat or drink nothing but milk. As she lay alone in the heavily draped, dark sickroom Katherine suffered agonies of feverish sleeplessness and, when she did briefly rest, hallucinations—some of which may have been induced by the drugs she was given. She talked incessantly of death but told her mother that she was not frightened because "then Katie will have wings" and pointed at the corner of the ceiling where she believed Jesus would burst through in the night to take her away. Katherine's vivid descriptions of Jesus and his angels, whose beating wings filled her room with feathery cascades of sound, astonished Kate Pease more than anything Aunt Jane had ever conjured up in Meeting. Even after her recovery, Katherine was still morbidly preoccupied with death and told her mother, "I wish we could all die together so that no one would have to pity us."

Kate Pease became convinced that Katherine's brush with death had produced a weak constitution that needed constant watchfulness for the rest of her life. The disease, she thought, had filled her daughter with restless and unpredictable energy that irrevocably changed her disposition and behavior for the worse. The Victorian medical profession supported Kate in this belief and, in fact, suggested that such a severe response to disease was due to the "peculiarity of the individual attacked." Kate routinely referred to her daughter for years as "the poor child," but Katherine, with Aunt Jane's encouragement, became equally convinced that her illness had triggered latent psychic abilities that manifested themselves in "voices." This belief was absolute and unshakable, and throughout her adult life Katherine consciously sought out others, particularly women, who had had similar experiences.

In retrospect it appears that Katherine's childhood illness may have altered her brain chemistry or impacted brain development to trigger auditory hallucinations. Schizophrenia and tinnitus each create a strange ringing, rustling, or rattling in one or both ears. The brain, not the ear, creates the sounds, and there is virtually no escape from them. Beethoven suffered from tinnitus, as did Michelangelo. In addition to hearing "voices," Katherine complained throughout her life of having supersensitive hearing. Music was sometimes painful to her, and some annoying sounds (such as the buzzing of insects) were amplified to the point of nervous distraction.

In June 1871 Gurney Pease abruptly and arbitrarily decided to move his family to Walworth Castle, an enormous, turreted stone building isolated from the Pease family on the outskirts of Darlington. His only explanation was that a move to the country and a change of air might benefit everyone's delicate health. Kate Pease had taken up her "wifely duties" again after her recent breakdown and was pregnant with John Henry, her fifth and last child. Katherine's uncle Joseph Whitwell Pease, who was himself living "in a rather more elevated style of home and estate than any previously embarked upon by other members of the family," dryly called Walworth Castle "a biggish place" and agreed with Gurney that it was in need of a massive remodel. Work began immediately.

Six months later and three months after the birth of their last child, Gurney's father, Joseph Pease, died at Southend on February 8, 1872, forty years to the day after he had first entered the House of Commons. Although he was blind and bedridden and his death was not unexpected, the loss of the paterfamilias was overwhelming to Gurney Pease. He was unable to find the strength to teach or to minister to his growing Quaker congregation, and he took no interest in his newborn son. Doctors variously diagnosed scarlet fever, scarlatina, influenza, and Bright's disease, a kidney ailment. Confined to his bedroom in the bleak and unfinished Walworth Castle, Gurney Pease sank into melancholia that soon became suicidal depression. One morning, he calmly told his alarmed wife that he would be next in the family to die.

A famous physician named Dr. Kidd was called, and he ordered Kate Pease to take her husband to Malvern, where, it was hoped, intensive hydrotherapy treatments would banish his willingness—even eagerness—to die. On June 9, 1872 Kate frantically wired Gurney's brother Arthur to bring Katherine and the other children, including baby John Henry, to Malvern. There they said a final, emotional good-bye to their father, and Gurney Pease, aged thirty-three, died on June 11, 1872. Katherine was two months from her sixth birthday.

Kate Pease brought her husband's body home to Jane and Emma at Southend, where the house was still shrouded in memory of Joseph Pease.

On the day of the funeral the sky was overcast and a weak, mid-June sun was incapable of warming the scene. Gurney's casket, surrounded by the entire Pease family, was conveyed in solemn procession to the Friends Meeting House at Skinnergate. Hundreds upon hundreds of silent people followed, including delegations of workmen from the Hutton Ironstone Mines Gurney had managed.

The huge crowd assembled in front of the Meeting House as Kate and her close relatives entered the burial ground. Katherine, dressed in a mourning costume that was a miniature replica of her mother's, joined Kate at the open grave. Quaker silence descended, and Katherine stoically endured. Then, no longer able to contain her sorrow, Katherine threw herself, crying and screaming, on her heavily veiled mother. Confronted with Katherine's loss of composure, Kate Pease was shocked and Katherine was whisked away.

Katherine's tearfully honest explanation for her behavior was that the magnitude of her loss had completely and spontaneously rushed upon her. Kate Pease—unable to express her own emotions with such honesty— regarded Katherine with trepidation for literally the rest of her life. At home or among friends and family, Kate was constantly "on the jump" in fear of an emotional "outburst" or "bombshell" by her impulsive daughter. From this point on, Kate often equated Katherine's behavior with Harold's and used the same language to describe it. The hardest thing for her, Katherine said, was that "I will never again hear my beloved father's voice on earth." The terrible irony, however, is that the opposite would prove to be true.

After the funeral Kate Pease and her children returned to Southend for the reading of Gurney's will. They remained there, in an atmosphere of confusion and grief, for three days, with Kate Pease confined to her room and the children forbidden by Jane and Emma to see her or to make any noise. Three days later, Kate insisted on taking her fatherless children home to Walworth Castle—still being remodeled and in chaos. Reeling from the emotion of Gurney's loss and unable to nurse her new baby, Kate withdrew physically and emotionally from all of her children, then collapsed. "All of the joy and love" had gone out of her life, and everything, Kate said, was now "a terrible blank." Joseph Whitwell Pease echoed her feelings of despair. The family deaths, he said, "have shaken my hold on life." Katherine, wanting nothing more than consolation in her own loss, received only pity and rejection.

It took Kate over a year to get back on her feet. She mercilessly repressed her emotions and withheld all intimate or even personal memories of Gurney from Katherine and her other children, all of whom were desperately hungry to know about their father. After Kate died in 1915 her children were touched to find Gurney's shaving things and his silver pencil and pocket knife in her bedside table. In 1916 Katherine was surprised to receive a letter from a man she did not know, Mr. James N. Richardson of Ireland, who had been a classmate of Gurney Pease's brothers Charles and Frank in the Quaker school at Tottenham. Her father's "merry nature," he wrote, was "like a breeze off the North Sea at Marske." He had seen her photo in the newspaper, and remarked that Katherine bore a striking likeness to her father, and to the Pease family in particular. Katherine cherished this pathetic crumb of information and repeated it to her brothers and sister.

Waiting for Change:
Woodside, 1872

✦

GURNEY PEASE LEFT KATE AND THE CHILDREN A LEGACY of loneliness and an estate worth, in terms of today's purchasing power, about £14 million, or approximately $21 million. One month after Gurney's death his executors and older brothers—Joseph Whitwell Pease and Arthur Pease—rescued Kate and her children from Walworth Castle and purchased Woodside, one of Darlington's more impressive estates, for them. A fine, vaguely Italianate brick and stone mansion, Woodside was set in fifty wooded acres surrounded by a brick wall. The family's nearest neighbors were Jane and Emma at Southend and, at Blackwell Grange, Sir Henry Marshman Havelock-Allan, Darlington's most distinguished non-Quaker citizen, and his family. Woodside was the Gurney Pease family home until Kate Pease's death in 1915. It gave order to family life but also confined Katherine in a closed world of stifling domestic routine.

Joseph Whitwell Pease supervised a massive remodel of the house, clashing with Kate on many architectural details. Work went on for an almost unbearable five years, and by 1878 Kate Pease was "invalided" again for eight months with "palpitations." Katherine was then twelve years old, and this was the third major breakdown an exhausted Kate Pease had had in just nine years. Her illnesses were, by now, deeply imprinted upon Katherine's childhood. To top it all, Kate had gone beyond her budget, forcing Sir Joseph to frantically juggle resources. Such extravagance was not unusual in the Pease family and went essentially without consequence.

When it was finally finished, Woodside house had a pleasing, orderly facade with lovely, big windows overlooking a rolling green park. Massive beech and elm trees were comforting old friends to Katherine, and as an adult she insisted that they never be cut down. She loved the changing natural drama the trees created, especially in autumn when they became a mass of gold. In the winter their branches were stripped down to only the black smudges of rooks' nests, and a fierce "Woodside wind," which Katherine hated, blew out of the west, driving snow and sleet before it and rattling windows and doors. On those blustery days Woodside's conservatory—with its hundreds of potted palms, ferns, and lilies punctuated by comfortable wicker chairs plumped in bright red cushions—made a cheerful corner.

On summer afternoons, wearing a white pinafore and hair ribbons, Katherine raced with her cousins through the "children's gardens" that rolled down to the croquet lawn, scrambling back up a steep bank to have tea in a summerhouse surrounded by terraces. From Woodside house's upper floors Katherine could look down on her mother's colorful beds of purple hyacinths and red tulips, nasturtiums, geraniums, and lobelia, all creating the illusion of a bright Turkish carpet thrown down on the green lawn. Kate laid out kitchen gardens and a vineyard that were so prosperous they lasted as commercial market gardens until 1984, well after Woodside house had been demolished.

Woodside's dining room, framed by red marble pillars setting off walls papered in a motif of green leaves with tiny red apples, was Kate Pease's domain. She presided over her vast mahogany dining table dressed all in black, with only a gold watch and long gold chain as ornament. Meals were informal but punctual and repetitiously lavish, with heaping platters of meats, fish, and cheeses. At least three different sugar-laced "puddings" (dessert) were lined up in front of Kate, and she spooned them out with accompanying custards and sauces. From the age of about eight, however, Katherine was always on some sort of diet dictated by doctors "for the blood" and, in spite of such heavy meals, was often tormented by hunger. Red meat was either denied or prescribed according to medical whim. Kate firmly enforced the rules, but when her mother was not watching, Katherine used to stuff unwanted food down the throat of a bronze dog that stood on the dining room mantel.

Katherine's bedroom windows faced west, with views toward rolling fields and misty hills. She suffered all of her life from insomnia and was often wide awake until the early-morning hours, only falling into a fitful sleep near dawn. Every morning she heard her mother rise early, noisily slam doors to wake the servants, and then go back to bed to await her tea. Breakfast in bed was a habit Kate passed on to Katherine. Propped with pillows and wearing a pink bed-jacket, Kate Pease received her children at noon. They trooped in with their nurses and stood around their mother's bed, over which hung an embroidered text illuminated with a border of leaves and ferns. The words stitched on it, which Katherine read every day of her childhood, were "I will never leave thee nor forsake thee."

After Kate's death in 1915 an inquisitive cousin named Mary Anna Pease Hodgkin asked for a tour of Woodside before the house and furnishings were sold. Wilson showed her through the rooms and into his mother's bedroom. Mary Anna told him that the embroidered words were the last Gurney had spoken to Kate before he died. Stunned that his mother had never confided such an intimate and important bit of information to her children, Wilson realized his cousin knew his mother better than he did. Wordlessly, he took the framed piece from the wall and gave it to her.

Katherine's favorite place was the big downstairs library, which was filled with books of every description and dominated by a massive engraving of Joseph Pease. On rainy days she often sat under his gaze, absorbed in a favorite book, as the fireplace's gas jets hissed quietly and gardeners crunched past on the gravel driveway outside, their collars turned up against the cold. She graduated from *The Water Babies* and other nursery tales to the many novels of Dickens; the philosophical works of the Reverend Charles Kingsley; *Mr. Midshipman Easy* by Frederick Marryat; Johnson's massive *Lives of the Most Eminent English Poets;* the history of Captain James Cook's voyages and Charles Darwin's *The Voyage of the Beagle.*

Well before the age of eighteen Katherine had devoured Mrs. Marshall's novels, popular books that gave hints and social guidelines on how to snare a husband. These books, she later said, had "illusioned" her about men and marriage. George Meredith's famous comedic novel *The Egoist* was another favorite. Meredith was a champion of women, dramatizing the ideas presented by John Stuart Mill in his famous *Essay on the Subjugation of Women.* Katherine's bookish interests amused her mother, who read aloud to her children but never for her own enjoyment. Looking at Woodside's vast shelves of books Kate Pease said, "They seem just the sort of books I should like to read if I was fond of reading!"

Katherine met with her tutors in the Woodside library to study art, history, literature, geography, and mathematics. None of her tutors, unfortunately, was a real mentor capable of helping her to model her thinking or to find her true self, and she had few intellectual peers against whom she might judge her progress or test her ideas. Katherine's level of educational achievement reflected the vacillations of Woodside's domestic atmosphere, and she veered unpredictably between passionate curiosity and total involvement to lethargy and disengagement, from reason to sentiment and from rational to irrational judgment.

Katherine was taught elocution and spoke in a round, clipped, prewar Oxford accent standard throughout upper-class England of the time. Her inflection began somewhat high and then lowered toward the end of a sentence, and she had the "ability to talk very firmly to horses and other animals." Katherine had a fine vocabulary and was familiar and comfortable with all the anachronistic verb forms of the Quaker idiom and the eccentricities of various Yorkshire dialects. Although she had no great affinity for foreign languages, the word games she and Wilson played with Harold taught her how to detect and use hidden meanings or secret metaphors. Katherine was admonished *never* to raise her voice, although she had a hearty laugh.

In her youth Katherine wrote in a clear and decorative hand, but after Oxford her flowing script, written in black ink with a thick pen nib, was hurried. The tone of her existing letters, even those to her closest relatives, was formal and she signed her full name. The actual presentation of the content, however, was informal and occasionally reached scribbled indecipherability. Scratched-out words, whole sentences sometimes running up and down the margins, and shorthand spellings are all typical. She learned to type at some point, but was never adept at it and usually omitted punctuation. After 1925 Katherine, who was then nearly sixty years old, experienced episodes of severe psychic detachment prompted by mental illness, and she rationalized them through participation in séances or other Spiritualist practices. Signs in her writing of such episodes include looping together nearly all words in a sentence or on a page and the use of multiple sets of quotation marks.

Katherine was raised with a huge household staff at her beck and call. Anonymous hands laid and lit fires, scrubbed floors, polished silver, dusted pictures, did laundry, made and mended clothes, cooked every meal, and emptied every chamber pot. Maids and nurses came and went, but two special people held places of intimacy and trust in the Gurney Pease family. Their butler, "Bossy" Bossomworth, a devout Quaker whom the children called the conscience of the family, oversaw everything and was devoted to Kate Pease. He retired reluctantly, as an old man, to a small farm she purchased for him in Richmond. Katherine's nanny, Mrs. Hopper, lived with her husband, who was Kate's coachman, and her son, Alfred, in a cottage at Woodside until Kate's death in 1915. On Sunday evenings Katherine walked Mrs. Hopper home and, from 7 P.M. until the gong sounded for supper an hour later, sat with her and heard stories of childhood and "theories of life and conduct."

Kate Pease managed her home and staff efficiently and taught her daughters to do the same. Katherine, however, flatly hated all domestic chores or burdens. She never trusted anyone who worked for her, had a limited ability to inspire loyalty, and was nearly incapable of rewarding competent service. Keeping house for migratory male relatives, as Jane and Emma had done, was anathema. Katherine said there was "no excuse for household cares," and only once in her life did she take housekeeping very seriously. That was for a short time in 1908 when she and her husband, William Scoresby Rout-ledge, were living in London after their return from British East Africa.

Katherine's warmest childhood memories were not of Southend or Wood-side but of Christmas festivities at Underfell, her Wilson grandparents' home at Kendal, Westmorland. Aunt Sarah, white cap tipped to one side and her spectacles crooked across her nose, welcomed Katherine and the other chil-dren into the big house with affectionate kisses. More than thirty adults and twelve children sat down at one enormous table for Christmas Eve dinner. They prayed, then feasted on roast chicken and duck, "wigs" (buttered tea cakes), oranges, figs, and pastry while a whole choir of schoolboys sang hymns and carols in high, clear voices. At the end of the evening Katherine and the other children were bundled off to cozy, fire-lit bedrooms, shadowy tree limbs dancing in snowy darkness beyond the windows. In the early-morning dim before sunrise they were awakened by the sound of an entire brass band playing "Christians Awake" in the hall below.

The contrast between such memorable experiences and Woodside's per-vasive gloom created two separate spheres of emotional existence for Kate Pease's children. This dichotomy was partly responsible for the oddly sad and emotionally disconnected adult lives of Katherine's siblings. Lilian had few intellectual interests, married a man who was cruel and then kept an obses-sively neat and orderly home in which, it appears, she developed a healthy taste for port. John Henry graduated from Cambridge, married a sociable and lighthearted woman, and had two children. They lived at Carlbury near Dar-lington in a home that his wife hated and his own brother called a "house of gloom." Wilson, whom Katherine adored, was admitted to the bar but never practiced law, married a woman he loved but then lived an aimless life of golf and endless social calls. He was a kind and thoughtful man with a mild addic-tion to opium and an unfortunate compulsion for gambling.

Only Katherine among the Gurney Pease children developed Joseph Pease's intellectual ambitions and political "concerns." She was sent to school at Sevenoaks in Kent, between the ages of either thirteen and sixteen or sixteen and eighteen (her school records appear not to have survived). Thereafter Kate, who professed satisfaction with her own limited home edu-cation, developed an intellectual and social competitiveness with her daugh-ter. Katherine, who had little patience with topics not up to what she considered her own intellectual standard, became convinced that her mother deliberately turned dinner conversation into an intellectual tug-of-war, mak-ing provocative statements and then sitting back, "waiting to be challenged."

After Sevenoaks Katherine watched with envy as her male cousins, some of whom were far less capable than she was, went off to university. Even

Harold, with all of his problems, departed for Cambridge. Proud of her intellectual abilities but painfully aware that displaying them caused unpopularity and dislike in the Pease family, Katherine was even less sure of her femininity. Her clothes were always of the best quality and her shoes custommade, but she never developed the art form of self-display.

When Joseph Whitwell Pease was created a baronet in 1882 and became known, thereafter, as Sir Joseph, the Pease family acquired a coat of arms. Darlington life grew progressively more elaborate, and all Peases were, to varying degrees, plunged into a glittering social whirl of dinners, balls, garden parties, and London theater events. Katherine and other Pease women were expected to achieve a high standard of flippant wit, charm, and glamorous dress. In 1884, at the age of eighteen, Katherine and some of her female cousins were presented at court during one of Queen Victoria's traditional early-afternoon "drawing-rooms." Katherine wore the Victorian fashion required for presentation to the monarch: a frilly dress, a string of pearls, and an enormous ostrich-plume fan. In the standard debutante photograph her typically frank and intelligent gaze is tentative, her awkward pose uneasy.

In the social season of 1884–85 Katherine joined shooting parties and, in August of 1884, competed in the Third Annual Cousins' Lawn Tennis Tournament, where she made a respectable showing. She and her cousins, dressed in fashionable white, sipped champagne and flitted about the green grass like flirtatious butterflies. As old social barriers fell, male cousins brought home eligible bachelors from among their university friends, and non-Quakers joined the family circle. Aunts and uncles watched from the sidelines, but snaring a suitable husband was no longer a Pease family enterprise—even though Katherine and her cousins faced a new and challenging social and sexual world.

Katherine's usual escort was her brother Wilson or cousin Reginald Pease, and her closest female friend—but also her competitor in the marriage market—was her much prettier cousin, the orphaned Beatrice Mary Pease. Born in the same year as Katherine, from the age of fourteen Beatrice had lived with Sir Joseph and his wife as one of their own children. On paper Beatrice was an heiress worth millions, but her estate was also burdened by huge and worrisome debts. Sir Joseph and his brother Arthur managed Beatrice's inheritance, just as they managed Kate Pease's. Beatrice played a pivotal role in Pease family history that had serious repercussions for Katherine.

The chain of events began when Newton, Sixth Earl of Portsmouth, was introduced to Katherine, Beatrice, and their cousin Helen at a Pease garden party. Portsmouth flirted with Katherine until someone cynically said, "You're on to the wrong one—that isn't the heiress." In the blink of an eye he set his sights on Beatrice. Within a few months Sir Joseph and his wife visited Hurstbourne Park, the Portsmouth family seat in Hampshire. Set within six hundred sweeping acres landscaped by Lancelot "Capability" Brown, the estate suggested considerable wealth but, unfortunately, was mortgaged to the hilt and in dire need of expensive repair. Although he was not a Quaker, the Pease family was dazzled and flattered by Portsmouth's exalted social rank and failed to see him as the gold digger he was.

Beatrice and Portsmouth became engaged, and his family entered immediately into aggressive negotiations for a substantial marriage settlement (a cash gift, much like a dowry, given by the bride's family to the intended groom). Red flags immediately went up with Sir Joseph, who recognized ruthlessness in business when he saw it. In addition Beatrice, encouraged by Portsmouth, requested a substantial amount of cash to remodel and redecorate Hurstbourne. Laying hands on the money meant that Beatrice's stocks in Pease family enterprises would have to be sold at the inflated value they were given by her trustees whenever they used them as collateral, for example, in other business deals. Sir Joseph was forced to liquidate his own assets in collieries and ironstone businesses on the open (non-Quaker) market.

This set the stage for the later collapse of the Pease empire and precipitated a clash between Katherine and her uncles when her sister, Lilian, fell in love with Charles Leslie Fox of Somerset, gave up her Quaker religion, and was baptized and married in a "very splash" ceremony in St. Cuthbert's Church, Darlington. Katherine, deeply saddened and suffering the indignity of having her younger, prettier sister married first, nevertheless "looked splendid" as one of the bridesmaids. Sir Joseph, who could see the Pease fortune unraveling before his very eyes, could not bear another marriage of a niece to a non-Quaker and bolted from Lilian's extravagant wedding by the vestry door.

In the weeks leading up to Lilian's wedding, Wilson and Katherine negotiated her marriage settlement. In a thoroughly nasty confrontation with Sir Joseph and Arthur Pease, they accused their aghast uncles of going beyond the powers of Gurney Pease's will and purchasing property in a risky real estate development called Newport Estate. Further, they said that they "had a claim against Arthur" for other unprofitable investments he had made. Sir Joseph was deeply insulted—"one belligerent niece is enough in any family"—Kate was appalled, and Arthur removed himself as a trustee of Gurney Pease's estate.

No evidence of wrongdoing by either Arthur or Sir Joseph has come to light, but unfortunately, the damage was done. On Black Friday, August 22, 1902, the J. & J. W. Pease Bank crashed. Pease family members—including Kate Pease, who loaned the bank a substantial amount of money—rushed to

Sir Joseph's aid, but it was futile. Beatrice's actions had utterly ruined Sir Joseph, who lost his entire fortune and Hutton Hall, his family home. His sons, Alfred and Jack, next in the direct male line of inheritance, were, effectively, bankrupted. Ironically, Beatrice and Katherine came out of the shambles far better than the rest of the family. The assets of their fathers' estates remained intact, and at Kate Pease's death, Katherine became a lavishly wealthy woman. Sir Joseph, who had done his generous best to carry the burdens of the Pease family fortune, died at Kerris Vean, Falmouth, late in the afternoon of his seventy-fifth birthday. His body was brought home to Darlington, and Kate Pease, in a gesture of love and respect, opened Woodside to family and friends for the funeral of Joseph Pease's eldest son.

The winter of 1890–91 was one of the coldest ever in Darlington. Conversations were even more boring and trivial than usual and Katherine, who at twenty-four was considered an aging spinster by Darlington standards, escaped Woodside for Potsdam and Berlin, where she fell in love with German philosophy, poetry, and opera. Katherine returned to Woodside with an attitude of forthright independence that her family frankly thought was "tactless." Not happy to be home, Katherine was frustrated, judgmental, and critical. She grumbled at the way her mother had brought her up and regretted that she had not been coached well in the marriage game. She was not alone in her feelings—her female cousins had similar resentments—but she was more vocal than others. Katherine blamed Kate Pease for her social failure and bitterly noted that Quaker parents "look less to the advancement of their children & more to the filial services which they require from them."

The anger Katherine felt at having to provide "filial services" in Woodside's gloomy, claustrophobic atmosphere soon plunged her into deep depression. Health problems, real or imagined, were always acceptable reasons for withdrawal in the Gurney Pease family, and Katherine retreated into a maze of dietary phobias. She slept late, often not rising until midday, and then acted either "prickly" or "slack," depending upon her mood. Katherine participated only reluctantly in Quaker charity work and told her mother that "in giving money away you are giving it to those who have not earned it, while in spending it you are giving it to those who have." Kate Pease flatly said that her unhappy daughter made her own problems because "it's in her that ills her."

This was, in fact, one of the lowest moments in Katherine's life. The prospect before her was not only uninviting, it was unbearable. Woodside offered no opportunity to grow and she found it hard to think straight while she was living there. She desperately wanted to use her intellectual gifts in the outside world and recognized how unhappy family life made her. Nonetheless, Katherine professed a deep attachment to the people and the place and felt terribly guilty about acknowledging her negative feelings. Then, surprisingly, her backbone straightened. She called upon an impressive reserve of inner strength and announced her intention to pursue an advanced education.

Everything done in the Pease family quickly became a matter of gossip, and Katherine's decision was widely discussed, challenged, and judged. Few appreciated the courage it took for Katherine to extricate herself from Woodside and its entangling family bonds. Her strongest supporters were Aunt Emma and an accomplished and independent cousin named Lucy Pease Fowler. Ten days after she had announced her decision in January of 1891, Katherine and her reluctant mother departed Darlington for Oxford. The following October Katherine Maria Pease, spinster, aged twenty-five, passed her entrance examination and was accepted at Somerville Hall (now Somerville College), Oxford.

Escape:
Oxford and South Africa, 1891

◆

"SOBERLY DRESSED AND DECOROUSLY BEHAVED," KATHERINE arrived in Oxford just a dozen years after women students were first admitted. Women had gained access to most of the lecture halls, laboratories, and libraries of the university, but the unspoken, stubborn policy was still to ignore them as much as possible. Gertrude Bell (1868–1926), who was a Pease family friend, attended Lady Margaret Hall, which was affiliated with the Anglican Church. One of Gertrude's tutors, unable to deal with changing times, required her to sit with her back to him because she was not a man. Gertrude fumed and then, years later, had her revenge when she rose to international prominence as a desert explorer, archaeologist, diplomat, and winner of the Royal Geographical Society's Gold Medal.

Women's halls, at this date, were not yet an official part of the university. Katherine chose nondenominational Somerville because of its connection to Liberal politicians and to the wealthy Quaker community. Its founder, Mary Somerville, was a scientist and an early, presuffragette feminist. In 1868—two years after Katherine was born—Somerville was the first to sign John Stuart Mill's famous petition to Parliament on behalf of women's rights. Katherine would spend four challenging years of her life at Somerville, in a conflicted but idealistic and energetic atmosphere, pursuing a degree in modern history. Her academic years were divided into demanding three-month terms of Lent (spring), Summer, and October, with holidays each August through September.

Oxford women were allowed to take the same exams required of men in a very limited range of subjects, including Katherine's field of modern history, but the degrees earned were withheld. Katherine's residence at Somerville coincided with intense political efforts to gain university degrees for women, and she passionately supported the cause. Somerville principal

Agnes Catherine Maitland was forty-one years old when Katherine Pease met her, a brilliant, idealistic, energetic, rigid, and autocratic Liberal who never married. While strongly in favor of women's rights, Maitland demanded "appropriate" feminine behavior at all times. In Maitland, who became her mentor, Katherine recognized the usefulness of some of her own personal characteristics, long regarded as unladylike by her family.

Twenty "presentable" young women, ages nineteen to twenty-five, joined Katherine in her first October term at Somerville. They competed intently for each other's attention and affection, and social jealousy was rampant, but Katherine made two or three fast friends and several interesting acquaintances at Somerville. Among the latter was Cornelia Sorabji, who was the first Indian woman to study at an English university. Her physical beauty— she cut an exotic figure in diaphanous Indian drapery—masked fierce determination, and she went on to become barrister-at-law and legal adviser, Court of Wards, Bengal, India. There she became a colleague of Sir Richard Harington, William Scoresby Routledge's closest friend, and may have been an introductory link between Katherine and her future husband.

Two of Katherine's closest friends were Gertrude Pesel and Ethel Hurlblatt. Gertrude was a leader in Somerville politics and a student advocate of degrees for women. She and Katherine belonged to the same Oxford organizations and suffragette societies and had, it seems, similar taste in men. They agreed that a strong man of the world was exceedingly charming company, and Katherine told her brother, "reliability is the charm of strength." Ethel Hurlblatt, nicknamed "Hurly" or "Hurly-burly," had a commanding presence and a hearty handshake. She became a distinguished educator, and in 1923 Katherine traveled all the way across Canada on her return from Mangareva to see Ethel at Royal Victoria College, McGill University.

Katherine's private Somerville room had a window, a desk, and a bed cleverly disguised as a sofa and later became the model for her cabin on *Mana*, the yacht she and Scoresby built that carried them to Easter Island. She read by malodorous lamplight and took turns with other Somerville women bathing in a tin tub that doubled as the housekeeper's bed. Elaborate meals were served in the communal dining room on long tables laid with linen and, on special occasions, adorned with flowers. On Wednesdays the women hosted afternoon tea for Oxford society and gave regular salons and "at homes." Katherine joined a debating society called Sharp Practice and developed an effective public-speaking style.

Other than her strong commitment to women's rights, Katherine did not embrace many of Oxford's more radical political ideals or aesthetic tastes. She was serious, afraid of failure, and sometimes quite lonely. She and other Oxford women were still forced to live with a typically Victorian code of behavior, discouraged from going anywhere alone and required to attend lectures in groups of two or three. Often in need of an escort, Katherine called upon Wilson to come from London and take her out to dinner or the theater. On some Sunday evenings they spent hours together in her room, talking and reading. Katherine enjoyed being with her brother and in his absence sought the company of older professors and her male tutors.

R. R. Marett (1866–1943), a scholar of comparative religion and Fellow of Exeter College, Oxford, was a profound influence on Katherine. He was strikingly handsome, and one of his male students said that Marett was "a first-rate and inspiring teacher and a vivid personality, and he was also a most likeable person." He had a wide range of interests and enthusiasms, a modern outlook on the world, genuinely liked women, and supported their presence at Oxford. Marett became Katherine's closest professional mentor and adviser, and everyone who knew her, even after her marriage to Scoresby, considered her to be spellbound by him. Katherine was deeply attracted to Marett and, quite likely, in love with him. It is possible that at least some of the repetitive health issues she faced while at Oxford were due to the strain of her unrequited infatuation with him.

Furthermore, Marett's intellectual influence on Katherine was substantial. Katherine learned from Marett that culture could be shaped through the power of individuals upon tradition and became convinced that equitable personal relationships between modern men and women were the key to reforming the moral climate of society. She accepted Marett's theories on "primitive" religion, which were elaborated from the work of Quaker scholar Sir E. B. Tylor. Marett defined the Polynesian religious concept of *mana* as supernatural "electricity" emanating from a supreme power and capable of entering objects and beings, including visionaries. Katherine refined this into her own notion of *mana* as a profound "inner light" and life force, an ideal that rested easily upon the foundation of her Quaker upbringing.

Professor Edward B. Poulton, newly appointed Hope Professor of Zoology, became Katherine's friend in 1893 through his feminist wife, Emily, who was the daughter of a wealthy and substantial Quaker member of Parliament. Poulton's lectures proved to Katherine's satisfaction the viability of the new science of evolution, and through his influence she came to accept Harold's medical condition as evidence of hereditary mental illness in her own family.

In spite of R. R. Marett's influence, Katherine was not able to study anthropology—Oxford's first diplomas in anthropology were not awarded until 1908, more than a decade after she had departed. Oxford's first female anthropologist was Barbara Freire-Marreco Aitken (1879–1967), who received her B.A. with distinction from Henry Balfour. In 1909 Freire-

Marreco became a Somerville Research Fellow and, from 1912 to 1929, edited *Notes and Queries in Anthropology*, a journal Katherine read regularly, and both women contributed articles independently to *Folk-lore*. Marett included Katherine Routledge and Barbara Freire-Marreco Aitken in his personal stable of standby scholars who could always be "counted on to produce a number of interesting papers."

Oxford prepared Katherine intellectually for many things, and the people she met, Marett above all, were instrumental in turning her attention toward anthropology. Archaeology was then in its infancy, and Katherine never received any formal training in surveying, excavation, or artifact analysis. Before she departed for Easter Island in 1913, Katherine asked Marett for advice about excavating. He responded with a few rules on a single sheet of notepaper, and she carried it as a talisman in the pocket of her field jacket. Katherine boldly—and quite messily—plunged into excavating forty or more Easter Island statues and many other archaeological sites. In the beginning she approached the work with some order and discipline. Rather soon, however, she abandoned herself to hasty and ill-conceived rummaging that, when confronted today in the pages of her fieldnotes, causes a modern archaeologist to cringe.

At Oxford Katherine discovered that she had a substantial ability to deal with people of varying social and economic backgrounds. Later, in British East Africa, her storytelling skills gave her an edge in collecting tribal legends and myths. On Easter Island she refined and developed a solid strategy for interviewing ethnographic consultants that produced incredibly valuable results. Marett cautioned her against recording and validating hearsay when in the field, and she diligently sought accuracy, consistency, and corroboration. In his autobiography, published six years after Katherine's death, R. R. Marett named Katherine among eight "women anthropologists, of whose achievements the Oxford school was particularly proud." Marett said that she and the other women had "brought me much satisfaction and perhaps some credit" with their outstanding work. High praise, indeed, from a man as demanding as he was generous.

Katherine spent Christmas of 1892 at Woodside, where there was fresh snow and frozen ponds for skating. She attended a gala masquerade party and flaunted her university status, wearing a brilliant red dress and her undergraduate's cap and gown. Wilson and Harold, accompanied part of the time by a physician, had spent nearly two years touring Egypt, India, and the Near East. The journey, it was hoped, would cheer Harold and change his behavior. Instead, both men contracted malaria, and the disease, apparently, triggered renewed symptoms of schizophrenia in Harold.

During all of 1893 the Gurney Pease family lived "under the cloud of

Harold's illness." He was alternately depressed, irrational, and violent and, in Wilson's words, went "in pursuit of the Holy Grail" or followed "wandering fires" into the dark of many nights. He took to drink, and his doctors tried to control him with heavy doses of drugs. Wilson favored hospitalization, but Katherine, who was living at Somerville, argued for keeping Harold at Woodside, even though it was clear that Kate Pease was unable to cope.

In April the famous Victorian physician Dr. Clouston diagnosed a "nervous condition" aggravated by recurrent symptoms of malaria, and a full-time nurse was hired. In an attempt to euphemistically explain the hereditary nature of Harold's illness to Kate Pease, Clouston told her that "Quakers had in the course of generations acquired a certain cast of mind" and that Harold was suffering "for the mental activity" of his forebears. Fresh air and an active life, with continued residence at Woodside, were prescribed. Within weeks it was obvious that such treatment was an abject failure, and Harold was dragged off against his will to Clouston's clinic in Edinburgh. A large family party traveled north and settled there in a hotel. The night before he was due at the clinic, Harold went to bed and cunningly pretended to be asleep, then disappeared.

Wilson, desperate with worry, engaged detectives and placed an advertisement in the newspaper. Harold was eventually found, but Wilson was sick to death of his brother's antics and willing, he said, "to do anything for a quiet life." Wilson believed that Harold's only hope was to commit himself. After two futile months in Edinburgh, however, Harold remained stubbornly unwilling—or unable—to do so. Wilson took the train to Oxford, hoping to persuade Katherine to join him in convincing Kate Pease to institutionalize Harold once and for all.

The weather was hot, and Katherine and Wilson ate strawberries and cream and talked for hours. They wanted to love their brother, but the shared burden of Harold had bound them all of their lives in a harmful cycle of anger, denial, and heart-wrenching sadness. Institutionalization was an awesome decision, and Katherine and Wilson went around and around, trying to find a way out that would allow Harold a decent life with some freedom.

Katherine was convinced that narrow Quaker superstition was at the heart of Harold's confusion, and that they had failed by "not placing wider views of religion before him." Katherine's incredibly inappropriate plan for her mad brother was as absurd as Dr. Clouston's prescription of fresh air: she suggested reading the biography of the Reverend Charles Kingsley aloud to Harold, hoping it would release him from his religious delusions and encourage habits of observation, skepticism, and criticism. Yet she recognized that, for too long, the Gurney Pease family had refused to face the truth of Harold's illness. "It has been a great lesson to me," Katherine said, "never to hesitate to proclaim what one holds to be the truth." In the end the family backed away from full institutionalization, and in November of 1893, Harold was sent to yet another spa-like hospital in Harrogate.

Peace descended, and in the early spring of 1894 Katherine's Somerville work was "very strong and sensible," although, as the term progressed, she "could not get above a Second." On April 5, 1894 Aunt Jane, who was sixty-seven years old, died at Wroxhall, Torquay. Kate Pease, Aunt Emma, and other family members escorted her coffin north to Darlington, and at her funeral it was cloaked in primroses, ivy, and sprigs of cypress from Southend's gardens. Katherine, who was then twenty-seven years old, and her brothers and sister placed a wreath on Jane's grave bearing the words "in memory of childhood." A distinguished, gray-haired old clergyman stood bareheaded in silence next to Jane's open grave for a long time, then slipped away from the Quaker burial ground without joining the family at Southend, as was customary.

Half a century before, Jane, a dreamy maiden of seventeen, had gone with her family to Cliffe House, the Pease summer home in Marske-by-the-Sea. There she had met a handsome youth, and they had fallen in love. He was destined to become the Church of England's respected archdeacon of Cleveland, and she was a Quaker. Joseph Pease blocked his heartbroken daughter's marriage and threatened her with being "disowned" for "marrying out" of her faith. Jane was forced to give up her heart's desire and the young couple went their separate ways, but she never loved another and he never forgot her. On the day of Jane's funeral the elderly clergyman became transformed, in Katherine's eyes, into a youthful and romantic lover saying a last, adoring farewell to the dream of his past.

For months after Jane's death Katherine veered between extreme nervousness and depression. Doctors advised rest, distraction, and a restricted diet. Wilson escorted her on a brief holiday to Normandy, France. Each morning the sun shone brightly through the lace window curtains of their rented holiday rooms, but Katherine stayed under the feather quilts until nearly noon, then had breakfast in bed. Forbidden to eat red meat, she anxiously scanned the menu each evening for chicken or fish and, afterward, sat silently with Wilson in front of a wood fire, reading tales of Joan of Arc.

Throughout the journey, in fact, Katherine was preoccupied with Joan of Arc. Near Rouen she and Wilson encamped in a field amidst clouds of butterflies and heaps of violets, and Katherine imagined Joan as a sturdy country wench, striding toward them in a swirling cacophony of birdsong, church bells, and Joan's ever-present "voices." One of their diversions was to write descriptions of architecture and then to compare them for accuracy. Katherine was incredibly critical and a stickler for minute detail, making the exercise odious for Wilson. If he, on the other hand, criticized her, she would burst into uncontrollable tears. Perhaps seeing some of Harold's behavior in Katherine, Wilson was alarmed and deeply concerned for his sister.

Katherine did not return immediately to Oxford, but went home to Darlington and stayed with Aunt Emma, who was alone at Southend. Like Wilson, Emma saw that Katherine's mental health was precarious. Her long and intimate experience with Jane had sharpened Emma's powers of observation, and in July of 1894 she was the first in the Pease family to recognize that Katherine was plagued by "voices." In August Katherine was persuaded to join her family in Scotland, where Kate Pease had taken a lodge on the shore of a salmon-filled stream. The hills echoed with gunfire, and Wilson, sun-browned and wearing a cozy flannel shirt, smoked opium-laden cigarettes while tramping with Katherine for miles along the loch.

In December of 1894, wearing an elaborate garden-party frock, a large black velvet hat, and carrying a bouquet of violets and a Chinese fan, Katherine walked down the aisle as a bridesmaid in her brother Wilson's wedding party. During their stay in Scotland, Wilson had confided his love for their cousin Joan Fowler, the daughter of William and Rachel Fowler of Moor Hall in Essex. Katherine told him that he had no chance and that Joan—who was three years older than Wilson—thought of him as her little brother. Katherine was wrong, however. Joan adored Wilson, and though she was plain, to his eye Joan was "an epic poem in petticoats." Katherine, who had known Joan all of her life and was fond of her, was jealous and felt Wilson's loss keenly. It is a measure of the maturity of both women, and of their mutual devotion to Wilson, that Katherine and Joan were able to forge strong sisterly ties in this intimate triangle.

Katherine's work was prospering if not always thriving at Oxford, and one of her tutors noted that "if she keeps her health she ought to do extremely well" in her forthcoming exams, where she hoped to achieve a First. Keeping her health, however, was touch and go. On Easter Sunday, 1895 Katherine attended sunrise services at St. Hilda's, the Anglican church in Darlington. The altar was banked with lilies and palms, and waves of daffodils drifted down the sides of the chancel. As Katherine watched from the side aisle, white lines of choristers followed the glittering cross and banners toward the altar. When the sun came up the whole scene was lit with brilliant white light, and Katherine was completely overcome by the exotic pomp of the "heathenish sight."

For a year after Jane's death Emma had suffered a bereavement of deep loneliness, and Southend had remained draped in black. On July 2, 1895 the enormous engraving of Joseph Pease hanging in the Woodside library crashed to the floor. The next day, as if in response to her stern father's command, Emma Gurney Pease died in her sleep. Kate had checked the picture's fastenings the night before, and Katherine and the rest of the family were impressed with the superstitious coincidence. Drawing on letters she and her daughters had received from Emma at emotional turning points in their lives, Kate wrote a touching portrait of her for the Quaker *Annual Monitor*. A small contingent of Pease family members walked in a broiling sun behind Emma's casket to Skinnergate burial ground, where it was laid in the same grave as Jane's. Their names are chiseled into the smooth, white surface of a single gravestone.

Katherine's Victorian aunts had lived in thrall to their stern father's sickbed without love, sex, or family of their own. Their lives were sacrificed to Joseph Pease's selfish ideal of female servitude, and their subordination bred frustration, disappointment, anger, and guilt. Katherine responded with a vivid determination to stand on her own two feet, but also developed an elusive, romantic, and finally unattainable image of true love.

Kate Pease's grown-up children were now without the constant love and support of both eccentric and "interfering" aunts. Almost immediately after Emma's funeral, Katherine suffered what the Pease family frankly regarded as a breakdown: chills and fever followed by bleak depression. Her symptoms were all remarkably similar to those that once had afflicted her father, Gurney Pease, but more severe than those triggered by Lilian's marriage three years earlier. Katherine's doctors prescribed rest and a restricted diet, but a bromide of potassium, quinine, morphia, chloral, or other mood-altering drugs with known side effects was probably given.

At the beginning of July Katherine joined Harold at Charleton—an old, ill-kept country house shaded by thick trees with barred windows overlooking the Firth of Forth and Bass Rock. Often in restraints, Harold suffered violent outbursts of temper, religious obsessions, and suicidal impulses. Katherine's family maintained that she was just visiting her brother, but it is highly probable that she was being treated for depression. Katherine hated Charleton—she called it "charlatan"—and thought the nurses and attendants were incompetent.

Did Katherine recognize any similarity between Harold's more severe illness and her own repeated depressions? Quite possibly she did, but without doubt she understood the hereditary implications of his disease. Pondering her brother's religious obsessions, Katherine concluded that Quakerism had failed him, and that her own upbringing had not given her the deep personal faith she sought. She appears not to have discussed her "voices" at this time with anyone, including Wilson, but in an effort to explain them she took up an intense, almost obsessive interest in alternative "sciences" and treatments, including mesmerism, homeopathic medicine, and Christian Science. Finally, she turned to Spiritualism.

In 1865, just one year before Katherine was born, the Association of Progressive Spiritualists was formed in Darlington. It was based on the belief that, after the death of the mortal body, an immortal spirit and personal identity continued to exist. When the spirit left the body, it entered one of seven levels of the "spiritual plane," from which it was able to communicate with the living either directly or through mediums. By 1882 a distinguished group of academics—including Edmund Gurney, one of Katherine's relatives—had founded the British Society for Psychical Research to investigate hundreds of Spiritualist claims of telepathy and clairvoyance. In 1894, the year before Katherine's stay at Charleton, the society published an influential survey of seventeen thousand persons; three hundred of them claimed to have experienced spirit "sightings." Because eighty of these "sightings" occurred within twelve hours of the otherwise unknown death of the person "sighted," they were judged "inexplicable" and, therefore, valid spiritual encounters. In Katherine's opinion, this "scientific" evidence validated Spiritualism.

Florence Marryat's *There is no Death* and *The Spirit World* were the basic texts of Spiritualism, and Katherine read both books. They provided anecdotal accounts of meeting departed spirits not through Aunt Jane's world of personal visionary experience but, instead, by channeling during organized séances. Sometime between 1894 and 1896 Katherine embarked upon a quest to reach the spirit of her father, Gurney Pease. Her companion during these séances was her orphan cousin Beatrice Mary Pease, spoiler of the Pease fortune.

Individuals who claim to channel spirits enter into a light trance that can deepen into a state similar to hypnosis. Their real personality is pushed aside and "another presence" speaks words that come spontaneously in a "stream of consciousness" mode. Beatrice claimed to have heard her father's voice, harsh and disapproving of her behavior toward her family. Beyond a doubt, Katherine also believed herself capable of reaching the spirits of deceased relatives, most notably that of her stern Quaker grandfather, Joseph Pease.

Katherine rallied from her breakdown, departed Charleton, and returned to Oxford. She took her exams and then, like other Somerville women, was bitterly disappointed when the student body's petition to grant degrees to women was denied. Toward the end of July 1895 Katherine received her exam results: Honors 2nd Class in Modern History. She had expected more and, Wilson said, "if it had not been for her breakdown just before the exam she would have been a certain 1st." Katherine felt she had failed, but she was being too hard on herself. Of the twenty women who had been part of

Katherine's Somerville class of 1891, only twelve sat for exams and *none* of them received anything higher than a Second, perhaps by tacit agreement of the male teaching establishment. Six exams were given in modern history, with Katherine and four others each taking Second and one woman a Third. Katherine's performance, as erratic as it obviously was, was competitive.

Katherine took a position as extension lecturer in history at Darlington Training College, where she applied herself "uncommonly well." Not long afterward she and her cousin Alfred Edward Pease, eldest son of Sir Joseph Whitwell Pease, began a major tug-of-war over Harold, who was then thirty-two years old. For several months Harold had bombarded members of the family with letters pleading to be rescued from Charleton, and in truth, he seemed more calm and rational than in the past. Alfred, apparently at Kate Pease's request or at least with her consent, paid a visit to Charleton and, taken in by Harold's charm, found him "quite sane." Alfred ordered Harold's restraints taken off and the bars removed from the windows, then began negotiations to return him to Darlington.

Katherine had suffered a breakdown only six months earlier, but she now became, Wilson said, "the backbone of the family." She flatly refused to allow Harold to come home to Woodside, but Alfred, who meant well, persisted. Kate Pease saw a conflict looming and withdrew to her bed with "palpitations." The rest of the Pease family found Katherine's forceful behavior "unbecoming in a woman," yet she held her ground. Harold went to live with Alfred and his family, who helped him lead the "healthy outdoor life" with such success that Harold rather soon graduated to his own home in Great Ayton, Teesside.

In September of 1896 Harold's marriage to his cousin Gwendolen Margaret Butler of Ayton House, Great Ayton, was somehow "arranged." Everyone who knew Gwen, who was twelve years younger than Harold, described her as attractive and warmly affectionate. The question, of course, is why would this desirable, optimistic young woman marry such a dark, sad, and dangerous man as Harold? Why, in fact, would her family allow the marriage? When Harold was at his best in the country life of dogs and horses he seemed eccentric and tender, and perhaps Gwen felt herself capable of saving his dispirited life. A business arrangement was certainly involved, and Kate Pease's will generously provided for Gwen. After Harold's marriage Katherine no longer considered herself responsible for her brother's fate and firmly closed the door on that part of her life.

By the summer of 1897 Katherine had "a craving after some new thing" that, her brother Wilson thought, "does not satisfy when she gets it." After a tense holiday in September of 1898 Kate Pease and her daughter were unable, in Wilson's words, to "hit it off," and Katherine, at last, asserted her independence—symbolic and real. She demanded that henceforth her family address her as Katherine, not with the diminutive of Katie as they had all of her life, and announced that she intended to leave Woodside and take up residence in London. The sale of Southend had made her financially independent, and Katherine took an apartment at Queen Anne's Mansions, overlooking St. James' Park. She joined the Ladies' Empire Club, became actively involved in the suffragette movement, and spent increasingly more time with Eliza "Lyle" McAllum.

Katherine had known Lyle since at least 1893. Slight and fragile, she was about five years older than Katherine, had never attended university or married, and led a sheltered life. On the surface it appears remarkable that she interested Katherine at all, but Lyle soon replaced all but Wilson in Katherine's affection and outlasted all of her Oxford friendships. The Pease family thought the relationship was unequal, and in economic ways it certainly was. The daughter of a minor customs official, Lyle had no income of her own. In the classic Victorian spinster manner she lived with her younger sister Barbara Lucy and Colonel Sir Albert Edward Bingham, her extraordinarily wealthy husband, at Ranby House in Nottinghamshire. Lyle had a little north-facing room, curiously placed halfway up the main staircase of the house, and while she was loved and respected within the family, she had the status of a poor relative.

In other ways, however, Katherine and Lyle had a great deal in common. Both were respectable watercolorists, and their holidays with the Pease family in Scotland or bicycle rambles through the English countryside were carefree times of painting and sight-seeing. Like Katherine, Lyle had a playful imagination, a gift for storytelling, and a warm relationship with her sister's children. Her intellect challenged Katherine in some ways and flattered her in others. Very early in their friendship Katherine and Lyle jokingly created the "Sensible Women's League." They were the only two members, and their goal was to form only platonic friendships with men—no woman, they felt, could be both a free person and a sexual being.

At Oxford there had been "raves" and "crushes" between women students thought to have "sapphist" tendencies, and sexual naïveté, repressions, and anxieties are all recurring themes of Victorian female life. Close, even ardent, attachments between many "new" or "odd" women, including leading artists and intellectuals, are widely evident in memoirs, letters, and journals of the time. One woman's physical attraction to another, depicted so lyrically in Virginia Woolf's *Mrs. Dalloway*, might be erotically expressed but not, in fact, acted upon. Yet some loving Victorian same-sex friendships were also love affairs, and Katherine and Lyle may well have been lovers. Katherine kept a careful record of the letters she wrote to Lyle from Easter Island but, unfortunately, none has survived among either woman's papers. That, in itself, is suggestive. While the full parameters of their friendship cannot be defined, the obvious truth is that the emotional attachment between the two women was strong and lasting.

Lyle had "ceased to believe in religion" and, like Katherine, was intensely superstitious. In darkened, draped rooms they attended séances conducted by their closest friends, Quaker spinster sisters named Elsie and Louie Fletchers. Both women were gifted mediums with a strong dose of larceny, and they channeled a female spirit named Julia. As Katherine and Lyle watched in fascination, Julia communicated in a spontaneous stream of consciousness. The Fletchers' thick pens moved across blank sheets of paper and formed words in "automatic writing." William Scoresby Routledge, who met the Fletchers in 1910, disliked them intensely and Wilson Pease was extremely skeptical. He saw them in Monte Carlo in 1909, "hot and eager" at the roulette table but failing to win with the numbers Julia had predicted.

As early as 1930 psychiatrists recognized that automatic writing tapped into subconscious knowledge and feelings, and that a major component expressed is paranoia. Louie Fletchers, like Katherine, had been desperately ill as a child and, afterward, experienced "voices." She interpreted her "voices" as spirit communication, encouraged Katherine to do the same, and taught her a valuable control technique. The key was to focus completely on a steadily burning candle flame, blocking out all daily thoughts and any pictures in the mind's eye. An act of will far greater than mere contemplation or meditation was required, but Katherine became extremely adept at it. When she practiced it along with a healthy lifestyle of rigorous exercise and intellectual involvement, as she did on Easter Island, the technique provided welcome relief.

On May 3, 1902, twenty-eight days before the defeated Boers signed the formal peace agreement with England that ended the bloody Second Anglo-Boer War, Katherine set sail from Southampton aboard *Kinfaun's Castle* on the first of two voyages she would make to Cape Colony, South Africa. Like other privileged, romantic, and patriotic women of the age, Katherine was on a mission. Her goal was to investigate resettlement of single, working women from England to South Africa after the war. In South Africa Katherine witnessed history firsthand—from the hideous degradation of the prison camps to the seductive danger of the Empire's most powerful men.

In Johannesburg Katherine met General Baden-Powell (1857–1941), defender of Mafeking. She was starstruck enough to ask for his autograph, then corresponded with him for years, including from Easter Island. Viscount Alfred Milner (1854–1925), the brutal and uncompromising governor of South Africa, made a similarly vivid impression on Katherine. At a garden party at his redbrick villa outside Johannesburg, she looked over her teacup into the "piercing brown eyes" of this ruthless man and found him alluring. She was shamelessly flattered by his "delightful knack" of making her feel involved, "helping to govern the country for the time being!"

In Pretoria Katherine became deathly ill and required hospitalization. She suffered paroxysms of high fever, chills, and anemia followed by sleeplessness and depression. Doctors suggested influenza, but Katherine convinced herself she had malaria. Ever since Wilson and Harold had contacted malaria in India, she had attributed all such recurrent physical symptoms to that disease. Katherine recovered slowly and then returned to England, bringing with her a pure enthusiasm for South Africa—which she revisited in 1903. Whatever her feelings were for Lyle, Katherine's Oxford ideal of a strong, reliable man now included his living a purposeful life in a wild, dramatic setting.

Scoresby:
"a true British barbarian," 1904

♦

SIX FEET TALL, TANNED AND FIT, WILLIAM SCORESBY Routledge strode across the elegant dining room of London's Carlton Hotel with a commanding presence. His dark hair was slicked back and he was wearing an expensive suit made by a fashionable London tailor. Wilson Pease stood to greet him and, as Scoresby reached to shake his hand, was amused to see that wire bracelets made by African craftsmen incongruously encircled his wrist. Katherine, her thick hair swept up, looked her very best in a slim Parisian gown of gray silk with thousands of tiny pink beads sparkling in the warm candlelight. She had personally attended to every detail of this lavish dinner party in Scoresby's honor, and when he seated himself next to her, he found gifts tucked into his napkin: an old silver box to use as a cigarette case and a gold matchbox. The crisp sauternes being poured into chilled crystal goblets was his favorite.

Katherine was plainly infatuated, but Wilson and his wife, Joan, were less impressed with the forty-six-year-old raconteur—although, they thought, he played the evening's "game of conversation" with skill. Katherine's new life philosophy, she boldly told Wilson, was to "get as many contrasts as you can. Lead the simpler, the luxurious, the sensuous, the strenuous, the intellectual lives till you have as many, or nearly as many, lives as a cat."

In August of 1902 Scoresby had been in British East Africa (Kenya) with only vague plans. On the voyage out he had struck up a friendship with a young couple: Dr. Sidney L. Hinde and his linguist wife, Hildegarde. Hinde was a promising government official who served as district subcommissioner at Fort Hall (now Murang'a), sixty-eight miles northeast of Nairobi in the wild, newly opened Central Highlands of Kenya. In the bar of a Nairobi hotel Hinde introduced Scoresby to Richard Meinertzhagen, an energetic twenty-four-year-old officer in command of the army in the region surrounding Fort

Hall. His mission was to quell any native African disturbance that threatened the safety of European newcomers, and he did it ruthlessly. A complex and vulgar man, Meinertzhagen was capable of appreciating lilting birdsong and then, in the next moment, coldly executing an entire village in retaliation for the death of a single white man. His impression of Scoresby was that he was a globe-trotter, "out to see the fun."

In early December Scoresby accompanied Hinde and his wife on safari in the vicinity of Fort Hall, camping out in the bush with Meinertzhagen's forces. Kikuyu warriors fiercely attacked Meinertzhagen's men when on patrol, and upon their return to camp he demanded that the "civilians"— Scoresby and Hildegard Hinde—return to the greater safety of Fort Hall at once. After a tense confrontation between Hinde and Meinertzhagen, Hinde relented, and the next day, Scoresby and Hildegard reluctantly accompanied the wounded back to Fort Hall under strong escort.

Less than a week later Scoresby became one of the earliest homesteaders in Kenya's Central Highlands when Meinertzhagen founded another fort at Nyeri, thirty miles north of Fort Hall in the fertile valley between Mount Kenya and the Aberdares. The customary lease allotment at the time was 640 acres (with a maximum of five thousand acres possible without approval by the secretary of state for the colonies in London). Homesteading did not necessarily carry with it an obligation to settle personally, but an investment of about £1,000 per year for five years was usually required to avoid confiscation. This amount was more than three times Scoresby's yearly income, all of which was generated from a modest inheritance. It is likely Scoresby acquired his property on the promise of payment—funds that he then had to raise.

On New Year's Eve of 1903 Scoresby was to have joined Meinertzhagen on safari but, Meinertzhagen said, "never turned up on account of the rain. As he had arranged to bring food, I missed him." Within months of standing up Meinertzhagen in the bush, Scoresby was back in England. His intent, he said, was to learn surveying at the Royal Geographical Society, but he also needed to secure investment capital to retain ownership of his homestead. Katherine's background and Scoresby's could not have been more dissimilar, but before the end of 1904 their paths had crossed.

Known to his family as Will, Scoresby always used his middle name, given in honor of the Reverend William Scoresby (1789–1857)—whaler, arctic explorer, natural scientist, inventor of the "Scoresby compass needle," and Routledge "family friend." William Scoresby went to sea for the first time at the age of ten aboard his father's ship *Resolution,* then entered the University of Edinburgh to study chemistry, natural philosophy, and anatomy. In 1810, at the age of twenty-one, he became captain of *Resolution* and the most successful hunter of polar whales (bowheads) in history. In 1820 he published an influential book on the history of whaling, and when *Moby Dick* appeared in 1851, Herman Melville acknowledged William Scoresby as the model for the character Charley Coffin. In 1825 he was ordained a clergyman in York and, in September of that year, joined Katherine's great-grandfather Edward Pease on the maiden run of the Darlington and Stockton Railway.

Married twice to women he considered partners "in the matrimonial excursion," the Reverend William Scoresby was a widower when, in the summer of 1848, he met Anne Sophia Twycross—Katherine's future mother-in-law—in Brampton. Anne was in her early twenties and living with her widowed father, and William Scoresby, by all accounts, was charming, dynamic, vital, and many "young ladies were susceptible to his charm." The Reverend Scoresby had developed challenging theories about mesmerism, and one day Emma Twycross, Anne's younger sister, eagerly stretched out on a couch in the darkened family parlor to act as a subject in his hypnotism experiments. After many futile attempts he gave up trying to hypnotize Emma, and Anne took her place. Anne promptly fell, quite literally, under his spell.

Her love was unrequited, however, and Anne was devastated when William Scoresby remarried for the third time in 1849. In 1853, still unmarried, she emigrated to Melbourne with two male relatives and, three years later, encountered the Reverend and Mrs. Scoresby in Melbourne. At his death in 1857 Anne's decade-long dream of him ended. Very soon thereafter she married a Melbourne merchant named William Routledge, who also had emigrated from England and was in a modestly successful business partnership with his brother James. In 1859 Anne's only son—William Scoresby Routledge—was born and named after the great, lost love of her life.

William Scoresby Routledge spent the first seven or eight years of his life in Melbourne, where Anne Routledge delivered two more children, Elizabeth Louisa ("Bessie"), born four years after Scoresby, and Agnes Mary, born in 1865. In 1863 James Routledge died in Melbourne and his wife and only child left Australia for England. Sometime between 1865 and 1867— the time frame encompassing Katherine's birth in Darlington—William Routledge sold their joint holdings in Melbourne and followed with his own family. Anne's fourth and last child, dreamy and artistic Anne Georgiana Haliburton Routledge, was born and baptized in Reading in 1867, although the Routledges eventually settled in Eastbourne.

Emma Twycross also married, and both she and Anne Routledge absolutely doted on their sons, filling them with dreams of the sea and an interest in natural science. Emma's only child, John Milne, William Scoresby Routledge's first cousin, was born in 1850 and was known in the family as

"Earthquake Johnny." He was a brilliant scientist who invented the modern seismograph and founded the Seismological Society of Japan in 1880. He established seismological stations from British Columbia to Calcutta and, in 1906, successfully monitored the great San Francisco earthquake from his home laboratory on the Isle of Wight. Married to an exotic Japanese woman, he was a charismatic international celebrity with a rugged, open-air face, thick mustache, piercing blue eyes, and a ready laugh.

William Scoresby Routledge graduated from Christ Church, Oxford, in 1882. Victorian social critic Matthew Arnold wrote that the typical Christ Church man was "a true British barbarian." Friendly and straightforward, Arnold's "barbarian" had "no nervous self-assertion, but the careless ease and self-confidence of an assured position—easy-going and pleasant-spoken, yet not a fool to be taken in, or to put up with liberties." In actuality, however, the affable John Milne fit Arnold's description far better than Scoresby ever did and many people, including his own nieces and nephews, found Scoresby unlikable, prudish, and terribly pretentious.

The Reverend William Scoresby's legacy to both men was a love of science. William Scoresby Routledge's fieldwork in British East Africa is a commendable inventory of tools and other artifacts, which he described in intricate detail. He tinkered constantly with machinery, experimented with compasses, survey instruments, guns, and ammunition, and concocted an endless variety of ways to cook and eat the exotic breadfruit, of which he was enormously fond. Even as a very old man Scoresby was still a scientific hobbyist, writing his sister Agnes Mary about his experiments with apple dumplings and detailing the extensive test procedures he used to bake them in a gas oven.

In 1882–83 Scoresby enrolled at University College London to study medicine. He lived on a modest allowance and worked hard. In 1883 he received the physiology prize and, in the same year, was elected to fellowship in the Royal Geographical Society. A photograph taken in September 1884 shows Scoresby, a handsome and eligible twenty-five-year-old bachelor, sitting on the grass in front of a bevy of young females including two of his sisters and several Milne cousins. Although surrounded by so many women, Scoresby appears to have been curiously asexual, and there is no mention of a love interest in his life at this point or at any time before he met Katherine.

In 1887 Scoresby received an M.A. degree from Oxford and, in 1888–89, won the coveted Erichsen Prize for Practical Surgery. He was awarded a certificate and a surgeon's case of operating instruments valued at "at least Ten Guineas," and referred to himself for the rest of his life as "Erichsen Prizeman." In spite of such obvious promise and significant accomplishments, Scoresby left University College London in June 1889 without attaining the doctor of medicine degree. His father was ill and perhaps there were family obligations, but it also seems that he was not disappointed with leaving.

On his father's death in 1891—the year Katherine entered Oxford—Scoresby came into a modest net income from stocks, funds, and securities "not exceeding three hundred pounds per annum." This was the only income he ever had in his life until he married Katherine, and it was inadequate to finance either his homestead in Kenya or his later, more elaborate dreams of travel. Sometime in early 1900 Scoresby left England and struck out for eastern Canada. There he lived "with the Micmacs in Central Newfoundland to learn hunting and woodcraft." He walked, he said, in dense forests carrying "a heavy load almost daily for four months." Scoresby always described his sojourn among the Micmacs in anthropological terms, but his interest appears to have been more entrepreneurial than cultural. He was certainly not the first to see the commercial value of Micmac quillwork, lacquerwork, furs, and pelts, all of which were sold through wholesale mail-order catalogues. He left Canada at an unknown date, then turned up in Africa.

William Scoresby Routledge was not a country gentleman, horseman, hunter, or farmer, but British East Africa gave him the opportunity to invent a new persona. Scoresby established his Nyeri homestead as a fixed camp on high ground; built a "long drop" latrine; dug a deep, encircling trench; and strung a barbed-wire fence to keep out lions and rhino. He was an interested but not avid photographer and constructed "a rough stone room for photographic work." He pitched tents on cement floors to discourage the ever-present rats, ticks, and vicious ants and raised protective thatched structures over them called *bandas*. He improvised, took risks, and surely experienced feelings of isolation and freedom, exhilaration, euphoria, and fear, as he wandered the bush "shooting, photographing, collecting and taking notes" among the Kikuyu.

Scoresby did not speak Bantu, the language of the Kikuyu, and learned only a little pidgin Swahili, Africa's lingua franca. Instead, he used his medical knowledge to open doors and then documented and collected tools, ornaments, and weapons. Patience and politeness were essential, and Scoresby described the "campfire strategy" he used to draw people to him: "I made it a practice to have a big fire in front of my tent and everyone was welcome. They sat around it in order of social consideration, talking amongst themselves. I presently joined in the conversation, perhaps asking a question, and so induced one man to give an explanation which would be corrected and amplified by the others."

Scoresby attained a certain degree of bushcraft and self-reliance, but he also depended greatly upon the society of the generous Kikuyu. He penned descriptions of his first sojourn in Africa that show a deeply romantic turn of phrase and a strong natural ability as a cultural observer. He had an appreciation for the commercial market value of tribal objects and was drawn to the mechanics of their uses and minute descriptions of their characteristics. Sadly, Scoresby eventually lost his connection with the sensory richness of Africa, and his attention to descriptive detail overwhelmed the childlike sense of adventure that was one of his most attractive qualities. Eventually, the line between the objective reality of science and his own subjective experiences would become blurred.

Scoresby found Kikuyu women charming, friendly, musical, sensual, spontaneous in expressing their emotions, and often wreathed in smiles. At frankly erotic ceremonial dances in sacred groves "where the African moon poured her flood of light," Scoresby admired "well oiled bodies" glistening with the "sheen of velvet." Many years later, Scoresby's enemies accused him of "going native" and having sexual liaisons with African girls. If so, he would not have been the only white man of the time to do so, or the first to suffer guilt and recriminations afterward.

Most of the military officers and virtually every railway official in Nairobi kept a native African girl. They were, Richard Meinertzhagen said, "usually a Masai, and there is a regular trade in these girls with the local Masai villages. If a man tires of his girl he goes to the village (munyatta) and gets a new one." Meinertzhagen bragged that he had three very young Kikuyu "dancing girls" himself. Girls—or sometimes young boys—were bartered by chiefs or forcibly abducted from their homes by unscrupulous Europeans, and having churchmen in the vicinity did not necessarily make things any better. In one particularly notorious case a missionary named Smith told "converted girls that they cannot be true Christians until they have slept with a Christian."

The year before Katherine introduced Scoresby to her bemused family, he had been elected to membership in the Anthropological Institute of Great Britain and Ireland and had presented his first group of thirty-eight African ethnographic objects to the British Museum. Mutual friends or contacts within the Oxford community, the Museum, or the Institute may have introduced him to Katherine. An African travel connection through Katherine's uncle Frank and aunt May Wilson, daughter of the famous explorer and missionary Dr. David Livingstone, is possible but unlikely. The only positive evidence of an intermediary comes from Dr. Arthur Cayley Headlam, bishop of Gloucester, who told Katherine's sister, Lilian, that "my wife and I were a little involved in the matter of her marriage."

However their introduction took place, on April 1, 1906 Katherine, Scoresby, and Dr. and Mrs. Headlam joined Wilson and Joan Pease at Bertolini's Hotel in Naples. With no apparent sense of irony Wilson referred to Scoresby, then forty-seven years old, as Katherine's "young man Routledge." Scoresby had proposed marriage, and it fell to Wilson "to act the parent, to inquire into prospects etc., a job that brings black lines under the eyes." Wilson and Katherine walked silently through the museum at Pompeii "with our eyes on the statues and our thoughts on the great 'to be or not to be' of marriage."

Children certainly were not part of these deliberations. Katherine was still physically able to bear children but did not want any of her own, although she needed the feeling of a common past that her large family provided and lavished attention on Lilian's little girls in the manner of her own "interfering aunts," Jane and Emma. Katherine had not, apparently, confided in Wilson the full scope of her fears about her own mental health, but they both worried about the implications of hereditary mental illness in their family. On April 8, 1906 Vesuvius erupted, sending up a great pillar of black smoke nearly three times as high as the mountain. Katherine superstitiously saw this historic natural disaster as a personal bad omen and promptly fled Naples. She abandoned Wilson, Scoresby, and her tortured marriage discussion, cut short her holiday, and drove to the railway station under dark skies raining the ash of centuries.

Less than four weeks later Wilson and Joan were in Tunbridge Wells at Toys Hill House, a lovely, secluded house built of native stone by Margaret Sewell, daughter of Anna Sewell, the author of *Black Beauty*. Into this idyllic retreat, the blackness of Naples far behind them, came Katherine and her "young man" William Scoresby Routledge. Walking on a sunny May morning through leafy colonnades of wind-shimmering birches, Scoresby pressed his case and offered Katherine an engagement ring. Without any further hesitation, she accepted.

Wilson obligingly went down to Yelverton to see Scoresby's sister Agnes Mary and her husband, Major Ernest Townsend, to get a character reference. He liked the Townsends well enough, but was not impressed with the Routledge family background in "the shop." Although he often criticized Katherine for being pretentious, Wilson had his own nasty Victorian brand of bigotry and, he said, "pride of birth, for at least there is no shopkeeping blood in my veins." If Wilson had the traditional Englishman's disdain for hardscrabble Australians, certainly Scoresby did not care much for Wilson either.

The announcement of Katherine's engagement was met with skepticism by her relatives, who were unimpressed with Scoresby. The financial disaster caused by the unfortunate Beatrice Portsmouth and her greedy husband was still an open wound in the Pease family, and while some saw Scoresby as a "rough diamond," others frankly considered him to be a fortune hunter.

Katherine's cousin Sir Alfred Edward Pease, who was an internationally recognized game hunter, never liked Scoresby and saw him as an African pretender. The best Alfred's very kind wife, Nellie, could say about Scoresby was that he was a "very scientific man, an African traveller." Katherine's niece Rachel Pease Chaytor uncharitably remarked that Katherine was "lucky to get" Scoresby and that "he was as mad as she was."

Scoresby's financial incentive to marry was strong, and Wilson's major goal was to protect Katherine's inheritance. He negotiated a settlement payment to Scoresby of £20,000, a fortune by Routledge standards but modest by those of the Pease family. Katherine was a handsome, intelligent woman with an adventurous spirit, status, and lavish means—in the words of the Reverend William Scoresby, a perfect traveling partner in the "matrimonial excursion." Was Scoresby in love with Katherine? Katherine's brothers Wilson and John Henry Pease thought Scoresby was tolerable enough as a husband, even loving and respectful. The Routledge family more realistically recognized that "Uncle Willie" was marrying "a rich wife who wanted to travel."

Marriage was the key, within Katherine's traditional family, to a life of greater freedom, but it was not really necessary. South Africa had given her a new natural landscape to explore on her own and, at the same time, an energetic social purpose to embrace. Katherine was a forthright, modern woman who idealistically sought a "companionate" marriage—a relationship that provided intellectual recognition, social equality, and sexual freedom without sexual pressure. To Katherine's eye, Scoresby was her Oxford ideal: the strong, reliable man living a life of purpose in an interesting place.

In mid-July of 1906 seven Somerville women, including Katherine Pease and Ethel Hurlblatt, journeyed to Dublin and triumphantly claimed their ad eundem degrees from Trinity College. Katherine did so, in part, to gain parity with Scoresby and to advance their plans for African fieldwork. She rushed back to Darlington and plunged into whirlwind arrangements for her August 6 wedding. Kate Pease was suffering "palpitations"—as she often did when something went against the grain—and Katherine's jubilance quickly turned into a major case of prenuptial jitters. Joan fitted her gown and struggled to calm her, in spite of Katherine's annoyingly "imperious manner." Then, out of the blue, the disaster known in the Pease family as the "Grosvenor Hotel incident" exploded into Katherine's life.

Harold Gurney Pease was on leave from Holloway Sanatorium, St. Anne's Heath, Virginia Water, when he violently attacked his wife, Gwen, in a room at London's Grosvenor Hotel. He beat her badly and Gwen required months of care. The Pease family rushed to calm her terrified and angry parents and to keep the incident out of the newspapers. Harold was returned to Holloway

Sanitorium immediately, with no prospect of ever again being released, and died there twenty-two years later at the age of sixty-three. Gwen, who meticulously managed Harold's financial affairs for years, generously wrote that she was "very sad at the thought of his suffering and the long years of his wasted life. The awful part was that I could do nothing for him."

Katherine Maria Pease wed William Scoresby Routledge in a traditional Quaker ceremony at Skinnergate Meeting House, Darlington, on the afternoon of Monday, August 6, 1906, just five days before her fortieth birthday. Katherine's niece, Lilian's daughter Evelyn (Eve) Leslie Fox, entered first, wearing white muslin and lace tied with blue ribbons and carrying a bouquet of pink carnations. Katherine followed in a magnificent, virginal gown of rich, white crepe de chine trimmed with hand embroidery and lace, wearing a matching white hat and carrying a mass of white carnations. Her only jewelry was on her left wrist—an exquisite gold bracelet, the gift of Lyle McAllum.

Katherine sat stiffly next to Scoresby on a raised platform in the middle of family and friends, few of whom were practicing Quakers. The expectant and uneasy silence of the room must have been uncomfortable for Scoresby, who was certainly unfamiliar with Quaker wedding ceremonies and was surrounded by people he barely knew. Katherine's childhood Meetings had always achieved long silences born of family unity and deeply held communal beliefs, but on this day the visionary voice of Aunt Jane was missing. Duty, not the Inner Light, finally prompted friends and relatives to rise and bless the couple.

Silence again descended until Katherine stood abruptly and Scoresby, taking his cue, rose to face her. He made his marriage declaration first, but there is no record of what he said. "I take thee, my Friend . . ." is typical, but it is doubtful that such words would have fallen easily from Scoresby's lips. Without warning the afternoon light falling through the clear panes suddenly deepened from pearl to gray, dark shadows were cast over the wedding couple, and a tremendous thunderstorm burst over Darlington. Katherine spoke hurriedly and the wedding certificate, beautifully illuminated in an album, was signed by the newlyweds and witnessed by Wilson Pease and Scoresby's sister Bessie Crick. Gathering her gown around her, Katherine led the wedding party out of the Meeting House into torrents of rain and flashing bolts of lightning.

The garden reception at Woodside was moved indoors, and while Kate Pease remained upstairs in her room, guests were served champagne and a huge buffet, photos were taken in the conservatory, and heaps of silver, silver plate, books, prints, and crystal were admired. Kate Pease's gift was an elaborate camera outfit—chosen personally by Katherine. Anne Sophia Twycross,

Scoresby's absent mother, sent the oddly impersonal *Murray's Oxford Dictionary*. Scoresby presented Katherine with an expensive diamond and ruby ring, a diamond necklace, a parasol with an ivory and silver handle, and a wristwatch. She gave him two gifts that symbolized their union with perfect, if unconscious, humor: a leather suitcase and a sovereign purse.

In the best Pease family tradition, at the end of the reception Mr. and Mrs. William Scoresby Routledge departed Darlington by private railroad carriage. Katherine wore an elegant dress of black-and-white-striped French tweed and a green embroidered vest. Determinedly refusing to live out the Victorian script handed, so long ago, to her spinster aunts, Jane and Emma, Katherine's future lay in a distant country with a man who was still a stranger but, she hoped, would become a friend. She looked forward, eager eyes on the horizon, to a partnership in life that would be interesting, imaginative, and exciting. Katherine and Scoresby, in a mysterious way, had independently arrived at points in their life where each was willing to change and then came together, with perfect psychological timing, in optimism and even some empathy. Seventeen years and thousands of miles later, however, Katherine Routledge remembered her wedding day with melancholy, telling her niece Hilda that "life cannot be all happiness" and "weddings are never all joy."

British East Africa:
Love, Sex, and Empire, 1906

✦

KATHERINE AND WILLIAM SCORESBY ROUTLEDGE SAILED
into Mombasa harbor on the morning of December 11, 1906, four months
after they were married. They departed the chaotic port town four days later
for the overnight journey to Nairobi via the pioneer railway known as the
"lunatic line." The Routledges settled into the newly completed Norfolk
Hotel, and Scoresby returned to Mombasa the next day to bring back two
expensive Arabian horses just arrived from Bombay. Feeling comfortable
and curiously at home, Katherine took the opportunity to explore Nairobi, a
rough-hewn frontier town built of wood and tin. She wandered down dusty
dirt roads shaded by groves of messy, fragrant eucalyptus trees, taking in the
sights and smells and the babbling cacophony of languages.

When Scoresby returned he was appalled at what Katherine had done and
promptly instructed Dosa bin Mishámi, his head groom, to keep a closer eye
on her. Katherine was flattered and Dosa became her shadow, "a delightful
person" who, "if he received orders to see I did not leave" during Scoresby's
absence, would "emphatically obey them!"

The central motivation of the Routledge marriage was travel, but they
were not aimless wanderers. They planned to spend two years in Africa and
had structured their journey as a scientific expedition. Thomas Athol Joyce,
assistant keeper in the Department of British and Medieval Antiquities and
Ethnography, British Museum, encouraged Scoresby to collect Kikuyu tribal
artifacts for the British Museum. (Joyce would later take a central role in
sparking the Routledges' interest in Easter Island.) Scoresby had a zoological kit from the British Museum of Natural History and a botanical kit from
the Royal Botanical Gardens, Kew. His main objective was to collect plant
specimens on the slopes of Mount Kenya, where, Katherine excitedly said, it
"is all new country."

Katherine was never greatly interested in artifacts or natural history, however. Scoresby said that, when he presented his Kikuyu friends to Katherine, "she found them so interesting that she devoted herself to gathering information in directions that I had passed over." Katherine was, in fact, a natural-born ethnographer, insatiably curious and intuitively skilled, and in Africa those elements of her personality that usually alienated people worked in her favor. Her attentiveness, usually taken for suspicion, directed her attention and made her a keen and often quite penetrating observer. Her obsessive and repetitive nature was transformed from authoritarian rigidity into a searching inquisitiveness that rooted out valuable information.

The Routledges practiced setting up their tents first in the Norfolk Hotel garden, and then, to test the rest of their equipment and make sure everything was in order, they established a shakedown camp a few miles outside Nairobi. Katherine's tent was pitched alongside Scoresby's and connected to it by an awning. It accommodated a cot, a portable writing desk that doubled as a dressing table, a folding safari chair, and Katherine's luggage. A small, attached tent served as her personal bathroom, complete with a canvas tub and tin washbasin cleverly balanced on tripod legs. Stable tents and servants' tents were pitched a distance away from the sleeping and cooking compounds, and at dusk, campfires and lanterns cast a romantic glow over the scene. When night fell, Katherine found that the African darkness brought back "nightmares of one's early days." Cries of hyenas and other beasts seemed uncomfortably close. Once a leopard was shot over a quarter of a mile away but Katherine, terrified, erected a protective barricade at the entrance to her tent. Amused, Scoresby told her that "no animal not in the furniture removing business would think of attempting to enter."

Katherine provisioned her first safari, from Nairobi to Fort Hall, with virtually no experience but the training in household management Kate Pease had given her. An analogy has long been drawn between a safari going into the bush and a ship going to sea—both are self-contained adventures into the ocean of nature. The requisite food and water, cooking pots, enamel dishes and utensils of every description, weapons and ammunition, books, and wardrobes of clothes were all assigned to numbered baskets, tin boxes, or specially constructed wooden crates. In addition to Katherine's modest camera outfit, Scoresby brought along a number of special lenses provided by the famed Dalmeyer, Ltd. of London and glass plates, chemicals, camera bodies and tripods, dry-plate negatives, silver bromide, and albumen paper. He intended to set up a field photo lab in a tent that acted as a makeshift darkroom or, when in camp, in the stone building he had constructed years earlier. Astonished at how much was needed by an English couple in search of the "simple life," Katherine nevertheless saw no irony in lamenting that it was "depressing" how openly the camp staff envied their wealth.

Katherine's wardrobe in the field was simple and practical. She knew "the blessings of a good thick skirt," but usually wore a more fashionable, shorter one topped off with a white shirt, jaunty sun helmet, gloves, puttees, and a safari jacket or long khaki coat with roomy pockets. When she rode horseback, she shed the skirt for trousers. The freedom from restrictive social convention that Katherine's wardrobe offered her was one of the things she loved best about Africa and, later, Easter Island. Modesty and vanity were of little concern to her, but the informal look she achieved was flattering to her figure and comfortable. She tried always to avoid insect bites and the threat of fever and protected her skin from the sun with rosemary creams, potions, and lotions of every description.

The day before the Routledges departed on safari to Fort Hall, seventy native African men dressed only in animal skins, their bodies glistening with red ocher and mutton fat, walked solemnly into camp. The men patiently lined up while the Routledges packed and unpacked repeatedly to achieve carrying balance and to bring each man's load to between forty and fifty pounds. Sometimes, Katherine said, she "looked on in agony" while Scoresby "with positive glee put cartridges in with 'respectability' clothes, and household belongings in the stationery box."

At 3 A.M. on the day of departure Katherine arose and, in the still-cold night air, pulled on khaki knickerbockers and a safari jacket, packed her personal things, and put them outside her tent. By 5 A.M. she and Scoresby had breakfasted and were silently watching the remains of the campfire, listening to the babble of tribal languages as the tents were struck. Then, she said, "to boot and horse" to make the most of the cool morning hours. Scoresby took the lead, followed by his gunbearers. Then came Katherine with Dosa and, in their wake, a caravan nearly one hundred strong.

The road had been widened from the 1902 track Scoresby remembered, and wound up and down through undulating grass flecked with acacia trees. The entire party proceeded at a walk until Katherine grew impatient and urged her high-strung Arabian horse to a gallop, only to have him toss her into the long grass, injuring nothing but her pride. As the sun climbed in the cloudless, equatorial sky, the day grew unbearably hot and the party halted near the Nairobi River. Exhausted and exhilarated, Katherine watched the unearthly amber and opal sunset, and then she and Scoresby dined together by firelight under a canopy of stars.

The second night out was a good deal less romantic. Beetles rained down on her tent, and then droves of mosquitoes attacked in a thick, black cloud.

Katherine, who obsessively feared malaria and was always troubled by high-pitched sounds, found their buzzing din hard to bear. She and Scoresby raised a mosquito net inside the largest mess tent and had dinner there, their food handed inside through a small flap. At 1 A.M. thousands of swarming red ants joined the fray. The Routledges fled ignominiously to one of the servants' tents and then moved camp well before dawn.

The Routledge safari made the sixty-eight miles between Nairobi and Fort Hall in five days, losing one day to a sudden rainstorm. Then they trekked another thirty miles over Jambo B'wana road, a rough track from Fort Hall to Nyeri. Nyeri had scarcely changed since its founding by Meinertzhagen in 1902 and was still nothing more than a few Indian shops (*dukas*) and some round mud huts. As they drew close to the territory of a local chief named Mun-gé, Katherine was treated to the sight of her husband being welcomed by laughing crowds of Kikuyu. Mun-gé presented them with a live sheep in honor of Scoresby's return, and Katherine was thronged to the point of embarrassment, welcomed with gifts of bananas, eggs, and a lovely native basket. Katherine was as delighted as a schoolgirl, and in her newlywed eyes, Scoresby cut a romantic figure. Her husband, Katherine said, "goes by the Swahili name of 'B'wana M'refu,' which being interpreted is Mr. Long. They are very anxious to know how many goats I cost!"

The Routledge homestead was in the "white highlands" about six thousand feet above sea level and only thirty miles south of the equator, set in a breathtakingly beautiful green and gold landscape studded with flame trees that rolled away from Katherine's eyes on an immense scale. Cuckoos, larks, sunbirds, and thrushes warbled and cooed at dawn, and starlings flashed iridescent in the midmorning light. Eland, wildebeest, and rhino were everywhere, and what sounded like rolling thunder at night was the rumble of lions in the dry grass. The Routledges took long rides together in the shadow of Mount Kenya and lived under a constant sense of the ancient, majestic mountain's presence. Whenever its craggy peaks were veiled in mist, Scoresby said, "there is a felt need in the landscape till it again appear. No wonder that the god of the Kikúyu lives on Kénya."

Katherine found that Africa imparted to her a "sensation of rest and space and freedom, of in some mysterious way 'coming into one's own.'" She felt a sense of simplicity that, she said, was either a "half unconscious recollection" of her own childhood innocence or a genetic memory of when "our forefathers also lived in simple communion with nature, in the childhood of the world." Kenya was a raw, richly sensuous environment; the air in the "white highlands" was exceptionally clear and pure, and breezes scented with exotic spices were said to cause sexual euphoria in *wazungus*—white people. Great love stories and scandalous liaisons, some of them immortalized in literature, were born in Kenya.

Katherine and Scoresby might have become lovers in Africa—for a time. They pitched their separate tents under the same thatched *banda* roof and shared crisp nights in front of a big fire, gazing at crystalline stars in a luminous sky. They rose at dawn and drank tea from Katherine's silver service at a little camp table covered with a cheerful cloth, then lingered over conversation. Katherine stayed out of the sun each day from eleven to four and then, after a formal tea, ventured out in the cool of the evening. Twilight was Katherine's favorite time, and each day ended with a hot bath and then a ritual glass of wine at sundown. In June of 1907 she wrote an admiring birthday letter to her niece Hilda. Written in Katherine's customary loopy scrawl, it is essentially one long, breathless sentence describing a hunt in which Scoresby shot a zebra and had the hide made into a rug for her tent.

Katherine wrote her family that the "gipsy outdoor life grows upon one for its own sake, and after all if one lays in nothing but numberless fresh impressions and interests, the time will not have been wasted." The Routledges, in fact, accomplished a good deal in Africa. They met their goal of collecting artifacts for the British Museum, where records show 116 entries for tools, weapons, and ornaments gotten in the vicinity of Mount Kenya and donated by Scoresby in 1910. Their main objective, to collect plants for Kew Gardens on the slopes of Mount Kenya, was only partially met, but for reasons beyond their control. The region was still considered unsafe, and to climb the slopes of the Kikuyus' sacred mountain, the Routledges were required to hire an armed escort. They chose, instead, to keep more or less within the boundaries of tribal lands belonging to chiefs whom they knew well.

The Routledges had sharply different interests and skills, and their interactions with native Africans reflected their unique personalities. Scoresby, for example, once asked a chief if he might be allowed to sacrifice a sheep to a major god "in the orthodox Kikúyu fashion." This astonishing request was reluctantly granted, but the location on which the sacrifice was enacted was deliberately chosen to prevent such an odd ceremony from contaminating the ancestral site that, for generations, had been used to honor Kikuyu gods. In the midst of the old chief's prayers, Scoresby interrupted, produced a recording machine, and asked the chief to repeat everything into it. Scoresby then insisted on having it all translated before the ceremony could proceed.

Katherine, in contrast, was more sensitive and effective. She simply tried to be a good neighbor to the Kikuyu, who, in turn, were considerate and friendly. "A tribute is due," Katherine wrote, "to the chivalry shown by Kikúyu chiefs to a white woman." One of the chiefs begged Katherine, when

Scoresby was absent, to move her tent nearer to his camp as "he would not like a white woman who was visiting him to be eaten by a lion." After six months in Africa Katherine had only learned a little "kitchen Swahili," but her main skills were directness, courtesy, and patience. She did not hesitate to show her dependence upon the Kikuyu and was grateful for the many favors they did her. Her reward was openness, and Katherine's observations of Kikuyu daily life and her collection of folktales comprise the earliest anthropological fieldwork by a woman in British East Africa. "My first introduction to a Kikúyu home," Katherine wrote, "was by means of an old lady who came to our camp to sell bags. I went back with her to her hut to pay a return call.

The winding path led along the hillside, with wide views over the smiling, undulating landscape, sinking away in the distance to the great Athi plains. We skirted the edge of the sacred grove, passed between patches of cultivated ground, to where, near the homestead, the young men of the party were sleeping in the sun, then down through springing corn to the little huts standing among a grove of bananas. My friend was a widow, and lived in one of them with her remaining child; another hut close at hand was the home of her elder and married daughter, who came with her baby to help to receive the visitor. We sat under the shade of the hut, and discussed the weather, the crops, and the grandchild, and felt that human and feminine interests were of more importance than the colour of skin.

Katherine walked with young women, their babies strapped on their bodies, to their *shambas,* or plots of cultivated ground, and helped them tend plants. She learned to prepare *posho,* a maize staple, and to roast meat on a spit. Sometimes she let her notebook and pencil lie idle and simply absorbed her surroundings. Katherine's relationship with the Kikuyu was quite different from Isak Dinesen's more celebrated one, but both women were moved by their "dignified ways . . . with a laughter like silver bells."

Each day, it seemed, Katherine crossed new cultural boundaries. She inquired into all manner of "things a woman wants to know," including betrothal and marriage, sex and childbirth. Kikuyu women, some of whom had surely known Scoresby as a single man, turned the ethnographic tables on her, and Katherine fielded many searching questions. Some wondered why she allowed her hair to grow so thick and long and did not shave her head in the Kikuyu manner. Others wanted to know why Katherine was childless and pitied her. It was a matter of intense curiosity that Katherine not only did not do heavy work, she had no co-wives to do it for her. Finally she had had enough, and Scoresby explained to a very skeptical Chief

Mun-gé—who was convinced Scoresby kept a harem in England—that he would not take a Kikuyu co-wife because "a white woman preferred to have her husband to herself."

In the spring of 1907 Katherine was the first white woman, so far as can be determined, to witness circumcision operations performed on boys and girls in British East Africa. She and Scoresby rode some distance to attend the initiation ceremonies and pitched their tents near the dancing ground. Not knowing quite what to expect, Katherine watched for two days as the youngsters, adorned with white paint and garlanded with cowrie shells, danced to exhaustion and then collapsed. In the early dawn of the third day the boys were operated on first, then taken away by their fathers and sponsors. The girls, who were about twelve years old, were then arranged in a row, two women seated behind each girl. One held the child's legs tight in the grip of her own, and an old woman, wielding a razor used for shaving the head, performed the operation on each girl in turn. Katherine watched this bloody ordeal but soon found it unbearable, and the Routledges pulled up stakes and departed at midday.

In Scoresby's words, female circumcision slices away "the nymphae and clitoris," causing great pain and considerable loss of blood. Katherine, who certainly understood the physiology of sexual pleasure, said that the "strain and excitement" of the rituals, not to mention the actual pain of the operation, had negative effects on personal development and changed young girls' lives "for the worse." By the 1970s, 74 million females had suffered genital mutilation and thousands more have, since then, risked their lives to speak out against it. The practice, nonetheless, is still part of contemporary African tribal life.

Katherine's health in Africa was generally good, but beginning in late August of 1907 and lasting through the rainy season until Christmas of that same year, she suffered what she said was a "somewhat severe illness." She had just celebrated her forty-first birthday, and the biology of fluctuating estrogen and progesterone may have produced anxiety and general malaise, but her other symptoms included the familiar ones of chills and fever, pain and sleeplessness, associated with stress. Katherine, as always, attributed these symptoms to malaria—then rampant in British East Africa—and assumed she had first encountered the disease in South Africa.

Medicines based upon opium were commonly used to treat malaria, or five grams of quinine were taken at the appearance of the first symptoms. Scoresby carried a full medicine chest on safari and kept both laudanum and quinine on hand. Quinine caused a constant, high-pitched ringing in the ears, a distressing side effect that was well-known but impossible to prevent. Katherine would have been driven to absolute distraction by such noises.

There is no direct evidence that she experienced episodes of auditory hallucination—her "voices"—during the two years she lived in Africa, but there is certainly the possibility that she did. She had her tent ritually purified, consulted a spiritual healer, and wore a charm he gave her to ward off evil.

Katherine's spirituality was based upon her unique synthesis of inner soul and intellect, but for at least ten years Spiritualism had helped her to account for and deal successfully with auditory hallucinations. One day when Katherine was alone in camp, Chief Mun-gé invited her to his village. Curious, she followed a dusty path to the chief's hut, where a large group of women were settled in the shade. Without a word, one of them pulled back the hide covering the door and beckoned Katherine to enter. Dust glimmered faintly in thin bars of pale and brittle light, and out of the darkness, one male voice after another rose in supplication, calling upon the spiritual power of the Kikuyu to provide rain and increase fertility of their herds and women.

Katherine took a place in the circle and, as her eyes became accustomed to the dimness, realized that she was the only female present. As a cup of mildly intoxicating, ceremonial beer was passed slowly from hand to hand, Katherine drank from it. Then the group sat for a long time in the "gathered silence" that, she wrote, "resembled precisely" a Quaker Meeting. Finally, the chief rose to leave the hut and Katherine followed. He handed the ceremonial cup again to her, and she passed it to the eldest of the assembled women. Intellectually, Katherine saw no difference between the Inner Light of Quakerism and the spiritual power of the Kikuyu. She was deeply impressed with the Kikuyu recognition that she deserved a central role in their ceremony.

By the spring of 1908 Katherine's romantic excitement had given way to malaise and disillusionment. As always there seems to have been a constellation of disappointments, but one of them may have emerged when she sought a more intimate relationship with her husband than he cared to have with her. Katherine wrote her brother Wilson, after just two years of marriage, that "I am so wretched" and "so tired," and he compared her to a lazy, unpleasant female character in a popular London play called The Mollusc. When Katherine referred to Scoresby as a "black sheep," Wilson speculated on the pain of what he considered to be her failed romance and replied, "Any husband is better than none. Most old maids are miserable."

Katherine pressed Scoresby for a meeting with a Kikuyu "medicine man," and the Routledges participated in what they called a séance in the shade of some big trees near their camp. The medicine man used "second sight" to commune with spirits of the dead, channel spiritual power, and predict the future. As a young boy he had suffered a severe illness that revealed his mystic calling—an event eerily close to Katherine's own childhood experience.

Scoresby, who was variously a religious skeptic, an agnostic, or an atheist, thought Katherine overly superstitious but, nonetheless, believed that African diviners and mystics "acted in good faith." In response to queries from the Routledges about whether their future lay in Africa or England, the Kikuyu medicine man invoked the gods of Mount Kenya, held aloft a calabash with incised designs, and then cast its stones, seeds, and other charms on the ground. He saw the shadows of past deaths on Katherine, he said, and predicted that Scoresby was going back to England "because of wives or war." He was right on all counts.

In the best tradition of her grandfather Joseph Pease, and perhaps with some prompting from his ancestral "voice," Katherine developed a "concern" for native Africans, who, in increasing numbers and at an alarming pace, were being taxed and evicted from ancestral lands. Though she held the patronizing opinion that native Africans were childlike in their need of English parental supervision, Katherine urged Scoresby to give up his homestead. She boldly and quite openly put forth the radical opinion that all white settlers were squatters.

This did not sit well with the insular white community in Nairobi nor, in fact, with Katherine's Pease relatives. In 1906, at about the time Katherine and Scoresby married, her cousin Sir Alfred Edward Pease had leased 4,998 acres of land at Kilima Theki, near the Kamba Reserve, on which he planned to start an ostrich farm. Alfred then acquired 1,010 more acres on supposedly inviolate native African lands, displacing hundreds of people. Without directly referring to Alfred—who was not, of course, the only one involved in such land speculation—Katherine said that she had made a "solemn promise to point out to the people of England that all reclaimed land in Kikúyu, whether under cultivation or lying fallow, is private property" and should not "be given to others."

An incident of sexual exploitation known as the Silberrad Affair then erupted. It began when Wombúgu, a chief whom Scoresby had known since 1902, officially complained to him about Mr. Hubert Silberrad, acting district commissioner at Nyeri. Silberrad—who held the post once filled by Scoresby's friend Hinde—had forcibly removed a thirteen-year-old girl named Wameisa from her village and taken her into his home as his concubine. He then ordered a second girl, who was a year younger and "belonged" to a native African policeman, to his home as well. The girl escaped and the policeman protested, but he was promptly beaten and jailed. Katherine, in what her critics considered a parody of outraged motherhood but which, in fact, was a gesture of great personal courage, marched alone on Nyeri and publicly claimed custody of Wameisa. She returned the girl to Chief Wombúgu, and Scoresby rode four days through the rain to report the entire incident to the governor.

Scoresby brought formal charges against Silberrad and forced the High Court to hold an inquiry at Nyeri from March 25 to 29, 1908. During the proceedings Scoresby, rather bizarrely, personally confronted Silberrad in his garden after dark. Silberrad begged him to drop the charges but Scoresby upbraided him and refused. The next day in court, as Katherine watched, Wameisa gave her evidence in a clear, credible way and the judge believed her. Silberrad was removed from his position at Nyeri and deprived of the right to govern a district for two years. His duty pay and seniority were lost and so was his opportunity for career advancement. A confidential memo was sent to the various government departments in British East Africa warning other officers against similar behavior, and the matter, it was assumed, was closed.

Scoresby, whose actions seem to have been motivated by more than mere animosity for corrupt bureaucrats, was not placated. In December of 1908 he wrote a righteous letter to *The Times* of London disclosing the entire event and naming Silberrad as the guilty party. He maintained that Silberrad's sexual morality was irrelevant—the issues were abuse of governmental power, infringement on chiefly authority, and destruction of tribal society. Prostitution on the streets of Nairobi was, Scoresby said, the only future for Wameisa and girls who, like her, were removed from chiefly protection.

Silberrad's colleagues—some of whom had their own sexual and homosexual skeletons in African closets—rushed to defend him. They publicly heaped scorn on Scoresby, saying he was a "youngish man" who did "nothing in particular." He was branded as an "officious, loquacious, self-important prig." Because he had described Wameisa as a child when, by African standards, she was a woman capable of marrying, Scoresby was said to misunderstand African culture. In fact, Scoresby knew perfectly well that Wameisa, like all native African females, was regarded within her culture as property. A blizzard of internal government correspondence accused Scoresby of being a jealous mischief-maker, suborner of witnesses, teller of lies, bearer of grudges, dictator of morals, and an "ignoramus who tries to gain the confidence of the natives" by speaking to them in a "vile jargon he calls Swahili." Scoresby was damned as a drinker and a hypocrite who had "intercourse with native girls."

Were Scoresby's enemies right in their assessment of his character and sexual behavior? The conspicuous lack of evidence supporting their claims—and their obviously self-serving need to discredit him—strongly suggests that they were not. Although she *had* described Scoresby privately as a "black sheep," there is no hint that Katherine ever, in all the years of her marriage, felt betrayed by infidelity. Whatever Katherine's original hopes for a "companionate" marriage had been, in the romantic world of Africa she had become infatuated with her husband and, quite probably, had sought a sexual relationship with Scoresby. If they had achieved intimacy—or even if they had not—by the time they departed Africa Katherine was resigned to a platonic relationship.

Scoresby's behavior during the Silberrad Affair was arrogant, aggressive, and self-righteous and created profoundly personal enemies who haunted him for many years. Surely sparked by issues of principle, the incident nonetheless reveals him as an extremely rigid and defensive man who assumed a highly critical and deeply parental, judgmental attitude. The Silberrad incident is only one of several well-documented instances in which Scoresby attempted to control the sexual behavior of younger men, and the impression is inescapable that he repressed and projected upon others what he found most shameful in himself. Tender feelings or sentiments were all intellectualized in Scoresby's life, and his own sexual fears were transformed into vigilance against the sexual weaknesses of others.

Katherine used her impressive political connections to have all of the documents pertaining to the Silberrad case brought before Parliament in open forum. The ensuing debate was heated. Her influential cousin Lord Daryngton declared that Scoresby had performed a "signal service, not only to the cause of morality, but to the people of this country." Daryngton indignantly asked if the defenders of Mr. Silberrad were "aware that Mrs. Routledge went to the house of this Silberrad and took these girls of twelve and thirteen away from him?" Another MP said, "We must all be grateful to the lady for the action which she took," and the House erupted in loud and sustained cheers for Katherine Routledge.

Katherine's return from British East Africa was a mixed blessing for the Gurney Pease family. Wilson found his favorite sister to be "no older, or redder, or thinner, just the same loving sister Katherine," but the notoriety of the Silberrad Affair was unwelcome to the entire Pease family, and Wilson did his best to keep it from Kate. The Routledges took a house at 36 Bedford Square, London, Scoresby wrote an article for *Man*, the journal of the Anthropological Institute, and they began a coauthored book about their African experiences.

Katherine renewed her friendship with Lyle, and the two women again became inseparable. Lyle took Scoresby's place at Pease family get-togethers and on holidays in Scotland, events he had always shunned. Katherine and Lyle attended séances conducted by the Fletchers and Spiritualist meetings in London. Katherine also renewed her acquaintance with friends active in the feminist cause. In June 1908 a crowd converged on Hyde Park to demonstrate in favor of votes for women, and Katherine, resplendent in Oxford cap and gown, marched in the procession. Three years later she joined yet another suffragette procession, but this time behind the blue banner of Somerville College and in company with over forty thousand other men, women, and children.

In December 1908 Katherine went home to Woodside for the Christmas holiday. A costume ball was planned at a neighboring estate, and Katherine got herself up in native African dress. On the morning of the party she made a grand entrance into her mother's sitting room: an antelope wraparound skirt painted in red ocher skimmed her bare knees, a hide cape was thrown around her shoulders, and dozens of wire, glass-bead, and cowrie-shell necklaces lay on her bare breasts. Her thick hair was piled high on her head, and ropes of beads and leaves were wound through it. As she stood barefoot on the hearth rug, the butler walked in and dropped a fully laden coffee tray in stunned surprise. Katherine went off to the ball that evening in African regalia, escorted by Wilson and Joan. Darlington society was properly shocked and Katherine was the hit of the party.

Katherine, who had long ago found acceptance and support within the feminist world, obviously brought home from Africa a new and irresistible feeling of expansive horizons, an enriched sense of self, and a healthy ability to express her sexuality—although she no longer professed a strong romantic interest in Scoresby. The Routledges' platonic, "companionate" marriage appeared to outsiders to be unequal, and some in Katherine's family recognized that she had the upper hand. A few thought that she treated her husband—the "poor chap!"—as a doormat. Scoresby, in contrast, led a life for the next nearly fifteen years that can only be described as asexual. Sir Richard Harington, his wife, and family were his closest friends; he was distant but not estranged from his sisters and their children. Scoresby's marriage formed his major touchstone.

In the late spring of 1910 the Routledges celebrated the publication of their book, *With a Prehistoric People: The Akikuyu of British East Africa,* and made the rounds of book-signing parties. Like their marriage, the book is a rather tentative union of forceful styles. Katherine's breezy, personal writing was more successful with the public than was Scoresby's careful, dull descriptions. He astutely noted the "stupendous change" in the African natural environment between 1902 and 1908 and spoke out with prescience against deforestation, water pollution, the hut tax, forced labor, and the disruption of tribal life by Europeans. Katherine presents the folktales she had collected and states her sources—admitting the problems created by translation. She preserved variations in the narratives but resisted the temptation to polish or embellish.

Katherine very quickly discovered that she was attractive to the news media. She hired a clipping service and filled albums with reviews, including some from prestigious journals such as *Nature* (where their book was favorably compared to E. B. Tylor's work). R. R. Marett lavished praise on Katherine. Oceanic scholar A. C. Haddon said Katherine had brilliantly provided "the woman's point of view" to the book. Remarking on the land issue, the Quaker publication *The Friend* pointed out that Katherine's "sympathy with the oppressed is hereditary." Harsh criticism, reflecting the nastiness surrounding the Silberrad Affair, came from the *East African Standard*, which accused the Routledges of being superficial, inaccurate, and sloppy. Katherine's unfortunate habit of describing the native Africans as "children" was condemned—although a Kikuyu man later said about Isak Dinesen, "We children called her our mother." Louis S. B. Leakey later referred to the Routledge book at least a dozen times in his *The Southern Kikuyu Before 1903*, but it is rarely cited today.

Katherine, whose illness remained in control if not in check, had gained a remarkable degree of self-knowledge and self-acceptance in just four short years as a married woman. Her interests in the field—and her voice in the book she and Scoresby had produced—were not reduced to second place or rendered invisible. In fact, *With a Prehistoric People* is living proof of Katherine's self-confidence and Scoresby's willingness to treat her as an equal partner. The fallout from the Silberrad Affair had damaged their reputations, but it also encouraged them to envision themselves as standing together against the forces of moral ambiguity and corruption. Their shared attraction to a migratory life was made stronger by Scoresby's disdain for London society, but the Routledges were uncertain about their future and unsure about their next move. A path then opened, as so often in Katherine's life, more by serendipity than deliberate choice.

◆

EASTER ISLAND

◆

Mana, 1910

✦

KATHERINE'S DREAMS OF ISLANDS AND SCORESBY'S OF
the sea were imparted to them as children on their nursery hearth rugs, but
not until "Ewers" came so fortuitously into their lives did they realize
how treasured—and attainable—those dreams were. In 1910 Katherine and
Scoresby rented a house for the summer in Bursledon, a little village situated
on a bay of the Hamble River near Southampton. There they stumbled upon
Ewers, a famous riverside cottage with a romantic history that enchanted
them. Scoresby bought the house in his own name, and the Routledges
entered the tightly knit community of sailors, fishermen, and yachtsmen.

Philemon "John" Ewers, a shipbuilder who constructed seven large ships
for the Royal Navy during England's war with France and Spain, had built
the house sometime before 1750. Perched so close to the river that, at high
tide, water washes over the brick terrace, Ewers endures today as a ship-
shape brick cottage facing cheerfully into the morning sun. Right next door,
on the downriver side, is the centuries-old Jolly Sailor Public House. Many
of today's pub customers arrive by boat, just as they did in Katherine's day.

Scoresby, who loved to bake, often prepared breads and pastry in a huge
fireplace in Ewers' roomy kitchen. The master bedroom has a charming view
of bustling river traffic and is connected by a clever wooden "bosun's pipe"
to the sitting room and kitchen downstairs. Katherine loved having breakfast
in bed, the wet, green smell of the river entering open windows and underlying the scorched scent of Scoresby's baking. She simply whistled into the
pipe, and coffee and warm rolls were brought up from the kitchen. In the
garden below were apple trees and roses, and Scoresby eventually converted
one of the boatyard storehouses into a Victorian-style "home museum"
housing Micmac "curios," African artifacts, and eventually, objects from
Easter Island.

The Hamble River flows into Southampton Water, where the tempting
shadow of the Isle of Wight—John Milne's home—rides the horizon and,

beyond, the open sea. The river's pull outward to adventure is so strong even landlubbers feel it, and for Scoresby, who had always dreamed of a sea journey, it was irresistible. Ewers was his starting place, but he had no fixed destination in mind. Kenya was out because Scoresby had given up his homestead claim and the Silberrad Affair had poisoned Africa for him. He considered going to Peru or the Canary Islands, but neither grabbed him. Then one day Thomas Athol Joyce, assistant keeper in the Department of British and Medieval Antiquities and Ethnography of the British Museum, suggested a destination to Scoresby that struck a resonant chord: Easter Island, a sixty-four-square-mile speck of land in the Pacific's Southern Hemisphere, midway between Tahiti and the Chilean coast of South America. Joyce enticed Scoresby with a profoundly alluring—even slightly reckless—dream he shared with A. W. F. Fuller, a London solicitor who became an internationally known collector of Pacific artifacts.

Fuller and Joyce believed that Easter Island's labyrinthine web of lava tubes and "secret caves" concealed priceless collector's items called *kohau rongorongo* (literally, "talking wood"), pieces of wood covered with tiny, incised characters representing an elusive "script" unique in the Pacific. The first of these objects only became known in 1868, and only about twenty-five examples of *kohau rongorongo* survive in various museums throughout the world today. Most of the inscriptions are short, but one example collected in 1870 has over two thousand characters. None of the inscriptions is dated, so no one knows when they first appeared on the island. A few roughly equivalent symbols are found carved on the island's rocks as petroglyphs, or superimposed on fallen statues (called *moai* in the Rapanui language). The meanings of the symbols have always been matters of scholarly controversy.

Joyce was convinced that *kohau rongorongo* held the secrets of who had discovered and settled Easter Island, and how and why they had carved the statues. He stressed to Scoresby that, if surviving old people on the island could be convinced to hand over hidden examples of *kohau rongorongo*, it would be an accomplishment of worldwide notice. Scoresby was intrigued with the South Seas as a refuge from English society, but he was also seduced by the idea of secret treasure and fame. His chief goal on Easter Island, from the beginning, was to discover and decipher examples of *kohau rongorongo*.

Not exactly sure where Easter Island was, Scoresby plunged into historical and yachting literature and read reports of early visits to Easter Island, compiling a chronological record of ships' calls. Katherine described her husband as "a keen yachtsman," but he had no maritime credentials. Neither did he have command of the sailor's rich vocabulary needed to communicate on such diverse topics as trawl nets, rigging, and navigation. Scoresby was, however, a quick and determined student, and he spent a lot of time talking to fishermen and sailors beneath the smoke-grimed rafters of the Jolly Sailor pub. By August of 1910 he was immersed in sea lore, lingo, and history, and he introduced the idea of Easter Island to Katherine.

"I was out certainly for fresh experiences," she later said, and she responded eagerly when Scoresby took her to the British Museum to see a superb Easter Island statue called Hoa Hakananai'a. Brought back by HMS *Topaze* in 1868, the statue is carved of smooth, dark basalt and stood then at the museum's entrance. To Katherine's eye it had a tremendous presence: power, dignity, and authority. In short order, she learned that on Easter Island there were vastly bigger statues still standing on the slopes of the volcano— called Rano Raraku—where they had been carved. Katherine's imagination was captured by the grandeur of vision and the strength of religious dreams that the statues conveyed. She failed at first to see the intricacies of the statues' disarmingly obvious design, but was immediately touched by their timelessness.

From the start, the Routledges framed four basic questions—all of which were then genuinely perplexing mysteries: Who were the original people who had discovered and settled remote and nearly inaccessible Easter Island? Where had they come from, and when? What, exactly, did the statues mean? How are the statues linked to the present inhabitants of the island? This was not the first time—or the last—that such questions were asked, but in their simplicity and directness, they were right on target.

The large size and number of the statues—there are 887 of them— contrasted sharply with the island's landscape: It was virtually treeless at the time of European contact and remained so when Katherine saw it. This apparent gap between culture and nature was the greatest mystery of all. Captain James Cook, whose ship *Resolution* called at Easter Island in 1774, was the first to state clearly the puzzling disparity between the magnificence of the built environment and the apparent paucity of available wood resources.

Writers of the fantastic rushed to fill the gap. One of the more bizarre tomes claimed that Easter Island was part of the mythical lost continent of Lemuria. When Lemuria supposedly disappeared under the sea, a reincarnated, clairvoyant Third Race of Giants said to live there also vanished, "leaving Easter Island and the statues as its witness." Although she found such fantasies interesting, it is to her everlasting credit that Katherine resisted the seductive pull of paranormal mystification.

Scoresby's opinion was that the real discovery of Easter Island by its original Polynesian settlers was a far greater mystery than anything concocted by pseudoscience. T. A. Joyce (whose scholarly expertise was in New World prehistory) was drawn to the possibility, suggested by a Catholic missionary as early as 1803, that the Pacific may have been settled from Peru. Several Fellows of the Royal Geographical Society put great store in the notion, and language, Joyce believed, would resolve the question of whether Easter Island culture was Polynesian or South American. Scoresby put greater store in physical anthropology. His major field goal, therefore, became twofold: to collect examples of *kohau rongorongo* and, as well, human remains.

Writing in 1920 and preparing for a return to the Pacific in search of Easter Island origins, Katherine anticipated the comparative strategy of historical anthropology used today in Polynesian studies. "In dealing with any scientific problem," she said, "the first step naturally is to find out all that can be discovered . . . while the second is to co-ordinate that material with similar examples elsewhere, so that knowledge which may fail from one source, can be supplied from another." The Routledges now prepared to take the first step.

Mounting an international scientific expedition meant that bureaucracies were the first hurdles to be faced—but here Katherine excelled. She fired off dozens of letters to friends and relatives soliciting introductions, affiliations, funds, and assistance in cutting through red tape. For scholarly support and justification she turned first, as always, to R. R. Marett. He and Joyce helped her form an advisory committee made up of experts in the cultures of the western Pacific. The committee's direct involvement in pre-expedition planning was limited to letters of introduction or advice.

W. H. R. Rivers was then one of the more influential figures in British academia. A psychologist, he had spent 1907–8 doing fieldwork in Melanesia (Pacific islands northeast of Australia). A. C. Haddon was a Cambridge scholar who, in 1898, had led an expedition to the Torres Strait Islands (between Queensland, Australia, and Papua New Guinea). C. G. Seligman, a pioneer survey ethnographer, had published *The Melanesians of British New Guinea* in 1910. The work of each of these men, to varying degrees, influenced Katherine's postexpedition thinking. Bolton Glanville Corney (who was an expert on early European contact with the island) lent his expertise as well.

Katherine went up to London, ensconced herself at the Ladies' Empire Club, and haunted the Reading Room at the Royal Geographical Society— where book checkout slips in her own hand are still on file. She amassed her own library of Oceanic history and, throughout the fall and winter months of 1910–11, read it all. Katherine was not able, given the preliminary state of Polynesian research at the time, to pull together a complete picture of Easter Island history, and the Routledges were not fully aware of what they were getting into.

Katherine's thumbnail sketch of Easter Island began with a physical description. Isolated in the East Pacific, in an extreme windward position, the island lies at latitude 27°9' S, longitude 1090°26' W. It is 2,340 miles west of Chile and 1,400 miles southeast of Pitcairn, its nearest neighbor and home to *Bounty*'s famous mutineers. Mangareva lies beyond Pitcairn, and the Rout-ledges considered both islands to be probable starting points for Easter Island's Polynesian settlers.

Easter Island, Katherine learned, has no protective coral reef. Its roughly triangular shape was created by the coalescing flows of three massive submarine volcanoes—each of which marks a point of the triangle. Smaller volcanic cones punctuate a landscape of gently rolling hills and grassy, rock-strewn slopes. Soils are reddish-brown clays and loams, weathered but rather fertile. Winds are changeable but nearly constant. The climate is subtropical and rainfall is moderate, but Easter Island is no South Seas par-adise. Environmental hazards include drought and tidal waves.

Katherine surveyed the broad strokes of customs, arts, and languages in Oceania, then extended her research to the megalithic cultures of Indonesia, returning eastward to try to get a better look at the Austral Islands and the Gambiers (of which Mangareva is a part). Frustratingly little information was available, although she read Christian missionary accounts of Tahiti and Hawaii. Easter Island was stumbled upon on Easter Sunday, 1722, by the three ships of Dutch admiral Jacob Roggeveen, who named the island in honor of the day. He was followed by a Spanish expedition led by Felipe Manuel González y Haedo in 1770 and, four years later, by Captain Cook. In just fifty-two years, therefore, two generations of Easter Island people had encountered the languages, material culture, and behavior of three distinctly different European nations. The impressions these visitors made, and the effects they had on island culture, were significant.

From their first contact with Europeans, islanders had bartered food for nails, mirrors, tools, and other European goods. They traded away precious art objects and snatched hats and other items of clothing off unsuspecting sailors. It is notable, however, that they never perpetrated a single known incidence of bloodshed. Europeans, in contrast, inflicted random incidents of violence and, in 1805, vicious kidnappings. Between 1862 and 1863 islanders experienced trauma and disaster society-wide. In that year some twenty to thirty Peruvian slave ships called at the island—with as many as eight anchored off the coast at one time—and an estimated fifteen hundred islanders (approximately half of the population) were abducted. These unfortunate people were sold at auction into household service and manual labor in Peru, and others were destined for work in the guano mines. In partial response to this horrific situation, Eugène Eyraud, a French Catholic lay brother, established a mission on the island in 1863. He became the tormented target of an enraged Rapa Nui war chief named Torometi, and Eyraud's superiors, fearing for his life, removed him.

In 1864 about twelve to fifteen islanders were returned to the island from Peru. Their grieving families naturally took them in, but they brought a variety of diseases with them that blossomed into epidemics and killed many. Eyraud stubbornly returned to the beleaguered island in 1866, bringing with him another priest and three Mangarevan assistants. Joined later in the year by two additional priests, Eyraud's formidable team established two missions. The main one was in Hanga Roa, the island's only village, and a smaller station was at Vaihu, on the southeast coast. Within a year they had converted the islanders—at least superficially—to Catholicism, and by 1868 they had baptized every person.

The year 1868 was a watershed in the nineteenth-century history of Easter Island. Ostensibly converted to Christianity, islanders traded away important objects (including the first-known *kohau rongorongo*) and abandoned the practice of an ancient religious ritual—the *tangata manu,* or birdman ceremony. Then, with uncanny serendipity, two ships destined to figure prominently in Easter Island history appeared on the horizon. HMS *Topaze* put a crew ashore and, with the cooperation of the missionaries and Torometi, removed the basalt statue Hoa Hakananai'a—a centerpiece of the birdman rituals—to England. The other ship carried a French sea captain, a man in the old and unscrupulous privateer tradition: Jean-Baptiste Onèsime Dutrou-Bornier (whom the islanders dubbed Pitopito).

Driven by ambition and a nasty personality, Dutrou-Bornier terrorized missionaries and islanders alike. One of the Catholic priests, Father Roussel, was ordered by the Church to leave, and he took more than 150 Rapa Nui people with him to Mangareva. By the end of 1872 another 250 had departed for Tahiti. Only about 111 islanders remained, out of a contact-era population conservatively estimated at about 4,000. Dutrou-Bornier took an island woman as his "queen" and established a despotic little empire at Mataveri, a fertile plain at the base of Rano Kau (spelled *Rano Kao* by Katherine), one of the island's three formative volcanoes. Mataveri, as Dutrou-Bornier probably knew, had been the traditional staging ground for the birdman ceremonies. Finally, the islanders had had enough of Dutrou-Bornier and murdered him.

John Brander, an entrepreneur who was married to Titaua, the daughter of prominent trader Alexander Salmon and a Tahitian princess, had backed Dutrou-Bornier. At Brander's death his brother-in-law, Alexander Salmon Jr. (1855–1914; called Arii Paea), became partner/manager of all Rapa Nui enterprises. He established himself at Vaihu, on the southeast coast of the island, on land Dutrou-Bornier had confiscated from the mission, but the Catholic Church (in the person of Bishop Etienne "Tepano" Jaussen) asserted its right to 1,482 acres in Hanga Roa. This land became a refuge, a tiny island within an island, and most of the population relocated there, huddled around the abandoned mission. In a move that would resound forty years later and impact Katherine's work on Easter Island, the Church also claimed one-third ownership of all Brander livestock.

Salmon's stay on Easter Island precisely bracketed two important expeditions: a German group led by Lieutenant-Captain Wilhelm Geiseler and the USS *Mohican* survey, spearheaded by Paymaster William J. Thomson. Salmon, who avidly excavated caves and other sites and brokered sales of artifacts, served as go-between for both. In 1888 the government of Chile officially annexed the devastated island, and the Brander interests sold out to a Chilean naval family. Salmon departed and a remarkable islander named Nicholás Pakarati Urepotahi returned from French Polynesia, where he had trained to be a Catholic lay preacher, or catechist. He established his ministry in Hanga Roa, raised a family, became a central figure in the community, and played an important role in Katherine's work on Easter Island. Ten years later "the whole of Easter Island" was the property of one Enrique Merlet, an individual destined to be hated with as much passion as Dutrou-Bornier ever was.

Merlet eventually formed La Compañía Explotadora de la Isla de Pascua (the Company—literally, "the company to exploit the island") with Williamson, Balfour Co., an immensely successful, Valparaíso-based Scottish shipping and trading firm. The Company imported a starter flock of four hundred to five hundred merino sheep and took over the Dutrou-Bornier stronghold at Mataveri as its headquarters. A Chilean named Alberto Sanchez, accompanied by his family, managed the island for five years until Merlet decided he was too soft on the islanders and replaced him with Horace (Horacio) Cooper. Cooper strong-armed the islanders into building miles of stone walls and wood fences that locked them into the village and made the rest of the island off-limits. He also hunted down sheep poachers mercilessly until he was forced to flee the island in well-deserved fear for his life. Before doing so, Cooper handed over the manager's job to another Englishman: Percival (Percy) Henry Edmunds.

Edmunds, a traveler, amateur photographer, and dealer in artifacts, was born in Hampton on January 23, 1879. He was the son of John Edmunds and Ida M. Thornley, and his grandfather had founded the Midland Bank. Before arriving on Easter Island in 1908, Edmunds' last stop had been Argentina, where he had lived for about seventeen years and, some said, left behind a wife and at least one child. Because he was the "sole representative of both Company and government," Edmunds held complete power over the islanders. As enterprising, in his way, as Scoresby had been among the Micmacs, Edmunds energetically excavated caves for examples of *kohau rongorongo* and collected and commissioned artifacts, forwarding them to his mother for sale in England. Ironically, it was Edmunds' stories to collector A. W. F. Fuller that had sparked T. A. Joyce's interest in Easter Island, and he, as we have seen, encouraged the Routledges.

Edmunds communicated with islanders in a mixture of English and Spanish until he learned Rapanui. A capable and tough rancher, he was not afraid to get his hands dirty. In everything, however, he relied heavily on an islander named Juan Tepano, his foreman. Tepano, who was just one year younger than Katherine, had been set apart years earlier by his adaptability to outsiders and willingness to participate in larger Chilean culture. He was destined to become an indispensable, central figure in Katherine's work and later became famous as a prominent ethnographic "informant" or consultant for several cultural anthropologists who followed in her footsteps. The cost of such prominence to Tepano's life, however, was not inconsequential.

The Routledges, of course, recognized that colonial rule on Easter Island had an unsavory side, but they were not fully aware of the more sordid and tragic details. That is, in part, because Peruvian slave-raid records were in Spanish, and Catholic missionary documents were in French. Katherine did not read the most important missionary papers until 1917, a year after her return to England. Perhaps if the Routledges had been better informed, they might have reacted more sympathetically to some events they later lived through or caused on the island, but that is impossible to say. In any event, to land on Easter Island and then remain there for the planned six months, the Routledges needed permission and logistical support from Chilean officials, Williamson, Balfour Co., and Enrique Merlet. Most important, they needed the goodwill of Percy Edmunds.

Over the next two years Scoresby corresponded often with Merlet and Edmunds from Ewers, Bedford Street, and the Conservative Club. Most of the letters were sent out in Scoresby's name, but Katherine typed and signed them. To introduce the serious intent of the expedition they sent a copy of *With a Prehistoric People* to Williamson, Balfour Co. Merlet and the company had been strongly criticized in Chile because of their heavy-handed ways with impoverished islanders, and it is somewhat of a mystery why they so openly accommodated the Routledges. Part of the reason, certainly, was that Katherine lined up an impressive array of endorsements, and when that was combined with the influence of Pease business and political connections, the expedition was hard to resist.

Scoresby drew up a list of seven basic queries, including means of communication and type of accommodation available, cost of labor, type of land transport, varieties of food, and the nature of seasonal weather variation. The Company responded promptly that the manager's house was available, a "large roomy bungalow with six rooms, capable of lodging 12 persons. It would probably require a thorough scrubbing." They did not, however, mention that Edmunds was occupying it. Caves were recommended as suitable camping places when they were in the field, but it was also suggested that the Routledges bring good tents to protect against the rain. Horses were available but the Routledges needed to provide their own saddles and tack.

Scoresby asked if fever or other diseases existed on the island. He was flatly told that there were none, but in fact extremely serious respiratory diseases were common, and leprosy (Hansen's disease) had been introduced in the mid-1800s. About a dozen islanders were confined, without medical care, to a squalid leper colony set some distance apart from the village of Hanga Roa. A similar number of islanders without the disease also lived there, choosing to risk exposure rather than to be separated from family members or friends.

The Routledges were told that all of the islanders were "in service to the Company" at "very low wages." About forty men were in the available labor pool, but women and children also worked. "Payments will not be made in money, which is of no use to the natives, but in articles from the Company's store." Families shared as a group in the food or goods received or traded by individuals and cared for their own old or infirm members. Juan Tepano, however, looked after a small group of old men who were alone in the world. The Routledges found out rather quickly after their arrival that the Company's age-old system of debt enslavement held the deeply resentful islanders in an iron grip.

Easter Islanders were always referred to in the Routledge-Company correspondence as *Kanaka* (*Canaca* in Spanish), the Hawaiian variation of *tangata*, meaning "people." Even in Katherine's time "Kanaka" was considered improper (if not racist) when used by Europeans, and it certainly is today. In 1912 William Churchill pointed out that the indigenous name for the island, if one had ever existed, was not known. Instead, in the 1800s repatriated islanders had coined *Rapa Nui* (Big Rapa) to distinguish it from another island, Rapa Iti. Katherine's fieldnotes show that islanders referred to themselves as *Rapa Nui* or as *Pascuense* (from the Spanish Isla de Pascua), but she inexplicably persisted in the offensive colonial term *Kanaka*.

A wide range of political and organizational difficulties and the Routledges' own inexperience made the expedition, in Katherine's words, "a much larger undertaking than had been contemplated; we had our doubts of our capacity for so important a venture; and at first the decision was against it but we hesitated and were lost." Once they had committed themselves to Easter Island the biggest decision the Routledges faced was how they were going to get there. Williamson, Balfour Co. owned *Falcon*, a small schooner that could be chartered, complete with an experienced crew, from Chile to Easter Island. After seeing a photo and plans, Scoresby offered to purchase *Falcon*, but was turned down.

The Routledges then made a risky and adventurous choice: They decided to build their own yacht, hire an English crew, and sail to Easter Island. It was an incredible stretch for them, a daunting and even dangerous, impractical proposition. Katherine was immediately met with a discouraging range of objections from nearly everyone she knew, including some women friends who considered themselves quite avant-garde. Only the ever-supportive R. R. Marett never hesitated to show enthusiasm and provided unfailing encouragement once the decision was made. Katherine's willingness to undertake such a South Seas challenge is a direct and positive measure of her self-confidence and the driving power of her vision.

By January of 1911 Katherine had arranged the necessary financing for their dream ship's design and construction. The first set of plans drawn up for the vessel proved frustratingly unsatisfactory, and they turned to Charles Nicholson of Gosport, a famous (and costly) designer. He completed a second set of plans in the summer of 1911 (a real work of art still on file with Lloyd's of London). Built to Lloyd's highest standard by Whitstable Shipping Co. Ltd., the vessel's owner was listed only as W. Scoresby Routledge, although Katherine paid the bills. The keel was laid in the fall of 1911, and Scoresby wrote to Percy Edmunds that the expedition would set sail in time for Katherine's birthday on the eleventh of August 1912. They planned, he said, to stop en route in Rio de Janeiro to witness a total eclipse of the sun on October 10, reaching Easter Island by February 1913.

Serious delays in the yacht's construction, however, resulted from Scoresby's obsessive attention to detail and frequent disagreements over the installation of such comforts as steam heat and electric light. He spent months researching a state-of-the-art auxiliary paraffin (kerosene) engine that would allow him to escape exorbitant towing charges in foreign ports. He finally purchased one in Glasgow that was encased in a steel box with a complex water-cooling system and had a theoretical speed capability of 5.5 knots. Not satisfied, Scoresby meddled with every aspect of the engine's design and construction, suggesting modifications and changes that ate up time and Katherine's money.

At Scoresby's insistence Nicholson also designed four costly galvanized-steel watertight bulkheads. Convinced the yacht was "unsinkable," Scoresby was shaken when *Titanic* went down in April 1912, her double-bottomed hull and sixteen watertight compartments unable to prevent the loss of 1,513 lives. Scoresby demanded repetitive redesigns of the yacht's bulkheads, finally driving Katherine into a lawsuit against the builders (which she won). In spite of so many problems, Katherine proudly watched as the yacht blossomed and then matured into a lovely product of her intimate, creative collaboration with Scoresby.

Shortly before noon on a Thursday in late May 1912, a small knot of people shuffled around the boatyard of Whitstable Shipping Co. The sky was overcast, but as Katherine climbed a shaky wood ladder, the sun came out brilliantly. She broke a bottle of red wine against the vessel's side and, with a lump in her throat, intoned, "I name this ship *Mana*, and may the blessing of God go with her and all who sail in her." Scoresby had lobbied to have the yacht named after the Reverend William Scoresby, but Katherine took R. R. Marett's suggestion and chose the Polynesian word *mana* because of its brevity—but more important, because of its spiritual meaning and good-luck connotations. A somewhat scruffy, droll, and very bright young Oxford man named Osbert Guy Stanhope (O.G.S.) Crawford, present that day as a working member of the crew and the expedition's official anthropologist, disparagingly whispered that *mana* was an "untranslatable" word and that Katherine had simply "picked it up" from Marett in an effort to flatter him.

In August, probably to celebrate her forty-sixth birthday, Katherine went north to Woodside to say good-bye to her family. She was free of her usual health problems, happy, and, it seems, at peace with her marriage. Katherine invited her family to see *Mana*, but the weather had been constantly rainy for weeks and no one wanted to make the journey. Wilson finally agreed to visit as soon as the skies cleared, and Katherine later wrote a gracious note to his wife, Joan: "You and Wilson . . . are the nicest couple I know. Scoresby and I have our good points. Still, I think that you & Wilson are nicer." Katherine hired a Darlington photographer to take a formal Gurney Pease family portrait that echoed others taken at Woodside in years past. Harold and Gwen had disappeared from the family circle, but Katherine and Lilian dutifully sat on either side of their mother. Two of Kate Pease's daughters-in-law stood behind her, and three of her four grandchildren arranged themselves at her feet. When Katherine left Woodside it was the last time she ever saw her mother.

A month or two later Wilson Pease arrived in the little village of Hamble. As the cab pulled up in the square, Katherine's radiant face suddenly appeared at the window. Her cheeks were rosy with sea air and she was breathless, her hair escaping in tangles from a yellow oilskin cap. Wilson alighted from the cab and hugged her, then walked with his happy sister down to the river's edge.

Katherine and Wilson climbed into a launch that plowed downriver toward Southampton Water, then pulled abreast of *Mana*, her new red-and-white Royal Cruising Club burgee fluttering in the breeze. Scoresby, in a heavy wool jacket and with a cigarette clamped between his teeth, welcomed them aboard. Katherine proudly took Wilson around the sturdy, ninety-foot schooner, oak decking gleaming and copper and brass polished to a warm gloss. She climbed agilely over cargo boxes, nautical equipment, and drums of fuel, then took him into the deckhouse. Piles of paperwork were stacked neatly on her little desk, and Katherine explained how she had painstakingly calculated the provisions they would need to feed themselves and the crew on the first leg of the voyage out. Using all of the skills she had mastered on safari, Katherine had crated, labeled, and then stowed everything in exactly the same order it was to be removed from the hold for use, and Wilson marveled at his very organized sister.

Katherine took her brother below and into the pine-paneled saloon with its sofa, table, and bookshelves. She would be sharing this tiny space with her husband and three other men, and Wilson was astounded that his normally demanding sister was dealing so cheerfully with such cramped quarters. Just as they had had separate tents on safari, Scoresby and Katherine each had a cabin aboard *Mana*. Hers was lovingly modeled after her Oxford student sitting room and had three photographs framed and mounted on the wall. One was of her family just taken at Woodside in August, another of Kate Pease with all four of her grandchildren, and the third was Wilson's pensive pose enlarged from the family photo. On the wall at the foot of her bed a local carpenter had carved and painted one of Katherine's favorite biblical texts: "Though I take the wings of the morning and dwell in the uttermost parts of the sea, even there shall Thine hand lead me, and Thy right hand shall hold me."

The Routledges prepared lunch together and Wilson thought the food was very good. After lunch he and Katherine again got into the launch so she could show him Ewers. They alighted right at the front doorsteps of the house and Katherine led Wilson inside. Seeing his proud sister so happy, Wilson told her he thought the house was charming, and that "I would be happier living in this cottage than in any Surrey villa."

They walked through the garden and up the path to the road at the back of the house. A quarter of a mile down the lane they came to St. Leonard's church and crossed the leaf-strewn grass of the burial ground. They wandered about and read aloud to each other the quaint phrasing on the tombstones, then entered and sat in one of the pews in front of an ancient tablet erected to the memory of John Ewers. Katherine tried to express to her brother the complex feelings of reverence, closeness to history, and homely pride of place that Ewers had given her. Her riverside life—and the vessel she and Scoresby had created—was a genuinely sublime moment in her marriage. Perhaps, as well, she shared with Wilson her fears: of the drudgery, boredom, loneliness, and dangers of a long voyage, or of ignoble failure on Easter Island. As dusk fell and it got closer to train time, Wilson found himself walking hand in hand with his sister into the station and not knowing when, if ever, he would see her again.

The Mana Expedition:
Sailors, Scientists, and Spies

✦

KATHERINE WAS THE ONLY WOMAN ON A TEN-PERSON crew composing two very different types of men: paid sailors and unpaid scientists. From the start, her presence was resented and some disliked her. This might have been avoided if personnel had been selected with a sharp eye to group dynamics. Unfortunately, that was not done and the Routledges' personalities complicated everything. Scoresby tended to see things only in black and white while Katherine usually tried to see the other fellow's good points. She tried to avoid unnecessary conflict and believed she was evenhanded. Others, however, saw her as stubborn and narrowly opinionated. Neither Scoresby nor Katherine had strong interpersonal skills, and Scoresby, who was intractable and could be incredibly petty, lacked leadership ability.

The Routledges advertised for Mana Expedition crewmen and interviewed dozens of applicants before hiring a captain and full crew that, for reasons not entirely clear but certainly as a result of massive dissatisfaction, deserted en masse just before Christmas of 1912, while *Mana* was still in Southampton. After that nasty setback, the Routledges began again. The most important position was that of sailing master, or captain. They needed a resourceful and patient man, capable of facing down everything from fogs and gales to ugly tempers and shipwrecks with nothing but a strong cup of tea, a vast storehouse of knowledge, and an ability to make decisions— whether *Mana* was becalmed or caught in a whirling chaos of water and wind.

Seamanship is equal parts intelligence and experience, and Henry James Gillam had ample stores of both. When he read the Routledges' advertisement for a sailing master, Gillam was in Kobe, Japan, and had spent the previous year as captain aboard a private yacht that called at far-flung ports from

Venice to Singapore. Born in Emsworth, Hampshire, in 1876, he was the thirty-six-year-old son of a miller. His mother had died before Gillam was five years old, and that loss accounted, in part, for his later resourcefulness in life. His father had raised him and his younger sister, Sarah, with the help of his late wife's sisters. When Gillam was old enough to leave home he joined the merchant marine and then married Ada Maria, settled her in their modest home in Portswood, Southampton, and went back to sea.

When Katherine met Gillam he had crisp, reddish hair with a touch of gray curl. His face was lined from exposure to sun and sea and his eyes crinkled lavishly at the corners whenever he flashed his warm smile. Pensive and usually reticent, he had a modest, assured manner that inspired confidence. Gillam had a colorful accent—dropping every *h* in the manner of Eliza Doolittle speaking to 'enery 'iggins—and his even temper was evident to Katherine from the start. Although they had disagreements throughout the voyage, Katherine never criticized Gillam and said flatly that "the successful achievement of the voyage" was due to his skill.

In addition to Gillam there were five other paid, regular crew members. Mate Frank Preston was forty-nine years old, with a lush mustache and graying hair. Hired as deck officer, one rank below Gillam, he had years of experience on private yachts. He was not loquacious but was loyal, with a real dedication to the sea. Albert Light was a burly, skillful Brixham seaman "with a face just like an apple." Liked by everyone, he was expert at any rigging or sailing tasks, but would have nothing to do with the ship's engine or power supply. Katherine was uncharacteristically open and willing to listen to what she considered Light's "intelligent criticism" and thought that his sense of humor added a great deal to the "amenity of the voyage."

Frank T. Green, from Glasgow and twenty-five years old, was not a professional seaman, but was recommended by the builder of the yacht's engine for the post of ship's engineer. He was a keen and very good photographer and, for six months on Easter Island, acted as official Mana Expedition photographer. Green, who never learned the seaman's lesson of avoiding or ignoring land-based differences, caused unnecessary friction with his outspoken Socialist views. Scoresby (always a Conservative) never liked him. Green considered Scoresby to be an annoying yachting pretender and inept meddler in mechanical things and disliked Katherine. By the end of his time on Easter Island Green flatly despised Scoresby, and the Routledges rightly regarded him as a manipulative, gossipy troublemaker not above sabotaging the yacht's engine.

Charles Giffard Jeffery joined at Whitstable. Just eighteen years old, he was an eager young man with a round face, ready smile, and high hopes for the future. Brought up with the fishing fleet, he yearned to spend his life in the merchant marine. He looked to Gillam as a mentor but Katherine, like her aunt Jane before her, enjoyed the company of bright young men and affectionately regarded Jeffery as her protégé. Jeffery spent a few weeks ashore on Easter Island, but his assistance to the expedition was limited by his responsibilities to Gillam.

This core crew remained throughout most of the voyage, although cooks and stewards changed in nearly every port. F. W. Shephard was the first to take the job of cook, and George Smith, who was the last man hired before sailing from Falmouth, replaced a steward fired after only a matter of weeks. At least seven other men were discharged, while three chose to desert rather than labor under Katherine's exacting eye. She outlined daily duties literally minute by minute from the crack of dawn. Stewards reported for duty at 5:15 A.M. promptly, cleaned cabins and the bathroom, scrubbed decks, polished brass and did laundry and then, at last, took their first morning break at 11 A.M. At 1 P.M. each day they served luncheon, at 4 P.M. tea, and at 7 P.M. supper. The rest of the time was divided into tedious and very specific tasks at fifteen-minute intervals until 9 P.M.

Easter Island is small and absolutely isolated in the wide-open southeast Pacific, and while Gillam had superb "rule of thumb" navigational skills, greater abilities were required. Scoresby requested the loan of a navigator from the Admiralty. The first man he engaged is not known, nor is his reason for leaving the expedition. The second was Lieutenant R. Douglas Graham, Royal Navy. Graham was willing and enthusiastic but quite eccentric. His main hobby was dancing, and he was an expert on the pseudoscience of Atlantis and Lemuria. Katherine initially liked Graham and described him as "brilliant," but he clashed with Scoresby and Gillam over the chain of command and use of the titles captain and sailing master. After he departed the expedition, Graham never forgave Scoresby and followed news accounts of the voyage with scathing distaste. Lieutenant David Ronald Ritchie, Royal Navy, replaced him.

When he first laid eyes on *Mana*, Lieutenant Ritchie saw a vision of his own double-masted dream ship and fell in love. Ritchie approached *Mana* with his heart on his sleeve, and Scoresby saw it immediately. Tall, slight, with fine, light reddish brown hair, wire-rimmed glasses, and a serious demeanor, Ritchie was twenty-six years old and single, a career naval officer just home from China. Born in Glasgow, he was the son of a wine merchant. Lieutenant Ritchie had joined the Royal Navy as a midshipman in 1903, passed nine seamanship exams (including gunnery and torpedo), qualified as a navigator, and attained the rank of lieutenant by 1908. His conduct reports include words like *zealous, capable, careful and observant, skillful, trustworthy,* and *methodical.* Katherine found Ritchie dull and lacking in interests, but by the time they parted company on Easter Island she was fond of him. Scoresby immediately offered him the job.

Ritchie was a regular (full-time and active) Royal Navy officer during his stint with the Mana Expedition and never considered himself to be under the command of either the Routledges or Gillam. Ritchie kept his own counsel and maintained social distance from the Routledges, and by the time *Mana* reached Talcahuano, Chile, heartily disliked them both. On February 24, 1913 (just four days before *Mana* departed Southampton for Easter Island), Royal Navy paperwork lending Ritchie for special service to the Mana Expedition—on full pay—was finally completed.

This unusual arrangement was due entirely to the fortuitous timing of the Mana Expedition, which overlapped the increasingly tense, pre–World War I naval rivalry between Germany and Great Britain. The most powerful German surface force in the Pacific was the East Asiatic squadron of fast cruisers under the celebrated Admiral Graf Maximilian von Spee. The Germans, to the far-thinking Admiralty, might one day threaten merchant shipping on Britain's Pacific trade routes, and Lieutenant Ritchie's official business, in exchange for his services as a navigator, was to gather intelligence in South American ports on the movements of von Spee's ships.

With the crew more or less settled, the Routledges continued their quest to add two qualified scientists to the Mana Expedition: an archaeologist and a geologist. Katherine was a frugal person—most people considered her stingy—and the cost of building and fitting *Mana* was soaring. Scoresby responded by offering the scientific posts for sale at a massive £500 per year each. Her advisory committee had essentially no advice to offer on funding grants or hiring scientific personnel, and Katherine turned, as always, to R. R. Marett and to T. A. Joyce.

Joyce flatly told Katherine that it was not necessary to hire an experienced archaeologist. There was, he said, "no need to use the care in excavation there that is necessary in Egypt; you don't expect to find stratified remains which it is possible to date by their position, & as for results I feel that you would do more with a spoon there than a spade elsewhere." Marett disagreed and urged Katherine to seek someone with excavation experience. In the face of such conflicting advice, she concluded that it was essential to hire a person with a broad natural history background and surveying skills. She wanted men—women were not considered—with solid, practical knowledge of photography and plane table surveying. They would share the yacht's double cabin and, Scoresby said, bear hardship and disappointment and "enter with whole hearted interest into the life & work."

In the late summer of 1911 Oxford geographer A. J. Herbertson recommended O. G. S. Crawford to Marett. Born in Bombay in 1886, Crawford was the twenty-five-year-old son of a minor British civil servant. His mother had died a few days after his birth and he had been sent home to England to be raised with "moral fervor" by two doting spinster aunts. During his fourth academic year at Keble College, Oxford, he took up the study of geology. He met the archaeologist Harold Peake and his wife, Carlie, who, at this late stage of Crawford's life, filled the role of surrogate parents. The Peakes were upright agnostics who encouraged Crawford to have skepticism in all things, and he was devoted to them. Peake—who nicknamed him Mog—influenced Crawford toward archaeology, although no regular instruction in archaeological excavation was given at any British university at this time, and as an obvious consequence, no teaching positions in the subject existed.

When the Routledges met Crawford he was working as a junior demonstrator (a kind of assistant teacher) in geography at Oxford. By the end of 1911 Scoresby was corresponding informally with him, giving advice and trading books. Crawford was quite honest about his financial circumstances, which were sharply limited. Scoresby, in turn, was helpful but firm—almost fatherly—with suggestions about how Crawford might come up with the required expedition contribution of £500. Katherine tentatively accepted Crawford on the condition that he undertake a course in surveying, study with Marett, and pass Oxford's Diploma Examination in anthropology.

On April 23, 1912 Katherine, her brother Wilson, and Crawford attended a meeting of the Oxford University Anthropological Society, which Marett had founded sometime earlier. She was the only woman in the bare, shabby room filled with "underdressed, earnest men" gathered in a thick, smoky atmosphere that reminded Wilson of a Nihilist meeting. Crawford, writing in the 1950s, was dismissive of Katherine, saying that she had simply "come under the spell of Marett and was taking his course, or had taken it," and "picked up" an interest in anthropology from him. Such a negative opinion could not have been obvious to Katherine, whose frequent correspondence with Crawford was gracious and friendly. She invited him more than once to luncheons and weekends at Ewers and, on at least one occasion, paid some of his university fees.

Scoresby eventually cut the contribution he had asked of Crawford from £500 to £100, and Crawford raised half of it. The deal he struck with the Routledges was that Crawford's expenses would be covered by the expedition and he would work off the other half of the contribution as purser, a paid member of the crew. Under these very clear conditions, Crawford signed on. Crawford thought he had entered a "curious three-sided bargain by which Marett got a pupil for his course, Mrs. Routledge got an excavator for nothing," and Crawford would gain field experience and three years expenses.

At this point a cheerful, twenty-three-year-old Cambridge man and promising geologist named Frederick Lowry-Corry signed on, also as purser. He intended to join the expedition in Punta Arenas, Chile, after completing jobs in India and Argentina. Lowry-Corry and Crawford, both of whom had heard about Scoresby from several earlier, failed members of the crew, had trepidations but were excited beyond words about Easter Island. They began a course in surveying together, and everything seemed ready to go.

Continued delays, however, kept *Mana* in Southampton, and Crawford grew increasingly anxious and worried about money. He had no salary coming in and was spending money hand over fist on clothing and equipment. Scoresby loaned Crawford money, and Katherine encouraged him and Lowry-Corry to live on board *Mana* at no cost. Worry gave way to resentment as days turned into weeks, Scoresby continued to fuss with details, and Crawford became increasingly indebted to him. In the final weeks there was a flurry of activity.

Katherine supervised the loading of six months' worth of staple provisions. The cabin got stores of Dutch cheese, Westphalian ham, tinned French pâté, marmalade, Devon cream, chocolate, and other wonders. Crew rations for the voyage—which included two years' supply of tea and tobacco—were at three-quarters the legal requirement per person, but to hear Katherine tell it, the expedition was so well provisioned that she never ran short of anything essential. Some *Mana* crewmen, however, would later beg to differ. Their food included ham packed in charcoal to keep out the rats and damp; beans and oven-dried root vegetables; sausages and veal covered with thick layers of butter and fat and stored in wood casks, and boiled tripe in vinegar.

The Routledges bought tents, saddles and tack, and cooking utensils. Katherine ordered camp beds, safari furniture, and two prefabricated metal and wood buildings of the type widely used in Africa from Humphrey's Ltd. of Knightsbridge and had it all shipped to Chile. Scientific gear included all of the photographic supplies and equipment the Routledges had taken to Africa, as well as surveying instruments and supplies to preserve human bone. They also carried coal and tanks of oil and water, cases of wine and champagne, several rifles and ample ammunition. Crates of "alarming size" arrived from the Admiralty and Royal Geographical Society "containing sounding machines and other mysterious articles." With his medical training—albeit with no formal degree—Scoresby took on the role of ship's doctor and arranged for huge quantities of bandages, splints, and medicines. "Judging from the quantity of bandages," Katherine said, "we were each relied on to break a leg once a month."

In July 1912 Katherine assembled a small group of friends at the Hans Crescent Hotel in Southampton for a party because, she said, "you must advertise your departure if you wish for a welcome on your return." She invited O. G. S. Crawford, Frederick Lowry-Corry, and Lieutenant Graham, who had not yet been replaced by Lieutenant Ritchie. Wilson Pease watched his sister as she moved about the large hotel banquet room, welcoming guests, offering champagne, and "doing the honours splendidly." Spencer Havelock-Allan, Katherine's Darlington neighbor and friend since childhood, told her that the best cure for seasickness, which she was sure to suffer, was laughter.

Delays of every sort continued—most of which Crawford attributed directly to Scoresby, a "gadget fiend." The relationship between the two men had soured, then had deteriorated sharply and was breaking down. At this point, however, Crawford was completely caught up in the dream of Easter Island, where, he told family and friends, he hoped to write an "epoch-making book" and "solve the riddle & become famous!" In his enthusiasm he offered to collect photos, measurements, sketches, and samples for a number of scholars, including Henry Balfour—an infringement on the expedition's time and autonomy that, when Scoresby later discovered it, made him furious. Confining Scoresby and Crawford aboard *Mana* was a recipe for disaster.

Seven unbearable months later, on February 28, 1913, *Mana* at last sailed for Dartmouth. She anchored there for five days, with Katherine's sister, Lilian, and her husband as guests. Bad weather delayed final departure from Falmouth yet another three weeks, and Crawford "began to despair of ever sailing in the open ocean." Katherine, who had nurtured *Mana* since the beginning of the project three years earlier, was more sanguine. She calmly attended the funeral of Dr. Thomas Hodgkin, a famous Quaker scholar who was the father of Lucy Violet Hodgkin, a friend and distant relative. Then, seemingly without any warning, she came down with what, as always, she thought was a relapse of malaria "after six years' complete immunity." Reluctantly, Katherine began a course of quinine treatment, stoically enduring the drug's awful side effects.

Katherine received a farewell letter from her favorite niece, Beatrice Evelyn (Eve) Leslie Fox, that cheered her up and responded, "Uncle Scoresby is still packing things into cupboards as I write & I don't know how the poor thing can swallow any more." Such last-minute rearranging of supplies was the sort of confusion that, whenever it was inflicted upon her, Katherine hated. The crowning, nerve-racking inconvenience was Scoresby's latest, eccentric experiment: he had paid the local baker to prepare dozens of loaves of fresh bread baked into the unusual shape of huge buns. Absurdly too large and awkward for any of the galley shelves, the buns had to be stacked floor to ceiling in the yacht's bath, which was then impossible to use until the bread had been eaten.

The winds refused to cooperate and the clock ticked as *Mana* crewmen watched the skies, smoked, and nervously paced the decks. A letter arrived from Katherine's brother Wilson saying, "It is now up to you to show that Durham can produce a great woman." *Mana* tossed. Scoresby scowled. Crawford fretted. The crew rumbled darkly. Katherine stubbornly went ashore to send a telegram of farewell to her mother. Gillam felt the wind stirring about, ready to shift, and told the men to stand ready. Katherine returned from shore. On the morning of Tuesday, March 25, 1913, the wind finally changed, blowing fresh and strong. *Mana* motored out of Falmouth Harbor in the early-evening darkness, hoisted sail, and spread her wings for Easter Island.

Atlantic to the Pacific:
an "archaeological fiasco"

✦

AFTER LESS THAT TWENTY-FOUR HOURS AT SEA *MANA*
was caught in a huge gale. She pitched and rolled, pummeled by huge
waves. Katherine lay frightened and sick in her bunk, the skylight over her
head leaking cold droplets of salty water. She was ill from the din of the
storm, the constant screaming of the rigging, and the groaning and crashing
of waves. Her whole body and mind felt black-and-blue. In the long-ago
habit of her Quaker childhood she sought to create stillness within, the
silence that would bring solace. She meditated on the reassuring Bible verse
carved in the wall by her bunk and recalled the fatalistic philosophy of a
young Swahili porter when she had asked him if he feared lions. "Frightened?" the porter had asked. "No, he eats me, he does not eat me; it is all
the will of Allah."

In the morning Gillam reduced sail and turned his ship's head to the wind,
allowing *Mana* to proceed southwest across the Bay of Biscay. Within hours
the glass rose and fell again and another storm hit. This one lasted an interminable thirty-six hours and the seas ran high—but not nearly so mountain-
ous as in the first storm. The wind moderated; *Mana* found her pace and
made sixty to seventy miles a day for the next three days. The wind gradually died away and the weather alternated between squally and dead calm.

Somewhere off Gibraltar, Scoresby discovered that all the bread, baked in
the shape of huge buns and stacked in the bathroom, had rolled around like
pinwheels and was wet and moldy. Rather than admit his mistake to the
crew, Scoresby decided they could eat green bread. This was the first of what
would become many subsequent disagreements over food, and the crew,
naturally, saw it as an ominous beginning to a three-year voyage from which
there was no honorable escape. Crawford said that "mutinous talk" began,
and the grumbling finally forced Gillam to lead a deputation to speak to the

Routledges. Their protest was ineffectual and Crawford "saw red rather than green."

Lieutenant Ritchie steered a tense course for Puerto de la Luz, the harbor below the town of Las Palmas, Grand Canary. Squalls hit again, and Gillam heaved to overnight while a third major storm passed over *Mana*. When the rocky coast of Madeira came into sight it was decided to put in at Funchal, but *Mana* was suddenly becalmed in dense mist and a heavy swell. Rocking idly, she drifted dangerously and inexorably toward disaster. Green struggled valiantly to get the engine going, but it was soaking wet and failed to start. After tense and frightening minutes a breeze finally rose. The engine turned over and then kept time with the ship's rolls, alternately racing and stopping almost dead. The crew chalked up the stubborn engine and moldy bread to Scoresby's stupidity.

This was not Katherine's first time in Madeira, but before the Routledges could explore what she called its "sunshine and smiling houses," Scoresby needed to organize repairs to the vessel and the engine, and she needed to purchase fresh provisions. Her shipboard menus were all drawn from *15 Books of Old Recipes as used in the Pease and Gurney Households in the XVIIIth Century*, and Katherine planned every meal with care. Crawford, as purser, was clearly obligated to help her, but the island was enticing. Finally, he made time to buy fresh vegetables. "I was cross-examined by Mrs. Routledge about the cost of each purchase," Crawford said, "to make sure that I had bought at the cheapest rate; and after one there was a very careful counting of the change I handed back." Crawford was insulted, refused to do any more provisioning, and had, he said, "the full moral support of everyone else on board except Routledge, who took no part in the affair."

Mana departed Funchal, caught a good breeze, and made a fast run to Grand Canary Island, three hundred miles away, arriving at dusk on April 18; she took a berth in the harbor about two miles outside the town of Las Palmas. Leaking skylights in Katherine's cabin were sealed shut. The desk in the chart room was removed. Major repairs to the engine and the engine's cooling pipes were made, and then a leak was discovered. The hold was full of seawater and dozens of supplies were brought up on deck to dry out. Among them were boxes and boxes of tea, all of which had to be opened and the tea arranged on trays in the sun. The crew now imagined themselves washing down moldy bread with seawater-sodden tea and groaned in despair. *Mana* was in port for three miserable weeks.

Crawford acted as if he were a lucky tourist disembarking from a cruise ship rather than a working member of the Mana Expedition. He found the delay "rather nice as it will enable me to explore the island." He blithely left *Mana* and her troubles, refused to help Katherine with the provisioning, and went off to climb mountain peaks, explore Las Palmas, collect artifacts and lunch with Lieutenant Ritchie at the British Club. As a Royal Navy officer on full pay, Ritchie had freedom from responsibilities not specifically included in his role of navigator, while Crawford was obviously in a different position. Petulantly, Crawford "did not see why, if Ritchie could be allowed to enjoy himself in his way, I should not do so in mine."

Five days before departure Crawford and Green got roaring drunk on the local rum and were hauled on board *Mana* by the watch. Scoresby was furious and "had a great row" with Crawford in front of the entire crew. Ugly words, impossible to take back, flew. Crawford told the Routledges "things about themselves that I don't think they knew," including their "extraordinary lack of courtesy" and "appalling stinginess," and said that Scoresby was "a complete fraud" as a yachtsman. Crawford demanded personal time in all ports of call and freedom from provisioning duties, on threat of resignation. Katherine desperately negotiated a generous resolution that, essentially, gave Crawford three or four days per week off duty when in port. Even so, Crawford wrote home for money, just in case he needed to clear out.

The weather from Grand Canary Island to St. Vincent (in the Portuguese colony of Cape Verde Islands) was delightful, the sea unchallenging, and much to Katherine's relief, the noisy, smelly engine was silenced. *Mana* flew with confidence and grace on the track of Sir Francis Drake, the first Englishman to circumnavigate the world (aboard *Golden Hinde* in 1577). This was everything the Routledges had planned, dreamed about, and worked for, and it should have been perfect. It was not, however. Crawford was not speaking to the Routledges, meals were taken in uneasy silence in close quarters, and tempers were stretched thin. Scoresby had discovered what he considered Crawford's secret agenda—a pact with other researchers to benefit personally from the Mana Expedition. One night Scoresby crept stealthily on deck and angrily accused Crawford of sitting down while on watch. Crawford lost his temper and told Scoresby that he had had enough of both him and his wife and wanted to leave *Mana* and the expedition at St. Vincent.

A meeting was held the following day to discuss the matter. Katherine, trying to prevent the loss of the Mana Expedition's only scientist, sat at the table in the saloon and read a formal statement asking the men to forgive and forget. Crawford refused to apologize. Scoresby, who had roughed out a letter describing Crawford's behavior in the most unflattering terms, threatened to send it to everyone involved with the expedition—a gesture that would have damaged Crawford's budding career terribly—and dramatically entered "discharged" in the logbook after Crawford's name. Crawford snatched at least one page of Scoresby's damning letter and fled the saloon. The entire episode was childish in the extreme, but *Mana* crewmen (according to Crawford, at least) were "entirely sympathetic and not a little envious."

At St. Vincent, Scoresby stiffly shook Crawford's hand and said good-bye. Crawford ran to the British consul for help and wrote a hasty letter home from the Hotel Central, asking for money.

> I have had to resign my position on board the Mana. The behaviour of the Routledges has been perfectly impossible & no one in my position would continue to tolerate it. Everyone on board completely agrees that I have taken the right course & wonder that I have put up with them so long. There is not a soul on board whom the R's have not exasperated beyond bearing, but with the exception of Ritchie they are all in their pay & therefore clutches & unable to get out of it. . . . He dislikes the Routledges as intensely as I do, & can hardly bear to speak to them.

Katherine was deeply concerned for the future of the expedition, feelings made worse by her intense dislike of St. Vincent. It had, she wrote, a "marvelous bleakness," with rugged hillsides bare of "any trees, any grass, any green on which to rest the eye" and a "constant tearing wind" that must have reminded her of the Woodside wind of her childhood.

O. G. S. Crawford finally made his way to Liverpool on a cargo boat and then told his story to everyone who would listen. Katherine wrote to Marett, Lowry-Corry, R. Douglas Graham, and others, explaining her view of what had happened. To Lowry-Corry she simply said Crawford did not like the life, but she frankly told Marett that Crawford was sullen, harbored grudges, and nursed grievances to make trouble. Marett sensibly replied that he wished to hear both sides of the story, although he felt "dreadfully sorry for having so strongly recommended a man who evidently was not the right man for the job." Katherine asked Marett to find a replacement for Crawford but he was unable to do so. Marett, who now shared Joyce's opinion that cave excavation was the most important goal, encouraged a worried Katherine to do the job alone: "Other things—survey of islands, photographs of remaining monuments, descriptions of modern islanders, etc— seem to me quite secondary compared with discovery and investigation of caves. There lie the treasured secrets—Good luck." Armed with little but Marett's encouragement and her own determined grit, Katherine faced the daunting prospect of conducting an archaeological field project on Easter Island with no training.

Between 1914 and 1938 archaeology matured tremendously as a science, and ironically, one of the important leaders to emerge was none other than O. G. S. Crawford. He referred to the Mana Expedition as "an archaeological fiasco," but was haunted by Scoresby's threats to dash his career hopes. He avoided R. R. Marett for a long time, finally asking a mutual friend to intercede. He secured a post excavating in the Sudan (for which Marett recommended him) and eventually, to his great relief, repaid his debt to Scoresby. He became a navigator in the Flying Corps and prisoner of war during World War I, then head of the Ordnance Survey. His distinguished career included work as a professional archaeologist, photographer, and founder and editor of the influential journal *Antiquity*.

Katherine undoubtedly knew of Crawford's work, but never referred to him by name in any of her fieldnotes or publications. In 1937 Scoresby was an elderly widower on the island of Cyprus, preparing to build a home there. Crawford was also on Cyprus, looking for property. One night they nearly collided with one another as both men entered the restaurant of the Nicosia Hotel for dinner. Scoresby was quite alone and might have liked company, but Crawford, who later disingenuously said he bore Scoresby no ill will, thought "he was a terrible bore and had few friends, and it would have been difficult to avoid his company if we had made up the old quarrel." Katherine, it turns out, was on target in her assessment of Crawford: he held a grudge.

Mana raced across the Atlantic, the newly caught trade winds filling her voluptuous white sails. The full moon hung overhead in a bruised, navy blue sky, and sparkling foam spit from the yacht's bows. Katherine emerged from her hot and humid cabin and stumbled on deck. Each watch was four hours on and eight off, and Katherine had come up to take her turn. She had stripped off layers of heavy, khaki clothes as they approached the equator and was dressed in wrinkled white linen. Her thick auburn hair was pulled back and tied up with one of her husband's bootlaces, and she carried the worn Bible of her childhood. Scoresby's tall figure was alone against the sky. One hand rested lightly on the ship's rail, and in the other, he held the lighted cigarette he was never without. At 9 P.M. Katherine, a spectral figure in blowing white skirts, was on watch for'ard as *Mana* crossed the equator and turned toward the Atlantic coast of South America.

A day or two later Scoresby took it upon himself to ration the crew's water consumption, although, it seems, there was no need to do so. When the steward, George Smith, and F. W. Shephard, the cook, helped themselves to more water than he had allowed, there was an angry confrontation. Scoresby, according to the account given by Frank T. Green, upbraided both men: "He started to accuse both Smith & Shepard [*sic*]of stealing water, calling them a couple of wastrels and a few other uncomplimentary names, one of which happened to be worse than the others & a disgrace to anyone's mother, on which Smith spoke back and got his ears boxed." Smith defended himself and Gillam rushed in to stop the fight. Later, Gillam told Scoresby that he was completely out of line and needed to apologize, and Scoresby did so. Within days, however, he got in a shouting match with the inoffensive Albert Light and nearly came to blows with him as well.

Such violence among men was not unknown to Katherine, who had grown up with Harold's hot and threatening temper, but it was exceptionally ugly. In the close quarters and isolation of shipboard life, it was imperative that everyone behave in a civil manner, and Scoresby's actions were dangerous. The problems aboard *Mana* always seemed to stem from the same two issues: Scoresby's inadequacies and the need to protect his status and authority, and the crew's complaints about food. By the time *Mana* reached Pernambuco, Brazil, morale was so low that, when Scoresby offered the men part of a large birthday cake his sister had sent and the gift of a Dutch cheese, they promptly threw it all in the sea. *Mana* had become, in the words of Green, a "Floating Hell."

Sailing along the coast toward Rio de Janeiro, *Mana* struggled hard against strong head winds for more than five days. Scoresby wanted to shelter in Cabral Bay, Brazil, for some relief, but Lieutenant Ritchie disagreed. The entrance to the bay, in his opinion, was risky and they had no official permission from Brazilian authorities to land. Scoresby persisted. Tight-lipped, Lieutenant Ritchie requested written orders before complying. The crew stood silently by, watching the tense confrontation between Scoresby and the prudent and stubborn young naval officer. The minutes ticked away, the sails strained, and waves passed under the bow. Finally, Scoresby stomped angrily below, wrote the order as requested, and handed it wordlessly to Lieutenant Ritchie. *Mana* put in at Cabral Bay without incident for two days of welcome rest. With the atmosphere on board only slightly less nasty, *Mana* set out again under a sunset rainbow and flew along the coast toward Rio.

On July 14 Katherine awoke in her cabin to look out upon Rio harbor, overwhelmed by what, to her eye, was a magical scene from the pages of *Arabian Nights*. In the "wonderful transparent light" of morning the city shone "pure and soft, blue and green, like an opal." The Routledges went ashore to dine with the British minister and consul, visited the botanical gardens, and saw the sights of the city. Katherine sent out her laundry and then went shopping, purchasing new uniforms for her crew. She bought them white-and-blue-striped sweaters, some with the name *Mana* emblazoned on the front, and white-and-blue caps. For Gillam and Scoresby she purchased tropical white suits and caps.

Mana departed Rio harbor on August 2, 1913 in weather that grew increasingly ominous and threatening. Lieutenant Ritchie and Gillam anxiously watched the skies for signs of a *pampero*, a gale they had been warned might sweep down from the Andes with uncommon ferocity. *Mana* was soon overtaken by a particularly vicious storm; the Routledges rushed on deck, which was bucking and tossing insanely, and pitched in to stow sails. Pummeled by rain and waves, Katherine struggled until both Gillam and Scoresby forced her to go below. Katherine was humiliated and the incident still rankled more than six years later. "The next generation of females," she hoped, would not be so ill-treated.

On August 17 *Mana* anchored in the bustling, crowded port of Buenos Aires. Her berth was in the shadow of huge warships—duly noted by Lieutenant Ritchie. Needing a breather from *Mana*, Katherine checked into Buenos Aires' luxurious Avenida Palace Hotel. She booked a large suite with a marble tub, ate three big meals a day, and went shopping, buying herself five expensive pairs of custom-made, brown leather boots.

When Katherine discovered that Scoresby had, in her absence, given members of the press a tour of *Mana* "with her hatches up and the floor covered with packing-cases," she was angry and her pride, which almost sounds maternal, was injured. Then, opening the paper at breakfast one midmorning, Katherine was stunned to see a large headline in the English-language Buenos Aires *Herald*: "The Riddle of the Pacific: What does Easter Island mean? Scientific Expedition Under Mr. Routledge to Attempt Solution." Making no mention of Katherine as his expedition partner, Scoresby disregarded his previous reticence with the English press, ignored the expedition's lack of scientific staff, and brashly overstated his accomplishments in Africa.

On August 31 Scoresby joined Katherine at the Avenida Palace Hotel, where he took a separate suite, and the Routledges faced a crisis in their marriage. Katherine felt that the agreement she had made with her husband was clear: She would fund the construction of *Mana*, and they would work together to assemble a well-qualified team and then co-lead a scientific expedition. Katherine believed that, for three years, she had kept her end of the bargain, but the expedition team had not been carefully constructed and then had fallen apart; the crew was disgruntled and angry; the scientific work was in jeopardy; and Scoresby was now undeservedly tooting his own horn in the press. Katherine, who was never good at examining or reflecting on her own shortcomings, blamed Scoresby for everything. The Mana Expedition to Easter Island was on the verge of self-destructing.

In *The Mystery of Easter Island* Katherine's anger and disappointment are obvious and projected fiercely onto all of Argentine society, which she hated. She castigates the country's antiquated double standard, "almost that of the

East," that keeps women in bondage to male ambition and forces them to become concubines. It may be a stretch to assume that Katherine equated her domestic role with that of a concubine, but there is more than a hint of such bitterness in her tirade. In spite of everything, however, Katherine was not willing to give up either her marriage or the expedition. Somehow, the Routledges resolved their differences for the moment and *Mana* departed Buenos Aires, sailing southward.

On October 15, 1913 *Mana* entered the labyrinthine Straits of Magellan and began her dangerous, more-than-three-hundred-mile passage from the Atlantic Ocean to the Pacific. The South American mainland ends there in gray-green water, deep and cold. Southward lies the island of Tierra del Fuego and then, eventually, only the blue and white wilderness of Antarctica. The Straits are, even today, a major navigational challenge, but Lieutenant Ritchie rose to the occasion. Only once, at a place called English Narrows (widely considered the most difficult area to navigate), did he ask Gillam to take the helm. The crew pulled together, and the tensions of their passage were punctuated with vistas of incredible beauty.

On the second full day into the Straits, Scoresby spied several rhea—South American ostriches—on a small promontory. He insisted on going ashore to shoot them, not for fresh meat but simply for sport. After a comic chase that included Lieutenant Ritchie and Gillam brandishing revolvers as they scrambled, laughing, over wave-washed rocks, Scoresby shot two and then had one of the unfortunate birds strung up on the deck of *Mana*. Katherine took a photograph of her husband standing triumphantly next to the carcass.

When *Mana* reached the tiny Chilean town of Punta Arenas, Frederick Lowry-Corry, who had signed on in Southampton, joined the expedition as geologist and purser. Completely up-to-date on the details of Crawford's angry departure, Lowry-Corry was keenly aware that he was the only scientist on board. He got on immediately with everyone, including Scoresby. Katherine's hopes soared. Unfortunately, *Mana* was delayed in Punta Arenas for six long, dull weeks while much needed repairs to her engine were made. The crew was frustrated with disappointment, and the costs of repair work mounted beyond reason. Fumes and noise disturbed Katherine's sleep and she hated the engine unreservedly. To escape she took up Spanish lessons in Punta Arenas.

Steward George Smith, cook F. W. Shephard, and an understeward known only as Luke fled *Mana* at Punta Arenas. Luke took with him Katherine's cherished Pease family cookbooks and all of her favorite recipes. Katherine rightly called the theft "mean" and was devastated. The abandoned duties of steward and cook were taken over by F. F. Gray and L. Bailey, both hired in

Punta Arenas. Gray deserted in Talcahuano, but Bailey (as he was always known to Katherine) endured in the post of cook for two years, finally leaving *Mana* in Tahiti. A man with no roots who had knocked about the world for years, Bailey liked to drink and play cards. He was not, on the surface, the sort of man one would imagine Katherine getting on with, but she liked him, enjoyed his brash company, and developed a real fondness for him.

At last, the engine seemingly repaired, *Mana* departed Punta Arenas for the Patagonian Channels, following the tracks of explorers, whalers, and scientists through, in Katherine's words, "a bewildering labyrinth of waterways and islands," where "fresh passages open up from every point of view, till the voyager longs to see what is round the corner, not in one direction, but in all." The revolutionary ideas of Charles Darwin, formed so long ago on the voyage of HMS *Beagle* through these same waters, filled the crystalline air with their brilliance. One early morning Scoresby shouted to Katherine to come topside and see a small group of native Patagonians coming out in canoes to greet them "just like in the picture-books."

On November 30 Katherine and Scoresby, together with Gillam and Lowry-Corry, packed compasses, notebooks, tinned beef, and a big thermos of hot coffee into the yacht's launch and headed for Lobo Arm, an inlet on Desolation Island, where they found a portage 160 yards long that cut the island in two. All hands, Katherine said, carried the launch over the portage "cut through the thick forest undergrowth. [It] had the appearance of a long and brilliant tunnel between the two waters, [and] was carpeted with bright moss and overhung with trees . . . covered with lichen. The bottom was soft and boggy, and I at one time became so firmly embedded that I could not get out without assistance."

Once in the water on the other side of the island, the little exploring party was out of sight of *Mana*. If they lost her they would be in grave danger. To keep track of their position, relative to hers, they needed their compass direction, of course, and a watch, but it was also necessary to know the speed at which the launch was being rowed through the water. Gillam calculated speed by using a device called a log line (a wooden board attached to a line). He threw the board overboard and assumed it to be dead in the water. As the launch moved forward he paid out the line and timed it. In this ancient manner they successfully mapped an uncharted channel connecting the Pacific Ocean with the Magellan Straits. Scoresby proudly christened their discovery Mana Inlet, and under midnight's icy stars, they made their way back to *Mana*.

In 1916 Katherine gave a paper about Easter Island at the Royal Geographical Society and, in passing, mentioned their discovery. A Fellow named Mr. B. W. Stainton, Esq., wrote to Mr. Arthur Hinks, secretary of the society, to challenge her. He said that in 1876 Paymaster R. Richards, of HMS *Challenger,* had described in his private diary the same channel the Routledges called Mana Inlet and that, therefore, the discovery was not theirs. Katherine held her ground and Hinks, who characterized Stainton as "a rather persistent critic anxious to make a point against Mrs. Routledge," sent the diary on to Pacific scholar (and Routledge friend) Bolton Glanville Corney to get his opinion. Corney agreed that a *Challenger* party had, indeed, reached the head of Mana Inlet, but no one had reported it officially to the Hydrographic Office of the Admiralty. The Royal Geographical Society, therefore, concluded that the Routledges could claim discovery of Mana Inlet. The name is found today on English and Spanish maps as Mana Canal or Canal Mana and stands as a lasting tribute to the Routledges' beloved vessel.

Mana spent Christmas of 1913 lying at the foot of steep cliffs in Hale Cove, Patagonia Channels. The weather was overcast and then poured cold rain all day. In fond memory of all her happy childhood Christmases at Kendal, Katherine and Bailey prepared a gala four-course Christmas Day dinner. In the cabin she served vegetable soup, roast beef with potatoes, and festive Christmas pudding garnished with "Holly Antarctic." Bonbons and coffee followed cheese, bread, and biscuits. She presented each of the men with a tin of tobacco, and then the whole crew raised their voices in Anglican hymns and cheery carols. It was a genuinely happy Christmas, and the next day, Katherine turned out all hands to do a massive laundry onshore.

Mana was then forced to lay in Hale Cove for nearly two tiresome, rainy weeks. The land's ragged silhouette emerged from the drizzly mist only occasionally, and the barely visible gray-brown trees tossed morosely in the cold, wet wind. Wandering alone one day in a small cove adjacent to where *Mana* was moored, Katherine came upon the remains of a European-style homestead and a burial. On the spur of the moment she undertook what she called, years later, her "first experience in scientific body-snatching." The grave was shallow and there apparently had once been a rough wooden coffin, but the broken skull and other bones were so tangled with earth and tree roots that Katherine fell to her knees and dug them out with her fingers. Back on *Mana* she dumped the bones unceremoniously on the saloon table, bits of earth and plant still clinging to them. Scoresby examined the fragments and concluded they were the remains of a "civilized man." In Katherine's chagrined opinion, this was off-limits to science, and she gathered up the bones and went ashore again. Feeling "a little weird being thus in contact with the dead in his lonely resting place," Katherine reburied the bones without marking the grave but read over it a poem and a Bible verse.

On January 14, 1914 *Mana* arrived in Talcahuano, Chile, her last continental port before moving out into the far reaches of the Pacific. The Routledges claimed the massive shipment of ninety-six crates, boxes, and packages that awaited them, and the ship's mailbag. It carried news of the death the previous July of Scoresby's famous cousin "Earthquake Johnny" Milne, and letters from O. G. S. Crawford for Green, Lowry-Corry, and Lieutenant Ritchie. Everyone on board *Mana*, including the unflappable Gillam, was "thoroughly fed up" with unending delays, squabbles, and tensions. Lieutenant Ritchie was nearing a point of exasperation that, considering his even temperament, was quite extraordinary. He wrote to Crawford, saying:

> Things go on in much the same way as they did before in this—ship, only
> more so. . . . Progress has been slower than a snail's funeral . . . life on board
> is to me almost unbearable now. Thank Goodness we get to the Island soon
> & the change may make the rest of the time go faster. Only 6 months more—
> Thank God. Poor Gillam is fed to the neck & isn't the only one. I wish I had
> left at St. Vincent and come home with you, old card, & taken whatever con-
> sequences might have arisen.

There is no solid evidence that the Routledges planned to abandon the expedition in Talcahuano, but if they had, it would have been a logical place to do so. They took an inventory of the talents available on their crew: Frederick Lowry-Corry was their major asset, but Frank T. Green had revealed himself to be a fine photographer, and Lieutenant Ritchie's skills as a navigator would transfer well to the task of cartographer. While in Hale Cove they had broached the subject to him, and Ritchie had agreed. They very nearly hired on a man to serve as the expedition's artist-illustrator, but unfortunately that failed. When Mr. Hope-Simpson of Williamson, Balfour Co. threw the substantial logistical power of his little colonial empire behind the expedition, things looked brighter. They met with Enrique Merlet of La Compañía Explotadora de la Isla de Pascua (the Company), eagerly pored over maps, and made plans.

The Chilean public was gradually becoming aware of the Company's harsh treatment of the Easter Island community and was increasingly outraged. A year earlier *Knight of the Garter*, cruising from Valparaíso to Australia, had called at the island and publicized the "extreme poverty of the inhabitants." Lady Grogan, wife of Sir Richard Grogan, the British military attaché, and Captain Enrique Larenas, of the Chilean navy, had spearheaded a drive to collect clothes, shoes, food, and equipment for the islanders. Katherine promised that *Mana* would carry everything to Easter Island but then changed her mind, perhaps because she was afraid of complicating or rupturing negotiations with Merlet. Undaunted, Lady Grogan—who was later hugely successful at World War I fund-raising efforts in England—scrambled to send everything aboard *Jenaral Baquedano,* the Chilean navy's training vessel.

Mana departed Talcahuano for Juan Fernández Island on Friday, the thirteenth of February—a date that always brought Katherine superstitious shudders. Frederick Lowry-Corry had a slight fever and Katherine had a premonition of disaster. His fever quickly developed into a full-blown case of typhoid, which he had picked up in a restaurant in Talcahuano, and Scoresby came down with dysentery. After a very rough passage of four hundred miles, *Mana* moored head and stern in Cumberland Bay, Juan Fernández Island, and then tossed for four miserable days in heavy squalls. Katherine gamely attended to both men, surely a major ordeal. Everyone agreed that the only hope was to turn around and race back to Valparaíso. Scoresby recovered and Lowry-Corry was transferred to the British and American Hospital. *Mana* departed again for Juan Fernández Island, and although Katherine held out hope that Lowry-Corry would rejoin the expedition, he failed to recover and returned to England. The Mana Expedition was now completely committed to Easter Island but without any professional scientific staff.

Mana anchored for the second time in Cumberland Bay, Juan Fernández Island. Apparently never inhabited by Polynesians—although it may have been known to them—it is one of three islands, separated by about ninety miles of water, at latitude 34° south. Juan Fernández, a merchant seaman, was the first to sight the islands in the mid-1500s and named the two largest Más a Tierra (Nearer Land) and Más a Fuera (Farther Out). The name Juan Fernández Island stuck to Más a Tierra, and in 1914 the island boasted a neat little Chilean fishing village of some three hundred people. A mail schooner called twice a month, and a wireless station was under construction.

In 1704 an insufferable British seaman named Alexander Selkirk had been unceremoniously marooned on Juan Fernández Island after a disagreement with Thomas Stradling, commander of *Cinque Ports,* a privateer. Selkirk had only his sea chest and bedding, a gun, some rum and tobacco, and a prayer book, but he survived for four years and was then rescued. Daniel Defoe idealized and romanticized Selkirk as the shipwrecked Robinson Crusoe—one of Katherine's favorite stories. One day she and Scoresby decided to go in search of Defoe's story and rowed to a small cove, passing under a rocky cliff just as hundreds of white pigeons took flight. The flock wheeled out overhead and then, seemingly, paused to look down on the interlopers before turning away in a fluttering, cooing cloud of white and gray.

The Routledges landed the cutter on a minuscule beach, boulder-strewn and slippery, and scrambled through a wave-cut stone arch. Inland lay a little, turf-covered meadow that formed the mouth of a small valley, and a stream, fresh and clear, splashed down from above. About sixteen feet above the little beach and overlooking the blue Pacific, just as Katherine had hoped, was Selkirk's Cave. It held a cozy fireplace hearth and storage niches in the rock. Katherine sat down and imagined the fictional Crusoe, dressed in goatskin clothes and swinging his umbrella, coming homeward down the valley.

On the day before they departed Juan Fernández Island, Katherine sat in the deckhouse with the door open to the warm breeze, gazing up at the steep, rocky cliffs poured out centuries ago by volcanoes that bloomed with fire and streamed lava. At her feet was a tank full of seawater holding dozens of live lobsters. The mailbag, full to bursting, was ready to be dropped off in anticipation of the mail schooner's next call. Inside was a long letter to her nieces and nephews that enclosed a charming sketch of the island, the bay, and *Mana* lying at anchor.

At the eleventh hour—the morning of the day *Mana* departed Juan Fernández Island—Scoresby hired Henry MacLean, a handsome, eighteen-year-old Chilean citizen who spoke Spanish and English. He was not a crew member but, instead, would act as translator on Easter Island. He stayed with the Mana Expedition for four months and twenty-nine days and was a vital asset to Katherine. At 6 P.M. on Monday, March 9, 1914 *Mana* quietly slipped anchor in Cumberland Bay, Juan Fernández Island, and motored out to sea on the last leg of her journey to Easter Island.

Toward Easter Island:
Ecology and History at Sea

✦

THE SOUTHEAST PACIFIC THAT *MANA* SAILED INTO WAS not uncharted water, but after departing Juan Fernández Island she was on her own in the midst of a vast emptiness. The Pacific covers over eleven thousand square miles of the earth, and a volatile seascape lies beneath the surface. Mountain ranges and canyons inch along on moving tectonic plates, and liquid rock sometimes emerges at midocean rifts to create volcanic "hot spots." In 1835 Talcahuano was the epicenter of an earthquake that ran four hundred miles along the coast of Chile. The sea drained out of the bay and then returned in three massive tidal waves of death and destruction. From the deck of HMS *Beagle,* Charles Darwin reasoned that the earth's crust lay upon a raging inferno and that basaltic "high" islands—such as Easter Island (Rapa Nui)—had risen out of the sea. Rapa Nui is, in fact, volcanic, and located on the Pacific Rise at the unstable juncture of the Pacific and Nazca plates. By 1914 seismic research was an established field, thanks largely to Scoresby's pioneering cousin John Milne.

Plankton—minute animal and plant life—are fed by nutrients that flourish on the sea bottom or are flushed from the land by rivers and streams. In the open sea, plankton species float in layered zones. These are the subtropics, and fairly constant temperatures keep the water permanently divided between a warm upper layer and a cold lower layer. Surface weather, winds, water currents, and eddies vary—sometimes a great deal—within generally predictable patterns. Most of the time eastern Pacific winds and currents flow from the east, but from September to May they often shift toward the west or southwest. These marine patterns define the environmental reality of all islands, and they had a profound effect on all ancient voyagers. Fish, marine mammals, and birds migrate through the region in a complicated dance of water and air that coincides with the movements of the floating planktons and water temperature. American whalers respected, and were often frightened of, the lack of marine life in this part of the Pacific—they dubbed it the Desolate Region.

In 1520 Ferdinand Magellan, circumnavigating the globe in command of a five-vessel fleet of triple-masted caravels led by *Trinidad,* emerged from the strait that bears his name to enter the Pacific. He then sailed for ninety-eight days, his men suffering severe thirst, hunger, and scurvy, from one side of the Pacific to the other without sighting a single island. Many centuries earlier—between 2500 and 2000 B.C.—a horticultural, pottery-making people, speaking an Austronesian language, had expanded from Taiwan and was sailing the warm waters of island Southeast Asia. Their descendants fared better than Magellan and his unfortunate crew, and by 1500 to 1400 B.C. a cultural entity that archaeologists call Lapita had emerged.

Within about two hundred years, Lapita colonists were making long-distance voyages to islands that were increasingly distant from one another. Scattering southward and eastward, they reached Fiji by about 900 B.C. and then Tonga and Samoa, where Lapita culture was gradually transformed into Ancestral Polynesia. Over the following generations they perfected their marine technology and discovered, settled, and sometimes abandoned nearly 350 islands—from Hawaii to New Zealand (Aotearoa) to Rapa Nui. By at least 150 A.D., but perhaps earlier, they had reached the Marquesas Islands and their vessels were plying the waters of the Desolate Region.

On islands possessing large hardwood trees, sailing vessels evolved into double-hulled, double-masted canoes from forty-nine to seventy-two feet long. Their masts, sails, and steering paddles were proportionately huge. A living platform straddled the two hulls, a community of people lived aboard it in the same manner they had lived in their land-based villages, and each person had his or her place and task. In 1865, at the same time the decimated Rapa Nui culture was being missionized, a Western sailor described a trip he made in a Fijian double-hulled canoe.

> Up went the huge sail, down went the great steer oars, splashing into the sea, and away we shot like a racehorse. The breeze was strong. Every timber of the canoe creaked again, while the mast bent like a reed and cracked in its socket, as if it would split the deck in two . . . the sea was like a hissing cauldron on either side of our course, and the vessel, instead of having time to mount over the smaller waves, cut its way through them.

Other types of Polynesian vessels, however, are also well known, including massive log-platform rafts with triangular sails.

The most famous seagoing raft in the Pacific is not Polynesian, however.

In 1947 the late Thor Heyerdahl built *Kon-Tiki,* a balsa raft with a square sail that also had modern (for the time) survival gear and communications equipment. He theorized that the Pacific islands were settled from Peru, and basic to this premise was his understanding of the easterly direction of the prevailing winds and currents. Heyerdahl and his five-person crew boarded their raft, which was then towed about fifty nautical miles out to sea from the Peruvian coast, and set out. They rode out storms and fought off sharks, collected rainwater for drinking, and feasted occasionally on flying fish that landed on deck. The South Equatorial Current forced them farther to the west than they had anticipated. Finally, after more than three months at sea, *Kon-Tiki* landed, hard, on a reef in the Tuamoutus. Heyerdahl's bold adventure caught the public imagination, but it did not prove that any Polynesian island—and certainly not Rapa Nui—had been settled from Peru. Heyerdahl, it is unequivocally clear, "got it backward."

The large Polynesian sail-bearing rafts and double-canoes of the Pacific-settlement era have virtually no parallel in Peruvian precontact culture, and the lack of either light woods or large trees along the continental coast was an obvious hindrance to building such vessels. South American rafts—the earliest, tenuous evidence for which comes from about A.D. 700 in Chile—were extremely modest with little seagoing capability. Notwithstanding a general proclivity to hug the continental shoreline, however, the craft of northwest South America were more advanced: Heyerdahl found prehistoric pottery fragments in the Galápagos Islands, some six hundred miles off the coast of Ecuador.

It is archaeologically certain, however, that Polynesian double-canoes or rafts moved between Pitcairn and Mangareva, in the distant vicinity of Rapa Nui, to exchange pearl shell and basalt. It is ethnographically suggested that Rapa Nui mariners, in search of birds and birds' eggs, sailed 260 miles eastward to a small, isolated rookery called Sala y Gomez. It is plausible that, generations earlier, either a raft or a double-canoe, crewed by Polynesian voyagers who were the beneficiaries of thousands of years of maritime knowledge, had sailed within sight of the South American coast—by accident or design—and then met and traded with offshore vessels before turning homeward. That would explain how the sweet potato *(Ipomoea batatas),* domesticated in South America, and the gourd *Lagenaria* were introduced into the Pacific. The sweet potato—which had been carried westward into Central Polynesia by at least A.D. 1000—was introduced to Rapa Nui, where it became a staple food and fueled the statue-carving industry.

Polynesian navigators lacked modern instruments and charts, but they were men of intellect, skill, and prestige who had been trained in organized schools of learning. Rote memorization of rhythmic chants taught them patterns of waves, swells, and winds; the arc of the sun; and the paths of stars. They understood latitude but, like all seamen until John Harrison invented a reliable marine clock in 1762, couldn't calculate longitude. While that was a hardship, it was not a fatal shortcoming, and Polynesians had methods that compensated for this gap in knowledge. They tracked the idiosyncratic but interrelated movements of birds, fish, turtles, whales, and dolphins, judged their vessel's speed through the water by the passage of waves under the bow, and kept a lunar calendar. On outward voyages they steered a course across, against, and down the wind, a prudent strategy that maximized the chances of returning on a following wind. Navigators had the mystique of secrecy, the emblems of beauty, and the power of *mana* and were given status and responsibility commensurate with their skills. Some became heroes linked with gods in stories and songs.

Alone in the sea before its discovery by Polynesians, the island that became Rapa Nui began as barren rock and ash, but as it was colonized by seabirds it slowly greened with deposits of plant seas and guano. Rapa Nui winds are capricious, but southeast trade winds blow throughout the austral (Southern Hemisphere) summer, and westerly winds—preferred by Polynesians for long voyages—only occasionally dominate. The island has an embarrassment of volcanic stone riches: dense, hard, and dark basalt; black volcanic glass; and porous tuffs, some stained the deep, rich red of oxidized iron. Sunset-hued clouds give way to a glistening nighttime canopy of stars, then return through morning mists and rainbows to cast scudding daytime shadows. Rooted in cool, unbelievably turquoise waters more than a thousand fathoms deep, the island's ragged and rocky coastline is punctuated with a few small landing spots, a pink-sand cove, and one large beach.

Isolation and small size shaped Rapa Nui history, but so, too, did latitude, altitude, geology, rainfall, soil quality, and other factors—making it so environmentally challenged as to be ecologically unique in the Pacific. Only about 126 species of fish are seasonally present. Stands of palm (*Jubea* sp.) once blanketed the island but only forty-eight indigenous plant species are known. Although there is only moderate, seasonal rainfall, abundant freshwater lies in deep crater lakes carpeted with reeds that have flourished naturally for at least thirty thousand years. The island's richest resource was birds: at least six types of land birds and twenty-five species of seabirds (from subarctic to tropical) were once present.

The identity of the navigator who guided the settlement party to Rapa Nui is a mystery, but the name of the paramount chief (*ariki mau*) who led it is vividly remembered: Hotu Matu'a (Great Parent). Descended from the gods Tangaroa and Rongo, he was the ancestral head of the aristocratic Miru clan. The patron god of Hotu Matu'a was a creator named Makemake. Born from a skull in the care of an ancient priestess, his voice was heard in thunder and he ate the souls of the dead. Makemake was linked with the migrations of birds, especially the sooty tern, and with food.

The voyagers departed from Marae Renga in Hiva (literally, a "foreign place"), and Katherine believed their starting point was Mangareva. The motivation for embarking upon such a hazardous, life-threatening adventure is not known, but heroic feats in all cultures have been accomplished for many romantic, melodramatic, and mystical reasons. Rapa Nui legends say they were on a quest to find the island that had appeared in a vision to Haumaka, the royal tattooer. More practically, environmental disasters such as hurricanes, droughts, or tidal waves, or the related social problems of famines or diseases, may have encouraged flight. Overpopulation or family disputes over land leading to violence are other possibilities. Whatever the underlying causes, the Polynesian world was connected, not separated, by the ocean, and cultural traditions and ancient myths provided the courage to take risks.

How did Hotu Matu'a, or his navigator, find isolated Rapa Nui? There is no way of knowing, but surely he prevailed through a combination of original intent and fortunate accident, and by having a stout vessel, a strong crew, a thorough understanding of marine ecology, and good luck—*mana*. A major clue to the island's location, certainly, was migrating birds: Rapa Nui was once the largest migratory seabird destination in the Desolate Region. During the months of July, August, and September the skies between Sala y Gomez and Rapa Nui were black with clouds of birds, and their screams created a din that masked even the thunderous waves. It is no coincidence, then, that some legends say Hotu Matu'a found Rapa Nui during their month of Anakena—right in the middle of the southeastern Pacific migration season.

Migrating seabirds layer themselves in formations and plunge-dive, sometimes from considerable height, to feed on euphausiids—shrimplike crustaceans—and smaller fish forced to the surface by schools, often more than fifty thousand strong, of streamlined, fast-swimming skipjack (*Katsuwonus pelamis*) and yellowfin (*Thunnus albacares*) tuna migrating through the Desolate Region. Aggregating schools of dolphins and sharks swim through, over, and under the tuna as they speed through the water. Birds such as shearwaters (*Puffinus* sp.), tropic birds (*Phaethon* sp.), and terns (*Sterna* sp.) fly at the rear of the school and plunge into the water in front of it. A constant stream of diving, rising, flying, and settling birds sweeps in and out of the scrimmaging mass. Frigate birds (*Fregata* sp.) float high above the whitecap fray, seizing fish thrown into the air or robbing them from the beaks of smaller birds. From time to time formations of birds veer off, heading for land.

Such a violently explosive ecological pageant is usually visible or, at the least, audible for many miles. If Hotu Matu'a—deliberately seeking Rapa Nui or blown off course en route elsewhere—had encountered such an event, the birds, the fish, and the miraculous provision of food would have become intimately, mystically merged with the *mana* held in his person. Hungry people would have scrambled to spear fish or club the biggest birds from the sky. More practically, the navigator would immediately have marked the birds' track to land, converted their "flight path into a star compass heading," combined it with other environmental hints, and if they were within fifty to seventy-five miles of Rapa Nui, sailed directly there.

Terns are related to gulls, but are smaller and daintier. Adult terns migrate vast distances, flying in graceful, bouncy patterns and spending nearly all day on the wing. Once settled down in a rookery like Rapa Nui, they form a deafening colony of activity. In the 1930s a visitor to a Pacific tern rookery described it:

> The air was filled with uncountable thousands of screaming Terns. The ground was covered with uncountable thousands of blue-gray brown-spotted Tern eggs, while over the surface in every direction flopped, or fluttered, stumbled or ran, other uncountable numbers of birds in their dark gray youthful dress. It was almost impossible to walk about without crushing eggs or knocking young birds over. If you strolled about, a curtain of birds rose in front of you, leaving a margin of a dozen or twenty feet between themselves and you. If you sat down, mother Terns came quickly back to their nests and sat and watched you six or eight feet away.

The enemies of nesting seabirds are humans, rats (the Pacific rat, *Rattus exulans*, was transported on Polynesian canoes), and frigate birds—huge, hulking, predatory hawks with wingspans up to seven feet. Each of these predators, to varying degrees, negatively impacted the Rapa Nui bird population. The frigate bird and the sooty tern *(Sterna fuscata)*, Katherine would later discover, were Rapa Nui icons of the birdman religion.

Rapa Nui settlers took shelter beneath the hulls of their overturned canoe, but also in caves, probably first in the vicinity of Anakena. They established a modest ceremonial site right away: a cleared space with an upright stone or, perhaps, a woodcarving. Women gathered sea urchins from coastal tide pools; men snared land birds and caught near-shore fish. Families began to clear scrub trees to plant gardens. Some of their starter plants—perhaps including breadfruit and coconut—and animal stock that they had hoped to establish had perished at sea. Transplants such as bananas and sugarcane, chickens (the red Asian jungle fowl), and rats, however, flourished.

The subtropical climate could turn suddenly cold, but men of learning gradually understood and could predict Rapa Nui's pattern of seasonal change by attending to the stars, the tides, and the sun. The island's richness of stone resources produced fine tools, and trees were felled and burned to open up more space for planting, but also for timber to build houses, canoes, and rafts. Old people died, babies were born, families thrived, and a richly elaborate ceremonial life evolved. Over time, Hiva and Marae Renga receded in memory, but remained in myth. The royal lands at Anakena were reserved in perpetuity for the paramount chief, but Hotu Matu'a divided the rest of the island among his six sons, according to their birth order, and an early, impressive site was established at Tahai, on the western shore. As he neared death, Hotu Matu'a ascended the slope of Rano Kau to gaze westward, and then was buried near Akahanga.

As *Mana* made her way through the Desolate Region, of course, Katherine knew none of this. Rapa Nui was just a dot on Lieutenant Ritchie's chart, as it had been a vision in the mind's eye of that long-ago Polynesian navigator. The Southern Cross hovered above, flying fish sprang out of ripples and wavelets, and the days hurried by. The surface of the ever-changing Pacific was calm and clear on one side of the yacht, reflecting crisp, white trade-wind clouds. On the other side of *Mana* the sea was cast in a deeper, vaguely uneasy, grayish tint.

"Easter Island at last!"

✦

AT TWILIGHT ON MARCH 28, 1914 LIEUTENANT RITCHIE came up from the chart room and took the yacht's position by the evening star. Katherine, wrapped in a warm sweater, watched while the lights were hung out on the fore-rigging. As night fell she restlessly paced the deck. At daybreak on Sunday, March 29, Gillam sighted Easter Island off the starboard bow. It was 5:30 A.M. precisely, and the dawn was shrouded in mist. Katherine and the others gazed out upon the distant island in "awed silence." At seven, *Mana* was close enough for Katherine to sketch the island from the southeast.

At ten-thirty *Mana* swung around Motu Nui and two other tiny islets off the western shoulder of Rano Kau volcano. The skies were bright and the Southern Hemisphere sun was already hot. Katherine picked out a horse and rider winding their way down the windswept side of Rano Kau and reached for her binoculars. The rider's frame was strong and lithe, but a wide-brimmed hat shadowed his face. She watched as he reined in his horse and then turned to gaze down on her. *Mana* passed along the rugged coastline and Katherine lost sight of the rider.

Gillam brought the yacht into Cook's Bay (as it was called on Lieutenant Ritchie's English navigation charts). Hanga Roa, the island's only village, was about one square mile in area; scattered huts set in tiny garden plots huddled around a single flagstaff, its Chilean colors flapping wildly in the wind. Gillam took a bearing off the village church, dropped anchor at 12:45 P.M., and then made his customary terse entry in the logbook: "Arrived Easter Is. Anchored Cook's Bay."

The dry earth and smoky scent of the island wafted on the offshore breeze toward *Mana*, but the sensuous pleasure of it did not last long. Katherine and Scoresby watched in mounting alarm as a huge crowd, nearly all of the island's approximately 250 residents, materialized on the shore. Rapa Nui people shouted, laughed, and called out with an enthusiasm bordering on hysteria. Men, women, and children piled into fishing boats while others, who were equally curious but more wary, kept their distance, children and dogs swarming around their feet. Katherine scanned the scene, anxiously seeking the reassuringly white face of Company manager Percy Edmunds. Finally, to her relief, Edmunds appeared on horseback. He cut through the crowd and dismounted, then got into one of the boats and came out to *Mana*.

Edmunds was a rugged, suntanned man with a black mustache. He wore a tropical white shirt and pants and a wide-brimmed straw hat and spoke in friendly, colorful phrases. Katherine ushered him below for tea, but as the thermometer climbed steadily the heat, in Edmunds' words, "took the ginger off the biscuit" and they retreated topside. The uproar ashore had not diminished when Edmunds disembarked, but soon the crowd on the beach settled down to watch and wait. When darkness fell they built fires along the shore, talking and singing late into the night.

The biggest problem Gillam faced was finding a safe anchorage for *Mana*, and he kept her constantly on the move to avoid crashing on the rocky coastline. Lights were set out and the watch posted, but no one aboard *Mana* slept. The biggest problem Bailey could see was the treeless landscape: There was no wood at all to make a cook fire.

The next morning Katherine was awake at daybreak. She dressed hurriedly and then watched from the deck as Scoresby got the ship's launch in the water and went ashore. Percy Edmunds had sent two oxcarts to transport *Mana* supplies and stores, and the Rapa Nui men who had been selected as a workforce stood ready. One man was obviously in charge: Juan Tepano, Edmunds' ranch foreman and *jefe* or "headman" of Hanga Roa village. Katherine recognized Tepano as the man she had seen riding the crest of the island the day before.

The Rapa Nui people who greeted *Mana* in 1914 were living in a repressed and desperately impoverished state. They were confined to Hanga Roa and a surrounding, tiny patchwork of about six acres. The rest of the island—more than 90 percent of its surface—was deserted of human life but used by the Company as pasture for thousands of sheep and other livestock. Ceremonial centers (*ahu*) with toppled statues (*moai*) and family graves, as well as extensive and once productive plantations and the best fishing grounds, were all inaccessible to islanders. The only crop foods were bananas and sweet potatoes grown in small household plots. Big, deep-sea fish were rarely available, and smaller coastal fish and sea urchins were commonly eaten. Milk was rare and meat so expensive that Company sheep and cattle were regularly poached.

Mana sailed blithely into this history like a butterfly fluttering into the eye of a typhoon. The expedition promptly off-loaded a massive amount of cargo—enough to feed and probably clothe the entire island community—and it was small wonder that a drumbeat of excited gossip rolled over Hanga Roa. Survey equipment, tools, rope, saddles, tack, clothes, blankets, and especially food poured from the yacht's hold. Live chickens and ducks, bags of flour and rice, crates of English ham and bacon, butter, marmalade, tea, fresh produce of every description, and exotic tinned foods must have seemed like manna from heaven to the poverty-stricken Rapa Nui people.

Juan Tepano's job was to supervise the workers and keep the rest of the people at bay, but everyone wanted to help; everyone wanted to see what the boxes and crates contained. In spite of Tepano's stern warnings and constant watchfulness, within hours it became clear to an unnerved and angry Scoresby that Mana Expedition supplies were being pilfered and spirited away. Scoresby may not have blamed Tepano personally, but his impression of Rapa Nui people, from this first encounter, was negative.

Everything was stacked and loaded on an oxcart. Straining against the heavy wooden yoke, two lumbering beasts pulled the cart over the dirt road that wound along the coastline to the bay of Hanga Piko, a mile south of the village. There the supplies were locked in a sturdy wool shed for safekeeping. When the shed was full to capacity, the rest of the goods were taken a mile inland to the Company compound at Mataveri. When the storage building there was also filled, the overflow went into the attic of Mataveri house, Edmunds' home.

Three days after arrival Katherine finally disembarked *Mana*. She handed down a locked, white tin trunk with "Mrs. S. Routledge" painted on the lid in black block letters, then climbed into the launch with Charles Jeffery and another crewman. A few strokes of their oars and the Pacific breakers carried her toward the island whose history had consumed her attention for over four years. The water was crystal clear and bluer than any she had ever seen. The black rocks that loomed ahead were pitted, almost embossed or engraved, with the burst bubbles of ancient lava. Once they made the tiny beach, Katherine hitched up her skirts as hands reached for hers, and before the next wave hit, she was on the Rapa Nui sand.

Katherine stood alone in a small circle of eager, amiable people who were surprised to see a European woman come ashore. Looking around, she saw "a handsome race" of people "possessing attractive manners." While their clothing was eccentric and shabby, the children bounced with energy, the women had flowers in their hair, and some men wore garlands of fragrant leaves. Katherine felt immediately comfortable and, oddly, at home. She climbed aboard the oxcart to sit next to Tepano. He knew some English and Katherine had studied Spanish, so they must have greeted one another. Surely she noticed that Tepano was a handsome man, lean and slightly built with intense eyes and a strong, thoughtful presence. He was just a year or so younger than Katherine and had nut-brown skin, black hair, and a lush mustache. In contrast to the poverty the other Rapa Nui men displayed, Tepano was well dressed in a wool riding jacket and good, polished boots.

He drove the oxcart along the rutted road, and Katherine looked back over her shoulder to catch a last glimpse of *Mana* lying restlessly in the bay. Ahead of her loomed the smooth, grass-covered slope of Rano Kau volcano while, on her right, the sea crashed against the island's rocky coast. If Tepano and Katherine spoke again to one another it would have been at her initiative, and if she did not understand his replies, she would not have displayed her ignorance. She probably simply smiled or nodded as she used to do when, as a young Oxford student, she and her brother Wilson toured the Brittany countryside with a talkative but unintelligible French guide. The oxcart rolled noisily along, and then turned inland and up the long lane to Mataveri farm and Percy Edmunds' house.

Mataveri is a flat, fertile plain backing up to the steep slope of Rano Kau, and the 1,742-acre farm lay on land that stretched from the slopes of the volcano to the bay of Hanga Piko. The house was set in a small compound of paddocks, stables, and overgrown gardens. The simple, wood-frame building was elevated on a foundation of ancient and beautifully carved stones that, long ago, had supported a Rapa Nui ritual structure. Glass-paned windows looked toward the sea, and a wide veranda ran along the front. There were six sparsely furnished rooms and a detached kitchen.

Katherine climbed down off the oxcart and went up the steps to the veranda. No one greeted her, so she sat down in a creaky wicker chair to wait for Scoresby, Edmunds, and the others. Tepano turned the oxcart to go back down the road, and when the rumbling of its wheels died away, Katherine felt for the first time the total, enveloping silence of Rapa Nui. The wind dropped, the grass ceased stirring, and not even a bird called. She sat for a long time in the perfect silence she had sought so futilely in Quaker Meeting until, finally, she became aware of the far-off roll of the sea. In this Mataveri silence, Katherine met Rapa Nui in a private and personal encounter that moved her deeply.

The little watch pinned to the lapel of her khaki jacket ticked and, too soon, Katherine became aware of the sounds of horses coming up the lane. Scoresby, Lieutenant Ritchie, and Edmunds rode into her reverie and dismounted in a cacophony of male voices and boots thumping on wood planks. For the next several hours Katherine dealt with the details of settling down and then, in the early evening, watched a glorious sunset. With Scoresby and Lieutenant Ritchie, she joined Percy Edmunds in Mataveri house for her first meal on Rapa Nui.

The door on to the veranda was open, for the night was hot, and the roar of breakers could be heard on the beach; while near at hand conversation was accompanied by a never-ceasing drone of mosquitoes. The light of the unshaded lamp was reflected from the clean rough-dried cloth of the table round which we sat, and lit up our host's features, the keen brown face of a man who had lived for some thirty years or more, most of it in the open air and under a tropical sun. He was telling us of events which one hardly thought existed outside magazines and books of adventure, but doing it so quietly that, with closed eyes, it might have been fancied that the entertainment was at some London restaurant, and we were still at the stage of discussing the latest play.

Mataveri farm—on land that had been, until 1867 to 1868, the staging ground for ancient, exotic birdman ceremonies—and the village of Hanga Roa were worlds apart, and their isolation was geographical, cultural, economic, and profoundly symbolic. Hanga Roa's small, dark houses, built of stone or cast-off wood with thatched roofs, clustered together haphazardly. Dirt floors were strewn with straw, there was no furniture, and families slept crowded together on the floor. There was no school, no medical care, no sanitary facilities, and only one or two water cisterns. Mataveri was strictly off-limits to all but a chosen few, like Tepano. Workmen were given seasonal work shearing sheep or running stock, and wages of about twenty to forty centavos a day were credited against purchases in the Company store. Most families were enslaved by debt, and a man's entire yearly salary was just enough to buy a simple cotton dress for his wife.

The link between Mataveri and Hanga Roa was Juan Tepano, a pragmatic and adaptable man of many talents. The son of Victoria Veriamu and Rano, her third husband, Tepano was baptized Catholic and had served in the Chilean military, where he had acquired a sense of personal discipline, punctuality, and familiarity with weapons. Upon his return to the island in 1901 he was named "headman" of the community and, in 1902, appointed "mayor" by the Company. He had police power in the village and freedom to travel all over the island, making him the natural target of resentment. Nonetheless, Tepano commanded respect.

Tepano initially knew nothing about the scientific purposes of the Mana Expedition, and nothing had prepared him for a woman like Katherine. She, however, immediately grasped Tepano's central role in island society, although he only worked sporadically with the expedition until December 1914. Then, after Scoresby was unexpectedly detained in mainland Chile for over four months, Tepano and Katherine worked alongside one another nearly every day. They communicated in a patois of Spanish and English, but by the last few months of her fieldwork, they had added Rapanui to the mix.

After Katherine praised Tepano in *The Mystery of Easter Island*, visitors and researchers who followed in her footsteps avidly sought him out. Famed Swiss anthropologist Alfred Métraux of the 1934 Franco-Belgian Expedition to Easter Island was among them. Tepano not only gave Métraux information gleaned from Rapa Nui elders, he also *repeated what he had learned from Katherine*. Métraux said that Tepano was Katherine's "interpreter" and had "retained" from his contact with her "a keen interest in the past. He is intelligent, quick, and proud of his reputation as the *maori* [expert] of the old folklore. When other natives are asked about their ancestors they always refer to Juan Tepano."

In fact, Tepano was far more than a mere interpreter. He took a firm stance between Katherine and Rapa Nui society, and Katherine said that he was her "escort" who prevented her from being "imposed on." His role as protector was as much for his own prestige and economic benefit as it was for her comfort and safety, but as time passed, Tepano became a real link between Katherine and the island—her companion in the field, chief collaborator, and friend. Though from two completely different and distant cultures, Tepano and Katherine were surprisingly alike. Sensitive, savvy, and ambitious, their innate gifts and dominant personalities caused other people to perceive them as odd, and to resent them. Each of them was an outsider within his or her own culture—and in recognizing that they found a kind of kinship.

Katherine came to Rapa Nui because, she told her brother Wilson, she wanted to experience "the sensuous, the strenuous and the intellectual" challenges and excitements of a free but engaged life. Katherine was a harsh judge and a critical observer, but she was also sensitive and sought unconventional relationships with interesting people. "Any real success" she had on the island, Katherine later said with uncharacteristic humility, was "due to the intelligence of one individual known as Juan Tepano."

First Impressions
and Plans

✦

THE ROLLING, GRASS-COVERED HILLS OF EASTER ISLAND, the breaking surf and endless sky entranced Katherine. In the deep mists of time, she said, "great lights and flowing lava must have gleamed across the expanse of water, then gradually lessened and died away, leaving their work to be moulded by the wind and tide." Three massive volcanoes rose from the sea bottom to create the island's triangular shape and remained as landmarks. Maunga Terevaka (1,674 feet above sea level) anchors the northern point of the island. To the east lie the smooth, grassy slopes of Poike headland, and to the west, Rano Kau marks the extreme southwest point of Rapa Nui. Rano Kau rises 985 feet over Mataveri and hides, deep within its crater, a freshwater lake nearly a mile wide.

The deserted ruins of Orongo—a ceremonial "village" that was once the epicenter of the birdman religion—balance precariously on the precipitous brink of Rano Kau. The stone buildings are expertly made of cantilevered basalt slabs and face a dangerous cliff that plunges nearly one thousand feet into the sea below. Hundreds of exotic petroglyphs are cut into the surfaces of the boulders so skillfully that they seem to move and breathe in the sunlight and shifting shadows. Below, the Pacific rolls in from the faraway, crystalline shores of Antarctica, slowly eating away at the volcano's base and battering three tiny offshore islets clustered like ducklings around their island mother. The largest of these is Motu Nui, an ancient sooty-tern rookery.

Orongo was the first place Katherine wanted to see. It was home to Hoa Hakananai'a, the statue she had seen in the British Museum. Carved of basalt, it had been planted in the ground, buried to its chin, inside one of the Orongo buildings. The English had removed it, along with another, smaller statue that had been stuck upright in the ground near Mataveri. Katherine hoped to accurately pinpoint the original locations of both statues.

One early morning soon after the Mana Expedition's arrival Percy Edmunds guided Katherine, Scoresby, and Lieutenant Ritchie up a winding trail from Mataveri to the top of Rano Kau volcano, where they dismounted to gaze down into the caldera. The wind filled Katherine's ears and tore words out of her mouth. She planted her feet as firmly as she could on the ground, but the deep darkness of the crater's lake and the sweep of the Pacific horizon gave her vertigo. Suddenly the wind dropped and silence descended. It was an immediate relief but almost too deep, Katherine thought, a "silence which may be felt," the utter stillness of death. The sudden, distant cry of circling seabirds brought her out of her reverie, and Katherine retreated a short distance away to solid ground, scribbling her thoughts in her journal. Orongo, she wrote, surpassed "the wildest scenes depicted in romance." It would become the site of her best work.

Early the next day Edmunds took the Routledges to Rano Raraku—the volcano that is the ancient statue (*moai*) quarry. They explored eastward along "Brander's road" for nearly two hours until, one by one, massive statues implanted upright in the crater's grassy exterior slopes gradually emerged from the distant shadows. Others lay scattered about on their face, back, or side like so many discarded toys. Uncounted hundreds more rested high above, layered in quarried tiers on the cliff face and not yet cut loose from the rock. Katherine was "overcome by the wonder of the scene."

Edmunds rode ahead along a narrow pathway that wound through a forest of sculpture, and the Routledges followed, calling out to one another as they discovered, one by one, each new statue. They dismounted and scrambled dangerously on foot over the quarries, encountering statues in all phases of completion. Each statue was truncated at the waist, and none of them had carved eye sockets. Some were only roughed out, but others had elongated ears and carefully delineated arms clasped tight to their sides; graceful hands rested low on their bellies in a uniform posture. A few lay so close together that it was impossible to imagine how carvers and other workmen had toiled amidst dust and debris without stumbling over one another. Entering the crater's hidden interior, Katherine looked down into a huge eye of water, its upward gaze reflecting the silently moving clouds overhead. She plopped to the ground and pulled off her riding duster. Not a breath of air was stirring.

Orongo had impressed Katherine with its bold natural setting and the precariousness of its perch on the lip of wave-lapped cliffs. The statue quarry, in contrast, was an auditory experience, humming in her imagination with creative human industry and vast ambition. Katherine imagined the thunk of heavy stone tools on the soft, compressed volcanic ash and the creaking of enormous wood timbers straining against tightening lines as statues were lowered, pushed, and pulled. Here, she thought, deep in Rano Raraku, was the once-beating heart of the island, the profound and mysterious vision that had driven the Rapa Nui people so relentlessly forward.

In the depths of one of Katherine's duster pockets she carried handwritten notes Scoresby had taken from a publication by Paymaster William J. Thomson of USS *Mohican*. It described a brief period between December 19 and New Year's Day, 1886, when Thomson had led American sailors on a rapid but remarkably productive reconnaissance of the entire island. With Alexander Salmon Jr. as intermediary they had purchased artifacts for the Smithsonian Institution—including priceless *kohau rongorongo* and a basalt statue similar to Hoa Hakananai'a. Thomson's report, although flawed by hearsay and his inability to deal with the Rapanui language, was the only account of the island in existence at that time, in Katherine's opinion, "with any pretension to scientific value."

Now, Katherine leafed through her notes. There were, Thomson said, ninety-three statues on the interior of the crater, of which forty were lying on slopes or propped up, partially buried, in holes. The rest lay in quarries. He estimated their average weight at between ten and twelve tons, but also guessed that some probably weighed up to forty tons. He had excavated in Rano Raraku, but Katherine had no idea where—his descriptions were unclear. Putting it all together, she thought there must be about 250 statues in Rano Raraku, all just waiting, sightlessly and still, for her. Katherine made up her mind: She would start her own investigations on the interior, snug between the lake and the crater's ancient, crumbling cliffs.

Back at Mataveri, Katherine spent a restless, nearly sleepless night as the wind rose and fell. In the light of a new day the Routledges realized that they faced a huge task impossible to accomplish in the six months they had planned to stay on the island. Katherine, however, was stubbornly optimistic and argued in favor of beginning work in Rano Raraku right away. Scoresby wanted to find and explore hidden caves—and the opinions of T. A. Joyce and R. R. Marett were on his side. Finally, they agreed to establish two expedition outposts: their "town house" would remain at Mataveri, convenient to Orongo and Hanga Roa village. Their "country establishment" would be set up at the base of Rano Raraku.

On April 26 they began a detailed reconnaissance of the island. Gillam sailed *Mana* back and forth along the coast while Katherine and Lieutenant Ritchie studied every cove or isolated rock with binoculars and sketched prominent geographical features. This was a clever move that saved a good deal of time. The island, Katherine said, had its own marked individuality—yet it reminded her not of a South Seas dreamland but, surprisingly, instead brought to mind the wild rocks of the Scilly Isles or the Cornish coast. The subtropical climate suited her; the landscape's strikingly sensuous beauty invigorated and challenged her. She was extraordinarily happy, and each new day brought broader horizons.

Katherine and Scoresby rode over the island's rock-strewn landscape, deserted of human life and eerily quiet. They crisscrossed one another's paths repeatedly and then doubled back along the coast toward Mataveri. They encountered literally hundreds upon hundreds of stone ruins: hearths, circular garden walls, and house foundations. Usually, Scoresby dismounted and, using the metal tape measure he and Katherine had received as a wedding gift, measured the remains. Alternatively, he paced off the distances, each of his long strides counting as three feet. He called out the measurements to Katherine, who sat astride her horse and took notes in a field book. Often, they reversed roles. Gradually the Routledges learned to "read" the lay of the land and the pattern of archaeological remains, to discern the history of Rapa Nui on the ground.

Outside of Rano Raraku, no matter where they went, they found that not a single intact statue remained upright. Most were lying facedown and broken, their bases still resting upon flat pedestal stones atop rectangular stone platforms called *ahu*. It was obvious that the statues had once stood upright on the platforms, facing inland over fields and homes. As the Routledges knew even then, *ahu* are the Rapa Nui version of ceremonial centers (*marae*) found throughout Central and East Polynesia. Not all *ahu* had statues, and Scoresby dubbed those that did "image *ahu.*"

The most important image *ahu* were built along the coastline—massive structures made of multiton, impressively fitted basalt stones. Ahu Tongariki, lying in the curve of a large bay less than a mile from Rano Raraku, was the island's largest *ahu*. Thomson had collected human bones and skulls from many *ahu* and described the island as "one vast necropolis." Scoresby removed bones from partially exposed burials, stuffed them in saddlebags, and carried them back to Mataveri. Some were very recent, and once the hair and European clothes of a male skeleton were discovered still intact. Another time he found over thirty European glass trade beads buried with a woman's remains. Katherine, who took a morbid glee in "scientific body snatching," said that it was "impossible to go for more than a few hundred yards without coming across" a burial.

Ahu Tongariki possessed fifteen statues—but now only one broken fragment remained upright. Thomson, who had trenched through the central portion of the platform, found that it was honeycombed with tombs and filled with hundreds of human remains, some of which were obviously recent. Katherine's imagination was fired, and she envisioned Tongariki as a vast, occult stage:

The back of the stage, which is thus the highest part, is occupied by a great terrace, on which are set up in line the giant images, each one well separated from his neighbour, and all facing the spectator. Irrespective of where he stands he will ever see them towering above him, clear cut out against a turquoise sky. . . . The stone giants, and the faithful dead over whom they watch, are never without music, as countless waves launch their strength against the pebbled shore, showering on the figures a cloud of mist and spray.

The dramatic ceremonies that took place on image *ahu*, she said, could only be imagined. "Every day, as the power to see increased," Katherine experienced a "greater sense of wonder and marvel."

One of the expedition's first guides was a personable young man named Maanga, who was from the Tuamotu islands. Although he was trustworthy and a good worker, he had no ancestral connection with the land. When Katherine questioned him for place names or the functions of certain archaeological features, he could provide little. She quickly concluded that the expedition needed guides who knew the identities and histories of Rapa Nui families as well as the names of sites. Slowly, she began to make contacts and tried to establish trust—just as she had done in Africa.

Rapa Nui legends say that, as he lay dying, Hotu Matu'a divided the island among his six sons. Each plot of land was commensurate in value with each man's birth order within the family. The eldest inherited the greatest share of his father's *mana*, the royal estate lands at Anakena and the powerful title of paramount chief. The youngest son, called Hotu Iti, was his father's favorite and received the entire eastern portion of the island—including Rano Raraku. This legacy acknowledged that Hotu Iti, although outranked by his brothers, was somehow gifted. About ten known lineages evolved from this first division, and Katherine, like Thomson before her, called them clans.

One of Katherine's most important ethnographic discoveries was that individual families, many of whom had members still alive in Hanga Roa, were traditionally connected with specific parcels of land. If she could determine boundary lines it would be possible to forge again the broken links between image *ahu*, the statues that had once stood upright on *ahu*, and clans. That would enable her to address one of the Mana Expedition's basic research questions: How are the statues linked to the present inhabitants? In Africa she had championed native land rights, and on Easter Island she became driven to discern the human history that framed the island's archaeological remains.

She began the tedious work of naming the clans and then sorting them into one of two major political divisions, each with a long history of animosity for the other. The western alliance ("greater tribes") was called Ko Tu'u—it contained the Miru lands of Anakena. The eastern alliance ("lesser tribes") was Hotu Iti. Unwittingly, the Routledges positioned the Mana Expedition at Mataveri in Ko Tu'u and, in the east, at Rano Raraku, which Katherine dubbed Camp Hotu Iti. Such an apparent acknowledgment of ancient political divisions set the stage for dramatic events to come.

Faced with a complex social and historical situation and a formidable treasure trove of sites to study, and with no way of knowing what they might still discover, the Routledges began tentatively. One of the expedition's first projects was to document the heavy, red stone cylinders that had been balanced on the heads of some statues. Scoresby made careful, useful drawings and measurements of some at Ahu Tongariki. He explored Puna Pau, the quarry in which the cylinders were carved, and then assigned Lieutenant Ritchie the task of mapping it. Ritchie and two men produced the map in just nine days, then began to survey the largest image *ahu* lying between Vinapu and Tongariki.

Following his "shakedown" practice with tents in Nairobi, Scoresby experimentally set up the expedition's prefabricated wood and iron houses in Edmunds' garden. They were enormously complicated, heavy, and hard to manage, and Scoresby realized he would need capable help to erect them. Edmunds recommended hiring a French carpenter named Vicente "Varta" Pont, who was married to a Rapa Nui woman named María Heremeta. Varta set up the houses in Camp Hotu Iti and, as Scoresby's arthritic shoulder grew more painful, carried his field equipment and saddled and unsaddled his horse.

Scoresby turned his determined, methodical attention toward finding secret caves and, he hoped, stashes of *kohau rongorongo*. Countless thousands of caves are on Rapa Nui, and Thomson and all Company managers including Edmunds had excavated dozens of them without finding anything of real value. Rapa Nui people had ransacked many others in the hope of finding something to sell to the crewmen of visiting ships. Scoresby groped his way through pitch-dark caverns and crawled through lava tubes filled with rainwater, but got nothing for his effort except banged-up shins and a major case of what, in retrospect, was probably bronchitis. He blamed the Rapa Nui men for leading him astray and refused to pay them. They turned away in disgust.

The Routledges had been on the island about two months when *Mana* left for her first of what, in the end, became three round-trips to the Chilean mainland. Gillam's task was to purchase new provisions in Talcahuano, make repairs to *Mana*, and collect the mail. On May 23, 1914 Gillam deposited Frank T. Green, along with his bedding, cameras, and photographic gear, on the beach at Anakena. The Routledges rode across the middle of the island to deliver their dispatch bag to *Mana*. It contained a report to the British Association for the Advancement of Science; the first of several newspaper articles Katherine would write for the *Spectator;* her letters to Sir Baden Powell, Lyle McAllum, Wilson Pease, Scoresby's sister Bessie and his mother, and a charming birthday note to her niece Hilda:

> The statues here can't go through the post & I don't think that there is anything else to send. What you would like is one of the ponies. There are 500 of them running wild, more than any one knows what to do with so every body rides, even the lady who does the washing rides up a volcano & washes her clothes in the crater where all the hot ashes used to come out, there is a lake there now. There is one foal that walks about all over here & comes & pokes its head into our pockets, it lost its mother. . . . This is a lovely [island] quite like a story book . . .

Katherine, Scoresby, Green (now expedition photographer), and the Rapa Nui men with them watched and waited, their horses' legs deep in the sands of Anakena beach. *Mana* moved out quickly and then, all sails full to bursting, disappeared over the horizon in the gathering twilight. Then they set off, safari style, for Mataveri, but were losing the light. Stumbling along the rock-strewn trail, they arrived at Mataveri, exhausted, at 9 P.M. With *Mana* gone, the expedition's link with the outside was severed.

Orongo:
The Eleventh Hour

✦

KATHERINE REACHED INTO THE POCKET OF HER KHAKI
field jacket and pulled out a folded paper: R. R. Marett's note describing
how to excavate in caves.

> Fix a base line by means of a firmly moored tape, and with two sticks nailed
> across each other exactly at right angles you can plot out the ground plan in
> squares of a foot (or yds. if a big cave, or better still, perhaps, metres). Then
> when each object is found put it in [a] separate envelope or packet and mark
> at time of finding the space in which it was found and the depth. In a big
> cave, of course, it may be impossible to cover the whole area, but in that case
> choose a likely spot and make a broad trench—broad enough to allow free
> work, and light—and carry it right across the cave, and down to the bottom,
> if you can reach it; get a perpendicular section, and examine it carefully for
> evidence of stratification. If different soils, bring away specimens of each
> (labeling [sic] each carefully). Bone, implements, etc. can be identified at
> leisure afterwards; but the man on the spot must locate exactly.

The "man on the spot," if excavations were done properly, was sup-
posed to be either Katherine or Scoresby. Unfortunately, they didn't follow
Marett's perfunctory advice.

Islanders always used the word *ana* (cave) rather than *hare* (house) when
talking with Katherine about the Orongo stone buildings, and she could see
why. To enter them she wriggled on her stomach through doorways that
were actually low, narrow tunnels. The air inside the dark, dank interiors was
close, and with every breath Katherine seemed to take in the heavy, shadowy
essence of past occupants. Sometimes the light of her flickering candle stub

glanced off lifelike red and white paintings of birds in flight and European ships in full sail.

Katherine mapped out a plan to investigate Orongo. She started preliminary work almost immediately after the Mana Expedition arrived and continued until July of 1914. Then, after a long break until December she began investigations that lasted until March of 1915, with follow-up work continuing until the expedition's departure five months later. Lieutenant Ritchie, who had the benefit of plans of Orongo buildings created by Lieutenant Dundas of HMS *Topaze* and Lieutenant Symond of USS *Mohican,* mapped the entire complex with the help of Antonio Haoa Pakomio.

Frank T. Green took photographs but also cleared and "partially excavated" at least two of the Orongo buildings; Katherine dug at least four and Scoresby excavated another half dozen. She found paintings in nine houses and carvings in ten and collected seashells, moss, stone spear points, and beach cobbles from the floors. In or in front of three buildings Henry MacLean, Antonio Haoa, or another Rapa Nui man, Carlos Teao Tori, found and then removed engraved stones. One of them was a fabulous "doorpost" carved as a human face. These and other objects were carried down to Mataveri to be crated for removal.

Rapa Nui workmen reported everything back to the villagers at Hanga Roa—where the expedition was working, what they had found, and what they were removing. Three *moai* had been removed from the island in the past fifty years, and important objects associated with Orongo had been sold or traded to missionaries and ships' crewmen. No one was surprised that these newcomers were ransacking Orongo or other Rapa Nui sites, but the people resented the Routledges' sense of entitlement and were angry that they paid nothing for the objects taken.

From time to time Juan Tepano joined the crew working at Orongo—mostly to keep a sharp eye on what was being removed. He watched as Katherine scrambled around on the very edge of Rano Kau, sketching and counting the petroglyphs carved in stone. It was dangerous work, and the wind was a constant threat. Somehow, Katherine discovered that Tepano was, she said, "an able native draughtsman." After Katherine had made notes on more than 368 petroglyphs, Tepano sketched representative examples of major design categories for her. She counted over a hundred carvings of frigate birds, all with human hands and feet, and labeled them "ducks," but he told her they were *tangata manu,* or birdmen—and she was on her way to uncovering the secrets of Orongo.

For weeks Katherine futilely attempted to pinpoint the Orongo building in which the British Museum statue, Hoa Hakananai'a, had been found. Rapa Nui workmen provided conflicting answers to her questions, but finally everyone agreed that building 11, which belonged to the highest-ranking Miru clan from the western part of the island, was the right location. Failing to make sense of J. Linton Palmer's confusing report, and puzzled as to why Hoa Hakananai'a would be hidden in a dark Orongo building rather than placed on an *ahu*, Katherine needed to talk to someone who knew the statue's history. When Tepano introduced her to Victoria Veriamu, his mother, Katherine found a gold mine of information.

Veriamu's age in 1914 is uncertain, but she was probably the oldest Rapa Nui woman then living. Even so, Veriamu's strong character and intelligence still shone in her eyes. She had been born on the eastern part of the island, literally in the shadow of the great statue quarries of Rano Raraku, and had been a beauty in her youth. Veriamu had had three husbands, but all of her children except Juan Tepano and a daughter—who lived in the leper colony—had perished in the mid-1800s. Her last husband, Rano (baptized "Iovani"), was Tepano's father and Veriamu's favorite. Rano was from the eastern district, and it was through him that Tepano claimed the lands around Tongariki.

Katherine learned that Rano had been an eyewitness to the removal of Hoa Hakananai'a from Orongo. Torometi, the tough Rapa Nui war chief who had tormented missionaries, had arranged the whole thing. The English had demolished part of the stone building to remove the statue, then dragged it, facedown, all the way to the sea, where it was floated out and hoisted aboard HMS *Topaze*. Sometime later, Rano left Veriamu and his family and departed for Tahiti.

Now outsiders were again at Orongo and none of the Rapa Nui people, including Tepano, trusted the Routledges or the Mana Expedition—for good reason. Yet Katherine had something to offer them: her intellect, her intense curiosity, her almost perverse inability to relinquish her demand for detail, and her spirituality. These qualities, once some of them became known, were eccentricities that transformed her in Rapa Nui eyes. When the men who worked for her saw Katherine bring a large, black-and-white photograph of Hoa Hakananai'a to Orongo and crawl with it into building 11, she symbolically returned the *moai* to his rightful place on the island. All Rapa Nui people tell and retell such interesting events, and for a while at least, Katherine was linked to Hoa Hakananai'a—certainly to his history and possibly to his *mana*.

Slowly, doors began to open. Katherine made the acquaintance of Jotefa Maherenga, the oldest man on the island at the time. His memory was sharp, but the details he recalled of Hoa Hakananai'a and Orongo did not jibe with those of Veriamu, and the two old people quarreled frequently. Katherine sometimes came away from these meetings on the veranda of the

Mataveri house or in Veriamu's garden more frustratingly confused than enlightened, but she stubbornly returned and asked the same questions over and over again. Katherine realized that she was getting details that probably did not go back further than about one hundred years, although some of the overarching themes were surely far older than that.

Veriamu remembered best the Orongo initiation rites for little girls, while Jotefa told Katherine about rituals for young boys. Virginal "bird children"— fledglings like the downy, white-feathered terns in the offshore rookery of Motu Nui—were confined in special houses and, perhaps, in the "caves" that were Orongo buildings. They were pampered and fed to produce white skin and portly bodies. After about three months they were brought to the most sacred part of Orongo. The girls—and sometimes other "fine women" of the island—stood on the carved rocks, their legs wide apart. Priests standing just below them examined their genitals and then carved petroglyphs of vulva (*komari*) in their honor.

The boys' coming-of-age ceremonies were less exotic. Jotefa's parents arranged the one that he and ten other children had participated in, and his father paid the officiating priests—called *ivi atua*—with chickens. Some priests were women, and all spoke prophetically with the voices of gods and the ancestors. Jotefa was about seven years old and not yet baptized by the missionaries. His sturdy little body was adorned with designs in white paint, some of which Katherine later recognized were similar to those on wood carvings. He wore special wooden ornaments and a loincloth called a *hami*.

Jotefa and the other children gathered in a semicircle in front of the doorway of building 11, their backs to the sea. Hoa Hakananai'a waited silently inside the dark building, buried up to its chin in the earth and facing away from the doorway. Like the boys, the *moai* was painted in red and white, and he was said to have worn a special belt made of bark cloth and rubbed with red pigment. The priests chanted, the wind swirled, and distant birds called as the children raised tremulous voices and sang to the *moai*.

Hoa Hakananai'a had presided over these and probably other rites for at least two generations. No wonder the statue's removal was wrenching to some Rapa Nui. No wonder Katherine lay awake nights, counting the hours until dawn when she could go back to work. Mindful of Marett's advice to seek corroboration, Katherine set out determinedly to locate others who, like Jotefa and Veriamu, could share with her their youth. It was a painstaking process. She tried everything she could think of to gain trust, but only began to make real progress after Scoresby had gone to the mainland from December 5, 1914 to March 15, 1915.

Almost immediately her relationships with Rapa Nui people improved. Tepano looked after a small group of elderly men who were without family, and he brokered or arranged fruitful contacts with them and a half dozen others. Each of these colorful old Rapa Nui endeared himself in some way to Katherine, and each contributed nuggets of priceless information to her growing understanding of the island and its past. Aside from Antonio and Maanga, however, Katherine had poor social relationships with younger Rapa Nui males. They kept their distance because Juan Tepano, Katherine said, had "assumed the attitude of watch-dog" over her.

From January 1915 until the Mana Expedition's departure on August 18, 1915, Tepano was on a completely different footing with Katherine than were all other consultants or field-workers. The number of days he spent in the field with her steadily increased, as did his salary—which she negotiated personally, without going through Percy Edmunds. Katherine's financial records are careless, but even allowing for a wide margin of error, Tepano worked on many occasions without receiving a salary. This suggests several possibilities: that Tepano received benefits in trade or privileges instead of cash; that he deferred his salary to his mother or his wife (who also worked for Katherine); or that he was not paid fairly. Alternatively, Tepano's salary may have become somewhat incidental to his own quest.

Younger Rapa Nui men, if not the entire community, naturally assumed that sex was part of the bargain between Tepano and Katherine. Sex had always played a religious and economic role on Rapa Nui, just as it had in all other early island societies. When Jacob Roggeveen's men landed on Rapa Nui in 1722, they encountered young women and boys seductively arrayed along the shoreline like Sirens, and the Dutch sailors were encouraged to respond in ways appropriate to their own desires. Katherine noted that "sexual morality, as known to us, was not a strong point in life on the island."

Tepano's proprietary, "watch-dog" relationship with Katherine benefited him and enriched her work, but it also curtailed it. Headstrong, blunt, and turbulent, Katherine had rebelled against the constraining, provincial notions of Darlington society—but she did not, it seems, resent Tepano's control over her. She was flattered and beguiled by his masculine attentions and reacted to his demands in the same pliant way she had when Scoresby, so long ago in Africa, had appointed Dosa her guardian in the bush.

Katherine lived her life on the island—whether Scoresby was there or not—with a sense of enjoyment, self-expression, and personal freedom that challenged the Victorian norms that had shaped her life. She also held some quite startlingly conventional beliefs about personal morality and conduct. Tepano's life was equally conflicted. As *jefe* or headman of the village, Tepano acted as a kind of policeman. Some say he was, like Scoresby, a prig and zealous enforcer of sexual morality in others—people in Hanga Roa sang a song, a little ditty, to warn others when he was nearby. Embodying such conservative notions of sexual propriety was part of the role Tepano played in the European world. His private life, however, was not necessarily so constrained. Both Katherine and Tepano had lived deeply ambivalent lives before they met, and were equally susceptible to charm and challenge. Perhaps that was part of the attraction they had for one another.

The creative process, it is said, requires that the mind be "given the blessing of silence and the gift of sequence." Katherine spoke often of the joy she found in Rapa Nui silence, and most of the time she was in a state of complete intellectual and emotional connection and purpose. Vibrant and involved, she enjoyed good health and occasionally experienced moments of splendid perception. This is an exciting way to live and work in the field, and it is magnetically attractive to others who are drawn into such an intense quest—and for a myriad of reasons, Tepano was assuredly drawn in.

He, in turn, drew in others. "Kapiera" (Gabriel Revahiva), "Porotu" (Hongi Atua a Ure Auviri), "Te Haha" (Ramón Te Haha), and others met with Katherine in what anthropologists call veranda interviews. Katherine gave them tobacco, and they talked and laughed with her for hours. Sometimes they grew aggravated or annoyed, became bored with the topic or got fiercely angry at being criticized or disagreed with by others, and stomped off. Then Katherine changed her tactics and coaxed them back.

"Langitopa" (Matamu'a Rangitopa I Ka'i) was the source of names that had been given to quarries and some statues; he also told her several important legends and many less credible stories. Katherine brought Langitopa out to Camp Hotu Iti often from July 1914 to December 1915. They explored Rano Raraku together and then sat in her tent, at night, talking. Katherine took down his words phonetically in Rapanui, but then labored for countless hours with either Varta or Henry MacLean to translate them into Spanish and English.

Langitopa was an eccentric old man with a wry sense of humor and Katherine liked him a lot. In his eagerness to help her, he once set fire to the grass on the slope of Rano Kau, hoping to expose sites Katherine could not find. The fire advanced so fast that, by two o'clock in the morning, all of Mataveri was in danger of being engulfed. The next day Katherine paid Langitopa for his services and reluctantly dismissed him.

Katherine painstakingly traced genealogies and connected a family web of almost two hundred Rapa Nui people. She considered information from a single source to be "inadmissible evidence," as she had in Africa, and tried to banish discrepancies through corroboration. Her methodology was to seek two individuals who could support a given point, thus giving her three statements. She rarely got that, but was able quite often to validate a statement with one other confirming opinion.

Katherine's personality was perfectly suited to this work, and she went relentlessly about her interviews in the same manner that Kate Pease had long ago gone around and around over a single topic during Woodside dinner conversations. In many ways the odd, repetitive manner that had so irritated her family was one of Katherine's best qualities as an ethnographer on Rapa Nui. It is possible, in fact, that anyone lacking this legalistic quirk might have given up on many important questions.

Scoresby, even though his pockets were always filled with trinkets and treats for children and elders, failed to establish rapport with Rapa Nui people. He had no respect or even liking for them and was convinced that Jotefa, Langitopa, and the rest of Katherine's consultants were dishonest, making up stories to either please or mislead her. Tepano, to a certain extent, shared his cynicism—he once characterized one of his own relatives as "a liar." One of the younger Rapa Nui women working at Mataveri derisively told Katherine that the old men did not know what they were talking about.

Katherine realized, of course, that some old people were only telling her what she wanted to hear, or what would bring them increased attention or personal reward. Yet she also knew that one hundred years of scattered dreams and stories still filled the dark corners of memory. Stubbornly poking and prodding, Katherine rescued and scribbled down virtually everything she was told. She became obsessed with the inexorable passage of time. Sometimes, alone in her tent, the sound of the waves and wind were paced to the remembered sound of her mother's black-and-gold wall clock, and Katherine's every moment became a determined effort to stave off the eleventh hour.

The old people with whom Katherine had the deepest connection provided her with an important part of the inducement she needed to persist so tirelessly in her quest. Katherine had an almost mystical belief that memory was not only history, but proof of being alive. As pages and pages of field-notes mounted, confirming her view of herself as a "seeker" in the Quaker tradition, Katherine stashed everything in her white tin trunk.

On Rapa Nui Katherine was removed from the "gathered" security of Quaker communal spirituality and responded by attending services conducted in the village church by Nicolás Pakarati Urepotahi, a catechist or trained Catholic lay preacher. Pakarati came into Katherine's sights only reluctantly, and she never established more than a limited rapport with him. Pakarati, she discovered, had information that went far beyond the puberty rites described by Veriamu and Jotefa. He had been a direct participant in the final stages of the central religion of Orongo: the birdman ceremonies. Porotu, too, had participated. Pakarati told Katherine that he and six other men had once spent a month on the islet of Motu Nui, waiting for the migrating waves of sooty terns and other birds to arrive.

When Katherine knew him Pakarati was a dignified, literate man. He showed his age in his face but was lean, strong, and healthy. His unique personal style was expressed in a proclivity to keep his fingernails quite long and to wear an earring in his right ear. He favored European suits and interesting caps and had a crisp mustache laced with gray. Pakarati was born into the Tupahotu clan at Mataveri and grew up near Hanga Piko, where he lived with his mother and grandmother. In his youth he had been baptized Catholic and was then selected from among several candidates to travel to Mo'orea in Tahiti, where he took up residence in an isolated, mountaintop enclave and trained as a catechist. He met and married eighteen-year-old Elizabet Rangitaki Temaki, who was from the Tuamotus. Tahitians, it was said, feared the women of her island as witches.

Pakarati and his bride returned to Rapa Nui in 1888, the same year that Chile annexed the island. Twenty years had passed since Hoa Hakananai'a had been removed from the island, the birdman ceremonies had ended, and all islanders had been baptized in 1867. Traditional beliefs, however, had not been eradicated. Rapa Nui people depended upon male and female healers and diviners to ease the pains of childbirth or the agonies of death, and Pakarati did not directly challenge those practitioners of the old ways. He also accommodated some Orongo concepts in his Catholic teachings, as he had been taught to do, and both of the Routledges recognized that.

Tepano had been baptized Catholic, but like all islanders his spiritual life was a complex mix of past and present belief systems. He told Katherine that he "firmly believed" in dangerous personal spirits called *akuaku*, and in the predictive power of dreams. Rapa Nui souls, he said, appeared at the moment of death to friend and foe alike. Katherine understood Tepano's beliefs completely, accepted them, and, in her own eccentric way, shared them.

One day in late May, just two months after the Mana Expedition's arrival on Rapa Nui, Katherine traded a blanket and some paint to Tepano for a rough, odd little stone *moai* he (or someone else) had taken from a cave on the offshore islet of Motu Nui. Tepano told Katherine it was the "boundary marker" that anchored the line dividing Rapa Nui into east/west districts. The line ascended the cliffs of Orongo and divided the buildings there, as well, into east/west sides. It ran right through building 11 and past or through Hoa Hakananai'a.

Before Scoresby left Rapa Nui in December of 1914, he drilled Tepano with questions and become convinced that there were more objects to locate in caves on Motu Nui. Scoresby failed twice to land there but, on the third try, succeeded. He found petroglyphs on the walls of one cave, some of them painted in brilliant red, a few odd little charm stones, but nothing else. When he attempted to remove a human skull from one of the caves, Antonio and Tepano firmly stood in his way until, abashed, Scoresby backed down. This was not the first confrontation Scoresby had with Tepano, nor the last.

Katherine went out twice to Motu Nui. Her boat edged up to the wave-washed rock and then poised restlessly alongside, rising and falling with the enormous swells rolling in from the open sea. A Rapa Nui man leaped onto the rock with a rope. His job was to watch the bow of the boat and, at the same time, the swells behind it, then signal when the boat would be lifted to its highest point and it was time for the next person to jump. Katherine stood up in the middle of the boat, waiting. The boat rose and fell, rose and fell, and then, without warning, she was literally picked up and flung on the rock by the Rapa Nui man behind her. She clung there, then crawled up and over, finally lying on the dry grass unable to breathe.

A few birds circled forlornly overhead, so close she could hear the wind under their wings. She found her way to the narrow entrances of two little caves, each of them choked with grass. Crawling inside, Katherine came out in a small, circular room about ten feet in diameter with a low ceiling. She found four skeletons lying side by side on the floor, and the bones of a fifth scattered haphazardly near the entrance.

> On the walls were three heads, carved in relief, the only ones encountered; they were adorned with touches of red paint. The one which was best wrought was twenty inches in length, and projected some two to three inches from the surface of the wall. . . . The sides of the cave were also adorned with incised drawings of birds. In order to copy these carvings by the light of a small candle, it was necessary to encamp among the damp mould of the floor in contact with the remains of the dead. The proceeding felt not a little gruesome, even to a now hardened anthropologist.

The drawings Katherine made are hurried and sketchy, and one can almost sense her need to get what she could and get out fast.

The Mana Expedition made both a mistake and a discovery about death on Rapa Nui. Scoresby, who had studied medicine, failed utterly to see archaeological evidence of the widespread practice of cremation at image *ahu* sites, but Katherine discovered cannibalism—not the actual practice of it, but stories about people who, it was said, had eaten human flesh. One day, she encountered the remains of a human skeleton said to be that of Ko Tori, the island's lavishly tattooed "last cannibal." Riding on Rano Kau, one of the old

Rapa Nui men with her suddenly jumped from his horse and vanished into a crevice in the rocks: "I dismounted, scrambled into a little grotto, or natural cave, where a skeleton was extended; the skull was missing, but the jaw-bone was present, and the rest of the bones were in regular order." Katherine collected the bones and passed them out the mouth of the cave. She then wrapped them in grass and packed them in her picnic basket. Sitting down on a rock, she primly asked to be told the story of Ko Tori. He had died an eccentric but respected old man, and one of his friends sitting there with Katherine had actually helped carry his body to this very cave for burial. "I had then undone this last pious work and committed sacrilege. To my great relief, however, strange sounds soon made it clear that the humourous side had appealed . . . they were suffocating with mirth. 'And now,' they said, gasping between sobs of laughter, 'Ko Tori goes in a basket to England.' "

Over many months Katherine painstakingly pieced together the recent history of Orongo from the flotsam of memory, broken traditions, and garbled history. This was no small task, and she performed a major service to science. Katherine recorded a mass of conflicting detail told not by experts but, instead, by old people who, as children, had been wide-eyed participants in scary initiation ceremonies. Details of the birdman ceremonies were equally confusing, but she got those from old people who had participated as adults. Importantly, Katherine was the first researcher to note that Rapa Nui people understood that an ecological reason underlay the birdman rituals. Seabirds, they told her, "used to be on the land but became frightened of being killed & went to live on the islands."

Fit, young athletes—Pakarati and Porotu had been among them—represented chiefs in the sacred birdman contest. When the signal was given the athletes descended Rano Kau, plunged into shark-infested waters, and swam for their lives. Those who successfully made it to Motu Nui settled down to await the birds. The first man to secure a sooty-tern egg swam with it back to Orongo, scaled the cliff, and presented it unbroken to his chief. The reward given the athlete is not known, but the lucky chief was designated birdman for one year.

Taken in procession to Anakena, the birdman lived in seclusion until the next year's gathering at Orongo. His diet, clothing, speech, and sexual activities were all surrounded by sacred restrictions. When the priests consulted him, he intoned his wisdom in a voice that was not his own but that of a creator god called Makemake. The community feared the *mana* the birdman contained—and, in effect, channeled—and heeded his pronouncements and predictions. He and his family received honors and gifts of food.

It is quite likely that, from its inception, the birdman competition was limited to the aristocratic Miru. The rites were gradually broadened to include more western clans, and more stone buildings were built or enlarged at Orongo, just as *ahu* had been refurbished to hold bigger and heavier statues. When the eastern district of Hotu Iti—Tepano's district—joined in, the bird-man ceremonies blossomed into a pan-island phenomenon. If the victorious birdman was from the eastern district he was taken in procession to Rano Raraku, where he lived for the required year. In this intricate, innovative, and highly creative way, Rapa Nui society channeled not only spiritual power but social competition and conflict over resources as well.

Katherine was less successful in her *rongorongo* quest, but her information, nonetheless, is incredibly valuable and unique. Jotefa was her first source, but then Ramón Te Haha, who had enjoyed a long association with the last paramount chief of Rapa Nui, told her that *rongorongo* was a carefully guarded secret of the Miru. Experts or *"rongorongo* men" passed on their knowledge and skill to their sons or apprentices in organized schools of learning. They gathered together and recited chants—oral history, creation legends, genealogical information, names or lists of people slain, dates of ceremonies conducted, and much more—for the paramount chief's approval at Anakena. At other times the paramount chief visited schools established at other image *ahu* in the western district, teaching and critiquing. Katherine was told that a similar expert—apparently not the paramount chief—did the same in the eastern district, but she couldn't corroborate that.

In the mid-1800s, a Catholic lay brother, Eugéne Eyraud, gave the first *kohau rongorongo* to fall into European hands to Bishop Tepano Jaussen. A Rapa Nui man named Metoro, who was living in Tahiti, is said to have been a *maori*, or expert, who knew the meanings of some symbols and translated them for Jaussen. Others thought Metoro was a fraud. Another old man refused to recite them for Paymaster Thomson of the USS *Mohican*, but not willing to take no for an answer, the Americans invaded his house, got him drunk, showed him some photographs of *kohau rongorongo*, and got him to recite nearly fifty lines or verses that, apparently, were not decipherments but stories.

The first person Katherine met who, it was said, could actually "read" *rongorongo* was "Kirimuti" (Timikore "Timoteo" Keremuti). One of Tepano's relatives, he had been born on the island and was about eighty-six years old. Some said he was taken to Tahiti to work on the plantations when he was about twenty, but others knew only that he was away from the island for a long time. He was on the island in 1886, and when Katherine knew him Kirimuti sometimes lived in the isolated leper colony (though he was free of the disease). Kirimuti was involved in many artifact-hunting excavations with Percy Edmunds, and Katherine came to believe that he was the most intelligent of her consultants. Scoresby's fieldnotes say that when Kirimuti was "shown a picture of [rongorongo] tablets he and other old men began at once to sing them . . . it was a prayer to god & in Reply to Request for its name gave Ko-how. . . . Promises to show cave & tablets in it. Promises small statue over 300 years old." These were big promises. Tepano thought the old man flatly lied or misled on many things, but believed there was a good chance that in this instance he was telling the truth. Scoresby held out hope that Kirimuti would reveal his cave.

Te Haha told Katherine that the first settlers had brought rongorongo to the island, and that it was originally written on bark cloth, a material associated with the highest ranked and most privileged. Feather crowns and feather standards were their emblems of rank and authority. He remembered hearing snippets about rongorongo experts chanting at some Orongo ceremonies. Langitopa recalled hearing a congregation of rongorongo experts chanting all day from the cluster of petroglyph rocks at the eastern end of Orongo. Everyone agreed that the elder statesman of rongorongo was Vaka Tuku Onge a Teatea ("Tomenika"), an old man living in the squalid leper colony north of town.

Somehow, Katherine discovered that Nicolás Pakarati Urepotahi had in his possession a piece of paper that had about seventy-five rongorongo signs written on it in ink. Pakarati told Katherine that the signs had come from Tomenika, who later "acknowledged the figures as his work." Growing up, Tepano had often seen the old man making marks on banana leaves, but never carving them on wood or writing them on paper. On July 6, 1914 Katherine persuaded a very reluctant Pakarati to loan her the paper. She reciprocated by giving him one of Scoresby's collars and a tie, one of her skirts for his wife, and sugar for their children.

Katherine first showed the paper of signs to Kapiera, who said he had learned to read a form of rongorongo from Tomenika's adopted father. Kapiera "read" four lines from right to left for her. On his second attempt he associated fifteen to twenty-two Rapanui words or phrases with the same number of carved symbols. Kapiera was not consistent, however, and Katherine thought that only twelve identifications might be reliable. She lost sleep for several nights and then asked another old man to read the same paper. He haltingly recited words and phrases that were completely different from Kapiera's and, even more disappointing, changed each time he was asked to repeat them. Katherine realized that her only hope was Tomenika, and that she would have to brave the leper colony to talk to him.

It was known as early as 1873 that a bacillus caused leprosy, and in 1914 some natural oils and other substances were used as tentative treatments for the incurable illness. Because Merlet had not disclosed the presence of the disease on the island, however, Scoresby's medical kit lacked anything then available. Katherine was absolutely terrified of contracting any "fever," but Tepano visited his half sister who lived in the leper colony and Katherine took heart in that. "How could one allow," she asked, "the last vestige of knowledge in Rapa Nui to die without effort? So I went, disinfected my clothes on return, studied, it must be confessed, my fingers and toes, and hoped for the best." Katherine's bravado fails to mask her vividly determined courage and willingness to risk her life in hope of discovery.

On the morning of July 8 she rode out to the leper colony with Scoresby, Antonio, and a reluctant Henry MacLean and talked with savvy old Kirimuti. She showed him a catalogue she had made of photographs of wood carvings and other artifacts in the British Museum collection. Katherine asked him to discuss the pictures, but learned little, then asked him questions about his family. Scoresby quizzed the old man less gently and more relentlessly—in the same high-handed way he had once demanded information from old Kikuyu chiefs. The interview was uncomfortable and unproductive, Kirimuti was confused and trying to please but, Scoresby's notes say, he "declined to show his cave."

They left, and two days later, Katherine passed through Hanga Roa on her way again to the leper colony. She stopped long enough to return the original paper of signs to Pakarati, then rode on. She found Tomenika, wearing a long coat and felt hat, seated on a blanket in the sun outside his house. He was tired and suffered from painful lesions on his legs. Katherine's notes say: "quite bright and capable but legs bad. gave him paper of signs. he claimed to be the last man who cd write them but got no satisfactory explanation— must try again but difficult, interpreters naturally afraid of infection—." Tomenika asked Katherine for a paper and pencil. He put the paper on the ground in front of him and grasped the pencil. He drew circles and check marks as he recited rapidly, keeping count in that way of his words or phrases. Katherine asked him to go more slowly and he grumbled but began again.

MacLean and Antonio refused to go near Tomenika. At this point Katherine had only memorized lists of Rapanui nouns and was just beginning to wrestle with pronouns and adverbs. Sitting between Tomenika and MacLean, who stood some distance off, she asked her questions of MacLean in English. He conveyed them in Spanish to Antonio, who, in turn, translated them into Rapanui for Tomenika.

The interview was really more like the children's game of Chinese Whispers or Telephone than good anthropology. Though she was not sure, Katherine thought Tomenika was reciting the years in which certain Rapa Nui men had hosted feasts (*koro*) in honor of their fathers. She left the paper and pencil with Tomenika in the hope he would write something more, then went away. That same afternoon, her notes say: "got <u>Juan</u> to come up to *Orongo* beautiful aft. & considerable amount information from him."

The information she got was about Kirimuti's "secret cave." Juan had given Scoresby no help at all, but shared the little he had been able to glean from the old man with Katherine. They got horses for Kapieri, Varta, and Porotu and, Katherine says, rode out to Poike "cave hunting" according to Kirimuti's directions, but "in vain." Tepano, his mother, and Varta then worked for a full day with Katherine, trying desperately to translate Tomenika's notes. Tepano went back out to the leper colony to talk with Kirimuti many times, but without any luck.

Katherine did not see Tomenika again until the late afternoon of December 22, 1914. Tepano and Varta accompanied her, but Scoresby was detained on the Chilean mainland (where he had gone to see what was keeping *Mana*, long overdue on her second round-trip voyage). Katherine returned on December 26, again with Tepano and Varta, but then didn't see Tomenika again until May 16 and 17, 1915. Realizing that the old man was near death, Katherine became quite desperate, and desperation made her bold. She bravely entered Tomenika's dark hut and sat next to him on his blanket.

He drew two signs that, he said, were always used to designate the name of a man who was giving a feast in honor of his father. He described other ceremonies at which *rongorongo* was chanted, but he was tired and confused. He talked about his adopted father, who was his teacher, and rambled on about other people and places.

> I left the hut for a moment, and leant against the wall outside, racking my brains to see if there was any question left unasked, any possible way of getting at the information; but most of what the old man knew he had forgotten, and what he dimly remembered he was incapable of explaining. I made one more futile effort, then bade him good-bye and turned away. It was late afternoon on a day of unusual calm, everything in the lonely spot was perfectly still, the sea lay below like a sheet of glass, the sun as a globe of fire was nearing the horizon, while close at hand lay the old man gradually sinking, and carrying in his tired brain the last remnants of a once-prized knowledge. In a fortnight he was dead.

Katherine was humbled and felt a great sense of despair, even guilt, over Tomenika's death. She shared her feeling of loss with Tepano, who was filled with his own self-blame. He told Katherine that Tomenika had offered to teach him *rongorongo*, but he had been "anxious to learn Chilean & declined." Katherine and Tepano had failed to capture Tomenika's memories, but they had learned something about the meaning of mutual dependence and moral obligation in fieldwork.

Words, numbers, phrases, and stories in Rapanui contain many veiled meanings filled with innuendo and dense with metaphor. Katherine believed that *rongorongo* was a cultural tradition of real antiquity, but that the signs etched in wood were a more recent innovation. She recognized that there was probably a pattern to the signs, and that recitations were probably given in a certain order. She had a profound and firmly held belief in her own ability to solve problems but, in the end, was forced to conclude that *rongorongo* was forever a mystery. It was, she wrote, a system "of memory," and the signs themselves were but "aids to recollection, or for keeping count like the beads of a rosary."

Katherine's rosary metaphor may have been intuitively correct. Perhaps, faced with the loss of cultural memory after so many damaging contacts with Europeans, "aids to recollection" were precisely what Rapa Nui spiritual leaders needed. Many investigators have suggested that the carved symbols of *rongorongo* were inspired by contact with outsiders.

For example, in 1770—less than fifty years after Rapa Nui's first contact with Europeans—a Spanish expedition claimed the island for the king of Spain. Soldiers marched in armor; drummers, standard-bearers, and chanting Catholic priests in full ceremonial regalia followed in procession. They raised three crosses on three Poike hillocks in the eastern territory of Hotu Iti, far from the traditional Miru seat of power. Rapa Nui chiefs who witnessed this impressive pomp then "signed" a treaty, which they obviously could not read, by drawing symbols. Katherine was told that Rapa Nui clans had no distinguishing marks or emblems, and the symbols may have been copied from the island's rock art.

Katherine did not suggest that *rongorongo* symbols emerged or were inspired by this event, but she did consider imitation of European behavior to be a logical impetus for many Rapa Nui cultural innovations. Tepano showed her several curious sites that consisted of longhouse foundations and mounded-up piles of earth that represented, he said, European ships. He told her that poles were once raised upon the mounds to symbolize masts, while groups of people, dressed in European hats and clothes snatched from visiting sailors, performed ceremonies. To Katherine's great amusement, Tepano comically marched around the "deck" of one of these earthen "ships," gesturing and shouting commands as he had seen his elders do.

From 1722 until the missionaries collected the first *kohau rongorongo* in 1868, individual Rapa Nui people (including Kirimuti) had gone aboard foreign ships. Any one of them could have seen open logbooks or charts or heard some sort of a counting or sounding system in use that, back onshore, inspired the notion of associating symbols with *rongorongo* text.

One possibility that comes immediately to mind is the log line that Gillam used when discovering Mana Inlet. Many sailors, when paying out the log line, recited rhythmic sentences to measure a block of time. Similar to the child's method of counting "one thousand one, one thousand two," the recitations were often amusing nonsense chants or, occasionally, prayers. If a Rapa Nui person had witnessed such a mystifying little ritual it would have been just as interesting as seeing a Spanish captain put pen to paper.

Katherine didn't attempt to account for the origin of *rongorongo*, but looked for its meaning in the Rapa Nui culture as she understood it. Eventually, she looked beyond Rapa Nui, toward Mangareva, and found there a class of intellectuals and educators, called *rogorogo*, who were of noble birth and responsible for keeping genealogical lists, myths, legends, and other history. These experts formed a kind of choir, intoned sacred texts during secret rituals on important ceremonial sites, and presented an obvious parallel with Rapa Nui.

The Rapa Nui world of 1914 was an uncomfortable and confusing place for the elders who were Katherine's consultants. Destitution and death were familiar, and they understood very well the fleeting nature of time. They also had a wry humor, dark fatalism, a sense of place, and an awareness of history. If they had had more to offer on the subject of *rongorongo*, Katherine believed, they would have given it to her. "Day by day they were dropping off; it was a matter of anxious consideration whose testimony should first be recorded for fear that, meanwhile, others should be gathered to their fathers, and their store of knowledge lost for ever." In April Kirimuti died, and Katherine attended his funeral feast with Tepano, Varta, and Kapiera. Her final link with *rongorongo* was gone forever.

Troubled Waters

✦

LESS THAN A FORTNIGHT AFTER THE MANA EXPEDITION
had established base camp at Mataveri, Scoresby found that two separate
attempts had been made to break into their Hanga Piko storage shed. Quantities of food, soap, tools, nails, and other goods had all been spirited away.
Upon the expedition's arrival, some Rapa Nui people had "pilfered every
loose article on which they could lay their hands," but this was more than
petty theft. Scoresby called together a more or less random group of islanders
and demanded the immediate return of Mana Expedition stores. He threatened dire punishment from the government of Chile, but in spite of his blus-
ter, nine days later the same thing happened again. Katherine said that Rapa
Nui people "steal freely from one another, as well as from white men," and
the "greatest barrier to progress" was the "absence of security of property."
Stealing and poaching were commonplace, but understandable when the distribution of property was so astoundingly unjust.

The Mana Expedition faced myriad other difficulties as well. All of the
ugly tensions that had accumulated during the voyage had been transferred
ashore intact, and to top it all, Scoresby's relationship with Percy Edmunds
was on shaky ground. The Routledges were using Mataveri house as expedition headquarters while Edmunds still maintained it as his private residence.
The walls were paper-thin and there was a complete lack of privacy—a situation Katherine had handled well as the only woman aboard *Mana*. At
Mataveri, however, things were different.

Sofía Hey Rapu, Pakarati's niece, lived with Edmunds at Mataveri, and
Scoresby, in a dismal echo of the Silberrad Affair, found this cohabitation by
an "administrator" with a "native" islander personally distasteful and
bureaucratically inefficient. To further complicate matters, Edmunds also
had a budding relationship at the same time with Victoria Rapahango
Tepuku, who lived in Hanga Roa and would have been fifteen or sixteen years
old. Victoria was a lovely and intelligent young woman and traced her aris-

tocratic Miru ancestry directly to the legendary Hotu Matu'a, the founding ancestor and paramount chief of Rapa Nui.

Rapa Nui men of rank—including Tepano—had frequently married more than once, and Edmunds behavior was not judged. Traditionally, Miru married only within their own lineages and territory, while others married within a defined group of several lineages (called *tumu*). Katherine asked rather intimate questions of a few men, but her close contacts with women were limited to Veriamu and a half dozen women in the younger generation, including Dutrou-Bornier's granddaughter Parapina, whom Katherine employed as a maid. Katherine thought she understood Polynesian sexual mores, but held Edmunds to a higher standard.

On May 30, 1914 Katherine and Edmunds had a "breakfast difficulty" that was the last straw. As a result, she and Scoresby moved into separate tents in the garden, although they both retained rooms in the house. Katherine's tent was pitched on a slight rise about a hundred yards west of the house and nearly on top of the grave of the murdered Dutrou-Bornier, a fact that did not escape the superstitious islanders. Mataveri, as the staging ground from which the sacred birdman ceremonies were traditionally launched, was filled with ghosts and spirits. Katherine was told that cannibals, like the venerable Ko Tori, whose bones she had gathered into her picnic basket, had once camped on her tent site.

Each evening after dinner Scoresby would light a camp lantern and escort Katherine to her tent by a little path that ran through thick grass and a small eucalyptus grove. He would, she said, "see that all was well, put down the light, and leave me with the mystery of the island." The mystery, as far as the Rapa Nui people were concerned, was how Katherine could bring herself to sleep alone so near the restless and angry ghosts of Rapa Nui cannibals and Dutrou-Bornier. Such conduct was strange but also intriguing and marked Katherine in Rapa Nui eyes as certainly as Edmunds' living arrangements may have condemned him in hers. Katherine's proximity to the dead logically suggested to the islanders that she might be a witch in touch with spirits, a woman with *mana*.

Another Rapa Nui point of view was more pragmatic: the Mana Expedition was a source of employment and, therefore, personal gain. The expedition needed men who knew the island and were capable, willing workers, but Edmunds seasonally employed the forty or so men who fit that description. Throughout the Mana Expedition's stay on the island, this inherent competition between the needs of ranch work and those of fieldwork was never resolved.

The Routledges had promised Merlet that they would hire only the men and women recommended by Edmunds. This, in theory, would allow the

Company to maintain control of the workforce and assure Edmunds the economic upper hand after *Mana* departed the island. Although Scoresby and Edmunds did the hiring at first, Katherine was always the one who actually paid out wages in Chilean pesos to Percy Edmunds. He, in turn, held back a fee as required by the Company and then paid the Rapa Nui in supplies from the Company store. Katherine made the first payment for wages to Edmunds in April 1914 and then monthly thereafter. The women began at a salary of ten centavos per day and the men at forty. Tepano's salary began at seventy centavos and ended at more than two pesos per day. All salaries increased several times and were seriously inflated by September of 1914.

In addition to salary, however, the Rapa Nui people expected to be provided with food during the workday. This was a traditional way of working but also a necessity, as many of them reported to work hungry. The Routledges now made the grave mistake of treating Rapa Nui workmen as they had *Mana* crewmen: they were stingy. The food they took into the field for themselves was better and more ample than that which they gave their Rapa Nui workmen, just as cabin food had been better than that served to the crew aboard *Mana*. This, in itself, would not be unusual for the time, but everything depended upon discretion, a quality neither of the Routledges had in abundance. They provided sweet potatoes but no meat or milk, then openly indulged themselves with tinned meat, cheese, sugar, and other unheard-of delicacies. On an island that teemed with off-limits Company sheep, cattle, and horses, the major issue was meat.

Katherine established a small vegetable garden with seeds donated to the Mana Expedition. Bailey baked breads and made rice puddings filled with sugar and cinnamon, and their tantalizing scents wafted out over the garden. When Katherine was in residence, meals were served promptly and tea was *always* at 4 P.M. The Mataveri kitchen, which was detached from the house, was amply stocked, but supplies mysteriously disappeared. Schooled by her mother to keep a sharp eye on the household help, Katherine fretted constantly over thievery.

In the field she presided over the picnic baskets Bailey prepared with the ceremonial manners of Kate Pease on long-ago Scottish holidays. She personally opened each basket, sorted and handed out the food in the order of seniority. She was impressed with the gracious manners of the older Rapa Nui workmen, who waited patiently, ate some of the food, and put the rest away to take home. Katherine was not only the purser of the expedition but the keeper of the larder keys, and her power was obvious.

The Mana Expedition's staggering display of wealth created problems from the beginning, but so too did *Mana*'s cargo of ill will. Lieutenant Ritchie took the first opportunity, upon landing, to distance himself from the Routledges. He loved the island and its landscape and camped out while doing fieldwork. He got along well with Rapa Nui men like Antonio Haoa and took a deep and abiding interest in mapping. His maps of Orongo and Rano Kau are superb for the time and tools he had at his disposal, and his survey of the southeast coast is valuable. He manipulated his schedule so that whenever the Routledges were in Mataveri he was in Rano Raraku, and vice versa. He read every novel aboard *Mana* to pass the time, but also socialized amicably with Percy Edmunds and several Rapa Nui families.

Henry MacLean, who was just a youngster, had joined the Mana Expedition, as we have seen, in Juan Fernández Island. His primary role was interpreter. On the day after Katherine came ashore "for good," MacLean asked the Routledges "to be left on shore because of girls." At eighteen "girls" seems a good reason for a sailor to go ashore, but when Edmunds "warned" Katherine of "15 or 20" unmarried girls on the island, Scoresby immediately took on the role of a watchful, extremely critical parent. MacLean naturally bristled at such a priggish—almost voyeuristic—preoccupation, and the two men were at odds for the duration of the expedition.

The Rapa Nui people knew Lieutenant Ritchie as "el teniente" (the lieutenant), Frank T. Green as "el mecánico" (the mechanic), and Scoresby as "el caballero inglés" (the English gentleman). The young, attractive Henry MacLean, in contrast, was more familiarly and simply called Enrique. As he made friends quickly in the Rapa Nui community, he spoke freely of his dislike of Scoresby. Frank T. Green—who spewed venom constantly and, at this point, can only be described as a habitual troublemaker—gossiped about salaries and undercut Scoresby's fragile authority at every opportunity. Green and Edmunds became fast friends, and long after the Mana Expedition had departed the island, Green was still criticizing Scoresby to Chilean authorities.

From at least the second week in June and possibly earlier, a young Rapa Nui man named Carlos Teao Tori ("Charles" or "Charlie") and an unnamed Rapa Nui "boy" worked with Scoresby in the field. Carlos also worked with Katherine at Orongo, but he lied or exaggerated often and she did not trust him. Carlos removed carved stones and other artifacts from Orongo to Mataveri and saw Rapa Nui bones and skulls stacked haphazardly and with an astonishing degree of insensitivity in Scoresby's tent. The irony, of course, was that the Routledges, who condemned the Rapa Nui for thievery, were doing their own—arguably more detrimental—kind of stealing, though they would have been shocked to hear it called that.

On June 23 there was a "food row" in which Edmunds suggested (at Frank T. Green's instigation) that Mana Expedition members and Rapa Nui workmen were not getting enough meat. Just six days earlier Katherine had discovered that a large tin of biscuits had been taken from the Mataveri kitchen, and Scoresby fired Carlos. Within a day or two all of the expedition's Rapa Nui workmen but Juan Tepano and Antonio had disappeared. Scoresby was stubbornly unwilling to compromise, but a truce was declared when Katherine agreed to provide milk every morning and one full meal at midday for all workmen. The stage, however, was set for a drama that, in retrospect, was the culmination if not the direct result of everything that had happened since *Mana* had arrived on Rapa Nui almost three months before.

Beginning on June 21 Katherine left Mataveri every day to walk alone along a narrow path to Ana Kai Tangata, the so-called cannibal cave, a huge cavern cut into the rock on the water's edge. Islanders and others in search of treasure had ransacked it more than once. The Routledges excavated it again, but found little. Above their heads, on the vaulted ceiling, were red and white paintings—images of swooping and soaring sooty terns. Katherine spent many days sketching the paintings, diverted by the play of light on the tumbling breakers.

On June 30, just as Katherine was climbing down the cliff side to the cave, Edmunds was alone on the veranda at Mataveri. He looked down the road to see three figures slowly approaching. In the middle, supported by two Rapa Nui men, was an aged, crippled woman he knew as Angata. Barefoot and leaning on a staff, she had walked from Hanga Roa with the determination of a biblical prophet. Edmunds watched in fascination as the minutes ticked by and the figures grew larger. Angata's dark hair was cropped to her shoulders. Her face was sculpted in sharp, bold contours with high cheekbones and thick brows, and her dark eyes looked straight ahead as she walked. She wore a flowing, rough wool robe and a chain of beads or seeds with a large, red-painted cross swung from her neck. The trio stopped in front of the steps leading up to the veranda. Angata's eyes found Edmunds' and then never left them as she announced, with firm conviction, that she had had a vision, a "dream from God."

"Katarina"
and the Prophetess Angata

✦

ANGATA WAS, LIKE PAKARATI, A TRAINED CATECHIST. Unlike him, however, she was probably not literate—although she often "read" from missals written in Tahitian. She wore an elaborate rosary and went door-to-door in the village, refusing to enter but counting her beads and intoning an eccentric and unintelligible language that was a mixture of Rapanui, Tahitian, and made-up words. Angata was a woman in a long tradition of Rapa Nui spiritual practitioners. She was respected, but her behavior was spooky and many people feared her as a witch.

In 1888, the year the island was annexed by Chile, a chief named Simeón Ririroko went to the mainland with Juan Tepano, who was then in his twenties, and other Rapa Nui men. Simeón's mission was to speak to the president of Chile and protest against the unfair treatment of the Rapa Nui people by Enrique Merlet and the Company. Valparaíso officials received them and Simeón was invited to have dinner at the home of a confidant of Merlet. The next day, the Rapa Nui men learned that Simeón had died mysteriously of "poisoning."

With a wave of her hand, Angata said that God had told her Enrique Merlet was dead. The island now belonged to the hungry Rapa Nui people, and God commanded them to kill cattle, cook the meat, and eat their fill. A written declaration was ceremoniously handed over to Percy Edmunds. It bravely stated the obvious and completely true fact that Merlet "took this possession of ours" and "gave nothing for the earth, money or goods or anything." The message had been at least partially dictated by Angata, but was written and signed by Angata's son-in-law Daniel and by Carlos Teao Tori, Scoresby's disgruntled former employee.

Later the same day—June 30, 1914—Carlos ominously predicted "great winds coming." The very next night a stupendous gale blew over the island.

Katherine was alone in her tent at Mataveri, and the ferocity of the wind threatened to rip its stakes right out of the ground. Three times during the night she awoke from a restless slumber to get up and go outside into the teeth of the howling wind, fighting to tighten ropes. Katherine listened to the wind's almost human sound, waiting apprehensively for the burst of squally rain that never came. Exhausted and with dark circles under her eyes the next morning, Katherine dressed carelessly and went into the house for a late breakfast with Scoresby, who had slept soundly through the night.

Just as the Routledges were finishing breakfast, Edmunds stomped into the house in muddy boots. He told them that, sometime during the night, the Rapa Nui people had made good their threat of the previous day by "carrying off cattle." Ten or more head of the Company's cattle had been rustled, driven into the village of Hanga Roa, and at that very moment were being slaughtered quite boldly in front of the church. Smoke was rising from at least a dozen fires as the hungry villagers prepared for a feast. Katherine was convinced that the nocturnal Rapa Nui thievery had been communicated psychically to her as she fought the wind the night before.

Scoresby grew increasingly indignant when he was told that the Rapa Nui were going to give the Routledges one of the Company's cows in payment for the goods stolen from the wool shed. Edmunds, quite understandably, was feeling an uncomfortable similarity between his situation and that of his despised and murdered predecessor, Dutrou-Bornier. He immediately took on a kind of siege mentality and warned the Routledges against going into the village. The Mana Expedition had ample firearms and ammunition, and Edmunds intended to employ all of it in his defense. Bailey was posted as an armed guard outside Mataveri house. Antonio and Parapina stayed at Mataveri rather than return to the village, and Katherine moved out of her tent and back into the house. Tepano came back from Hanga Roa.

Scoresby flatly refused to allow the Rapa Nui to hold him an unwilling captive at Mataveri and rode unchallenged into Hanga Roa and back. Henry MacLean, in the meantime, told Katherine that some Rapa Nui women interpreted Angata's vision to mean that they should take Katherine's extensive wardrobe. She was incredulous, amused, and then indignant. More seriously, and in the best Quaker tradition, she argued vigorously against the use of violence. The Mana Expedition split into three factions: Katherine was passionately against the use of firearms; Scoresby was willing to employ them if necessary; and Lieutenant Ritchie, Frank T. Green, and Henry MacLean believed that gunplay was inevitable.

Cooped up in Mataveri with so much tension, worry, and dissent caused Katherine to feel like her childhood self, frightened and trapped in the gloom of Woodside. To escape, she packed up some food and her field gear and turned intently toward her work at Orongo. High on Rano Kau she was above all the turmoil. Fresh sea winds blew, immense vistas stretched to the horizon, and Katherine felt safe and unafraid. She worked intently until nearly sunset, then rode back to Mataveri. Nothing had changed. As the day drew to a close, Scoresby sent Frank T. Green into Hanga Roa to see what was going on. Green walked his horse through the deserted village and up to the little wooden church. It was filled to overflowing with Rapa Nui men, women, and children, and the strong, intense voice of Angata rhythmically singing or chanting could be heard. Green listened for a while and then galloped back to Mataveri.

When Katherine was frightened, as she surely was now, she focused on details that were controllable, trying to build a structured framework that would allow her to feel safe from her own emotional chaos. She referred to the law, to the Bible, and to history: greed was at the root of things on both sides, she said, and the Rapa Nui conflict was no different from other "risings in many lands and all ages." She recognized clearly that the people who worked at Mataveri, especially Tepano, were under substantial pressure to align themselves with the villagers. Their own self-interest, however, required them not to alienate Edmunds. On July 3 Parapina told Katherine that Angata had had another "dream from God," a mystical vision that she had recounted to the entire village in a rousing church meeting. God had told Angata that He was greatly pleased that the animals had been killed and eaten. God was, in fact, so pleased that He said to kill more. Angata's words were no more out of her mouth when about fifty Rapa Nui men rushed into the countryside to rustle more cattle and sheep.

Fear at Mataveri was now palpable and it was perfectly clear that, if the Rapa Nui chose to do so, they could attack Mataveri, destroy the Mana Expedition, and take lives. Yet Katherine continued to go to Orongo and passed through the village on horseback twice en route to the leper colony. At some point she either witnessed one of Angata's visions—they were public events and many people saw them—or learned the exact details of them from Parapina or another Rapa Nui woman. Whenever the skies clouded and rain was about to appear, Angata placed a large, black, coffinlike box in a cleared area and lay down under it. Then she entered what appeared to be a trance state, listening to the amplified sound of the wind and the droplets of rain falling on the top of the box. The whooshing and drumming, Angata said, communicated the clear, strong voice of God directly to her.

On July 8 Katherine and Antonio were riding in the village and saw elaborate preparations being made for a joint wedding of five couples, planned for 9 A.M. the following day. Apparently, it was hoped that the nuptials would save the Rapa Nui bridegrooms, who were among the rustlers, from being arrested and taken to the mainland when the Chilean warship *Jeneral Baquedano* (usually called simply *Baquedano*) finally arrived. Juan Tepano told Edmunds that the brides' families intended to boldly raid the sheep pen, taking animals enough to provide meat for a traditional, celebratory feast.

Edmunds decided to stand guard at the target stock pen and shoot the first man who tried to enter. Katherine believed he was placing himself in mortal danger, threatening the islanders with bloodshed and bringing international scandal to the Mana Expedition. Yet she could see both sides and argued the case with herself in notes scribbled in black ink up, down, and sideways on pages of her various field journals. The combination of occult fear and impending physical violence terrified Katherine. Throughout all of the events leading up to this sorry situation, however, and until its final denouement, Katherine never seemed to have considered that the Routledges' own behavior and the expedition's wealth had sparked the dry tinder of Rapa Nui discontent and inflamed the community to rebellion.

Scoresby, in fact, never budged from the position that the uprising was caused by politics and a very long history—and that if Edmunds had been a better colonial administrator things would never have reached the point of armed confrontation. Edmunds, who wanted positive assurance of Mana Expedition backing against the islanders, played what he thought was his trump card: a paper from the president of Chile appointing him *subdelegado marítimo* (port captain), along with instructions from the captain of the *Baquedano* giving him administrative powers.

Katherine and Scoresby rather disingenuously claimed later that they "had always understood from him he had no official position." They could simply not have been in the dark as to Percy Edmunds' political power—even if they did not know the *exact* nature of his official status as a representative of the Chilean government. Scoresby called Lieutenant Ritchie, Frank T. Green, Henry MacLean, and Bailey into the room and asked them to officially witness the fact that Edmunds, as a legal representative of the Chilean government, was now requesting, in writing, armed assistance from the Mana Expedition:

I would ernestly [sic] request that you would give me the benefit of your armed assistance in the protection of human life in the event of trouble arising through my endeavours to enforce law & order, or through other causes, and that you would place this assistence [sic] at my disposal at such places & times as may be hereafter agreed upon. I would ernestly [sic] request that you would not make use of firearms except in the case of it being necessary for the protection of human life, and further that you would use your own discretion as to the time of opening fire . . .

Scoresby then issued his own written directive to members of the Mana Expedition:

> No member is to take part in any killing of natives with the object of protecting livestock, if however the personal safety of Mr. Edmunds is in danger they shall give him armed assistance, & if there is no opportunity to refer the matter to me they shall act in the same at their own discretion.

Lieutenant Ritchie replied, in writing, that he was responsible for his own actions "so long as I remain an officer of the British Navy on Full Pay, to my Lords Commissioners of the Navy." Edmunds sent Tepano to warn the villagers one final time that Company property would be defended by all necessary means, including arms. Tepano, who had always been in the middle between Mataveri and Hanga Roa, was now in a terrible position.

At seven-thirty the next morning Edmunds, Scoresby, Lieutenant Ritchie, and Henry MacLean rode down the lane and out of Mataveri, drawn by reports of marauding Rapa Nui rustlers. They were all very visibly armed with rifles and shotguns. Katherine got up early to see off the "gallant little band," but the thought of taking Rapa Nui lives turned her "suddenly sick." She wandered anxiously around the Mataveri house all day, moving from veranda to detached kitchen and back again. Isolated and unable to influence the outcome of potentially tragic events, Katherine retreated to her tent in the garden and tried to work on her fieldnotes, but her mind was unsettled. She read her Bible, but was tormented by fear.

Finally, she heard the sound of horses coming up the lane and ran from her tent to greet Scoresby and the others. They dismounted and trooped into the house, and a disgusted Percy Edmunds reported that they had been outsmarted, tricked into following cunning decoys while other Rapa Nui men stealthily scaled walls and stole sheep. Katherine, whose nerves were raw, found the whole thing hilariously and uncontrollably funny. The men were not amused.

Throughout the following days Katherine continued going into the village. She bartered with various people, including Nicolás Pakarati Urepotahi. She was astounded at the complicity of the entire village in the rustling adventure, including nearly everyone who worked at Mataveri except Tepano. Katherine saw "10 or 12 sheep skins pegged out to dry & any quantity of sheep being cut up in the Frenchman's [Varta's] kitchen." She did not, apparently, confront or lecture Varta. Neither did she hold it against him once the crisis had passed and continued to employ him. Katherine, in this and in other ways, adopted the pragmatic Rapa Nui ethic as her own. On July 11 she gave up sleeping in the Mataveri house and returned to her tent unafraid.

The Mana Expedition was, however, terribly behind schedule, and Katherine resented it. The pecuniary interests of the Company, she thought, were intruding on the scientific goals of her work. She wanted to get on with things. Like Tepano, she was trying to steer a middle course, separate herself from the actions of the men at Mataveri, and avoid rupturing personal relations with people in the village. In that effort she was quite alone, but not lonely. Removed from the "uniting" circle of her family and the "gathered" spiritual experience of Quaker community, Katherine found comfort and control in solitary meditation.

On July 18 Katherine was in her tent alone, sorting her notes from Orongo. The early-morning air smelled of wet soil and sea salt. Katherine's clothes clung to her body, the curl in her hair was unruly, and the papers in her hand were limp. Everything felt vaguely heavy. Suddenly, a Rapa Nui man whom she did not know appeared. Startled, she lost the few Rapanui words at her command and simply stood there. He then ceremoniously presented her with two chickens and some raw sweet potatoes. The present, he said, was from Angata. For the first time, Katherine was drawn personally and directly into the conflict.

The old men of Orongo had taught Katherine that Rapa Nui people prized chickens as presentation and feast foods. They had told her that chickens were given to male and female priests in the birdman and other ceremonies. Katherine intuitively knew that singling her out for this private, symbolic gift of food was an important gesture. Scoresby and Edmunds had been self-importantly and aggressively posturing for weeks and the Rapa Nui men, inspired by Angata, were equally demonstrative. Angata, however, had ignored them all and turned to Katherine. It was a simple, woman-to-woman gesture of political and spiritual recognition. Angata, who had never spoken to Katherine before, was addressing her now as one woman of *mana* to another.

Katherine was "puzzled what to do." Unwilling to imply approval of what were, in her estimation, serious trespasses against property, she made the awkward gesture of offering to pay for the food. Refusing, the Rapa Nui man told an abashed Katherine that Angata had said, "Food was from God, she did not wish for money or thanks." Katherine found this spooky confrontation with Angata's power far more frightening than the threatening, thieving, and posturing of the Rapa Nui. After the man left, she wandered restlessly about Mataveri. Finally, unable to bear being alone, she impatiently walked out the gate and down the road, hoping to encounter Scoresby. She finally did. "For the first time," Katherine wrote in her journal, "it feels terribly lonely. Not only do we have no help but no means of knowing if help is coming."

The next two days were unbearable. Rapa Nui men embarked upon an orgy of destruction, killing cattle and oxen and leaving them to rot where they fell. Edmunds discovered fifty-six oxen had been destroyed, but there was no hope of using the meat before it spoiled. July 20 was Katherine's longest day ever. In the morning Scoresby wrote a letter "To The Jefe & all the Kanakas of Easter Island," offering the Rapa Nui people a personal gift of two bullocks a month if they would refrain from further destruction and await the coming of the *Baquedano*. Katherine, who may or may not have agreed with his course of action, typed it.

Juan Tepano—the *jefe* to whom Scoresby referred in his letter—assembled the men on a hillside, to the east of the church. Scoresby stood before them and read his letter in a loud voice, and Henry MacLean translated. It is not known how Scoresby's use of the word *Kanaka* was received, but his offer was flatly rejected and it was made quite clear that the bullocks were not Scoresby's to give. A letter to the captain of *Baquedano*, written in a mixture of Spanish and Rapanui by Nicolás Pakarati Urepotahi, was then read. In it, Pakarati described Angata's visions as commands to action that faithful Rapa Nui believers could not ignore. Scoresby countered by stating that his main concern as a "neutral" was Edmunds' safety. Unfortunately, he also made an ugly threat to join in gunplay if Edmunds was attacked. Pakarati responded that Angata's visions assured them God would not allow any of them to be injured or to die, no matter what Scoresby did. The gulf between Mataveri and Hanga Roa was as wide as the sea, and neither faction was capable of crossing it.

Having accomplished absolutely nothing, a disgusted Scoresby returned to Mataveri. He insisted on writing yet another letter, demanding to know why the Rapa Nui had refused his offer. Katherine typed it up, but when Edmunds saw it he refused to allow Scoresby to deliver it. The lines that had been drawn earlier between Scoresby and the other men of the Mana Expedition were now completely set: Lieutenant Ritchie, Frank T. Green, and Henry MacLean rejected Scoresby's authority completely, intending to take up arms and stand with Edmunds. Scoresby used words like "insubordination" and "refusing orders" and suffered a complete loss of rapport with Green and MacLean that was never mended.

Katherine was wrestling alone with "much anxious thought," realizing that "we can only hope & pray & watch" for the coming of the *Baquedano* "before there is bloodshed." Angata's gift to her—which Katherine took as a sign of recognition, respect, and an open invitation to talk—encouraged her to try to reason with Angata. She had been taught the arts of feminine manipulation, but Katherine had resisted that course of action at important turning points in her life. In Africa she had taken honest, direct action to rescue Wameisa, and now she made up her mind to see Angata in person. She retreated alone into her tent, opened her Bible, and meditated for some time on the text "Lo, I am with you always even unto the end." In the late afternoon of this same eventful day, Katherine put on a broad-brimmed straw hat and her best boots, took Parapina and Henry MacLean, whom she insisted had to be unarmed, and rode into Hanga Roa.

Katherine slowed her horse to a walk and entered the village as inconspicuously as possible. It was, she thought, "a horrible sight, a shamble." Joints and strips of meat hung from doorways, and hides were pegged out on the ground to dry. More happily, the church and its outbuildings, once badly in need of repair, were being reconstructed, and there was an air of hope and directed energy. A small group of Rapa Nui women sat in front of Nicolás Pakarati Urepotahi's house. Leaving Henry with the horses, Katherine and Parapina approached them. Seated in the middle of the group, Angata wore a long, shapeless garment and was barefoot, her feet tucked under her in the posture of a child. Around her neck hung the ever-present string of beads or seeds and a heavy medallion. Angata appeared frail but not terribly old, her hair only barely touched with gray and her strong face unlined. Her eyes were intense, focused, and expressive. Katherine was immediately drawn to her, and to her "distinctly attractive and magnetic personality." The Rapa Nui women made room and Katherine and Parapina sat down in the grass.

Katherine reached out her hand and Angata took it, holding it in her own throughout the entire conversation, which MacLean tried to interpret. Angata looked deep into Katherine's eyes and asked her name, addressing her from then on as "Katarina." Katherine began by thanking her for the gift of chickens and potatoes she had sent and offered her payment in return. Angata repeated her belief that "food came from God & she wished for no money." Katherine presented her with a long knitted scarf, which Angata simply handed to her daughter.

Angata, gesturing toward meat cooking on a nearby fire, offered some to Katherine, who refused it politely. This, Katherine said, gave her the "opening" she needed, and she tried to explain that "God did not wish men to be killed." She begged Angata not to let Rapa Nui men go out again on raids or Edmunds would have them shot. Angata's "face hardened for a moment and her eyes took the look of a fanatic & she said something about God with the upward gesture she always uses when speaking His name." Angata was speaking in a mixture of Rapanui and her own made-up words, and neither Katherine nor MacLean could have understood her. They, in turn, depended upon pantomime to make themselves understood.

When Angata's voice died away there was utter silence. No one spoke a word for a long time, and then Katherine "hastened to relieve the tension by saying 'we must all do the will of God.'" Angata's voice and manner softened and there was silence again. Finally, Angata cast her eyes toward heaven with "a confidence that was sublime" and said *"ine he maté, ine he maté"* ("no one is dead," or "no one will die"). It is beyond doubt that Angata frightened Katherine, but she also thrilled her in a childlike way that harkened back to Aunt Jane—that other "prophetess" of the "inner light."

The ancestors of Hotu Matu'a, the old men had told Katherine, "came with him in his boat, and he knew they were there though the others did not see them." The island was inhabited, in Rapa Nui eyes, with the wandering spirits of the dead, and Katherine had a strong connection with the concept of family ghosts. Not long after she returned to England, the Pease family concluded that Katherine had dramatically changed. They were convinced that Angata—"the witch doctor on Easter Island"—had so much power that, after meeting her, Katherine was never the same again. Now, she returned to Mataveri and frantically insisted that the Mana Expedition immediately pack up and ride for Camp Hotu Iti.

Katherine's plan was met with argument and strong resistance from everyone but Scoresby, who saw the wisdom of prudent retreat, and Bailey (who always took Katherine's lead). Lieutenant Ritchie, without discussion, remained at Mataveri. He intended to support Edmunds and, if possible, to continue work at Orongo. Henry MacLean and Frank T. Green, who made a strong case for "working up" his photographic negatives in his Mataveri darkroom, basically refused to leave. Katherine, normally obsessed with sorting, packing, and labeling everything perfectly, now veered sharply from her usual ways. She simply threw clothes, expensive survey equipment, and ammunition haphazardly into two bullock carts. Without thinking, she hurriedly stuffed a bag filled with Chilean peso notes and £50 in gold under the blankets in one of the carts. She was at the breaking point, and the expedition had fallen apart.

Katherine left Mataveri at four-thirty on the day after meeting with Angata and "rode as fast as possible" toward the east. Behind her, red sunset clouds were settling over Hanga Roa, bringing nightfall at an alarming rate. Ahead of her lay Rano Raraku, its giant statues standing patiently in the gathering dusk. She arrived as a starless night was falling and settled into her prefabricated metal and wood house. Scoresby bunked in the roomiest of the tents and Bailey took over the cook tent. The distance Katherine had put between her and Angata was significant, but she was now encamped near the quarry that was, according to the Rapa Nui, overflowing with the spirits of the dead. The night was heavily overcast and silent. There was no wind, and the distant breakers on Tongariki's shore rumbled. Katherine balanced a dozen can-

dles on her camp table and clustered others on packing crates, filling the
night with their tiny flames.

At breakfast the Routledges faced facts. The Mana Expedition was now
irrevocably separated into two camps—one in the west and one in the east—
just as the island had been traditionally divided between the same two antag-
onistic districts. Tepano moved back and forth between the two camps, just
as he had always mediated between Mataveri and Hanga Roa. Without workmen, excavations were impossible. Scoresby was suffering from rheumatism
in his shoulder and even simple tasks were blindingly painful. Surveying was
essentially in the hands of Lieutenant Ritchie, whose work in the quarry was
incomplete—but he now labored alone at Mataveri. The future looked bleak.

It rained steadily for three days, and the oxcart loaded with Mana Expedition cash got mired in the mud halfway to Rano Raraku. Under dark,
early-morning skies on July 23 Tepano rode out to Camp Hotu Iti. He had
been sent by Edmunds but also carried an enigmatic message from Angata
to Katherine. As Tepano passed a hastily erected stone barricade, Bailey
emerged from a patrol tent and then, recognizing him, waved. Seated at a
table with a mug of hot tea steaming in front of him, Tepano delivered
Angata's simple message: She had had a vision of *Mana* on the high seas and
was certain the yacht would return to the island before the Chilean warship
Baquedano arrived. Then, Tepano added, Angata had seen the Routledges
embark and *Mana* disappear over the horizon. The message sounded threatening. The skies grew increasingly dark and then opened up and poured
cold rain.

On July 26 MacLean braved the deluge to tell the Routledges that
Edmunds refused to be responsible for the safety of the stranded oxcart,
which was now a target for thieves, and that the Rapa Nui were planning
another raid, this time to steal horses from Camp Hotu Iti. There was nothing anyone could do, as darkness was falling, but the following morning
Scoresby got up early. The rains were pounding thick and heavy on his tent
and the road to Hanga Roa was awash in red mud. Scoresby threw a heavy
poncho over his shoulders, then went into the prefabricated house, where
Katherine was asleep. He got her up, made thick, black coffee, and shouted
for Bailey. For the next half hour he instructed them both in the loading and
firing of his best rifle, a Holland & Holland weapon that could bring down
an elephant. Scoresby armed himself with a pistol, mounted up, and rode
alone along the coast toward Mataveri. He found the oxcart at Vaihu and
rescued the Mana Expedition's cash, but was forced to leave everything else
behind.

Later that same day—July 27—Varta came into camp with yet another
message from Angata. Unlike Tepano, he delivered it in formal terms, almost

as an emissary from a queen. Standing in front of Katherine, he removed his hat and then intoned that he brought "greetings from God." Angata's vision, he told Katherine, was again of *Mana*, but this time she was bringing letters of great importance for Katherine. Within hours of Varta's departure, a Rapa Nui woman materialized in front of Katherine, bringing eggs and potatoes from Angata. She asked Katherine to give her two large, tin storage containers and told her that, in return, Angata would send more potatoes and chickens. Now thoroughly alarmed at the attention directed at her, Katherine nevertheless searched through her things and found the containers Angata wanted. The minute the woman left camp Katherine got on her horse and went looking for Scoresby.

She found him down near Tongariki, the ruins of the island's greatest image *ahu*. Katherine and Scoresby sat on rocks near the sea, talking. Katherine, who had left Mataveri in the hope that she could sever contact with Angata, found herself again the almost obsessive focus of the old woman's attention. Scoresby, who believed that "medicine men" in Africa acted in good faith, did not feel the same about Angata. The overtures she had made toward Katherine, Scoresby said, were simply manipulative and aggressive acts designed to extort goods. Scoresby also recognized the terrible effect the old woman had on Katherine and remembered it years later when he compared it to the similar influence of Spiritualists, whom he despised.

Katherine turned and started back toward camp alone, then heard Bailey shout, "The Kanakas are coming!" Looking toward Mataveri, Katherine saw twenty or thirty Rapa Nui men on horseback, silhouetted against the sunset sky and less than half a mile away. She shouted for Scoresby and they ran to Katherine's house, where they closed the bottom half of the Dutch door and Scoresby leaned his rifle against the wall, out of sight but close at hand. The Routledges waited at the half-closed door as the minutes ticked away and the horsemen approached.

When they entered camp Katherine recognized Nicolás Pakarati Urepotahi at the front of the group. Wearing his best jacket and cap, Pakarati carried a prominently displayed picture of the Virgin Mary and a Bible. As they walked their horses within a few feet of Katherine's house, the horsemen raised a rousing "Hip, hip, hooray!" in English. Then Pakarati formed them into a semicircle facing the Routledges, who remained behind the half-closed door. As the next few minutes unfolded, an astonished Katherine lost all fear. She realized with a thunderclap that Pakarati had led what was essentially a religious procession to her camp. He was about to conduct a ceremony here, in the shadow of the great statues, and Katherine was the object of it.

Almost as one, the Rapa Nui men dismounted and removed their hats. Their mounts breathed and stomped, flies buzzed about, and the strong smell of sweaty horse hung on the wet but suddenly still air. Not a word was spoken, and the only sound was the rumble of breakers on Tongariki's shore. Finally, Pakarati opened the Bible and began to read a verse. When his voice died away the entire company of Rapa Nui men crossed themselves. Silent seconds ticked away and then, incongruously, they raised another cheer.

Ignoring Scoresby, Pakarati looked directly at Katherine and spoke only to her. As was by now customary, he first said that he brought her greetings from Angata, who had had another vision of *Mana* approaching the island in full sail. Then some of the men opened their saddlebags to bring out eggs, potatoes, and at least a dozen lifeless chickens, their necks wrung and feathers drooping. This gift was, by Rapa Nui standards, an astonishing wealth of food. Katherine took it without hesitation and placed it on the table in her house. She looked frantically about for something to give back in ceremonial exchange. Her eye fell on a large tin of tea biscuits, and she handed it back over the door to Pakarati.

Katherine often quoted one of R. R. Marett's favorite phrases, "The past is the present," but on this day she understood for the first time the profound meaning of those words. Nicolás Pakarati Urepotahi was an emissary from a woman who, like the traditional birdman of ancient times, spoke with the voice of God. Once that god had been Makemake, the creator. Today Pakarati had appropriated the God of Angata's visions. He had conducted the ceremonial presentation of food to Katherine in nearly exactly the same way he had, as a small child, seen similar ceremonies conducted in front of the Orongo stone house within which Hoa Hakananai'a had silently waited. By the time Pakarati had finished and the horsemen had turned away, the Rapa Nui uprising had dramatically been transformed, in Katherine's eyes, into "a war of independence."

At two o'clock that morning Katherine awoke from a troubled sleep and scribbled nearly indecipherable notes in her journal: "worried night thinking about the situation & desire to do straight thing . . . to receive gifts like this seems to compromise ourselves—to receive a big gift like this . . . W. [Scoresby] feels increasingly [Edmunds'] position madness . . . the place will be in a blaze." Such fears had been with her nearly constantly for weeks, and all of Katherine's journal entries during her experience with Angata and the Rapa Nui uprising are tension-filled, disjointed, hurried, and messy. They reveal powerfully the tremendous isolation Katherine felt, not just on the island but from Scoresby and the other men of the Mana Expedition as well. Emotionally, she was utterly alone.

There was no longer even the pretense of cooperation among Scoresby, Green, and MacLean, and the Mana Expedition was in a shambles. MacLean and Green worked several days at Rano Raraku until MacLean defied one of

Scoresby's orders, then was fired and barred from Camp Hotu Iti. Absurdly, Scoresby threatened to press charges of mutiny. Green formally resigned, abandoned his photographic duties, and went back to Mataveri. Both men saw Scoresby as a coward, hiding out at Rano Raraku while Edmunds was endangered at Mataveri. The weather was a mess, the camp was waterlogged, the days were passing, and Katherine was alternately terrified, angry, and depressed. To her enormous relief, there was a break in the rain and Juan Tepano turned up at Camp Hotu Iti.

Tepano brought Veriamu, his elderly mother, with him. Katherine and the two of them wandered over the muddy ground from Rano Raraku to Tongariki. Veriamu chattered happily, recalling her girlhood, the men she had loved and lived with, and the stories she had been told. On this day, it appears, Katherine first realized fully the profound connection the older Rapa Nui generation still felt with the ancestral lands now off-limits to them. She scribbled a note in her journal that demonstrates her skeptical yet understanding opinion that an economic injustice had been done to Tepano and his family: "½ of Tongariki and ½ of Rano Raraku 'belonged' to his mother & the other ½ to his father. They wd belong to him if they had not been taken away." For Katherine, the desperate uprising that she had recently characterized as a war of independence now wore a more human face.

As three weeks of steady rain slowed to a trickle, the Chilean warship *Baquedano* drew ever closer, and Angata heard the voice of God less often. Her dreams and visions grew dark, and she predicted danger for the Rapa Nui people. On August 2 the winds changed and the rains abruptly stopped. For the first time in nearly a month silence fell over the entire island, and Katherine at last got a good night's sleep. During that same night Angata had a brilliant vision of *Baquedano*'s arrival. On the morning of Monday, August 3 Angata sent a messenger to Camp Hotu Iti with a special request: She wanted Katherine to give her some material for a flag but, in a gesture completely out of character, had sent nothing in exchange. Katherine scoured her camp and came up with a piece of white cotton used by Lieutenant Ritchie as a survey flag, some red cloth from her camera outfit, and an old blue shirt of Scoresby's. She rode obediently into the village and personally handed the fabric to Angata. It was quickly sewn into a tricolor and hoisted on the Hanga Roa flagpole.

A day or two later Henry MacLean, in spite of having been fired by Scoresby, surprised Katherine with a willingness to go back to work. She needed MacLean's language skills desperately, but Scoresby refused to leave his tent and speak to him. He made Katherine do the dirty work of telling MacLean to get out of Camp Hotu Iti and never return. MacLean left and never looked back. At five in the morning on August 5 some of the more hotheaded Rapa Nui men, having heard from Angata that *Baquedano* would soon appear, decided they had nothing to lose and prepared to attack Mataveri.

Then the seemingly impossible happened. As if, Katherine later wrote, it was the third act of a bad comic opera, *Baquedano* appeared. She was spotted in the early morning, and by midafternoon, four Rapa Nui men were in irons. "I almost broke down with pure joy & relief," Katherine wrote. "I had not known till then <u>how</u> great the strain had been." The Routledges left immediately for Hanga Roa, where they boarded *Baquedano*, met with the second-in-command, left their cards, and received the shattering news that England had declared war on Germany. *Baquedano* was carrying the clothes sent out by Lady Grogan for the Rapa Nui people, and Katherine volunteered to distribute them. She planned to use them as a reward for Rapa Nui friends and as a stick over the heads of others.

Katherine found Mataveri house filled to overflowing with newcomers. Enrique Merlet, Angata's nemesis, had arrived with *Baquedano*, accompanied by three men. One of them, Pedro Adams, intended to evaluate the island for future investment. A German called "Gomollo" was more mysterious. He said he was a "tobacco planter," but Scoresby thought he was an overly shrewd man of considerable colonial experience—certainly an agent of the German government. To Edmunds, in contrast, Gomollo seemed a fool. Katherine spent an uncomfortable night tossing on a cot on the Mataveri veranda, covered only by a large ship's signal flag. The next morning she cleared out early and went aboard *Baquedano*, where she promptly gave the *Comandante* "the whole history of events," saying that the rebellion was not only economic but "much deeper."

The *Comandante* was amiable and agreed that Katherine could distribute the clothes. At about 3 P.M. she rode down to Hanga Piko and waited patiently for about three hours. At last she saw two small boats headed in her direction, but to her complete surprise, they suddenly veered off toward Hanga Roa. Katherine galloped along the coast road and pulled up in time to find the clothes being handed out to a whirlwind of happily jostling people.

Outsmarted, Katherine demanded a seat in one of the boats returning to *Baquedano* and saw the *Comandante* alone. By this time he had conducted detailed interviews with the Rapa Nui prisoners and other men, including Juan Tepano. He was informed about the conflicts within the Mana Expedition, was fully convinced that the Rapa Nui people were justified, and said that Edmunds should consider himself lucky that he had not been killed. There was nothing more to say, and not wishing to spend another night on a cot at Mataveri, Katherine departed Hanga Roa alone for the long ride back to Camp Hotu Iti. She crawled into her own bed at nearly midnight, but could not sleep. The island's crisis may have been over, but England was embroiled in war.

Over the next few days Chilean authorities questioned about a dozen Rapa Nui men ranging in age from seventeen to their late thirties, including Carlos Teao Tori and Daniel María Teave. The same questions were asked of each man, and the answers were all similar, almost rehearsed. Each of them dispassionately told real tales of economic deprivation, unfairness, and cruelty at the hands of the Company. Some men made the eminently reasonable case that Edmunds, as a non-Chilean, should not hold the post of *subdelegado marítimo*, although they pragmatically realized he would remain on the island with the Company. Almost to a man, they turned their wrath on Tepano. They criticized him for having ample food and clothes, keeping himself apart at Mataveri, and working for Edmunds while turning a blind eye to their suffering.

When Tepano was interviewed, he honestly replied that the work given by Edmunds to the Rapa Nui was good but wages were too low and supplies too costly. He also pointed out that the younger men were hotheads, and several women, including Angata, had taken advantage of that to instigate the uprising for their own ends. In this, Tepano's opinion was similar to Scoresby's. Chilean authorities kept scrupulous records of everything and concluded that the causes of the uprising were Merlet's sorry character, the Company's unfair policies, new ideas of equality imported from the Continent, and religious fanaticism. They did not question neglectful government policies toward the island and pointed out that Tepano's lifestyle and separation from the community created jealousy.

The upshot of the investigation was that only one man, Angata's thirty-six-year-old son-in-law, Daniel María Teave, bold writer of the Rapa Nui declaration of war, was taken to the mainland to face the authorities there—justifying, in Katherine's opinion, Angata's promise to protect the Rapa Nui. Edmunds was removed from his position as *subdelegado marítimo*, and a Chilean journalist-turned-teacher named J. I. Vives Solar assumed the post. Edmunds stayed on, as the Rapa Nui had predicted, in his position as Company manager, and his powerful influence on the island economy and society was essentially unchanged.

The *Comandante* of *Baquedano* wrote an official letter to Scoresby warning him that the Chilean navy could not guarantee the Mana Expedition's safety after *Baquedano*'s departure. Scoresby responded with a lack of restraint and in a manner calculated to make the *Comandante* his enemy for life. Four pages, typed by Katherine, poured out a bitter litany of complaints about the Rapa Nui people's laziness, dishonesty, thievery, and violence. They were, he said, "with rare exceptions, an unsatisfactory people," and "no value can be attached to their word." Scoresby criticized the *Comandante* personally, saying that "the vessel . . . has been unable to deal with the 250 natives" and implying that, if anything happened to the Mana Expedition after the departure of *Baquedano*, it would be a consequence of the *Comandante*'s actions.

Lieutenant Ritchie, whose time with the Mana Expedition had officially ended on July 24, saw *Baquedano* as his escape. He was, he wrote Scoresby, "very keen" to return to Chile and then home to wartime duty. He asked Scoresby to lend him money and bedding, which Scoresby did. Ritchie wanted to take the incomplete maps he had diligently drafted and finish them in England, but Scoresby refused. Ritchie and Henry MacLean were both granted passage on *Baquedano*, and Ritchie, at least, intended to go out to camp to say good-bye to Katherine. As the hour of departure approached he decided, instead, to stand by his gear, and Katherine rode into Hanga Roa on August 14 to say farewell.

As she stood on the shore and watched Lieutenant Ritchie and MacLean being rowed out to *Baquedano*, Katherine surely realized that the Mana Expedition was, on one level, finished. Ironically, however, Ritchie's desperate dislike of the Routledges had worked in the Mana Expedition's favor. He had buried himself in his work, accomplishing plans of Orongo and Puna Pau and beginning a complex survey of the south coast. He had made detailed notes of the major statue transport road between Rano Raraku and the south coast. His preliminary work on the interior and exterior of Rano Raraku created the solid foundation on which Katherine built her follow-up work. Ritchie's skills as a cartographer, his orderly attention to detail, and his dedication to mapping the island's remains, even in the face of conflict, disorder, bad feelings, and finally, islander rebellion, were absolutely invaluable and completely irreplaceable.

On August 23, 1914 *Mana* finally returned. Katherine delved into the mailbag that carried "important letters" from her family, just as Angata's vision had predicted. Wilson described the mounting chaos of war and wrote that now "the tables are turned" and it was Katherine who was "peaceful in the Pacific" among "old, forgotten far off things."

Katherine saw Angata at least once again after the end of the Rapa Nui rebellion, and perhaps several times. Although her journal is silent on what transpired between them, it is possible that she sought advice or predictions from Angata or met with her for healing, just as she had done with seers in Africa. There is no question, however, that Angata held a strong place in Katherine's imagination. After the old woman died and long after *Mana* had departed Easter Island, Angata's memory haunted Katherine's restless journeys.

Camp Hotu Iti:
Living Faces

✦

LIVING IN CAMP HOTU ITI AND WORKING IN RANO
Raraku brought Katherine into contact with a wondrous spiritual landscape of striking beauty.

> Immediately above the camp towered the majestic cliff of Raraku, near at
> hand were its mysterious quarries and still erect statues; on the coast below
> us, quiet and still, lay the overturned images of the great platform of Ton-
> gariki, one fragment of which alone remains on its base, as a silent witness
> to the glory which has departed. The scene was most wonderful of all when
> the full moon made a track of light over the sea, against which the black
> mass of the terrace and the outline of the standing fragment was sharply
> defined; while the white beams turned the waving grass into shimmering
> silver and lit up every crevice in the mountain above.

As Katherine walked over the plain between Rano Raraku and Tongariki
the sound of the sea was constant, part of the very air she breathed. She
moved through the sound, walking in an undulating island landscape that
ended abruptly in front of the encircling horizon. An acrid and scorched
smell, like molten lava bubbling up from the depths of the sea, rose from
the sun-warmed soil. The island's continued existence seemed precarious
to her, but also audacious. Winds buffeted and rolled over the land, swirling
in interesting patterns around fallen statues or small *ahu* and enveloping
each place in a distinctive environment of sound and movement. They
joined with the sea to become an all-enveloping auditory experience, ending
the island's watery isolation and connecting it to whatever lay beyond the
horizon.

Shadows of clouds flew over the blowing grass, and if she concentrated,

Katherine could make the horizon disappear. She could visually melt land and sea seamlessly into one entity, and for a moment, the ever-present feeling of complete isolation was gone. Then the island, floating on the seascape, gave her a sense of moving toward something new and waiting. That promise of destination—of the pursuit of the irrecoverable—was the tantalizing, seductive secret of Easter Island.

The statues never failed to arouse awe in Katherine, especially at sunset. Standing in the impenetrable calm of Rano Raraku, they had "quiet dignity" and a presence "of suggestion and of mystery." The statues still lying in quarries, unreleased from the rock, were recumbent giants so like ancient effigies that "the awed spectator involuntarily catches his breath, as if suddenly brought face to face with a tomb of the mighty dead." Rapa Nui people didn't see them as dead, however, and wouldn't go near them at night. They acknowledged their masculinity as phallic fertility gods, and Veriamu joked about their seductive attractiveness to women.

Tepano taught Katherine the Rapanui names of a hundred different things: the winds—*tokerau*—and the nights of the moon. She repeated them until she got them right and then scribbled them down, slowly building a vocabulary. She was amused by his linguistic tricks and she, in turn, teased him with the jabberwocky rhymes of her childhood. He read the sky by the colors of the clouds and warned her when a squall was about to blow over. Thanks to Tepano, as the months passed, Katherine's fieldnotes became less spattered with inky raindrops.

As early as July 1914 Tepano had begun, Katherine said, to take "a real interest in the work." After *Baquedano* departed in August and Angata's reign ended, Tepano was not popular in the village. He removed himself from Hanga Roa often and began to spend more time at Camp Hotu Iti. Usually he rode out with his small daughter, eight-year-old Amelia (TeTe), on the saddle in front of him. More than fifty years later, Amelia remembered two important things about Katherine: She worked hard and had beautiful boots.

One late, cloudy afternoon Katherine and Tepano sat together at the table in her prefabricated house, Lieutenant Ritchie's unfinished survey map of the southeast coast spread out in front of them. Tepano was intensely interested to see his island sketched so vividly in black and white and realized how vital it was to get everything down correctly and completely. The Rapa Nui people had just engaged in a desperate but futile effort to reclaim their island, and the legal and historical value of locating, naming, and authenticating ancient family boundaries was completely apparent to Tepano from the moment he laid eyes on Lieutenant Ritchie's map.

Thus began a mutually beneficial collaboration between Katherine and Tepano that grew and deepened into a quest that lasted for the rest of her seventeen-month stay on Easter Island. By the time the Mana Expedition departed, they had covered every inch of the island and were a field team of two—working together on the same task or separately pursuing the same elusive bit of information. Scattered throughout Katherine's fieldnotes and journals are dozens of pencil sketches by Tepano with her notes in pen attached; pages torn from his Company account books and scribbled on by her hand; names of places, families, statues, and clans given to her by old people and then scratched out and corrected by Tepano. It's almost as if, at times, they impulsively snatched pencils and pens from one another's hands to complete a sentence or a thought and then hurried on to something else.

Katherine's days in Camp Hotu Iti were crowded with statues and sites, and the bracing sea air and exercise were astoundingly good for her. Bailey cooked up fresh fish every day and she ate well. The only problem in camp life was the ever-present flies—at dinner, crowds of them, she said, "committed suicide in the soup." She still did not sleep well, but she was used to that and more or less resigned to it. She was hopelessly sunburned and windscoured, but filled with energy.

At the end of a day or a week Katherine transcribed and sometimes typed her notes with Tepano beside her, correcting names and phrases. At these times her handwriting is more clear, her sentences precise and complete. It is as though his presence and focus were keeping her on track. She liked to work at night, with a hurricane lamp lit and candles all around her. Sometimes the pages of her field books are covered in large, loopy words strung together like fish flopping on a line. The pages almost turn themselves, breathing with the palpable rush of passing time.

Rapa Nui elders could shed little direct light on the statues—but Katherine did glean important facts from Porotu and Kapiera and, to a lesser extent, from Langitopa. They told her that many statues had names and gave her a list of about a dozen, on which, unfortunately, they rarely agreed. Second, they told her that many statues in the quarry, like those on *ahu*, had been toppled on purpose. Kapiera showed her one that, he said, had been "pulled down in his father's time."

In the weeks after the Mana Expedition first arrived on the island, the Routledges had made a fairly detailed reconnaissance of Rano Raraku, turning over their notes every few days to Lieutenant Ritchie, who drew up a plan—a bird's-eye view—of the crater. Working with *Mana* crewman Albert Light, Ritchie accomplished a triangulated survey of Rano Raraku using a theodolite loaned by the Admiralty. They measured the base of the volcano twice, once using one hundred feet of steel chain, and Ritchie used a sextant and station pointer to complete a topographical survey of the adjacent coastline, locating the positions of statues and *ahu*. He surveyed the interior of Rano Raraku as well, increasing Thomson's statue count by twenty-four.

After Ritchie's departure the exacting and physically taxing job of mapping fell to Katherine and Scoresby. They didn't use the expedition's survey equipment, but relied instead upon a compass, a tape measure, and a camera. Katherine created a large, very rough, and occasionally proportionately inaccurate watercolor sketch of the crater's interior and the southeastern portion of the exterior, then scrambled up and down slopes to find statues. Sometimes she sent Maanga, Antonio, or another workman up to locate them and then, using binoculars, pinpointed them on her sketches.

Katherine divided Rano Raraku statues into four discrete areas: interior and exterior slopes and interior and exterior quarries. A fifth, related area was made up of statues lying in a circular pattern at the exterior base of the crater, and a sixth consisted of statues along roads leading to and from Rano Raraku. She described statues in terms of eight different levels of carving, from the first roughing-out stage to final finishing. Once back in London the Routledges handed over panoramic photos, compass orientations, fieldnotes, and sketches to professional draftsmen at the Royal Geographical Society. They, in turn, produced finished plans and diagrammatic sketches.

The goal of the Mana Expedition's statue inventory was to systematically document what each statue actually looked like—something never done before—and to make notes on carving and transport procedures. Katherine told her family that she was "having a happy time over final work on the statues—we have measured & described every one in the quarries—(7 measurements for each)." Quarries on the exterior were numbered with Roman numerals and statues with Arabic numbers, but on the interior that system was reversed and the numbers were also assigned to an "A" and "B" series corresponding to west and east. The rock art found in Rano Raraku was noted, and a few statues were matched with the quarries in which they had been carved.

The expedition used nautical terms like *gangway* and *launch* and described such features as the stone ridge that connects partially undercut statues to bedrock as a *keel*. Scoresby chose a single statue to represent the majority, then painstakingly calculated volume and weight and estimated time and manpower ratios. Katherine observed that many statues were being moved out and over others that were unfinished. She noted the directions of tool (*toki*) marks and places where tools of different sizes or types had been used. She recognized design details and observed that the best-executed statues had been smoothed to a fine finish. All of the information she collected is hard to decipher, collate, summarize, or compare.

In the first week of September the Routledges decided "what statues to dig out," but pinpointing them today is not easy. While numbers were assigned to each statue, Katherine's excavation notes often refer to statues by shorthand, descriptive names such as "tall," "leaning," "fat giant," or "statue with collar." To find the excavation description of a particular statue among the Mana Expedition papers, a list of statue names must be constructed from three field books. A similar list of statue numbers must be drawn up using her fieldnotes and a chart she constructed, then both must be matched with her rough sketches. Coordinating that information with yet another renumbered sequence that she used later at the prepublication stage may lead to actually uniting a given statue with its excavation notes.

The excavations themselves are also a big problem. They were usually done with little or no supervision, and trenches were left open for weeks or filled in and then reopened. Sometimes heavy rain caused the holes to fill up with mud or collapsed them completely. This terrible situation was a function of time and labor shortages, but also of carelessness and an unfortunate belief the Routledges had brought with them to the island: that they did not need to worry about stratigraphy. Stratigraphic levels—if they could be identified—were sometimes noted as rough measurements, but usually not. They dug out twenty statues on the exterior and another twelve on the interior. They found human bones, stone carving tools, burned wood and charcoal, lumps of red pigment, and on at least one occasion a portable stone figure.

On September 21 Scoresby, Katherine, Antonio, and three other men dug out two statues in the interior of the quarry that turned out to be, in Katherine's opinion, her single most important archaeological finds on the island. One of them was buried up to its chin and the other to midtorso. Langitopa told her that one of the statues—or the nearby quarry from which it was carved—was called Papa Haa Puré. He named the other statue "Papa's wife" as a joke, and that is how they are identified in Katherine's fieldnotes.

The Routledges, Antonio Haoa, and three other Rapa Nui men dug out Papa on two separate occasions—once just so Frank T. Green could take photographs. The first excavation was made about four feet from the back of the statue, the second was about ten feet, and one of them was about sixteen feet deep. At eighteen inches Katherine noted red pigment and a well-made stone carving tool near the statue's shoulder, and then more charcoal—some was burned sugarcane, used for body paint, and some the remnants of a grass fire. On September 24 Tepano was at Mataveri and heard gossip that many *toki* had been taken from the excavations of Papa and Papa's wife when Katherine's back was turned. He reported it immediately to her, and two days later, Katherine refused to pay the men until the tools were returned.

Both statues' backs had intricate, bas-relief carvings Katherine dubbed "sash" or "ring and girdle." She had seen remnants of the design on a few statues fallen from image *ahu,* but no one could tell her what it was called or what it meant. On the back of Papa, however, she was astonished to find something even more interesting: secondary carvings had been superimposed *after* the "ring and girdle" had been carved and the statue finished. Everything, of course, had been done *before* the statue was buried.

Kapiera had given Katherine specific details of similar body paintings or tattoos on the backs of children during the Orongo rituals. She did not realize, however, until she was back in London that Hoa Hakananai'a, the British Museum statue from Orongo's building 11, had both a "ring and girdle" design on its back and, as well, carvings of birdmen and other Orongo-type petroglyphs. Putting it all together, Katherine concluded that the designs she had discovered were the product of an integrated and long-lasting Rapa Nui culture. Katherine was the first researcher to see the underlying continuity in Rapa Nui culture, and her genius for synthesis produced a groundbreaking interpretation of island history: Orongo in the west—and its ceremonies and beliefs—was directly related to the statue-carving tradition that had reached its greatest expression in the east.

The statues were the "living faces" of Rapa Nui ancestors, and the more intimately Katherine lived on the island, the more she was able to see a family resemblance between people and statues. Whatever fears they had struck into the hearts of the ancients who had made and moved them, in Katherine's eye the mute and majestic statues peopled the island with friendly faces. She told her Darlington family that, after the first few months on the island, she was never lonely or afraid, and that the statues comforted her in times of trouble.

A Spy Story

✦

MANA DEPARTED FOR HER SECOND ROUND-TRIP VOYAGE
to the mainland on September 4, 1914. Gillam was expected to pick up the
expedition's mail in Valparaíso, purchase some supplies, make repairs to the
vessel, and return within a month. Scoresby promised that, on Gillam's
return, the expedition would be packed up. Whatever was left undone would,
Scoresby said, remain that way. He was suffering terribly with rheumatoid
arthritis in his right shoulder and, to make matters worse, had injured his
knee in a fall from his horse. Scoresby was, in fact, thoroughly sick of Rapa
Nui.

The Routledges intended to remain in Camp Hotu Iti for the duration of
their stay on the island, but conditions were miserable. It rained nearly all
day and night and the winds were fierce. Dozens of Rapa Nui people, including Antonio and Parapina, were sick with influenza brought ashore by sailors
off *Baquedano*. Throughout most of August 1914 everyone in Camp Hotu Iti
was down with colds and fever, and on September 11, Katherine was the last
to collapse.

Sheep-shearing season was almost upon them, and the best Rapa Nui
workers were all employed by Edmunds on ranch work. He and Scoresby
were at odds, as usual, and Katherine, once back on her feet, kept her distance from them both. She invited Langitopa, Kapiera, and Porotu to Camp
Hotu Iti, hoping they would tell her more stories of the statues. Now that
MacLean was no longer available, she pleaded with Edmunds to allow Varta
to act as her translator. She had, she said, "under great difficulties" learned
"a certain amount of Kanaka, but I cannot follow long legends or explana-
tions." Desperate, she offered to double Varta's wages and pay "any reasonable sum" to compensate the Company for his loss. The old men, she
frantically told Edmunds, were "dying fast."

From September to December 5, 1914 Scoresby single-mindedly focused
on exploring lava tubes that emerged at the water's edge and made, he

thought, perfect hiding places for artifacts. He hit upon the clever idea of constructing a small boat out of the reeds that filled Rano Raraku's crater lake. Varta was a good carpenter and the two of them, with the help of Antonio, built the kayak-like boat and took it to the beach at Anakena, where Scoresby paddled it along the shore looking for caves. He carried a small, postcard-sized, embossed red leather notebook and wrote an excruciatingly detailed, but ultimately useless, description of beach cobbles.

By October Katherine was working all day, staying awake half the night and then rising early with a fresh sense of each moment as precious. Late in the morning of October 12 the Routledges learned that a squadron of ships had suddenly appeared off Hanga Roa. All of the Rapa Nui workmen dropped their tools and rushed back to the village. At nine o'clock in the evening the mysterious visitors were identified: nine German ships, including four men-of-war and five transports. By Sunday it was learned that the celebrated German admiral Graf Maximilian von Spee was aboard his flagship, *Scharnhorst*, and that the fleet was part of twelve vessels crossing from the China station to Valparaíso.

Since early August the fleet had been set on a devious course, snaking its way from the China station through the Caroline Islands in the far-western Pacific and all the way to the Chilean coast. Now they steamed round Easter Island at night with their lights off, and rumors flew. Katherine wrote in her journal that "there is something mysterious about the fleet." Edmunds and Vives Solar (the Chilean schoolmaster in Hanga Roa who also held Edmunds' former Chilean government position of *subdelegado marítimo*) rowed alongside *Scharnhorst* and were taken aboard. Hoping to be offered a whiskey, they didn't even get a cup of tea. Edmunds asked for news but the German captain and paymaster, both of whom spoke English, were tight-lipped. A deal was struck to slaughter 150 cattle and sheep and provide the Germans with the meat.

The officers disembarked in the afternoon to explore the island, and Katherine was certain they would come out to Rano Raraku and photograph her work in progress. Frank T. Green, she said, "worked like a slave covering up our best things." Katherine and Green pitched shovelfuls of earth against the backs of Papa and Papa's wife, and Katherine did not know whether the spectacle was "more amusing or pathetic." She stayed up all night typing up an article for the journal *Man* about the designs on the backs of the statues, saying that they were "entirely unsuspected" and of a "striking character" and pleading for protection of the statues from the "lamentable destruction" of time and the elements.

The next morning Edmunds and Tepano presided over a bloodbath on the beach at Hanga Roa. Rapa Nui men lassoed and drove livestock into the corral, and Edmunds, with the help of German sailors wielding axes and knives, killed and cut them up—surrounded by the entire population of the village. To this point, Edmunds later said, they had heard no war news, but a Rapa Nui man learned from one of the sailors that the Germans had bombarded Papeete, Tahiti. The next day the ships departed for the other side of the island. Upon their return Gomollo, the German living at Mataveri, was taken aboard one whole day and, when he returned, carried wild war tales of Europe in flames and England in chaotic defeat. Katherine filled pages and the margins of pages in her journal with fears and frantic plans.

> How much is true? The officers are forbidden to say anything but . . . they are in fighting trim . . . so here we sit & it sounds like a Jules Verne novel or story . . . the greatest struggle since the days of Napoleon & one can do nothing but pray, pray, pray for victory . . . but, Oh, the suffering hearts everywhere! And we can only go on with our work here & wait & wait—I say to myself it is God's will we should be here . . . and yet in the very distance is a certain rest one can do nothing.

Finally she got her hands on some newspapers that had been smuggled off the ship and read that German armies were advancing into France. "One sits and writes calmly," Katherine said, wondering how one can do "archaeology in the face of such realities & yet—we can & do take interest in it & in every sunset & and in moonlight nights—though the shadow is always there."

On October 18 the Germans departed Easter Island as suddenly as they had arrived. The light cruiser *Dresden* joined the fleet, and on November 1 von Spee engaged the British force in the Battle of Coronel, inflicting a humiliating defeat—much later Katherine learned that the husband of one of her friends went down with the entire crew of *Monmouth*. On November 10 Wilson Pease, frantic for news of his sister and afraid that "the German cruisers might have got her" or that she was "marooned on Easter Island," inquired for news of *Mana* at Williamson, Balfour Co.'s London office. Sir John Balfour told him that he had secret "intelligence" that von Spee's fleet had called at Easter Island, purchased fresh meat, and then moved on. There was no wireless on Easter Island, and Wilson was stunned.

Unfortunately, Balfour had no specific news of the Routledges, but promised to wire Valparaíso immediately. Four days later Balfour received a return wire: Gillam had sailed *Mana* safely to Talcahuano on September 28, but was "detained through war" and then officially ordered by the British consul not to return to Easter Island. Exactly one month later, Gillam received word from the British consul that the sea was clear of enemy warships, and he had permission to sail. However, when he applied for his dispatches from Williamson, Balfour Co., Gillam was surprised to learn that he was to be detained still longer—until a release was sent from the Valparaíso office.

The Routledges, who naturally knew nothing of the Battle of Coronel, were also in the dark about Gillam's plight and growing increasingly frantic about *Mana*. Not certain if she was still in Talcahuano, they feared she would be captured or sunk by the Germans. To further complicate matters, Scoresby believed that the yacht was grossly underinsured. On December 2 Edmunds sent word that a yacht flying the Chilean flag, but captained by an Englishman, had arrived from the mainland. It was *Aranco*, and Captain Walker's mission, he said, was to check on Williamson, Balfour Co. interests and deliver letters to the Routledges. In fact, Captain Walker's real mission was "to spy on the Germans." The Routledges' mailbag contained newspapers reporting the sinking of *Monmouth* and a letter from Gillam saying that *Mana* was stranded in Talcahuano. Katherine received a letter from Wilson, who tried to describe the disaster that had struck their safe and ordered world.

Darlington had been turned into a military post and all horses had been conscripted into service. Tents were rising on the rolling green lawn of Woodside and other great estates, and Seaforth Highlanders and Munster Fusiliers marched in formation down the same country lanes Wilson and Katherine had once driven pony carts. The railway had been taken over by the government, and already there were shortages of petrol and other goods. The press was filled with panic but, Wilson said, as long as the German fleet was contained, there seemed no danger of starvation. "Spy mania" was everywhere.

Captain Walker told Scoresby that the Company wanted them to abandon the Mana Expedition at once, pack up, and leave the island aboard *Aranco*. Scoresby agreed but Katherine flatly refused to pull up stakes. Frustrated beyond endurance, Scoresby decided to go back to mainland Chile aboard *Aranco*, insure *Mana*, and bring her back. Frank T. Green had been looking for a way out for a long time, and he talked himself aboard *Aranco*. On December 5 Scoresby and Green, who could not have looked forward with much pleasure to a month together on shipboard, left Easter Island and sailed for mainland Chile. Katherine and Bailey were now the only members of the Mana Expedition left on Easter Island: "a very quiet day absorbed in papers til tea time & then did notes, etc . . . a soaking wet evening & could not allow myself to think—bearing my small share of trouble brought by war. Epistle = God of Patience, Consolation and Hope."

On the morning of December 8 Katherine and Bailey moved back to Mataveri. She set up an office in one of the Mataveri house bedrooms, pitched her tent in the garden, and was, by all indications, quite happy to be alone and quietly absorbed in her work. Bailey took up his duties in the kitchen and Katherine her work with the old people of the village. Unknown to anyone on the island, Admiral von Spee and the crew of *Scharnhorst,* along with most of the German fleet, went down in a battle in the Falkland Islands. *Dresden* escaped and began a dangerous game of hide-and-seek with the English.

On December 23 Edmunds was having breakfast at Mataveri and Katherine was alone in Ana Kai Tangata, the "cannibal cave," working on her sketches. As she climbed back up the pathway out of the huge cavern she looked seaward to discover a ship, flying no colors, in front of Hanga Roa. The ship continued northward and then returned to anchor. Edmunds and some Rapa Nui men rowed out, a rope ladder was lowered, and he went aboard. The ship, he soon discovered, was a German armed cruiser named *Prinz Eitel Friedrich.* Edmunds made a deal with the paymaster to provide meat, answered some questions, and as he was going off met the German Gomollo coming aboard.

The cruiser sailed away the following morning—only to return towing *Jean,* a small French ship loaded with coal. As the two ships lay side by side in Cook's Bay, the Germans transferred the coal to the hold of the *Prinz Eitel Friedrich.* The village was puzzled and Katherine watched the strange goings-on with interest. She spent Christmas alone, unaware that a German bombardment thundered less than twenty miles from her brother John's home, or that Kate Pease watched every day as hundreds of recruits she called "my khakis" drilled in Woodside's fields.

A German officer and three sailors landed, got horses from the Rapa Nui, then established a signal station on top of the island's highest point. Katherine rightly considered it a breach of Chilean neutrality and international law and promptly "put her oar in." On December 28 she and Tepano rode up to the signal station to confront four wary Germans. Even though Katherine spoke some German, she stayed on her horse and let Tepano, as *jefe* of the village, do the talking. Tepano said his piece, then returned to tell Katherine that the Germans did not want her there. Discretion being the better part of valor, she retreated. The signal station remained.

Gomollo, in the meantime, had "let off steam" to the Germans, ranting that Edmunds was anti-German and conspiring with the islanders to kill him. Edmunds responded by saying that Gomollo was "off his head" and the Rapa Nui people were "quite pleasant." The Germans finally settled accounts with the Rapa Nui for renting their horses and with Edmunds for the meat they had purchased. Katherine wrote a formal letter protesting not only the establishment of the signal station but the provisioning of the German ships. She delivered the letter to Vives Solar and copied it to the British minister in

Santiago. She handled this crisis straightforwardly, but also deferred to Tepano's authority in the matter.

Midday on New Year's Eve, 1914 Katherine was riding back from the field when she saw *Prinz Eitel Friedrich* steaming from her anchorage "like a great blot on the radiant sea" and towing *Jean* "in a last Judas embrace." For nearly three hours Katherine sat on the shore, watching spellbound as the cruiser "swooped round in great circles like an evil bird of prey, and every time that she came broadside on she fired on her victim." As *Jean* sank she drifted within the three-mile limit, and then "suddenly the end came, and where there had been two vessels on the blue sea only one remained."

Captain Joseph Dillinger and his crew had been taken off *Jean* and put ashore by the Germans—along with Captain Sharp and the surviving crew of *Kildalton*, another vessel sunk earlier by *Prinz Eitel Friedrich*. Edmunds provided nearly fifty marooned men with food, clothing, and shelter for about two months—straining Company supplies and island resources to the breaking point—until they were taken off by a passing Swedish vessel. Katherine cleared out of her room in Mataveri so the English captain could take up residence there. She shared her supplies, Bailey cooked ample meals, and Katherine enjoyed diverting conversations at dinner, trying to ignore a terrible truth: *Mana* would surely meet the same fate as *Jean* if she crossed paths with a German ship.

During the time Katherine was alone on the island—from Scoresby's departure in December until his return in March—she was engaged and productive, but occasionally found it hard to keep her course. During part of January and February Katherine was feverish and ill, feeling "slack," sleeping late, and "fighting the blues" of depression. She took refuge in quiet days with Kapiera, Porotu, Veriamu, and some of the other old people in their homes or at Mataveri, usually in company with Tepano or Varta but also often on her own.

Some days Katherine rode into the field. Once she camped alone on the remote northwest coast, and another time she spent a week among the silent statues at Rano Raraku. These forays may have been attempts to seek meditative silence and, possibly, to still voices that, for the first time since she had been on the island, were a problem. The only two occasions on which Katherine was part of a large social gathering were funerals: one for a friend's child and, on January 29, 1915, the other for Angata.

Angata's funeral service took place in the village church. Katherine walked with others behind her "pathetically tiny" casket, a black box covered by a strip of black-and-white calico. From the church door the procession wound toward the village's small burial ground. Men and boys, mostly members of Angata's family, dug her grave. As each man tired he handed off his shovel to another—and the work proceeded without halting. Throughout it all women intoned a steady flow of cheerful song and prayer. Katherine noted, "I stood at a little distance watching gleams of sunshine on the great stones of the terrace of Hanga Roa and on the grey sea beyond, and musing on the strange life now closed, whose early days had been spent in a native hut beneath the standing images of Raraku." They lowered Angata's prayer benches into the grave with her and then, to Katherine's surprise, raised three English cheers—hip, hip, hooray! Dirt fell thuddingly on her coffin, a great feast in Angata's honor was prepared, and Katherine rode away alone.

Three days before Angata's death Wilson Pease had again called at the office of Williamson, Balfour Co. to inquire after his sister. They told him that they had no news from Easter Island but that *Mana* was in Talcahuano "afraid to cross back to the island." Not satisfied, Wilson went to the Admiralty and demanded that a warship be sent out to "see that the Routledges were all right." The Admiralty put him off, but a few days later Williamson, Balfour Co. told him they had received a wire from the Routledges in Valparaíso saying "all well." Persistent questioning finally revealed that it was Scoresby, alone, who was in Valparaíso and that *Aranco* had, indeed, been sent out "to spy on the Germans under excuse of visiting their ranch on Easter Island."

At that very moment, Scoresby was flat on his back in the British and American Hospital in Valparaíso suffering from acute dysentery. He had nearly died on the crossing from Easter Island to mainland Chile, unable to eat and lying helpless "with the rats eating his clothes." To make matters worse, Captain Walker was a raging alcoholic—drunk and utterly out of control day and night—forcing Scoresby to sleep with a pistol under his pillow for protection.

Frank T. Green also went into hospital in Valparaíso, then returned briefly to *Mana* to instruct a new Chilean engineer named Eduardo Silva on the eccentricities of Scoresby's unreliable engine. Green was paid off and left once and for all on February 5. An extremely professional navigator named C. Hector Jones joined the crew as mate—perhaps assigned by the Chilean navy. Scoresby insured *Mana* for a fortune, took sailing clearance for Tahiti, and set out for Rapa Nui—fully intending to uproot Katherine from the island once and for all and set out for French Polynesia. On March 15, 1915 Charles Jeffery sighted Rapa Nui from the foremast, dead ahead. *Mana* hove to off Hanga Roa awaiting daylight, and Gillam set out her lights according to regulations.

In the midmorning Scoresby went ashore and met Katherine, Edmunds, and Bailey at Mataveri. Unknown to anyone on Rapa Nui, the previous day the German light cruiser *Dresden,* a remnant of von Spee's squadron, had taken refuge in Cumberland Bay, Juan Fernández Island, and then was trapped by *Glasgow.* The Germans abandoned ship and then blew her up rather than lose her to the British. That evening three Rapa Nui women reported excitedly that they had seen a "steamer with two funnels" off the southern coast, and Scoresby, Bailey, and Edmunds were convinced it was *Prinz Eitel Friedrich* returning to the island to replenish her provisions. Bailey, in fact, had seen the same ship from Rano Raraku just two days earlier. The next morning Gillam reported that he and Hector Jones had seen the German signal light—the one Katherine had futilely demanded be removed—flash several times during the night.

Scoresby immediately wrote a detailed letter to the British minister in Santiago containing a full description of *Prinz Eitel Friedrich,* the loss of *Jean* within the three-mile limit of Easter Island, and everything else that Katherine told him had transpired during his absence. He said that Edmunds ("an Englishman") was ordered by Merlet to provide provisions to the Germans, and that the Company had installed a spy at Mataveri— the German Gomollo—who took "an active part in the arrival of German war vessels & obviously gave them every assistance & information & generally acts as their agent." Scoresby described Katherine's attempt to remove the German signal light and the vital importance of Easter Island as a stopping-off place for wartime vessels. His words eventually resounded all the way to London.

Mana, in the meantime, was lying off Hanga Roa with no signal lights, in clear violation of international maritime regulations. Gillam and Hector Jones were on watch all night, prepared to run if *Prinz Eitel Friedrich* turned up. In the late afternoon of March 17, Scoresby handed Gillam sailing orders and a dispatch bag containing the unsealed letter to the British minister. Gillam was to make his way—for the third time—to mainland Chile and deliver the dispatch to the British consul general in Valparaíso. At 6:45 P.M., in heavy and threatening weather, Gillam weighed anchor under full sail, without sailing permission and showing no lights. *Mana* moved so fast away from Rapa Nui that Gillam spilled a whole mug of tea over his open log.

Gillam fulfilled his mission and delivered the dispatch to the British consul in Valparaíso, then traveled to Santiago to see the British minister personally and to "answer questions." What exactly transpired in these meetings is not known, nor is it clear if Gillam was given a reply to Scoresby's letter. Scoresby's instructions to him were to remain in Chile no longer than ten days, and he departed on April 27 in extremely bad weather for a rough run to Rapa Nui. The ship's log says *Mana* arrived May 28, but Katherine's journal has her appearing off Hanga Roa on May 29, probably from a different anchorage along the coast. Possibly coincidentally, *Baque-dano* also arrived on May 28 and then departed May 30. For the next nearly interminable ten weeks *Mana* dodged uneasily and endlessly, waiting for Katherine to finish her work and get off Easter Island.

During the first ten days of July *Mana* kept moving, trying to keep out of sight of any German vessels that might be in the vicinity, but Gillam set her lights every night. On July 10 the engineer Silva started the ship's engine and the cylinder cracked vertically. On July 11 *Mana* hove to along the northern coast and sighted what appeared to be a warship to the northeast, making a course that would take her to the south side of the island. At 1 P.M. the newcomer was identified as British. She anchored and, by 7 P.M., vanished. From that evening until the expedition's ultimate departure on August 18, Gillam never again set the yacht's lights.

Mana Expedition papers do not reveal the identity of the British ship, but it apparently was HMS *Orama*. F. W. Wilsden went ashore and met Scoresby and Edmunds, who showed him quickly around the island. The presence of *Orama* in the vicinity could have been coincidental or related to the recent British action against *Dresden,* but it is more probable that Gillam brought back some sort of a dispatch from the mainland to be handed off to either *Baquedano* or *Orama*. If so, Henry James Gillam and *Mana* had gallantly fulfilled their wartime mission.

Legacy

◆

ON MARCH 15, 1915, KATHERINE NOTED, "MANA ARRIVED in the morning," but made no mention of her husband, from whom she had been separated for more than three months. She started to pack but then abandoned it, went briefly aboard *Mana,* and then, a week later, "Moved to Hotu Iti." Katherine worked like a demon, hardly taking time to make even perfunctory notes in her journal. She completed her watercolor sketch of a portion of Rano Raraku's exterior slopes and wrote to her faraway family on Easter Sunday, April 4, 1915—eight days before her mother's death. Seated at a table in her tent Katherine began a long, rambling "circular" letter that she did not complete until June. She told her family how sorry she was to leave, and how deeply she had grown to love the island's quiet, moonlit nights that brought her "dreams of beauty." She regretted "leaving this immense stillness for the bustle of life." With dead certainty and profound sadness, Katherine Routledge knew she would never see Easter Island again and, she wrote, "simply daren't to think of it."

Scoresby, in sharp contrast, was frankly desperate to get off the island as quickly as possible. He turned his full attention to crating artifacts and organizing photographic plates and negatives. Katherine commented rather dismissively that he was writing "elaborate essays on the subject of stone chisels," a topic that he found "sufficiently absorbing" but which left her "somewhat cold." He drafted a letter to Mana Expedition advisers as a follow-up to the one he had written in May 1914 and outlined their accomplishments. He oversaw some final digging of statues in Rano Raraku, but Tepano handled most expedition details: "Did I make clear," Katherine wrote Edmunds, "that if you have not got the 2 men to dig for us on Monday I should be so much obliged if you would *hand the matter over to Juan* [emphasis added] & [ask] him to find them if possible. Wages of $1 a day & mutton if they want potatoes etc they had better bring them."

The weather was squally but Katherine and Tepano rode over the entire island and revisited nearly two hundred *ahu* until, at last, she was convinced that the general survey work was "satisfactorily finished." She drove herself with intense concentration, talking to every islander she knew and filling page after page with words, phrases, and place-names. Running out of paper, she tore out pages of her yacht's log and used them. She wrote so fast her pen gave out and her flying hand struck her inkpot, splaying black ink, in a great blob, across the cover of one of her worn blue field books. She awoke in the middle of the night, lit a candle, and scribbled last-minute instructions and reminders to herself for the next day. Katherine (in a modest understatement not typical of her) wrote her mother that "if people ask you if we have 'solved the riddle,' you can say that we do not claim to have done that, but we have found much that is new & interesting."

On April 12 Kate Pease and her daughter Lilian traveled by train from Darlington to London and checked into Brown's Hotel. That evening Kate had a slight heart attack. The doctor was called and she was confined to bed. In the morning she seemed bright and cheerful but then, without warning, fell unconscious and passed quietly away. Wilson Pease pulled his family together to escort their mother's body home to Woodside, and on April 19 Kate was laid to rest in the Quaker burial ground behind Skinnergate Meeting House. A high "Woodside wind" blew, a small crowd of family and friends attended, and an honor guard of her beloved "khakis" stood by. Her will left numerous wartime charities greatly enriched and Katherine and her siblings enormously wealthy. Within days an almost ritualistic burning of letters and journals began, and hundreds of letters from Katherine—except a few on which she had written "Save"—were tossed into the fire.

On April 28 Wilson Pease placed a bunch of yellow daffodils in Katherine's name on their mother's grave and, for all of the next month, tried repeatedly to get word of Kate's death to her. On May 21 Katherine scribbled, "Believe K. Pease is gone," in her journal. She grew listless and preoccupied, slept badly, and when she did sleep, had nightmares. Camping in Rano Raraku, amidst the restless ghosts of Rapa Nui ancestors, Katherine had a sense of disconnectedness, of being afloat. About to leave forever a place she had come to love, Katherine found herself confronted with the recurring existential crisis of her life: the never really forgotten personal losses of her distant childhood.

In material ways Katherine was surely blessed, but all of her life she had been told that her problems were within her and of her own making. The solution to any unhappiness, she had been taught, was prayer and the simple *choice* to be happy. The absence of love in Katherine's life was the result, her mother had always said, of the lack of charity in her heart—but Katherine was genuinely in love with the island. It was, in many ways, not unlike her in character: stubborn and separate, half-superficial and half-concealed. Its boundedness was liberating, its isolation was filled with possibilities. It had encouraged both forgetfulness and discovery in her and held out an almost erotic promise of independence that had encouraged her imagination. She had been Crusoe for a time, but now that time was gone.

At home in Darlington, Wilson settled Kate Pease's affairs with efficient dispatch. He found new places of employment for the servants, chose mementos to give relatives, and sold off the horses and livestock. Katherine's many personal belongings were stored in her Woodside room, along with Kate's silver, jewelry, and paintings. These would await Katherine's return to be divided. Wilson had labels made for all of the furniture being offered for sale and prepared catalogues for the printer. Woodside house was destined for demolition; the trees Katherine loved would be harvested and the parkland developed.

Alone in the garden on his last morning at Woodside, Wilson sat for a little while in the summerhouse on the terrace, then wandered down to "the children's gardens" and across the lawn. Here was the playground where he and Katherine and so many others had learned croquet, cricket, archery, and finally, tennis and flirtation. Cars filled with strangers began to arrive, and people walked around his childhood home as though it belonged to them— it was time to go. Steps led up from the lawn to his parked car in the drive, but the quickest way, the way he and Katherine had used as children, was up a steep, fifteen-foot bank. Wilson ran up it, something he had not done in twenty-five years.

Katherine and Scoresby, on that day, were at Mataveri. The weather was wet, cold, and miserable, and fierce winds kept shifting. Scoresby was methodically crating and organizing while Katherine pored over her field-notes. Her journal for June and July of 1915 is a scribbled series of extremely brief, disjointed shorthand entries not unlike the vague "list of doings" Kate Pease once kept. With Kapiera and Tepano she revisited Orongo many times, concentrating on getting information on body paintings and tattoos, trying to make comparisons between them and the designs on the back of Papa and to decipher their meanings. In June she took photographic portraits of Tepano and her other consultants and made molds of Orongo petroglyphs. She negotiated for artifacts with the old men and collected some important feather crowns they said were once used in Orongo ceremonies. Her last pair of boots were still in good shape, but her wardrobe was nearly completely exhausted and she began to give most of her things away, keeping only a white dress for Tahiti, some shirts, and two skirts.

By mid-July Katherine had spent sixteen months living on Easter Island. She had worked, eaten, and slept in tents, prefabricated buildings, under the stars, and in the relative comfort of Mataveri house. She had sailed around the island countless times, crawled into caves, climbed down the sides of cliffs, dug up human remains, and excavated statues. She had confronted her fears, braved discomfort, and risked her life to disease in the hope of discovery, filling many hundreds of notebook pages with stories, observations, speculations, myths, legends, lies, and memories. She had made sketches and watercolors, taken photographs, bought or bartered for hundreds of objects. Her work had repeatedly been interrupted or redirected by competition, aggression, and the arrival of each new ship, and her papers were a mass of valuable but conflicting detail—but still she persisted.

The human bones Scoresby was labeling and crating for removal were the ancestors of Rapa Nui people Katherine had come to know. Though she was a woman who wandered the world, Katherine's own family ties were binding. She saw the Easter Island family of statues and people in the context of Pease family traditions, a sympathetic understanding of the past, and her own Quaker belief in standing up for the underdog. The island landscape was peopled for her with myriad shadows that needed to be anchored in place. It was but a small step from lists of place-names and genealogies to linking whole families to ancestral lands—uniting "locality and memory."

Katherine placed Veriamu, Kapiera, Porotu, and other old people in the context of their families or clans, assigned their clans to one of the east-west political divisions, and tried to link both to *ahu* sites. Tepano's original list of family groups, written in his own hand with the proper Rapanui spellings and accents all carefully included, is in her fieldnotes. He made inquiries as to where, exactly, the boundaries of family lands were located, then they rode out to places as far away as Anakena and Ahu Tepeu to locate the actual stone boundary markers and judge them with their own eyes. She worked backward—from ethnography to archaeology, from the people to the statues—and then forward again. Although the boundaries Katherine was able to draw are inexact and sketched in broad strokes, her map of political divisions provides the first graphic, public statement ever made of Rapa Nui land ownership.

The patterns of structures, trails, and fields laid down a template of land use, and the Orongo ceremonies opened a tiny window onto beliefs. Katherine synthesized her information into a workable, interpretive theory that had four basic points: the ancestors of present-day Rapa Nui people had produced the statues; at some point Orongo had emerged as the center of a new but directly related religion; that new religion was itself interrupted by the evils of slavery; and finally, what was left of it was reshaped by commerce and missionization.

Katherine Routledge and Juan Tepano, though worlds apart, had created a legacy of enormous and lasting value. Men like Tepano are rare. Only a few dozen men and women around the world have gone down in history as invaluable and irreplaceable cultural sources, guides, and interpreters. For each of them, however, there are dozens more who are nameless. In Katherine, Tepano found an admirer, an intellectual equal, and a partner; an unusual woman in an unusual place. Her gift of storytelling, her ability to accommodate superstition, her obsessive attention to detail, and her sense that history and myth are compatible all made her the perfect person for the ethnographic job she took on—the right woman in the right place at the right time.

Katherine and Tepano were each complex characters with real needs. Katherine was no shrinking Victorian violet, and she liked and admired men in whom, like Tepano, "reliability was the charm of strength." Her partnership with Tepano—not with Scoresby—salvaged the Mana Expedition from the brink of disaster. Katherine's personal feelings about Tepano are clear: She respected him, depended upon him, and trusted him. Katherine bonded with few people in her life—Wilson Pease and Lyle McAllum were among them—and she did not take orders from anyone. With Tepano, however, she was quite willing to subordinate her way of doing things to his.

The island and some who lived there—especially Tepano—melted something in Katherine and stirred emotions that were pure and direct, intense and unfamiliar. Her feelings were those of being in love, but in Katherine's eyes she and Tepano had achieved the genuinely precious, challenging, and rewarding "companionate" ideal she had sought all of her adult life. In *The Mystery of Easter Island* Katherine said that "the whole voyage of the *Mana* is a tribute" to Henry James Gillam, and the success of the Mana Expedition "was due to the intelligence of one individual who was known as Juan Tepano."

Did Tepano ever read those lines? He had mastered Katherine's language and the manners of her culture. He had assumed responsibility for the success of her work and, in fact, indelibly stamped it with his own interpretations. He had invested time in being her protector and companion and thrived on being her sounding board. If he was disappointed, felt a sense of accomplishment, or a feeling of abandonment after her work was over and Katherine sailed away, there is no way today of knowing. Through Katherine's published praise of him other investigators, employers, patrons, and benefactors sought out Tepano and gave him recognition. He rightly came to be regarded as an authority on Rapa Nui culture. He was not, however—nor did he pretend to be—the embodiment of it.

Tepano's relationship with Katherine was rewarding while she was on the island and made him famous afterward, but it also cost him. Unconventional and set apart from his own community long before she met him,

Tepano's aptitude for languages, his striking intellectual ability, and his reflective nature were important assets, but his moralizing, ambition, and economic success all made him the target of envy and suspicion. The delicately self-sustaining Rapa Nui world constantly tried either to save itself from outsiders or to benefit from contact with them, and the community guarded its resources carefully. Because Tepano received so much support from outsiders, he, in turn, lost some familial support. Like others who have served as consultants in other cultures, Tepano came to believe that anthropologists and archaeologists were building reputations and getting rich from his hard-won knowledge.

On July 16 boxes, baskets, and crates from Mataveri were hauled down to the shoreline, where they were inventoried and then loaded on *Mana*. Tepano, who had been so indispensable when off-loading *Mana* on her first arrival over a year earlier, did not participate in this work. Instead, he spent days and most evenings with Katherine at Mataveri, usually in company with Veriamu or Kapiera. At the end of the day on August 6, 1915—the Routledges' ninth wedding anniversary—Katherine left Kapiera and Tepano and went aboard *Mana*. She stowed her white tin trunk containing her fieldnotes, then went ashore the next day. As preparations for departure swirled and eddied in hectic currents around her, she calmly sat on the Mataveri veranda with Kapiera and Pakarati. With a notebook in front of her, she asked every question she could think of, went back over familiar ground, and raised new issues. The next morning she rode up to Orongo alone for the last time, then spent the afternoon and evening with Pakarati and Tepano.

Squalls and heavy rain blew in on August 9, but Gillam had set no lights since July 11, and *Mana* pitched and rolled in the darkness. On Tuesday, August 10 the weather cleared a bit and Katherine disembarked *Mana* at the crack of dawn to spend the entire day in Tepano's garden. Jotefa and Veriamu were with her for at least part of the time, but she had no questions for them. In fact, they seem to have talked little. Katherine wandered distractedly about in the village, saying good-bye to friends, giving and receiving gifts as tents and equipment were moved in a steady stream of chaotic shore-to-ship activity. She stayed ashore as *Mana* dodged along the coast at night, still without lights, and Scoresby on the 6 to 8 P.M. watch. The next day was Katherine's birthday, and though she did not know it at the time, Friday, August 13—a date she was always superstitious about—was to be her last day on Easter Island. When she went aboard *Mana* at the end of the day Katherine fully expected to get back on shore at least once more.

The seas were rough and the wind constantly changed. *Mana* dodged skittishly off the west side of the island, then hove to, and Gillam checked the positions of landmarks for the expedition's map. On the south coast he checked the heights of hills, then *Mana* moved along the eastern cliffs and around again to dodge off Hanga Roa. On Wednesday, August 18, *Mana* bucked and then, suddenly, bore away from Easter Island. Scoresby, preoccupied with the potential threat of German warships to *Mana*'s safety, abruptly gave the order to sail without proper sailing clearance.

Katherine had no opportunity to say a last good-bye to either the island she loved or to Tepano, the man who was her closest friend there. She stood at the rail and watched until "the last vestige of the long coast of Easter Island dipped below the horizon." Even today, many islanders mark the hour a good friend or family member leaves the island to the minute, noting the exact direction of the wind or the precise phase of the moon. Falling rain on the day of departure is a good-luck sign, an indication one will return. When Katherine Routledge last saw Easter Island, the wind was blowing from off-shore and the sun was setting in a gray but remarkably cloudless sky.

✦

AFTER EASTER ISLAND: ADRIFT

✦

Voyage Home

✦

MANA MADE THE 1,350-MILE JOURNEY TO PITCAIRN ISLAND, Easter Island's nearest neighbor, in ten days. She arrived in Bounty Bay, where, 126 years earlier, HMS *Bounty* had sunk in flames set by the most famous mutineer in Western history: Fletcher Christian, master's mate to Captain William Bligh. On August 27, 1915 sturdy descendants of the mutineers welcomed *Mana.* The island was lush with tropical flowers, and neat houses were connected by shady lanes of palms and bananas. Katherine attended a church service where a missionary darkly predicted the imminent end of the world and found "it was depressing."

For two days the entire village pitched in to dig enthusiastically on two or three nearly destroyed prehistoric *marae* (temple) sites, built by Polynesians who had abandoned the island long before the arrival of the mutineers. Human bones and statues had been associated with some of the *marae.* One site, Katherine glumly said, "resembled to some extent" the *ahu* of Easter Island. She was shown the remains of one broken, headless red scoria statue that had "a certain resemblance to that of Easter Island, but the workmanship is much cruder." Scoresby asked for stone tools and villagers parted with about eighty of them.

The British Association for the Advancement of Science had asked Scoresby to make skeletal measurements on Pitcairn, and Katherine to collect genealogical information. She did not pursue it, but Scoresby neatly solved his assigned research problem by taking aboard two Pitcairn Islanders, Charles and Edwin Young, as living specimens. *Mana* made for Rapa Iti, some seven hundred miles away, but because of strong winds, the Routledges could not land. *Mana* lay off Rapa's precipitous coast, sailing back and forth in thick rain and heavy seas until her forestays gave out. Katherine sketched the rocky profile of the island, then they went on to Tahiti.

In the afternoon of September 16, 1915 *Mana* anchored in front of the bustling town of Papeete, Tahiti. The British consul came aboard and a messenger delivered two large mailbags bulging with a year's worth of letters and newspapers. Katherine sat at the table in the saloon, stacking everything neatly in chronological order and separating out Pease family letters. She found twenty letters from her mother, which she placed together in a pile. Expecting the worst, she opened the most recent letter from Wilson— and discovered that Kate Pease had died on April 15, 1915.

Katherine's experience of Tahiti was clouded in a haze of stifling, humid heat, sleeplessness, and tears. She moved into a hotel and went to bed, reading and rereading her mother's letters and the daily war news that arrived by wireless from Honolulu and New Zealand. She wrote a letter to Wilson and Joan that suggests she may have been troubled with the auditory hallucinations she called her "voices." She went on a food binge that continued for the rest of the journey and resulted in a huge weight gain. Because Scoresby insisted, she paid a reluctant call on the wife of the French governor and on the queen of Tahiti, widow of Pomare V, and was guided around the island by the queen's daughter, Princess Takau Pomare. Katherine found brief amusement in conversations with an American geologist, who was out to disprove theories of mythical sunken continents.

> He had found himself involved in the everlasting quarrel between geologists and biologists, who each want the world constructed to prove their own theories. In this case a biologist wished for continuity of land to account for the presence of the same snail in islands far removed. Our friend had contended that the mollusks might have traveled on drift-wood, but was told in reply that salt water did not "suit their constitution." He had then argued that they could easily have gone with the food in native canoes. "Anyhow," he concluded, with a delightful Yankee drawl, "to have the floor of the ocean raised up fifteen thousand feet, for his snails to crawl over, is just too much."

Katherine saw the ruins of a famous *marae*, but took little interest. She visited a small colony of Rapa Nui people, descendants of laborers removed there by John Brander more than thirty years earlier, but did not interact much. Then her old friend Bailey, the Mana Expedition cook who had stood by her so well on Easter Island, decided to leave the crew in Tahiti. He had not collected his wages during the voyage and was, Katherine said, "quite a millionaire" when he was paid off. He took up residence in Katherine's hotel, bought a luminous new suit of ice cream white, and had his photograph taken, which he then ceremoniously presented to her. Before Bailey departed for England aboard a commercial vessel, Scoresby arranged to have an English officer look after him. He made it safely home (although he had lost, or spent, nearly all of his wages), then joined the Royal Navy. Sadly, Katherine said, she "saw his name subsequently, with most sincere regret, in a list of the 'missing.' "

On October 3 Katherine drafted, but apparently never sent, a strange, messy letter to an unnamed bishop that reveals her extreme emotional vulnerability. Her experience on Easter Island, "the loneliest spot on the globe," had, Katherine wrote, given her "both food & time for reflection." Those living in the midst of "fresh thoughts literature & contact with others have no idea of the mental & spiritual hunger of those in lonely places." Katherine makes the extremely odd suggestion that a committee be formed that would, somehow, make periodic addresses "to the Empire" and banish loneliness.

Mana departed for the Hawaiian Islands on October 8, 1915, sailed within sight of the Tuamotus, then was becalmed in the Doldrums, her engine again useless. It was stifling hot and everyone was either bored or short-tempered. Katherine, who had suffered increasing sadness and isolation since her departure from Rapa Nui, now settled into the "mean blues," a depressive state that remained with her for the rest of the voyage. Nothing pleased her, very little interested her, and no one was capable of raising her spirits.

In September Scoresby had begun to draft the final Mana Expedition report, and he worked on it throughout this leg of the voyage home. On November 11 *Mana* reached Oahu and the Routledges went ashore in Honolulu. They toured the island with the British consul and Dr. William T. Brigham, first director of the Bernice Pauahi Bishop Museum of Polynesian Ethnology and Natural History. Founded in 1889, the Bishop Museum already had a significant collection of Polynesian objects, a library, and a publication program. A huge model of an ancient Hawaiian temple *(heiau)* constructed by John F. G. Stokes, curator of ethnology, dominated the exhibits. Unimpressed, Katherine said it had "no resemblance either to the marae of Tahiti or the ahu of Easter Island." Brigham took them to see the ruins of a *heiau*, but Katherine found that "the art of building never seems to have approached" the high level of Easter Island. Everything, in fact, failed to compare to Easter Island.

Scoresby had a photo of *Mana* printed as postcards and, on November 30, cheerfully sent them off to friends and family. Katherine's Christmas greeting, in contrast, was a small, six-page leaflet in memory of her mother. Printed on heavy cream paper and bound in black satin cord, its cover is adorned with a cross (unusual for a Quaker) and the last page with Kate Pease's embossed initials. Inside are stanzas from two hymns that, Katherine said, her mother had sent to her the previous December with "for 1915" written on the margin. Katherine firmly believed that Kate had had an accurate premonition of her death, and had "heard the voice bidding her cease her wanderings."

On November 28 *Mana* departed Honolulu for San Francisco without the Routledges, who took a steamer to the Big Island of Hawaii and then embarked on a long motor trip. They arrived in San Francisco aboard a commercial liner on December 14, 1915, and *Mana* sailed through the Golden Gate on Christmas Day, 1915. She anchored off the Panama Pacific Exposition Building. Scoresby was ill with bronchitis, but Katherine went to Berkeley, settled in the Victorian-style Hotel Claremont, and attended a luncheon in her honor arranged by E. W. Gifford, a young ethnologist at the University of California. She met A. L. Kroeber, head of the university's museum and department of anthropology, and his ebullient assistant, Thomas T. Waterman.

At the museum on Parnassus Heights, Gifford gave Katherine a photo of an Easter Island dance paddle, which, she said, "was a great joy and also most useful." She was taken on a private tour of the museum and caught a glimpse of California's legendary Ishi, the "last Yahi." Ishi's entire tribe had perished with the coming of white men to the Sacramento Valley, and he had been alone since childhood. One day, as a middle-aged man starving to death, Ishi walked into the white man's world—a place filled with danger and diseases that threatened his life. Kroeber moved bureaucratic mountains to provide a safe haven for Ishi, who came to live in the museum among the artifacts of his past. He taught the anthropologists how to hunt and fish in the Yahi manner and sang the songs of his childhood.

Waterman gave Katherine a pamphlet about the Yahi entitled "The Last Wild Tribe" and she found it "positively <u>thrilling</u>." She asked to meet Ishi, but he was ill and she was only able to stand at the door to his room. Ishi was in bed, covered up and shivering. His eyes, bright with fever, were all she saw of the "hero" who "greatly impressed" her. In 1916 Katherine learned that Ishi had died of tuberculosis. He had begged his anthropologist friends not to "dissect" him in the manner he had seen museum scientists study biological specimens, saying that to do so would injure his spirit. They had promised him they would not, but sadly, the pull of scientific curiosity was too strong and an autopsy was performed.

Katherine, who had not been aboard *Mana* once since disembarking in Honolulu harbor, decided to travel overland to New York, where the Routledges planned to sell *Mana* rather than take her across the submarine-infested Atlantic. With Scoresby, Gillam, and a rather sketchy crew, *Mana* left San Francisco harbor on January 20, 1916, and headed south. On January 16 Katherine, whose mood can only be described as bleak, left by train for Los Angeles ("a winter resort for various Central American millionaires"), the Grand Canyon ("more impressive than beautiful"), and Chicago (where she "got as far as admiring the outside of the Field Museum"). She detoured to

Washington, D.C., to see the Easter Island collections of the USS *Mohican*, then went on to New York, where she crossed the Atlantic with "no submarines in sight!"

Katherine landed in Liverpool on February 6, 1916. Wilson and Joan Pease met her in Bournemouth, "where we could all three be alone together and get over her sad home coming."

> When the train from the North drew up at the platform, I saw a very round and short lady alight. She was dressed in deep black, and her luggage was baskets, parcels and canvas sacks. She was standing with her back to me and I walked round her before I was sure the lady was my sister. Not that three years have altered Katherine much except that she is even stouter than she was.

Their hotel sat high on a cliff and looked obliquely across the bay. Joan, Wilson, and Katherine each had a tiny bedroom and a sitting room, where blazing fireplaces fought off bitter cold. The skies were gray and Wilson and Joan escaped each afternoon while Katherine slept.

> Poor Katherine was always very near her tears. It is a most awfully sad home coming for her. I am naughty enough to think she rather enjoys her sadness, and finds luxury in self pity. What Joan calls our "family feelings" are terribly developed in Katherine. She looks about for slights, and tries not to forget them. She burst into tears as she told us that she had had no letters of sympathy from her friends when they heard of Mam's death. "I was lonely and in sorrow and none of my friends wrote to me."

Katherine told and retold stories of Angata and the "native rising," the German squadron, and the sinking of *Jean* by *Prinz Eitel Friedrich*. She gave a lecture on Easter Island—her first ever—to a few hotel guests. Free from later second-guessing, Katherine described continuity in Rapa Nui culture and clearly stated her findings. Wilson took notes.

> The Islanders say their ancestors made the statues and there seems no reason to doubt it. Similar statues are found on other islands in the Pacific. They are not so large as those on Easter Island but the Easter Island stone is most easy to work. The statues ceased to be made in the 18th Century. That is about the time Europeans first visited the island. K's theory is that then the Kanakas changed their religion to the worship of the whitemen and their ships. The statues stood on terraces, looking inland. They seem to have been thrown down by man not by earthquake. Probably this was done in tribal

wars. How they transported these statues and set them up, and how the people originally crossed 2000 miles of sea to reach Easter Island, are secrets to which K. has not found the answers.

Katherine, nonetheless, was in culture shock. She was miserably unhappy, endlessly critical, and "terribly hard on sinners."

K. could make no allowances for poor young Edmunds . . . for living with a native girl. She could not realise his temptation or his loneliness. I wish the "poor child" (as Mams used to call her) had more "love, joy, peace," I wish that her mind of which she is so proud was a broader one.

Katherine admitted to her brother that she had "quarrelled with nearly all the company on the Mana."

I may go through life too easily on the anything for a quiet life principal. But K. certainly goes to the other extreme. She is . . . so sure she knows what is just and her right, and so determined that it is her duty to put the world right, and yet so morbidly anxious to be loved and liked that she must live on the rack. For a person of her sized brain K. is curiously conventional. She could hardly control her fury to find that 9 months after Mams death Jo . . . was out of mourning. I nearly said "It's better to do all you can to help and make happy your dear ones when they are alive, than to wear mourning for them when they are dead." But I'm glad I refrained for it would be too terrible if K. ever realised how much unhappiness she had caused poor dear Mams.

She considered herself an expert on everything, but just beneath the surface lay self-doubt, a sense of loss, and profound unhappiness.

The fact of the matter is that she has a swelled head. She puts mentality before magnanimity . . . yet she is a loving and loyal sister to me. But I do wish for her own sake she could "study to be quiet" and take pleasure in the beauty and joy of the world.

Katherine was fast approaching breakdown. The loss of Kate Pease was a genuine source of distress, but another sadness was Katherine's unacknowledged loss of Easter Island. Katherine's sojourn on Rapa Nui had been the most engaged and vital time of her life, and her work there had given her great gifts of self-expression and self-realization. The price she paid for such freedom was, in Katherine's melodramatic and guilt-ridden judgment, Kate

Pease's death. Her fury at Edmunds' island life—even though she remained in friendly contact with him for years after the Mana Expedition departed— is extremely odd and bears the stamp of self-hatred so evident in Scoresby's behavior during the Silberrad Affair.

On February 11 Wilson, Joan, Joan's maid, Katherine and her bags, baskets, and canvas sacks all took the train to London, where Lyle McAllum met them at Fleming's Hotel. Lyle saw the state Katherine was in and immediately took her home to Ranby House in Nottinghamshire. Katherine walked in the winter garden, wrote letters, and talked incessantly to anyone who would listen. She regained her bearings and then, two weeks later, moved into the Ladies' Empire Club on Grosvenor Street, London. There was snow in the streets one early morning when Katherine and Wilson drove to Westminster Abbey to attend the ceremony investing Katherine's friend, the Reverend Harold Ernest Bilborough, as suffragan bishop of Dover. This impressive event took place at the same time she was experiencing a religious awakening that, eventually, took her far from her Quaker roots and deep into the occult.

Katherine, who had not heard a word from *Mana* since she had left San Francisco, received a cable from Scoresby in Colón saying that they had been allowed to pass through the Panama Canal. He was, he said, somewhat regretful of that stroke of luck. Had *Mana* been forced to sail around Cape Horn, she would have been at Punta Arenas in time to help Sir Ernest Shackleton rescue his men after *Endurance* went down on November 21, 1915—"a job for which *Mana* was eminently fitted." He decided not to sell the yacht but to "trust to our good luck, which invariably follows Mana" and risk encountering German submarines in their run across the Atlantic. The weather was alternately overcast and gloomy or blowing huge gales, and the crew was filled with so much tension that even Gillam was uncharacteristically "bad tempered and feeling generally fed up." In spite of it all, *Mana* bravely crossed without mishap and arrived in Southampton on June 25, 1916.

The Story of an Expedition,
1916–1920

✦

THE MANA EXPEDITION, HOWEVER LIMITED AND FLAWED, was the first true attempt to conduct an archaeological survey of Easter Island. Pacific island anthropology was only nascent, and the Routledges' exposure to archaeology was sharply limited. Yet Katherine, like a few other women of her time, combined a brilliant mind, a solid education, diverse life experience, and a quirky personality to make up for the training she lacked. Her strong, highly personal motivation, combined with her serendipitous association with Juan Tepano, gave Rapa Nui its voice as well.

The Routledges were not institutionally based, but they had astutely affiliated the expedition with the British Association for the Advancement of Science, the British Museum, and the Royal Geographical Society. Scientific hypotheses and goals, however, had not figured prominently in their pre-expedition planning. This was both good and bad. It gave, on the one hand, freedom from intellectual constraints and institutional expectations. On the other, analysis and interpretation of findings had to be accomplished within an intellectual framework constructed in retrospect, and that is difficult for anyone to do well.

Once back in England, the isolated nature of the Routledges' fieldwork disappeared. They were required to begin a new phase of their collaboration with each other and to enter into certain kinds of cooperative associations with other researchers. The blank page loomed before them, and critics lay in wait. Their massive Rapa Nui data demanded a much more strenuous writing effort than had their more limited African material. The years from 1916 to 1920 were challenging, even trying in some ways, but they were Katherine's most productive post–Rapa Nui years.

Scoresby paid off his crew in Southampton in early July of 1916, and the men of *Mana* dispersed, most going immediately into uniform. On July 28 the king and queen received the Routledges with Charles and Edwin Young, the direct descendants of the mutineers of the *Bounty,* as "representatives of England's smallest colony." In September Scoresby sent the Youngs to Sir Arthur Keith, Royal College of Surgeons. They represented the sixth gener- ation of progeny arising from the union of British sailors with Tahitian women, and Keith saw it as an opportunity to study the genetic effects of iso- lation. In his opinion, "they were a most docile pair of young men, helpful in every way, but the impression they left on me . . . was that their mentality was of a low grade." Katherine, in sharp contrast, thought the Youngs "had proved themselves very intelligent."

The adventures of *Mana* received massive publicity, and Scoresby's ene- mies thought that he had "returned with some pretty tall yarns." Gossip swirled, and then Scoresby became embroiled in a professional disagree- ment. Both he and Katherine planned to give illustrated papers at a meeting in Newcastle of the Anthropology Section of the British Association. Hers was entitled "Recent Culture on Easter Island and Its Relation to Past His- tory," and Scoresby's was "Megalithic Remains on Easter Island." He high- handedly demanded that a large lecture hall be reserved for the massive crowds he expected to attend his presentation, and members of the associa- tion, including O. G. S. Crawford's father figure Harold Peake, refused.

Scoresby's report to the association ran to forty-seven handwritten pages and was edited by Katherine, who disagreed with some of his points. Scoresby gave up on the question of statue transport, saying, "We failed to find any image undoubtedly in the process of being moved and therefore are unable to throw any light on the methods used." Caves had been explored with "no notable results" because the "natives have always been in the habit of hiding property" and are "aware of the value of all antique objects and have eagerly sought to sell them." The meaning of the statues, he said, required more study, and "comparative study in the Pacific can alone eluci- date this matter."

On October 3 the Royal Geographical Society announced that Mr. and Mrs. Routledge would deliver a paper entitled "Easter Island." The society did not, at this time, accept women as Fellows, and Arthur R. Hinks, secre- tary of the society, expected a jointly authored paper delivered by Scoresby. The Routledges, however, intended all along to have Katherine write and deliver the paper. It meant facing a critical and informed audience, and she wired Hinks to ask "what is latest date for paper delayed by illness." Reply- ing to the telegram signed simply "Routledge," Hinks extended the deadline but didn't know which Routledge he was addressing. Katherine, who was staying at a hotel in Devon, did not clarify when she responded: "Thank you so much for your kind telegram & letter. It is kind to give us a little space. I have been having horrid headaches & generally feeling . . . overworked I suppose & I've come here for a little rest. But the lecture is half done & I think may be safely promised for the 15th."

On October 15 Katherine mailed her paper to Hinks, although she was "ashamed to send you a ms in this condition—but perhaps it is better than to fail again." Believing that her lecture was too convoluted to understand, Katherine sent a synopsis, "which I hope will make its drift clearer," and reminded Hinks that she had been, after all, "one of the Lecturers for Oxford University Extension . . . !!!" He tactfully replied that it was "pleasant to be assured that you will not suffer from stage fright. How is the reading of the paper going to be divided between your husband and yourself?" Without waiting for a response, Hinks sent Katherine's paper to Alfred P. Maudslay as referee, and his official report stated, "The paper is original and should be accepted for [presentation and] publication." His unofficial opinion, which he sent to Hinks privately, was that "it will make a splendid paper for an evening meeting if someone will rearrange it & partly re-write it."

That odious task fell to Hinks, who complained that it was a "sad prospect" since he had already "spent much more time than I can afford re-arranging and partly re-writing" it. At Hinks' request Maudslay's wife agreed to "look after" Katherine during the meeting, now scheduled for November 20, when it was fully expected that Scoresby would deliver the paper to the society. Katherine must have gotten a letter from Mrs. Maudslay and com-plained to Scoresby, who wrote to Hinks: "I gather from my wife that I failed to make my wishes clear to you at our last interview—What I wished you to understand was 1. That Mrs. Routledge will address the Society on the sub-ject of Easter Is and not me. 2. That I desire to speak for from 3 to 5 minutes prior to her beginning her address and following on the President."

At Burlington House on November 20 Katherine stood before a large, nearly all male audience and delivered her paper to the Royal Geographical Society. She preceded her remarks by vividly describing Angata and her pow-ers over the Rapa Nui community, and environmental damage to the statues and the destruction of archaeological sites by ranching, then talked in detail about the archaeological survey conducted by the Mana Expedition. A demanding question-and-answer period followed in which, as we have seen, B. W. Stainton challenged the Routledges' right to name Mana Inlet. This ini-tiated a flurry of correspondence and was, in part, responsible for subsequent delays in the publication of Katherine's paper.

Katherine's Royal Geographical Society lecture was widely reported in the press, and ten days later the Routledges held a triumphant "At Home" reception at the Hyde Park Hotel, Knightsbridge. Katherine was now fully aware of how attractive she was to the press as a woman who dared to travel and work in a man's world, and she realized that Easter Island was a dependable attention getter. She reveled in being at the center of such a storm of popularity.

In January 1917 Scoresby delivered a paper at the Geological Society dedicated to Frederick Lowry-Corry, a war casualty in 1915. He began to prepare another presentation (which he never gave) on fifty-eight Rapa Nui skulls, some decorated with incised lines, that he had given to Sir Arthur Keith to study. Keith produced a preliminary report noting that most of the specimens were from the latter part of the nineteenth century, but that, in his opinion, they approached "the Melanesian more than the Polynesian type." This was a thunderclap: Melanesians, of course, inhabit the Solomons and other islands in the distant west Pacific and are culturally and linguistically different from Polynesians. Keith's findings, with which T. A. Joyce cautiously concurred, contradicted Mana Expedition findings and raised serious questions about Rapa Nui origins.

On May 16 Katherine spoke at a meeting of the Folk-Lore Society on the topic of Orongo and continued to speak of Rapa Nui culture as Polynesian. That paper was published in May, as was Katherine's Royal Geographical Society article. Some respected male scholars immediately built on Keith's theory of Melanesian connections to question her conclusions more sharply, and to draw interesting comparisons between the birdman designs of Rapa Nui and similar ones in the Solomon Islands of Melanesia.

Katherine, however, did not discern the sharp break in religious beliefs, social structure, and material culture that would signal direct or recent Melanesian influence. Neither did she conceptualize contact between Rapa Nui and the distant Solomon Islands. Lines were drawn and two scholarly camps formed: the first was made up of eminent academics with experience in Melanesia and the western Pacific, nearly all of Scoresby's enemies, and most of O. G. S. Crawford's cronies. They argued that Katherine's evidence revealed a Melanesian presence on Easter Island prior to the coming of the ancestors of the present-day Rapa Nui. The second camp was much smaller, and Katherine was their standard-bearer. She and R. R. Marret, B. G. Corney, and one or two others held that the modern Rapa Nui residents were descendants of ancient Polynesian statue makers. Nipping around the heels of those in both camps were believers in sunken continents and other fantastic theories.

Katherine did not easily give way in this competition, and some of the old guard at the Royal Geographical Society thought she was a bit much. Someone took umbrage when she frankly said everyone "from the earliest inhabitants to the recent ranch managers" had damaged or destroyed Easter Island archaeological sites. At an unknown date between 1916 and 1920, the offended person inserted into Royal Geographical Society files a copy of a Chilean document marked "Strictly Confidential" that ferociously attacked Scoresby.

He was accused of being a correspondent of *The Times* of London who "might make unjust accusations against a country" in which "he was particularly well treated." The Mana Expedition's difficulties on the island were said to have been due to "Mr. Routledge's objectionable character," his "lack of scientific training," and "incorrect and ungentlemanly conduct towards all who had to deal with him." It was, however, true that "the collaborators and employees with whom he sailed from England gradually left," and in return for Chilean hospitality he had "sailed from the island without notifying the authorities of his departure."

In a completely separate and more positive event, Scoresby was awarded the Royal Cruising Club's Challenge Cup "for his cruise in the Pacific in 'Mana' and exploration on Easter Island." He was immensely proud of the honor, which had last been awarded to the famous yachtsman Lord Brassey for the 1876 voyage of *Sunbeam*. Katherine, meanwhile, was gathering copies of letters she had written to family and friends, newspaper articles she had authored, professional correspondence, and other bits of writing for use in compiling a book. While fieldnotes documented the nucleus of the Mana Expedition story, Katherine intended to knit it together with entertaining traveler's tales.

In August 1917 Katherine celebrated her fifty-first birthday and did a strange thing: she told her family that she wished to be addressed by her mother's name, Kate, in the same manner that she had long ago demanded to be called Katherine and not Katie. She was, Wilson said, in a "state of nerves about losses at sea and talk of invasion," and the cloud of war hung over all of her conversations. She took up a "concern" that put her at "loggerheads" with her sister, Lilian, insisting that her niece Evelyn, who was then eighteen years old, should be taken from school for war work. Katherine wrote a note to Wilson, thanking him for his birthday wishes, but also telling him something he found "morbid": "There came again wonderfully to me on my birthday a promise I had once before in the first dark days, that as I was the first of her conscious children to say goodbye, so I should be the first to be with her again. I hope I hear aright, anyway it warmed me all right through." Katherine was again hearing the voice of Kate Pease.

For the rest of 1917 and through all of the next two years, Scoresby and Katherine lived like nomads, sometimes apart but often together. Scoresby was preoccupied with the Mana Expedition's image collection. His poor relationship with Frank T. Green had, apparently, resulted in some of the expedition's negatives going to Percy Edmunds—who also had taken his own photographs. This raised issues of ownership between Scoresby and Edmunds that took a long time to resolve. To Green's credit, book reviewers maintained that "its photographs alone would justify the Expedition."

Scoresby assembled a team to produce Katherine's book. He hired a secretary to take dictation and type their fieldnotes, a draftsperson (E. F. Ridgway) to render field sketches into diagrams, an artist (A. Hunter) to turn sketches and watercolors into drawings, and a cartographer (F. Batchelor) to review Lieutenant Ritchie's maps. One of the maps Batchelor produced showed the clan boundaries and land divisions Katherine and Tepano had uncovered.

Katherine's book was originally entitled *Easter Island: The Story of an Expedition,* but she decided to make the title more romantic and changed it to *The Mystery of Easter Island: The Story of an Expedition.* She worked rapidly to check page proofs twice and, in February of 1919, wrote the preface. By the end of the year she had hired a clipping service and was basking in the glow of a highly favorable reception for her privately published book.

A large number of reviewers pointed out that this book would be followed by another, more "scientific" Mana Expedition report. Pacific scholar A. C. Haddon said it was a "delightful book of travel" and put forth his own speculations about Melanesian connections. It was called "substantial," "noteworthy," "handsome," and "fascinating," "as spacious a book of voyaging as we have had in years" giving "a remarkable body of data for the study of a strange archaeological problem." If the Routledges had not solved the mystery of Easter Island, to most critics they had gone a long way toward doing so.

By the beginning of 1920 Katherine's book was a resounding popular success and, in April, went into a second printing. This offered, she wrote, "a chance to repair shortcomings." She bowed to the scholarship of the day, which maintained that pre-European contact culture was "derived from a union of the two great stocks of the Pacific, the Melanesian and Polynesian races." Notwithstanding that, however, her most important point was that the Mana Expedition had rescued "at the eleventh hour much of high value, more especially that which points to a connection between the only recently expired bird cult and that of the images." The Rapa Nui, she stubbornly maintained, "are connected by blood with the makers of the statues; this is, of course, the crucial point."

The Mana Expedition's "more scientific" book was now number one on Katherine's agenda. Scoresby amassed an annotated bibliography; they divided the island into geographical areas and then into topographical sections such as inland or coast. Sites were divided into type categories, and the Orongo buildings were described individually. Based upon examinations of

260 *ahu*, or ceremonial platforms, and 231 statues fallen from image *ahu*, Scoresby drafted valid *ahu* prototypes and estimated that image *ahu* represented about one third of the island's total. Katherine attached Tepano's information on clan identities and land ownership whenever possible.

The paper trail the Routledges followed through their fieldnotes is well marked. They made excellent progress through the "Northern" and "Western" divisions of the island, Orongo and "Rano Kau and Adjacent Islets." When they got to Rano Raraku and the statues, however, the Routledges faltered. This happened for both personal and professional reasons. First, Katherine and Scoresby were unable to report their statue excavations with the degree of precision they now realized scholarly critics would require. Second, Keith's suggestion of a Melanesian influence in Rapa Nui skeletal remains had thrown them off, and now others had extended the theory to include material culture and art. The notion that "more than one native expedition [had] performed the miracle of reaching Easter Island" was strange and incredible to both Katherine and Scoresby, and they didn't accept it.

The enigma of Easter Island, Katherine noted, was complex, but all of the Mana Expedition's discoveries argued for cultural continuity. Her three basic assumptions were that the giant statues were carved by the ancestors of the present inhabitants, the birdman cult had been alive and functioning within the "living memory" of these same inhabitants, and important, that the two religious points of view were linked. This linkage, Katherine maintained, was made graphically visible by the similarity of "ring and girdle" designs incised into the backs of wood figures, painted on the backs of children during Orongo rituals, and carved on the backs of some statues in Rano Raraku. The placement of Hoa Hakananai'a, with its similar designs, "in the centre of the village of Orongo" provided, in Katherine's view, irrefutable proof of an integrated symbolism through time.

Katherine asserted that the island's impressive number of statues "does not necessarily imply that their manufacture covered a vast space of time." Oral traditions proved to her satisfaction that the last—and tallest—statue that had once stood on image *ahu*, a giant called Paro, was thrown down by about 1840. She thought that the overthrow of the first upright statues from image *ahu* had begun around contact with the Dutch in 1722. A fertile ground for research, she wrote, was "the part played by the advent of the white men" in culture change.

The Routledges' "companionate" partnership as travelers and researchers began to disintegrate while they lived in London, and the new wealth Katherine had acquired with Kate Pease's death complicated matters. Katherine's behavior toward her husband was not generous. Pettiness, combined with sharp mood swings and real symptoms of emerging paranoia, made her not only difficult to live with but almost incapable of doing serious research.

A solution to their unhappiness, as always, was wandering. The Routledges toyed with the idea of moving to Jamaica, where, on the voyage home in 1916, Scoresby had met a Dr. Campbell, whose company he enjoyed. They visited him for a month or so, but Katherine hated the place and returned to London. Scoresby remained to mount a costly, ten-man expedition with Campbell to cross the John Crow Mountains, which, he said, were completely unknown territory and ripe for exploration. His first assault failed because of unending torrents of rain, and he wrote Katherine a description of his second attempt.

> I and two men succeeded in packing through yesterday. The Rest of the party are still in the mountains: tomorrow at daylight I shall Return on our tracks in order to make sure that they are all right . . . I hope you got my cable asking you to arrange for 50 [pounds] to be put to my credit . . . with much love and hoping you have been having a pleasant if tame time of it at home . . .

Katherine cabled the money, and Scoresby responded with gratitude.

> Many thanks . . . Jamaica as I have seen it since your departure is a difficult world . . . you could never have cut it. . . . It has suited me however and I have never been more fit. The maroons complimented me on my walking & staying power saying they never could have believed I could have held out so long. Of course I neither smoked nor drank. They did. With much love . . .

Scoresby returned to England, officially advanced his claim to be the first man to cross the John Crow Mountains, began an ambitious publicity campaign, and prepared to write an article about his adventure for the Royal Geographical Society *Journal*. He soon discovered, however, that he was lacking the necessary maps and photographs. He planned an immediate return to Jamaica and, abruptly, sold *Mana*. The buyer was Lieutenant General Douglas Mackinnon Bailie Hamilton, the twelfth Earl of Dundonald KCB KCVO.

Dundonald is the titular name of a long line of distinguished Scottish nobles whose reigning heir is known as Lord Cochrane. Thomas Cochrane, tenth Earl of Dundonald, was a famous admiral who served with distinction as commander of the Chilean navy, 1818–22. His ties to Chile and acquaintance with the Pease family made the earl, in Katherine's eyes, the perfect new owner for *Mana*. He had the vessel completely refitted, remodeled the Routledges' cabins, rewired all of the electrical connections, and replaced

Scoresby's old, recalcitrant, and smelly engine. These substantial and costly improvements allowed *Mana* to retain the coveted Lloyd's of London "15 A1" insurance classification that Scoresby had worked so diligently to get in 1914.

The Earl of Dundonald took *Mana* on a successful shakedown cruise to the Portuguese coast and then, in September of 1922, sailed for Brazil to participate in centenary celebrations in Rio de Janeiro. *Mana* swiftly crossed the Atlantic via Madeira, following her old track, and one month later sailed proudly into Rio harbor, all flags flying. After the festivities the earl and his crew departed aboard a mail steamer, leaving *Mana* anchored alone in Rio harbor.

In November the Earl finalized the sale of *Mana* to a Mr. D. C. Klugman of Rio de Janeiro. The unfortunate Mr. Klugman, who appears to have been involved in the import-export business, did not enjoy *Mana* for long. On the night of September 1, 1923, fire inexplicably broke out on board and *Mana* was destroyed. Subsequent investigation found no cause of the blaze, and a disgruntled—perhaps even suspicious—insurance agent reluctantly authorized a substantial payment to Mr. Klugman. News of the mysterious accident was widely reported in yachting circles, and Scoresby and Katherine surely heard of the lonely demise of *Mana*, their brave and beautiful, much loved, good-luck dream ship.

By July 1920 Scoresby and Katherine had decided to return to the Pacific. They intended to take a steamer first to Jamaica—allowing Scoresby to get the maps and photos he needed to substantiate his claim to having crossed the John Crow Mountains—and then to charter a yacht. Their goal, stated years earlier, was to find links between Easter Island and other islands in the East Pacific. Katherine busily contacted Pacific scholars and governments to smooth her path but, uncharacteristically, did essentially no preparatory research. The Royal Geographical Society again loaned Scoresby surveying instruments. Their first destination was Rapa Iti, but they also planned to visit others of the Austral Islands, Mangareva, and the Gambiers. In retrospect, however, it seems clear that Katherine—now Kate—was retreating from an increasingly distressing inner collapse, and that Pacific islands offered sanctuary.

Links, Sidetracks, and Dead Ends,
1921–25

✦

IN JANUARY OF 1921 THE ROUTLEDGES WERE IN JAMAICA, camped in the shell of a stone building damaged months earlier by a hurricane. Three months of steady rains pounded them until, in May, Katherine insisted that they leave for New Orleans and make their way overland to San Francisco. Scoresby wrote to Arthur Hinks of the Royal Geographical Society from Berkeley, California, describing his failed second attempt to cross the John Crow Mountains. He also told Hinks that he was "glad to accept my wife's kind offer to edit & condense" his article on the crossing for the society *Journal*.

Scoresby left the job undone in Jamaica because, in fact, Katherine was funding it and had put her foot down. Her "kind offer" to edit was the price she was willing to pay to abandon a project in which she had no role or interest. Katherine frantically scribbled masses of confusing edits on her husband's dense manuscript, packaged it up, enclosed a watercolor sketch of her own and a complex set of instructions for typing and preparing illustrations and maps. She sent everything off by sea post from San Francisco to poor Hinks, who must have shuddered when he opened the package.

> I am writing for dear life for our Tahiti vessel sails in 40 minutes—wd I have not left it to the last! I have been working like 3 Trojans for weeks boiling down this mss. If you can leave it as it is (though I fear longer than you wanted) we should be grateful—I wish I cd have finished it myself. It is maddening to send off things like this. My comfort is I know you will kindly see it through without frightful cataclysms. . . . The article is his not mine!

Once aboard the steamer to Tahiti, Katherine realized that some fence-mending was in order. She and Scoresby, apparently unknown to each other, penned separate apologies to Hinks. Katherine's tone is that of a woman in flight:

> I must really apologise for the condition of my scribbled notes, with no ink or typewriter available at the last I have been working at it so hard to get it off before we left, that I could not bear to be defeated in the end, so I was up practically all night & registered it forty-five minutes before the ship actually left the docks. . . . We hope to get to Rapa Iti as soon as we can. . . . Our further plans are quite uncertain, whether we shall be there three months or twelve or eighteen depends on how things turn out!

Katherine wrote to A. L. Kroeber, at the University of California, asking him to contact H. E. Gregory, Brigham's replacement as director of the Bernice P. Bishop Museum in Honolulu, and find out where Bishop Museum anthropologists were working. Gregory responded eagerly, offering to pool resources and join in publication. The year 1920 has been called a "watershed in Pacific anthropology," and archaeology a "virgin field" requiring island-wide surveys revealing "hints of time relations and local variations." Gregory was launching the prestigious Bayard Dominick Expeditions to the Marquesas Islands, Tonga, the Austral Islands, and Hawaii, and his goal was nothing less than to resolve the problem of Polynesian origins—the very question plaguing Katherine about Easter Island. Unhappily, the exciting opportunity to collaborate with Gregory came too late in Katherine's life and work.

She replied that, while there were surely advantages to such an association, the practical difficulties were just too great. She even asserted a certain territoriality and a prior claim to working on Rapa Iti. The Routledges intended to explore all four of the Austral Islands, she said, and had received official permission to investigate Rapa nearly a year ago. Kroeber communicated Katherine's negative response to Gregory, confiding his own opinion that the Routledges "appear to be well-to-do people who do their work as a form of amusement."

> You will remember that their Easter Island book was preceded by one on the Akikuyu. They got into this through big game hunting. While their ethnology is remarkably excellent, it therefore always represents a vacation. Naturally they prefer to remain free. Such a thing as tying up with an institution or binding themselves in their arrangements would offer them no returns, nor would they consider taking on [W. C.] McKern [an archaeologist who worked on the Tonga team] or anyone else. They are not endowing science but pleasing themselves.

Under the circumstances, Kroeber said, it was best to simply let them proceed. "Where they find that [ethnologist R. T.] Aitken or [John F. G.] Stokes has done an island intensively they will probably pull out and concentrate on those which your men have covered more hastily. The net outcome promises to be comparatively little duplication and some valuable checking."

The Routledges arrived in Tahiti on July 4, 1921, and Scoresby immediately began making charter arrangements for the Austral Islands. They spent two or three weeks on the neighboring island of Mo'orea, where they documented four *marae*—ceremonial centers with stone platforms—and two *ti'i* or small stone images. Scoresby took measurements, photographs, and compass bearings and made sketch plans. None of these sites recalled Rapa Nui, but that was because they had yet not developed, in Katherine's words, "intelligent eyes." The Routledges were ahead of the archaeological game in Tahiti—not until 1923 was a preliminary reconnaissance of sites accomplished in the Society Islands, and only in 1925 did Bishop Museum archaeologist Kenneth P. Emory conduct an in-depth survey. Emory, in contrast to the Routledges, had the benefit of broad experience and saw a relationship between the stonework of Tahiti, Mo'orea, and Rapa Nui.

Scoresby chartered *Vaite*, a double-masted, 150-foot schooner, and the Routledges prepared to embark on a cruise through islands that were then little known—and which still have large archaeological question marks associated with them today. On August 24 the Routledges, a French-speaking secretary-interpreter, their Tahitian captain, a seven-man crew, and someone's pet pig named Antoinette departed Tahiti and headed southward for what Katherine later called "a delightful cruise" through the Austral Islands to Rapa Iti. *Vaite* made for Rimatara, the westernmost of the Australs, but somehow turned up at Tubuai instead—a navigational error of about two hundred miles.

Vaite lay in the Tubuai lagoon for six days. The Routledges conducted a quick survey of four *marae*, and Scoresby spent three days clearing and carefully mapping one he called Harii. Here again, he saw differences rather than similarities to Rapa Nui structures. They called next at Rurutu, where they surveyed the remains of about ten *marae* from horseback and made a good sketch plan of one structure. On September 9 they arrived at Rimatara, got a guide, and went out on horseback to document three more *marae*. Sailing eastward again, *Vaite* reached Ra'ivavae on September 15 and remained there for a week.

Ra'ivavae has the finest stonework in the Austral Islands, and Scoresby employed laborers to clear the thick growth of trees and shrubs from ancient paved pathways and five major religious sites. He spent four days on one site alone, taking careful measurements and photographs and noting the use of red scoria in architecture. The Routledges documented five big statues carved of red scoria and discovered seven fragmentary figures and two statue bases. Katherine sketched them hurriedly, but two impressively tall, companion statues—one male and the other female—held her attention for an entire day. She photographed them and noted their similarities to the one broken statue she had seen years before on Pitcairn, but found them inferior to Rapa Nui statues.

> They throw no light on the origin of the statues on Easter Island . . . they were obviously made to be regarded at close quarters, whereas those on Easter Island were carved for broad and distant effects. These statues, together with others found in the undergrowth, seemed to have had a religious purpose, and even now the natives will not interfere with them.

Although Katherine said that "folklore was outside our sphere in the time at our command," she was tantalized by two geographical names on Ra'ivavae that caught her attention. A mountain peak called Hotu Atua recalled the Rapa Nui ancestral chief Hotu Matu'a, and another peak was named Hiro, the Rapa Nui god of sky or rain. In the end, however, she was perplexed, and the links she had expected to find eluded her. Yet with each watery mile through the Pacific the weight—on her mind and body—lightened.

Rapa Iti—the most southerly island in the Australs group—had been the Routledges' first destination after leaving Easter Island and was the main objective of this voyage. Like *Mana* in 1915, *Vaite* arrived in driving rain and heavy seas, then anchored in the bay for ten days. John and Margaret Stokes of the Bishop Museum had been on the island for three or four months when the Routledges turned up. Stokes—whose career at Bishop Museum was stalled by criticism and his own insecurities—and his wife "spent two years in virtual isolation, studying the material culture and customs of the people." The Stokeses, Katherine said, were "most kind to us but they had done the work most thoroughly & also it proved not to be quite in our line or what we had thought."

Katherine Routledge and Margaret Stokes apparently did not strike up a friendship. John Stokes and Scoresby compared notes on stone tools, which Scoresby avidly collected and on which he was, by now, an expert. Stokes showed the Routledges about twenty fortified strongholds called *pale*, and they examined eight of them. They climbed to the impressive fortified ridge-top village site known as Morongo Uta (Katherine had checked the hilltops at Anakena on Easter Island for fortifications, but found none). A few days later she settled on the deck of *Vaite* and produced a beautiful watercolor

Gurney Pease (1839–72),
Katherine Routledge's father, c. 1863.
(Darlington Borough Council, Darlington Library
and Art Gallery)

Kate Wilson Pease (1840–1915),
Katherine Routledge's mother, c. 1863.
(Darlington Borough Council, Darlington Library
and Art Gallery)

Walworth Castle, the "biggish place" that was Katherine's family home when her father
died in 1872. *(Darlington Borough Council, Darlington Library and Art Gallery)*

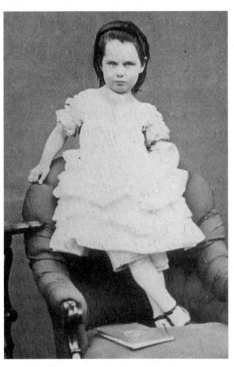

Katherine (Katie) Maria Pease, c. 1870. A little girl with a "serious amount of self-will," she was stricken with scarlet fever at about this age. *(Peter Bucknall)*

Katherine Pease: bookish, pensive, and eager to please, c. 1874. *(Peter Bucknall)*

Katherine Pease on her pony at Woodside, her beloved childhood home, c. 1875. *(Peter Bucknall)*

Katherine Pease *(left, front)* and her family, Woodside, c. 1882. Standing behind her are Harold Gurney Pease, Lilian Pease, and Wilson Pease. Kate Wilson Pease is seated *(front, ight)*, and John Henry Pease is in the center. *(Darlington Borough Council, Darlington Library and Art Gallery)*

The Gurney Pease family twenty years later at Woodside, just prior to the Mana Expedition's departure to Easter Island. From left, Wilson Pease, Beatrice Evelyn Leslie Fox *(seated, in front)*, Katherine Pease Routledge, Louisa Lambert Pease, Kate Wilson Pease *(seated, center)*, Caroline Joanna Fowler Pease, Lilian Leslie Fox, John Henry Pease, and seated in front, John Charles Gurney Pease *(left)* and Rachel Pease. This photo, and an image of Wilson enlarged from it, was among three framed pictures mounted on the wall of Katherine's cabin aboard *Mana*. *(Peter Bucknall)*

William Scoresby Routledge,
age three, Melbourne, Australia,
c. 1862. *(Pauleen West)*

Scoresby after his father,
William Routledge, had relocated
the family to Reading, c. 1867. *(Pauleen West)*

Scoresby as an adolescent, c. 1875,
after his family had settled
in Eastbourne and before entering
Christ Church, Oxford.
(Chris Lopez and the Twycross Burrell Collection)

Katherine Pease, age eighteen, at her debut presentation to Queen Victoria, 1884.
(Peter Bucknall)

William Scoresby Routledge's favorite portrait of himself, recovered among Mana Expedition papers in Cyprus, 1960. *(Eve Dray Stewart)*

Katherine and William Scoresby Routledge, c. 1910, after returning from safari in British East Africa (Kenya). Gossip surrounding the Silberrad Affair, a nasty colonial sex scandal, dogged them for years. Scoresby was viciously criticized, but Katherine triumphed. *(Peter Bucknall)*

Ewers, the Routledges' Hamble River honeymoon cottage, home museum, and favorite residence, as it looks today. *(Peter Bucknall)*

O. G. S. Crawford, Portsmouth, 1912. He quit the Mana Expedition in the Cape Verde Islands, never realizing his dream of "solving the riddle" of Easter Island.
(O. G. S. Crawford Photographic Archive, Oxford University)

The core crew of *Mana* throughout the voyage: Albert Light *(left);* Charles Jeffery *(rear);* Captain Henry James Gillam; Mate Frank Preston; Bartolomeo Rosa *(rear, right)* joined in St. Vincent, Grand Canary Island (Scoresby entered him in the ship's log as "Negro"); and William Marks.
(O. G. S. Crawford Photographic Archive, Oxford University. Photo by Frank T. Green.)

The Routledges' favorite photograph of *Mana*, off the misty cliffs of Charua Bay, Patagonia Channels, December 1913.
(O. G. S. Crawford Photographic Archive, Oxford University. Photo by Frank T. Green.)

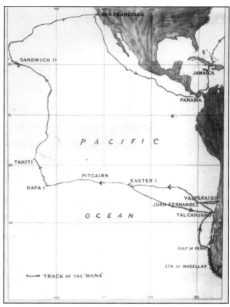

Scoresby aboard *Mana* with a rhea (South American ostrich) shot on the second day into the Straits of Magellan, October 18, 1913.

(The Royal Geographical Society [with the Institute of British Geographers])

The track of *Mana* beginning in the Gulf of Peñas. The expedition's emergency return from Juan Fernández Island to Talcahuano is shown on the map, but subsequent round-trip voyages between Easter Island (Rapa Nui) and the Chilean mainland are not.

(The Trustees of the British Museum)

Scoresby with two young men who boarded *Mana* from a dugout canoe, Indian Reach, Patagonia Channels, December 1913–January 1914.

(The Trustees of the British Museum)

Lieutenant David R. Ritchie on the veranda of Mataveri house (raised on carved stones taken from the foundations of prehistoric houses), Easter Island, 1914. *(The Trustees of the British Museum)*

Percy Edmunds, Mataveri ranch manager and Easter Island's port captain. Gracious to Katherine and helpful to the Mana Expedition, his life was in danger during the "native rising." *(Jorge Edmunds)*

The Mataveri ranch wool shed, set in the startlingly deforested Easter Island landscape, 1914. Mana Expedition equipment and supplies stored here became the target of clandestine raids that set off a dangerous "native rising."
(Bernice P. Bishop Museum Archives. Photo by Percy Edmunds.)

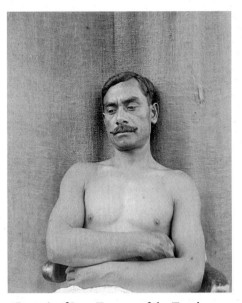

Portrait of Juan Tepano, of the Tupahotu. Photo taken at Mataveri by Katherine Routledge, July 23, 1915.
(The Royal Geographical Society [with the Institute of British Geographers])

Portrait of Victoria Veriamu (Paulina), of the Ureohei. She was Juan Tepano's mother and Katherine's most reliable female consultant, 1914.
(The Royal Geographical Society [with the Institute of British Geographers])

Juan Tepano standing at the upturned base of one of the fallen statues of Ahu Tongariki, July 1914. Tepano told Katherine that, through his father, he claimed the lands between Tongariki and Rano Raraku. *(The Trustees of the British Museum)*

The only known field photograph of Katherine Routledge (*right,* dressed in duster and hat) on Easter Island, 1914–15. She and her Rapa Nui assistant are measuring the foundation of an elliptical house *(hare paenga).*
(The Trustees of the British Museum)

Rapa Nui man, frequently but wrongly said to be Juan Tepano, with a fragment of the last upright statue on Easter Island, Ahu Tongariki, July 1914. A tidal wave destroyed the site, since restored, in May 1960.
(The Trustees of the British Museum)

Scoresby at a Chilean holiday festival in Hanga Roa, May 5, 1914. The mask, painted on white cloth, is made to look like an eel *(koreha),* a creature represented in Rapa Nui portable stone carvings and petroglyphs. *(The Trustees of the British Museum)*

Carlos Teao Tori, one of the instigators of the "native rising," with the carved "doorpost" he excavated from an Orongo building, June 2, 1914. Rapa Nui people were infuriated when Scoresby crated this and other objects for removal to England. *(The Royal Geographical Society [with the Institute of British Geographers])*

Bailey, the Mana Expedition cook whom Katherine considered a good friend, on guard with a loaded rifle at Mataveri during the "native rising," July 1914. *(The Royal Geographical Society [with the Institute of British Geographers])*

The charismatic and visionary Angata, leader of the "native rising," with her staff and rosary, August 1914. *(The Royal Geographical Society [with the Institute of British Geographers])*

Back view of Hoa Hakananai'a,
removed from the island by HMS *Topaze* in 1868.
Although the statue inspired Katherine,
she didn't actually see this view before sailing
for Easter Island. The curved line and circle,
which she later dubbed "ring and girdle,"
represents the sash *(maro)* of chiefly authority.
Superimposed carvings of birds, vulva *(komari)*,
and dance paddles on the head, and of birdmen
on the shoulders, are emblematic of Orongo's
famous birdman religion. *(The Trustees
of the British Museum)*

Sketch by Lieutenant M. J. Harrison, HMS *Topaze*, of Hoa Hakananai'a in situ,
Orongo, 1868. Katherine never saw the sketch, but it validates what Victoria Veriamu
told her: The statue looked toward Miru land. *(The Trustees of the British Museum)*

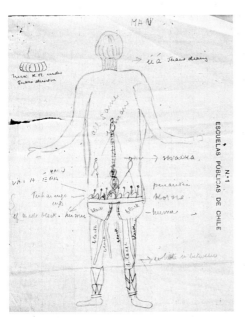

Field sketch of tattoo designs made by Katherine "under Juan's direction." Jotefa told her that the "ring and girdle" was a *maro*. Katherine astutely related tattoo to superimposed carvings on the backs of statues, petroglyphs, wood sculpture, and Hoa Hakananai'a. *(The Royal Geographical Society [with the Institute of British Geographers])*

Lieutenant Ritchie and a statue on the southeast side of Rano Raraku. The fingertips of the beautifully carved hands meet at the *hami,* the loincloth that covers the male genitals.
(Royal Geographical Society [with the Association of British Geographers])

The statue Langitopa dubbed "Papa," October 1915. Katherine said that the incised carvings on its back were "entirely unsuspected." She likened them, all superimposed after the "ring and girdle" was carved and before the statue was buried, to tattoos. Katherine and Frank T. Green rushed to hide these carvings when German warships arrived.
(The Trustees of the British Museum)

Standing, partially buried but complete statues on the exterior slopes of Rano Raraku, 1913–14. The prone statue in the foreground was mapped by the Mana Expedition as one of their "circular statues." *(The Trustees of the British Museum)*

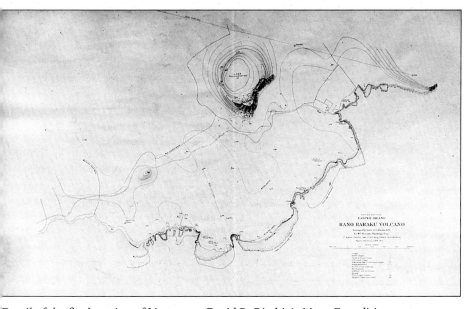

Detail of the final version of Lieutenant David R. Ritchie's Mana Expedition survey map, Rano Raraku and environs. Drafted by F. Batchelor, Royal Geographical Society, for William Scoresby Routledge. *(The Royal Geographical Society [with the Institute of British Geographers])*

Katherine Routledge (1866–1935),
co-leader with William Scoresby Routledge
of the Mana Expedition to Easter Island,
c. 1919. *(Peter Bucknall)*

Juan Tepano (1867–1947),
chief consultant to Katherine Routledge,
toward the end of his life, on Rapa Nui.
(Bernice P. Bishop Museum Archives)

White tin trunk belonging
to Katherine Routledge
and used to store her Rapa
Nui fieldnotes. Items shown
include a drafted version
of her statue transport road
map, photo and newspaper
albums, and a watercolor
of a ritual *(koro)* house.
These and other irreplaceable
materials are the legacy
of the Mana Expedition
to Easter Island. *(The Royal
Geographical Society [with the Institute
of British Geographers])*

panorama of the Rapa Iti coast, her best work on this voyage. Rapa Iti was, Katherine wrote, "not quite what we had expected. . . . Hill forts only, nothing to do with Easter Is & little else." She was willing to give up any official claim or permission to work on Rapa Iti and left it to John and Margaret Stokes. Sadly, their work resulted only in a manuscript report that was never published.

Vaite set off for Mangareva, the largest inhabited island in the Gambier group. Mangareva is about nine hundred miles from Tahiti and, with three other inhabited islands and many smaller, rocky islets, lies within an encircling coral reef. It was not, Katherine said with relief, "in the Bishop Museum programme." A few days out from Rapa Iti, she wrote, "The Polynesian Capt. overshot his mark & we wandered for 13 days—nothing so exciting ever happened on *Mana!*" Scoresby took it upon himself, as he had on *Mana*, to ration food and water. Even so, it seemed that the pet pig would have to be sacrificed until, miraculously, rain came, Mangareva was sighted, and Antoinette's porcine soul was saved.

Once safely inside Mangareva's outer reef the Routledges went ashore with their baskets, boxes, and bags—their secretary-translator, unlike long-ago *Mana* crewmen, had not yet deserted. They settled in a small hut with a raised wood floor and corrugated metal roof that was perched on the sandy shore and shaded by tall palms. The island atmosphere was still and the tiny village almost silent. Mangarevans—unlike the Rapa Nui—were shy and retiring. The Routledges had entered, at last, a real South Seas dream world.

Katherine was immensely happy right from the start and found her neighbors to be exceptionally beautiful people. Women were dressed in colorful *pareu* wraps and wearing flowers in their lustrous hair; energetic young men paddled small outrigger canoes and old men smoked in front of their homes. Children, dogs, and chickens ran about everywhere, and a Catholic cathedral, with a pearl-shell-inlaid altar, dominated the scene. A French gendarme, his wife, and two Catholic priests completed the small community.

On November 4, 1921 *Vaite* departed and the Routledges began their longest sojourn on an isolated Pacific island since leaving Rapa Nui in 1915. *Vaite* carried pleas for help from Katherine to Arthur Hinks at the Royal Geographical Society and to B. G. Corney, who had done extensive research on the early records of French missionaries in Polynesia: "We find ourselves planted here instead of Rapa! . . . Would it be trespassing too much to ask you to look through the Mangarevan literature? Much you need not bother about, for simply historical matters we can look up at home, what we want is anything that will put us on the track of things to hunt up here. There may of course be nothing." On January 9, 1922 Hinks faithfully replied that

Corney was seriously ill, but that he would look for the materials. Corney, however, gallantly responded with "just the help we needed."

Mangareva, like Rapa Nui, was divided into two major political districts, and a central razor-backed ridge of peaks separated them. A well-trodden footpath traversed the ridge and connected the main village of Rikitea, where the Routledges lived, with the Gatavake district. Katherine collected vocabularies, folktales, stories, songs, chants, and myths, writing them all down on index cards. Mangarevans speak a Central Polynesian dialect—and Katherine recognized many words that were similar to Rapanui—but they also spoke French. Katherine's French had never been good, and she turned to Father Vincent-Ferrier Janeau, a missionary who spoke some English and shared her interest in what was "an almost wicked amount of folk lore," she said. "Some of it at the instigation of the French priests has been reduced to writing & with the help of the capable French-speaking native I have struggled through the translation of about 50000 words of Mangarevan Mss."

The manuscript that Katherine "struggled through" was a partial copy of an oral history recorded by Father Honoré Laval, a missionary of the same Catholic Congregation of the Sacred Heart that had trained Nicolás Pakarati Urepotahi and Angata. It contained stories about warring chiefs forced to make long settlement journeys on rafts or double canoes from Mangareva to other islands. Tantalizing clues, she thought, connected Mangareva with both Pitcairn and Rapa Nui and hinted at "three different migrations from here to Easter."

The people of Mangareva, Katherine discovered, came from Hiva—as did the Rapa Nui—in the direction of the setting sun. On Mangareva a class of experts or intellectuals, called *rogorogo,* formed a specialized choir during *marae* rituals, and their relationship to the *rongorongo* of Rapa Nui was obvious. Chiefly children were sequestered high on the peaks of Mount Duff in a manner reminiscent of Orongo practices. Mount Duff and Rano Kau were landmarks of evident and similar importance on their respective islands— Katherine even toyed with the idea that they were navigational landmarks. There were essentially two levels of society on Mangareva, and these divisions were maintained after death. Katherine was intrigued by a belief that the soul left the body at death and walked westward. Mangarevans believed that the spirits of the dead roamed ancestral lands within strictly defined territories, as did the Rapa Nui. Perhaps drawn by memories of Angata, Katherine was beguiled by the voices that rose in three-part harmony during gatherings Mangarevans called *himene*—feasts with Christian-inspired singing that clearly recalled the *rogorogo* choirs of old. Katherine attended mass, but Scoresby most definitely did not share her interest, and thought Polynesia was becoming depressingly "priest-ridden."

The genealogy of Mangarevan kings included the ancestral chief Atu-motua—his name recalled Hotu Matu'a, the legendary discoverer of Rapa Nui, as well as Hotu Atua of Ra'ivavae. Katherine recognized the names of other mythic Polynesian figures and gods on Mangareva, but the most intriguing was Miru. She traced a complex, wandering saga of two deposed royal brothers who had voyaged among many islands. In search of their bur-ial place, the Routledges visited the inhabited islands of Taravai, Akamaru, and Aukena, but found nothing. Then, on the north end of a tiny, three-quarter-mile-long, uninhabited island they found a rock shelter containing the remains of two burials. Unlike their casual rooting through caves on Rapa Nui, they examined and measured these bones with care and noted the presence of bark cloth and cordage but, in the end, could not be certain of any connection between the bones and the legend.

Scoresby, Katherine wrote, "has been photographing & surveying such sites as there are [with] a telescopic aledate [sic]" lent by the Royal Geo-graphical Society. Archaeological sites in Mangareva had been decimated by the priest Laval. He had fanatically burned wooden idols and carried off stone and coral blocks to build his own monuments, half-finished church buildings, and the cathedral.

The large marae on the atoll of Temoe, twenty-five miles southeast of Mangareva, had escaped damage, and although it had previously been described, the Routledges were the first to document it in detail. They were in the exciting vanguard of East Polynesian archaeological survey and, for the first time in their wanderings, saw a distinct resemblance between the stonework of that marae and Easter Island ahu.

Wilson Pease, on the traditional August holiday in Scotland, wrote his sis-ter a letter that she received in time for Christmas. It is a revealing work in which he thanked her for the "picturesque picture of your 'Retreat.'" The Retreat at York was an early Quaker institution that provided rest and rehabilitation—and treated mental illness—and Wilson seems to be acknowledging that Mangareva and, perhaps, Rapa Nui and all Pacific islands were Katherine's very own "Retreat." Wilson told his sister that he was "so glad you are happy" and "I look forward to enjoying the fruit of your folk lore labours. I believe you will be quite sad when the time comes to leave your island. But it's years since we've seen you."

There is no doubt that Katherine was happy in Mangareva, and that she was at peace. She wandered about barefoot, wearing a broad-brimmed hat and wrapped in a pareu. When the pearl-diving season opened three Tahitian merchants arrived with suitcases stuffed with francs, and Katherine, who wanted pearls enough for a necklace, was gleefully swept up in the divers' competitive excitement.

Ever since departing Rapa Nui, Katherine had told many people and lots of reporters that she wanted to return, but without *Mana* or another yacht it was impossible. Surely she could have chartered *Vaite* or a similar vessel— she had the funds to do so. She did not, however, and it is a puzzle why not. Perhaps she was afraid of some shadow. The Pease family thought that, in some way, Angata was responsible. It is as if Rapa Nui was held intact in Katherine's memory, but separate, apart, and purposefully out of reach. She called her work on Easter Island "love's labour lost" and, perhaps, was waiting to return until she had something special to offer. Wherever she voyaged, however, nothing quite matched up for her—she could find no parallels, no comparisons, no links. In her mind and in her experience, there simply were none.

In November of 1922 Katherine sent off letters and notes to friends with holiday greetings, including one to the family of Frederick Lowry-Corry, late geologist of the Mana Expedition. "We shall follow I expect, or I shall anyway, not far behind this. S. may wait for warmer weather." Christmas and the New Year came and went. Katherine wrote to Arthur Hinks that "we have had a pleasant fourteen months here, much more comfortable & not nearly so thrilling as Easter Is, to which by the way I am beginning to long to return."

Percy Edmunds wrote to say that J. Macmillan Brown had been living on the island for about five months and had "brought forward a very satisfactory solution of its problems." Katherine was distressed to think that he might have solved the "riddle of the Pacific" where the Mana Expedition had failed. Her fear that he had discovered things she had missed was a heavy burden and may have been part of her reluctance to return. Though she could not have known it at the time, Brown's work was fanciful and deeply erroneous.

The Routledges departed from Mangareva on board *Curieuse,* a French mail vessel that offered no conveniences. They cordoned off the one available deck cabin by hanging a blanket from the middle of the ceiling and shared the space with the captain and his wife. Katherine said, "We were really quite comfy & enjoyed it." In Papeete on February 5, 1923 she picked up their mail and, once again, was shattered by news of family tragedy: Wilson's beloved wife, Joan, had died on October 25.

Oh Wilson, Wilson what can I say? It has just been a whirl of thought & heart-break since I opened the cabin at the Post Office, when I went to fetch our letters on our arrival here six days ago. You & she were "not two persons at all" . . . you had every daily thought & interest in common & the separation must be grief inexpressible. We were all so proud of Joan too, & never had a woman a more true & loyal sister than I had in her. How often have I said in the last months "I will talk that over with Joan when I get back!" and so it went round & round in confused agony . . . I do not know whether God sends or only permits such sorrows as yours, but I do believe that through them we can learn something we did not know before.

Katherine hinted at her own problems. "I have not had your terrible shock or grief, but I have had some pretty hard times in life at some of which you know or can guess, others perhaps not." She did not "know about the future," but then, without missing a beat, imposed upon her bereaved brother to go apartment hunting for her in London: "I really don't think I can face housekeeping & write a book . . . for it looks as though I might be alone next winter. I have got to go over to Belgium as soon as I can & try to persuade the . . . Priest of the 'Sacrés Coeurs' [sic] to let me see their early records of Mangareva." Being "alone next winter" meant, it seems, that Scoresby intended to return to Jamaica and finish what he had started.

In Papeete, Katherine met a Rapa Nui woman who had been born near Tongariki "after the statues had fallen" and had left the island for Mangareva and Tahiti—Katherine interviewed her but took only a few lines of distracted notes. On February 19 the Routledges sailed for Sydney via New Zealand, and on March 5 the telephone rang at Swarthmoor, the lovely country home of prominent Quakers John Holdsworth and his wife, Lucy Violet Hodgkin. Because Lucy was deaf, a cousin answered and spoke to Katherine, who said that she and her husband were in New Zealand for ten days and wondered if she might visit. Lucy, who was the daughter of Thomas Hodgkin—the man whose funeral Katherine had attended on the eve of the Mana Expedition's departure for Easter Island in 1913—was delighted to receive an "English visitor . . . almost a relation!" She rushed to get the spare room ready, then recorded her impression of Katherine:

She looks much older—in a touristy blue coat & skirt with a squashy gray hat and travellers blue veil. And alas! I found her almost impossible to lipread . . . nevertheless, in spite of everything her visit was a real success: a restful time I hope to her & a great pleasure to me . . . we sat over the fire in the drawing room . . . & with the aid of pencil and paper a good many things were said . . . she likes to walk with a stick—from rheumatism—likes to go to bed at 9 p.m. . . . K.R. has become a great talker—how I longed to hear what she was saying. . . . We took her on a stroll around the garden & lemon grove but I did not feel she really saw or noticed things much . . . she was most easy & sweet & understanding. After a rest (she can't do without her rest!) we ran her up in the car a few miles . . . that she might see the tall overhanging hills . . .

Lucy and John took Katherine to Napier to meet W. W. Moore, a doctor with an interest in local archaeology and history. They left her there with him, "the 2 archaeologists talking hard," and Scoresby joined her that evening at The Masonic (the best hotel in Napier). The next morning they drove to Taupo and then Katherine and Scoresby parted ways.

On March 28 reporters interviewed Katherine aboard *Makura* in Sydney harbor. The story says Mangareva is a "link" to Rapa Nui, that Katherine "may visit Easter Island again," and that Scoresby had been "obliged to return at once and had already embarked for London from New Zealand." On April 21 Katherine was in Vancouver. Newspapers there said she would "shortly publish" her Mangarevan research and that she "would very much like to go back to Easter Island." All of this publicity, which Katherine courted, paints a picture of a woman with a sense of direction—and her compass set on Rapa Nui.

She traveled cross-country to Montreal and stayed at Royal Victoria College as the guest of her old Oxford friend and classmate Ethel Hurlblatt. On May 17 she sailed alone for England after nearly two years living an island life in the remote Pacific. In her bag she carried a mass of fieldnotes documenting Mangarevan folklore, myth, and oral history. Katherine intended to go to Belgium to research Laval's original Mangarevan texts, planned a book about Mangareva, and intended to return to Easter Island. None of this, however, was meant to be. Just two weeks after Katherine's return home, Wilson Pease, aged fifty-five and a widower for only eight months, died alone in his London town house. Katherine now faced, in the long-ago words of her mother, Kate Pease, "a terrible blank."

Spooks and Voices

✦

LOVE, IT HAS BEEN SAID, FURNISHES THE VITAL SENSE OF purpose that is the polar opposite of depression. Those of us who are loved learn to love in return, sometimes passionately. We learn to love ourselves, others, our home—and then our work, our country, our world, or our God. We can abstract our love to ideas, causes, or beliefs. In modern society, working and loving are clear indications of emotional stability. In Katherine's life the two realms of love and work blended memorably and productively when she was living in isolation on Rapa Nui. The work she did and the love she felt for the island allowed her to achieve, for a time, real happiness. To a lesser extent, she had the same experience on Mangareva.

The quality of happiness felt at any moment in any life is fragile, but love is the greatest contributor to it. Love, in fact, can create a biochemical reaction in the human mind and body that acts as a shield against depression. Those who knew Katherine best recognized the lack of love in her life and understood how much of her unhappiness stemmed from her need for it and quest to find it. Katherine needed love as much as *Mana* had needed ballast, and when she lost Wilson she was, in many ways, at sea.

Katherine's Woodside world had been, on the surface and in the eyes of the outside world, exceptionally stable. Inside the family, inside the house, and inside her, however, there had been turmoil. Remarkable life events—her father's death, her mother's withdrawal, Harold's violence, desperate illness, and deep insecurity—had all triggered emotional reactions and depressions that were, to varying degrees, influenced by Katherine's own biochemistry. Yet the compelling contradictions that haunted and shaped her world had, at the same time, propelled her on a life quest and a unique voyage of discovery.

Studies show that the earliest episodes of major depression in people like Katherine are almost always tied to life events, but that as time passes depression becomes a living thing—a monster that no longer needs outside nourishment but that can live inside quite well on its own. Katherine's profound needs and erratic behavior inevitably caused negative reactions in others. The level of affection, understanding, and tolerance others had or could muster for Katherine decreased with time. Throughout it all, however, Wilson had always been there.

Wilson was the appreciative audience Katherine demanded, the sounding board she trusted, and the reality check she needed. Her sisterly love for him, like all love, had a huge helping of selfishness. He told Katherine that she had "the grit of all Pease women," and his confidence in her helped her to adjust and alter her course through life—even though it had been set a long time ago. Loss, or the fear of loss, created stress and depression in Katherine— loss of people and places, of course, but also of other, less tangible things as well—the very passage of time and, above all, loss of love. Grief resulted, and Katherine grieved inordinately for Wilson.

Mangareva had been a respite for Katherine, a place of peace in which her inevitable decline was slowed and she had been, in many ways, her island self. Wilson's death propelled Katherine toward chaos. Her return to England can be viewed through two lenses: private and public. As in the family dichotomy she had lived with as a child, Katherine's private world was gloomy but she presented a cheerful, "businessy" image to the public. There was a great deal of publicity when Katherine and Scoresby returned— most of it purposefully generated by them. Katherine told exciting tales of being lost at sea, but also recounted slightly weird stories of Mangarevan myths and legends. Mangarevans had shown her what they called the "footprints of the dead" along an isolated beach. The belief was that the footprints had been left by souls of the dead journeying westward. Katherine was, she said, perplexed that the prints "certainly were different" from "ordinary ones."

Scoresby essentially separated from Katherine for a time, living at Ewers and the Union Club. She, in turn, moved restlessly from hotel to apartment to her club to a London town house and then back again, never settling long in any one place. Too often, it seemed, melancholy fell on her "sudden from heaven like a weeping cloud." On her niece Hilda's twenty-first birthday Katherine revealed her own emotional struggle: "Life cannot be all happiness, for some reason we do not altogether understand it is not made like that, but if we find that the dark times have something to teach us, & that we can, if we will, become more our best selves for going through them, then we shall begin to realize that they too are worthwhile."

In September 1923 Katherine rallied. She joined eighteen other women scientists at the annual meeting of the British Association in Liverpool and presented a paper entitled "Mangarevan Folklore" in the Anthropology Section. Katherine was living a double emotional life at this time, trying to maintain her role in the real worlds of science and society while struggling with grief and depression. This was taxing, and Katherine was lonely. Long ago, the Pease family had believed that Harold's marriage to Gwen would salvage him. Modern medicine suggests that "the best defense" for people with mental health vulnerability is a "good enough" marriage that lends stability, absorbs external stress, and minimizes isolation. Katherine's marriage had always done those things for her, and she retreated to it now.

Katherine threw out her anchor in London, buying a hugely expensive, seventeen-room mansion with a lovely view at prestigious 4 Hyde Park Gardens. She spent a fortune to fill it with expensive furniture, art, family heirlooms, and every modern amenity, including lavish bathrooms. Scoresby was persuaded to move into a private apartment in the house, for which he agreed to pay a portion of her monthly expenses. In December of 1924 Katherine gave a newspaper interview in her new home: "Mrs. Routledge looked out of the window at the fog and talked about sitting on a coral strand while a native woman told her the ancient legends of the islands of the Pacific. I should like to be back there again, said Mrs. Routledge, still looking out of the window . . ."

Returning to Easter Island—or anywhere in the Pacific—sounds like a wistful, longed-for dream, but, in fact, Katherine had the means and the opportunity to do it. What she lacked was the strength. She told the press that she had "just started seriously to work on my new book," which would be "based on the results of the last expedition my husband and I undertook in the Pacific." She needed diversion, however, and during the Christmas season of 1924 presented a series of inconsequential but popular public lectures about Easter Island and Mangareva to young people. In March 1925 she was elected a Fellow of the Royal Geographical Society. Scoresby began to dismantle their home museum at Ewers, donating objects to the British Museum and the Pitt-Rivers Museum, University of Oxford.

Katherine had never had a will, but her enormous wealth since Kate Pease's death and her new property, the lawyers said, required one. In December of 1925 she had one drawn up, with Scoresby as her chief beneficiary. She left 4 Hyde Park Gardens and all of its contents to him and appointed him trustee—with her brother John Henry Pease and her cousin Lord Darynton. She provided major legacies to Lyle McAllum and Ethel Hurlblatt, annuities to servants, and contributions to women's political organizations. Katherine's central concern, however, was her "scientific researches." She set aside funds sufficient for the publication of her Mangarevan book and directed that her Easter Island and other fieldnotes were to be deposited with either the British Museum or the Royal Anthropological

Society. In a confusing move that caused family discord and forced Lilian to dispute her will, Katherine left "all other" property to her sister and nieces.

In June 1926 Katherine became a great-aunt when Lilian's daughter, Eve, gave birth to a son. The little boy became an obsession of Katherine's—and the major topic of conversation for an imaginary chorus of Pease family "voices" that filled every room of 4 Hyde Park Gardens. The triggering mechanism in this situation is not known, but Katherine's life pattern reveals that her voices most often appeared during great stress or accompanying an illness. There is no record that the symptoms she usually self-diagnosed as malaria occurred at this time, but they may have. In any case, her great-nephew became the focal point of Katherine's now nearly overwhelming anxieties, and his mother the target of her exaggerated need to control and manage the people and events in her environment.

In July, from Switzerland, Katherine wrote Eve a letter responding negatively to the news that she had chosen the name Peter for her son. Katherine gave a long list of alternative choices that, she said, had been told to her by beings that had passed "out of the children's sphere" or "up into the 3rd sphere," a reference to Spiritualist concepts. Even while reporting such obviously odd and disturbing things to her baffled niece, Katherine went on to say that "the book prospers."

The book, in fact, was not prospering at all. Books and papers spilled out of her study to virtually every room in the Hyde Park Gardens house, but her fieldnotes were more or less in one place. She and Scoresby were living almost as strangers, making appointments to see one another and engaged in a major tug-of-war about virtually everything. She was proprietary, petty, and jealous and spent nearly all of her time with Spiritualists, whom Scoresby despised. Even Lyle refused to engage in some of the séances Katherine attended and recognized that the women she had fallen in with were gold-digging frauds and charlatans.

By December 1926 Katherine's hold was slipping badly, and her reason was shouted down by "voices"—the ghosts of long-ago Darlington Pease family members—that raised a nearly constant clamor. Her long-dead grandfather Joseph Pease, her great-grandfather Edward Pease, many deceased aunts and uncles, Kate and Gurney Pease, Joan and Wilson, all refused to be silenced. The subject of their discourse with Katherine was nearly always Eve's son, Peter, his upbringing, education, and future. In an echo of the stern admonishments she had received as a little girl at Southend and Woodside, Katherine was obsessed with every detail of Peter's appearance, character, behavior, and prospects for the future. Each time after poor Eve visited her aunt at 4 Hyde Park Gardens, she waited anxiously for the inevitably strange letter that followed. On one occasion, Katherine wrote:

Pete was a great social success on Monday! Scoresby quite took my breath away by volunteering twice over what "a nice little Kid" he was—and then, dear, we had a loving admiring other world audience . . . quite a number of them had been here . . . then Wilson came later in the evening . . . (They see through my eyes so to speak—the pictures in my brain).

Alone in her Hyde Park Gardens house one evening, Katherine faced a terrifying onslaught of voices that refused to be stilled until nearly dawn. She wrote Eve six pages filled with sadly disjointed words and thoughts "channeled" through her pen as automatic writing.

Wilson came after I was in bed & was very excited & delighted to hear you had written . . . Joan tells me I am to write this . . . Joan came after luncheon today & asked to have your letter read . . . we were always so confident of your love dear Katherine she said . . . Wilson can't write he is engaged on his Master's business . . . Wilson is here now . . . uncle and aunt Arthur told me to say . . .

Lilian turned to her brother John Henry for help, and the two siblings were now in the same position Katherine and Wilson had been with Harold. Eve continued to receive a stream of missives from Katherine, including a lengthy one about Peter's future in January 1927 that included, Katherine wrote, a message "from her great grandfather Joseph Pease dictated to me as I wrote a few words at a time by clear mental impression."

The vivid Polynesian and African folklore Katherine was once steeped in did not translate into tribal voices but, instead, gave her the framework within which she saw herself as a "seeker" or visionary. Katherine believed herself to be a woman of ancestral *mana*, a woman with spiritual power. Angata did not speak to her—but Katherine believed they shared the same sort of psychic powers. She slept only minutes at a time, ate nothing for days, and could not behave in a civil manner. Nothing could stop the voices that buzzed day and night. She tried desperately to reassert control using the tricks of concentration that had once worked miracles for her, but to no avail. In early 1927 a new challenge arose: the obsessions of Katherine's voices were made worse by her alarmingly paranoid fears and behavior.

Katherine suspiciously challenged every act, word, and intention of Scoresby's and began, one by one, to turn her back on anyone who tried to reason with her. The first to suffer her rejection was Lyle, who begged Katherine to allow her to live with her and take care of her. Scoresby favored the arrangement, but Katherine suspected a conspiracy and would not hear of it. She then turned her full wrath on Scoresby. They stopped having meals together; Katherine moved his desk out of their shared study, opened his mail, and went through his personal papers. Finally, she gave him written notice "to remove his things from Hyde Park Gardens."

Katherine's complaint against her husband was a failure to help her research her Mangareva book and "a want of sympathy and assistance in her pursuits." Scoresby turned to the other executors of Katherine's estate for help. John Henry was sympathetic to Scoresby:

> This spook business seems to be practically sending her off her head though no doubt the fact that she has a big income compared with his also makes things difficult as she thinks she ought to boss everything as she pays most. At the bottom I think he would like to cut the whole business and go away for good but his conscience will not let him do so freely.

Scoresby's conscience very likely resisted the thought of deserting Katherine at such a terrible time in her life, but his financial interests were also at stake. Scoresby was paying room and board at 4 Hyde Park Gardens "as a lodger might," as well as a portion of the taxes Katherine incurred when his income raised hers into another bracket. Nonetheless, to move out of the house would be tantamount to desertion and he would risk being cut out of her will. Scoresby described to Katherine's brother John Henry how he tried to reason with her:

> At the brief and infrequent interviews she has granted me to talk over this business I have done my best to get her to see that, in justice to herself and to me, she should not assume the joint roll [sic] of Judge, Jury and Prosecution . . . but all in vain. It only irritates her. All the same I have gradually got her to come to meals, and to talk and to behave graciously at table, and even to take me to a studio to have my portrait painted for her as a keepsake! The line I am taking is to speak and to act as if our joint life was, and had been, undisturbed . . .

Katherine responded by accusing Scoresby of "greed" and energetically "turned him out of the house by force, throwing out some of his things . . . into the street after having ransacked them." She changed the locks on the doors and refused to accept or forward his mail. Publicly humiliated and furious, Scoresby moved into the Union Club, put his things in storage, sent Katherine the bill, and instructed his lawyer (who had been advising him all along) to initiate proceedings against her. Katherine calmly wrote to her sister and broke the news.

Did I tell you Scoresby and I have parted? It has been hard but I am not
unhappy. It was better so for many reasons. At the last it came from me—
Please don't write about it—I shall understand your sympathy—

Katherine became utterly estranged from John Henry and, having so
violently severed her relationship with Scoresby, remained connected
only with her sister and nieces. In January 1928 Katherine's niece Hilda
became engaged. In wistful denial of the way her own marriage had gone,
Katherine told Hilda that marriage was a partnership of "happy and restful
companions—united interests, united outlook on life . . . and love the best
foundation of all."

A major crisis was precipitated when Katherine flatly refused the terms
of a judicial separation (essentially, a divorce) offered by Scoresby's lawyer.
She then met in dozens of fruitless planning discussions with her own
lawyers—all of whom reported everything back to Scoresby and her other
executors. Presumably they had Katherine's best interests at heart, but the
obvious fact is that her paranoid suspicions of conspiracy were borne out by
their behavior. They were more or less sure that Katherine would end up
institutionalized as Harold had been and were working toward minimizing
the financial implications of such an event. John Henry and Lord Darynton
both thought that Scoresby was shrewd and original in his business negotiations, but not necessarily greedy. Money, Scoresby told them, was at the
root of his marriage problems, and everything had been fine until Katherine
became rich after her mother's death. John Henry got the impression that
Scoresby was not a materialist.

> My opinion is that K. is upset really that she has no one to manage now that
> she has turned off S. and that though she would not admit it even to herself
> is really beginning to wonder whether she has not done the wrong thing. That
> is what S. hoped she would never realize as he says it would make her
> remorseful for the rest of her life. . . . The outlook is very sorrowful; she won't
> be happy without her husband, she was not happy with him, her money
> hasn't helped her and she is a deplorable sort of wreck.

On June 1, 1928 Scoresby acted. Demanding that Katherine pay the minor
but overdue storage fees on his warehoused belongings, he secured a High
Court order and froze multiple thousands of pounds of Katherine's assets,
including all properties, securities, bonds, stock dividends, and bank
accounts. This left her flat broke, with overdrafts on her accounts, overdue
bills, little cash on hand, and no credit. Saying "I will not submit," she dis-

missed her servants, canceled all tradesmen's deliveries, and stubbornly locked herself in her house, where she began "camping out in the bathroom." She rose to a majestic level of indignation, called in the press, and showed them her quarters in the bathroom, where she was cooking on a small camp stove and sleeping in the tub: "I am taking this action as a protest on behalf of women. The administration of the law today seems to me to be heavily weighted against women. If an attempt is made to force an entrance into my home I shall not resist, though I shall not admit them voluntarily."

Within days, Katherine had received hundreds of letters of sympathy from outraged women across England, some sending money. Katherine promptly announced she would keep the money as the first donations in her "Society for the Reform of the Administration of the Law." She sold her Mangarevan pearls to get funds to pay the grocer, and Scoresby, reading about it in the papers, offered to "take steps to recover them for her." Lilian found the entire matter dreadful and also offered to pay Katherine's bills or to give her money, but John Henry sided with Scoresby. He lectured his sister that, since Katherine "cannot or will not manage" her financial affairs "without injustice to others," the sequestration order was a good way to get her "out of the tangle."

Scoresby made his next move, securing two more High Court orders. One of them allowed a portion of Katherine's assets—far exceeding the warehousing fees—to be placed into a special account to which Scoresby had access. Technically, this discharged the financial obligation she had and should have ended the action, if not the dispute. The second, much more questionable order permitted the seizure of 4 Hyde Park Gardens. When a court official delivered the orders, Katherine led him politely through the house and then locked him in an upstairs room for an entire day, letting the poor man go only after he promised never to return.

Shortly after midnight a day or two later a taxi drew up in front of 4 Hyde Park Gardens. The driver honked his horn four times. Katherine opened the door and the driver loaded six or eight large trunks into the taxi. Katherine got into the taxi and was driven away. An hour later she returned. The next day, at about nine-thirty or ten in the morning, a garbage man removed a pile of paper and parcels from behind a locked gate near the entrance. Katherine pulled down all of the blinds in the house, slammed the front door, and walked down the street carrying two attaché cases. She stopped at the home of a neighbor and said, "I am going away. I have left the house in charge of the men." Somehow it became known that her trunks had been delivered to Paddington railway station for the night, and that Katherine had gone "abroad."

The following Monday at about 4 P.M. Scoresby, two court officials, a lawyer and his clerk, a male and a female bailiff, and a locksmith approached 4 Hyde Park Gardens. Obviously, Scoresby knew Katherine had gone. The locksmith climbed over the black iron railing, descended a few steps, and took a pane from the scullery window. Within five minutes he was in Katherine's house, unlocked the door, and admitted the others. They searched every room "expeditiously and neatly," took an inventory of the contents, and found, the papers reported, that "everything inside is in order." Notwithstanding that opinion, however, the papers or other belongings Katherine had packed in the six or eight trunks—including all of her Easter Island field-notes stashed in the white tin trunk—were certainly missing. After a while, they locked everything up and departed.

Where Katherine went or what she did between summer and early fall is hard to trace, but there is a strong suggestion that she traveled all the way to Damascus, or at least tried to do so—her voices had told her Wilson was there. Katherine had always been a take-charge woman, and for a few months she lived a horrible parody of her previous existence, traveling and making notes on what she saw and did. In none of her existing papers does she acknowledge any similarity between her plight and what Harold had gone through, but when lucid, she surely understood her situation.

The decline of Katherine's personality from intermittent but increasingly longer bouts of depression—alternating with manic episodes—into deepening paranoia is a downward trajectory unique to her particular illness and her own personality. She was disabled on some days, stabilized and then invigorated on others. Sometimes she could function through anything, and at other times she took to her bed for days. There is no suggestion of overt suicidal feelings, but she may have experienced them. What Katherine was going through was unimaginable—only Wilson might have understood, but even he might have turned away in his own constant search for a quiet life.

By October of 1928 Katherine had managed to move some funds into new accounts and, apparently, had drafted a new will. She secretly returned to 4 Hyde Park Gardens, "barricaded" herself inside the house, and prepared for a "siege." The suspicion, distrust, and fear that afflicted her blossomed into the solid conviction that she was being poisoned. Katherine had hated the nauseating fumes and sounds of the engine aboard *Mana* and now believed that the same gases were being pumped into her home. She was often up all night trying to find the sources of smells, and she flung open every door and window during the day, no matter what the weather. She became convinced that her food and water were laced with arsenic. She was afraid to leave the house and, when she did, suffered severe "palpitations" born of pure terror. Sometimes she fainted dead away in taxis and hotel lobbies.

With the cleverness and will to survive that is frequently characteristic of the schizophrenic person, Katherine sent out a blizzard of letters begging for help from people in high places. She sought the protection of the Home Office, claiming Williamson, Balfour Co., and especially Archibald Balfour—publicly accused of collaborating with the Germans—were trying to kill her. She collected samples of food or drink in glass containers, stored them on special shelves throughout her house, and had some chemically tested for arsenic. Lilian prevailed upon her to see two separate doctors, thinking that they could prove she was free of arsenic and Katherine would be at peace, but that tactic failed.

The terrible, lonely ordeal Katherine faced just getting out of bed every day became increasingly trying. She wrote a friend that her life was "strenuous," that she was in "desperate trouble" and "not strong," but "I see people from time to time and I am not dead yet!" She kept a journal, in a pathetic echo of her long-ago fieldwork, entitled "Things Unknown told to me by 'The Spooks.' " She still wrote to her sister, Lilian, who responded with vague assurances that enraged her.

Beatrice Portsmouth, Lilian and her daughters, and a neighbor woman were all able to get Katherine to open the door to 4 Hyde Park Gardens, but only on a chain and not for long. One by one, even they were turned away. In November Katherine turned her back, with finality, on Eve, unfairly accusing her of never offering "to help in any way though I am ill & alone." With finality and the terrible cruelty of the mentally ill, Katherine told Eve that she refused to allow her to go on "waiting for my death so your name does not appear in my new will."

That was the last straw for the family, but there was little they could do. Chemical imbalances of the brain were considered possible causes of mental disorders, but the strength of reason in controlling behavior was emphasized and intervention greatly circumscribed by law. Several doctors implied that Katherine had simply fallen apart in the face of external tensions that others with stronger internal control might have endured. John Henry thought that "the arsenic craze" might simply "settle down" and advised doing nothing until some action of Katherine's gave them the excuse they needed to have her committed. When she posted public notices on her front door claiming that she was engaged in a struggle with death by poisoning and accusing prominent government officials and agencies, Scoresby and John Henry—with the knowledge of Lilian and the official orders of two physicians—took action.

Katherine was never an early riser, but because she did not sleep anymore at night she frequently dozed off in the early morning. On a cold, wet day in February of 1929 she had fallen asleep at her desk, her head on her arm. The street outside 4 Hyde Park Gardens was quiet, and she was awakened by the sounds of footsteps. Eight men, including two locksmiths and two doctors, were on the pavement in front of the house. One of the men knocked on the door and waited. Katherine, not sure what to expect, opened it a few inches. The man placed his foot firmly in the door, and then all of the others joined in forcing it wide open. There was a fierce scuffle and shouts as Katherine fought hard against the intruders. Finally she was dragged out and down the front steps to two nurses, who bundled her into a waiting ambulance disguised as a motorcar and then sped away.

Katherine was committed to Ticehurst House, an asylum in Sussex, south of London, for a crime she believed she was not guilty of: insanity. Writing to Lilian from what she defiantly called "The Lunatic Asylum," Katherine did not blame Scoresby but accused her sister of an "appalling wickedness in lending the whole of your influence to consign me, a perfectly sane woman, to this place." Katherine wrote dozens of letters begging for help, but Ticehurst staff destroyed most of them. At least one made it to Sir Alfred Edward Pease, who had tried to help Harold so many years before. He found Katherine's letter perfectly sensible and wrote immediately with empathy to advise her.

Katherine's illness was diagnosed as "systemized delusional insanity." Within about two months Katherine's contact with the world outside of Ticehurst diminished, and then she became completely isolated. There is no evidence she ever saw Scoresby again. Books were kept from her for a long, long time, and she despised the boredom and conformity imposed upon her. When she was given "parole" to pursue her own interests, such as walking in the garden, she overstepped her bounds and told her doctors "she had done it on principle." Katherine never gave up her belief that she was illegally detained at Ticehurst and never stopped writing letters.

Eventually she calmed down and became less voluble but no more malleable. She was awakened every morning at 7 A.M., an impossibly early hour for her and an imposition she must have hated. She saw a doctor daily, took tea at 4 P.M., and was locked in her room at 10 P.M. every evening. She came to believe that her food was safe to eat, but still worried about poisonous gases. Her doctors regarded her fear as intractable and her illness as incurable, yet she soldiered on. Ticehurst doctors practiced radical interventions such as electroshock therapy and prefrontal lobotomies, but whether Katherine was subjected to such tortures is not known. If she had, it would have altered her personality and damaged her memory.

She was not, however, forgotten by others. Her sister, Lilian, widowed in 1933, continued to be concerned about Katherine's welfare, as did her nieces. Her great-nephew Peter cherished vague but warm memories of his aunt Katherine. The memories of Pacific islanders are long, and in 1932 the famous modernist painter Robert Lee Eskridge said that, during six months on Mangareva, he "came across many stories concerning Mrs. Routledge." Her fellow researchers continued to seek out news of her, and T. A. Joyce discreetly fielded requests from those interested in using her photographs, quoting her work, or reviewing her fieldnotes. Scoresby, who had tried but failed to recover all of Katherine's hidden boxes and cases, lamented the loss of some of the Mana Expedition's papers "in consequence of my wife's insanity."

The great voyage that was her life ended on December 13, 1935 when Katherine Maria Pease Routledge, explorer, author, and brilliant, brave-hearted woman, died of a cerebral thrombosis. Ironically, Beatrice Portsmouth, her cousin and partner in Spiritualism, died the same day. Katherine's death, at age sixty-nine, was essentially painless, the doctors said, but it did not go unremarked. There were dozens of obituaries, and every one of them mentioned Easter Island. Her fieldwork was described in great detail, *Mana* was sometimes pictured, Scoresby was mentioned, and her research and writing were lauded.

Katherine's body was cremated, and as her will had instructed, no marker or memorial was erected. Her Easter Island ethnographic and genealogical fieldwork remains Katherine's legacy to science and gift to the island's future. She had been, in the words of England's great poet Shelley, "a traveler from an antique land," a seeker and sojourner in exotic, enigmatic islands. According to ancient Polynesian beliefs, Katherine's spirit would have headed westward after appearing, at the precise moment of her death, to someone close to her. Juan Tepano was still very much alive in 1935. Perhaps he saw Katherine's footprints in the sands of Anakena.

Cyprus, 1961

✦

THE SMALL STONE HOUSE IN TJIKLOS, CYPRUS, WAS DARK and cool. Outside, aged carob and olive trees shimmered in the warm moonlight. Archaeologist James Stewart and his colleagues sat at the heavy wood dining table, bathed in lamplight. Bottles of red wine and the remains of a good Turkish dinner were pushed aside to make room for overflowing ashtrays and a large archaeological map of a Bronze Age cemetery near Karmi, west of Kyrenia.

The conversation was animated, only slightly less than argumentative. Jim dominated, and even though his health was failing, his excited, opinionated confidence was attractive. Eve Dray Stewart watched her husband for a while and then idly pushed back her chair. She walked outside and stood on the terrace. The sea breeze cleared the scents of wine and cigarette smoke and she looked down on the few lights far below, remembering.

In 1936, the year after Katherine had died at Ticehurst, Eve was just a teenager, slight and very pretty. Traveling from England to Cyprus aboard a large cruise ship, she played deck tennis and flirted. Her father, Thomas Dray, and William Scoresby Routledge sat in nearby deck chairs. Scoresby was a mysterious figure who had lived on Malta for a while and then wandered about the Mediterranean. Even though he was nearing eighty he was still tall and lean, with a quick intelligence and sharp tongue. Eve cast a glance their way, hoping the two men were watching, but they were oblivious—completely engrossed in each other and the plans they were making.

When the ship docked in Cyprus Eve went home to her mother. Tom Dray and Scoresby returned to Go Down, a dramatic old house in Kyrenia complete with gardens, servants' quarters, and a Turkish bath. Scoresby and Tom had shared Go Down for several years, and after Katherine's death, Scoresby had filled it with Hyde Park Gardens furniture, paintings, books, and papers shipped out from England. He and Tom were always together, to the exclusion of anyone else. They went to the horse races, dined at the English Club, and toured everywhere in Scoresby's big, open car. They were absorbed in their own projects, one of which was the building of a small yacht.

Tom had come to Cyprus at the age of eighteen to work for the Survey Department. He was an expert on the tortuous Turkish inheritance laws, and when Scoresby fell in love with Tjiklos, a magnificent hilltop plateau with sweeping views of the Mediterranean, Tom negotiated its purchase. He designed a stone mansion and drew up the architectural plans, but Scoresby kept making revisions and delayed its construction. Scoresby rode up to Tjiklos every day on a donkey to supervise work, and they managed to build rows of mud-brick henhouses, a circular gravel drive, a two-tiered garage, and a house for their chauffeur. Scoresby imported a gardener from Scotland, and he and Tom laid out orchards and an English garden filled with stocks and snapdragons. The rains failed and the flowers died, but carob and olive trees thrived.

On July 31, 1939 Scoresby was in the office of J. Burleigh & Co., Ltd., a manufacturing company in Paddington. He was pitching an ambitious import-export idea to one of the office assistants when he collapsed across the man's desk and died within minutes. Tom Dray was bequeathed Tjiklos and nearly all of Scoresby's other property on Cyprus. To fulfill the explicit instructions of his will, Scoresby's body was placed in a cheap, rough wood coffin and buried in unconsecrated ground in Putney Vale Cemetery, London. No religious official, of any kind, was allowed to participate in the brief burial ceremony.

Scoresby had never located all of the papers Katherine had hidden during the final stages of her illness, but those he had recovered—which included hundreds of photographic negatives, glass slides, maps, and plans made on Easter Island by the Mana Expedition—were stored with his other possessions at Ewers and the Union Club or scattered elsewhere in closets, desk drawers, and boxes. Scoresby's executors struggled valiantly to sort everything out. Clothes, books, paintings, and household furnishings were donated to charities, given to relatives, sold, stored, discarded, or simply abandoned. In 1948 John Charles Dundas Harington, one of Scoresby's executors and the son of his best friend Sir Richard Harington, miraculously recovered a batch of Mana Expedition negatives. He sent them to the Royal Geographical Society, where Scoresby had deposited, on loan, a major part of Katherine's fieldnotes and other papers in 1929.

Now, a slight chill overtook Eve and she turned to go back into the house. Jim and his colleagues were still at the dining room table. Their conversation had fallen to a low murmur, ebbing and flowing around thoughtful silences.

She went into the large living room, picked up a book, then put it down. Tom Dray had died the year before and Eve had spent her idle hours every evening going through the last of her father's things, all stored haphazardly in cupboards and bookcases in the Tjiklos house. She settled down on the floor in front of a massive, ornate wood cabinet with a glass front.

Eve opened the lower doors and out tumbled a mass of papers. On top was a photograph, and she picked it up. A dreamy young Englishman, depicted in soft sepia tones and dressed with a romantic flair, gazed out at her. Looking closer, she recognized Scoresby. The papers, as she unfolded them, were maps and plans of Easter Island archaeological sites made over fifty years earlier. There were also rolls of blueprints of the yacht Scoresby and Tom had been building on Cyprus, and of *Mana*, the yacht that had carried Scoresby and Katherine Routledge to Easter Island, and—oddly—a large sparkplug from *Mana*'s engine. Reaching deep within the cabinet, Eve found a small, heavily tarnished silver cup mounted on a black base. The plaque said it was the Challenge Cup, awarded in 1917 by special resolution of the Cruising Club to "W. Scoresby Routledge for his cruise in the Pacific in Mana and Exploration on Easter Island."

Within a year of Eve's discovery and rescue of irreplaceable papers from the Mana Expedition, they joined Katherine's other fieldnotes in the archives of the Royal Geographical Society. The recovery and preservation of these scattered papers are great gifts to scholarship, and John Charles Dundas Harington and Eve Dray Stewart are real heroes—but much is missing. The other objects Eve found—the photograph, the sparkplug from the yacht's engine, and the Challenge Cup—reveal what Scoresby cherished in life: his adventurous youth, his inventiveness, and his Pacific voyaging accomplishment.

Epilogue

✦

MERLET'S LEASE ON RAPA NUI EXPIRED ELEVEN DAYS after the Mana Expedition departed. A political tug-of-war resulted in its renewal and, at the same time, the final legal and judicial incorporation of the island into Chile. In 1916 Catholic bishop Rafael Edwards arrived aboard *Jeneral Baquedano* to assess the conditions under which islanders were living. He was utterly appalled at what he found and spearheaded a campaign to rid the island once and for all of tyranny. Williamson, Balfour Co. strongly protested what it considered unfair accusations, and Frank T. Green and Percy Edmunds wrote letters in support of the Company. Not until the 1950s was the Company lease finally revoked.

Percy Edmunds' descendants prospered honorably in the twin worlds of Rapa Nui business and politics. He retired from the Company and moved to Tahiti, where he established a new family. He died in Mara'a, Tahiti, on September 8, 1958, and is buried there. Victoria Rapahango raised her children, ran a small business, and worked with the ethnographer Alfred Métraux of the Franco-Belgian Expedition to Easter Island (1934–35).

On May 9, 1916 Henry James Gillam contemplated his future and cautiously anticipated the worst as *Mana* prepared to run from Bermuda to the Azores and then across Atlantic waters infested with German submarines. Gillam hated submarines and found them an unnatural environment for any self-respecting sailor. *Mana*'s luck held, however, and he returned safely to his wife, Ada Marie Gillam, of Portswood, Southampton, near where *Mana* was laid up in the Itchen River yards. Then, Katherine wrote, volunteers were needed for "especially dangerous work in capturing submarines; Gillam responded—it is impossible to picture his doing otherwise."

Given the rank of lieutenant in the Royal Naval Reserve, Gillam was assigned to HMS *Egmont*, a decoy ship. He was killed on Sunday, April 7, 1918 during an encounter in the eastern Mediterranean with one of the submarines he so despised. Henry James Gillam, who was forty-two years old, is buried in Porto Empedocle Communal Cemetery, a little graveyard on a hill above a village on the southwest coast of Sicily. He is not alone, but rests with others lost in the Great War. For Katherine, "the loss to his country is great; to us it is very real and personal. . . . One can only think of him in that other life as still keen for some new work or enterprise, and carrying it out with perfect loyalty and success."

Lieutenant David Ronald Ritchie returned safely home from Chile and was posted to the light cruiser *Charybdis*. On January 30, 1916 he was promoted to lieutenant commander, and on July 31 he married Phyllis Gurney, the twenty-three-year-old daughter of Dr. Harold Gurney and his wife, Cecelia, in St. Augustine's Church, Dovercourt, Essex. In 1928 he was granted the Legion of Honor, and on June 30, 1932 he retired with the rank of captain. He returned to active duty with the Royal Navy during World War II, retiring again in 1947. By 1955 he had received the Chadwick Gold Medal, a naval prize. He and Phyllis had a son, Major William David Ritchie. On March 13, 1963, seventy-six years old and suffering "senile degeneration," David Ronald Ritchie, RN, navigator and cartographer extraordinaire of the Mana Expedition to Easter Island, died of cardiac failure in his wife's encircling arms.

Members of *Mana*'s crew scattered to the four winds. Engineer Eduardo Silva went back to Chile. Mate Frank Preston went home to Burton Street in Brixham and then immediately into the Royal Navy. He was assigned to HMS *Victory* as an able seaman and, less than six months after *Mana* returned to England from Easter Island, died in battle. Charles Giffard Jeffery, who idolized Gillam and wanted to follow in his footsteps, also joined the Royal Naval Reserve. On April 27, 1917 he was killed while serving aboard the trawler *Agile* on minesweeping duty off Harwich, leaving behind a grieving mother, sister, brothers, and Lily, his heartbroken fiancée. Katherine wrote sadly that he "grew from boyhood to manhood on *Mana*" and then "met with a hero's death" on the sea he passionately loved. The Chatham Naval Memorial, Kent, commemorates his sacrifice and that of over eight thousand others.

As it turned out, Katherine was justified in racing Easter Island's ticking clock to prevent its striking "the eleventh hour" and carrying off her informants. Tomenika and Timikore Keremuti ("Kirimuti") had died while she was on the island; Maanga died the same year the Mana Expedition departed. Less than three years later both Jotefa Maherenga and Ramón Te Haha were dead. Matamu'a Rangitopa I Ka'i ("Langitopa") died in 1922 and Juan Porotu in 1924. Their generation's personal memories of Orongo and its past glories, however, were preserved for posterity by Juan Tepano's enlightened self-interest and Katherine Routledge's tenacity. Antonio Koropa Haoa Pakomio, one of Katherine's most trusted fieldworkers, died of pneumonia on June 30, 1918. He was only thirty-one years old.

Nicolás Pakarati Urepotahi died in 1927, his name forever linked with the Catholic Church and the spiritual lives of Rapa Nui people. He is buried in a carefully tended plot next to Hanga Roa church, and tourists regularly snap photos of his grave. Recently, Angata's remains were removed from the old Hanga Roa cemetery and reburied in a place of honor next to him. The famous Mana Expedition picture of her, taken either by Katherine or Frank T. Green, adorns her grave.

Veriamu, Juan Tepano's mother, outlived Katherine by one year and died, at the age of about one hundred, in 1936. Tepano's children grew into very interesting individuals. Amelia learned many things from her father, married into the Pakarati family, raised her own children, and became an honored authority on traditions. Tepano's son, Jorge, who worked at Orongo in 1955 with archaeologist Edwin N. Ferdon Jr. (of the late Thor Heyerdahl's Norwegian Archaeological Expedition), told Ferdon that Swiss ethnographer Alfred Métraux challenged his memory often. Their disagreements finally came to a head one evening when Tepano, deeply annoyed and angry, shoved Métraux out of his house.

Yet Tepano's generous spirit had guided and enriched Katherine Routledge's fieldwork, and he had endured, usually quite patiently, the searching and apparently endless personal questions of those who, like Métraux, had followed in her footsteps. He left a profound legacy to world history, and his life on Rapa Nui was a personal journey through his island's past. Juan Tepano died in 1947 at about the age of eighty, and he is buried, surrounded by his family, in Hanga Roa cemetery.

AFTERWORD

✦

ON MAY 22, 1960 AN ENORMOUS TIDAL WAVE, CAUSED BY a massive earthquake off the coast of Chile, rose out of the Pacific and slammed into Ahu Tongariki. The last fragment of an upright *moai* was battered to the ground, and older statues once buried in the *ahu* were flushed into the open. The sea forced its way almost half a mile inland and, as it retreated, stranded thousands of fish, lobsters, and other sea life—all left to flop forlornly in the sun.

Five years earlier Thor Heyerdahl, leader of the Norwegian Archaeological Expedition to Easter Island (1955–56), had raised a *moai* upright on an *ahu* near Anakena. At virtually the same time the tidal wave struck, American archaeologist William Mulloy, one of Heyerdahl's original team members, was erecting seven statues at Ahu Akivi. Archaeology came into its own with the Norwegian Expedition, but the years between it and the Mana Expedition were not scientifically uneventful.

The Franco-Belgian Expedition arrived in July 1934 and departed in January 1935. The expedition's unfortunate archaeologist had died in Patagonia, but like the Mana Expedition, the shorthanded team—ethnologist Alfred Métraux, museum curator Henri Lavachery, and a Chilean doctor intending to study leprosy—carried on.

There were 456 Rapa Nui or part–Rapa Nui people living on the island then—nearly double the number of Katherine's time. Métraux and Lavchery, who had tried and failed to locate Mana Expedition papers through the British Museum, sought out Juan Tepano and everyone else still alive who had worked with Katherine.

Glumly, Métraux found the island "distressing." "I know of few places in the Pacific where so little remains of the ancient culture. The rare traditions that linger in the memory of a small group of natives have been recorded over and over again by visitors to the island."

Unlike Katherine, who never felt she had asked the last question, Métraux was certain that his ethnographic survey was thorough ("I doubt that a longer visit would have added much to my material"), then stamped "finis" to any further attempt to capture traditional history on Rapa Nui. "No important source has escaped my attention," he said, adding that his published report held "all the available documentation on the island." Métraux suggested that a team of archaeologists might spend a year on the island— although "no new information could be expected."

Padre Sebastián Englert (1888–1969) arrived within months of the Franco-Belgian Expedition. While sternly tending to the islanders' souls, he studied the Rapanui language and *rongorongo*, recorded myths and stories, and inventoried archaeological remains—including an incomplete account of many *ahu* and *moai*. Marking a significant departure from the methods of both Katherine and Métraux, Padre Englert replaced Tepano, who had died in 1947, as liaison between the Norwegian Archaeological Expedition and the Rapa Nui community.

Like the Mana Expedition, the Norwegian Archaeological Expedition was privately funded by its leader. Unlike the Routledges, however, Thor Heyerdahl brought with him a team of archaeologists who used up-to-date methods. They used the published versions of Lieutenant Ritchie's maps and Katherine's diagrammatic sketches to locate and excavate statues—this time in a professional manner. The expedition collected pollen samples; carried out time and manpower tests for carving and moving statues; developed a three-period sequence or time frame for island history, and obtained a series of radiocarbon and obsidian dates.

Heyerdahl and his colleagues believed that the Mana Expedition was a "milestone" that had thrown "a great deal of light on the problems surrounding the statues." They, like Métraux and Lavachery, did not know that Katherine's fieldnotes were on file with the Royal Geographical Society and did not have the benefit of consulting them. The expedition's incomplete but useful report offered hard evidence that the Rapa Nui culture was assuredly Polynesian—a finding that has been repeatedly validated.

Scientific life on Rapa Nui, after the Norwegian Archaeological Expedition had departed, progressed slowly but purposefully. In the 1970s the Chilean air force conducted an air reconnaissance to create contour maps, and then an initial archaeological survey pinpointed more than two thousand sites. Orongo, Rano Raraku, and other areas were placed under the care of the Chilean National Park Service.

At Anakena, a team led by Sergio Rapu Haoa made what T. A. Joyce would have called an "epoch-making" discovery: a near-perfect example of a coral and red scoria eyeball that, Rapu correctly deduced, had once been set into the carved socket of an *ahu* statue. Priests inserted the eyeballs to ritually

"open" an individual statue's eyes, perhaps during chiefly mortuary ceremonies, and to warn the community that the *moai* was alive with dangerous
power *(mana)*. Certain activities on the lands as far as the *moai* could see
would have been *tapu*, or forbidden. In the absence of open eyes *moai* were
neutral, lands were more accessible, and activities were less circumscribed.

In the 1980s Chilean archaeologists collaborated further with American,
French, and Italian researchers to extend the survey, conduct more excavations, study human remains, and reconstruct more sites. At this time, the
Royal Geographical Society made Mana Expedition fieldnotes available on
microfilm to several institutions. Katherine's journals, *Mana* logbooks and
expedition accounts, and hundreds of pages of sketches, site descriptions,
and measurements were now accessible—but if they were consulted, they
were rarely cited.

From 1992 to 1996 Chilean archaeologist Claudio Cristino raised fifteen
moai onto the rebuilt platform of Ahu Tongariki, said to be the largest ceremonial site in Polynesia. Today's visitors can see about fifty standing statues
on various *ahu* sites—none of which were erect when Katherine was on the
island. The Rapa Nui people live daily with the reborn *moai* of their ancestors, and the past is truly the present.

Astonishingly, more than twenty thousand archaeological sites have been
located to date on Rapa Nui. Ceremonial architecture orders the division of
the landscape: There are some 300 *ahu*, and about 113 of them had upright
statues. A dozen major image *ahu*, built over several generations by combined lineages led by powerful chiefs, dominate the coastal region and represent the island's most impressive building accomplishment. The majority
of surface finds, however, are gardens, shelters, and stone foundations, distributed in repeated patterns and revealing how ordinary people lived.

Elliptical houses, many of which Katherine documented, are called *hare
paenga*. They were built two or three hundred feet inland from major image
ahu, and sometimes clustered in small groups. The finest of them had terraces paved with round beach cobbles, superbly dressed basalt foundation
stones, and upright carved images at the sides of thatched, tunnel-like doorways. Poles, inserted into holes in foundation stones and arched, supported
a thatched superstructure. More modest elliptical houses, with or without
stone foundations, and some having pavements, are found at greater distances from image *ahu*.

Resembling the hull of an overturned canoe, *hare paenga* had symbolic
meanings associated with their material and shape, and are directly related
to Orongo stone buildings. The placement of *hare paenga* relative to image
ahu, and the observations made by Katherine and earlier explorers, clearly
show that these unusual houses were reserved for high-status priests and

chiefs. Twenty-eight *hare paenga* foundations ring the base of Rano Raraku, suggesting that the statue quarry was monitored as a sacred space.

Other types of houses also exist, however. Some were temporary, seasonal, or ceremonial houses. Square or rectangular buildings were clustered in large groups near Terevaka and Rano Kau, and were used by specialists who cut trees, quarried stone, transported raw materials, or built structures.

All basic households include roughly circular, stone-outlined cooking ovens *(umu pae)* that stand apart from the house and were sometimes sheltered from the wind by a thatched screen; subterranean or circular, stone-walled garden enclosures *(manavai)* that create microenvironments by collecting water and protecting plants from the wind; solidly built, rectangular stone structures *(hare moa)* said to house and hide chickens—sometimes with chiefly skulls placed inside in a ritual effort to increase egg yield—and water basins *(taheta)*.

Deep-sea fishing was never highly successful on Rapa Nui, and decreased over time. Expert fishermen used two-piece fish-hooks and large canoes to fish for chiefs, who acquired, consumed, or redistributed migratory and seasonal long-line fish, such as tuna, as well as turtles, large crayfish, and dolphin. Nets of plant fiber weighted with stone sinkers were used to take certain kinds of fish, and one early bone harpoon fragment, similar to those used in the Marquesas, was found at Anakena. Coral files and obsidian drills were used to make fishhooks of bone, but large, smooth, beautifully crafted hooks of basalt and were ceremonial. The only known parallel for such hooks is one example from Pitcairn.

All of these sites, features, and artifacts reveal a flourishing Polynesian society once humming with industrious activity. At least ten thousand people once crowded the island, and perhaps thousands more. Most of them lived in hamlets interspersed among plantations close to the coast, and on the interior they settled near water sources and on high ground. The archaeological record teaches us two clearly visible truths: ordinary people did the heavy work of food production and resource exploitation; chiefs and priests controlled access to sacred places and the use of high-status resources.

There is, without doubt, a basic cultural continuity on Rapa Nui from settlement—perhaps as early as A.D. 100–300 but certainly by A.D. 600–800 —to European contact in 1722. When language is added to the mix, a strong case may be made for the Marquesas as the primary East Polynesian distribution source, with Mangareva/Pitcarin as the Rapa Nui voyagers' probable home region—just as Katherine theorized. Some investigators have suggested that two Polynesian contacts occurred, and that the oral traditions of Hotu Matu'a date to the more recent event.

The basic outline of Rapa Nui prehistory known today is the enlightened product of intense, collaborative, and highly competitive research by international teams of scholars. When I began my fieldwork on Rapa Nui in 1982, however, a good deal less was known. My goal was to inventory the *moai* within a specific region, describe them through measurements, maps, drawings, and photographs, then to plot their relationships to the landscape and to change over time.

Initially, I consulted the microfilm copies of Mana Expedition fieldnotes, but they were frustratingly difficult to decipher. I didn't know enough about the island then to make sense of what I was reading, and I abandoned trying to integrate my work with Katherine's. In 1986 I compiled and analyzed the field data I had collected on three hundred statues and their sites to produce a stylistic analysis of the *moai*—and within a year, I had returned to the island.

Turning again to Katherine's fieldnotes, I decided to work only with the original Mana Expedition papers, not with microfilmed versions. In 1987 I made the first of many subsequent pilgrimages to London and the Royal Geographical Society. Katherine's handwriting, in the original, was still impossibly difficult. As I began to excavate my way through her papers, however, I became as interested in the woman who had produced them as I was in what she had turned up about the *moai*.

In 1992 I found a torn scrap of paper that suggested Katherine or someone else had selectively edited or censored her fieldnotes—and then I discovered the full and tragic story of her mental illness. I almost gave up, fearing that by detailing her life history I would discredit or damage her scholarship. Instead, I discovered that on Easter Island she was engaged, invigorated, and in control of her illness. This fact—which took me years to establish—guides my use of her fieldnotes, and it should encourage other researchers who use them.

I continue to move toward my final goal of documenting every statue. In this, I suppose, I have been as obsessive as Katherine was in scribbling down the memories of the past. The *moai* are unique objects for archaeological study. They contain within them hard evidence of how artisans shaped them and how ancient engineers moved and erected them. Their placement on the landscape and in relation to other structures discloses their function, and their aesthetic reveals belief.

In 1989 Cristián Arévalo Pakarati, the great-grandson of both Juan Tepano and Nicolás Pakarati Urepotahi, joined my project. Cristián's first job was nothing more than holding the ladder while I climbed statues—today he is Easter Island Statue Project co-investigator. We have trod the same paths Katherine and Tepano did, gazed at the same statues, and pondered the same questions.

As of this writing, we have collected full descriptions of 887 statues (some reconstructed from fragments) and mapped the interior of Rano Raraku quarry using the latest in GPS technology. We have filed thousands of photographic images, line drawings, field sketches and notes, maps, and statue measurements in interactive, computer-based records; sorted the statues into groups based on location, shape, material, and other variables. Statue groups have been arranged into a developmental series, and although *moai* cannot be directly dated, they can be integrated into a slowly unfolding time line.

Moai appeared first in the vicinity of Ahu Nau Nau (Anakena) by at least A.D. 1000–1100, and perhaps several centuries earlier at Ahu Ko Te Riku (Tahai). They spread tentatively, and then quite rapidly, on Miru coastal sites. Certain *moai* attributes, including spiral carvings on the buttocks, neck details, and dorsal designs, are unique to Anakena and emblematic of the paramount chief. The *moai* is an icon that merges Rapa Nui's mythical, ancestral founder with that of individual, deified chiefs.

In the early stages of *moai* development carvers experimented with basalt and red scoria as sculptural materials, but diagnostic details were established quickly and then innovated only rarely—demonstrating their role as key metaphors in a fundamental belief system. The rounded contours of early *moai* were refined and then streamlined until nearly all curved lines were lost. Within about one hundred years *moai* had been reshaped into a simplified, utilitarian, largely rectangular form carved nearly exclusively from Rano Raraku stone.

Image *ahu* platforms began as modest structures, settled into a general architectural pattern, and proliferated. At the most important bayside sites, they increased in complexity through continuous rebuilding and enlargement. The *moai* increased in size and weight over time, and their features became increasingly but proportionately elongated—their entire forms stretching, as it were, toward the sky. The reerected *moai* visitors see today all evolved out of earlier, smaller statues, and the most interesting of them are carved of red scoria.

Katherine did not see the red scoria statues we have found—some of which have her "ring and girdle" design representing the *hami* (loincloth) and sash *(maro)* of chiefly authority. Neither did she discern any points of comparison between Rapa Nui *moai* and the single known red scoria statue fragment of Pitcairn, or others in the Austral Islands—but there are commonalities. Red scoria statues are a minor but persistent counterpoint to *moai* development, a parallel strand of art with a long history. The transference of the early *moai* concept from—or, perhaps, to—the Pitcairn/Australs region is traceable through red scoria statues.

How *moai* were transported from Rano Raraku to *ahu* was one of the basic questions that the Mana Expedition attempted to answer, but Scoresby finally admitted he was stumped. He felt more certain about carving procedures, and proposed that a master carver and a crew of fifty-four men could carve a thirty-foot-tall statue in fifteen and a half days, using stone tools.

Scoresby suggested that thirty men first isolated a rectangular stone block, then undercut it to balance on a stone "keel." Simultaneously, twenty-four other men could sculpt details of the upper surface, sides, top, and base. The amount of stone to be hewn, by his careful calculation, was 1,690 cubic feet, with each man able to remove about two cubic feet per day. Even if the workforce were reduced by 50 percent, Scoresby noted, the task could still have been accomplished in one month.

His understanding of work steps was correct, but our interior quarry map illustrates that the standing space there for individual carvers—in canals averaging about a foot wide and sloping twenty-four to thirty-two degrees—was too limited to accommodate even his most conservative number of twenty-seven workers. Reducing it by at least 10 percent, and increasing the number of days proportionately, would result in a more accurate estimate.

We actually carved a full-scale replica statue (representing the statistically average height of thirteen feet), and discovered that detail work was most efficiently accomplished with one master craftsman in control and one or two assistants. Throwing a fishnet over a supine statue created a measurement grid. Unfinished projects clearly show that heads and faces were carved first, and the nose was used to align all features.

Since the Norwegian Archaeological Expedition's attempt to move a statue at Anakena by dragging it—and Heyerdahl later "walked" a statue a few feet by manipulating it upright—other theories have been advanced and other tests conducted. It is highly unlikely that one method worked in all cases, and strategies certainly varied with terrain, statue size, and resources. We will never know for sure how it was done, but we can speculate within what is known about Polynesian preindustrial technology. Builders of houses and makers of canoes used a defined range of tools and techniques to cut and move massive stone or coral blocks, or to lift and carry tree trunks.

In 1998, on a plot of land midway between Rano Raraku and Ahu Tongariki, my colleagues and I used our full-scale statue replica to test the validity of our transport hypothesis. We conducted a series of replicable and fully evaluated pretests and experiments, one of which was filmed and broadcast by PBS Nova.

Our replica moai was placed horizontally on a specially rigged, pegged, and lashed A-frame log sled. The sled was based on simple design principles of flexibility and balance known to precontact Polynesian outrigger-canoe makers. Horizontal cross beams, which we originally thought might be used as rollers, were lashed under the sled to create a "canoe ladder," an ingenious device used by Polynesians to haul heavy canoes up and over rocky cliff sides. Two rope crews pulled the replica statue, on its transport frame with attached beams, over parallel wood logs on relatively flat ground.

We demonstrated that fifty to seventy Rapa Nui men, women, and children could efficiently, even relatively easily, do this work. We calculated that the statue, in this manner, could traverse nine miles in about five to seven days—an event that was certainly accompanied by feasting and ceremony. In all, the average chief mobilized about 395 to 435 people (eight and half extended families) for this task. They, in turn, produced, consumed, and used (in rope making, for example) the surplus agricultural and available timber resources of at least fifty acres of land—but foods such as crayfish and tuna were reserved for the high-status chiefs, priests, and master craftspeople.

Twenty expert workmen raised our replica statue, still on its transport frame and with topknot in place, upright on a replica *ahu*. This work—based, in part, on methods used restoring Ahu Akivi—required more time and patience, an orderly exchange of information along clear lines of authority, and a high degree of expertise. In addition, carving, hauling, lifting, and raising stone to build and expand *ahu* consumed even more massive amounts of energy. Expending such human and natural resources in prehistory created a passionately transforming social force inspired by the gods, demanded by the chief, and channeled by the *moai*.

The stone giants—in Katherine's time and now—stand at the heart of the allure of Easter Island. The destiny of a seafaring people isolated on a small island was to shape their beliefs into an image in human form and then, for at least twenty generations, to repeat that image until they had reshaped their island. Control of statue form, conformity of design, and consistent use of material all demonstrate the continuity of a stable internal social structure. The large number and island-wide distribution of *moai* reveal the successful production of surplus food. The overall pattern of the natural environment was predictable and, therefore, conducive to statue production, from at least A.D. 1100 to A.D. 1500.

Rapa Nui society had achieved a high degree of internal integration, but by 1500 the energy output demanded by ambitious and competitive chiefs—all but one of them in Hotu Iti territory—had escalated. In part because of this pressure, archaeologists infer the gradual disintegration of major multilineage alignments, although family unity on the household level remains apparent. By European contact in 1722 the island was essentially deforested—although there were still productive plantations and gardens—and toppled statues and conspicuous warrior chiefs revealed conflict and violence.

Archaeologist Patrick Kirch has pointed out that deforested island environments were often the inevitable result of ancient Polynesian practices of clearing and burning vegetation to create living and gardening space. Forest clearance caused the erosion of thin island soils, especially on hillsides, and destroyed land-bird habitat. Easter Island tantalizes because it represents the enigma of passion: profoundly creative energy can raise rational individuals—or reasonable societies—to new heights, but why does it also cause excess that sweeps everything away to destruction?

Recent, interesting Pacific environmental research holds part of the answer: nine variables, among them small size, isolation, altitude, latitude, soils, and rainfall levels, define the ecological fragility level of eighty islands in a database—and *Rapa Nui possesses every variable*. That remarkable revelation describes not only a crucial part of the island's natural condition but sets out a hypothesis of its destiny: Rapa Nui's deeply vulnerable ecological deck, metaphorically speaking, was stacked against Polynesian settlers.

Rapa Nui holds the dubious distinction, alone among eighty environmentally fragile islands identified, of having been completely deforested and transformed into grassland. Necker, Nihoa, and Niihau in the Hawaiian group are the only other islands studied to have approximated that dismal condition.

Scoresby pointed out the negative environmental and social impact of deforestation in Africa, and he certainly recognized it on Easter Island. Today, while narrow-viewed political experts endlessly argue the economic nuances of forest depletion, most schoolchildren recognize that the inexorable pace of worldwide deforestation threatens planetary ecology.

Deforestation—whether it is to clear ground for planting crops, to provide fuel for cooking, to stoke the raging fires of chiefly crematoria, or to build transport rigs and lay rails to move mighty statues—leads to soil depletion, a decrease in fertility, a lessening of productivity, and a decline or permanent loss of plant species. Palm forest was harvested as early as A.D. 147–676 at Rano Kau, and by A.D. 950 it had been cleared there. It has long been known that, in the vicinity of Poike, vegetation was burned as early as A.D. 235–615.

The full extent of soil damage on Rapa Nui, however, and our understanding of the social change it may have caused, remains tentative. Nonetheless, it is probable that a decreased crop yield encouraged the perception that there was a loss of chiefly *mana*. Over time, such perceptions create negative attitudes that can destabilize a tradition-based social system and cause conflict.

Ravaged soils can be rejuvenated by lying fallow or by enrichment with fertilizers. Less obvious is the natural restorative power of fallout from tephra volcanic ash, burning vegetation, or continental dust clouds—yet another indicator of island fragility. The eastward-moving Southeast Asia dust cloud floats across the Pacific as a plume, decreasing in size as it deposits trace ions that enrich soils. Those islands that are forested fare better from such fallout than those that are not: trees capture ten to twenty times more dust than do grasslands.

Rapa Nui is on the outermost, impoverished edge of the Southeast Asia dust cloud, and the island's deforested state made it impossible for its soils to benefit from the small chance of fallout. Given the marginal environment of Rapa Nui, researchers have naturally assumed that deforestation was detrimental. Ominously, it is now clear that the damage it caused was irreversible.

Standing today, as Katherine so often did, on Rano Raraku's highest vantage point, and gazing out over the island's treeless and once densely populated southeastern plain of Hotu Iti, one can see a region once alive with building, remodeling, and reconstruction. Sites such as Tongariki grew out of powerfully effective and far-reaching, challenging political alliances. The tempo of statue carving reached a crescendo in Hotu Iti, and it is clear that the region produced—but also consumed—the lion's share of food and resources.

From the 1500s, however, statues destined for Hotu Iti were abandoned along the roads from Rano Raraku; others were toppled from *ahu*. Image *ahu* construction on lands belonging to all but the island's most united and tradition-bound families slowed and then gradually ceased—the stubborn Miru chief at faraway Ahu Akivi was one of the last to erect *moai*. Deforestation, coupled with soil depletion, slow plant regeneration, and the depredations of human-introduced rats to land-bird populations and to the palm nut (required for reforestation), created plant and bird extinctions and food shortages. What did Rapa Nui people do?

In empirical studies it has been consistently found that individuals, and whole societies, choose or innovate religious strategies to cope with disturbing stress, change, and loss. On Rapa Nui, Orongo birdman ceremonies placed strong emphasis on nontraditional access to the gods through revealed knowledge, rather than through hereditary ancestry, and through the channeling of supernatural power by seasonally anointed priests.

Orongo emerged in an atmosphere of environmental unpredictability, resource overuse, alliance dissolution, and a crisis of confidence in Miru *mana*. The *moai*, however, didn't disappear. The tallest and most impressively elegant *moai* were carved in the exterior quarries of Rano Raraku. Tall statues in a kneeling posture, a form that had been slowly evolving, emerged at Rano Raraku and elsewhere. At Poike, a few statues were carved of trachyte. Most important, Hoa Hakananai'a became a centerpiece of Orongo.

Orongo ceremonies, and their symbols, evolved on the island out of a complex web of motivation and necessity, but Mother Nature probably also played a part. Prolonged floods and drought in South America, and marked environmental change in the Desolate Region surrounding Rapa Nui, are often caused by El Niño–Southern Oscillation (ENSO) events. In such cases, the migratory patterns of birds and fish are interrupted or diverted.

In the Moche Valley of Peru, for example, the Miraflores Flood Episode of A.D. 1350 caused house and infrastructure loss on a massive scale. The immediate aftermath was disease and famine; the long-term results were settlement abandonment, population decline, and important changes in ideology and art. In the same area, at another time, severe drought created heightened competition, increased movement of people, and the emergence of new disaster management strategies by the ruling classes.

Twenty-two ENSO events described as "strong" occurred from 1525 to 1722—the period encompassing the expansion of Orongo. Eight "strong" ENSO events happened in the 1500s alone, and one described as "very strong" took place in 1578. Although none of them, alone, would have altered the course of Rapa Nui history, any of them, in the context of stress, might have induced change or demanded adjustments.

Manavai, stone mulching in agricultural fields, and other inland farming adaptations were small-scale technological attempts to conserve water and protect plants from wind damage. There is, as yet, little evidence, however, of societywide, nonideological adaptive coping strategies. Rapa Nui chiefs were proven successes at organizing great public works. Why didn't they build extensive irrigation systems to deal with drought, as on Hawaii? Why didn't they build fortified defenses to deal with aggression, as on Pitcairn?

Such responses, if needed, demand social organization, political order, and a unifying ideological principle, as well as an institutional ability to recognize crisis as long-term rather than occasional. Timing is also of vital importance. While it is certain that Rapa Nui society unraveled, contact with the West in 1722 interrupted, ruptured, redirected, and nearly destroyed it. We will never know, as a result, how internal history would otherwise have played out.

Katherine Routledge's Easter Island work, like my own and that of all others, is flawed and incomplete, but I believe important aspects of it will stand the test of time. She made two contributions that will certainly last: her book, *The Mystery of Easter Island,* is a significant tool of public education that has recently been reborn through reprinting, and she salvaged extremely important, fragmented memories of island traditions that otherwise would have been lost. While it is completely true that Katherine's association with Juan Tepano shaped, to a certain extent, the information she collected, it just as surely enhanced her effectiveness.

Katherine came to the island in the wake of many ships and many people, bringing along her family history, unique gifts, and profound troubles. Wilson Pease, Katherine's beloved brother, noted that "blood is thicker than ink and a relationship to historical characters must introduce an intimate touch to history." I have tried to bring such an "intimate touch" to this story, to illustrate the significance of the Mana Expedition's work and the monumentality of Katherine Routledge's life struggle.

Writing Katherine's biography has interrupted, for five years, my research, but it has also enriched it. The island, however, is a very different place from what it was in Katherine's day; it is also quite changed from the time when I began my fieldwork. Tourism, archaeology, and technology have fueled cultural growth and rediscovery. Three thousand or more people now live on the island—a large portion of them not Rapa Nui—and they own homes, vehicles, fax machines, computers, telephones, and televisions.

There are paved roads, hotels, shops and restaurants, arts festivals, and sports clubs. Government leaders, teachers, and citizens alike see their island changing, and as Rapa Nui's past becomes clearer, the unfolding lessons of history gain immediacy. Deforestation was the product of ancient cultural behavior, and it caused irreversible environmental damage on an ecologically fragile island. Conflict and chaos resulted, but so did extremely creative attempts to restructure and reinvent religion and society.

Irreversible, human-created environmental damage and destruction, wherever it occurs, is a cultural calamity. Instructive parallels can be drawn, of course, between continental environments and island ecosystems, between states and chiefdoms, between the past and the present—but taking preventative or mitigating action requires time and vision. The challenge to the island, however, is personal and immediate. Tepano would be gratified to know that a repatriation program is returning hereditary lands to their rightful owners, but he would also point out that stewardship of the land is vital.

Archaeological site preservation often conflicts with community land use, affecting the island's most important cultural resource and economic asset: the moai. Our records are essential to statue preservation, and it is hoped that Rapa Nui people will use them to restore and conserve family sites. It is impossible to save all the moai, but they will continue to exist in Katherine's fieldnotes and in our more detailed inventory.

Even as the *moai* change and the island moves inexorably forward, the sea is still a deeper blue than anywhere else on earth, and the clouds still move breathtakingly fast overhead. The seductive promise of discovery is still there, and I can wander the grassy slopes in silence. The wind, as in Katherine's day, still communes with the stone giants and the spirits that haunt them. They wait, in stoic silence, for someone or something we can never know.

Jo Anne Van Tilburg
Malibu, California, 2002

NOTES

✦

ABBREVIATIONS OF MANUSCRIPT, ARCHIVE, MUSEUM, AND FAMILY COLLECTION SOURCES FREQUENTLY CITED

BGS British Geological Survey, Kingsley Dunham Centre, Keyworth, Nottingham. Correspondence on file between WSR and J. A. Howe, 1916.

BL The British Library Map Room.
1. 97300 (1) Easter Island, "one of the draughts to Captain Cook's second voyage."
2. 147.e.10 (31) Easter Island, Paris 1790(?).
3. H.F. SEC. 15 (541) Easter Island, Paris 1840(?).
4. SEC. 15 (1386) Easter Island, Lieutenant C. M. Dundas, HMS *Topaze*, 1868.
5. H.F. SEC. 15 (3028) Easter Island, *O'Higgins*, 1782.
6. SEC. 15 (1386) Easter Island, Chilean Government Survey, 1870; British Admiralty Chart, 1876.
7. Additional MS. 15,500.7 Easter Island, Cook's second voyage, pl. 9.

BL UCB Bancroft Library, University of California, Berkeley. Department and Museum of Anthropology Correspondence Records hold letters between KSR and T. Waterman, H. E. Gregory, E. W. Gifford, and A. L. Kroeber.

BM British Museum, London. Katherine and William Scoresby Routledge.
1. Glass lantern slides (369 slides in six boxes, each slide currently being numbered individually) taken by members of the Mana Expedition to Easter Island, 1913–15, and during the second Routledge voyage to the South Pacific, 1920–23. Received from unknown source in the 1970s. From these, negatives (with MMOO numbers) and prints have been made.
2. Ethnodocs. Numbered and filed correspondence and other papers related to Katherine and William Scoresby Routledge and the British Museum, beginning in 1921. Some earlier correspondence is filed by year and alphabetically (with no index) and held by British Museum, Department of Medieval and Modern Europe.
3. Af1904, 0613.1–38 shows thirty-eight East African objects donated in 1904 by WSR, Conservative Club, London.
4. Af1910, 0305.1–13 and Af1910, 0604.1–103 show 116 descriptive entries for objects from East Africa donated in 1910 by WSR, Waterside, Bursledon, Hants, and four additional descriptive entries (Af1979.01.2439, 2450, 2454, 2449).
5. 1920, 0506 shows 197 descriptive entries for objects from Easter Island donated in 1920 by WSR. T. A. Joyce was invited by WSR to select the objects personally.

6. Ethnography Department Register, vol. 5, shows descriptive entries with accompanying sketches for objects (Oc 1925 1019.1–117) from Mangareva and other islets in the Gambier Islands, the Australs, and Pitcairn including about thirty adzes, donated in 1925 by WSR.

7. Presentation copy of *With a Prehistoric People: The Akikuyu of British East Africa.*

BMNH   British Museum (Natural History), now known as the Natural History Museum (NHM), London. Keeper of Zoology Out-letters to WSR include DF 201/8, 28 Oct. 1916, and DF 201/9, 11 Oct. 1917. Keeper's letter register DF 204/8, 28 Oct. 1916, describes "Mass of Vermetus" presented by J. F. Bartram from Bermuda with letter from WSR.

BOD MS   Bodleian Library, University of Oxford, Department of Special Collections and Western Manuscripts. "Uncatalogued Papers of O. G. S. Crawford." Six boxes of papers containing twenty-nine bundles of correspondence written or received by Crawford, his sister, and two aunts, and nine sealed envelopes enclosing various notes and memorandums by Crawford. Included are letters to or from the Routledges, Lieutenant Ritchie, Frank T. Green, R. R. Marett, and encompassing the period of the Mana Expedition to Easter Island. Access derestricted in 2000.

BPB   Bernice Pauahi Bishop Museum of Polynesian Ethnology and Natural History (Bishop Museum), Honolulu, Hawaii. Correspondence and objects concerning Easter Island (Rapa Nui) on file, including about 150 negatives and/or photographs taken by PE.

D/GP   Durham Record Office/Gurney Pease family of Darlington. Estate and Family Records, Gurney Pease Collection. Diaries and letters of Gurney Pease [GP] of Woodside, Darlington, and his son, Wilson Pease [WP], deposited by J. C. Gurney Pease, Holdip Hill, Headley, Newbury, Berkshire, 11 Nov. 1972.

1. D/GP 46288. Letters.
2. D/GP 46289–90. Articles and stories written by GP and WP, 1874–1924.
3. D/GP 46291–92. Papers concerning the estates of GP and WP, 1874–1924.
4. D/GP 3–15 46293–315. Diaries of GP (13 vols.), 1860–72.
5. D/GP 16–54 46216–54. Handwritten diaries of WP (39 vols.), 1890–1918; 1921–22. These are referenced in my text as D/GP, followed by my item no. 5 (diaries).
6. D/GP 57–75 46257–275. Transcripts of diaries of WP, 1890–1918, by Humphrey Allen Bucknall. These are referenced in my text as D/GP, followed by my item no. 6 (transcripts), followed by volume number and page number.
7. D/XD 63. Abstract of a conveyance, Arthur Pease as trustee of the will of GP (1 file).
8. D/XD 5. Records of the Pease family deposited by N. A. Pease, Esq., 24 July 1979.
9. E/Da. Logbook of the Gurney Pease School.
10. D/PS. Papers of Pease/Stephenson.
11. D/GP 76. Index of persons, places, Peases, in D/GP 57–75.
12. D/XD 64/1/1–17; D/XD 64/2/1–61; D/XD 64/3/1–37. Miscellaneous documents, Darlington: Gurney Pease correspondence.

D/GMP   Durham Record Office/Gwendolen Margaret Pease (GMP) papers, 297 pages, 1905–56 (D/XD 64/4).

D/KP   Durham Record Office/Katherine Pease (KP) (née Wilson). Miscellaneous journals and diaries, Darlington (D/XD 64/7/1–4).

1. Journal of John Gurney of Keswick, b. 1716.
2. Torn scrap referring to KSR, Dresden to Coblentz (n.d.).
3. D/XD 64/7/4. Sketch of the last illness of Francis Richard Pease by JWP.

4. Papers of Katherine Pease, née Wilson, 1863–74. Three small volumes bound together, including
    4a. D/XD 64/7/1. Book possibly compiled by KP, 1 vol. and 2 pp., 1846–1905, "Some dates of family doings."
    4b. D/XD 64/7/3. KP's memories of family life, 1 vol., 5 unnumbered pp., 1863–74.

D/PE   Durham Record Office, Pease family of Darlington. Estate and family records, correspondence, and papers.

DPL   Darlington Public Library, Local History Study Room, including Pease family photographic albums (U418ePEA), news cuttings, and Durham County Local History Project audiotapes.

DQB   "Dictionary of Quaker Biography." Unpublished typescripts of collected biographical details and some published references for various members of the Society of Friends, including Pease, Wilson, Whitwell, and other KSR family. Religious Society of Friends in Britain, Friends House, London.

DTC   Darlington Training College records held at Durham County Record Office, including:
    1. Staff Register.
    2. DTC *Magazine* (E/DAR/2/81).
    3. "Some Experiences of South Africa," written by KSR (E/DAR/2/83).

JGP/JVT   Correspondence between Joseph Gurney Pease (JGP) and Jo Anne Van Tilburg (JVT) on the subject of KSR, the Pease family of Yorkshire, and WSR, 1995–98, including extracts from the original letters, diaries, and journals of Joseph Whitwell Pease (JWP), Alfred Edward Pease (AEP) and Lady Pease (Helen Ann Fowler), Maud Pease, and others in the collection of JGP. Copies on file, JVT and JGP.

MPSE   Museo Antropológico Padre Sebastián Englert, Hanga Roa, Isla de Pascua (Easter Island). Colección Fotográfica. Ethnographic and archaeological photographs by Percy Edmunds and others. Prints of some photos in the British Museum Mana Expedition collection were included in a special exhibit, *Katherine Routledge y la Expedición Mana a Isla de Pascua, 1914–1915* (Hanga Roa and London, 1995).

OGSC   O.G.S.C. Photo Collection, University of Oxford. Uncatalogued photographs, including a few from the Mana Expedition, en route to Easter Island, taken by Frank T. Green and sent to Crawford as postcards or enclosures.

PB   Peter Bucknall (PB) private family papers, selected letters, news cuttings, and photographs pertaining to the family lives of KSR and WSR, including correspondence between PB and JVT and photos. Copies on file, JVT.

PE   Percy Edmunds selected letters and other documents on file, Routledge collection, RGS.

PRM   Pitt Rivers Museum, University of Oxford. 694 objects (beginning 1916.36.1, see object catalogue 14.1.02, on-line) donated by WSR from February of 1913 to 1934 and collected in Africa, Easter Island, East Polynesia, Patagonia, John Crow Mountains, and elsewhere. Henry Balfour was invited by WSR to personally select Mana Expedition objects. East Polynesian objects include stone implements, among them about twenty adzes and assorted obsidian spear points. In 1951, his heir, John Charles Dundas Harington, donated objects collected by WSR.

PRO   Public Record Office, London.

RBG   Royal Botanic Gardens, Kew. Archive holds three letters to the director from WSR in 1906 and a list of plants received from WSR in British East Africa, 1909.

RB/JVT   Correspondence between Reggie Barnes and JVT regarding the Routledge yacht *Mana* and their journey to Mangareva, and photos. Copies on file, JVT and RB.

REB   Rosemary Elizabeth Blair private family papers held by Pauleen West (PW), and photos. Selected copies on file, JVT.

RGS LBR   Royal Geographical Society (with the Institute of British Geographers) Library (see PE above and WBCO below).
1. Library Y 222.4. Copy of interview given to *The* (London) *Times* by WSR about his Jamaica expedition.

RGS MR   Royal Geographical Society (with the Institute of British Geographers) Map Room, London.
1. The "Mana Expedition to Easter Island, Track of the 'Mana,'" 18 May 1917.
2. Pacific OC.S/S.101. "Rapanui or Easter Island" by Lieutenant Colin Dundas, RN, HMS *Topaze*, 1868, showing J. L. Palmer's route and locations of two monolithic statues removed and presented to Queen Victoria, who, in turn, presented them to the British Museum.
3. Pacific OC.S.117. Rough survey map of Easter Island south coast with notes on sites 19A to 41A by Lieutenant D. R. Ritchie, RN, 7 June 1961.
4. Pacific OS.S.117. Rough survey map of Easter Island south coast, including Tongariki and Rano Raraku, along with key to symbols, by Lieutenant D. R. Ritchie, RN, 7 June 1961.
5. Pacific S 95. Finished, large-scale survey map in three parts, including Rano Kau (showing outlines of stone buildings and pathway inside the crater) and Rano Raraku, by Lieutenant D. R. Ritchie, RN, for WSR, Esq.
6. Sheet 5375, Isla de Pascua, Chile G2. Santiago de Chile: Instituto Geográfico Militar, 1954. Showing Canal Mana.

RGS PL   Royal Geographical Society (with the Institute of British Geographers) Picture Library, London.
1. Items numbered A 19675–723, A 26632–715, B 7897–908, consist of 142 negatives of photographs (of which 40 prints are on file) taken on Easter Island by members of the Mana Expedition. Presented by J. C. (Dundas) Harington, 7 June 1948 (Routledge PR/055183). For cross-reference see descriptive letterpress for certain photographs offered for newspaper reproduction with captions by WSR and edits by KSR, RGS Routledge Collection item 4/14/8.
2. Items numbered X677/024261–104273 consist of matted photographs taken in Chile and on Easter Island by members of the Mana Expedition and presented by WSR. Acc. 27 Feb. 1917.
3. Items numbered PR/055184–7 and PR/042881 consist of photographs taken on Easter Island by Major A. J. A. Douglas, 1924–25.
4. Numbered items PR/055188–PR/1055226 consist of photographs taken on Easter Island by the Reverend E. Stockins, 1953.
5. Item F30 is an album of pen-and-ink and chalk drawings, and watercolors done by J. Linton Palmer while serving aboard HMS *Topaze* when it called at Easter Island, 1868.
6. Items Chile (Chl) 2–5 are photographs of maps and plans (see RGS Map Room above) made by Lieutenant D. R. Ritchie for the Mana Expedition to Easter Island.

RGS PMB   Royal Geographical Society (with the Institute of British Geographers), Pacific Manuscripts Bureau. The Routledge Collection filed as Papers of Katherine Scoresby Routledge, relating chiefly to Easter Island, 1911–12 (microfilmed version of the Routledge Collection for PMB, Research School of Pacific Studies, The Australian National University, Canberra, A.C.T. 2600 [PMB 531]). Referenced by reel designation. Copies held at the National Library of Australia, Canberra; the State Library of Victoria, Melbourne; the National Library of New Zealand, Wellington; Auckland Public Library, New Zealand; the Library of the University of Hawai'i, Honolulu; and Instituto de Estudios de Isla de Pascua, Universidad de Chile, Santiago. Paper copy only held by the Rock Art Archive, The Cotsen Institute of Archaeology at UCLA (R1–R12).

RGS WKR   Royal Geographical Society (with the Institute of British Geographers) Archives: The Routledge Collection, including the Mana Expedition to Easter Island papers, together with some papers concerning WSR's expedition to cross the John Crow Mountains, Jamaica. Because Items 1 through 6 below were left at the RGS in 1929 by WSR, on loan, the collection is referenced under his name as 402/WSR and included as such in the national "Access to Archives" listing (www.a2a.pro.gov.uk). The reference employed here (WKR), however, was suggested by A. Tatham and more accurately reflects the joint authorship of the materials.

    1. Logbooks of yacht *Mana*, 1913–16 (15 vols.).

    2. Burgee of the yacht.

    3. Lists of *Mana* stores and accounts.

    4. Correspondence, collection of source material, rough notebooks giving vocabularies, genealogies, ethnological notes, drawings, photographs, etc. of Easter Island. Catalogue of Easter Island collection given to the British Museum. Manuscript copy of *The Mystery of Easter Island: The Story of an Expedition*. Material divided into subcategories 4/1 to 4/22. KSR's chronological journal is marked 4/9. KSR gives dates as, for example, April 26, 1914. Some correspondence is dated as, for example, 26 April 1914. Other papers are undated or only partially dated. This lack of consistency is reflected in the footnotes here. Items 4/12, 4/14, 4/17–18, 4/20 are in a white tin trunk labeled "Mrs. S. Routledge."

    5. Tracings of rock carvings, sketch plans, lantern slides, from Easter Island. Divided into subcategories 5/1 to 5/2. In tin trunk (see above).

    6. One folder of notes and correspondence on WSR's crossing of John Crow Mountains, 1920–33.

    7. Two albums of news cuttings, chiefly reviews of *The Mystery of Easter Island*. Two albums of news cuttings, chiefly reviews of *With a Prehistoric People: The Akikuyu of British East Africa*. Presented by Professor James R. Stewart, 1961 (see Director's Corr files, 1961).

    8. Box of index cards: vocabulary of Mangareva and of proper names on Mangareva showing relationships. Presented by Professor James R. Stewart, 1961; for notes on photographic negatives, Mangareva, see item 4/14/4.

    9. Journal MS Islands 402/JMS/1917. Discussion notes after lecture by K. Routledge on Easter Island, and letters, B. G. Corney.

    10. Campbell, Commander A. B., 402/CB/1921–30, includes one letter from K. Routledge.

    11. Routledge, W. S., and Mrs. K. Routledge, 402/CB/1881–1910; 1911–20; 1921–30.

RH   Sir Richard Harington private family papers and collections, held by Sir Nicholas Harington; correspondence between Sir Nicholas Harington and JVT. Copies and photos on file, JVT.

SCO   Somerville College, Oxford, library holds presentation copies of various Routledge and Pease family volumes.

WBCO   Williamson, Balfour & Co. Selected letters on file, Routledge papers, RGS. Company archives contain duplicates of some Mana Expedition letters on file, RGS, and a few others referring to the Mana Expedition or to the Routledges.

ABBREVIATIONS OF PUBLISHED SOURCES FREQUENTLY CITED

BCEI   Routledge, Katherine. 1917. "The bird cult of Easter Island." *Folk-Lore* 28 (4): 338–55.

EI   Van Tilburg, Jo Anne. 1994. *Easter Island Archaeology, Ecology and Culture*. London: British Museum Press.

JGP   Pease, Joseph Gurney. 1992. *A Wealth of Happiness and Many Bitter Trials: The Journals of Sir Alfred Edward Pease, a Restless Man.* York: William Sessions Ltd., The Ebor Press.

MEI   Routledge, Mrs. Scoresby. 1919. *The Mystery of Easter Island.* London: Sifton, Praed & Co. Ltd.

OEI   Routledge, Katherine 1920. "Survey of the village and carved rocks of Orongo, Easter Island, by the Mana Expedition." *The Journal of the Royal Anthropological Institute of Great Britain and Ireland* 50: 425–51.

WPP   Routledge, W. S., and K. Routledge. 1910. *With a Prehistoric People: The Akikuyu of British East Africa.* London: Frank Cass & Co. Ltd.

A NOTE ON SPELLING AND PRONUNCIATION

xi. The modern Polynesian name—I am following my own standard orthography in this matter (as previously stated in Van Tilburg 1994:10 and Krupa 1982:43–119). *Rapa Nui* is the official Chilean spelling of the island and is used nearly unanimously by islanders (cf. Hotus y Otros 1988), making it rather confusing at the moment to use the linguistically more correct *Rapanui*. Precedents for the practice of employing Westernized spellings of island names exist in many places in Oceania (cf. Hawaii/Hawai'i [Kirch 1990:51 n. 5]; Englert 1978; Green 1988); Finney and Alexander 1998 discuss the Rapanui language and recent changes in it.

PROLOGUE

xiv. "Half sunk, a shatter'd"—Shelley 1994.

xv. Today we know—Preliminary results of the modern statue inventory, a follow-up to three earlier, incomplete projects (Thomson 1891; Routledge 1919; and unpublished Mana Expedition fieldnotes [RGS WKR]; Cornejo and Atan [Van Tilburg and Vargas 1998]; and Englert 1948), may be seen in Cristino et al. 1981; Van Tilburg 1986, 1987, 1988, 1993, 1994; Van Tilburg and Vargas 1998; Vargas 1993.

ANCESTOR WORSHIP: SOUTHEND, 1866

3. "It was my misfortune"—This phrase is taken from the transcribed diary of Wilson Pease (hereafter, WP) (D/GP 6, v. 2, p. 79) and cross-checks with the original handwritten diary (D/GP 5, 7 Aug. 1892).

3. "I'm thinking of"—D/GP 6, v. 1, 15 Jan. 1891, 20 Jan. 1891.

3. "I can quite understand"—D/GP 6, v. 1, 15 Jan. 1891.

4. "an eternal stone armada"—Fowles 1978:5; the Scilly Isles comprise more than 150 islands, islets, and rocks located about thirty miles off Land's End. Five of them are inhabited.

4. "that of God"—The term *Quaker* was used by early critics in mockery, because "the early Quakers urged people to tremble at the Word of the Lord" (Glover 1984:12; Hufton 1996:418–20). The movement has had several names, including Friends in Truth. The name Religious Society of Friends came into use by 1800, but today the terms Society of Friends and Quakers are used interchangeably (Brayshaw 1982:44). *Historical note:* At Fox's death in 1691 there were 50,000 Friends in Britain. Today the membership is 20,000 in Britain and Ireland and about 240,000 worldwide.

5. "priesthood of all"—Individual testimony in Meeting may be given by anyone, male or female, young or old. This has been recognized since the inception of the religion. By 1697 women ministers were granted the right to sit in official meetings.

5. "studying to be"; "gathered"—D/GP 6, v. 6, p. 11.

5. "child of God"; "Inner Light"—Ibid.

5. "all the ecstasy"—Ibid.

6. Quakers of the—The promise of obedience was omitted from Quaker marriage cere-

monies on the grounds that it was not "in accordance with the Quaker ideas of perfect equality" (Raistrick 1950:24; Brayshaw 1982; Samuel 1998:304).

6. "and that one person"—Samuel 1998:204.

7. "spooks"; "voices"—After Easter Island, Katherine Scoresby Routledge (hereafter, KSR) routinely referred to her auditory hallucinations as "spooks" and channeled them through the Spiritualist practice of "automatic writing." See also Leudar and Thomas 2000.

7. "father of English railways"—DQB, Pease, Joseph (1799–1872); Sir Alfred Edward Pease (hereafter, AEP) 1907 showed that the first Pease was of Baddow, Essex, in Henry VII's time (D/GP 6, v. 25, p. 28); Emden 1939; Raistrick 1950; Joseph Gurney Pease (hereafter, JGP) 1992:viii–xvi gives an overview and background of Pease family enterprises; "The Peases of Darlington" in The British Workman, Special No. Jan. 1873 (DPL U418ePEA PB 19). Edward Pease's (1767–1858) brick and cobblestone home at 146 Northgate is still noted on Darlington tourist maps. WP interviewed workers who remembered his father, Gurney Pease (hereafter, GP) and great-grandfather, Edward Pease, an impressive figure "with his white tie & walking stick" (D/GP 6, v. 3, p. 109; JGP 1992:1–4). The world's first train (the Stockton and Darlington Railway), in which Edward played a prominent financial and developmental role, consisted of six wagons loaded with coal and a coach with the directors and their friends aboard. It started on September 27, 1825, from Darlington and traveled twelve miles to Stockton in three hours, seventeen minutes (Emden 1939:47); Foster 1981; Kirby 1984:28–9; Simmons 1975. Ironically, William Scoresby (1789–1857), the man for whom WSR was named, was on board.

7. For generations all—After 1833 Quakers took more of an active part in government. Historical note: In 1854 Joseph Sturge, who had a "concern" to prevent the looming Crimean War, headed a Quaker peace delegation to Russia. With Robert Charlton and KSR's relative Henry Pease, he called on the emperor of Russia in St. Petersburg. Upon their return, the non-Quaker community humiliated them as traitors (Steere 1984:43–44; The Illustrated London News, Sat., 11 Mar. 1854 [DPL U418ePEA]; reprint of "Address of the Society of Friends to Nicholas I, Emperor of Russia" [DPL U418e 36347]; Hufton 1996:418–20).

8. "a very scientific man"—AEP's wife, Nellie, to her son Edward, 24 Aug. 1906 (JGP/JVT, 12 Sept. 1995).

8. "I would have liked"—D/GP 6, 1906.

8. Joseph Pease amassed—Oppenheim 1991:184–86. Joseph Pease and Emma Gurney had twelve children, of whom nine survived.
Historical note: The later phases of the Industrial Revolution in Great Britain produced a huge increase in manufactured goods, rapid growth in national income and population, and trade guilds. Movement increased from rural areas to expanding industrial centers. Darlington became one such center, and many Quaker families, including the Peases and the Gurneys, prospered enormously. Great wealth encouraged the abandonment of Quaker rules of behavior. Quakers were termed "worldly," "gay," or "in the world" if they strayed far from the strict rules of dress, speech, and behavior demanded by the Society of Friends. Edward Pease was considered the last of the genuinely "plain" Quakers in the Pease family. See also Samuel 1998:299–300; Raistrick 1950; Lloyd 1990c.

8. Darlington had a population—In 1896 Pease and Partners Ltd. owned Bowden Close, Esh, Roddymoor Drift, Saint Helens, Stanley, "Drift" and "Pit," "Sunniside," Waterhouses, Whitelea Drift, and Wooley coal mines, employing 4,196 underground and surface workers.
Historical note: The Pease family employed 5 percent of the total 72,614 in the South Durham mining industry at that time (Peak District Mines Historical Society Ltd.).

9. Joseph Pease's sons—Lloyd 1990a, 1990b; Wedgwood n.d.b. In 1857 a Darlington historian wrote that "the leading families of the Friends have made their fortunes with their own right hands, and have settled down in all the best and snuggest man-

sions in town. They love ample gardens and green plantations, plain houses and high walls, and there is an air of the quintessence of comfort in their grounds."

Historical note: In 1858 about eight hundred colliers struck for increased wages, better working conditions, and less personal extravagance on the parts of colliery owners in Staffordshire, saying that "it was the duty of their masters to give a fair day's wages for a fair day's work" (Golby 1986:12–13).

9. "thought they were"; "spoiling industrial hand"; "ash heaps and chimneys"—(JGP 1992:5 quoting AEP). The "huge and foul workshops" of the "big murky places" that were England's centers of manufacture in the nineteenth century were ridiculed by William Morris in 1890 (Golby 1986:306–7).

Historical note: In 1829 Joseph Pease and others formed a company called Owners of the Middlesbrough Estate. The company bought six hundred acres of sandbanks and pastureland to form "a seaport for the shipment of coals brought to the Tees by the railway" (Emden 1939:51). Ten years later, an industrial and shipping town of 5,500 people had been established, and within half a century, had grown to 120,000. In 1851 blast furnaces were erected and it was "one of the most important iron-working districts in the world" (ibid.). AEP refused to attend the jubilee celebration of the town in 1881, saying, "I don't see much to jubilate about. My grandfather and his contemporaries managed to lay the foundations of a huge hideous town, a den of misery, dirt and debauchery planted on the once green fields by the banks of the Tees. Out of this place have come huge fortunes and many more lost—we have never made much out of it" (JGP 1992:18). "Filth and noise characterized Victorian cities" (Matthew 1989:476).

9. Interestingly, though not surprisingly—Sylvia Calmady-Hamlyn to JGP, 28 July 1957; AEP, 3 May 1891 (JGP/JVT 19 Sept. 1995).

9. "uneducated and fervid"; "an ordeal in"—D/GP 6, v. 26, p. 8.

10. She was the daughter—Joseph Gurney and Jane Chapman of Lakenham Grove, Norwich.

Biographical note: Life at the Grove was in the tradition of "plain" Quakers, while Earlham, the home of Joseph's brother John Gurney and his wife, Catherine Bell, was "gay" (DQB, Gurney, Joseph, 1757–1830; Gurney, John (1749–1809); Anderson 1980:13 gives different birth dates). Earlham children were given a rich and "unguarded" education. One of John and Catherine's children, Elizabeth (Gurney) Fry, was greatly influenced by her uncle, Joseph Gurney of the Grove (KSR's great-grandfather), in her "concern" for prison reform (DQB, Gurney, Elizabeth, 1780–1845; Emden 1939:97–106; see also Rose 1980; Raistrick 1950:28–31; Dunbar 1953:29). The Gurneys of Earlham Hall were often cited by non-Quaker social critics of the time as a model Victorian family.

AEP, WP (D/GP 6, v. 25, p. 18) noted, had "satisfactorily proved the Norman descent of the Gurneys." Daniel Gurney, however, had established the relationship in 1845 in *Records of the House of Gournay.*

10. "it took Gerard"—D/GP 6, v. 20, p. 31, in which the transcription incorrectly gives "Gerald" (see JGP 1992:268,273).

10. "bush baby"; "little rat"—D/GP 6, v. 28, p. 60. AEP also kept a pet jackal brought from Africa. He treated it as he would a dog until one day it bit his son, Christopher, and was sent off to the zoo (JGP/JVT 22 April 2002).

10. "wonderful catch"—AEP Random Notes c. 1917 (JGP/JVT, 12 Sept. 1995, 17 Nov. 1995); James N. Richardson to KSR, 31 Aug. 1916, p. 5 (PB); relatives thought GP had a "merry nature" that, unfortunately, did not show well in his photos; DQB, Pease, Gurney (1839–72); KSR's niece Rachel Chaytor (née Pease, b. 1906) was taught to revere her Pease forebears by KSR's younger brother John Henry Pease (DPL audiotape 10, track 1 [U4184], Nov. 1973). GP was said to be a "shamrock," a combination of three rare qualities: "the perfect gentleman, the sincere Christian and the good man of business" (J. N. Richardson to KSR, 31 Aug. 1916, p. 2 [PB]); D/GP 12, D/XD 64/5/34).

10. "the handsomest and best"—D/GP 6, v. 36, p. 13. *Darlington and Stockton Times* noted in GP's obituary that "viewed from the public stand point his life was singularly uneventful." GP "was no good at business & made a mess of it" and "nearly ruined his show before ill health took him out of it & my father [Joseph Whitwell Pease, hereafter JWP] came to the rescue" (AEP in Random Notes, c. 1917). AEP says GP and his brother Charles were "useless" in business (JGP/JVT, 12 Sept. 1995); see also JGP 1992:201. On Kate Pease's (hereafter, KP) death Helen Pease wrote to WP that "your father had one of the finest and merriest of natures that I ever remember to have known" (D/GP 6, v. 34, p. 28).

10. "rattle"—AEP, Random Notes, c. 1917; JWP 3–8 May 1863 (JGP/JVT, 19 Sept. 1995).

11. Kate Wilson, who—DQB, Pease, Katherine (7 Oct. 1840–1915). Born at Underfell, Kendal, Westmorland, KP was the third of twelve children. The family home was broken up in 1891.

11. Kate Wilson's Quaker—The Wilson pedigree begins generations before Anthony Wilson (bap. 1672) and Dorothy Benson, who built High Wary House in 1728 (Somervell, J., 1924:13; Benson 1912; Benson and Benson 1962; Foster 1890). KSR's grandmother was "greatly loved" and helped many through her "ready sympathy in times of joy or sorrow" (DQB, Whitwell, Hannah Maria, 1866); Tessa Wilson, of Kendal, holds the diaries of Mary Wilson (b. 1786), KSR's great-great-grandmother, and an embroidered map tracing the sea routes of Captain Cook done in 1808 by Hannah Jowitt (KSR's great-great-aunt); Anna Braithwaite says that "the Wilsons, the Crewdsons, and the members of Isaac Braithwaite's own family were all descendants of Isaac and Rachel Wilson" and "held an influential position" and made a "deep impression" on their community (Braithwaite 1905).

11. "family circles"; "marrying out"—JWP, Sun., 21 Sept. 1862 (JGP/JVT, 19 Sept. 1996).

11. "shared, parallel"—JGP 1992:xii; D/GP 6, v. 24, p. 17; v. 36, p. 13; v. 25, p. 28; "we Peases all have a trace of Wilson blood in us" (D/GP 6, v. 28, p. 15–16); at the beginning of the 1900s the Gurneys, Peases, and Wilsons had pedigrees that went back more than nine hundred, four hundred, and three hundred years, respectively.

12. "hearts and minds prepared"—News cutting attached to the reverse of photo of Gurney/Wilson wedding party (DPL U418ePEA B96); "Marriage at the Friends Meeting House, Darlington" in *Darlington and Stockton Times*, 16 Aug. 1862, describes the similar marriage of Sophia Pease and Theodore Fry (DPL U418ePEA); Raistrick 1950:22–25.

12. In time, Gurney—In most English liturgies, well into the twentieth century, the bride promised to "love, honor, and obey" her husband.

12. "fat and flourishing"—D/KP 4b; all of KP's impressions of her children quoted here are taken from the same source, and some are corroborated in D/KP 4a. The former are found on five handwritten, unnumbered journal pages that are only occasionally dated. The notes appear to have been written in retrospect.

12. Katherine (Katie) Maria Pease—Before I began this research, I erred in giving KSR's birth date as c. 1880 (EI 1994:14; notes compiled by C. Kelly, RGS archivist, for J. Lipscombe, 11 April 1991). My research subsequently corrected the information (correspondence on file, RGS). KSR's birth date is found in D/KP 4a and 4b; see also Certified Copy of an Entry of Birth CJ947421, Darlington, County Durham; Certified Copy of an Entry of Marriage TE 262155, Darlington, County Durham; Foster 1890; Somerville College Register 1891; Benson 1912:192; Benson and Benson 1962.

12. The Gurney Pease family—D/KP 4b; KP nowhere records her reaction to Greencroft West, but may have been displeased with it. As early as September 21, 1865, she and GP were looking for another house (JWP, 21 Sept. 1865 [JGP/JVT, 4 Oct. 1995]).

13. "I am a very brainy"—Dr. Bernard Hart to Dr. McDowall, 24 Mar. 1929 (PB).

13. "What can I do"—D/GP 6, v. 25, p. 22.

13. "Charm is inate [*sic*]"—Ibid.

13. "outrageous pride"—John Henry Pease (hereafter, JHP) to Lilian Leslie Fox, 22 June 1928 (PB).

13. "interfering aunts"—D/GP 6, v. 3, 1892–93. DQB, Pease, Jane Gurney (1827–94), and DQB, Pease, Emma Gurney (1829–95).

14. She was preoccupied—The cookbooks are *15 Books of Old Recipes as used in the Pease and Gurney Households in the XVIIIth Century.* JWP and Emma planned to publish the cookbooks, later passed down to AEP, who finally compiled and published them privately (JGP/JVT, 17 May 1996). One copy is in the Friends' Library, London, and another in the library of JGP.

14. "Pease physique"—J. N. Richardson to KSR, 31 Aug. 1916, p. 2 (D/GP 12, D/XD 64/5/34).

14. Jane cherished Katherine—D/GP 6, v. 6, p. 10.

14. "saw the world"—Ibid. See also AEP, Random Notes, c. 1917 (JGP/JVT, 30 Apr. 1996).

"A TERRIBLE BLANK," 1872

16. "glimmer"—D/GP 6, 8 Aug. 1891, p. 17.

17. "glorious twelfth"; "bright little companion"—D/KP 4b.

17. "very amusing and very sharp"; "sociable, loving and verbal"—D/KP 4b; the Pease family was greatly influenced by Queen Victoria's *Leaves from the Journal of Our Life in the Highlands* (1877; first published, 1868). WP entitled a portion of his journal "Leaves from a Life in the Highlands" (D/GP 6, v. 12, p. 32); D/KP 4b; see also Golby 1985: 118–122;

    Historical note: John Ruskin likened the home and household to a castle, the husband and wife to "Rex et Regina" who "feed and clothe," "direct and teach," their children, who are likened to subjects. WP (D/GP 6, v. 13, p. 31) compared his "queenly" mother to Queen Victoria.

17. "family feelings"; "terribly insecure"—D/GP 6, v. 2, p. 13; D/GP 6, v. 35, pp. 59–60; DQB, Caroline Joanna ("Joan" or "Jo") Fowler (1864–1922); see also Benson 1912:192; Benson and Benson 1962.

17. "I must give you"—D/GP 6, v. 28, p. 15: "Mother jumped up out of her chair, as though a real weight had been taken off her shoulders, and throwing her arms round my neck said 'I must give you a kiss, you dear boy.' This is the first impulsive kiss that my mother had ever given me."

17. "stillness and darkness"—D/GP 6, v. 1, 1890.

18. "separate characters" and "true natures"—D/GP 6, v. 3, p. 103; Ruskin's *Sesame and Lilies* in Golby 1985:20; Kingsley's novels gave KSR a "healthy ideal." "This evening we read Ruskin's 'Lillies' [*sic*] aloud. . . . It was most important that when girls were at the susceptible age they should have suitable novels to read" (D/GP 6, v. 3, p. 103).

18. "cowardly" and "bilious"—D/KP 4b; JWP, 21 Oct. 1866, found Harold "not very civil" (JGP/JVT, 4 Oct. 1995); see also Wolman 1970; Poznanski and Zrull 1970.

18. One of the few things—On KP's death, her children found that she had saved nearly everything they had ever produced: maps, drawings, poems, and letters.
    Note on documentation: WP saved bundles of photographs and childhood papers, possibly including KSR's sketch of Balmoral Castle. His intention was to go over them later, when KSR returned from the Pacific. At least some of them were deposited by JHP in the Durham County Record Office, but only one of KSR's childhood papers, a letter to KP from Greencroft, 14 Nov. 1873, is included (D/GP 12, D/XD 64/5/17).

19. "Empty my heart"—D/KP 4b; lines from an untitled hymn reprinted by KSR in a memorial leaflet for KP, issued on Christmas, 1915, off Honolulu (PB/JVT).

19. "it was not nice"; "manly"; "they are much"—D/GP 6, 4 Nov. 1891.

20. He was locked—JWP, 21 Jan. 1887 (JGP/JVT, 26 Apr. 1996).

20. Today, his illness—The description of HGP's illness given here was drawn by JGP with JVT from family records (some of which had been censored or edited by family members, cf. D/KP 4a and 4b) and is filed with the author as "Chronology of Recorded Extracts [on the Illness of Harold Gurney Pease] From Diaries of Wilson Pease, Sir J. W. Pease, Sir Alfred E. Pease and Ethel Buxton (née Pease) Diary When Aged 17" (JGP/JVT, 30 July 1996).

Medical note: Winchester 1999:210; Claridge 1995. *Stedman's Concise Medical Dictionary* (1994) says that schizophrenia is "synonymous with and replacing dementia praecox; a common type of psychosis, characterized by a disorder in the thinking processes, such as delusions and hallucinations, and extensive withdrawal of the individual's interest from other people and the outside world, and the investment of it in his own; now considered a group of mental disorders rather than as a single entity." Within this current definition, eleven distinct types of schizophrenia are elaborated; see also Wolman 1970: 1,3,7, and on childhood schizophrenia; Williams and Dalby 1988 on the psychodynamics of schizophrenia and environmental stress; Romney (1988) on paranoid schizophrenia; for contemporary treatment of ambulatory schizophrenia in England, see Cooper 1996; Solomon 2001 on depression; Asbury 1996 on women's madness.

20. some Peases suspected—Rachel Pease Chaytor (DPL audiotape 10, track 1, U4184, Nov. 1973). The fear Rachel felt about passing on HGP's and then KSR's illness to any child she might have was repeated to me during interviews with a Darlington Quaker who knew Rachel and her family well.

20. "wifely duties"—JWP, 17 Apr. 1870 (JGP/JVT, 26 Feb. 1996), says, "Kate seemed wonderfully better."

   Medical note: On "wifely duties" Oppenheim 1991:190 notes that "advisors routinely told women that they were likeliest to conceive directly before and after their menstrual periods, the very time, in fact, of minimum fertility. Medical misunderstandings of this sort doubtless played a part in the production of large Victorian families."

20. Kate Pease, not—D/KP 4b gives KP's account of KSR's bout with scarlet fever, probably written sometime after the event. All quotations in this chapter that directly involve or cite KSR, KP, or others during that time come from this source.

21. "peculiarity of the individual"—Morris 1858:2; typhoid was another common and terrible disease at this time, and KSR's sister, Lilian, once had it.

   Historical note: St. Aubyn (1992) describes how Prince Albert died of typhoid, probably caused by the horrid sanitary conditions at Buckingham Palace and other royal family residences.

21. "the poor child"—D/KP 4b.

22. "in a rather"; "a biggish place"—JWP, 2 June 1871 to 31 Dec. 1872 (JGP/JVT, 26 Feb. 1996).

22. A famous physician—See AEP (Random Notes, c. 1917), who writes that GP, who was a strong temperance advocate, "died prematurely of Bright's disease. No doubt if he had obeyed doctors [*sic*] orders & taken wine, his life would have been prolonged (Arthur Pease had the same symptoms but was saved & cured)" (JGP/JVT, 12 Sept. 1995); on 18 June 1865, JWP records GP having severe migraine headaches (JGP/JVT, 4 Oct. 1995); JWP, 28 June 1865 (JGP/JVT, 4 Oct. 1995).

   Historical note: Dr. Benjamin Kidd was a social Darwinist of the 1890s. There is no indication that he is, or is not, the man noted here.

   Geographical note: Malvern is about 180 to 190 miles from Walworth Castle, and the journey was accomplished efficiently at this time by linked rail in a day.

23. "on the jump"; "outburst"; "bombshell"—D/GP 6, v. 35, p. 60.

23. "I will never"—D/KP 4b.

23. After the funeral—DQB, Pease, Gurney (1839–72); JWP, 29 Feb. 1872 to 31 Dec. 1872 (JGP/JVT, 26 Feb. 1996). See also "Death of Mr. Gurney Pease" in *The Northern Echo,* 12 June 1872; "Funeral of the Late Mr. Gurney Pease" in *The Northern Echo,* 15 June 1872; "The Late Mr. Gurney Pease" in *The British Workman,* Extra No., 1872. JWP thought GP died of scarlatina, AEP thought Bright's disease (see above), while others reported scarlet fever or influenza. See also D/KP 4b and D/GP 4, 1860–72.

23. "All of the joy"; "a terrible blank"—D/GP 6, v. 3, p. 23; D/GP 4; D/GP 5; D/GP 6, v. 20, p. 3; D/GP 2. Kate's indomitable sister Sarah Wilson came to take care of the children (D/KP 4a; D/GP 6, v. 16, p. 11). A few months before her death, Sarah told WP

that someone had said to her, " 'Sarah, thou art a very durable reader' . . . and I remember so well how she used to read to us children when she had charge of us during Mother's illness" (D/GP 6, v. 16, p. 11).

23. "have shaken my"—The death of GP and Charles Pease, both of whom "had been business partners with particular and separate spheres of responsibility," "placed great burdens on those remaining, through the survivors having to buy out deceased partners' shares" (JGP 1992:17; 24 n. 9). Edward Pease died, aged forty-five, on June 13, 1880 (D/KP 4a), and JWP and Arthur Pease were executors for all three men; JWP, 31 Dec. 1872 (JGP/JVT, 26 Feb. 1996).

24. "merry nature"; "like a breeze"—D/GP 6, v. 1, p. 23; D/GP 4; D/GP 6, v. 34, p. 31; James N. Richardson to KSR, 8 May 1916; KSR copied Mr. Richardson's letters and sent them to WP, Lilian, and JHP (D/GP 6, v. 36, p. 13, in which WP remarks that his cousin Helen and uncle David Howard "also told me of father's 'merry nature' "); copy of letters from Mr. James N. Richardson to KSR re " 'Memories of Gurney Pease' for L. Fox" in KSR's hand (PB) (D/GP 12, D/XD 64/5/34). Many Pease boys attended the Quaker school at Tottenham. The Richardsons were related to the Pease family through Joseph Pease's grandfather (also called Joseph Pease, 1737–1808), who married Mary, daughter of Richard Richardson of Hull.

WAITING FOR CHANGE: WOODSIDE, 1872

25. Gurney Pease left—Comments on the provisions of GP's will are given in JGP/JVT, 26 Feb. 1996 (JWP, 15 June 1872); on KP's will (JWP, 30 Jan. 1879); on KP's Kendal financial affairs (JWP, 15 Sept. 1879); on money advances to Wilson family members (JWP, 31 Jan. 1880; see also JGP/JVT, 10 Apr. 1996). Shares held by GP and his brother Charles in Pease businesses at the times of their deaths were among affairs that needed to be sorted out in 1902, when JWP was facing bankruptcy (JGP 1992:201); see also D/GP 3. See DQB, JWP (1828–1903); documentation on file, Friends Library, London: Annual Monitor, 1904, p. 104; Journal of the Friends Society, v. 25, p. 67; v. 8, p. 96 n.; v. 12, p. 148; v. 21, p. 10 n.; The Friend, 1903, v. 43, pp. 463–64; Friends Quarterly Examiner, 1904, v. 38, pp. 175–84; The British Workman, Spec. No., Jan. 1873 (DPL: U418ePEA PB19); Benson 1912; Benson and Benson 1962; Emden 1939; Foster 1890, 1891; Lloyd 1990b; Pease, A. E. 1907; JGP 1992; Raistrick 1950; Simmons 1975; Wedgewood n.d.a.; JWP 17, 21, 25 May 1863; 3 July 1863 (JGP/JVT, 4 Oct. 1995).

25. One month after—KP's father and JWP arranged purchase of Woodside from one Mr. Smithson for the cost of £9,500 (about $14,240); payment was to begin on October 1, 1872 (see Dean 1984: pl. 1; Meadows and Waterson 1993:65). Designed and built by Thomas Robson Jr. for J. C. Hopkins in 1842, it was remodeled in 1848 to include a square tower and conservatory for the Quaker civil engineer J. Harris by the Darlington firm of Richardson and Ross.

25. The family's nearest—D/GP 6, v. 2, Sat., 30 July 1892; JWP (18 Dec. 1886) says, "lunched at Woodside, two little Havelock boys there, very amusing" (JGP/JVT, 30 July 1996; see 28 Aug. 1996 for Havelock-Allan pedigree and further comment on adult lives); a tablet on the wall of St. Cuthbert's, Darlington, is dedicated to two generations of the Havelock-Allan family.

Biographical note: Sir Henry Spencer Moreton Havelock-Allan (2nd Bt) grew up with the Gurney Pease children and suffered at the heavy hand of his father, a famous military hero, who apparently had a terrible temper. The boy frequently ran to Woodside to hide from him. Spencer (as he was known to Wilson) was infatuated with Lilian and heartbroken when she married. He served as parliamentary private secretary to the undersecretary of state for India, 1910–14, and hosted WP and Joan when they were on holiday there. See Debrett's Illustrated Peerage 1990:B17.

25. To top it all—D/KP 4a; JWP (19 Feb. 1878) says that she had "overrun the constable owing to exceptional circumstances" (JGP/JVT, 10 Apr. 1996).

25. Massive beech and elm—D/GP 6, v. 16, p. 26, in which "the garden has been reduced

. . . several trees are to come down. Old friends like the poplar by the playroom steps and a wellingtonia on the croquet lawn." In D/GP 6, v. 18, p. 10, WP notes "taking advantage of K's departure from Woodside we have cut down one of the wellingtonias on the croquet lawn, and an elm on the south lawn. We have also cleared away the yews which made the little drive look like the entrance to a cemetery, and by so doing have opened up the fine fern leaved beech."

26. "I will never"—D/GP 6, v. 34, p. 30.

27. "illusioned"—D/GP 6, v. 5, p. 12 in which KSR notes also that the autobiography of the Reverend Charles Kingsley (1819–75) was a "revelation" to her.

27. "They seem just"—D/GP 6, v. 11, p. 50.

27. "ability to talk"—DPL, audiotape 10, track 1 (U4184), made by Mrs. Rachel Pease Chaytor (b. 1906), for Darlington Local History Project, Nov. 1973.
    Biographical note: Rachel was the daughter of KSR's youngest brother, JHP, and his wife, Louisa (Lou) Lambert. See D/GP 6, Sat., 30 July 1892; Benson 1912; Benson and Benson 1962.

28. Signs in her—The earliest handwriting sample I have been able to locate is a letter KSR wrote to KP at the age of seven (D/GP 12 D/XD 64/5/17). The next known sample is a scorecard for the Third Annual Cousins' Lawn Tennis Tournament, 1884 (DPL U418ePEA), written at the age of eighteen.
    Note on documentation: It is imperative that researchers wishing to use the direct data present in the Mana Expedition papers (RGS LBR MSS) familiarize themselves with the nuances of change in KSR's handwriting. Many examples are available, but compare, as an initial study, her journal entries (all 1914) for Tuesday, June 30 (neat, brief, few loops, separated words, some underlining, and general legibility); Wednesday, July 1 (less neat, more extraneous detail, more loops, words still separated but rewriting, overwriting, and insertion); Sunday, July 12; July 18; September 6; December 4, etc. The end point of this analysis is "Things the Spooks Told Me . . ." (PB), a record of KSR's communication with "voices." In this spectrum of material one may clearly see the handwriting attributes that signal, to a certain degree, her state of mind or indicate the moments when she believed herself to be "channeling" family spirits.

28. Anonymous hands laid—D/GP 6, v. 11, p. 48; Rachel Pease Chaytor (DPL, audiotape 10, track 1, U4184, Nov. 1973) was, like KSR, educated at home with "masses of servants" and a governess. She remembers her mother teaching her how to manage household stores.

28. "theories of life"—D/GP 6, v. 22, p. 48.

28. "no excuse for"—D/GP 6, v. 19, p. 37, in which, after returning from East Africa "K. takes housekeeping very seriously and finds it more difficult and time exacting than she expected."

29. Katherine's warmest childhood—D/GP 6, v. 11, p. 15–16; v. 22, p. 25.

29. Lilian had few—Lilian's affinity for port at this time of her life is described in D/GP 6, v. 23, p. 31, but does not necessarily signal a lifelong problem.
    Biographical note: Charles Leslie Fox, Lilian's husband, was sometimes quite peculiar and must have been a trial to live with. At the death of KP in London he made all the arrangements very efficiently. Afterward, however, WP (D/GP 6, v. 34, p. 38) noted with some concern that Leslie "trained to Richmond where he followed a dog to its home and tried to buy it. He walked on the Moors." Then, the next day: "Leslie again to Richmond. I wish he would go home. He worries Lil awfully." His behavior must have encouraged observers to say, "That chap wants locking up" (JGP/JVT, 13 Nov. 1996). Earlier, however, in 1912, "Leslie is much stronger, quite different, not tucked up and restless. He has taken to golf . . ." (D/GP 6, v. 28, p. 1). "Leslie is sweet to his mother" (ibid.); see also D/GP 6, v. 19, p. 33; KP visited Rumwell Hall for extended holidays, including Christmas, but WP rarely did, although Rumwell Hall was immaculate and Lilian hospitable (D/GP 6, v. 23 p. 1; D/KP 4a). Leslie had a filthy temper and once threw a slice of toast down the entire length of the din-

ing room table at his small, terrified three-year-old grandson (JVT/Peter Bucknall, Hampton, spring, 1996; PB also says that he once received a birthday gift from Leslie Fox: a slice of toast with a half-crown coin buried in it).

29. "house of gloom"—D/GP 6, vol. 35, pp. 19–20.

29. She was sent—Going away to school provided the GP children with a comparative window on their Woodside lives. "Staying away from home & seeing how nicely the men & women behave to one another always makes me come back with contempt for flippant Darlington, & I squirm at the invariable question 'I hope it was not naughty when it was away?'" D/GP 6, v. 1, 26 Sept. 1890; v. 8, p. 34; D/GP 6, Scotland, 1901, p. 48; D/GP 6, 2 July 1891; D/GP 12 D/XD/64/2/1–8, 9–13, 14–16. WP attended Oliver's Mount School, Scarborough (D/GP 12 D/XD 64/2/9–13).

29. "waiting to be challenged"—D/GP 6, v. 7; D/GP 6, v. 25, p. 36.

30. Aunts and uncles—JWP, 25 Aug. 1884 (JGP/JVT, 30 July 1996); see also DPL U418ePEA; AEP, 28 Dec. 1887; 9 Jan. 1889; 1 Jan. 1891 (JGP/JVT, 19 Sept. 1995); JWP, 23 Dec. 1885 (JGP/JVT, 30 July 1996). Ethel Buxton (15/16 Apr. 1885) describes a whirlwind of social activities (tennis, dinners) at Woodside over a few days. She notes, "we played lawn tennis on the grass which is very bad for it, but as Harold is soon going back to Cambridge, & Lillie to school, they do not mind it being spoilt" (JGP/JVT, 25 Nov. 1995; 30 July 1996); Reginald "Reg" Pease of Pierremont Hall was a frequent escort for KSR (including to Aunt Jane's funeral) and visited often when the family was on holiday in Scotland (D/PE 2/213–16; D/PE 6/82).

30. "You're on to the wrong one"—JGP 1992:25–26. The saga of Beatrice and Lord Lymington is succinctly and clearly told in JGP 1992: 25–75; (JGP/JVT); see also *Darlington Library Supplement*, n.d., p. 3. WP, 21 June 1880 (JGP/JVT, 20 Apr. 1996). The most severe financial losses in the Pease family as a result of the Lymington affair were felt in the direct hereditary line, i.e., JWP and AEP. Several women in the family (including Aunt Emma) whose assets had been managed by JWP gratefully and generously gave him access to whatever funds of their own they could provide. KP loaned J. W. Pease & Co. £5,000 at 5 percent interest (D/GP 3) and in 1903 released them from the debt (D/GP 12 D/XD 64/5/25).

31. Although he was not—JGP 1992:26; JGP/JVT, 1 July 1996; JGP 1992:28, 32–33. Eldest of twelve children and a Liberal MP, Portsmouth spoke with an aristocratic lisp, wore his red hair long, had a fabled temper, and was a shameless and calculating fortune hunter. Wilson Pease thought he was eccentric, and King Edward VII is said to have referred to him as "that supreme ass, Portsmouth!"

31. "very splash"—WP wrote to KP from Constantinople expressing tentative feelings about Lilian and Leslie (D/GP 12 D/XD 64/2/58).

   Biographical note: Charles Leslie Fox was born in Wellington, Somerset, 1865. Educated at Clifton and Clare College, Cambridge, Leslie held a B.A. and was a justice of the peace for Somerset. It is not known exactly when he and Lilian met, but he was introduced to her by J. A. Pease and is said to have gone "north to study banking" (inter. JVT/Diana Patricia Selina Cole-Hamilton [Diana Ford], Hampton, spring, 1996). If so, he was not at J. & J. W. Pease's Bank (JGP/JVT, 7 May 1996). The Somerset Foxes were not, so far as is known, Quakers, but "at some time in an earlier generation" presumably had been (ibid.). Leslie and Lilian were related as fourth cousins through the Crewdson branch of the Wilson family (Benson 1912; Benson and Benson 1962) and as third cousins once removed via Charles Leslie Fox's mother (Caroline Chapman). After a glamorous reception at Woodside the newlyweds left in a shower of rice, and Lilian later told Katherine that she enjoyed her honeymoon, "contrary to her expectations" (D/GP 6, v. 26, p. 36). Lilian and Leslie had two daughters, Beatrice Evelyn and Hilda Violet. KSR sent them presents every birthday and Christmas and gave them marriage advice in the best "interfering aunt" tradition.

31. "looked splendid"—D/GP 1, Oct. 1892, pp. 36–39; the wedding party, including KSR, was photographed in the Woodside conservatory, but the photos are lost or were destroyed; D/GP 6, v. 26, p. 36; KSR and her cousins learned the rhyme:

Shall I be carried to the skies
On flowery beds of ease?
Why yes I shall, of course I shall
My maiden name was Pease.

31. "had a claim against Arthur"—D/GP 6, v. 3, pp. 29 (1 Oct. 1892) "They now propose that before Lilian's marriage we should indemnify them from the loss incurred by these bad investments. The plan was first proposed to me in solemn conclave at the office on Monday morning. I demurred"; "We asked for time to consider & even hinted that perhaps Uncle A. might meet us half way in the matter. This rather annoyed Uncle J. who only saw the side from which we appear most ungrateful for their many voluntary services"; "I went to see Mr. Lucas about L's settlement concerning which we are considerably 'exercised'" (D/GP 3, p. 22); JWP, 26 Sept. 1892 (JGP/JVT, 25 Nov. 1995); D/GP 1, Oct. 1892; JWP, 12 Oct. 1892 (JGP/JVT, 25 Nov. 1995); JWP, 12 Oct. 1892 (JGP/JVT, 25 Nov. 1995).

31. "one belligerent niece"—See JGP/JVT, 25 Nov. 1995; 26 Feb. 1996; D/GP 6, v. 18, p. 11.

31. No evidence of wrongdoing—"Conditions of Sale and General Summary, Newport Estate Property, 1909" (M/5/132, document on file, JGP/JVT, 1996); JGP/JVT, 3 June 1996, estimated Newport Estate at about 3,500–3,900 acres, but it was certainly more; JGP/JVT, 10 July 1996 and 20 July 1996. Letters of sanction and approval from KP re investments are on file (D/GP 3). There were two sales of the property after KP died, with the 1916 "Newport Sale at Hereford" resulting in only three lots remaining in the hands of the trustees: the Public House (less than ten acres), the Great House, and Newchurch Farm (439 acres) (D/GP 6, v. 36, p. 29); JGP/Hereford and Worcester County Council, 16 July 1996; Land Registry Title No. HW122909, County of Hereford and Worcester, 25 Jan. 1923.

32. The assets of their—At the 1902 Pease Bank crash KP and her children "would have come out of the shambles with their assets all intact—except (possibly) cash balances. On 22nd August, 1902 when everything at the bank was 'frozen' pending the sort-out, that side of the family had credit balances at J. and J. W. Pease's Bank of 30,438.15.8d" (JGP/JVT, 18 Feb. 1996); "with their assets left intact, I imagine they were no less wealthy than the Arthur Peases" (ibid.); "the Gurney Pease descendants would most probably inherit shares in Pease & Partners Ltd., and be holders of North Eastern Railway stock" (ibid.); see also JGP 1992; Beatrice-Elizabeth Fell Pease stating distress at being blamed for the fall of J. & J. W. Pease (D/PE 3/141).

32. Sir Joseph, who—DQB, JWP; JWP received a birthday letter from KP on the day of his death. He died in the presence of his daughter Maud and a doctor, who treated his failing heart with "injections of strychnine and ether and hot sponges . . . but all was in vain and he passed away at 6 o'clock. He knew he was dying and said to the Doctor 'this is death,' and when I knew by the Doctor's face that the end was near, I kissed him and he said 'Good-bye'" (Maud Pease, courtesy JGP).

32. "tactless"—"Tact is not K's strong point" (D/GP 6, v. 20, p. 3).

32. "look less to the advancement"—D/GP 6, v. 2, p. 79; D/GP 6, v. 1, 2 July 1891; WP thought it was a mother's "first duty to get their daughters happily married and then she may launch out into philanthropy" (D/GP 6, v. 24, p. 28).

32. Health problems, real—D/GP 6, v. 2, p. 74; D/GP 6, v. 5, p. 68; KSR's dietary phobias often followed fashion, and Samuel (1998:304) says that the 1880s "saw the start of a wide-spread revolt against Victorian gluttony."

32. "in giving money"—D/GP 6, v. 11, p. 50.

32. "it's in her"—Ibid.

33. Everything done in—Ibid.; D/GP 6, v. 4, p. 18; KSR's uncle Gilbert Gilkes (DQB, Gilkes, Gilbert, 1845–1924), who married KP's sister Rachel in 1874 in a ceremony at Kendal in which KSR was a bridesmaid at age eight, was very critical of her decision; see also Benson 1912 and supplements; Rachel and Gilbert both spoke at KSR's wedding in 1906; "Gilbert Gilkes" in *The Friend*, 29 Aug. 1924, 751–52.

33. The following October—D/GP 6, v. 1, 26 Jan. 1891. End-of-term reports for KSR

copied for JVT by P. Adams, librarian and archivist, Somerville College, Oxford, 28 May 1991. Photocopied note with number 25 in the upper left is headed "October Term, 1891" and reads "K.M. Pease Passed First Examination. Oxford. Dec. 1891." KSR began at university in mid-January, 1892; copy of p. 173, Somerville College *Register*, "Pease, Katherine Maria (Mrs. Scoresby Routledge, 1906)." KSR's cousin Lucy Pease Fowler (her parents were Joseph and Emma Pease's daughter Elizabeth Lucy and John Fowler) and her uncle Colin Somervell were her "referees."

ESCAPE: OXFORD AND SOUTH AFRICA, 1891

34. "Soberly dressed and decorously"—Adams 1996:44; for a description of Oxford see Gerard Manley Hopkins, "Duns Scotus's Oxford" (1879), in Golby 1986:88.
34. Gertrude Bell (1868–1926)—Wallach 1996; see also review Wheeler, n.d. (1996), "Mesopotamian Miss," *The Times*, London; Champion 1998. Sir Hugh Bell, Gertrude's father, was well known to the Pease family through the Middlesbrough project; see JWP, 8–10 May 1897 (JGP/JVT, 10 Apr. 1996); D/GP 6, v. 26; WPP:xxii; Bell 1907, 1947.
34. Katherine would spend—End-of-Term Reports, K. M. Pease, Somerville Hall; copies requested for JVT by M. Stover, Department of Ethnography, Museum of Mankind, British Museum, and provided by P. Adams, 28 May 1991. Copy on file, JVT.
34. Somerville principal Agnes Catherine Maitland—Adams 1996:59; KSR left funds in her will for a portrait of Maitland, which hangs today in the college's dining hall (Routledge, Katherine Maria, n.d. [1925]. Last Will. Office copy without impressed court seal on file, Department of Ethnography, British Museum).
    Historical note: The first principal of Somerville Hall was Madeleine Shaw Lefevre. In 1906, when KSR's good friend, Ethel Hurlblatt, was leaving for Canada, Miss Shaw presented her with a jewel of tourmalines set in Portuguese silver, and Ethel wore it always. In 1931 Ethel Hurlblatt left it to Royal Victoria College as the "Warden's Jewel" (Vaughan 1934a:19).
35. "presentable"—D/GP 6, v. 2, p. 58; v. 4, p. 28; *Somerville College Register, 1891–1892*, pp. 12–13 (courtesy P. Adams, Somerville College Library); Adams 1996:110 n. 16, quoting a student (Ilbert on 10 Oct. 1895), says there was a good deal of jockeying for social position at Somerville.
35. There she became—Adams 1996:114; Sorabji 1916, 1935; de Villiers, Fox, Adams 1978:35; D/GP 6, v. 16, p. 35. Sir Nicholas Harington/JVT, 13 Mar. 1996. John Charles Dundas Harington, Sir Nicholas' son, was one of WSR's heirs and executors, along with REB, and recovered some of the Mana Expedition's papers.
    Note on documentation: Sorabji had a voluminous correspondence with family, friends, and colleagues, but there is no mention of KSR within her papers that I reviewed on file, Oriental and India Office Collections, British Library, MSS EUR F 165. Neither do any letters or papers from or about her exist in the extant KSR papers (as opposed to WP's papers) I have reviewed.
    Historical note: T. S. Eliot (1970:217) wrote "To the Indians Who Died in Africa" at the request of Cornelia Sorabji for *Queen Mary's Book for India.*
35. "reliability is the charm"—Gertrude Pesel Mayo (Mrs. Francis Carbutt Mayo), Last Will, 2 Feb. 1953 (official copy with impressed seal on file, JVT) and codicil to the Last Will, 18 Mar. 1953 (ibid.); died a widow at 21 The Mount, Malton, Yorkshire, 2 Dec. 1958; see also Adams 1996:126; D/GP 6, v. 7, p. 2.
35. "Hurly"; "Hurly-burly"—Ethel Hurlblatt in *Somerville Hall Register*, 1888, p. 8; Vaughan 1934a, 1934b; Last Will, 6 Aug. 1929; "Miss Ethel Hurlblatt Is Dead in France," undated translation of French newspaper story, McGill University Archives; Gillett 1981; "Hurly" or "Hurly-burly" is from Cornelia Sorabji, a friend at Somerville, as reported by Vaughan 1934a:20. Like KSR, Hurlblatt left written instructions that no grave marker or memorial be erected in her honor.
36. "a first-rate and inspiring"—Crawford 1955:79–80; Marett married Nora Kirk, a classmate of KSR's.

36. "primitive"—R. R. Marett in WWP:358. See, for example, R. R. Marett, "The Place of Kikúyu Thought in the Comparative Study of Religions," in WPP:359; Tylor 1871. *Historical note:* Not all scholars agreed with Marett on his notion of "magico-religious" thought. Some, like Sir James Frazer, felt there was a fundamental distinction, even an opposition, between magic and religion. By 1916 the debate on this issue was heated; see also MEI:240.

36. Poulton's lectures proved—D/GP 6, v. 2, p. 58; WP inaccurately referred to "Paulton [sic] . . . he is a science lecturer & interesting." "The Tragic History of a Butterfly," *Entomological Society,* 1916 (RGS WKR 7); MEI:152. In 1916 Poulton reported "his friends Mr. and Mrs. Scoresby Routledge" had captured a rare butterfly on Easter Island unknown to the natives, "who have no word for 'butterfly.' " The Routledges sent their specimen to him on one of the ships of the famous German admiral von Spee's Pacific Squadron at the beginning of World War I. The ship and the butterfly went down during the Battle of the Falkland Islands. Poulton later showed examples of *H. bolina* to a very disappointed KSR, who was convinced that their butterfly had been a male of that species.

    Historical note: Another interesting character in KSR's academic life was her tutor, Clara Pater, sister of writer and critic Walter Pater and Greek and Latin tutor to Virginia Woolf (1882–1941).

36. Oxford's first female—Babcock and Parezo 1988:20–23; Adams 1996:68, 206; Deacon 1997:239.

    Anthropological note: Barbara Freire-Marreco Aitken spent the summer of 1910 in Edgar Lee Hewett's Frijoles Canyon field school in the American Southwest, but her fieldwork was plagued by the difficulties of being a single woman, and she retreated (as did many others) to ethnography and folklore. Many women archaeologists are on record today with both opinions and evidence that little has changed.

37. "counted on to produce"—Marett, R. R. 1941:306; a search of the Exeter College Archives has failed to reveal any reference to a visit or lecture given by KSR (personal communication, Mrs. Lorise C. Topliffe, Sub-Librarian, Exeter College, 1998).

    Note on documentation: The Marett archive at Exeter is not large, and virtually everything relates to his activities as Fellow and then rector (personal communication, J. R. Maddicott, Exeter College, Oxford, 1998). Other Marett papers are on file at the PRM and with his family at Mon Plaisir, Jersey, Channel Islands (personal communication, S. Marett-Crosby, 1998).

37. "women anthropologists, of whose achievements"—R. R. Marett 1941:220.

37. "brought me much"—Ibid.

    Anthropological note: Marett's esteem for KSR is even more impressive since, in the 1920s, he encouraged other female social anthropologists who went on to significant achievements in their field. One such example is Beatrice Mary Blackwood, who earned a scholarship to Somerville College in 1908, was granted her diploma in 1920, and was then appointed demonstrator and lecturer in ethnology at Oxford, 1923–59 (Gacs et al. 1989).

37. "under the cloud"—D/GP 6, v. 4, pp. 11–13; JWP, 27 Apr. 1893.

38. "in pursuit of the Holy Grail"; "wandering fires"—Ibid.

38. "Quakers had in"; "for the mental"—D/GP 6, v. 3, p. 110.

38. "to do anything"—D/GP 6, v. 4, pp. 13, 17, 55; see also D/GP 6, Mon., 16 Nov. 1891; JGP/JVT, 1 July 1996:14; D/GP 6, Weds., 6 Jan. 1892; D/GP 6, 7 Nov. 1893–Dec. 1893.

38. "not placing wider"—D/GP 6, v. 5, p. 12.

38. "It has been"—Ibid.

39. "very strong and sensible"; "could not get"—End-of-Term Reports, Katherine Maria Pease, Somerville College, Oxford (P. Adams to JVT, 28 May 1991).

39. He was destined—What I call "Aunt Jane's love story" was a real puzzle, finally solved by JGP. Her disappointed lover was Henry Yeoman, archdeacon of Cleveland, who lived at Marske Hall, Marske-by-the-Sea, Cleveland, North Yorkshire. He attended

court (when AEP was justice of the peace) and "often defeated our intentions by paying the fines of the poorer offenders" (AEP 1931:64; JGP/JVT, 9 Oct. 1996).

40. Her long and intimate—Emma imparted "secret intelligence 'not to be revealed' of
'an affair'" to JWP. JGP is rather inclined to the view that this is "probably a reference
to Harold and Gwen. It's a thin line of reasoning, but it was about a month later (11
Aug. 1894) that JWP went to Ayton to see the Butlers and came away with "lots of
things to think about." Given Emma's close relationship with KSR, however, I tend to
believe it was KSR she was concerned about (JGP/JVT, 24 May 1996).

40. The hills echoed—D/GP 6, v. 6, p. 50; JGP/JVT, 10 July 1996:3; 20 July 1996:7; 28 July
1996:1; JWP, 18 July 1882; AEP took opium when in Asia Minor for stomach upset;
the Pease family cookbooks have a recipe for "black drop" or "Quaker black drop" (a
medicinal syrup of opium). WP smoked opium in JWP's unknowing presence (D/GP
6, v. 23, p. 31).

40. "an epic poem"—D/GP 12 D/XD 64/2/17–18, letters to KP from WP re his engagement to his cousin Joan Fowler; D/GP 12 D/XD 64/2/19–22, re engagement; D/GP 6,
v. 7, p. 8, for description of WP's wedding; WP's diaries are filled with loving references to his wife (and some pictures of her), to whom he was especially close all of
their marriage. It was, he thought, a "real English love match" when he married Joan,
and although they agonized over their childless state often in what WP called hours
of "midnight sentiment," WP did not really regret that Joan and he could not have
children. After her death he was incredibly lonely and died less than a year later.

40. "if she keeps"—End-of-Term Reports, Katherine Maria Pease, Somerville College,
Oxford (P. Adams to JVT, 28 May 1991). See also D/GP 6, v. 8, p. 4; KSR appears to
have been staying at Charleton for a rest cure but hated it. About the nurses, she said
it was "wonderful that people can be so satisfied with such empty heads."

40. "heathenish sight"—D/GP 6, v. 7, p. 41.

41. Pondering her brother's—Sylvia Calmady-Hamlyn (d. 10 June 1962), 28 July 1957
(JGP/JVT, 19 Sept. 1995).

42. "sightings"; "sighted"; "inexplicable"—Jenkins 1982:3; Britten 1884:90–91.

42. Their real personality—In 1914 Beatrice is said to have finally made contact, but the
absolution she sought was not forthcoming. Instead, the only words her father's spirit
said, in a harshly condemning tone, were "I wish to have nothing to do with you."
Beatrice was shattered, but the Pease family was not surprised. Tongue in cheek, WP
wondered if the unforgiving Edward "as a Quaker disapproved of spiritualism, or perhaps as a Pease disapproved of her lawsuit with the family?" (Hastings 1991:131).

42. "if it had not"—D/GP 6, v. 8, p. 12; D/GP 6, Mon., 12 Sept. 1892. Students graduat-
ing from Somerville customarily gave books in honor of the occasion. KSR chose to
give a full-length mirror nearly three years before graduation that, she said, the girls'
skirts needed. On other occasions she followed custom, as when she later presented
Somerville with a copy of MEI and other Pease family books.

43. "uncommonly well"—D/GP 6, v. 8, p. 37.

43. "quite sane"—Extract from journal of AEP, 5–6 Sept. 1895 ("Chronology of Recorded
Extracts from Diaries of Wilson Pease, Sir. J. W. Pease, Sir Alfred E. Pease and Ethel
Buxton (née Pease) Diary when Aged 17"), compiled by JGP/JVT, 30 July 1996.

43. "the backbone of the family"—D/GP 6, v. 8, p. 28; D/GP 6, v. 2, p. 14.

43. "unbecoming in a woman"—The phrase "unbecoming in a woman" was common in
Victorian times (cf. A. Fraser 1989:323), from George Buchanan, History of Scotland,
1571).

43. "healthy outdoor life"—D/GP 6, v. 4, pp. 28, 60; v. 6, pp. 10, 33; v. 3, p. 11.

43. "arranged"—Gwendolen Margaret Butler (hereafter, GMP) (1876–1957); Benson
1912; Benson and Benson 1962; D/GMP; Darlington and Stockton Times, 12 Sept. 1896
(DPL); JGP/JVT, 12 Sept. 1995. Copy of letter from KP to HGP describing the financial settlement she was making for him and GMP (17 Sept. 1896, D/GP 12 D/XD
64/5/21); letter from HGP to GMP's father, Theobold Butler, proposing to leave his
income and principal to GMP (26 Nov. 1896, D/GP 12 D/XC 64/5/22).

43. "a craving after"; "does not satisfy"—Extract of a letter from Helen Anne Pease (Nel-

lie, Mrs. AEP) to her son Edward Pease, 24 Aug. 1906 (JGP/JVT, 16 Oct. 1995); GMP to AEP, 7 May 1928, 12 Oct. 1913. D/GP 6, v. 8, Sun., 5 Jan. 1896; D/GP 6, v. 8, p. 37; "Lecture by Miss Pease at Darlington," *Darlington and Stockton Times,* 6 Feb. 1897 (DPL); "University Extension Lecture at Darlington," *Darlington and Stockton Times,* 13 Feb. 1897 (DPL).

43. "hit it off"—D/GP 6, v. 11, p. 50.
44. Katherine had known—D/GP 6, v. 3, p. 110; D/GP 6, v. 4, p. 60; Eliza McAllum, Last Will, 2 Dec. 1933, copy with impressed court seal on file, JVT; Family Tree 2, "The Binghams" (Peter Inchbald); Katherine Maria Routledge, Last Will, 1 Dec. 1925.
44. Lyle had a little—Peter Inchbald to JVT, 13 Feb. 1997, 7 May 1997.
44. "Sensible Women's League"—D/GP 6, v. 4, p. 63.
45. "ceased to believe"—*Biographical note:* KSR and Lyle had a connection through Lyle's older sister Frances Jane Fenwick Watson, who joined the Society of Friends in 1877 (DQB, Watson, F. J. F.). There was also a relationship by marriage through KSR's aunt May, daughter of famed African missionary Dr. David Livingstone.
45. Both women were—D/GP 6, v. 4, p. 63; v. 22, p. 27.
45. "automatic writing"—Hastings 1991:131.
45. "hot and eager"—D/GP 6, v. 22, p. 27, "It was not a pretty sight."
46. "piercing brown eyes"—Pease, K. 1903:97; "We also tender thanks to Miss Pease, at present in South Africa, for the kindness with which, in the midst of many claims upon her, she responded to our request to write an article" (E. F. Valentine, ed., DTC *Magazine,* 1903:96); D/GP 6, v. 14, p. 22. "Woman Barricaded Herself in Hyde Park Mansion," *Northern Echo,* Sat., 2 June 1928 (DPL, microfilm). Several other groups to which KSR had ties were active sponsors of South African programs, including the "South African Conciliation Committee" (through the Livingstone family connection) and the Friends South African Relief Fund, 1907–1908 (JGP/JVT, 20 Apr. 1996). WPP:125–26; KSR's positive impression of Lord Milner is bolstered by AEP, who found him to be "certainly a charming man" (Pease, J. G. 1992:220). Lord Milner was "kind and sympathetic," encouraging AEP before he took up his new administrative position (ibid., 221).
46. "delightful knack"; "helping to govern"—Pease, K. 1903:99–101.
46. In Pretoria Katherine—Pease, K. 1903:99–101; KSR from Retreat, Edzell, Forfarshire, to her niece Hilda Leslie Fox, 24 July 1920 (PB); KSR had a "bad attack" of "malaria" in 1913 after "six years complete immunity" (MEI:38). This may have been a relapse after encountering malaria in East Africa in about 1907, but the illness might also have been caused by an infection picked up in South Africa. How these illnesses related to KSR's first breakdown while at Oxford is not clear, except that the symptoms were always basically the same. Whatever the exact nature of her cluster of physical symptoms, the stress that resulted was debilitating and definitely produced or was linked to auditory hallucinations. WP and HGP were said to have contracted malaria when touring Egypt, India, and the Near East in 1891–92 (D/KP 4a; D/GP 12 D/XD 64/2/38–61).
    Historical note: The anopheles mosquito was recognized as the carrier of malaria in 1898.
46. Whatever her feelings—Pease, K. 1903:99–101.

SCORESBY: "A TRUE BRITISH BARBARIAN," 1904

47. Katherine was plainly—The scene described in these paragraphs is drawn from D/GP 6, v. 12, p. 9; v. 16, pp. 1, 13.
47. "get as many"—D/GP 6, v. 18, p. 8 (WP in notes to himself).
47. On the voyage—WPP:ix, in which WSR says he was in the area "by accident." This is probably an inaccurate statement in that, at this time, an early promotional effort to seek settlers for East Africa was being made and, quite likely, WSR responded. See also Meinertzhagen 1957.
    Historical note: The British East Africa Company was chartered in 1887, and the

East African Protectorate was established in 1895. In 1897 KR's cousin AEP and his wife, Nellie, were on safari in the deserts of Somaliland with Hugh Cholmondeley, third Baron Delamere (see Bull 1992:189 for photo). Soon afterward, Delamere abandoned the northern deserts for the crystalline air, rushing streams, and dizzying heights of the Central Highlands (see Huxley 1956). Dominated by the mystic presence of Mount Kenya, the Highlands were a largely healthful, congenial environment that Delamere fervently promoted as a white man's paradise. Kikuyu, along with wandering Masai herders who grazed and raided cattle, and smaller tribes such as the Dorobo, peopled the Highlands. Hereditary chiefs rightly perceived the white incursion as a threat, and blood was spilled. Nevertheless, by the end of 1902 the East African Syndicate had sold off more than five hundred square miles of tribal lands. On New Year's Day, 1902, the King's African Rifles was formed and "a multifarious collection" of white newcomers gathered to pour over British East Africa (Brown 1989:317). WSR was one of them.

48. "out to see"—Meinertzhagen 1957:54; see also Thurman 1995:134, Bull 1988:120.

48. After a tense—Meinertzhagen 1957:67.

48. "never turned up"—Ibid., 120.

Historical note: Meinertzhagen (1957:vi) held a substantial grudge against WSR and claimed that four or five of the photos in WPP were misrepresented by WSR as his own. Another photo credited to KSR and singled out by reviewers as exceptionally good was also, Meinertzhagen said, taken by him (WPP: photo facing pp. 307; 307–9; frontispiece, pl. CXI, pl. CIX). These accusations are untrue. Meinertzhagen is considered to be "a proven liar and a scoundrel" (John Hatt, publisher, Eland Books [1988 reprint edition of 1957 volume] personal communication, 19 Nov. 248; Meinertzhagen's biographer is Mark Cocker of Norwich). The reprint of Kenya Diary 1902–1906 was recently taken off the market because Hatt was convinced that Meinertzhagen had "doctored" the work (personal communication, 19 Nov. 2000). The original photos from WPP are, as of this writing, unavailable but still being sought (Autotype archives). Only laser-scanned photos from the original volume were used in the 1983 reprint.

48. Katherine's background and Scoresby's—D/GP 6, vol. 15, p. 45; the scant chronology of KSR's comings and goings during this period was kept by her mother in D/KP 4a. Five days before HGP was admitted to Holloway, KSR and Lyle went on a bicycle holiday in Tyrol.

48. Known to his—MEI:6. Regarding the yacht's name, KSR notes that "we had wished to give her one borne by some ship of Dr. Scoresby, the Arctic explorer, a friend of my husband's family . . ."

Historical note: In 1830 George Stephenson, Edward Pease's business partner in the fledgling Darlington and Stockton Railway, hosted his excited board members on a train journey from Manchester to Liverpool. With him, "on the footplate timing their progress," was none other than William Scoresby (Rolt 1984). Scoresby 1820, 1859:43; Stamp and Stamp 1976.

49. In 1820 he—Scoresby 1820.

49. "in the matrimonial"; "young ladies were"—REB, n.d., "Routledge" (PW); C. Stamp to REB, 16 Sept. 1981 (PW). "Poor Anne was by no means alone—I think many young ladies were susceptible to his charm." Transcription of the "Scoresby ms. on Miss Anne T." gave Stamp "striking proof of WS's utter innocence that he never seemed to guess at her real feelings" (C. Stamp to REB, 28 Dec. 1981). C. Stamp to REB, 16 Sept. 1981 (PW), in which "there are a few letters in this 1948 bundle (which obviously escaped Mrs. S.) in very affectionate terms from several young ladies." Anne Sophia Twycross to Dr. Scoresby, Lester's Terrace, 12 Aug. 1848. (PW); Anne Sophia Twycross to Dr. Scoresby, Bradford, 8 July 1848 (PW).

Historical note: In 1855 the Reverend Mr. Scoresby met the author Elizabeth Gaskell. He told her "many curious anecdotes" and tales of his hometown of Whitby, inspiring her to draw further from his works for her successful novel

Sylvia's Lovers (Gaskell 1996:479). It is not known if KSR read the book, but the historical setting of Whitby and the subject matter of women's relationships would have certainly interested her.

49. In 1853, still—James and John Twycross were aboard *Harbinger* in 1853, with Anne Sophia Twycross (Passenger List). The Reverend and Mrs. Scoresby and the *Royal Charter* sailed for Australia in early 1856 (Scoresby 1820, 1859):235.

Biographical note: The Twycross brothers formed a successful and prosperous partnership in the wool business in Australia. James returned to England (C. Lopez, personal communication, 2000).

49. In 1859 Anne's—WSR's paternal grandparents were James Routledge, a tanner of modest means, and Elizabeth Haliburton, daughter of Mr. Justice Thomas C. Haliburton (1829, 1838) of Nova Scotia, an MP, social critic, and published historian. See REB, n.d., "Routledge" (PW) and Family History Library Catalog, Aug. 1995, The Church of Jesus Christ of Latter-day Saints. Haliburton is also sometimes written as Halliburton (Certified Copy of an Entry of Birth, General Register Office, Reading, County of Berkshire, no. W008143/B) (copy on file, JVT); Davies 1988.

Biographical note: Anne Sophia Twycross, WSR's mother, was born May 25, 1821, in Wokingham, Berkshire. See also Lovell 1999a, 1999b. There is a conflict in the age of William Routledge, who, according to REB, would be thirty-three years old at the birth of WSR. The Registry of Births, Deaths and Marriages, Melbourne, Victoria, Australia, 94/152144, gives his age as thirty-two (copy on file, JVT, 9 Jan. 1996). William Routledge's brother James returned briefly to Brampton in 1857 to marry Anne Rennie. A family photo including WSR was taken at "Yarra Yarra Sept. 1884" (PW). Occasional references were made by WSR to his family's estate in Eastbourne being named Yarra Yarra, but no property with that name is given in his father's will. Members of the Twycross family, however, believe that William Routledge had two homes named Yarra Yarra, one in Australia and the other, perhaps later, in England (C. Lopez, personal communication, 2000). A family photo including WSR, two of his sisters, and two Milne cousins was taken in a garden and is labeled "Yarra Yarra," Sept. 1884, but the location of Yarra Yarra is not noted.

Historical note: Elizabeth Haliburton's brother Arthur Lawrence Haliburton served in the Crimean War, became undersecretary of state for war, and on retiring, received a baronet.

49. Sometime between 1865–881 Census Index, Sussex 1037/111/1. Copy on file, JVT.

Biographical note: James Routledge's daughter was Margaret Jane Routledge (Last Will, William Routledge, 2 June 1891. Office copy without impressed court seal on file, JVT).

50. "Earthquake Johnny"—Personal communication, C. Lopez, Twycross family, 2001.

50. "a true British barbarian"—*The Bookman*, Aug. 1910 (RGS WKR 7).

50. "no nervous self-assertion"—Ibid.

50. Even as a very—WSR to Agnes Mary Townsend, from Bursledon, 26 Mar. 1931 (PW).

50. He was awarded—K. Manners, assistant archivist, The Library, University College London, to M. Jacques, 21 Dec. 1995. Copy on file, JVT; Annual Report, University College London 1882/83, p. 14; Turk 1995:50–55.

51. "not exceeding three"—Last Will, William Routledge, court copy without impressed seal, 2 June 1891 (copy on file, JVT).

51. "with the Micmacs"—Routledge, Scoresby, in *Who Was Who, 1929–1940:* 1174; Last Will, William Scoresby Routledge, court copy without impressed seal, 27 Jan. 1938. See Jackson 1993, Upton 1979. It is probable that WSR went to Canada, in part, because of the region's connections with the Haliburton family.

Geographical note: Micmac territory covers the Canadian maritimes of Nova Scotia, New Brunswick, Prince Edward Island, Cape Breton, and Newfoundland.

51. "a heavy load"—WPP:104.

51. "a rough stone"—WPP: ix–xii; Meinertzhagen (1957) notes that WSR had come out to study the Kikuyu.

51. "shooting, photographing, collecting"—WPP:xii.
51. "I made it a practice"—Ibid.
52. "where the African"; "well oiled bodies"; "sheen of velvet"—WPP, 183, 185.
52. "usually a Masai"—Meinertzhagen 1957: 12–13; boys were also offered favors for sex by district bureaucrats, and one man committed suicide rather than face disclosure and disgrace.
52. Meinertzhagen bragged that—Meinertzhagen 1957: caption of plate facing p. 35; see also WPP: pl. CXI.
52. "converted girls that"—Meinertzhagen 1957:34.
52. "my wife and I"—Dr. A. C. Headlam, bishop of Gloucester, to Lilian Leslie Fox, 24 Mar. 1929 (PB). Deciphering Dr. Headlam's handwriting was no small task. It was accomplished by the combined efforts of M. Jacques, D. Lott, D. Bucknall, JGP, and JVT (JGP/ JVT, 19 Nov. 1997). Headlam Hall is described in Pease 1919:239, 300, 332, 346; D/GP 6, 5 Jan. 1896; for possible links to KSR and the Pease family, see JGP/JVT, 5 Jan. 1998; Dr. Headlam's family name and Headlam Hall appear to be coincidental; D/GP 6, v. 5, p. 12.
    Biographical note: There is a hint of a social link between WSR and KSR through the Pease Quaker connection in that WSR's maternal uncle James Twycross was married to Ellen Mounsey (1832–1921) of Lancashire, who may have been related to the Quaker Mounseys of Darlington, friends of KP. See also Jones 1996.
53. "young man Routledge"—D/GP 6, v. 16, p. 1.
53. "to act the parent"—Ibid. "Sometimes we long to be alone together on a South Sea Island, where relations and servants would cease from troubling" (D/GP 6, 1905, p. 25). WP quotes Chetwode that "friends are the gift of God, relations are the gift of the devil" (D/GP 6, v. 16, p. 1.).
53. "with our eyes"—D/GP 6, v. 16, p. 1; Pease, J.G. 1992:258.
    Historical note: In London's National Gallery there is a superb and evocative painting entitled *Vesuvius in Eruption, with a View over the Islands in the Bay of Naples* by Joseph Wright (1734–97).
53. Less than four—Lucy Pease Fowler (d. 1909) lent the house.
    Biographical note: Lucy was the same cousin who supported KSR's application to Somerville Hall and was the daughter of John Fowler of Leeds, "of steam plough [plow] fame" (Lucy B. Fleming, Sottelley Hall, Beccles, Suffolk, to Mrs. Henderson, 26 Jan. 1971 [papers of J. and P. Grey]). Her husband, Owen Fleming (d. 1955), was an architect and economist. See also Foster 1891, "The Descent of Pease of Hummersknott, Darlington, Etc."
53. "pride of birth"—D/GP 6, v. 24, p. 19.
    Historical note: The English prejudice against "shopkeeping" was quite persistent and deeply embedded in the conflict among capitalism, hereditary wealth, and social class. Wilson's attitude was especially unpleasant since it failed to recognize and give dignity to labor, something that his Pease, Wilson, and Gurney ancestors tried, in their way and at the time, to do.
53. "rough diamond"—PB to JVT, 29 May 1996.
54. Katherine's cousin Sir Alfred—AEP was considered "one of the finest hunters of the day" (Bull 1992:175).
    Biographical note: AEP hunted with Berkeley Cole (the husband of Karen Blixen) and U.S. president Theodore Roosevelt, among many noteworthies. AEP began as an avid "young blood," shooting charging lions on horseback. He then became an influential and eloquent conservationist (cf. Bull 1992:181–82). For an interesting photo of AEP and Nellie on safari with Lord Delamere, see Bull 1992:189.
54. "very scientific man"—D/GP 6, v. 16, p. 12; Lavender Pease wrote to her brother Edward, 29 July 1906, "I suppose you know Katie is engaged, her wedding next week & I suppose it will be a meeting of all the Pease family. She is going out to B.E. Africa immediately afterwards" (JGP/JVT, 29 Oct. 1995).

54. "lucky to get"; "he was as mad"—Sylvia Calmady-Hamlyn to JGP, 29 Mar. 1961 (JGP/JVT, 19 Sept. 1995).

54. He negotiated a settlement—Katherine's marriage settlement was difficult to unearth because her solicitor's files are no longer available. Neither are there any records I was able to find in the offices of WSR's former solicitors (JVT/R. M. W. Naylor, 28 Feb. 1996, 3 Apr. 1996; D. Walker/R. M. W. Naylor, 23 Feb. 1996). The probable amount of the settlement is deduced from KSR to her sister, Lilian, 20 Feb. 1929; see also JGP/JVT, 26 Feb. 1996; 10 July 1996; 20 July 1996; 13 Sept. 1996. As a comparison, WP lived on a "total income of about £1,700 sterling per year. He spent about £60 per year on clothes for Joan. On that income (at a rough calculation), Wilson would have probably paid about £56–57 income tax" (JGP/JVT, 10 July 1996). His total gambling losses varied but were often substantial.

54. "a rich wife"—Handwritten notes on the back of a photo of WSR and his mother, probably made by REB (PW).

54. In mid-July of 1906—The decision to grant degrees was made in 1904. KSR's delay in securing hers may have been the result of administrative issues, or it may have been because she did not apply until she had decided to marry. That suggests that the Routledges' travel goals of collecting and publishing were established.

54. "imperious manner"—D/GP 6, v. 16, pp. 11, 19.

54. Harold Gurney Pease—Sylvia Calmady-Hamlyn to JGP, 29 Mar. 1961 (JGP/JVT, 19 Sept. 1995). It is hard to piece together these events, and the "Grosvenor Hotel incident" could have been the first, rather than the second, of similar events. When HGP was "well," he was often released from whatever institution he was in, but once out in the world he often drank and his behavior worsened quickly to the point of violence, a rather typical situation for his type of illness. The force of his attacks on Gwen escalated over time.

54. Harold was returned—JGP/JVT, 17 May 1996; HGP requested substantial increases in his allowance from KP (14 Aug. 1903, D/GP 12 D/XD 64/5/26), and he was moving house frequently. He was admitted to Holloway on August 12, 1904, as patient no. 2779 in casebook B, p. 61.

   Note on documentation: The casebook is not on file either with the hospital or the Wellcome Institute (County Archivist, Surrey County Council/JGP, 23 Oct. 1996). Significantly, Harold was admitted without being legally certified in lunacy by the required hearing or "inquisition." This was probably to protect the family from scandal or to protect HGP's inheritance. No reports of HGP's attack on GMP were published in London or Durham County newspapers. The diaries of WP were "overcut rather than offend anybody's feelings" (Humphrey Allen Bucknall to JHP, 21 May 1930), explaining the brevity of D/GP 6, v. 15, autumn 1903 to spring 1906 (only nine pages for 1903–4). Patients admitted to Holloway could not "remain longer than twelve months, or return once having been discharged" (Taylor 1991:158). HGP, however, was officially there until his death on April 27, 1928.

55. "very sad at the thought"—GP to EP, 7 May 1928; see also 13 Oct. 1913, 23 Dec. 1913 (JGP/JVT, 29 Oct. 1995, 24 May 1996); AEP, 20 June 1905, 3 Aug. 1905, 14, 15, and 16 Aug. 1905, 10 Oct. 1905 ("Chronology of Recorded Extracts from Diaries of Wilson Pease, Sir J. W. Pease, Sir Alfred E. Pease and Ethel Buxton (née Pease) When Aged 17"), JGP/JVT, 30 July 1996. GWP's "entitlement" under HGP's will was protected (16 Feb. 1906, D/GP 12 D/XD 64/5/29; copy of HGP's will, D/GP 12 D/XD 64/9/7). GWP paid half of his expenses quarterly, about £250 per year, from HGP's stock dividends. KP paid the rest as a "voluntary allowance." Affidavit "In Lunacy" sworn 31 Jan. 1914 by GMP (DPL acc 40288; U418ePEA; D/GMP D/XD 64/4/1–134).

55. Katherine Maria Pease—"Wedding: Routledge—Pease," *Darlington and Stockton Times,* 9 Aug. 1906 (DPL); Benson and Benson 1912:191; AEP, 8 Aug. 1906 (JGP/JVT, 12 Sept. 1995); Nellie Pease to her son, Edward Pease, 24 Aug. 1906 (JGP/JVT, 12 Sept. 1995).

55. Duty, not the "Inner Light"—Addresses were given by Rachel (Mrs. Gilbert Gilkes), KP's sister, Mr. J. B. Hodgkin and Mrs. E. B. Mounsey, whose words "would have

arisen out of the Quaker silence & would probably have been asking for God's love and guidance to be with them in the years ahead, & a corporate blessing from all present at the great occasion" (Mrs. Dorothy Mounsey to JVT, 25 Mar. 1996).

56. "life cannot be"; "weddings are never"—KSR to (her niece) Hilda Violet Leslie Fox from Queen Anne's Mansions, London, 1923 (PB); KSR echoed verbatim the sentiments of Aunt Emma to her on the eve of Lilian's 1892 wedding, writing that "I know too, none better, what it means" to lose your sister when she marries (ibid.).

BRITISH EAST AFRICA: LOVE, SEX, AND EMPIRE, 1906

57. Katherine and William—WPP:335, Appendix I, KSR, 29 Mar. 1907; D/GP 6, v. 18, p. 10.

57. They departed the chaotic—Pease, J. G. 1992:262.

   Historical note: The Uganda Railroad ("Lunatic Line" or "Lunatic Express") was built by about fifteen thousand imported Indian workers, from 1894 to 1899, at a cost of £6–10 million (depending upon the source consulted. Bull [1992:186] gives £8 million). The goal was to carry passengers rapidly across Kenya (thought to be useless for development) to Uganda. To recoup the investment, Kenya was then developed, and "in 1902 the East African Syndicate sold 500 sq. mi. of prime highland real estate at low prices and as if it had been vacant. By 1915 over four and a half million acres" was in the hands of about a thousand white farmers (Thurman 1982:119).

   Biographical note: Just two years earlier Captain Charles Clutterbuck and his daughter, known later to the world as Beryl Markham, had made the same journey. In Wokingham, Anne Sophia Twycross (WSR's mother) had an older brother, John, who married a widow named Mrs. Clutterbuck. It is an unusual name, but the relationship to Charles Clutterbuck, if any, has not been established (REB, "Twycross," p. 4).

57. "a delightful person"; "if he received"; "emphatically obey them!"—WPP:337.

57. "is all new country"—Ibid., xiii; "Captain T. A. Joyce, O.B.E.," obit (P./D. Foster); see also Joyce 1905, 1906; WSR "proposes to spend about two years" in Africa (memo, C. H. Wright, RBG, 9 Nov. 1906).

   Collections note: WSR had a botanical kit from the Royal Botanic Gardens, Kew, and a zoological one from the British Museum of Natural History (now Natural History Museum), London.

58. "she found them"—WPP:xiii.

58. "nightmares of one's"—Ibid.: 337–38.

58. "no animal not"—Ibid.

58. An analogy has—Bull 1992.

59. "simple life,"; "depressing"—WPP:142, 339.

59. "the blessings of"—This was a favorite phrase of Victorians and is usually attributed to African explorer Mary Kingsley (for a famous photo of her see Bull 1992:131).

59. "looked on in agony"—WPP:338.

59. "to boot and horse"—Ibid., 339; KSR wrote, in early spring of 1907, to WP, who noted her many complaints and compared her first safari to his own journey through India. "It is easier to cross Africa than India. In Africa you have a healthy walk every day & eat the food you like, cooked by a cook of your own choosing—and at night you sleep in your own bed. In India you racket all day in a train, eat stomach-shattering meals & sleep on a back-breaking bed. I must point this out to Katherine of Aganda when we meet" (D/GP 6, v. 16, p. 34).

60. "goes by the Swahili"—WPP:340.

60. "there is a felt need"—Ibid., 341.

   Orthographical note: The Routledges wrote Kikúyu (the tribal nation and the land; also occasionally written Gikuyu) and Kénya, but the accents are not used today. Kikuyu (the people; also occasionally written Agikuyu) and M'kikú-yu (singular) are more usual.

For more on Kenya read Dundas, C. 1955:67 (related to WSR's heir John Charles Dundas Harington), who describes reforestation with eucalyptus in the Nyeri district.

60. "sensation of rest"; "coming into one's"—WPP:xxi.

60. "half unconscious recollection"; "our forefathers also"—Ibid.; the "childhood of the world" is a phrase KSR borrowed from Clodd 1914 (first published thirty years earlier).

60. Kenya was a raw—Thurman 1982:118.

61. In June of 1907—KSR to Hilda Violet Leslie Fox, Taunton, 27 June 1907 (PB).

61. Written in Katherine's—WSR "mourned over the departure of much of the game during the last three years" (WPP:343); see Thurman 1982:118, who, on the contrary, says "game abounded," and Pease, J. G. 1992.

61. "gipsy outdoor life"—WPP:343.

61. They met their goal—Tally from computer printout of objects from Africa donated by WSR, Conservative Club, London, to the British Museum (BM) (6–13–04), generated 23 April 1996, by the Department of Ethnography, British Museum; Departmental Register, v. 1, 1861–68 to 1903–7, BM 3.

   Collections note: The clay image WSR "subsequently acquired" is not in the BM collection. He may have kept it in his own home museum at Ewers or sold it. Its duplicate, collected by Mrs. Sidney Hinde, may be there, but I have not verified that (WPP:pl. cxvii–cxviii; see also WSR 1906:pl. A). Four shields of the many studied by KSR are in the BM collection. Photos in WPP of most artifacts are credited "Brit. Mus. [R]" and were probably taken by WSR, while a few that are unattributed cannot be further identified. None of the nonartifact photos, many of which were taken by KSR, are in the BM Photo Collection (J. Hamill, personal communication, 1996); Departmental Register, v. 2, 1907–13, shows items 1–13 given 3-5-1910; remaining items given 6-4-1910 by WSR, Bursledon, Hants. The names of some of the chiefs from whom some items were acquired are given.

61. Their main objective—WPP:343; "List of Plants collected in British East Africa by Mr. W. Scoresby Routledge" rec'd July 9, 1909 (RBG; see also KSR to "Dear Sir" (Curator, Kew Gardens) from Artillery Mansions, London, 7 Nov. 1906).

61. "in the orthodox Kikúyu"—WPP:229–35, 188–91; see also xiv–xv; Routledge, S. 1906.

61. "A tribute is due"—WPP:139.

62. "he would not"—Ibid.

62. "My first introduction"—Ibid., 120.

62. "dignified ways"—Beard 1990.

62. "things a woman"—Leicester *Mail,* 26 July 1910 (RGS LBR, MSS 7).

62. It was a matter—WPP:123.

63. "a white woman"—Ibid., 133, 272.

63. In the spring—Ibid., 154–67.

63. "the nymphae and clitoris"—Ibid., 64 n. 1; Dundas, A. 1924:177 (related to WSR's heir John Charles Dundas Harington).

   Medical note: Female circumcision is largely an Islamic or Islamic-influenced practice. In 1915 a circumcision ceremony was observed in which the operation was performed in two parts. In the first, the labia minora were cut and, in the second, the labia majora. The flow of blood was said to be "considerable" and the young girls were said to "suffer considerably," requiring many months to recover (G. St. George Orde Browne 1925: 65–68).

63. "strain and excitement"; "for the worse"—WPP:167.

63. "somewhat severe illness"—Ibid., 209.

64. "gathered silence"; "resembled precisely"—Ibid., 236.

64. Katherine wrote her—D/GP 6, v. 18, p. 21.

64. When Katherine referred—Ibid., p. 5; D/GP 6, v. 21, p. 23, in which a lifelong romance, when it is successful, "is bliss, but when it fails must be pergatory [*sic*]"; "a

black sheep makes the rest of the flock whiter" (D/GP 6, v. 31, p. 12); D/GP 6, v. 21, p. 23.

65. "acted in good faith"—WPP:250, 251–68.

65. He saw the—Ibid: 267; see also pl. CXXVII (2).
    Collections note: A gourd and pieces very much like that used to foretell the Routledges' future are in the collection of the Nairobi museum, with no record of donor (1912–69d, c. 1900).

65. In 1906, at—Pease, J.G. 1992:271.

65. Alfred then acquired—WPP:329; "Africa," AEP, The Morning Post, 13 June 1908 (written 12 June 1908 at Pinchinthorpe House, Guisbrough, Yorkshire).

65. "solemn promise to point"; "be given to others"—WPP: 329
    Historical note: The first settlers arrived in 1903 and, from the beginning, were "at sharp odds with the colonial authorities" (Bull 1992:187). The government's policy, said to have been ambivalent at best, was to "preclude racial conflict by restricting the acquisition of land by Europeans and Asians" and to "balance settler rights with native rights" (ibid.).

65. It began when Wombúgu—Nellie Pease to Edward Pease from Blackwell Grange, Darlington, 11 Oct. 1909 (JGP/JVT, 17 Nov. 1995); Pease, A.E. 1912; "An East African Official and Native Women," The (London)Times, 18 Dec. 1908.

66. "youngish man"; "nothing in particular"—"An East African Official and Native Women," The (London) Times, 7 Dec. 1908. Anonymous letter signed "Political Officer (West Coast of Africa)"; "An East African Official and Native Women," The (London) Times, 8 Dec. 1908, Comments; "An East African Official and Native Women," The (London) Times, 9 Dec. 1908.

66. "officious, loquacious, self-important"—Jacobson 1999:27; Meinertzhagen 1983:23.

66. "ignoramus who tries"; "vile jargon he"—Jacobson 1999:27.

66. "intercourse with native"—Jacobson 1999:27; Hyam 1992:163; see also WPP:272.

67. "signal service, not"—"The East African Protectorate." London: The (London) Times, 26 Dec. 1908; 30 Dec. 1908; letter by Mr. John G. Talbot, 29 Dec. 1908.

67. "aware that Mrs. Routledge"—"The East African Protectorate," The (London) Times, 26 Dec. 1908; "The Conduct of Mr. Silberrad," The(London) Times, 18 Dec. 1908.

67. "We must all"—"The East African Protectorate," The (London) Times, 26 Dec. 1908; "An East African Official and Native Women," The (London) Times, 18 Dec. 1908.

67. "no older, or redder"—D/GP 6, v. 19, p. 37.

67. Katherine renewed her—D/GP 6, v. 22, p. 20; v. 23, p. 40.

68. She hired a clipping—Four albums of news cuttings, some annotated in KSR's hand, were included in the papers of WSR salvaged in Cyprus by Mrs. Eve Dray Stewart and deposited with the RGS by Professor James Stewart, 1961 (RGS WKR 4/7); Leicester Mail, 26 July 1910; Daily Graphic, 16 May 1910; Scotsman, 25 Apr. 1910 (RGS WKR 4/7).

68. "sympathy with the oppressed—The Friend, 5 Aug. 1910 (RGS WKR 4/7).

68. "We children called"—Thurman 1982:127.

MANA, 1910

73. There they stumbled—The Routledges' addresses in Bursledon were "Waterside" and "Ewers," and it is not clear if they were one and the same. The Ewers property was in WSR's name and was managed by him (personal communication Mr. M. Richardson, present owner of Ewers and distant relative of KSR, 1997). John Charles Dundas Harington (son of Sir Richard Harington) inherited the property from WSR before selling it to Commander Richard Leigh, R.N. Mr. Richardson purchased the storehouse first in 1951 (now converted to a residence) and, in 1973, the cottage.

73. Philemon "John" Ewers—Memorial tablet on the wall of St. Leonard's church, Bursledon.

73. "home museum"; "curios"—WSR invited T. A. Joyce of the British Museum "to select what you want of the Gambier stuff picking against Balfour as you did in the case of . . . Easter Is." (WSR to Joyce, 4 Sept. 1925 [RGS WKR]).

Collections note: All objects donated to the BM and PRM are registered under the name of WSR. This is also the case at the RGS, although nearly all Mana Expedition fieldnotes were made by KSR. Objects collected by *Mana* crew members were considered property of the expedition. Osbert Guy Stanhope Crawford (hereafter, OGSC when citing unpublished documents) collected a "set of pot-making appliances" at Atalaya, Grand Canary Island (Crawford 1955:87). He "asked Routledge to be allowed to send them back to the [PRM], and he [WSR] consented on the condition that, as they were bought during the expedition, they should be recorded as presented by him. They are still on exhibition there." See PRM object catalogue 14.1.02. In 1934 WSR donated African objects he had collected in 1903 to the PRM (WSR to Henry Balfour, 26 July 1934, PRM), and in 1951, John Charles Dundas Harington donated African objects inherited from WSR, each precisely localized by original labels (PRM 1951.10.21.1–34). Very probably all of these came from the Routledge home museum.

74. Then one day—Captain T. A. Joyce, BM, to the Routledges, 1910 (RGS WKR 4/1/2); see also EI 1994:14. Total square miles or square kilometers given for Rapa Nui surface area varies considerably in the literature, from 160 km² to 173 km² and 62 square miles to 68 square miles (although *Webster's Geographical Dictionary* gives an inaccurate 46 square miles). This discrepancy results from the different accuracy levels of survey equipment or methods, paper shrinkage when values are taken off printed maps, and tidal variation. The figure I give here represents the mean value of the available data and is accurate within 2 percent.

74. Fuller and Joyce—Apparently, J. F. de la Pérouse was the first European to describe "secret caves" in a convincing manner (Ferdon 1958:146).

74. Most of the inscriptions—Barthel 1958; Fischer 1998:3.

74. He stressed to Scoresby—Joyce to WSR, 1910 (RGS WKR 4/1/2); Force and Force 1971 for data on A. W. F. Fuller; see also RGS WKR 4/1.

74. Not exactly sure—RGS WKR 4/2/3 has annotated bibliographies, references, and abstracts compiled by KSR, WSR, and a secretary who worked for them.

Note on fieldnotes: The Routledges did not consult missionary accounts of the island, it appears, until 1917 (WSR to Ferreir [Catholic missionary whom the Routledges later met in Mangareva] 1 June 1917, Ferreir to WSR, 13 July 1917 [RGS WKR 4/2/3]); see also RGS WKR 4/2/4. Some manuscripts were professionally translated from French, Spanish, or German, although KSR usually depended for such information on B. G. Corney. See also MEI:200–5.

74. "a keen yachtsman"—MEI:4, 9; Crawford 1955:81.

75. "I was out"—MEI:108.

75. She failed at first—While KSR visited and viewed Hoa Hakananai'a at the BM many times prior to her departure for the island, she never saw the carved back of the statue until her return (MEI:187, 263 n. 1).

Historical note: KSR's favorable impression of Hoa Hakananai'a was echoed many years later. Henry Moore (1981) singled it out as one of the pieces in the British Museum collection that impressed and inspired him when, as a young man, he was perfecting his art.

75. The large size—Feder 1999:v.

75. "leaving Easter Island"—"Lemuria" (RGS WKR 4/2).

76. "In dealing with"—MEI:xi.

77. In just fifty-two—With Captain Cook was the Tahitian Mahine, thus bringing the Rapa Nui people into contact, as well, with another Polynesian culture.

77. In that year—McCall 1998; see also Porteous 1981. There are a variety of conflicts inherent in such data, and specific numbers and dates in the literature vary.

78. The main one—Hanga Roa (Hangaroa) contains within its boundary a district adjacent to Mataveri known as Moe Roa (Moeroa).

78. Within a year—Zumbohm 1868; see also 1879, 1880; Van Tilburg 1992.

78. One of the Catholic—The estimate of 170 is sometimes given.

78. Only 111 islanders—Métraux (1940:3) gives the number 111, but 110 and 112 are also stated in the literature.

78. Dutrou-Bornier took an island—The last remnants of Mataveri house were demolished about two years ago. I visited the ruins several years earlier with Jorge Edmunds, Nikko Haoa, and Cristián Arévalo and videotaped an hour of conversation and reminiscences. The ruins were not of the house Brander had built (which was slightly to the rear of that site), but of the remodeled house Percival Henry Edmunds (hereafter PE) had constructed after the Mana Expedition had departed the island. Jorge remembered clearly many details of growing up in the house. It had a detached kitchen, a bath, and a separate latrine, as well as an office, a large dining room, and bedrooms.

78. Rano Kau—Rano Kau is spelled Rano Kao in KSR's published maps and texts.

78. Finally, the islanders—Jorge Edmunds told me a detailed story of the death of Dutrou-Bornier during our visit to the ruins of Mataveri house. He said that the motive was sexual jealousy, and that Dutrou-Bornier was injured by a serious blow to the head inflicted by a Mataveri employee who hid behind a door at the entrance to his house. Dutrou-Bornier lay outside from late afternoon until either later in the day or the next morning, then was stabbed to death by someone who took pity on him. Jorge also said that, when the remains of Dutrou-Bornier were dug up and moved, the hole in his skull was obvious. There are many variations on this theme, and the details of the story will probably never be fully clarified.

79. "the whole of"—Merlet to KSR on Rapa Nui, 25 Sept. 1914 (RGS WKR 4/4/3).

79. Edmunds, a traveler—PE's great-great-granddaughter (Elizabeth Edmunds) collected these data from family files. McCall (personal communication, 2002) says that Edmunds was born Percival Henry and died Henry Percy. He is known to his Rapa Nui family and to his half-Tahitian daughter as Percy. He signed many documents Percy Edmunds, but also Enrique Edmunds, Henry Percy Edmunds, or H.P. Major Thornley Edmunds (PE's nephew) told McCall that PE's preference for the initials H.P. was, perhaps, a joke inspired by the fact that they stood for Houses of Parliament. Major Edmunds also said that PE had a great fondness for a bottled meat sauce with a sketch of Parliament on the label and called H.P.

79. He was the son—Some family records have "Thronley," and I have not verified the correct spelling.

80. "sole representative of both"—Porteous 1981:166–67.

80. As enterprising, in his way—A. W. F. Fuller to KSR, n.d. pp. 6–7 of seven-page letter describing artifacts 5–7 (of seven) received from PE via Mrs. Edmunds (his mother). Letter received after KSR's return from Easter Island and during writing of MEI (RGS WKR 4/1/2). Mrs. Edmunds wrote a piece called "The Loneliest Briton" about PE and his isolation on Rapa Nui and submitted it to *The Daily Mail* to win a subscription to *The Over-Seas Daily Mail* for her son (Edmunds' archives; researched by Urbano Edmunds H.).

81. "large roomy bungalow"—WSR to WBCO, 11 Aug. 1910 (RGS WKR 7, 4/1). On the last page KSR added a question about previous or current expeditions on the island. WBCO to WSR, 26 Sept. 1910 (RGS WKR 4/1/1). The Mataveri house KSR stayed in was remodeled after the expedition left the island.

81. "in service to"; "very low wages"—WBCO to WSR, 26 Sept. 1910 (RGS WKR 4/1/1).

81. "Payments will not"—Ibid.

81. Instead, in the 1800s—The currently acceptable and official Chilean name of the people and the island is Rapa Nui, although some use the alternative spelling Rapanui (cf.Van Tilburg 1994:10). The name of the language is correctly written Rapanui (Churchill 1912).

81. *Kanaka*—Edmunds (1994; Oliveros 1994) used the term *Kanaka* when referring to islanders. KSR had read Palmer's 1868 report and probably Churchill (1912) on the Rapanui language prior to the voyage and was familiar with the variant spellings of Rapa Nui. Upon her return (and before her publications about the island) she read a newspaper article reporting that Albert P. Taylor, secretary and director of the Hawaii promotion committee, had sent a directive to all newspapers, magazines, and publish-

ers in Hawaii stating that *Kanaka* was a "slurring term" to be avoided (*Christian Science Monitor*, 24 July 1916 [RGS WKR]). Her continued use of the word after that date, in both Rapa Nui and Mangareva, is inexcusable and extremely puzzling in light of her fondness for both places and her earlier efforts in Africa to use the correct names of individuals and tribes. See MEI:209–10.

81. "a much larger"—MEI:4.

82. Williamson, Balfour Co.—WSR to WBCO, 11 Aug. 1910; WBCO to WSR, 26 Sept. 1910; WSR to WBCO, July 1911; WSR to WBCO, 8 Jan. 1911 (all in RGS WKR 4/1/1).

82. He completed a second—Eve Dray Stewart has a full set of plans for *Mana* and a spark plug from the yacht's engine that she found among WSR's papers in Cyrus (Stewart to JVT, 1998).

82. The keel was laid—WSR to PE, 3 Dec. 1911 (RGS WKR 4/1/1).

82. He finally purchased—One knot equals one nautical mile (6,080 ft.) per hour. A log was once attached to a rope with knots tied on it at evenly spaced intervals (47 ft. 3 in. apart). The log was thrown overboard to measure the speed of the ship by counting the knots let out in a specific time.

82. Not satisfied, Scoresby—KSR to "Dear Mr. Crawford" from Southampton, n.d. (BOD MS). *Mana* construction at this point was more than £1,000 over budget.

83. Scoresby demanded repetitive—D/GP 6, v. 29, p. 16. Over the course of two or three evenings KSR told WP and Joan about the lawsuit, which was obviously taking a serious toll on her nerves. She refused to compromise at £200 offered and eventually won a judgment in the amount of £800; Crawford (1955:81) says that "when the boat was finished Routledge was dissatisfied and sued the builders, obtaining quite a large sum from them by a judgment of the court." OGSC thought the complaint "frivolous" on the grounds that *Mana* was "thoroughly seaworthy." WP also hinted that KSR should not have brought the suit. KSR to "Dear Mr. Crawford" from Southampton, 17 Dec. 1912 (BOD MS); KSR to "Dear Mr. Crawford" from Woodside, 20 Jan 1913, "The arbitration concluded yesterday . . ." (BOD MS).

83. "I name this ship"—MEI:6; "An Interesting Launch," Whitstable *Times*, n.d. (RGS WKR). Only one superior piece of reporting marshaled facts and detailed challenges facing the Mana Expedition ("Easter Island: Aims of the Expedition," *The* (London) *Times*, 25 Dec. 1912 [RGS WKR]).

83. Scoresby had lobbied—Marett 1941:220. Edward Le Blanc, a steward and native of San Francisco, was the only crewman who made reference to *Mana* as anything other than a good-luck ship. He deserted in Honolulu harbor, saying he was "tired of living on a 'jinx' ship which carried the skulls of many South Seas tribes" (undated, unnamed San Francisco newspaper cutting, RGS WKR); Book 12, "Chief Officers Log Book of the Aux. Schooner 'Mana' from the Port of Southampton, England," Fri., 12 Nov. 1915, and Tues., 23 Nov. 1915 (RGS WKR 1/12).

83. "untranslatable"; "picked it up"—Crawford 1955:81.

83. "You and Wilson"—D/GP 6, v. 31, p. 15.

84. On the wall—D/GP 6, v. 28, pp. 52–53. "My day with Katherine and her Yacht" was written by WP as a journal entry and is the source for my sketch of KSR in Bursledon. All quotes are from that journal. With Reggie Barnes (hereafter RB) in 1997, I traced the path that KSR and WP took on the day he visited.

84. "I would be"—Ibid.

THE MANA EXPEDITION: SAILORS, SCIENTISTS, AND SPIES

86. The Routledges advertised—KSR to "Dear Mr. Crawford" from Southampton, 17 Dec. 1912, "they absconded during our absence on Sunday! So here we are stuck till we can get together a new crowd!! . . . So S. & I remain in charge" (BOD MS); OGSC to "Dear Auntie Do" from aboard *Mana*, n.d. (BOD MS); KSR to "Dear Mr. Crawford" from Southampton, n.d. (BOD MS).

86. Seamanship is equal—Gillam "has had a lot of experience in many ports of the world," "He is a very good man & a very nice one" and gives "very skillful guidance" to *Mana*

(OGSC to "Dear All" off Funchal, Madeira, 16 April 1913, BOD MS). Last Will, Henry James Gillam, 9 May 1916 (official copy with impressed court seal); Commonwealth War Graves Commission; 1881 British Census PRO RG11, Piece 1138, fo. 82, p. 13; personal communication, T. Gillam, 2000; personal communication, Peg and Dick Foster, 2000; Gillam's father was Henry Amos Gillam and his mother, Sarah Gillam. See also "Log Books of Yacht Mana, 15 vols. Commencing Febry. 20th 1913" for list of crew (RGS WKR 1/1–15).

87. "the successful achievement"—MEI:9; Crawford (1955:82). "Little Craft Braves Peril of Deep Sea," San Francisco *Chronicle*, 24 Dec. 1915 (RGS WKR). "Gillam says she is a splendidly built boat and 'very handy'" (OGSC to "Dear All," n.d. [BOD MS]).

87. "with a face"—OGSC to "Dear All," n.d. (BOD MS).

87. "intelligent criticism"; "amenity of the voyage"—MEI:9; Crawford (1955:84) says that Light was a chap "whom we all liked very much. He was a typical simple, efficient and stouthearted sailor, and he did his best to teach me." See also OGSC to "Dear All" from *Mana* off Hythe, n.d. (BOD MS).

87. Green considered Scoresby—Frank T. Green to "My Dear Crawford" from *Mana* off Buenos Aires, 19 Aug. 1915 (BOD MS).

87. Charles Giffard Jeffery—KSR (MEI:9) wrongly gives "Charles C. Jeffery" or, more correctly, "Charles Jeffery" (MEI:78, 390). He was the youngest son of Mrs. A. Hargraves of 78 St. Leonards Road, Lowestoft, and grandson of Edward Jeffery, M.D. His father died in 1894, and CGJ's mother had remarried to one James William Hargrave in 1906. Hargrave had also died by the time CGJ was killed (Mike and Carol Jeffery, personal communication, 2001). See RGS WKR 1/1/1–15 for crew list.

88. The second was Lieutenant—An elderly aunt of Lieutenant Graham's described her "Atlantis" theory regarding Rapa Nui (RGS WKR 4/1/1). KSR to "Dear Mr. Crawford" from 19 Wilton Street, S.W., 11 Jan. 1912 (BOD MS).

88. "brilliant"—Crawford 1955:82; see also Frederick [Lowry-]Corry to "Dear Crawford" from Lennox Gardens, S.W., 20 June 1912 (BOD MS); E. A. Reeves of RGS to "Dear Mr. Crawford," 9 July 1912 (BOD MS); KSR to "Dear Mr. Crawford" from *Mana* off Southampton, 13 Feb. 1913; OGSC to "Dear Corry" from Newbury, Berkshire, 8 June 1913 (BOD MS); R. Douglas Graham to "Dear Crawford" from Reading, 1 Feb. 1914, with cutting enclosed, "Images Carved by Giants," *Daily Chronicle* (BOD MS).

88. Lieutenant David Ronald—Registrar General for Scotland, 1886; certified copies of marriage (MXA 548335) and death (DXZ 657589) certificates, General Register Office; Last Will, David Ronald Ritchie, 27 Jan. 1960 (official copy with impressed court seal); personal communication, Peg and Dick Foster, 2000. Ritchie's father was William C. Ritchie and his mother, Margaret Agnes Eagle-Bott. He was engaged to Phyllis Gurney, who, apparently, was not a relative of KSR's. KSR's RGS paper (1917:322) erroneously gives "Lieut. R.D. Ritchie."

89. On February 24—PRO ADM 196/50 PT 2 E. The expedition was wrongly described as organized by the British Association for the Advancement of Science. The only involvement of that association was a contribution of £100.

89. The Germans, to the far-thinking—Whenever scholarly organizations pressed WSR for reasons why the expedition was so often delayed, or if the press asked him to clarify the scientific goals of the expedition, he darkly hinted that there was something about the crew or the voyage he was not at liberty to discuss. See, for example RGS to WSR at Ewers, 25 June 1912; KSR from 69 Grovenor Street to Dr. Keltie, 1 July 1912; R. Douglas Graham to WSR, 31 May 1912; KSR to Dr. Keltie, 18 Sept. 1912, "We are anxious that as little as possible appear in the press"; WSR to RGS from Tankerton Hotel, Whitstable, 9 June 1912 (all in RGS CB 8/3/73); A. W. F. Fuller to T. A. Joyce, 23 July 1912 (RGS WKR 4/1/1); WSR, 13 Oct. 1911 (RGS WKR 4/1/1); see also "Easter Island: Aims of the Expedition," *The* (London) *Times*, 25 Dec. 1912 (RGS WKR 6/1/1); "Physiography, etc., of Easter Island," *The Quarterly Journal of the Geological Society of London. Proceedings*, 1917:x–xi (WSR spoke before a meeting of the society).

89. Katherine was a frugal—KSR to "Dear Mr. Crawford" from Bedford Sq., 26 June 1912, re farewell party at Hans Crescent Hotel and his share of the cost (BOD MS).

89. Scoresby responded by—WSR but signed by KSR, 13 Oct. 1911 (RGS WKR 4/1).
89. "no need to use"—T. A. Joyce to WSR, 13 Oct. 1911 (RGS WKR 4/1). This opinion was widely held about Pacific islands well into the 1920s. When O. G. S. Crawford signed on as archaeologist, he shared it (cf. OGSC to "Dear Mr. R.," n.d. (BOD MS).
89. "enter with whole"—WSR but signed by KSR, 13 Oct. 1911 (RGS WKR 4/1). James H. Worthington, the son of a wealthy Liverpool shipowner, signed on after his father contributed £500. Worthington's consuming passion was astronomy, and he hoped to record the total eclipse of the sun predicted for October 10, 1912, in Rio de Janeiro. WSR sent Worthington to study with Marett and to the RGS to learn plane table surveying. Worthington, who thought WSR a bully, chose not to waste his time acquiring skills he did not want and resigned from the expedition. WSR promptly sued him in High Court for breach of contract.
90. "moral fervor"—Crawford 1955:40–41.
90. "underdressed, earnest men"—D/GP 6, v. 27, p. 41.
90. "come under the spell"; "picked up"—Crawford 1955:78.
90. "curious three-sided bargain"—Ibid., 77.
91. Continued delays, however—See, for example, KSR to RGS, 25 Mar. 1912, on *Mana* off Falmouth (RGS CB 8/73): "Here is the contribution to the Journal which it w[a]s promised to send before we sailed. As you will see other statements were premature. We have been subjected to a series of most vexatious delays in connection with the delivery of the vessel & lately from the weather but all seems now in working order & we intend to sail this afternoon."
91. Crew rations for—MEI:11; Crawford (1955:84) disagrees with KSR's assertion that "the quantity asked for by our men of any staple foods was always given."
91. "alarming size"; "containing sounding machines"—MEI:12.
91. "Judging from the quantity"—Ibid.
91. "you must advertise"—D/GP 6, v. 28, p. 9; see also MEI:9–10.
92. "doing the honours"—D/GP 6, v. 28, p. 9.
92. "gadget fiend"—Crawford 1955:77.
92. "epoch-making book"; "solve the riddle"—R. D. Graham to "Dear Crawford" from 30 Whitwell Road, Southsea, 3 Apr. 1913 (BOD MS); A. J. Herbertson to "My dear Crawford," 12 Mar. 1913 (BOD MS); C.M.A.P. to "Dear Mog," 8 Feb. 1913, "So its all hands to the pumps already, is it?" (BOD MS).
92. "began to despair"—Crawford 1955:82.
92. "after six years'"—MEI:38.
92. "Uncle Scoresby is still"—KSR to Beatrice Evelyn Leslie Fox, 8 Mar. 1913 (PB).
93. "It is now up to you"—D/GP 6, v. 30, p. 27.

ATLANTIC TO THE PACIFIC: "AN ARCHAEOLOGICAL FIASCO"

94. "Frightened?"—MEI:14. Crawford (1955:81–90) says that, for the period 1911–12, he kept no record and relied upon letters to write his memoir. See OGSC to "Dear All" from *Mana* off Funchal, 16 Apr. 1912 (BOD MS); see also OGSC notes on Marett's lectures in the Anthropological Archives at Oxford (which I have not personally examined) and Marett's notes from/for his lectures in the PRM archives, Oxford (also not personally examined); Marett 1941.
94. "mutinous talk"—Crawford 1955:84; OGSC also, at this point, raves about the comfort of his cabin, the skills of Gillam, and in general paints a favorable picture of the voyage (cf. Peake to OGSC from Westbrook House, 10 Mar. 1913, "I am glad to hear you find everything on board so comfortable; you will soon get your sea-legs" (BOD MS); C.M.A.P to "Dear Mog" from Lincoln's Inn Hotel, 5 Mar. 1913(?), "I was very glad to get the news that the Mana is such a seaworthy craft" (BOD MS).
95. "saw red rather"—Crawford, 1955: 84.
95. "sunshine and smiling"—MEI:18, 30.
    Personnel note: In Funchal, and for the rest of the voyage, KSR was responsible for overseeing employment of new crewmen and shore hands needed to under-

take work on *Mana* in port. Her duties included dispensing crew wages. The extant records are either incomplete or careless. KSR wrote each man's name and the amount paid in black ink on any available piece of paper, including store receipts. Each man initialed in pencil next to the amount received, and the paper was then simply tucked into a journal or record book filled with receipts for countless purchases. See also Crawford 1955:85–86.

95. Her shipboard menus—One of KSR's favorite recipes was for "rock buns," eaten in the morning and at tea. The recipe calls for flour, butter, sugar, almonds, and nutmeg. Other recipes were for stews, curries, and rich custards. KSR's diet was always heavily laced with sugar, and she relished dairy products. A postcard from OGSC to Miss G. A. Crawford from Funchal, 18 Apr. 1913, points out where *Mana* was anchored (BOD MS).

95. "I was cross-examined"—Crawford 1955:85–86; OGSC to "Dear All" from *Mana* off Funchal, 16–20 Apr. 1913, 9 pp. (BOD MS). He does not mention his problem with KSR.

95. "the full moral"—Crawford 1955: 86; see also OGSC to "Miss G.A. Crawford," 2 postcards, 22 Apr. and 5 May 1913, in which he says, "Am having a very good time . . . there is plenty to do" (BOD MS).

95. The crew now—Crawford 1955:31; for the tea episode, see OGSC to "Dear All" from *Mana* off Funchal, 16–20 Apr. 1913, p. 9 (BOD MS).

95. "rather nice as"—OGSC to "Dear All" off Funchal, 16–20 Apr. 1913, 9 pp. (BOD MS). "Am having a very good time & not a bit bored by being here as There is plenty to do" (OGSC to Miss. G.A. Crawford, *Mana* postcard, Las Palmas, 5 May 1913 (BOD MS).

96. "did not see"—Crawford 1955:87–88; OGSC to "Dear All" off Funchal, 16–20 Apr. 1913, 9 pp., in which he describes what he did in Las Palmas and notes the quarrel with the Routledges (BOD MS).

96. "had a great"—Crawford 1955:87.

96. "things about themselves"; "extraordinary lack of courtesy"; "appalling stinginess"; "a complete fraud"—Ibid., 89.

97. "I have had to resign"—OGSC to "Dear All" from Hotel Central, St. Vincent, 18 May 1913, 2 pp. (BOD MS); 2 postcards from OGSC to "Miss G.A. Crawford," 27 and 29 May 1913, one with photo by Frank T. Green (BOD MS).

Personnel note: In St. Vincent, WSR hired Bartolomeo Rosa and entered him in the log as "Negro." Rosa spoke Portuguese and, in an effort to help him learn English, KSR often engaged him in conversation. Rosa's goal was to save all of his wages from the expedition, return to St. Vincent, and find a wife. He would then buy and stock a shop and, while his wife attended to the customers, sit outside on a barrel and smoke. When KSR suggested that such idleness would lead to drink, Rosa told her that he would solve that problem by buying a boat as well and, from time to time, going fishing.

97. "marvelous bleakness"; "any trees, any grass"; "constant tearing wind"—MEI:28

97. "dreadfully sorry for"—R. R. Marett to KSR, 21 June 1913 (RGS WKR 4/1/1); see also R. Douglas Graham to "Dear Crawford" from Reading, 9 June 1913: "I should like to hear your version very much not that I credit anything from the Rs" (BOD MS); R. Douglas Graham to "Dear Crawford" from Reading, 4 June 1913 (BOD MS); H.D. (Herbertson) to "Dear Crawford" from Christchurch, Hants, 25 Sept. 1913: "he must be a bad man indeed who cannot get on with you!" (BOD MS).

97. "Other things—survey"—R. R. Marett to KSR, 21 June 1913 (RGS WKR 4/1/1).

98. He avoided R. R. Marett—OGSC to "Dear Dr. Marett" from The Grove, 23 June 1913 (BOD MS); the friend who intervened was Professor E. A. Hooten; "The reason I gave the Routledges for resigning was that I could not approve of the manner in which the expedition was being conducted; & when you hear some of the things they did you will be astonished. Their behaviour to everyone on board was perfectly scandalous . . . mismanaged . . . heartily sick of the whole affair . . . they persist in spreading inaccurate accounts."

98. He secured a post—OGSC to "Dear All" from (Wellcome Expedition) Excavation

Camp, Gebel Moya, Sudan, 22 Nov. 1913 (BOD MS); OGSC to "Dear All" from Ab Gyeili, 3 Feb. 1914 (BOD MS).

98. His distinguished career—In 1928, OGSC published *Wessex from the Air*, which included three hundred views of archaeological sites, and founded the professional journal *Antiquity*; Daniel 1981:166–67.

98. "he was a terrible bore"—Crawford 1955:239.

98. "He started to accuse"—Frank T. Green to "My dear Crawford" from Expedition Yacht Mana, Buenos Aires, 19 Aug. 1913, 6 pp. (BOD MS).

99. "Floating Hell"—Ibid.

  Personnel note: Green ridiculed KSR mercilessly, describing her in his letters as "K. Routledge (born Pease)"; "Mrs. R. made her appearance on deck and looked around with her fishy eyes"; "sitting in the deck house with a face like a Kilkenny Cat, mopping tears from her eyes with a hankerchief [sic] that would have been none the worse of some soap & water" (all in BOD MS).

99. Scoresby wanted to shelter—MEI:40.

99. "wonderful transparent light"; "pure and soft"—Ibid., 45

99. Katherine sent out—RGS WKR 3 (Mana Stores and Accounts); Shaw & Co.

  Medical note: The list of laundry sent out by KSR contains an item that she referred to as "2 diapers." *Diaper* was then, essentially, a term that referred to a "towel or napkin" of soft cotton or linen, usually white, with a distinctive woven, curvilinear pattern. It was a garment used by women during menstruation, suggesting that KSR was not yet, at the age of forty-seven, menopausal. This is significant in terms of understanding her general health and mental outlook while on Easter Island.

100. "The next generation"—MEI:50; KSR demanded her rights but was not above accepting special treatment. *Mana* crewmen were irritated that, on the basis of gender alone, she received double their water ration.

100. She booked a large suite—RGS WKR 3 (Mana Stores and Accounts, Simon Berg Shoemaker and Tailor, 4 Sept. 1913).

100. "with her hatches"—MEI:55.

100. "The Riddle of the Pacific"—Buenos Aires *Herald*, Wed., 3 Sept. 1913 (RGS WKR 4/13): MEI:3.

100. "almost that of"—MEI:61.

101. Luke took with him; "mean"—"Luke" is a mystery, as no one by that name appears in the crew list. On the voyage out KSR was so pleased with his services that she doubled his wages. Log Books of the Yacht Mana (RGS WKR1/1–15). F. W. Shephard was the cook, and George Smith, as steward, supervised "Luke." See also MEI:14, 73–74.

102. "a bewildering labyrinth"; "fresh passages open"—MEI:75.

102. "just like in the"—Ibid., 87.

102. "cut through the thick"—Ibid., 83.

102. Gillam calculated speed—The speed of *Mana*, in contrast, was determined by "the patent log, a mechanical screw which trailed behind the vessel and whose evolutions registered its rapidity" (ibid., 117).

102. A Fellow named—The entire account of the interchange between the RGS (Mr. Arthur Hinks, Secretary), KSR, B. W. Stainton, and B. G. Corney, which went on for at least six months (beginning 25 Nov. 1916), can be found in RGS CB 8/73. See also MEI:84 n. 1, 96.

103. Mana Canal or Canal Mana—Sheet #5375, Isla de Pascua, Chile, 1954, Instituto Geográfico Militar, Chile (Map Room, RGS Chile G.2).

103. "Holly Antarctic"—MEI:94.

103. "first experience in"—Ibid., 95–96.

103. "civilized man"; Feeling "a little"—Ibid.

104. "thoroughly fed up"—R. Douglas Graham to "Dear Crawford" from Reading, 26 Mar. 1914, "Cory [sic] says that if the R's are not already discredited they will be as soon as they begin lecturing on E.I."; "Ritchie's letter is almost pathetic, he is so sick of the whole affair" (BOD MS); Frank T. Green to OGSC, postcard from Talcahuano,

11 Feb. 1914, "Many thanks for your two letters & the Chambers Journals" (BOD MS).

104. "Things go on"—D. R. Ritchie to "Dear Old Crawford" from Talcahuano, Mar. 1914, "I hope never to come across the Routledges again after leaving this job. I can't conceive of anybody that I could personally dislike so cordially for any combination of reasons & to get two of them together at the same time is really bad luck" (BOD MS). See also R. Douglas Graham to "Dear Crawford" from Reading, 1 Feb. 1914, with enclosure "Images Carved by Giants," *Daily Chronicle,* n.d. (1914) (BOD MS).

104. "extreme poverty of the inhabitants"—"Scientific Expedition to Easter Island: The British Yacht 'Mana' in Valparaíso," *South Pacific Mail,* 28 Feb. 1914 (RGS WKR 4/1); MEI:148 n. 1. *Mana* was originally asked to carry the Australian bales of clothes but declined, and then, when approached again, Gillam agreed, but it was too late as they had been distributed to the poor of Valparaíso.

104. Undaunted, Lady Grogan—"Voyage to Easter Island: 'Baquedano' to Take Out Supplies," *South Pacific Mail,* 26 May 1914 (RGS WKR 4/1).

105. Katherine gamely attended—Frank T. Green to OGSC, postcard from Juan Fernández, 17 Feb. 1914, "Mr. R. taken ill also, but according to the quantity of food he eats he can't be very bad" (BOD MS).

105. Scoresby recovered and Lowry-Corry—A check for Lowry-Corry's medical records proved futile, and the British and American Hospital no longer exists.

105. Selkirk had only—WSR read *The Life and Adventures of Alexander Selkirk* (Howell 1829). *Historical note:* William Dampier, the controversial navigator and author of *A New Voyage Round the World* (1697), had commanded *St. George,* the sister ship to *Cinque Ports* before Dampier and Stradling had quarreled and separated their ships. Dampier was aboard *Duke,* the vessel that rescued Selkirk, as was surgeon John Ballett, also formerly of *Cinque Ports.*

106. About sixteen feet—Selkirk's Cave is not the same place as Selkirk's Lookout. Apparently, Selkirk never actually stayed in the cave KSR described.

106. Inside was a long—*Collections note:* Like so many of KSR's typewritten letters, this one is laced with typos. The sketches KSR drew for her niece are on the same notepaper, not enfolded separately. They are the basis for other, more elaborate sketches and watercolors KSR made of Juan Fernández (see also MEI:figs. 20, 22). KSR customarily gave her rough sketches and watercolors made in the field to various artists, including Miss A. Hunter, to be finished with the aid of comparative photographs. Typically, KSR kept copies of her letters or wrote "Save" on them so that the recipient would preserve them for her later use as notes. Virtually all of her published writing has clear antecedents or roots in her extant journals and letters or has been extracted whole from MEI (as was her *National Geographic* article).

106. At the eleventh hour—KSR never referred to MacLean by name in any of her published writing, but called him the "Juan Fernández boy" in MEI. The only way of identifying him in her fieldnotes was by matching a single, handwritten note in one of the *Mana* logs with KSR's journal entries (RGS WKR 1/1–15).

TOWARD EASTER ISLAND: ECOLOGY AND HISTORY AT SEA

107. The Pacific covers—Philbrick 2000:130, 144.

107. In 1835 Talcahuano—Moorehead 1969:137–38. *Historical note:* In 1960 another earthquake struck Chile. It caused a tidal wave that crossed the Pacific to Japan after striking the eastern and southeastern coasts of Easter Island. Ahu Tongariki, the largest ceremonial platform (*ahu*) on the island, was leveled, and fifteen multiton statues (*moai*) were tossed more than one hundred yards inland.

107. From the deck—Ibid. In 1891, G. Baur of Clark University suggested a rival hypothesis: that the Galápagos were "continental islands." KSR understood the geology of the Pacific, as it was then known, very well (cf. KSR to "My dear Children, Grown-up Otherwise" from off Juan Fernández Island, 8 Mar. 1914 [PB]).

Historical note: : Pseudoscientific theories of lost continents are centered on the long-ago discredited notion of the so-called continents of Lemuria or Mu. Easter Island was still seriously considered in the 1920s to be "the sole surviving remnant of an ancient land or oceanic continent—possibly an eastern extension of the fabled lost continent of Lemuria" (Wycherley 1928:223).

108. American Whalers respected—Ibid., 77, 120–21, 129–30; see also Fisher 1958 and, for a broad overview, *The Rand McNally Atlas of the Oceans.*

108. In 1520 Ferdinand Magellan—Ferdinand Magellan was the Portuguese navigator Fernão de Magalhães (c. 1480–1521). The Spanish explorer Vasco Núñez de Balboa (1475–1519) was the first to sight the Pacific, in 1513.

108. He then sailed—Withey 1987; Magellan landed on what is now Guam.

108. "Up went the huge sail"—Haddon and Hornell 1975 (I):326; estimated speed was ten to fifteen knots per hour.

109. "got it backward"—R. Green, personal communication, 2002 (Heyerdahl obit by JVT in *The Guardian*, 19 Apr. 2002), Kirch 2000.

109. It is archaeologically certain—Kirch 2000:241; see also Green 1988; Green 2001; Green and Weisler 2001; in addition to the sweet potato, a certain type of gourd was apparently also acquired and, perhaps, other goods not yet archaeologically known.

109. The sweet potato—Roger Green (personal communication, 2003) believes that the sweet potato was not introduced to Rapa Nui until about A.D. 1100 (about one hundred years after the current archaeological evidence of its presence in Central Polynesia). Prior to that, he feels, the yam was the major Rapa Nui crop.

110. On outward voyages—Finney (1994:59, 270–73) discusses routes southeast to Easter Island. See also Van Tilburg 1994. Speculated South American routes to Easter Island were published and discussed long before the Mana Expedition departed England and, obviously, long before T. Heyerdahl later promoted the concept. See *Illustrated London News*, 25 Mar. 1911; anon., 1909, *Scottish Geographical Magazine* xxv:196, in which Easter Island was "colonized by emigrants from Western America"; anon., 1910, "There were GIANTS in the earth in those days." See also *The London Magazine*, July 1910, 511–13.

> *Historical note:* Polynesian voyagers with fast vessels, assuming they had westerlies for at least a portion of the time and knew approximately where Easter Island was (as legends suggest they did), had a far better chance than the men of *Essex*, the American whaler that, in 1820, was a thousand miles west of the Galápagos when it was rammed and sunk by an eighty-five-foot bull whale (the incident inspired Herman Melville's *Moby Dick;* cf. Philbrick 2000). The men piled into thirty-two-foot whale boats and set out for the west coast of South America. They wandered around the Pacific for a month until, on the verge of death, they landed on Henderson Island, a coral and rock island that is part of the Pitcairn group and lies eleven hundred miles from Rapa Nui. Inhabited by Polynesians for about four centuries, by A.D. 1450 it had been abandoned, its inhabitants departing for other islands (Rapa Nui perhaps, or back to Mangareva?). Within just a week the *Essex* men had consumed all of the freshwater and killed or driven off all of the birds. Three men remained (and survived) while seventeen set out again, this time making for Rapa Nui. Nineteen days later they had been driven six hundred miles south of Rapa Nui. Wandering for another nineteen days, they resorted to cannibalism, and only five men survived when one boat made the coast of Chile and the other reached Juan Fernández Island.

110. Isolation and small—Jared Diamond, personal communication, 2002.

110. The identity of—The initial settlement of Rapa Nui might have been accomplished with one voyage of one or two canoes between A.D. 300 and A.D. 800. A second voyage, also of one or two canoes and bringing the sweet potato, may have arrived sometime soon after A.D. 1000. It is possible that Hotu Matu'a and his saga are remembered from this second voyage, which originated in Mangareva via Pitcairn. Sergio Rapu, who favored this theory at the time, discussed it with me over fifteen years ago.

111. The voyagers departed—MEI:277–80; Van Tilburg 1994:45 for discussion of Marae-
     renga as a place name in Rarotonga, Cook Islands; Van Tilburg 1996 for speculation
     on Rapa Nui voyaging canoe type, and 2001, notes. See also Métraux 1940, who
     relied on Tepano and KSR's other sources still alive; Barthel 1958:206–7; Arturo Teao
     provided most of Barthel's data on the subject of Hotu Matu'a. Buck (1938:40, 16, 19,
     418, 509) reports fragments of traditions that appear to suggest links between Man-
     gareva and Rapa Nui, many of them including references to the Miru.
111. A constant stream—Pinchot 1930:71.
112. "flight path into"—Finney 1994:271 and personal communication.
112. "The air was filled"—Pinchot 1930:404.
112. The enemies of nesting—See Steadman 1989 on bird exploitation in Polynesia; Hotu
     Matu'a was not allowed to eat rats, perhaps to prevent a loss of *mana*. Rats decreased
     the bird population, and Hotu Matu'a's positive, symbolic role was to increase bird
     and other food resources.
112. Rapa Nui settlers—Martinsson-Wallin 1994; Martinsson-Wallin and Wallin 1998; evi-
     dence of forest clearance by humans is suggested before A.D. 300, and linguistic evi-
     dence tends to agree with a settlement date prior to A.D. 800. The latter date, however,
     is currently suggested for Anakena and about A.D. 1000 for the apparent beginning of
     large-scale statue carving.

"EASTER ISLAND AT LAST!"

114. "awed silence"—MEI:124; EI:10; KSR's journal entry for Sunday, 29 Mar., is in RGS
     WKR 4/9. See also Log Books of Yacht *Mana*, 15 vols., commencing Febry. 20th 1913:
     "Chief Officer's Log Book No. 6 of the Mana on a Voyage from February 1st, 1914 to
     April 30th, 1914" (RGS WKR 1/1–15).
114. "Arrived Easter Is."—Log Books of Yacht *Mana*, 15 vols., commencing Febry. 20th,
     1913 (RGS WKR 1/1–15).
     Orthographical note: Regarding "Cook's Bay," note that place-names on Rapa
     Nui are affected by many variables, and maps in several languages are dotted
     with designations that are the result of imposed names, hasty recording, mis-
     information, or mispronunciation of Rapanui words. Rapa Nui people do not
     use the foreign-language names found on maps today (including Cook's Bay).
     Historical note: The present location of the Hanga Roa parish church is the third
     site it has occupied in the village. The parish cemetery occupied one previous
     site in the village, and there are at least two others, one at the leper station and
     the other at Vaihu.
     Two days after they arrived, Gillam noted in the ship's log that Scoresby
     went ashore "for an indefinite period." William Marks, Frank Preston, and
     Albert Light were typically ashore only a day or two at a time, and never more
     than seven to eight days. B. Rosa (referred to in KSR fieldnotes as "negro")
     worked at least one day in Rano Raraku. Bailey, Frank T. Green, and Henry
     MacLean were working members of the Mana Expedition onshore for several
     months. Henry James Gillam, in contrast, rarely set foot on Rapa Nui. One
     morning during the first week they were anchored in Cook's Bay, Gillam was
     rushing to bring *Mana* around and fell down the starboard wing hatchway. He
     was badly shaken and bruised down the entire left side of his body. Preston
     urged him to go ashore, but he refused. Scoresby bandaged his ribs and Gillam
     carried on.
115. "took the ginger"—Edmunds in Oliveros 1994:336.
115. *Mana* sailed blithely—While *Mana* may, in fact, have sailed unknowingly into a calm
     before the storm, there is another possibility. Archaeologist Robert Hommon has
     explored the notion of chaos theory in human societies. Meteorologist Edward
     Lorenz developed mathematical models of weather and once asked "if the flap of a
     butterfly's wing in Brazil could set off a tornado in Texas." According to chaos theory,
     such an event is theoretically possible when the molecules of air stirred by the Brazil-

ian butterfly's wings initiate an interactive, nonlinear atmospheric chain of events. *Mana* in this context is the metaphorical butterfly that set off a dangerous human "tornado."

116. In spite of Tepano's—*Historical note:* I once witnessed a similar event in the same place. A small yacht had been damaged on the rocks, and virtually everything aboard her was being off-loaded in order to bring her into dry dock for repairs. The American owners were retired, seeing the world on a budget, and their possessions were modest. Dozens of generous people rushed to help carry, stack, and store their goods in a nearby shed for safekeeping. Within hours it became clear that, while many honest Good Samaritans were working selflessly to help, a few others were spiriting away dozens of items as if by magic. Later an island-wide call for the items to be returned netted good results, but nonetheless some things were lost.

116. "a handsome race"; "possessing attractive manners"—MEI:140.

117. He was just a year—Tepano was born March 4, 1867, and died November 8, 1947 (Certificado de Defunción Servicio de Registro Civil on file, Esperanza Pakarati). There is confusion about his birth date. McCall (personal communication, 2001) doubts the veracity of the record held by the Pakarati family; Hotus y Otros 1988; Barthel (1958:297) says Tepano's birth date was "right around 1866."

118. "The door on to the veranda"—MEI:125.

Medical note: KSR's reference to the "never-ceasing drone of mosquitoes" suggests her typical auditory sensitivities. Frank T. Green ridicules her profound aversion to heat and mosquitoes in "Dear Crawford," 19 Aug. 1913 (BOD MS).

Collections note: KSR doesn't mention the presence of archaeological artifacts in the Mataveri house, but PE had many. He excavated dozens of sites on the island and was a serious collector and seller in the same way as was his friend A. W. F. Fuller. Other Europeans of the time, including Alexander Salmon Jr. and John Brander, also had extensive collections. A Danish carpenter named Christian Schmidt (who came with Dutrou-Bornier) and Vicente "Varta" Pont sold artifacts. KSR made a rubbing in pencil of an incised design on a human skull in PE's collection (RGS WKR 4/9).

118. There was no school—In August of 1914, J. I. Vives Solar arrived to set up a prefabricated building as the village school and assumed the role of teacher. According to KSR's notes, forty-seven children attended three hours per day. Vives Solar was a journalist who wrote prolifically (if not always accurately) about Rapa Nui. He spent about a year on the island and served for a time as *subdelegado marítimo* (port captain). On September 15, 1914, WSR, KSR, Antonio Haoa Pakomio; his wife, Parapina Araki Bornier; and "Maria" (may or may not be María Paoa Dutrou-Bornier) rode into Hanga Roa from Rano Raraku to attend a masked performance at the school marking a Chilean holiday. Earlier, on May 5 they attended an "evening dance" where the participants wore "white drapery & made wt masques one resembling lizard" (RGS WKR 4/9).

Collections note: The mask is now in the BM (Routledge photo neg. MM008341). From KSR's notes it is not altogether clear who actually made the lizard mask, and it may not have been a Rapa Nui person (Tuesday, 5 May and Friday, 15 Sept. 1914 [RGS WKR 4/9]).

118. The son of—Hotus y Otros (1988:302) says "Juan Tepano, Juan Araki Ti'a y de Pirivato, los tres últimos viajaban a cumplir con el servicio militar en el Regimiento No. 2 'Maipo' de Valparaíso." G. McCall (personal communication, 2001) says, "There is a nonsense story that he served in the Maipo regiment of the Chilean army in the 'War of the Pacific . . .'" "Republica de Chile Ministerio de Defensa Nacíonal Dirección General de Movilización Nacíonal" [Esperanza Pakarati]; see also "Juan Tepano Primer Militar Pascuense," unpublished poem by Nelson Ubilla Toledo.

119. "interpreter"; "retained"; "a keen interest"—Métraux 1940:304. For a different point of view, see Hotus y Otros 1988:357: "Tepano fue muy negativo para los pascuenses" ("Tepano was very bad for the islanders").

Historical note: The late Felipe Teao A., chief informant of the Universidad de Chile researchers and my own companion and guide in the field, spoke often to me of Tepano, attributing a good deal of information directly to him. José Fati, another consultant of repute, also said some of the information he gave me came from Tepano, as did Tepano's daughter Amelia.

119. "escort"; "imposed on"—MEI:158, 214.
119. Katherine came to Rapa Nui—D/GP 6, v. 18, p. 8.
119. "Any real success"; "due to the intelligence"—MEI:214.

FIRST IMPRESSIONS AND PLANS

120. The rolling, grass-covered—KSR, "The Riddle of Easter Island—First Impressions," *The Spectator*, 8 Aug. 1914 (Friday [May 15] A.M., written at the same time the first report to the British Association was drafted by WSR and edited by KSR; RGS WKR 7; RGS WKR 4/9). KSR (MEI:128) said that she wrote *The Spectator* article "in my tent, by the light of a hurricane-lamp, during the small hours of more than one morning." It was sent with *Mana* on her first return to the Chilean mainland.
120. "great lights and flowing"—MEI:131.
120. To the east—KSR 1921a:630.
     Note on fieldnotes: The map drawn by RGS for KSR shows different numbers than those given here for the height of Rano Kau (which erupted for the last time about 180,000 years ago) and Rano Aroi. See also BCEI and OEI.
120. Rano Kau rises—Thomson 1891; Cooke 1899; Roussel 1908; MEI:209–10.
     Orthographical note: In the 1800s the names Rapa Nui and Te Pito o Te Henua, "the navel of the earth," were both said to be the island's names, the latter suggested by the indented shapes of the three volcanoes. William Churchill (1912:4) doubted the truth of that assertion, and thought the name meant simply "land's end." Still, he showed a (unnamed) Rapa Nui man a map of the island and quizzed him about the origin of "navel of the earth." The man pointed to each of the volcanoes and said, "There are three."
120. Carved of basalt—Van Tilburg 1992; MEI:figs. 104, 106. J. Linton Palmer and Lieutenant Matthew James Harrison of HMS *Topaze* discovered the statue in 1868.
     Collections note: BM records show 272 entries in the Routledge Easter Island collection. There are sixteen objects in the HMS *Topaze* collection, of which fourteen are from Easter Island. Either Lieutenant Harrison or J. L. Palmer acquired them. The two monolithic statues are included in this total and were officially collected by Commodore Richard Ashmore Powell. A newspaper article states that Hoa Hakananai'a was "lowered undamaged 300 ft down the cliff at Rapa Nui with block and tackle," *The* (London) *Times*, 1956 (PB). Lieutenant M. J. Harrison recorded in his diary for November 5, 1868, that a "working party of 60 men" collected the image. It was hauled facedown, probably on the same sledge or "raft" used to float it out to the *Topaze*. It was apparently not covered all of the time it was stored on deck. Ample sailcloth, rope, pulleys, etc., were on board to move and store the statue. McCall (personal communication, 2002) says that José Fati and L. Tuki told him that "pillows" of grass supported the statue. There is no known evidence that they were used in statue transport, but they may have been.
121. "silence which may"—MEI:255; this phrase echoes another used by WP in his diaries and is one example of the recurrent use of imagery inherent in KSR's rich childhood experiences.
121. "the wildest scenes"—Ibid.
121. "overcome by the wonder"—Ibid., 184.
122. In the depths—Thomson (1891:493, 494, 497) counted 93 statues inside the quarry, of which 40 were upright, and 155 on the exterior. His count for the entire island was 555.
122. "with any pretension"—MEI:209.
122. "country establishment"—See Cristino F. et al. 1981 for contemporary survey strategy, Vargas C. 1993 for settlement pattern analysis.

Historical note: The USS *Mohican* survey crew did not interview elderly men directly but only with the help of Brander ranch manager Alexander Salmon Jr., who had also worked with Geiseler. Salmon was part Tahitian and spoke a mixture of Tahitian and Rapanui. WSR rightly dismissed or discounted as hearsay all information Geiseler and Thomson claimed to be ethnographic. WSR felt precisely the same way about Palmer's material: it was all secondhand (see Van Tilburg 1992: nn. 15, 23). See McCall (1998:fig. 2) for a picture of Salmon.

123. He called out—KSR was taught to ride in the manner Americans call sidesaddle, i.e., by sitting on her horse with both legs on the same side of an English saddle. In Africa and on Easter Island she rode astride on her own saddle, which she brought with her. She often threw a sheepskin over the saddle and by all accounts was an excellent horsewoman.

123. As the Routledges—See MEI:figs. 36, 40, for diagrams drawn by RGS and including details noted by Lieutenant Ritchie.

Expedition note: The Routledges intended to follow up on the work of two previous expeditions. Captain Wilhelm Geiseler had called at the island in 1882 for a brief (four-day) collecting foray officially requested by the German Imperial Museum and Navy (Ayres and Ayres 1995). His main goal was to secure examples of *kohau rongorongo* (which he failed to get), although he did collect over 250 artifacts, some from Orongo. The USS *Mohican* arrived in 1886, specifically to get a *moai* comparable to Hoa Hakananai'a (i.e., basalt). Paymaster William J. Thomson and his crew conducted a reconnaissance survey in just nine days, examined and described hundreds of sites, and purchased or collected a representative collection of artifacts. In both cases, Alexander Salmon Jr. acted as intermediary with the islanders. See also BCEI and OEI.

123. "one vast necropolis"—Thomson 1891:484.

123. "scientific body snatching"; "impossible to go"—MEI:166.

123. Ahu Tongariki possessed—Ibid., fig. 33.

Archaeological note: See Cristino F., C., and P. Vargas C. (1998) for discussion of restoration of Ahu Tongariki, about which there are dozens of international press articles detailing an intense controversy over methods; Van Tilburg (1986a, 1994) for statue data. From one to fifteen statues once stood on individual *ahu*, but fragments total many more. Most statues on *ahu* are four to five meters tall with four meters being average, and the tallest are at Ahu Hanga Te Tenga (it fell and broke before being erected) and Moai Paro on Ahu Te Pito Kura, which was the last to fall, c. 1840.

124. "The back of the stage"—MEI:171.

124. "Every day, as"—Ibid., 165.

125. The western alliance—Also written as Tu'uaro. Since KSR was consistent in her use of Ko Tu'u, that designation will be used throughout this volume.

125. Ritchie and two—Tues., 26 May 1914; Thurs., 28 May; 29 May 1914; Tues., 9 June to Wed., 17 June 1914 (RGS WKR 4/9).

Expedition note: Ritchie mapped Puna Pau with the assistance of Henry MacLean and Antonio Haoa Pakomio.

125. Edmunds recommended hiring—According to A. Padgett (personal communication, 21 Apr. 1999), who has married into the family but also has some details from published research, Vicente "Varta" Pont was born April 9, 1854, in Brest, France. He married María "Meta" Heremeta Make on August 12, 1912, and died April 28, 1947, of a heart attack in Hanga Piko. Varta (also called Bata) and María had one son, who, in turn, fathered thirteen children.

125. They turned away—KSR "The Riddle of Easter Island—First Impressions," *The Spectator,* 8 Aug. 1914 (RGS WKR 7): "It has been suggested that the secret [of the island] may be found in the caves. Caves there indeed are, literally by the tens of thousands . . . but all known ones have long ago been ransacked by the natives, anxious for curios to sell to passing ships, while the entrances to the hidden ones are concealed by intention and by the natural changes in the configuration of the

ground. Even where the general whereabouts are known these cannot be found. . . . The village for the last fortnight has been digging in a particular headland for a cave which belonged to a man who has died, and in which it is said more [*rongorongo*] tablets will be found, but without result. . . . Much may be attempted, something done, but if ever the caves give up the secret of Easter Island it will be the result of accident."

126. "The statues here"—KSR to "My dearest Hilda" from Easter Island, 21 May 1914, on *Mana* paper (PB).

ORONGO: THE ELEVENTH HOUR

127. "Fix a base"—R. R. Marett to KSR, 21 June 1913 (RGS WKR 4/1).

128. She found paintings—KSR's (1917a:342) first public statement of the number of houses was forty-six. She then gave "nearly fifty" (MEI:255).

Note on fieldnotes: KSR's handwritten fieldnotes state forty-five "houses," and she apparently accepted this number as it remains the same in her reviewed and corrected "first typed copy" of the expedition's draft survey manuscript (RGS WKR 4/2/1, Section VI, "Orongo Houses," p. 101). Ferdon (1961:fig. 137) shows forty-seven buildings, also called houses, including those clustered at the far-eastern end of the site. See also Ayres and Ayres 1995 for a discussion of Geiseler, his collection, and his notes on Orongo; Ferdon 1961 for explorations and excavations at Orongo; Mulloy 1975 for restoration of Orongo; MEI:256; RGS WKR 4/10/14, p. 9; see also BCEI and OEI.

Archaeological note: On the northwest coast a deep cavern has been structurally modified to resemble exactly an Orongo building and clearly supports the "cave" versus "house" distinction noted by KSR (JVT fieldnotes and video, 1998). RGS WKR 4/14/21 is WSR's three-page description of waterworn boulders or beach cobbles; Métraux 1940:figs. 42e, 42f.

128. "doorpost"—2 June 1914 (RGS WKR 4/9); MEI:fig. 107 shows one of two stones found "lying about" the building in which Hoa Hakananai'a had been placed. KSR thought that they had originally been foundation stones for a *hare paenga* before being "converted into doorposts for the house of the image" (MEI:257; OEI).

128. These and other—It was WSR's job to catalogue all portable objects collected, but he did not do it—in sharp contrast to his methods in Africa.

128. No one was surprised—WSR (RGS WKR 4/1/1) had written a high-handed letter to Edmunds before the expedition arrived, telling him to inform the islanders of the expedition's arrival and that, in the meantime, they were not to remove objects or disturb sites. There is a great irony, of course, in asking that of Edmunds, who was an indefatigable collector. It was not only the Rapa Nui people who perceived the Routledges as treasure hunters. Archibald Williamson, chairman of WBCO, wrote to his brother Harry in Valparaíso, 20 Aug. 1915: "I note that the Routledge's [*sic*] have been carrying off trophies. I think they should certainly have asked permission before doing anything of the sort. I doubt, however, if the British Museum would give much actual cash for them. They will give lots of thanks, but that is all, as a rule" (WBCO archives).

128. "an able native"—RGS WKR 4/10/41, p. 26; MEI:214. Tepano had a good eye and could draw with a pencil, but he was not an accomplished artist (neither was he a particularly good carver).

128. She counted over—Métraux (1940:313) points out that the birdman carvings of Orongo, "which even in early days were interpreted by the natives as symbolic of Makemake," are closely associated with another "carving showing a human face with huge eye sockets." The identification of the birdman and the human face carving as the birdman and Makemake, respectively, is recent and may not be reliable. More probably, as Métraux points out, the human face carvings represent the genesis of Makemake and the birdman represents his incarnation in human form. This is a very different and much more complex concept not explored in current research.

128. Rapa Nui workmen—Jotefa Maherenga Reva Hiva was the source of this information (see below). He also told KSR that "Taurarenga was the name of the moai Hahakananaia [*sic*]" (RGS WKR 4/3/2, p. 27, a dark blue ledger bound in maroon with the title "Notes Vol IV"), although "Taura-renga" was also given as the name of the house. Lieutenant Harrison wrote, "The natives say his name is Hoa Háka Nána Ia (the first two names being titles, as far as we could understand)" (K. Chettleburgh to BM, 1995).

Expedition note: KSR investigated a small structure near house 11 that she first thought might have been the *ahu* on which the *moai* had stood (4/9, Tues., 26 May 1914 [RGS WKR 4/9]: "investigated rocks w village e of path concluded not a terrace W found chips of Mataa)." KSR and WSR "provisionally concluded" that a smooth, dark stone in the wall of house 18 might have been the *moai* pedestal. Ferdon (1961:221, 234) has the "house of the god" as R-13; see also Routledge 1917a, 1919:257, 1920:436; Van Tilburg 1992:47. KSR to PE, Rapa Nui, 17 Nov. 1914 (RGS WKR 4/10). See also RGS WKR 4/21 for the "first typed copy" of draft survey manuscript of 105 pp. Section III is "Rano Kao and Adjacent Islets," Section IV, is "Orongo." Section VI, "Orongo Houses." Van Tilburg 1992; MEI:figs. 64, 65; see also OEI.

In Tahiti in 1923, KSR interviewed a Rapa Nui woman named "Kava . . . Kio" who was eighteen when she left Rapa Nui with Roussel. She was "8 or 10 years old when she participated in an Orongo ceremony . . . drawings of designs on the backs" and "lips outlined." She told KSR that "Tau ra Hanga" was neither the name of the house nor of the statue but "a great artist for tattooing." She also said that "her parents gave her presents" for being in the ceremony (RGS WKR 4/16; see also 4/8, p. 52, re Kapiera Maherenga). A sketch made by Lieutenant Harrison of HMS *Topaze*, long thought to have been lost, was recently found at the BM and validates Tepano's story.

129. When Tepano introduced—RGS WKR 4/6; Hotus y Otros 1988; McCall n.d. (1986).

Orthographical note: Viriamo (a)/Veriamo(a) were used interchangeably by KSR; Englert 1974:52 (see note "Slowly, doors began," below). It is spelled Veriamu in census and other records, and that designation is used in this volume. Her baptismal name was Paulina.

Personnel note: Besides Juan Tepano, Veriamu, and guides such as Antonio Haoa or Maanga, Katherine had regular contact with about fifteen to twenty people from whom she collected ethnographic data, but she knew many others. The women on her camp staff taught her Rapanui.

129. Veriamu had had three—Hotus y Otros 1988 reports Tepano's sister in the leper colony.

Note on fieldnotes: KSR very certainly recorded that Veriamu was married three times, with Juan Tepano the product of her third marriage to "Llano" (Rano, baptized "Iovani"). McCall (personal communication) agrees that Juan Tepano (b. 1867, d. 1947) is "the son of 'Iovani' Rano and Paulina or Victoria Veriamu" but says that "her marriage to Rano was her second marriage." By this, presumably, he means marriage sanctioned by the Catholic priests. KSR also recorded "Paulina" as the name of Tepano's mother (RGS WKR n.d., loose sheet of paper evidently written early in the expedition's stay on the island). Veriamu sang for KSR the song of the sailors as they hauled down Hoa Hakananai'a. Crippled and almost a century old in 1934–35, Veriamu witnessed the Franco-Belgian Expedition's removal of a statue called Pou Hakanononga. She composed a song to memorialize the occasion (apparently not the same as the song she had heard in 1868). That statue, which was located at Ahu Arongo, is described in RGS WKR 4/4/1, p. 100 (blue notebook); Forment 1983; Van Tilburg 1994. Veriamu died in 1936.

129. Katherine learned that—Stolpe (1899:214) shows "Tepano" in Tahiti with a scratched tattoo commemorating the removal of Hoa Hakananai'a (see below). See also Métraux 1940:fig. 32c; EI:117, fig. 91; Van Tilburg 1994 (perhaps misidentified as Tepano Rano) and Kaeppler 2001 (misidentified as Juan Tepano by copy editors).

129. The English had demolished—Van Tilburg 1992; MEI:figs. 104, 106.

129. Sometime later, Rano—Stolpe 1899; Métraux 1940:fig. 35a; Van Tilburg 1992.
    Historical note: Tepano and Veriamu both definitely told KSR three important
    things: that "Iovani" Rano was not tattooed; that he was on the island in 1868;
    and that he saw the removal of Hoa Hakananai'a. Veriamu also told KSR that
    "Iovani" Rano left the island "a few" years later. Census records, however, say
    that he was on the island twenty years later (i.e., in 1888 [McCall personal
    communication, 2002]). In any case, the tattooed man Stolpe depicted in
    Tahiti (who, judging by the scratched design on his arm of Hoa Hakananai'a
    being removed from Orongo, probably witnessed the event) cannot, therefore,
    be "Iovani" Rano (as I have earlier assumed, Van Tilburg 1994) unless he was
    tattooed after leaving the island, which is possible but probably unlikely.
      There are two other candidates for Stolpe's tattooed man. One is "Tepano
    Hakarevareva" (McCall n.d.), a Miru who, since he left the island in 1871, must
    have been baptized and probably saw the removal of Hoa Hakananai'a in 1868.
    He traveled in French Polynesia before purchasing a large plot of land in
    Pamata'i, Tahiti, in 1888. The arguments in his favor are (1) his presence in Tahiti
    is well documented, and (2) his wealth would have been commensurate with
    such lavish tattoos. The argument against him is that Stolpe's tattooed man
    worked on the docks in Tahiti, and that is unlikely if he was a wealthy landowner.
    The second candidate is a wild card—another, unknown Rapa Nui man who also,
    by coincidence, bore the name Tepano (a common baptismal name).
      There is no question that designs on Stolpe's tattooed man are Rapa Nui.
    Similar ones appear on *moai* and, with more precision, on bark cloth figures.
    Neither is there any question that the tattoos are of a high quality and that the
    scratched design on the man's arm is amateur. Stolpe's tattooed man may have
    scratched the depiction of Hoa Hakananai'a's removal on his arm because he
    had witnessed the event even though, for some reason, the English failed to
    note the presence of such a memorably adorned man. The scratched design,
    therefore, represents both a personal memory and a record of history. Alterna-
    tively (but far less likely), he may not have witnessed the actual event but
    recorded it when someone described it to him. In either case, the tattooed man
    seems to have had a personal interest in Hoa Hakananai'a, suggesting that he
    may have been Miru (which would be compatible with the designs). It is also
    possible that, in addition, his traditional role in Rapa Nui society was keeper of
    history. The basic questions are: Are the tattoo patterns—and, therefore, simi-
    lar patterns on other artifacts—associated with a part of the island, a time
    frame, a specific status, or a specific group? Did they belong to a man of the
    Tupahotu (east, i.e., "Iovani" Rano), or a Miru (west, i.e., Hakarevareva)? The
    jury is still out, but is leaning toward Hakarevareva.

129. Slowly, doors began—Jotefa Maherenga Reva Hiva was the "oldest man in the village"
    (MEI:266) (see above); RGS WKR 4/6, 4/4/1, 4/3/2. A sketch of Jotefa is in KSR's
    fieldnotes (RGS WKR 4/9).
      Historical note: Veriamu told KSR that the ceremony in which she participated
    took place in Rano Raraku because "there was a war on." Another time, she
    said she was "not manu nor her children" but that her first husband was a *poki
    manu* (RGS WKR 4/2/4). Nicolás Pakarati Urepotahi remembered being a *poki
    manu*, and his memories of the event were similar to Jotefa's.

130. "fine women"; *(komari)*—For KSR's confusion over the *komari* symbol and the word for
    it, see RGS WKR 4/9, "Rapa Nui Vocabulary," in which KSR gives "fig leaf"
    "hahamiro"; KSR to PE from Upper Fair Prospect, Priestman's River, Priestman,
    Jamaica, 20 Jan. 1921, asking "what is the native name for the design so often found on
    pillow stones & on the rocks at Orongo? Is it ko mari, ko marie, ko maria?" RGS WKR
    4/3/1. In house 41 "also a fig leaf" crossed out and written "ko mari" (RGS WKR
    4/12); see also RGS WKR 4/3/1; Thomson (1891:551) gives *Kannutu* as "vulva";
    Churchill 1912:218 gives *komari* as "pudenda." Once a translation for an *ahu* name was
    denied to KSR when her consultant "declined as 'improper'" (RGS WKR 4/21, p. 52;

MEI:263; RGS WKR 4/21, "first typed copy" of draft survey manuscript of 105 pages where "Summary of Types of Rock Carvings" is given). See also OEI; BCEI.

Historical note: KSR writes that "it was reported that women of the island, possessed of personal attractions, 'fine women' came up to this spot to be immortalized after this manner and that each of these designs represented a particular woman" (RGS WKR 4/21).

Note on fieldnotes: KSR did not, however, either record or suggest that *komari* were "portraits" of women, as Lee (1992:194) states. Rather, KSR (MEI:263) clearly argues that *komari* were conventionalized nonportrait representations and, furthermore, considers this important in understanding the similar use of monolithic sculpture. It is possible but not certain that KSR heard of the practice of elongation of the clitoris, which Métraux (1940) believes is a genuine part of Rapa Nui tradition. Tracing the exact source of that information is difficult, but wood carvings with exaggerated vulvae are known (Van Tilburg 1992:fig. 74), and the Rapa Nui practice of "trapping" sailors with feminine charms is well documented (Roe 1967). KSR is also not clear exactly which practices were associated with the seclusion of chiefly children and which were included in the more broadly available Orongo initiation rites.

130. He wore special—MEI:114. Churchill (1912:199) gives "clothing" for *hami.*

Note on fieldnotes: The designs said to have been painted on the *poki manu* were described to KSR by Jotefa. KSR confirmed these with Kapiera Maherenga and then compared them to carved designs on the back of the monolithic statues in Rano Raraku and at Anakena (see MEI:figs. 64, 65). Kapiera also gave her some names of the designs (RGS WKR 4/3/2); see also RGS WKR 4/3/1, pp. 59–60, in which Kapiera "was a Poki Manu head shaved & adorned with Pua painted in stripes of red, white, black on his back had white circles 2 on buttock." This strongly suggests that the "ring and girdle" designs on the statues are linked to a specific kind of (initiation?) ceremony or status that borrowed or related to their significance later in time.

Archaeological note: There is no doubt whatsoever that Hoa Hakananai'a had his back to the door and "looked at the island (quite clear on this)" (according to Kapiera and Te Haha as well as Tepano [RGS WKR 4/3/1]). Until recently it was thought that a sketch made of the statue in situ by Lieutenant M. J. Harrison had been lost, but the original is in the possession of K. Chettleburgh, Victoria, B.C., Canada, and a misfiled photographic copy of it was located by Dorota Starzecka after 1994 on file with the BM (Van Tilburg 2002). It confirms the information collected by KSR.

131. "assumed the attitude"—RGS WKR 3/1, "Mana Stores and Acc'ts, Places in Various Ports," and RGS WKR 3/2, "Mana Stores and Acc'ts," hold labels, receipts, and memos showing salary paid to crewmen, typical expenditures, and credit extensions during the voyage and while on the island.

Personnel note: Only one memo in this whole collection deals with Tepano, but scattered variously throughout are miscellaneous notes on Tepano's salary ($2 per day in her notes should be read not as U.S. dollars but, in all cases, as Chilean pesos) from January 1 to May 16, 1915. By my rough calculation, as of January 1, Tepano had earned $61 and, by May 1915, had earned another $76 for a total of $137. Thus, KSR paid Tepano for 68.5 days. Her journal (which is only partial) suggests he was present or working at least an additional 40 to 80 of the expedition's total 478 days on the island (i.e., 20–40 percent of total days, not just working days, which, at a maximum, were 340).

131. From January 1915—MEI:214.

131. "sexual morality, as"—Ibid., 226; "general morality" was "of a particularly low order" (ibid., 140); see also Van Tilburg 1986b. Métraux 1940:106–9; Ferdon (1957:227–29; 225, "advanced acculturation is . . . only material culture deep").

132. "given the blessing"—Cousins 1981:177.

132. veranda interviews—MEI:212–13; RGS WKR 4/3/1 clearly shows KSR's interview

strategy. Barthel (1958:298) calls a group of "old ones," some of whom were lepers, *korohua* and says that "Routledge enlisted her most important informants from among this circle." Some of this circle lived within the village, not just in the leper station as Barthel states. In both cases, however, Tepano was an important facilitator and provider. Some Rapa Nui old people may have given information to Walter Knoch in 1911. He was a German-speaking scientist sent out to establish a meteorological station.

132. "Langitopa" (Matamu'a Rangitopa I Ka'i)—A Universidad de Chile field team under the direction of P. Vargas excavated the Poike "ditch" (see Van Tilburg 1994 for photo). Langitopa told Katherine that seven sons of one Short Ears man, Ko Pepi by name, were murdered. He was avenged by his brothers, who killed many Long Ears and then drove the survivors to Poike, where they dug a ditch and filled it with brush to make a fire in self-defense. Betrayed by an old woman, the Long Ears were out-flanked and defeated, then immolated in the ditch. KSR doubted that the remnant of a ditch on Poike was man-made, and Vargas' excavation proved her right.

133. "a liar"—MEI:274, 282; RGS WKR 4/3/1.

133. One of the younger—KSR did not believe that her consultants deliberately invented stories, but did see the "tendency to glide" when "memory was vague" (MEI:212, 274, 282).

> *Note on fieldnotes:* RGS WKR 4/3/1, p. 46, gives in red ink the names or num-bers of volumes in which corroborative information and names of consultants are located. Note in upper-right corner says, "Cancelled as to accuracy." See also RGS WKR 4/3/2, "K.R. Notes Vol. III," and 4/3/3, "Notes Vol. IV." The names of KSR's consultants can be found in RGS WKR 4/3/1, p. 54, together with their maternal and paternal clan affiliations.

133. On Rapa Nui—Pakarati's birth name was Ko Ure Potahi A'Te Pihi a'Ure Atoro a'Pú Revareva (Englert 1974:46). At baptism he received the name Nicolás Pancracio, which later became Nicolás Pakarati (Hotus y Otros 1988:100; RGS WKR 4/3/1, p. 59–60).

> *Biographical note:* Elizabet Rangitaki was born on July 9, 1870, and died October 2, 1929 (personal communication, Cristián Arévalo Pakarati, 1999).

133. Pakarati, she discovered—Barthel (1958:295) points out that Pakarati's paternal uncle Veri Heka had important information about some Rapa Nui traditions, making him "instrumental in the transmittal of information" (ibid).

134. Tahitians, it was said—G. McCall (personal communication, 1999).

134. He also accommodated—Padre F. Nahoe (personal communication, 2000).

134. "firmly believed"—"This Juan firmly believed" (RGS WKR 4/3); Rano Raraku was believed to be haunted, and KSR was impressed with the intensity of that belief (MEI:140). Ferdon (1958:146) reports the continued belief in "dangerous personal spirits called *akuaku* who have the power to disable or kill."

134. One day in late—MEI:257; RGS WKR 4/21; see also Tues., 26 May 1914 (RGS WKR 4/9); MEI:fig. 111.

> *Archaeological note:* The statue came from Cave H (one of eight caves KSR examined on Motu Nui). It is now in the collection of the BM. Tepano was a prolific carver in both stone and wood, but this statue was probably not made by him nor of recent (i.e., c. 1914) manufacture. Three figures collected on Admiral Byrd's second antarctic expedition and attributed to Tepano are in my own collection, and his style is unmistakable (Byrd 1935).

134. It ran right—Van Tilburg 1992, 2001b.

135. When he attempted—RGS WKR 4/9, Saturday 13 June 1914.

> *Collections note:* Some artifacts collected on this site are in PRM.

135. She clung there—This description is based upon my own experiences landing four different times on Motu Nui. See MEI:257–58 for KSR's own hair-raising adventure, which took place not on arrival but departure, and her "tale was very nearly never written." KSR counted seven species of seabirds on Motu Nui (Routledge 1919:258; 1917a gives eight); see also McCoy 1978.

135. "On the walls"—MEI:275.

135. "last cannibal"—MEI:225–26.
    Note on fieldnotes: A sketch of Ko Tori showing his facial tattoos with their named components is given (without name of consultant, but the information probably came form Porotu) in RGS LBR MSS (PMB 531 REEL 1). RGS WKR 4/14/13 describes skeletal material taken from "Burial Cairns"; 4/8, p. 10, says, "Skulls bought"; MEI:fig. 96 of a "Miru skull with incised design"; "skull lies on left side, 36 from far end is silted up," in House 12, Orongo (RGS LBR MSS 4/12, in trunk); "found passage form No. 12 with skull" (RGS WKR 4/9, Sat., 4 July, at Orongo); twelve specimens of human craniums from Rapa Nui existed in the Museum of the Royal College of Surgeons. Fleet Surgeon W. S. H. Sequeira presented two lower "rocking" jaws in 1910.
    Note on collections: The Mana Expedition collected fifty-eight skulls, two of which were too fragmentary for study. Keith, Sir A., 1916, "Preliminary Report on the Collection of Human Skulls and Bones Made on Rapa Nui by Mr. and Mrs. Scoresby Routledge" (RGS WKR 4/10/42) refers to report by Dr. Volz of forty-nine skulls in *Archives für Anthropologie*. See below.
136. "I dismounted, scrambled"—MEI:225–26; KSR's consultant on cannibalism was the Miru Ramón Te Haha. Ko Tori's lavish head and facial tattoos were said to be for a cannibal only (RGS WKR 4/9); for Ko Tori's relationship to Carlos Teao Tori, see Englert 1983:51; KSR talked to Kapiera and Porotu (with Tepano translating) about Ko Tori and his life (Wed., 27 Jan. [RGS WKR 4/9]) (see above).
136. "I had then undone"—MEI: 225–26.
136. "used to be"—RGS WKR 4/9, p. 85.
137. They gathered together—I have gathered dozens of stories and tales on videotape from many Rapa Nui elders. I have asked them how they traditionally began a story (in the sense of "once upon a time" in English). They're baffled by the question and don't really consider themselves to be storytellers—that, they say, is for experts. Today, they often start with a few words in Spanish or English ("yeah," "well"), but otherwise they have no convention I have been able to discern.
138. "shown a picture"—Sunday, 26 Apr. 1914, p. 4 of nine pages in hand of WSR, "all conversations . . . were translated from the original Kanaka into Spanish by Ipollito [*sic*] & from Spanish to English by MacLean" (RGS WKR 4/4/3).
138. Somehow, Katherine discovered—RGS WKR 4/4/3; MEI:fig. 99; the old man's name was "Daniel."
    Historical note: Nicolás Pakarati Urepotahi is "said to have written down the traditions" of many old people, and these records are said to have then come into the possession of Zósimo Valenzuela, a Chilean chaplain, in 1916 (Barthel 1958:293). KSR's interaction with Pakarati over Tomenika's *ta'u* script took place immediately prior to Valenzuela's visit to the island. Barthel (ibid., 294) questions Tomenika's role in producing the script attributed to him, saying "his name may have been used to indicate (supposed) authorship or simply to give the appearance of authenticity to the copies of the rongorongo signs." Bancroft Library MSS P-N 16, "Evagerio no te mau Tominika o te tau," 69 pp., microfilm (96 exposures).
138. "acknowledged the figures"—MEI:250.
139. "fever"—Katherine (Catalina Te Hanga), who was Veriamu's daughter by Vaka Ariki (Hotus y Otros 1988:127), claimed to be an *ariki paka* or "aristocrat" through her father's clan (RGS KR 4/9, p. 96).
139. "How could one allow"—MEI:212.
139. "declined to show"—Wed., 8 July (RGS WKR 4/9).
139. She stopped long—RGS WKR 4/4/3, brown leather folder enclosing loose pages and "Native shots at Translation Tables." RGS WKR 4/8, p. 8, black paperback notebook; see also KSR's journal; McCall n.d. (1986), lamina 9; MEI:figs. 98, 99. Fischer (1993a:179), who apparently reviewed microfilm reels of KSR's fieldnotes, gives the wrong caption for "Tomenika's Script" in MEI:fig. 99 and lists "Priest's Paper of Signs" (that loaned by Pakarati to KSR) as an original *ta'u* found today in her field-

notes. In fact, the paper in her notes *is a copy*. The original was personally returned by KSR to Pakarati on July 10, 1914. MEI:253.

139. "quite bright and capable"—Fri., 10 July (RGS WKR 4/9).

140. "got Juan to come up"—Ibid. (RGS WKR 4/9).

140. "cave hunting"—Mon., 14 Dec.; Tues., 15 Dec.; Thurs., 14 Jan. (RGS WKR 4/9); see also MEI:272–76.

140. "I left the hut"—MEI:253.

140. She shared her—Barthel 1958, 1993; Tepano never represented himself to any investigator who followed KSR as an authority on *rongorongo*, although he rightfully did so in other areas. The Tepano family, members say today, has never laid claim to any special relationship to *rongorongo*. Nicolás Pakarati Urepotahi, partly as a result of his position as catechist (lay preacher), but also because of the nature of his personality and interests, became a keeper of traditions and, as we have seen, of some fragments of knowledge of *rongorongo*. The Pakarati family, until recently, has lived in a more traditional manner than many other families, and their interest in the past is genuine. However, their frequent interactions with researchers have had a huge impact on their stewardship.

140. "anxious to learn"—RGS WKR 4/9, p. 109.

141. "of memory"; "aids to recollection"—MEI:253.

142. "Day by day"—Ibid., 254.

TROUBLED WATERS

143. Quantities of food—RSS WSR 4/9, 9 Apr. 1914; MEI:141.

143. "pilfered every loose"—WSR to the *Comandante, Jeneral Baquedano* (usually referred to as *Baquedano*) from Camp Hotu Iti, Easter Island, 12 Aug. 1914 (RGS WKR 4/9); Ferdon 1958 explains exchange and barter during the post–Mana Expedition time he spent on the island.

143. He threatened dire—Wednesday, 17 June 1914 (RGS WKR 4/9).

143. "steal freely from"; "greatest barrier to"; "absence of security"—MEI:141.

143. Sofía Hey Rapu—D/GP 6, v. 35, p. 60.
    Historical note: In the census of 1916 Sofía was living with PE and had three children (Urbano, Enrique, and Ramon). Victoria had no children at this time and lived in Hanga Roa with her family (E. Edwards, personal communication, 1999), but frequently worked at Mataveri as a baby-sitter and in other capacities.

144. "breakfast difficulty"—Sat., 30 May 1914 (RGS WKR 4/9).

144. Katherine's tent was pitched—Dec. 10, 11, Mataveri "My tent=Pai a Tuke" (RGS WKR 4/4/1, p. 167; the source of this information was Langitopa). KSR gives "Houses at Mataveri" and Ko Te Pai a Tukí as "my house" (RGS WKR 4/3/1, p. 4). Alexander Salmon Jr. (see above) was also known as Ari'i Paea (McCall 1998:373, fig. 2). Dutrou-Bornier's remains were moved at least once from where they were originally placed (Jorge Edmunds, personal communication, 1996), and his grave is today plainly marked. The spot where KSR's tent was pitched is right above three little cavelike hollows. Its relationship to Dutrou-Bornier's original gravesite as well as to the present gravesite was shown to me by Jorge Edmunds. Even today, the place is spooky.

144. "see that all was well"—MEI:134.

145. Although Scoresby and Edmunds—RGS WKR 3, "Mana Stores & Acct's."

146. "for good"; "to be left"—RGS WKR 4/9, 1 Apr. 1914; WSR to "The Comandante 'Jeneral Baquedano' from Camp Hotu Iti, Rapa Nui, 12 Aug. 1914 (RGS WKR 4/9). WSR was particularly displeased with most of the men who engaged in cave hunting with him. "Ipolito" (Hipólito Ika Tetono) and "Casimiro" (Casimio Dutrou-Bornier) were among those he considered reliable. See Hotus y Otros 1988; Englert 1974:50, 53.

146. "food row"—Tues., 23 June 1914, "food row . . . end of Charles" (RGS WKR 4/9). Carlos Teao Tori was twenty-two years old. See also Hotus y Otros 1988:308–12.

146. Just six days—Wed., 17 June 1914 "found biscuits stolen"; Wed., 24 June 1914, "dismissed Charles" (RGS WKR 4/9).

147. Within a day—Thurs., 25 June 1914 (RGS WKR 4/9). A day later the Rapa Nui "boy" KSR often referred to in her notes (who has not been identified) gave notice, and then everyone else departed.

147. The Routledges excavated—"Mataveri Cave Ap. 22" (RGS WKR, two pages of hand-written notes). See also Wed., 24 June, A.M., 26 June, 27 June, 28 June (RGS WKR 4/9).

> *Archaeological note:* "WSR ran a trench, a couple of feet wide & 6″ deep along floor and carefully examined contents—below this was [*sic*] stones & mud other than cave earth found fish bones sheep bones whale bone needle (?). P.M. continued trench to mouth to a depth of 18″ found nothing indicating occupation . . . KR found arrowhead . . . found a vault made of slabs of slate faced on one aspect by vertical slabs roofed with other slabs superimposed cantilever fashion & floored with flattish oval sea pebbles size of soup plate this however had been disturbed."

147. In the middle—The old woman was María Angata Veri Tahi a Peno Hare Kohou, known as Angata (Hotus y Otros 1988:234). Daniel María Teave Haukena (thirty-six years old and of the Tupahotu) accompanied his mother, Angata. Matía Hotu Temanu (thirty years old), María Daniela Manuheuroroa and others (ibid., 303); see also Tues., 30 June 1914 (RGS WKR 4/9).

147. "dream from God"—KSR's journal says that in Angata's dream Merlet was "dead." In MEI:142 she quotes Angata as saying that Merlet was "no more."

"KATARINA" AND THE PROPHETESS ANGATA

148. Unlike him, however—Padre F. Nahoe Mulloy, personal communication, 2001; for KSR on Angata, see Mon., 27 July 1914, KSR diary notes (RGS WKR 4/9); MEI:145–49; D/GP 6, v. 32, Sun., Aug. 9.

148. "took this possession"; "gave nothing for"—MEI:142.

148. "great winds coming"—"Calendar of the rising" begins 1 July 1914, and are journal notes in sequence; one loose page in the back of the journal written on the back of the frontispiece of a 1909 popular novel is Lieutenant Ritchie's chronology of events (RGS WKR 4/9); RGS WKR 4/10/41, p. 16; RGS WKR 7; D/GP 6, v. 32, p. 40; v. 33, p. 221.

149. "carrying off cattle"—MEI:143; the number of cattle stolen at this point was variously estimated at nine, eleven, or thirteen (1 July 1914, RGS WKR 4/9).

149. Ten or more—It is quite probable that the Church's much earlier claim to a portion of the Company's herds, and Angata's role as a catechist, were part of the islanders' rationale for reasserting that right and taking cattle.

150. "risings in many"—MEI:142–43.

150. God had told Angata—Fri., 3 July 1914 (RGS WKR 4/9).

150. Then she entered—E. Edwards, personal communication, 1998.

151. "had always understood"—Wed., 8 July 1914. PE's predecessor Horace (Horacio) Cooper held the same position, and it was offered to Alberto Sanchez in 1900.

151. "I would ernestly [*sic*]"—PE to WSR, Mataveri, 8 July 1914 (RGS WKR 4/10).

152. "No member is to take"—WSR to "The Members of the Rapa Nui Scientific Expedition" (RGS/WKR/4/10). Typewritten with edits in hand of KSR.

152. "so long as I"—DRR to WSR, Mataveri, Easter Island, Wed., 22 July 1914 (RGS WKR 4/10).

152. "gallant little band"; "suddenly sick"—Thurs., 9 July 1914 (RGS WKR 4/9).

152. "10 or 12 sheep skins"—Fri., 10 July 1914 (RGS WKR 4/9).

153. "puzzled what to do"—Sat., 18 July 1914 (RGS WKR 4/9).

153. "Food was from"—Ibid.

153. "For the first time"—Ibid.

154. "To The Jefe"—WSR "To The Jefe & all the KANAKAs of Easter Island," 20 July 1914, typewritten letter with edits; original in the hand of WSR. A second letter under the same heading, typewritten on *Mana* letterhead and dated "Camp Hotuiti," July 22, 1914, was not sent. A note in the hand of KSR says "not delivered as objected to by

Mr. Edmunds." The letter essentially asks why the Rapa Nui had not responded to WSR's proposal. (RGS WKR 4/10). The *jefe*, of course, was Juan Tepano.

154. "much anxious thought"; "we can only"—Sun., 19 July 1914 (RGS WKR 4/9).

154. "before there is"—Mon., 20 July 1914 (RGS WKR 4/9).

155. "a horrible sight"—Ibid.; MEI:145.

155. "distinctly attractive and"—MEI:145.

155. Angata looked deep—KSR gives "Caterina" (MEI:145), but "Katarina" in her journal for Mon., 20 July 20 1914 (RGS WKR 4/9).

155. "food came from"—Mon., 20 July 1914 (RGS WKR 4/9).

155. "opening"; "God did not wish"—MEI:145.

155. "face hardened for"—Ibid.

156. "hastened to relieve"—Ibid.

156. "a confidence that was sublime"; *"ine he maté"*—Ibid. "It was impossible to argue further. As for myself, she said she would pray for me, and if I ever wanted chickens or potatoes I should be the first to have them. We parted the best of Friends but having accomplished nothing."

     Note on fieldnotes: The *Friends/friends* distinction may not be anything more than a function of rapidly noted impressions. However, KSR did not capitalize nouns in the Germanic way WSR consistently did. It is at least possible that it is an error based on KSR's recognition, conscious or unconscious, that what she was seeing in Angata was Quakerly, i.e., an echo of her aunt Jane's behavior.

156. "came with him"—Ibid., 280.

156. "the witch doctor"—Interview JVT/PB, Hampton, 30 May 1996.

156. "rode as fast"—Tues., 21 July 1914; (RGS WKR 4/9).

158. "greetings from God"—Tues. 4 Aug. 1914; Wed., 5 Aug. 1914 (RGS WKR 4/9).

158. "The Kanakas are coming!"—MEI: 146.

159. "a war of independence"—27 July 1914 (RGS WKR 4/9).

159. "worried night thinking"—WSR to the Comandante, *Jeneral Baquedano*, from Camp Hotu Iti, 12 Aug. 1914 (RGS WKR 4/10); see also Tues., 28 July 1914 (RGS WKR 4/9).

160. Green formally resigned—For Green's involvement in the "uprising" see Porteous 1981:76 n. 54; WSR to the Comandante, *Jeneral Baquedano*, from Camp Hotu Iti, 10 Aug. 1914 (RGS WKR 4/10); Sun., 16 Aug. 1914 (RGS WKR 4/9). WSR intended to bring formal charges against Henry MacLean for desertion, accusing him of leaving Camp Hotu Iti and going over to Edmunds without his permission. This nasty interchange over MacLean was one of WSR's worst moments, and he was encouraged in it by KSR (14 Aug. 1914 [RGS WKR 4/9]).

160. "½ of Tongariki"—MEI:214; Tues., 28 July 1914 (RGS WKR 4/9).

160. It was quickly—Mon., 3 Aug. (RGS WKR 4/9).

     Historical note: The exact form of the flag is not known. Porteous (1981:167) suggests it was a French tricolor that asserted the islanders' connection with Tahiti and French Polynesia, but that is highly unlikely and makes no sense as a conciliatory gesture, which was Angata's purpose. Edmunds (RGS WKR 4/9, Aug. 3) encouraged KSR to give the fabric and thought it would "set well with the Chilian [*sic*] authorities," supporting the notion that it was similar to a Chilean flag. Rapa Nui has its own official flag (Hotus y Otros 1988). It bears a *reimiro* or traditional crescent-shaped symbol of kingly authority and was frequently displayed inside the church. Today, it flies on a flagstaff in front of the church.

160. He made Katherine—Tues., 4 Aug. (RGS WKR 4/9); WSR "felt it was fatal to his word to the K[anaka]s that [MacLean] should ever be seen in the camp & told me to tell him to leave at once & if he had anything to say to him he wd meet him where the trail left the road. H.[enry MacLean] said he had 'nothing to say.' "

161. She was spotted—PE to WSR, 5 Aug. 1914 (RGS WKR 4/9).

161. "I almost broke"; "I had not"—Thurs., 6 Aug. 1914 "Before bkfast" (RGS WKR 4/9); D/GP 6, v. 32, Sun., 9 Aug. WP says that KSR's letters home "constantly refer to the peacefulness of our ordered stay at home lives. Now unknown to her the tables are

turned. It is she who is peaceful in the Pacific, and we who are living dangerously [in WWI]."

161. "the whole history"; "much deeper"—Fri., 7 Aug. 1914 (RGS WKR 4/9); MEI:146–47.

162. Over the next—Hotus y Otros 1988:312–16.

162. The *Comandante* of *Baquedano*—Capt de Fragata y Comandante *Jeneral Baquedano* to WSR, No. 1632 (RGS WKR 4/10).

162. "with rare exceptions"; "no value can be attached"—WSR to *Comandante, Jeneral Baquedano*, from Camp Hotu Iti, 12 Aug., 1914, p. 2 (RGS WKR 4/9).

163. "the vessel . . . has"—Ibid. Sentence in KSR's hand added that reads, "The effect of such an action is I fear bound to be of a most serious character."

163. "very keen"—Lieutenant Ritchie to WSR from Mataveri, Mon., 10 Aug. 1914 (RGS WKR 4/10); "List of Plans, etc" by DRR (ibid.); WSR to *Comandante, Jeneral Baquedano*, from Camp Hotu Iti, 10 Aug. 1914 (ibid.); DRR to WSR, Thurs., 13 Aug. 1914 (ibid.).

163. As she stood—KSR did not speak or understand Rapanui at this point, in spite of WSR's claim that she had "learnt the language" (WSR to *Comandante, Jeneral Baquedano*, from Camp Hotu Iti, 12 Aug. 1914 [RGS WKR 4/9]). See also KSR to PE, 17 Nov. 1914 (RGS WKR 4/10).

163. "the tables are turned"; "old, forgotten far off"—D/GP 6, v. 32, pp. 40, 41, 42; see also D/GP 6, v. 33, p. 22.

CAMP HOTU ITI: LIVING FACES

164. "Immediately above the"—MEI:136.

165. "quiet dignity"; "of suggestion and"—Ibid., 184.

165. "the awed spectator"—Ibid., 178.

165. "a real interest"—Ibid., 214; Tues., 28 July 1914 (RGS LBR MSS 4/9).

165. More than fifty—Lilian González N. (personal communication) recorded this information.

165. One late, cloudy—Tues., 27 Oct. 1914 (RGS WKR 4/9); PE added some place-names and site marks on the survey map.

166. Scattered throughout Katherine's—RGS WKR 4/9; RGS WKR 4/20/4.

166. "committed suicide in"—MEI:137.

166. "pulled down in"—KSR's notes on Rano Raraku statues are in three different journals and notebooks, and the researcher is required to coordinate them with handwritten tables, sketches, and finished drawings found elsewhere in her papers (RGS WKR 4/1).

167. Once back in London—The RGS was involved in many of WSR's preparations for manuscripts, photographic printing, and other publication chores. The draftsmen were F. Batchelor and E. G. Ridgway (MEI:x; RGS WKR 4/9).

167. "having a happy"—KSR on *Mana* stationery, Easter Sunday [April 4], but including to 15 June 1915, "My Dearests" (RGS WKR 4/10/34, four pages double-sided plus one).

167. "what statues to dig"—Sun., 6 Sept. (RGS WKR 4/9). Chronological journal record written by KSR and beginning Sunday, 26 Apr. 1914 (arrived 29 Mar.), and ending 25 July 1915 (departed 18 Aug. 1915).

168. Coordinating that information—To date I have only been able to correlate about one-quarter of the descriptions of statues dug in KSR's fieldnotes with journal entries and the expedition's maps.

168. Papa Haa Puré—"Papa" is statue I in KSR's notes and on her rough sketch, but no. 109 on the published diagrammatic sketch (MEI:fig. 17, and for back detail, see Green's photo MEI:fig. 64); "Papa's Wife" is statue II but no. 108 in the same sketch.

168. He named the other—*Archaeological note:* For excavation details see RGS WSR 4/9, Mon., 21 Sept.; Tues., 22 Sept.; Wed., 23 Sept.; Thurs., 24 Sept.; Fri., 25 Sept.; Tues., 13 Oct. "W., K. & Antonio & men worked in crater. dug out Papas back & much of Papas wife . . . found hieroglyphics & skeleton": Papa was "buried in almost immediate contact with the quarry wall & was submerged to a line midway bet the lobe of the ear & and the angle of the lower jaw. Its face is directed n. [and] half east. Excavated owing to tattoo [sic] marks being observed at exposed surface. The Back to a

depth of 16´ + from cranium to bottom. The level of the buttock . . . the front . . . the level of the navel. The figures had at level of elbow 2 disks in relief on either side the spinal groove immediately below & the triple raised band below wh again is a v shaped ornament"; "Skeleton long bones base of skull & patella were identified. It lay in wet soil crushed intermixed with large stones so the attitude cd not be determined beyond the fact that the head to the R. of the image & the long bones to the Left—the bones were extremely friable & cd only be identified by cleaning longitudinally cross section with a Knife"; "charcoal of grass fire, mahuté [bark cloth] and pungé [coral abrader]"; "The Back of the neck & the whole of the back of the figure also the . . . aspect upper part of upper arm covered with incised figures but so badly executed as to suggest they were made subsequent . . ."

168. On September 24—Thurs., 24 Sept.; Sat., 26 Sept. (RGS WKR 4/9).
      Collections note: Artifacts excavated in Rano Raraku are mostly in PRM.

A SPY STORY

170. He and Scoresby—RGG WSR 4/10, WSR to PE, Hotu Iti, 26 Aug. 1914; PE to KSR from Mataveri, n.d., Thurs.; PE to KSR from Anga Nui, n.d., Fri.; RGS LBR MSS 4/10, Thur., 5 Nov. 1914, Fri., 6 Nov. 1914.

170. "under great difficulties"; "a certain amount"—RGS WKR 4/10, KSR to PE, 17 Nov. 1914; Langitopa was telling KSR the story of the "Long Ears" and she could not make sense of it. See RGS WKR 4/9, Mon., 16 Nov., Tues., 17 Nov. On Wednesday, 18 Nov., KSR sent Langitopa back to Mataveri with Varta, who was required by PE, as it was "useless" to try to work with Langitopa without the help of Varta to translate. Tepano later helped with some of the language (see Fri., 20 Nov.).

170. "dying fast"—RGS WKR 4/10, KSR to PE, 17 Nov. 1914.

171. Varta was a good—RGS WKR 4/9, chronological journal record written by KSR and beginning Sunday, 26 Apr. 1914 (arrived 29 Mar.) and ending 25 July 1915 (departed 18 Aug. 1915). See Thurs., 10 Sept., and Sat., 10 Oct.
      Anthropological note: Rapa Nui people frequently make and use reed canoes in modern arts festivals, but there is no evidence they existed prehistorically on the island. All Rapa Nui canoes known were plank canoes of the traditional Polynesian outrigger type. The wood preferred was *hau;* the planks were sewn with vegetable-fiber cordage and caulked with moss from Rano Raraku (Métraux 1940:206). *Pora* were floats made of reeds and used as surf riders. They were seen by J. Linton Palmer of H. M. S. *Topaze* and were known to some of KSR's consultants, some of whom may actually have used them in the Orongo rituals (or adapted them as grass "pillows" to support Hoa Hakananai'a when it was removed from Orongo [McCall, personal communication, 2002]). It is entirely possible that WSR and Varta introduced the concept of a reed "canoe," a concept reinforced by T. Heyerdahl, who showed pictures of the South American version to some Rapa Nui people.

171. He carried a small—RGS WKR 1/14. Notebook is less than ½ full.

171. By October, Katherine—RGS WKR 4/9, Thurs., 22 Oct. 1914.

171. "there is something"—RGS WKR 4/9, Fri., 16 Oct. 1914.

171. "worked like a slave"—RGS WKR 4/9, Tues., 13 Oct. 1914.

171. "more amusing or pathetic"—Ibid.

171. "entirely unsuspected"; "striking character"; "lamentable destruction"—RGS WKR 4/10, untitled typescript, one page.

172. "How much is true?"—RGS WKR 4/9.

172. "One sits and writes"; "archaeology in the face"—RGS WKR 4/9, Mon., 2 Nov. 1914.

172. The light cruiser—D/GP 6, v. 33, p. 35. KSR's friend was Pamela Willoughby.

172. "the German cruisers"; "marooned on Easter Island"—Ibid.

172. "detained through war"—Ibid., 38; "Log Books of the Yacht Mana, 15 vols. Commencing Febry. 20th, 1913," Log Book 8, Fri., 25 Sept. 1914; Tues., 3 Nov. 1914; Wed., 18 Nov. 1914 (RGS WKR 1/1–15).

172. Exactly one month—"Log Books of the Yacht Mana, 15 vols. Commencing Febry. 20th, 1913," Log Book 8, Sat., 28 Nov. 1914; Mon., 30 Nov. 1914; (RGS WKR 1/1–15).

173. "to spy on"—D/GP 6, vol. 33, p. 63.

173. "Spy mania"—D/GP 6, v. 32, p. 41.

173. "a very quiet"—RGS WKR 4/9.

174. "put her oar in"—These words describing KSR appear frequently in D/GP 6.

174. "let off steam"; "off his head"; "quite pleasant"—Edmunds in Oliveros 1994.

174. She delivered the letter—KSR to Vives Solar, 25 Dec. 1914 (RGS WKR 4/10); I. Vives Solar to KSR, 11 Jan. 1914 (RGS WKR 4/10).

175. "like a great blot"; "in a last Judas"—MEI:158.

175. "swooped round in"—Ibid.

175. "suddenly the end"—Ibid.

> *Historical note:* More than sixty years later I witnessed a nearly identical incident. Riding with friends on the slope of Maunga Terevaka, I saw a Dutch vessel towing a cargo ship that had gone aground on the rocks a month earlier. She had been relieved of her cargo and was going to be sunk. As we watched, she tooted her horn in a sad, brave farewell, and it was almost human.

175. "slack"; "fighting the blues"—RGS WKR 4/9, Sat., 9 Jan.; Sun., 10 Jan.; Sun., 17 Jan.; Fri., 29 Jan.; Sat., 30 Jan.; Thurs., 18 Feb.; Thurs., 25 Feb.; Sun., 28 Feb.

175. "pathetically tiny"—The "black box" under which Angata had received the word of God may have been used for her casket, but that is not known for certain.

176. "I stood at a little"—MEI:149.

176. "afraid to cross"—D/GP 6, v. 33, p. 62; in fact, *Mana* was officially detained, just as Gillam had written the Routledges, on orders of the British consul (RGS WKR 1/1–15, "Log Books of the Yacht Mana, 15 vols. Commencing Febry. 20th, 1913," Log Book 9, 1 Nov. to 31 Jan. 1915).

176. "see that the Routledges"—D/GP 6, v. 33, p. 62.

176. "all well"—Ibid.

176. "to spy on"—Ibid.

176. "with the rats"—MEI:162.

177. Scoresby immediately wrote—WSR to HBM minister, British Legation, Santiago, 14 Mar. 1915 (RGS WKR 4/10).

> *Note on documentation:* There are two versions of this letter. The draft is eight pages and undated and bears comments by KSR. A neater, shorter version appears to be a copy of the final letter. It is marked "Confidential" and dated March 14 or 18, neither of which corresponds to the date in KSR's journal or *Mana* log. If it is a copy of the full letter, it had to have been written on March 17, 1915. The draft contains a truly extraordinary demand by WSR that the sum of £600 "be placed to the credit of the Easter Island Expedition with Messrs W & B & Co. Valparaiso in acknowledgement" of the "service" of *Mana* as a dispatch boat. He arrived at this sum because it was the same that was paid by Williamson, Balfour Co. to Captain Walker for *Aranco* when she was used as a "spy boat." This demand, if it was actually delivered in a letter or verbally by Gillam, is almost extortion and would surely have shocked the British minister and shown WSR up as a mercenary opportunist. Drafting his thoughts in this manner, by the way, was typical of WSR, and he drafted the speech he gave to OGSC before firing him.

177. "an active part"—Ibid., 4.

177. "answer questions"—MEI:163: "we have subsequently received kind acknowledgment from the Admiralty of our efforts to be useful." No written acknowledgment is in any of the expedition's papers, however.

177. The ship's log—KSR journal, Fri., 21 May 1915 (RGS WKR 4/9); see also MEI:317 n. 1.

178. Mana Expedition papers—KSR's journal has the cruiser arriving on Monday, 12 July (RGS WKR 4/9). The log of *Mana* has it 11 July (RGS WKR 1/1–15). "Ship arrived cruiser. Has gone without chance of posting." D/GP 6, v. 34.

178. F. W. Wilsden went ashore—"The Land in the Middle of the Sea" by Lieutenant F. W. Wilsden, H. M. S. *Orama,* 11 July 1915 (RGS LBR MSS).

LEGACY

179. "Mana arrived in"; "Moved to Hotu Iti"—RGS WKR 4/9.
179. "dreams of beauty"—KSR on *Mana* stationery, Easter Sunday (4 Apr.), but including to 15 June 1915, to "My Dearests" (RGS WKR 4/10/34, four pages double-sided plus one).
179. "leaving this immense"—Ibid.
179. "simply daren't to think"—Ibid.; "K. is sorry to leave Easter Island. 15 months have not sickened her of it" (D/GP 6, v. 35, p. 17). "In a circular letter K. tells of how sorry she was to leave Easter Island after 17 months there" (ibid., 38).
179. "elaborate essays on"; "sufficiently absorbing"; "somewhat cold"—KSR on *Mana* stationery, Easter Sunday (4 Apr.), but including to 15 June 1915, to "My Dearests" (RGS WKR 4/10/34, four pages doubled-sided plus one).
179. He drafted a letter—WSR to Royal Society with cover letter, 7 Nov. 1915 (RGS WKR 4/10/51).
    Note on fieldnotes: A good sample of the work WSR did on the Mana Expedition can be found in RGS WKR 1/14/11, Rano Raraku; RGS WKR 1/14/12, details of masonry with KSR edits; RGS WKR 1/14/13, burial cairns with finished drawing in RGS WKR 4/15; RGS WKR 4/2, outlines for survey report and book plus first-draft typed copy of survey report.
179. "Did I make"—Undated, unsigned note in KSR's hand to PE among out-of-order fieldnotes (RGS WKR).
180. "satisfactorily finished"—KSR on *Mana* stationery, Easter Sunday (4 Apr.), but including to 15 June 1915, to "My Dearests" (RGS WKR 4/10/34, four pages double-sided plus one).
180. "if people ask"—KSR to "My darling Mother," Easter Island, 8 June 1915 (RGS WKR 4/10/34). This is the cover letter to the circular of 4 Apr. 1915, above.
180. On April 12—D/GP 6, v. 34, p. 52.
180. "Believe K. Pease"—KSR Journal, Fri., 21 May 1915 (RGS WKR 4/9); see also MEI:317 n. 1).
181. At home in Darlington—D/GP 6, v. 34, p. 52.
182. "locality and memory"—WPP; MEI:214.
182. Although the boundaries—In 1821 Captain S. Chase of *Foster* is reported to have heard details of social organization, including the dual political organization and a "yearly ceremony" he did not describe but that may have been the birdman ceremony (McCall n.d.; Van Tilburg 1992:45).
183. "reliability was the charm"—D/GP 6, v. 7, p. 2.
183. "companionate"—KSR on *Mana* stationery, Easter Sunday (4 Apr.), but including to 15 June 1915, to "My Dearests" (RGS WKR 4/1034, four pages double-sided plus one).
183. "the whole voyage"; "was due to"—MEI:390, 214.
185. "the last vestige"—Ibid:306.

VOYAGE HOME

189. She arrived in—MEI:306.
    Historical note: Bligh and his men demonstrated remarkable courage and superb seamanship, sailing their open boat 3,618 miles from Tonga to the island of Timor in the East Indies. He returned to a hero's welcome in England. The mutineers, now marooned on Pitcairn Island, lived in utter isolation, warring with one another as the Tahitian men over women. In 1855 Queen Victoria relocated some to equally isolated Norfolk Island (until the preceding year a notorious penal colony).
189. "it was depressing"—Ibid., 308.

189. "resembled to some extent"—Ibid., 313.
189. "a certain resemblance"—Ibid., 314.
190. She wrote a letter—D/GP 6, v. 35, p. 38: "Nice private letter from Katherine. She has had the happy thought of how Mams must be enjoying 'Sarah and Susan.' K. thanks Joan for all she did for Mams, and wishes her to know how much Mams appreciated it."
190. "He had found himself"—MEI:318.
190. Katherine saw the ruins—Ibid., 320.
190. She visited a small—A map of land parcels maintained by Rapa Nui people in Pamata'i, Tahiti, in 1888 is in McCall n.d. (1986).
190. "quite a millionaire"—MEI:321.
191. "saw his name"—Ibid.
191. "the loneliest spot"; "both food & time"—KSR to "Your Grace" off Tahiti, Society Islands, 3 Oct. 1915, two pages incomplete (RGS WKR 1/10/40).
191. "fresh thoughts literature"—Ibid.
191. They toured the island—Stokes and Dye, 1991:4; see also "Three Years of Adventuring in War Sown Seas," Honolulu Advertiser, Sunday, 14 Nov. 1915; see also Honolulu Star-Bulletin, 15 Nov. 1915 (RGS WKR 7).
191. "no resemblance either"—MEI:323; Stokes and Dye 1991:fig. 71.
191. "the art of building"—MEI:323.
191. Scoresby had a photo—WSR to (his nephew) Colonel Howard Allen: "Wishing you all good luck in the Coming Year and assuring you of my Sympathy in present anxieties" (REB).
191. Inside are stanzas—Memorial leaflet, six pages exclusive of cover, from KSR "For Lilian Yacht Mana Off Honolulu Sandwich Islands Christmas 1915" (PB); "Empty my heart"—Ibid.; from hymn by C.F., published by E. C. Caswell.
191. "heard the voice"—Ibid.
192. On November 28—They visited Hikiau Heiau, South Kona (Stokes and Dye 191:fig. 44); MEI:326; see also Kirch 2192. "Megalithic Remains on Easter Island," unpublished paper read by W. Scoresby Routledge at the Annual Meeting, British Association for the Advancement of Science, Newcastle-on-Tyne, 1916. They also saw "Heiau Puukohoa" (Pu'ukohola Heiau in the Kohala District of Hawaii). See Stokes and Dye 1991:164–69; MEI:327, fig. 133.
192. Scoresby was ill—Gifford took from the Youngs a "full complement of anthropological measurements" (KSR to Gifford from Hotel Stewart, San Francisco, Wed. [BL UCB Correspondence, call no. 23, series 6, box 39, folder "Katherine Routledge 1916–1921; box 33, folder "Bishop Museum"]). Stan Louis to JVT, 8 Apr. 1997.
192. "was a great joy"—KSR to Gifford from USMS New York, 5 Feb. 1916 (BL UCB); KSR to Gifford from 69 Grosvenor St., London, 30 Mar. 1916 (BL UCB); Gifford to KSR, 20 Apr. 1916 (BL UCB).
   Anthropological note: Gifford worked on the Bayard Dominick Expedition to Tonga in 1920 and then went on to excavate in Fiji in 1947.
192. "last Yahi"—Kroeber 1976.
192. "positively thrilling"—KSR to Gifford from USMS New York, 5 Feb. 1916 (BL UCB); Gifford to KSR, 1 Mar. 1916 (BL UCB).
192. "hero"; "greatly impressed"—Ibid.
192. They had promised—Kroeber 1976 (originally published 1961); Buzaljko 1989.
192. With Scoresby, Gillam—WSR in MEI:Part IV, "The Homeward Voyage Continued San Francisco to Southampton," pp. 333–88.
192. "a winter resort"; "more impressive than"; "got as far"—MEI:332; KSR to Waterman from USMS New York, 5 Feb. 1916 (BL UCB); MEI:332.
193. "no submarines in sight"—Ibid.: "we hope all well to land tomorrow no submarines in sight!" "both Dr. Hough and Dr. Hodge were very kind particularly the former who spent much time showing me the collections under his care & made one or two very valuable suggestions about the articles there from Easter Island. I learned a great deal too about the Mohican collection."

193. "where we could"—D/GP 6, v. 35, p. 58.
193. "When the train"—Ibid.
193. "Poor Katherine was always"—Ibid.
193. "The Islanders say"—Ibid., 59.
194. "K. could make"; "quarreled with nearly"—Ibid.
194. "I may go"—Ibid., 60.
194. "The fact of the matter"—Ibid., 61.
195. Lyle saw the state—KSR to Gifford from (Ladies' Empire Club) 69 Grosvenor St., London, on Ranby House, Nr Retford, Notts paper, 30 Mar. 1916 (BL).
195. There was snow—D/GP 6, v. 35, p. 62.
     Biographical note: Appointed vicar of St. John Evangelist, Darlington, from 1897 to 1904, Bilborough was honorable chaplain to the bishop of Durham (1901–16) and a member of the House of Lords (1936–41).
195. "a job for which *Mana*"—MEI:361.
195. "trust to our"—"Log Books of the Aux. Motor Schooner 'Mana' from the Port of Southampton, 15 vols. Commencing Febry. 20th, 1913"; see logbook 15, Wed., 14 June 1916 (RGS WKR 1/1–15).
195. "bad tempered and"—Ibid.

THE STORY OF AN EXPEDITION, 1916–20

197. "representatives of England's"—MEI:389; news cuttings dealing with this event are from *The Times* of London, 29 July 1916, and others (RGS WKR 7, pp. 48, 49, of album).
197. In September Scoresby—Keith 1950:402–3.
197. "they were a most docile"—Ibid.
197. "had proved themselves"—MEI:389.
197. "returned with some"—News cuttings dealing with the return of *Mana* and all of the attendant publicity describe "Northern Lady's Feat," "A Small Yacht's Remarkable Voyage," and the "Wonderful Adventures" of *Mana* (RGS WKR 7, pp. 46–61 of album; see also 4/13). See also R. Winckworth to "My dear Crawford," 6 July 1916 (BOD MS).
197. He high-handedly demanded—Harold Peake to "My dear Mog," 22 Oct. 1916, 13 Sept. 1916, 29 Sept. 1916 (BOD MS).
197. Scoresby's report to—RGS WKR 4/10/42, "Easter Is Report to Royal Society," begun 10 Sept. 1915, forty-seven pages in WSR's hand with additions, edits, and corrections by KSR.
197. "We failed to find"—Ibid., p. 12.
197. "no notable results"; "natives have always"; "aware of the value"—Ibid., 14.
197. "comparative study in"—Ibid., pp. 19–28
197. "what is latest"—Telegram from Routledge at Fortfield Hotel, Sidmouth, n.d.; see also Miss M. E. Dalrymple Hay to RGS, 3 Oct. 1916; see also RGS response to KSR, 2 Oct. 1916 (RGS CB 1911–20).
197. "Thank you so"—KSR to RGS, 6 Oct. 1916 (RGS CB 1911–20).
198. "ashamed to send"—KSR to RGS on *Mana* stationery, n.d. (1916), probably part of KSR to RGS from Ewers, 15 Oct. 1916 (RGS CB 1911–20).
198. "which I hope"; "one of the Lecturers"—KSR to RGS on *Mana* stationery, 17 Oct. 1916 (RGS CB 1911–20).
198. "pleasant to be assured"—RGS to KSR, 18 Oct. 1916 (RGS CB 1911–20).
198. "The paper is original"—Reader's report, A. P. Maudslay to RGS (RGS CB 1922–20).
198. "it will make"—A. P. Maudslay to Hinks form Morney Cross, Hereford, 23 Oct. 1916 (RGS CB 1911–20)
198. "sad prospect"; "spent much more"—RGS to Maudslay, 24 Oct. 1916; RGS to KSR, 9 Nov. 1916 (RGS CB 1911–20).
198. "look after"—Maudslay to RGS, 27 Oct. 1916; RGS to Maudslay, 28 Oct. 1916 (RGS CB 1911–20).
198. "I gather from"—WSR to RGS, n.d. (RGS CB 1911–20).
198. A demanding question—The entire interchange on this issue is discussed in an earlier

chapter and is documented in a series of letters between Hinks, KSR, Stainton, Corney, and others beginning 25 Nov. (RGS CB 1911–20; see also Van Tilburg 1992).

> *Note on documentation:* Stainton based his claim, which was legitimate but had not been officially verified and was, therefore, considered invalid, on the diary of Paymaster-in-Chief R. Richards of HMS *Challenger,* a vessel Stainton erroneously thought had called at Rapa Nui in the mid-1800s. Notes by Richards about Easter Island were not made on the island, but were copied into his journal from a published account.

199. "the Melanesian more"—"Preliminary Report on the Collection of Human Skulls and Bones Made on Rapa Nui by Mr. and Mrs. Scoresby Routledge" by Arthur Keith, MDFRS, Conservator of Museum, Royal College of Surgeons of England, fifteen pages typescript (RGS WKR 4/10/45); MEI:295. In a slight echo of the eugenics debates, Keith says that the "Islanders are the largest-brained people yet discovered in the islands or shores of the Pacific," and KSR (ibid., 296) notes "their cranial capacity exceeds that of the inhabitants of Whitechapel."

199. Katherine, however, did not—*Historical note:* Not long after Katherine's RGS lecture, yet another controversy erupted. Dr. H. O. Forbes had maintained, during the discussion following Katherine's paper at the RGS, that Fleet Surgeon J. Linton Palmer of HMS *Topaze* had once brought actual examples of Rapa Nui *kohau rongorongo* to him at the Liverpool Museum. Katherine was extremely skeptical and, when Forbes' remarks were published with her paper, she received a letter from Palmer's widow, Frances, that clearly said Forbes was wrong. Katherine forwarded Mrs. Palmer's letter to Hinks, who, in turn, sent it on to Forbes. He responded by saying not only had he seen the boards, Palmer or some member of his family had offered them and other Rapa Nui artifacts for sale. When the museum had declined to purchase them, the artifacts were supposedly dispersed at auction. Katherine, again with Mrs. Palmer's support, suggested that Forbes had mistaken casts of *rongorongo* boards for the real thing. Forbes, whose tone toward both Katherine and Frances Palmer was patronizing throughout, was seriously offended. He promptly wrote to Hinks, saying that Mrs. Palmer was too old to be taken seriously and implying that Katherine was entirely too sure of herself. Hinks then wisely called a halt to the exchange. The interchange between KSR, Hinks, Forbes, and Mrs. Frances Palmer took place between July and December 1917 (with one letter marked 1920) and is in RGS WKR 4/19. The evidence is that KSR was right.

200. "Strictly Confidential"—RGS CB 8/73, item 74, n.d. (1915?): "Strictly Confidential Legación de Chile." Report from the Maritime Sub-Delegate of Rapa Nui to the Director of Maritime Territory concerning Mr. Routledge and the yacht 'Mana,' says he has learned in a conversation . . ." I. Vives Solar, who succeeded PE, is possibly the "Sub-Delegate" referred to here, but not certainly. How the document got in the files of the RGS is a mystery, but Frank T. Green, PE, OGSC (or any of his friends), or Lieutenant Graham are all possibilities (see below).

200. "might make unjust"; "he was particularly"—Ibid.

200. "Mr. Routledge's objectionable"; "his lack of"; "incorrect and ungentlemanly"—Ibid.; Frank T. Green and PE certainly maintained contact for some time, and it is possible that this synopsis of events and opinions could have been forwarded to the RGS by either of them. PE was in England in 1920–21 (cf. KSR to PE from Jamaica, 10 Jan. 1921 [RGS LBR MSS 4/19]).

200. "the collaborators and employees"; "sailed from the island"—Ibid.; PE charged WSR forty pesos each time *Mana* arrived at the island. This was done in his official capacity as a Chilean official. It is thus not credible that the Routledges were unaware of PE's official status (as they said during the "native rising"; see RGS WKR 4, Mar. 1915, for two receipts for these charges).

200. "for his cruise"—MEI:388.

200. He was immensely—Brassey 1879, 1885.

200. Katherine, meanwhile, was gathering—D/GP 6, v. 37, p. 46; the last division of KP's personal property was, apparently, on December 4, 1916.

200. "state of nerves"—D/GP 6, v. 35, p. 84; this volume has at least four pages missing.
200. "concern"; "loggerheads"—Ibid., 92
200. There came again—Ibid., 66.
200. Scoresby was preoccupied—See, for example, the exchange of letters between WSR, Cambridge University Press, BPB, and A. Métraux over use of maps and photos (RGS WKR 4/19).
201. This raised issues—Photos taken by both the Mana Expedition and PE are known. *Note on documentation:* Some of the latter are in BPB collection. Others have been privately offered for sale and I have reviewed them, including duplicates of some in the BPB. On June 7, 1915, WSR and PE both signed a statement written by WSR that says "I" am handing over to "you" 133 photographic negatives "left in my charge" by Green, "late photographer & Engineer to the Easter Is Expedition being Satisfied, from statements made to me by Mr. F.T. Green, that the copyright in & Right of Reproduction of these negatives is . . . in the Easter Is Expedition. I do the same on condition that, when finished with, the negatives will be Returned to my custody." A second memo says, "Edmunds handed to me 286 negatives . . . I have Retained temporarily to be Returned to Edmunds 133 negatives . . . I now hand back to E. 122 . . ."; KSR to PE from Jamaica, 20 Jan. 1921, "received the prints of the photos . . . I find however that there are seven not six negatives . . . enclose a cheque . . ." All of this suggests that PE had some negatives of his own or retained some negatives belonging to the expedition, made prints, and then sold negatives and prints to the Mana Expedition. Some expedition photos, therefore, could have been taken by PE as well as by Green and the Routledges (RGS WKR 4/19; RGS PC 1 142 negatives; see also BM collection).
201. "its photographs alone"—MEI:xii.
201. "scientific"—"Easter Island," *Pall Mall Gazette,* 5 Dec. 1919 (RGS LBR MSS 7; see also RGS WKR 4/13).
201. "delightful book of travel"—"Problems of the Pacific," n.d., in the *Observer* (RGS WKR 7 and RGS WKR 4/13).
201. "substantial"; "noteworthy"; "handsome"; "fascinating"; "as spacious a book"; "a remarkable body"—"The World of Books," *The Nation,* 22 Nov. 1919, and "The Mystery of Easter Island," *Scotsman,* 24 Nov. 1919 (RGS WKR 7 and RGS WKR 4/13).
201. If the Routledges—"Easter Island," *Westminster Gazette,* 6 Dec. 1919 (RGS WKR 7 and RGS WKR 4/13).
201. "a chance to repair"—MEI:xi.
201. "derived from a union"—Ibid.
201. "at the eleventh"—Ibid:xii.
201. "are connected by blood"—Ibid.
201. Based upon examinations—See, for example, MEI:166, 168, 186, 187, 189, 194, 199; one estimate of the number of statues recorded by the Mana Expedition was Thomson's earlier number of 555 and seems to have been given by WSR in "Yacht Covers 100,000 Miles," n.d. (1915), The (London) *Times* (Twycross-Raines n.d.).
202. The paper trail—See "first typed copy" manuscript of survey notes in RGS WKR 4/21. *Note on fieldnotes:* The paper trail is especially clear in KSR's Orongo rough notes: First version of notes was typed from dictation with KSR's handwritten edits, and corrections., and some of WSR's. Then a second typed version was produced, marked in some places "incomplete." Site descriptions were supplemented with ethnographic details including informant names. This rather full and interesting picture of the site, unfortunately, was not available when Orongo was later investigated (Ferdon 1961) and restored (Mulloy 1975); see also RGS WKR 4/14 and RGS WKR 1/14/2 for WSR notes on statue excavations, caves; see also tables of measurements and notes for Hanga Tee; RGS WKR 4/14/10; RGS WKR 1/14/11; RGW WSR 1/14/14; RGS WKR 12/14/14, second brown folder of twelve includes typed table of contents of

proposed book; RGS WKR 4/14/13, details on burial cairns intended to be part of final book, used in MEI; RGS WKR 4/15, finished drawings.

202. "more than one"—MEI:294.

202. "in the centre"—Ibid., 291.

202. "does not necessarily"—Ibid., 299.

202. "the part played"—Ibid., 300.

202. "companionate"—Emma Routledge Twycross Arnott's will was the focal point of a family disagreement and correspondence flew back and forth (solicitor's letter, London, 22 June 1915: "The eldest son, Mr. W.S. Routledge spends much time in the South Pacific in a Yacht on scientific investigation, he is very well off" (C. Lopez, personal communication, 2001).

203. Scoresby remained to mount—WSR to KSR, 18 Mar. 1920, "Proposed Exped Across John Crow Mtns," three pages, 4 Mar. 1920 (RGS WKR LBR MSS 6); the Routledges stayed with the Barclays, Quaker relatives of the Pease family, at Hummingbird House.

203. His first assault—WSR to KSR, 12 Apr. 1920 (RGS WKR 6).

203. "I and two"—WSR to KSR, 28 Apr. 1920 (RGS WKR 6).

203. "Many thanks . . . Jamaica"—WSR to KSR, 3 May 1920 (RGS WKR 6).

203. Scoresby returned to England—KSR and WSR met with a reporter at 9 Cadogan Mansions on a wire story entitled "Among the Maroons in Jamaica," 26 May 1920 (RGS WKR 6).

203. The buyer was—Boatman magazine, Nov. 1995, p. 18; Yachting World and Motor, 28 Feb., 27 Mar., 10 Apr., 24 Apr., 1 May 1920; Yachting Monthly, June 1920; Lloyd's Register of Yachts, 1912, 1914, 1919, 1920, 1922, 1923; J. C. G. Williamson, Surveyor to Lloyd's Register, Rio de Janeiro, 17 Sept. 1923; "List of Vessels Removed from the Register of Yachts for 1924 on Account of Being Broken Up, Lost, Etc.," p. 878; Royal Yacht Squadron Lists 1921, 1922. Mana's home port was London, then Campbeltown. For more on Dundonald, see Debrett's Illustrated Peerage; RB/JVT.

204. Their goal, stated—This was always part of their original Mana Expedition goal. "We felt that the work on Easter ought to be accompanied with the possibility of following up clues elsewhere in the islands" (MEI:4).

204. Katherine busily contacted—KSR's social calendar at this point was rather full. For example, she was one of the "one hundred representative women" who hosted a huge charity luncheon for "one hundred representative men" on behalf of the Royal Free Hospital and School of Medicine for Women. KSR represented "women travelers" (The Friend, 22 Oct. 1920, p. 676).

204. The Royal Geographical—WSR to RGS, 21 July 1920, from Cadogan Mansions; RGS to WSR, 23 July 1920 (RGS CB 1911–20).

LINKS, SIDETRACKS, AND DEAD ENDS, 1921–25

205. In January of 1921—Routledge, S. and K. 1921:438; they were in Jamaica "with the idea of doing a little more Satisfactory work of the Range, and to obtain photographs" (WSR to RGS from Upper Fair Prospect, Portland, Jamaica, 16 Jan. 1921 (RGS CB 1921–40). A photo of the building shell (a remnant left after a hurricane) in which they camped is misidentified in the BM collection.

205. "glad to accept"—"Our stay in Jamaica, en route to Tahiti has largely failed in its object. We gave the abnormal weather over three months to mend & then reluctantly decided that we give it up for the occasion & get on to Rapa Iti" (WSR to RGS, 2 July 1921, written while aboard ship en route to Tahiti [RGS CB 1921–40]).

205. I am writing—KSR to RGS, n.d., from San Francisco (RGS CB 1921–40).

206. I must really—KSR to RGS, 2 July 1921, en route to Tahiti (RGS CB 1921–40).

206. Gregory responded eagerly—KSR to A. L. Kroeber from Hotel Claremont, Berkeley, Calif., 18 June 1921 (BL UCB); A. L. Kroeber to H. E. Gregory, 20 June 1921 (BL UCB).

206. "watershed in Pacific"; "virgin field"; "hints of time"—Kirch 2206:21.

206. The Routledges intended—KSR to A. L. Kroeber from Hotel Claremont, Berkeley, Calif., 18 June 1921 (BL UCB).

206. "appear to be well-to-do"—A. L. Kroeber to H. E. Gregory, 20 June 1921 (BL UCB).
206. "You will remember"—Ibid.
207. "Where they find"—Ibid.
207. The Routledges arrived—KSR wrote an article entitled "The Frenchman Abroad" based on a conversation with a "vagabond" near the harbor in Papeete and sent it off to *The Spectator*, 26 Nov. 1921 (RGS WKR 7).
207. The Routledges were ahead—Emory 1933:102.
      Archaeological note: E. S. C. Handy accomplished the preliminary reconnaissance of stone structures in the Society Islands in 1923, and he gave his notes, etc., to Emory, who worked there from January 1925 to March 1926; Routledge 1921; Buck 1938.
207. Scoresby chartered *Vaite*—*Vaite* can be seen in EI:fig. 1, where it is incorrectly identified as *Mana*. My error was created because Love (1984:131, neg. MM008974) has misidentified this (and other) Routledge photos in the BM collection. RB and PB, both well familiar with *Mana*, pointed it out to me and then confirmed the error; see also "Island Secrets" in *The Evening Standard*, 21 May 1922 (RGS WKR 7). WSR to RGS c/o The British Consul, Papeete, Tahiti, 10 Aug. 1921 (RGS CB 1921–40).
207. "a delightful cruise"—KSR to B. G. Corney from Mangareva, Gambier Islands, 3 Nov. 1921 (RGS CB 1921–40).
208. They throw no—Routledge and Routledge 1921:452; "Rapa Nui Statues," 18 July 1923 (RGS WKR 7).
208. "folklore was outside"—Routledge and Routledge 1921:452
208. "spent two years"—Stokes and Dye 1998:17.
208. "most kind to us"—KSR to A. L. Kroeber from Mangareva, Gambier Islands, 3 Nov. 1921 (BL UCB); Stokes found it "difficult to complete reports on [this] research, probably because he was keenly self-critical and embarrassed by his lack of scientific training" (Stokes and Dye 1998:17).
209. "not quite what"—KSR to B. G. Corney from Mangareva, Gambier Islands, 3 Nov. 1921 (RGS CB 1921–40).
209. "in the Bishop Museum"—KSR to A. L. Kroeber from Mangareva, Gambier Islands, 3 Nov. 1921 (BL UCB).
209. "The Polynesian Capt."—KSR to RGS from Mangareva, Gambier Islands, 3 Nov. 1921 (RGS CB 1921–40).
209. "We find ourselves"—KSR to B. G. Corney from Mangareva, Gambier Is 3 Nov. 1921 (RGS/CB/1921–40).
209. On January 9—RGS to KSR, 9 Jan. 1922 (RGS CB 1921–40).
210. "just the help"—KSR to RGS from Mangareva, Gambier Islands, 9 Jan. 1923 (RGS CB 1921–40). Corney may have provided accounts of Mangarevan life by F. W. Beechey and J. A. Moerenhout, or another by an unreliable visitor named A. C. E Caillot. Most probably, however, he sent a dictionary or grammar of the Mangarevan language and, possibly, an overview of the Spanish in Tahiti. The Routledges had a copy of W. Ellis' *Polynesian Researches* and had read London Missionary Society (LMS) accounts.
210. "an almost wicked"—Robert Lee Eskridge, the famous modernist artist of Hawaiian folk scenes, said that "Père Feria" (actually, Father Vincent-Ferrier Janeau) told him "many stories" about KSR. She had, the old priest said, "completed a book" that was "an exhaustive study of the island and its peoples" (R. L. Eskridge to H. J. Braunholz, 26 June 1932 (BM).
210. "Some of it"—KSR to RGS from Mangareva, Gambier Islands, 9 Jan. 1923 (RGS CB 1921–40).
210. "struggled through"—*Historical note:* Father Honoré Laval lived on Mangareva from 1834 to 1871. After retiring to Tahiti, he worked with a priest or catechist named Tiripone, who was the son of a Mangarevan chief and ordained by Tepano's godfather, Bishop Tepano Jaussen (who had countless "godsons"). The original of Laval's manuscript, of which there were several copies (including at least one that was on Mangareva when KSR was there), is in Belgium.

210. "three different migrations"—KSR to RGS from Mangareva, Gambier Islands, 9 Jan. 1923 (RGS CB 1921–40).
211. "has been photographing"—Ibid.
211. "picturesque picture of"—WP to KSR, 12 Aug. 1922, from "John's Scottish Lodge" (PB).
211. "so glad you"—Ibid.
211. "I look forward"—Ibid.
212. "love's labour lost"—KSR to RGS from Mangareva, Gambier Islands, 9 Jan. 1923 (RGS CB 1921–40).
212. "We shall follow"—KSR to "My dear Alice" from Mangareva, 28 Nov. 1922 (REB). In this note KSR still referred to Polynesians, this time the Mangarevans, as "Kanakas."
212. "we have had"—Ibid.
212. "brought forward a very"—KSR to RGS from Mangareva, Gambier Islands, 9 Jan. 1923 (RGS CB 1921–40).
212. "We were really"—KSR to "My dear Alice" from Mangareva, 28 Nov. 1922 (REB).
212. "Oh Wilson, Wilson"—KSR to WP from Tahiti, 11 Feb. 1923 (PB).
213. "I have not"—Ibid.
213. "I really don't"—Ibid.
213. "after the statues"—"Informal no. obtained at Tahiti from an Easter Is Woman in the Year 1923" (RGS WKR 4/16). In the same notebook are notes on errands: "Money," "white clothes S.," and notes on Braine le Comte (address); service at Mormon church; some notes may have been made at an earlier stop in Papeete.
213. "She looks much"—Lucy Violet Hodgkin (Mrs. John Holdsworth). Excerpts from her "Journal" 1922–23, v. 2, pp. 56–59, included in a letter from Audrey Brodie to JVT from New Zealand, 12 Aug. 1995. Brodie and Brodie 2001:32.
214. "the 2 archaeologists"—Ibid. Dr. Moore practiced in Napier from 1925 to 1931. His private hospital was damaged in the earthquake of 1931 and then demolished. No diaries, papers, or artifacts are held in his name at the Hawke's Bay Cultural Trust.
214. "link"; "may visit Easter"; "obliged to return"—"Mangareva: Link with Easter Island," Sydney Morning Herald, 28 Mar. 1923 (RGS WKR 7).
214. "shortly publish"; "would very much"—"Spent Months on Lonely Easter Isle," Victoria Daily Times, 21 Apr. 1923 (RGS WKR 7).
214. In her bag—A handwritten note on a large file card reads: "Parcel of manuscript cards relating to Pacific Islands (Mangareva Vocabulary)." Sent to RGS, 2 Mar. 1961, by James R. Steward from Kyrenia (Cyprus) (RGS WKR 4/20/2).

SPOOKS AND VOICES

215. Love, it has—Solomon 2001:15.
216. "certainly were different"; "ordinary ones"—"The Footprints of Souls," Evening News, 26 May 1923 (RGS/WKR/7).
216. Scoresby essentially separated—WSR's illustrations and maps remained unacceptable to the RGS (John G. Gear, Esq., to RGS, 14 Aug. 1921; RGS to J. G. Gear, Esq., 6 Sept. 1921; RGS to KSR, 9 Jan. 1922; KSR to RGS, 9 Jan 1923; WSR to George Conway, Esq., 1921 (RGS CB 1921–40).
216. "sudden from heaven"—Keats (1911:232), "Ode on Melancholy."
216. "Life cannot be"—KSR to "My dearest Hilda" from Retreat, Edzell, Forfarshire, 24 July 1923 (PB).
216. "Mangarevan Folklore"—"Woman's Part in Science," Evening Standard, 27 Aug. 1923 (RSG WKR 7).
217. "the best defense"; "good enough"—Solomon 2001:63.
217. Katherine threw out—4 Hyde Park Gardens still stands, although greatly altered and connected to a similar adjoining building. It is painted white with black metalwork as it was when KSR owned it and has a modest portico entrance on the street but a large garden with a lovely view. The street is a quiet cul-de-sac with a taxi stand a few yards

away, and the location is prestigious. WSR may have bought Ewers at this time, if he had only been leasing it prior to this date.

217. "Mrs. Routledge looked"—"Coral Strands Preferred," *Daily Graphic*, 11 Dec. 1924 (RGS WKR 7).

217. "just started seriously"; "based on the results"—Ibid.

217. In March 1925—RGS Certificate of Candidate for Election, 15 Mar. 1925.

217. Scoresby began to dismantle—WSR to "Dear Joyce" from Hinton Manor, Farindon, Bers., 4 Sept. 1925 (BM).

217. "scientific researches"; "all other"—"Last Will," KSR, of 4 Hyde Park Gardens, 1 Dec. 1925, valid court copy with impressed seal.

218. "the book prospers"—KSR to "Dearest Evelyn" from Switzerland, 6 July 1926 (PB); see also KSR to "Dearest Evelyn" from 4 Hyde Park Gardens, 8 June 1926 (PB).

219. "Pete was a great"—KSR to "Dearest Evelyn" from 4 Hyde Park Gardens, 20 Jan. 1927 (PB).

219. "Wilson came after"—KSR to unnamed, but certainly Eve, from 4 Hyde Park Gardens, 4 Dec. 1926, and two addenda, both dated Sun., 5 Dec. 1926 (PB).

219. "from her great"—KSR to Eve from 4 Hyde Park Gardens, 17 Jan. 1927 (PB).

220. "to remove his"—JHP to "My dear Lil" from County Durham, 6 Mar. 1927, and quoting WSR (PB).

220. "a want of sympathy"—Ibid.

220. "This spook business"—Ibid.

220. "as a lodger might"—Ibid.

220. "At the brief"—Ibid.

220. "greed"; "turned him out"—JHP to "My dear Lil" from Carlbury Hall, 22 Jan 1928 (PB).

221. "Did I tell"—KSR to unnamed, but probably her sister, Lilian, undated, from 4 Hyde Park Gardens (PB).

221. "happy and restful"—KSR to "Darling Hilda!" from 4 Hyde Park Gardens, 9 Jan. 1928 (PB); see also KSR to "Darling Hilda" from 4 Hyde Park Gardens, 30 Jan. 1928 (PB), in which KSR talks about the obsessive repetition of even happy thoughts that "keep coming back . . . through all the work of the day like a lovely refrain."

221. "My opinion is"—JHP to "My dear Lil" from County Durham, 1 Mar. 1928 (PB); KSR to "Dear Mrs. Forman" (possibly her neighbor) from 4 Hyde Park Gardens, 6 Mar. 1928 (PB): "I am telling Lilian to let you know if anything very terrible happens to me!"

221. Demanding that Katherine—Press accounts conflict in details, but there is no question that WSR requested the sequestration order (JHP to "My dear Lil" from County Durham, 22 June, 1928 [PB]).

221. "I will not submit"; "camping out in"—"Woman Locked in Mansion," *Daily Mail*, 2 June 1928 (PB).

222. "I am taking"—Ibid.; see also "Lock House Woman," *Evening Standard*, n.d. (PB).

222. "take steps to recover"—WSR to "Dear Lilian" from Union Club, 6 July 1928 (PB).

222. "cannot or will not"; "without injustice to"; "out of the tangle"—JHP to "My dear Lil" from County Durham, 5 June 1928 (PB).

222. "I am going"—"Mrs. Routledge Leaves," *Daily Mail*, June 1928 (PB).

222. "abroad"—The definition of "abroad" is not clear, but there is a strong probability that KSR went to Damascus between July and the end of the summer (KSR to "Dear Lilian" from "The Lunatic Asylum," Ticehurst, Sussex, 20 Feb. 1929 [PB]). If that is the case, the reason may have been that, for some time, KSR had claimed that her "voices" told her that WP was in Persia.

223. "expeditiously and neatly"; "everything inside is"—"Bailiff at Mrs. Routledge's," *Daily Mail*, June 1928 (PB).

223. "barricaded"; "siege"—"Woman Barricades Herself in Hyde Park Mansion" and "Hyde Park Siege," unattributed, n.d., news cuttings (PB).

224. "strenuous"; "desperate trouble"; "not strong"; "I see people"—KSR to "Mrs. Forman" (possibly her neighbor) from 4 Hyde Park Gardens, 6 Mar. 1928 (PB).

224. She kept a journal—"Things Unknown told to me by 'The Spooks' and whether proving true or untrue," 18 Nov. 1928 (PB).

224. "to help in"—KSR to "Dear Evelyn" from 4 Hyde Park Gardens, n.d. (PB).
224. "waiting for my death"—Ibid. See also KSR to "Dearest L." from 4 Hyde Park Gardens, Wed., 12 A.M.; KSR to "Dearest Lilian" from 4 Hyde Park Gardens, 5 Nov. 1928; JHP to "My dear Eve" from County Durham, 14 Nov. 1928 (PB).
224. "the arsenic craze"; "settle down"—JHP to "My dear Lil" from County Durham, 1 Nov. 1928 (PB).
225. Katherine was committed—"Mrs. Routledge Taken to Nursing Home," *Daily Mail*, Feb. 1929 (PB).
225. "appalling wickedness in"—KSR to "Dear Lilian" from "The Lunatic Asylum," Ticehurst, Sussex, 20 Feb. 1929 (PB).
225. "systemized delusional insanity"—Dr. Percy Smith to "Dear Mrs. Fox" from Ticehurst House, Ticehurst, Sussex, 8 Mar. 1929; Bernard Hart to "Dear Dr. McDowall" from 94 Harley St., London, 24 Mar. 1929 (PB).
225. "parole"; "she had done"—Dr. Percy Smith to "Dear Mrs. Fox" from Ticehurst House, Ticehurst, Sussex, 8 Mar. 1929.
225. "came across many"—R. L. Eskridge to "Dear Mr. Braunholz" (of the BM), 26 June 1932 (BM).
225. Her fellow researchers—T. A. Joyce to Dr. Henri Lavachery (Franco-Belgian Expedition to Easter Island) from London, 1 Mar. 1932 (BM).
225. "in consequence of"—WSR to "Dear Mr. Braunholz" (of the BM) from Malta, 5 Mar. 1932 (BM).
225. "a traveler from"—"Ozymandias of Egypt" (Shelley 1994).

CYPRUS, 1961

226. The small stone house—WSR never completed his house in Tjiklos, although he amassed piles of the best building material. The British army built three small, stone houses on the property during the Second World War. JVT to Eve Dray Stewart, 5 Mar. 1998, 20 May 1998; Eve Dray Stewart to JVT, 9 Apr. 1998, 21 June 1998, 31 Jan. 1999, 17 June 1999, 4 Mar. 2000, 29 Dec. 2000; D. Frankel to R. C. Green, 2 Mar. 1998; L. Clougherty to JVT, 20 Jan. 1998; N. Stanley Price to JVT, 1 May 1998; R. S. Merrillees to D. Michaelides, 30 Jan. 1998; A. H. S. Megaw to JVT, 8 Feb. 1998, "Routledge was a legendary figure." Copies on file, JVT.
      Biographical note: The exact nature of the relationship between WSR and Thomas Dray (who had been married but was not living then with his wife and family) is not known. WSR had not formed such a close friendship nor lived with another man before this date, but it is clear that he and Dray had a singular relationship. It should be considered that WSR may have been a homosexual. If so, that would explain KSR's disappointment in him and refute accusations of sexual liaisons with native African women that were leveled at him by Silberrad and others.
226. Archaeologist James Stewart—Stewart was an Australian who held an M.A. from Cambridge.
      Biographical note: In 1937 Stewart was one of the first archaeologists to apply for a permit to excavate in Cyprus from the recently established Department of Antiquities in Nicosia (personal communication, A. H. S. Megaw). He and his first wife, Eleanor, dug at Vounous in 1937 and 1938 after arriving in Cyprus from Palestine, where Stewart had participated in Petrie's last excavation. Stewart was a POW during the Second World War and then married Eve Stewart. In 1960 he became the first professor of Near Eastern Archaeology at the University of Sydney. His health was failing in 1961, and he died the next year in Australia (personal communication, Eve Dray Stewart). See Stewart 1998.

EPILOGUE

231. Williamson, Balfour Co—Porteous 1981:270.
231. Gillam hated submarines—Henry James Gillam, Last Will, 9 May 1916, office copy,

District Probate Registry; 1881 British Census; notes on Gillam's wartime career were made by RB from Admiralty Register files at the Public Records Office (PRO), London, and by Peg and Dick Foster. See also Commonwealth War Graves Commission Web site.

231. "especially dangerous work"—MEI:390.

232. "the loss to his country"—Ibid.; RB to JVT, 1996.

232. Lieutenant David Ronald Ritchie—Notes on DRR's wartime career were made by Peg and Dick Foster; Registrar General for Scotland, 1886; certified copy of an entry of marriage B003171, General Register Office; certified copy of an entry of death B003171, General Register Office; Last Will, 27 Jan. 1960, certified copy with impressed court seal; PRO ADM 196/50 PT 2 E.

232. On January 30, 1916—Apparently, Lieutenant Ritchie's wife was not directly related to the Quaker Gurneys, but the surname is broadly connected.

232. Members of Mana's—MEI:385, WSR refers to the homeward bound crew as a "mixed lot."

232. "grew from boyhood"; "met with a hero's"—Ibid., 390; Jeffery's rank at death was deck hand; Lowestoft Journal, Apr. 1917; Mike and Carol Jeffery, Theodore Gillam to JVT, 2000; Frank Preston, see Commonwealth War Graves Commission Web site. Bartolomeo Rosa returned to St. Vincent, where, it is hoped, he opened the shop he dreamed of.

232. Less than three years—See Barthel 1958:298.

232. Antonio Koropa Haoa—Details on the Haoa family are from Hanga Roa parish church records and family history compiled by Nikko Haoa C.; see also McCall n.d. (1986).

233. Amelia learned many things—When she was an old woman, some in her family thought Amelia was a witch who had successfully cast injurious spells (Cristián Arévalo Pakarati to JVT, 2000); details on the Pakarati family are from Hanga Roa parish church records and family history compiled by Cristián Arévalo Pakarati; see also McCall n.d. (1986).

233. Tepano's son, Jorge—Edwin N. Ferdon Jr. to JVT, 1990.

AFTERWORD

235. On May 22, 1960—In 1946 an earthquake in the Aleutian Islands also created a tidal wave (tsunami) in the Pacific, but it was of small consequence to Rapa Nui.

235. At virtually the same time—E. R. Mulloy (1961) vividly describes the event; Mulloy and Figueroa 1978.

235. Métraux and Lavachery—T. A. Joyce to "Dear Mr. Lavachery" from the BM, 1932 (JVT/T. Lavachery).

235. "distressing"—Métraux 1940:3.

235. "I know of few"—Ibid.

236. "I doubt that a longer"—Ibid.

236. "No important source"; "all the available"—Ibid.

236. "no new information"—Ibid.

236. Padre Sebastián Englert—Englert 1964, 1974, 1978.

236. "milestone"; "a great deal"—Heyerdahl ("An Introduction to Easter Island") in Heyerdahl and Ferdon 1961:89; Skjölsvold 1961a:339.

236. They, like Métraux and Lavachery—Skjölsvold 1961a:339; the continuing misconception that KSR's fieldnotes were lost was not, so far as I can tell, based upon any real investigation. It was an oft-repeated but unvalidated notion that came to Heyerdahl via Métraux. WSR had told several people that KSR's illness had caused the loss of many papers. A simple check of RGS records, however, would have revealed them to the Norwegian Archaeological Expedition, and Heyerdahl could surely have done that (he was a Fellow). In writing his 1989 book he sent a research assistant to briefly consult them, but did not actually review them himself.

236. In the 1970s—Mulloy 1961, 1968, 1979, 1973, 1975; Ayres 1973; Ayres et al. 1998; McCoy 1976, 1978; see also Heyerdahl and Ferdon 1961; Cristino et al. 1981.

236. "epoch-making"—The Anakena work, which included the reconstruction of Ahu Nau

Nau (Naunau) and the reerection of its statues, was conducted under the supervision of Sergio Rapu, with the assistance of Sonia Haoa, also an archaeologist. Previously, fragments of the eyeballs had been revealed, but not recognized, on other sites, including Vinapu by W. Mulloy. See Van Tilburg 1994:Pl. 25, figs. 101–2.

237. In the 1980s—Ayres and Ayres 1995; Grau 1987, 1996; Hagelberg 1998; Klein S. 1988; Lee 1992; Martinsson-Wallin 1994, 1998, 2000; Oliveros 1994; Orliac 2000; Owsley et al. 1994; Stevenson 1986, 1997, 1998; Stevenson and Ayres 2000; Stevenson and Haoa 1998; Cristino et al. 1988; Fischer 1993 a and b; Kjellgren 2001.

237. From 1992 to 1996—Cristino F. and Vargas C. 1998. A mass of publicity is associated with this controversial project. Some structural difficulties have recently emerged; Van Tilburg 1994:Pl. 30.

237. Astonishingly, more than—P. Vargas C., personal communication; Cristino et al. 1981; Vargas C. 1993, 1998; Vargas et al. 1990.

238. There is, without doubt—See, for example, Métraux 1940; Heyerdahl and Ferdon 1960; Van Tilburg 1994; Kirch 2000; Stevenson and Ayres 2000; Kjellgren 2001; Kaeppler 2001.

238. When language is added—Green 1988, 2001; Weisler and Green 2001.

239. When I began—My project was initiated en convenio with C. Cristino F. of the Universidad de Chile. P. Vargas C. and L. González N. had developed the orginal parameters of the investigation. Her fieldwork and mine were not accomplished jointly, but both were undertaken within the context of the islandwide survey. For a full history, see Van Tilburg and Vargas C. 1998; Van Tilburg 1986 a and b, 1987, 1988, 1990, 1992, 1993.

240. Red scoria statues are—Van Tilburg 1986 a and b. I acknowledge a debt here to Felipe Teao, who showed me some scattered red scoria fragments.

241. He felt more certain—RGS WKR 1/14/20, 1/14/11.

241. We actually carved—Van Tilburg and Arévalo P. 2002.

241. In 1998—Van Tilburg and Ralston 1999; Van Tilburg and Ralston, in press.

242. By European contact—Flenley 1979; Flenley and King 1984: Flenley et al. 1991.

243. Archaeologist Patrick Kirch—See especially Kirch 2000.

243. Forest clearance caused—According to D. Steadman, at least six land-bird species and several dozen seabird populations were eliminated. Orliac's (2002) plant identifications illustrate that, in addition to the palm, sixteen tree species became extinct. The damage was irreversible.

243. Recent, interesting Pacific—I am indebted to Jared Diamond and Barry Rolett, whose report of this research is forthcoming, for this thumbnail sketch of island environmental fragility. See also Diamond 1995, 1997.

243. The full extent—Soil fertility is negatively affected when nutrients are leached out by erosion. Fertility levels are determined by measuring the presence and quantity of trace metallic ions. Existing pollen analyses are being amplified by new research. Modern levels of Rapa Nui soil fertility, or salvage soil enrichment methods, require study.

244. Less obvious is—Tephra volcanic ash fallout occurs west of the Andesite Line, not on Rapa Nui. This is made clear by the striking infertility of the Poike area, presumably because it has the island's oldest soils. Leached for two to three million years, they were not replenished by either Terevaka's two-hundred-thousand-year-old lava flow or the collapse of Rano Kau's caldera (also about two hundred thousand years ago) (J. Diamond, personal communication, 2003).

245. In the Moche Valley—JVT notes from Michael Mosely lecture, UCLA, 2002; see also Quinn and Neal 1987.

246. "blood is thicker"—D/GP 6 1892.

PHOTOGRAPH CAPTIONS

"biggish place"—JWP 2 June 1871 to 31 Dec. 1872 (JGP JVT 26/2/96).
"serious amount of self-will"—D/KP 4b.

"solving the riddle" to "become famous"—R. D. Graham to "Dear Crawford" from 30 Whitwell Road, Southsea, 3 Apr. 1913 (BOD MS).

"grand beyond description"—MEI:86.

"entirely unsuspected"—RGS WKR 4/10, untitled typescript.

"native rising"—MEI:142.

"circular statues"—MEI: 183–95.

SELECTED BIBLIOGRAPHY

✦

AFRICA

Beard, P., ed. 1975. *Longing for Darkness: Kamante's Tales from Out of Africa.* San Francisco: Chronicle Books.

Brown, M. 1989. *Where Giants Trod: Exploring Lake Rudolf (now Lake Turkana).* London: Quiller Press.

Bull, B. 1992. *Safari: A Chronicle of Adventure.* London, New York, Victoria, Toronto, Auckland: Penguin Books.

Clodd, E. 1914. *The Childhood of the World.* New York: The Macmillan Co.

Dundas, Hon. Anne L. H. 1924. *Beneath African Glaciers.* London: H. F. & G. Witherby.

Dundas, Sir C. 1955. *African Crossroads.* London: Macmillan & Co., Ltd.

Dundas, K. R. 1908. "Notes on the Origin and History of the Kikuyu and Dorobo Tribes." *Man* 8: 136–39.

Edwards, A. 1993. *A Thousand Miles up the Nile.* London: Parkway Publishing.

Hinde, H. 1904. *Vocabularies of the Kamba and Kikuyu Languages of East Africa.* Cambridge: Cambridge University Press.

Huxley, E., and A. Curtis, eds. 1980. *Pioneers' Scrapbook: Reminiscences of Kenya 1890 to 1968.* London: Evans Brothers Limited.

Jones, J. D. F. 1996. "Africa's 'dreadful old fogie.'" London: *Financial Times,* 20/21 April.

Joyce, T. A. 1905. "Steatite Figures from West Africa." *Man: Journal of the Royal Anthropological Society of Great Britain and Ireland.* London: Royal Anthropological Society 5 (57).

———. 1906. "Notes on a Series of Akikuyu 'Ndomi' in the British Museum." *Man: Journal of the Royal Anthropological Society of Great Britain and Ireland.* London: Royal Anthropological Society 3 (100).

Kingsley, M. 1897. *Travels in West Africa.* E. Huxley, ed. London: Everyman.

Leakey, L. S. B. 1977. *The Southern Kikuyu Before 1903.* London and New York: Academic Press.

Leakey, M. 1984. *Disclosing the Past: An Autobiography.* New York: Doubleday and Co.

Marret, R. R. 1910. "Appendix V: The Place of Kikúyu Thought in the Comparative Study of Religions." In Routledge and Routledge, *With a Prehistoric People: The Akikuyu of British East Africa,* 357–62. London: Frank Case and Co., Ltd. Reprint, 1968.

McGregor, A. W. 1904. *English-Kikuyu Vocabulary.* London: S.P.C.K. UCLA Special Collections.

Meinertzhagen, Col. R. 1957. *Kenya Diary, 1902–1906.* London and Edinburgh: Oliver and Boyd.

Orde Browne, Sir G. St. J. 1925. *The Vanishing Tribes of Kenya: A Description of the Primitive and Interesting Tribes Dwelling on the Vast Southern Slopes of Mount Kenya, and Their Fast Disappearing Native Methods of Life.* Philadelphia: Lippincott.

Pease, Sir A. E. 1898. *Hunting Reminiscences.* London: John Lane.

———. 1900. *South African Imperial Justice.* London: National Press Agency, Ltd.

——. 1913. *The Book of the Lion.* London: J. Murray.
Smuck, H. 1982. *Friends in East Africa.* Richmond, Ind.: Friends Illustrated Press. Originally published 1920.
Thurman, J. 1982. *Isak Dinesen: The Life of a Storyteller.* New York: Picador USA.
Trzebinski, E. 1993. *The Lives of Beryl Markham.* New York and London: W. W. Norton & Co.
Wallach, J. 1996. *Desert Queen: The Extraordinary Life of Gertrude Bell.* New York, London: Nan A. Talese, Doubleday.

ANTHROPOLOGY, ARCHAEOLOGY, AND RELATED AREAS OF STUDY

Aitken, B. Freire-Marreco. 1914. "Tewa Kinship Terms from the Pueblo of Hano, Arizona." *American Anthropologist* 16 (2): 269–87.
——. 1916. "Ethnobotany of the Tewa Indians." With W. W. Robbins and J. P. Harrington. *Bureau of American Ethnology Bulletin* 55.
Babcock, B. A., and N. J. Parezo. 1988. *Daughters of the Desert: Women Anthropologists and the Native American Southwest, 1880–1980.* Albuquerque: University of New Mexico Press.
Bateson, M. C. 1984. *With a Daughter's Eye: A Memoir of Margaret Mead and Gregory Bateson.* New York: W. Morrow.
Buzaljko, G. W. 1989. "Theodora Kracaw Kroeber (1897–1979)." In U. Gacs, A. Khan, J. McIntyre, R. Weinberg, eds., *Women Anthropologists,* 187–93. Urbana and Chicago: University of Illinois Press.
Champion, S. 1998. "Women in British Archaeology." In M. Díaz-Andreu and M. L. S. Sorensen, *Excavating Women: A history of women in European archaeology,* 175–97. London and New York: Routledge.
Charlton, J. 1999. "The Tale of Mr. Crawford and His Cap." *British Archaeology* 42.
Claassen, C., ed. 1994. *Women in Archaeology.* Philadelphia: University of Pennsylvania Press.
Crawford, O. G. S. 1921. *Man and His Past.* London: Oxford University Press.
——. 1953. *Archaeology in the Field.* London: Phoenix House.
——. 1955. *Said and Done: The Autobiography of an Archaeologist.* London: Weidenfeld and Nicholson.
Crawford, O. G. S. and A. Keiller. 1928. *Wessex from the Air.* Oxford: The Clarendon Press.
Dalton, O. M. 1910. *Handbook to the Ethnographic Collection.* London: The British Museum.
Daniel, G. 1981. *A Short History of Archaeology.* New York: Thames and Hudson.
Darwin, C. 1859. *On the Origin of Species by Means of Natural Selection or, The Preservation of Favoured Races in the Struggle for Life.* London: J. Murray.
Deacon, D. 1997. *Elsie Clews Parsons: Inventing Modern Life.* Chicago and London: University of Chicago Press.
Díaz-Andreu, M., and M. L. S. Sorensen. 1998. *Excavating Women: A history of women in European archaeology.* London and New York: Routledge.
Edwards, E., ed. 1992. *Anthropology and Photography, 1860–1920.* New Haven: Yale University Press in association with the Royal Anthropological Society, London.
Feder, K. L. 1999. *Frauds, Myths, and Mysteries: Science and Pseudoscience in Archaeology.* Mountain View, Calif.: Mayfield Publishing Co.
Flinders Petrie, Sir W. M. 1904. *Methods and Aims in Archaeology.* New York: Macmillan.
Freire-Marreco (Aitken), B., and J. L. Meyers, eds., 1912. *Notes and Queries in Anthropology, Edited for the British Association for the Advancement of Science.* London: The Royal Anthropological Institute.
Gacs, U., A. Khan, J. McIntyre, R. Weinberg, eds. 1989. *Women Anthropologists: Selected Biographies.* Urbana and Chicago: University of Illinois Press.
Hare, P. H. 1985. *A Woman's Quest for Science: Portrait of Anthropologist Elsie Clews Parsons.* Buffalo: Prometheus Books.
Hawkes, J., ed. 1963. *The World of the Past.* New York: Alfred A. Knopf.
Heizer, R. F., and T. Kroeber, eds. 1979. *Ishi the Last Yahi: A Documentary History.* Berkeley and Los Angeles: University of California Press.
Keith, Sir A. 1950. *An Autobiography.* London: C. A. Watts & Co.

Kroeber, A.L. 1923. *Anthropology.* New York: Harcourt, Brace and World.

Kroeber, T. 1976. *Ishi in Two Worlds: A Biography of the Last Wild Indian in North America.* Berkeley and Los Angeles: University of California Press.

Liliuokalanai, Queen of Hawaii. 1897. *An Account of the Creation of the World According to Hawaiian Tradition.* Boston: Lee and Shepard.

———. 1898. *Hawaii's Story.* Boston: Lee and Shepard.

Lutkehaus, N. 1990. "Refractions of Reality: On the Use of Other Ethnographers' Fieldnotes." In R. Sanjek, ed. *Fieldnotes: The Makings of Anthropology,* 303–23. Ithaca and London: Cornell University Press.

Lyell, C. 1990. *Principles of Geology.* Chicago: University of Chicago Press.

Marett, R. R. 1941. *A Jerseyman at Oxford.* London, New York, Toronto: Oxford University Press.

Ottenberg, S. 1990. "Thirty Years of Fieldnotes: Changing Relationships to the Text." In R. Sanjek, ed., *Fieldnotes: The Makings of Anthropology,* 139–60. Ithaca and London: Cornell University Press.

Rivers, W. H. R. 1906. *The Todas.* New York: The Macmillan Company.

Sanjek, R., ed. 1990. *Fieldnotes: The Makings of Anthropology.* Ithaca and London: Cornell University Press.

Sorabji, C. 1908. *Between the Twilights: Being Studies of Indian Women by One of Themselves.* London and New York: Harper and Bros.

———. 1916. *Indian Tales of the Great Ones Among Men, Women and Bird-People.* Bombay: Blackie & Son, Ltd.

———. *India Calling: The Memories of Cornelia Sorabji.* London: Nisbet & Co. Ltd.

Spier, L. R., and A. L. Kroeber. 1943. "Elsie Clews Parsons." *American Anthropologist* 45 (2): 244–55.

Stewart, J. R. 1992. "Corpus of Cypriot Artefacts of the Early Bronze Age." In E. Stewart and Paul Astrom, eds., *Studies in Medieval Archaeology,* v. 3, no. 1–2. Jonsered: Paul Astroms Forlag.

Syme, M. A. 1984. *Shipping Arrivals and Departures in Victorian Ports.* Melbourne: Roebuck.

Thompson, J. E. S. 1942. "Thomas Athol Joyce (1878–1942)." *Boletín Bibliográfico de Antropología Americana,* 252–59.

Trigger, B. G. 1989. *A History of Archaeological Thought.* Cambridge: Cambridge University Press.

Tylor, E. B. 1871. *Primitive Culture: Researches into the Development of Mythology, Philosophy, Religion, Art and Custom.* London: John Murray. First U.S. printing from second English printing, Boston: Estes & Lauriat, 1874.

Upton, L. F. S. 1979. *Micmacs and Colonists: Indian-White Relations in the Maritimes, 1713–1867.* Vancouver: University of British Colombia Press.

Wheeler, Sir M. 1954. *Archaeology from the Earth.* Oxford: Clarendon Press.

BRITISH CULTURE, HISTORY, AND WOMEN IN SOCIETY

Adams, P. 1996. *Somerville for Women: An Oxford College, 1879–1993.* Oxford: Oxford University Press.

Adams, R. M., ed. 1979. *George Meredith: The Egoist. An Annotated Text, Backgrounds, Criticism.* New York and London: W. W. Norton & Co.

Andrews, R. 1993. *The Columbia Dictionary of Quotations.* New York: Columbia University Press.

Arieno, M. A. 1989. *Victorian Lunatics: A Social Epidemiology of Mental Illness in Mid-Nineteenth-Century England.* Selinsgrove, Pa.: Susquehanna University Press.

Asbury, J. 1996. *Crazy for You: The Making of Women's Madness.* Oxford: Oxford University Press.

Baudelaire, C. 1989. *The Flowers of Evil.* Eds. M. Mathews and J. Mathews. New York: New Directions.

Bell, F. Lady (Mrs. Hugh Bell). 1907. *At the Works: A Study of a Manufacturing Town.* London: E. Arnold.

Bell, G. L. 1947. *The Letters of Gertrude Bell.* Ed. Lady Bell. London: E. Benn.

Black, E. C. 1973. *Victorian Culture and Society*. New York: Harper and Row.

Boucher, F. 1967. *20,000 Years of Fashion: The History of Costume and Personal Adornment*. New York: Harry Abrams.

Brittan, V. 1960. *The Women at Oxford*. London: George G. Harrap & Co., Ltd.

Britten, E. H. 1884. *Nineteenth Century Miracles; or, Spirits and Their Work in Every Country of the Earth. A Complete Historical Compendium of the Great Movement Known as "Modern Spiritualism."* New York: William Britten.

Brodie, A., and J. Brodie. 2001. *John Holdsworth and the House Called Swarthmoor*. Wellington: The Beechtree Press.

Busfield, J. 1986. *Managing Madness: Changing ideas and practice*. London: Hutchinson & Co.

Bynum, W. F. 1979. "Theory and Practice in British Psychiatry from J. C. Prichard (1786–1848) to Henry Maudsley (1835–1918). In T. Ogawa, ed., *History of Psychiatry—Mental Illness and Its Treatments—Proceedings of the 4th International Symposium on the Comparative History of Medicine—East and West*. Tokyo: Saikon Publishing Co., Ltd.

Calder, J. 1979. "The Insurrection of Women." In R. M. Adams, ed., *George Meredith: The Egoist: An Annotated Text Backgrounds Criticism*. New York: W. W. Norton & Company.

Cameron, J. M. 1926. *Victorian Photographs of Famous Men and Fair Women by Julia Margaret Cameron: With Introductions by Virginia Woolf and Roger Fry*. London: Hogarth Press.

Casteras, S. P. 1987. *Images of Victorian Womanhood in English Art*. Rutherford, N.J.: Fairleigh Dickinson University Press.

Chesser, E. 1956. *The Sexual, Marital and Family Relationships of the English Woman*. Hutchinson's Medical Publications. Watford, Herts, and London: Tayler Ganett Evans & Co., Ltd.

Chitty, S. 1974. *The Beast and the Monk: A Life of Charles Kingsley*. London: Hodder and Stoughton.

Christopher, M. 1975. *Mediums, Mystics and the Occult*. New York: Thomas Y. Crowell Co.

Claridge, G. 1995. *Origins of Mental Illness*. Cambridge, Mass.: ISHK Malor Books.

Clark, E., and L. S. Jacyna. 1987. *Nineteenth-Century Origins of Neuroscientific Concepts*. Berkeley and Los Angeles: University of California Press.

Clayton-Payne, A., and B. Elliott. 1988. *Victorian Flower Gardens*. London: Weidenfeld & Nicholson.

Collingwood, W. G., ed. 1891. *The Poems of John Ruskin*. New York: Charles E. Merrill & Co., and London and Orpington: George Allen.

Cook, B. W. 1999. *Eleanor Roosevelt*. V. 2. New York: Viking Penguin.

Cooper, G. 1996. "Schizophrenia is nothing to be afraid of." *The* (London) *Times*, Independent Section Two, 24 June, 4–5.

Cousins, N. 1981. *Human Options*. New York: W. W. Norton Company.

Davies, J. 1988. *The Victorian Kitchen Garden*. New York: W. W. Norton Company.

Debrett's Illustrated Peerage. 1990. London: Kelly's Directories.

Debrett's People of Today. 1990. London: Debrett's Peerage Ltd.

De Villiers, A., H. Fox, and P. Adams, 1978. *Somerville College Oxford 1879–1979: A Century in Pictures*. Oxford: Oxpress, Ltd.

Dunbar, J. 1953. *The Early Victorian Woman: Some Aspects of Her Life (1837–57)*. London: George G. Harrap & Co. Ltd.

Eliot, T. S. 1970. *Collected Poems, 1909–1962*. New York: Harcourt, Brace & World, Inc.

Ellis, H. 1926. *The New Spirit*. Boston: Houghton Mifflin.

Erickson, A. L. 1993. *Women and Property in Early Modern England*. London and New York: Routledge.

Ferris, P. 1993. *Sex and the British: A Twentieth-Century History*. London: Michael Joseph.

Fisher, T. 1995. *Scandal: The Sexual Politics of Late Victorian Britain*. Phoenix Mill, Far Thrupp, Stroud, Gloucestershire: Alan Sutton Publishing, Ltd.

Fraser, A. 1988. *The Warrior Queens*. New York: Alfred A. Knopf.

Fraser, F. 1987. *The English Gentlewoman*. London: Barrie & Jenkins.

Gaskell, E. 1996. *Sylvia's Lovers*. Edited with an introduction, notes, and appendices by S. Foster. London and New York: Penguin Classics.

Geller, J. L., and M. Harris, eds. 1994. *Women of the Asylum: Voices from Behind the Walls, 1840–1945*. New York, London: Doubleday.

Gillett, M. 1981. *We walked very warily: A history of women at McGill*. Montreal: Eden Press.

Gissing, G. 1890. *The Emancipated: A Novel*. London: Richard Bentley.

Goethe, J. W. von. 1957. *The Sorrows of Young Werther*. Trans. B. Q. Jones. New York: Frederick Ungar Publishing.

Golby, J. M., ed. 1986. *Culture and Society in Britain, 1850–1890*. London: BBC Open University.

Graubard, M. 1935. *Genetics and the Social Order*. New York: Tomorrow Publishers.

Greenfield, E. J. 1992. *One Hundred and One Classics of Victorian Verse*. Chicago: Contemporary Books.

Hastings, A. 1991. *With the Tongues of Men and Angels: A Study of Channeling*. London: Holt, Rinehart and Winston, Inc.

Hill, C. J. 1979. "Theme and Image in *The Egoist*." In R. M. Adams, ed., *George Meredith: The Egoist: An Annotated Text Backgrounds Criticism*. New York: W. W. Norton & Company.

Hopwood, D. 1989. *Tales of Empire*. London: I. B. Taruis & Co.

Horn, P. 1991. *Victorian Countrywomen*. Oxford: Basil Blackwell, Ltd.

Hufton, O. 1996. *The Prospect Before Her: A History of Women in Western Europe, 1500–1800*. New York: Alfred A. Knopf.

Hughes, J. S. 1993. *The Letters of a Victorian Madwoman*. Columbia: University of South Carolina Press.

Hyam, R. 1992. *Empire and Sexuality: The British Experience*. New York: Manchester University Press.

Jackson, D. 1993. *On the Country: The Micmac of Newfoundland*. Ed. G. Penney. St John's, Newfoundland: H. Cuff.

Jacobson, D. 1999. "Going Native." *London Review of Books*, 25 November, 27–30.

Jasper, R. C. D. 1960. *Arthur Cayley Headlam: Life and Letters of a Bishop*. London: Faith Press.

Jenkins, E. 1982. *The Shadow and the Light: A Defence of Daniel Douglas Home, the Medium*. London: Hamish Hamilton.

Johnson, S. 1781. *The Lives of the Most Eminent English Poets, with Critical Observations on their Works*. London: C. Bathurst, J. Buckland, etc.

Johnson, W. S. 1975. *Sex and Marriage in Victorian Poetry*. Ithaca, N.Y.: Cornell University Press.

Keats, J. 1911. *The Poetical Works of John Keats*. With an Introduction by Andrew Land. London: Ward, Lock & Co., Limited.

———. 1992. *The Poems*. Ed. G. Bullet. New York: Alfred A. Knopf.

Kingsley, C. 1877. *Charles Kingsley: His Letters and Memories of his Life, edited by his Wife*. New York: Scribner, Armstrong.

———. 1916. *The Water-Babies*. New York: Dodd, Mead & Co.

Kunitz, S. J., and H. Haycroft, eds. 1936. *British Authors of the Nineteenth Century*. New York: H. W. Wilson Co.

Laufer, G. A. 1993. *The Victorian Art of Expressing Yourself in the Language of Flowers*. New York: Workman Publishing Co.

Lear, E. 1893. *The Book of Nonsense*. Philadelphia: Wills P. Hazard.

Lee, S., ed. 1895. *Dictionary of National Biography*. V. 44. London: Smith, Elder & Co.

———. 1897. *Dictionary of National Biography*. V. 51. London: Smith, Elder & Co.

Leudar, I., and P. Thomas. 2000. *Voices of Reason, Voices of Insanity: Studies of Verbal Hallucinations*. London and New York: Routledge.

Longfellow, H. W. 1944. *The Poems of Longfellow*. New York: The Modern Library.

Lovell, J. H. 1999a. "A catalogue of archive materials associated with John Milne, F.R.S." London: British Geological Survey, Global Seismology Series *Technical Reports* WL/99/14.

———. 1999b. "Scientific visitors to John Milne's observatory at Shide, Isle of Wight." London: British Geological Survey, Global Seismology Series *Technical Reports* WL/99/17.

MacKenzie, C. 1992. *Psychiatry for the Rich: A History of Ticehurst Private Asylum, 1792–1917*. London and New York: Routledge.

Macleod, R., and P. Collins. 1981. *The Parliament of Science: The British Association for the Advancement of Science, 1831–1981*. Northwood: S. Rivens.

Marrell, J., and A. Thackery, eds. 1984. *Gentlemen of Science, early correspondence of the British Association for the Advancement of Science.* London: Royal Historical Society.

Marryat, F. 1892. *There is no Death.* London: Griffith, Farran.

———. 1894. *The Spirit World.* New York: Lovell Co. UCLA Special Collections.

Marshall, Mrs. L. A. 1821. *A sketch of my friend's family: Intended to suggest some practical hints on religion and domestic manners.* Wendall, Mass.: J Metcalf. Reprinted five times. UCLA Special Publications.

Martin, A. P. 1895. *The Withered Jester and Other Verses.* London: Dent.

Matthew, H. C. G. 1989. "The Liberal Age (1853–1914)." In K. O. Morgan, ed., *The Oxford Illustrated History of Great Britain, 463–522.* Oxford and New York: The Oxford University Press.

McColgan, J. 1983. *British Policy and the Irish Administration, 1920–22.* London: George Allen & Unwin.

McNeillie, A., ed. 1986. *The Second Common Reader: Virginia Woolf.* San Diego: Harcourt Brace Jovanovich.

Melville, H. 1998. *Moby Dick.* Ed. A. Robert Lee. London: J. M. Dent; Rutland, Vt.: C. E. Tuttle.

Meyerson, A. 1976. *The Inheritance of Mental Diseases.* New York: Arno Press.

Mitchell, K. n.d. "The Rising Sun: The First 100 Years of the Autotype Company." Manuscript on file with the author.

Moore, H. 1981. *Henry Moore at the British Museum.* London: British Museum Press.

Morris C., M.D., 1858. *An Essay on the Pathology and Therapeutics of Scarlet Fever.* Philadelphia: Lindsay & Blakiston. Rare Books, Biomedical Library, UCLA.

Morris, M. C. 1893. *Yorkshire Folk-Tales.* Privately printed.

Mott, F. W. 1910. "The Huxley lecture on hereditary aspects of nervous and mental diseases." *British Medical Journal* 2:1013.

Murphy, E. 1993. *Dementia and Mental Illness in Older People: A Practical Guide.* London and Basingstoke: PAPERMAC.

North, M. 1993. *Recollections of a Happy Life.* Introduction by S. Morgan. Richmond: University of Virginia Press.

Ogawa, T., ed. 1979. *History of Psychiatry—Mental Illness and Its Treatments—Proceedings of the 4th International Symposium on the Comparative History of Medicine—East and West.* Tokyo: Saikon Publishing Co., Ltd.

Oppenheim, J. 1991. *"Shattered Nerves": Doctors, Patients and Depression in Victorian England.* New York and Oxford: Oxford University Press.

Pankhurst, E. 1914. *My Own Story.* New York: Kraus Reprint, 1971.

Pantel, P. S., ed. 1992. *A History of Women in the West.* Cambridge, Mass., and London, England: The Belknap Press of Harvard University Press.

Pater, W. 1973. *Essays on Literature and Art.* Ed. J. Uglow. London: Dent.

Pearson, K. 1905. "On the inheritance of insanity." *British Medical Journal* 1: 1175.

Phillips, M., and W. S. Tomkinson. 1926. *English Women in Life and Letters.* London and Oxford: Oxford University Press.

Pictorial and Descriptive Guide to London, A. 1926. London: Ward, Lock & Co., Limited.

Plante, E. M. 1995. *The Victorian Home.* Philadelphia and London: Running Press.

Podmore, F. 1902. *Modern Spiritualism.* 2 vols. London: Methuen and Co.

Popenoe, P., and R. H. Johnson. 1935. *Applied Eugenics.* New York: The Macmillan Company.

Poznanski, E., and J. P. Zrull. 1970. "Childhood Depression: Clinical Characteristics of Overtly Depressed Children." *Archives of General Psychiatry* 23: 8–15.

Radford, E., and M. A. Radford. 1948. *The Encyclopedia of Superstitions.* Edited and revised by C. Hole, 1961. New York: Barnes and Noble Books.

Raeburn, A. 1976. *The Suffragette View.* Vancouver: Douglas David & Charles Ltd.

Randall, R. 1989. *The Model Wife, Nineteenth-Century Style.* London: Butler & Tanner, Ltd.

Reid, P. 1996. *Art and Affection: A Life of Virginia Woolf.* New York and Oxford: Oxford University Press.

Rolt, L. T. C. 1984. *George and Robert Stephenson: The Railway Revolution.* London: Penguin Books Ltd.

Romney, D. M. 1988. "Depression and Paranoid Schizophrenia." In R. Williams and J. T. Dalby, eds., *Depression in Schizophrenics.* New York and London: Plenum Press.

Ruskin, J. 1903–12. *The Works of John Ruskin.* Eds. E. T. Cook and A. Wedderburn. London: G. Allen; New York: Longmans Green & Co.

———. 1978. *Praeterita: The Autobiography of John Ruskin.* Oxford: Oxford University Press.

Samuel, R. 1998. "The Discovery of Puritanism, 1820–1914: A Preliminary Sketch." In A. Light, ed., *Island Stories: Unravelling Britain Theatres of Memory, Volume II,* 276–322. London and New York: Verso.

Scoresby, W. 1820. *An Account of the Arctic Regions with a History and Description of the Northern Whale-Fishery.* Edinburgh: A. Constable and Co.

———. 1859. *Journal of a Voyage to Australia and Round the World for Magnetic Research.* Ed. A. Smith. London: Longmans, Green, Longmans and Roberts.

Shelley, P. B. 1994. *The Complete Poems of Percy Bysshe Shelley.* New York: Modern Library.

Sidgwick, H. 1894. "A Report on the Census of Hallucinations." London: The British Society for Psychical Research *Journal.*

Small, H. 1996. *Love's Madness: Medicine, the Novel, and Female Insanity, 1800–1865.* Oxford: Clarendon Press.

Soloman, A. 2001. *The Noonday Demon: An Atlas of Depression.* New York: Scribner.

Spencer, H. 1969. *Principles of Sociology.* Ed. S. Andreski. Conn.: Archon Books.

Spitz, B. 1996. *Mill Valley: The Early Years.* Potrero Meadow: Barry Spitsh in association with the Mill Valley Historical Society.

Stamp, T., and C. Stamp. 1976. *William Scoresby, Arctic Scientist.* Whitby: Cademon of Whitby Press.

St. Aubyn, G. 1992. *Queen Victoria: A Portrait.* New York: Atheneum.

Stedman, T. L. 1994. *Stedman's Concise Medical Dictionary—Illustrated.* Ed. J. T. McDonough. Baltimore: Williams & Wilkins.

Stephen, Sir L., and Sir S. Smith, eds. 1921–22. *Dictionary of National Biography,* V. 8. London: Oxford University Press.

Stevenson, R. L. 1923. *A Child's Garden of Verse.* New York: Appleton.

Taylor, J. 1991. *Hospital and Asylum Architecture in England, 1840–1914.* London: Mansell Publishing Ltd.

Thomas, B. 1935. *Charley's Aunt: A Play in Three Acts.* First performed in 1892. London and Toronto: Samuel French.

Trendell, H. A. P., ed. 1912. *Dress Worn at His Majesty's Court.* London: Harrison and Sons.

Trombley, Stephen. 1981. *"All That Summer She Was Mad": Virginia Woolf and Her Doctors.* London: Junction Books.

Turk, J. L. 1995. *John Erichsen (1818–96): The Science and Art of Surgery: Nineteenth-century surgery in the immediate pre-Lister era. Journal of Medical Biography* (London) 3:50–55.

Vaughan, S. E. 1934a. "Ethel Hurlblatt, LLD., Warden of the Royal Victoria College, 1907–1929." *The McGill News* (Montreal) 15 (3): 19–23.

———. 1934b. "Memorials of Miss Hurlblatt at the Royal Victoria College." *The McGill News* (Montreal) 15 (4): 18–20.

Vicinus, M., ed. 1975. *Suffer and Be Still: Women in the Victorian Age.* Bloomington: University of Indiana Press.

Victoria, Queen of England. 1877. "Leaves from the Journal of Our Life in the Highlands." Ed. A. Helps. London: Smith Elder.

Williams, R., and J. T. Dalby, eds. 1988. *Depression in Schizophrenics.* New York and London: Plunum Press.

Winchester, S. 1999. *The Professor and the Madman.* New York: Harper Perennial.

Wolman, B. B. 1970. *Children without Childhood: A Study of Childhood Schizophrenia.* New York and London: Grune & Stratton.

EASTER ISLAND (RAPA NUI) AND OCEANIA

Agassiz, A. 1906. "Report." *Memoirs of the Museum of Comparative Zoology, Harvard College* 33.

Allen, F. A. 1884. "Polynesian Antiquities." In *Congrès International d'Américainists, Compte Rendu de la Cinquième Session, Copenhagen, 1883*, 246–57.

Anon. 1728. *Tweejaarige Reyze Rondom de Wereld* . . . Dordrecht: Johannes Van Braam.

Anon. (Powell, W. A.) 1869. "Easter Island." *The* (London) *Times*, 21 January.

Anon. 1870. "Die Steinbilder auf der Osterinsel." *Globus* 17: 248–50.

Anon. 1887. "Prehistoric idols." *Baltimore American*, 3 May.

Anon. 1892. "Easter Island." *Nature* 46: 258–60.

Anon. 1910. "There were GIANTS in the earth in those days." *The London Magazine*, July, 509–17.

Anuario Hidrográfico de la Marina de Chile: 1875 Hasta 1923. Santiago: Biblioteca Nacional.

Ayres, W. S. 1973. "The Cultural Context of Easter Island Religious Structures." Ph.D. diss., Tulane University.

Ayres, W. S., and G. S. Ayres. 1995. "Geiseler's Easter Island Report: An 1880s Anthropological Account." *Asian and Pacific Archaeology Series*, no. 12. Honolulu: Social Science Research Institute, University of Hawai'i at Manoa.

Ayres, W. S., S. M. Fitzpatrick, J. Wozniak, and G. G. Goleš. 1997. "Archaeological Investigations of Stone Adzes and Quarries on Easter Island." In C. M. Stevenson et al., eds., *Easter Island in Pacific Context South Seas Symposium*, 304–11. Easter Island Foundation Occasional Paper 4. Los Osos: Bearsville and Cloud Mountain Presses.

Baker, P. E. 1993. "Archaeological Stone of Easter Island." *Geoarchaeology* 8 (2): 127–39.

Barclay, Capt. H. V. 1899. "Easter Island and its colossal statues." *Royal Geographical Society of Australasia, South Australian Branch, Proceedings* 3: 127–37.

———. 1910. "The Lost Land of the Maoris: What We Found at Easter Island." *Life* 13: 373–76.

Barthel, T. S. 1958. *The Eighth Land: The Polynesian Discovery and Settlement of Easter Island.* Trans. A. Martin. Honolulu: The University Press of Hawai'i.

———. 1993. "Perspectives and Directions of the Classical Rapanui Script." In S. R. Fischer, ed., *Easter Island Studies: Contributions to the History of Rapanui in Memory of William T. Mulloy*, 32, 174–76. Oxford: Oxbow Books.

Beaglehole, J. C., ed. 1969. *The Journals of Captain James Cook on His Voyages of Discovery: The Voyage of the Resolution and Adventure, 1772–1775.* London: Cambridge University Press for the Hakluyt Society.

Behrens, C. F. 1908. "Another narrative of Jacob Roggeveen's visit." In B. G. Corney, ed., *The Voyage of Captain Don Felipe González in the Ship of the Line San Lorenzo, with the Frigate Santa Rosalia in Company, to Easter Island in 1770–1: Preceded by an Extract from Mynheer Jacob Roggeveen's Official Log of His Discovery of and Visit to Easter Island, in 1722.* The Hakluyt Society, ser. 2, no. 13, Kraus Reprint Ltd, 1967.

Belcher, Lady D. J. 1871. *The Mutineers of the Bounty and their Descendants in Pitcairn and Norfolk Islands.* New York: Harper & Brothers.

Belcher, E. n.d. (1825–27). "Pacific journal and remarks." PMB, ANU, Microfilm M51.

Benson, N. P. 1915. *The Log of the El Dorado.* San Francisco: J. H. Barry Co. UCLA Special Collections.

Bernice P. Bishop Museum. 1964. *Dictionary Catalog of the Library of the Bernice P. Bishop Museum, Honolulu, Hawai'i.* 9 vols., 2 supplements (1967). Boston: G. K. Hall & Co.

Bierbach, A., and H. Cain. 1996. *Religion and language of Easter Island: An ethnolinguistic analysis of religious key words of Rapa Nui in their Austronesian context.* Berlin: D. Reimer.

Bowditch, N. 1976. *Bowditch for Yachtsmen: Piloting.* New York: David McKay Company, Inc.

Branchi, E. C. 1934. *L'Isola de Pasque.* Santiago de Chile: Edizioni dell Istituto de Cultura Italiana.

Brander, J. A., and M. S. Taylor. 1998. "The Simple Economics of Easter Island: A Ricardo-Malthus Model of Renewable Resource Use." *American Economic Review* 88 (1): 119–44.

Brasseur, A. 1870. "Lettre de M L'Abbé Brasseur de Bourbourg à MVA Malte-Brun." *Annales des Voyages* (Paris).

Brassey, Baroness A. A. 1879. *Around the World in the Yacht 'Sunbeam' Our Home on the Ocean for Eleven Months*. New York: H. Holt & Co.

———. 1885. *In the Trades, the Tropics, and the Roaring Forties*. Leipzig: B. Tauchnitz.

British Museum. 1925. *Handbook to the Ethnographic Collections*. 2nd ed. London: Oxford University Press.

Brown, J. M. 1922. "Five articles clipped from The Press, Christchurch, N.Z., Sept. 9–Oct. 7." Honolulu: Bernice P. Bishop Museum Library DU Pam No. 228.

———. 1924. *The Riddle of the Pacific*. London: T. P. Unwin, Ltd.

Buch, P. 1995. *L'Île de Pâques, 1934–1935: Expédition Métraux-Lavachery*. Brussels: BUCH Edition.

Buck, P. (Te Rangi Hiroa). 1938. *Ethnology of Mangareva*. Honolulu: Bernice P. Bishop Museum Bulletin 157. Kraus reprint, 1971.

Byrd, R. 1935. *Discovery: The Second Antarctic Expedition*. New York: G. P. Putnam's Sons.

Byron, Lord. 1826. *Voyage of H.M.S. Blonde to the Sandwich Islands, in the years 1824–1825*. London: J. Murray.

Cavledes, C. N., and P. R. Waylin. 1991. "Anomalous Westerly Winds During El Niño Events: The Discovery and Colonization of Easter Island." *Applied Geography* 13: 123–34.

Churchill, W. 1912. *Easter Island: The Rapanui Speech and the Peopling of Southeast Polynesia*. The Carnegie Institution of Washington, no. 174. AMS Press reprint, 1978.

Codrington, R. H. 1891. *The Melanesians: Studies in Their Anthropology and Folklore*. Oxford: Clarendon Press. Reprint, New Haven: HRAF Press, 1957.

Cook, J. 1777. *A Voyage Towards the South Pole, and Around the World. Performed in His Majesty's Ships the Resolution and Adventure, In the Years 1772–1775*. London: W. Strahan and T. Cadel.

Cooke, G. H. 1899. *Te Pito Te Henua, Known as Rapa Nui, Commonly Called Easter Island, South Pacific Ocean. Report of the U.S. National Museum for 1897*. Washington, D.C.: Smithsonian Institution.

Corney, B. G., ed. 1908. *The Voyage of Captain Don Felipe González in the Ship of the Line San Lorenzo, with the Frigate Santa Rosalia in Company, to Easter Island in 1770–1: Preceded by an Extract from Mynheer Jacob Roggeveen's Official Log of His Discovery of and Visit to Easter Island, in 1722*. The Hakluyt Society, ser. 2, no. 13, Kraus Reprint Ltd, 1967.

Cristino F., C., and P. Vargas C. 1998. "Archaeological Excavations and Restoration at Ahu Tongariki." In P. Vargas C., ed., *Easter Island and East Polynesia Prehistory*, 153–58. Santiago: Universidad de Chile Facultad de Arquitectura y Urbanismo, Instituto de Estudios Isla de Pascua.

Cristino F., C., P. Vargas C., and R. Izaurieta S. 1981. *Atlas Arqueólogica de Isla de Pascua*. Santiago: Universidad de Chile Facultad de Arquitectura y Urbanismo, Centro de Estudios Isla de Pascua.

Cristino F., C., P. Vargas C., R. Izaurieta S., and R. Budd P., eds. 1988. *First International Congress, Easter Island and East Polynesia, 1984*, Vol. 1, *Archaeology*. Santiago de Chile: Universidad de Chile Facultad de Arquitectura y Urbanismo, Instituto de Estudios Isla de Pascua.

Cuming, H. n.d. (1827–28). "Journal of a voyage from Valparaíso to the Society and adjacent islands." ML, Sydney, CY REEL 194, A1336.

Dalton, O. M. 1904a. "Easter Island: Script." *Man: Journal of the Royal Anthropological Society of Great Britain and Ireland*, 78: 115–16.

———. 1904b. "On an Inscribed Wooden Tablet from Easter Island (Rapa Nui), in the British Museum. *Man: Journal of the Royal Anthropological Society of Great Britain and Ireland* 1: 1–7.

Daws, G. 1980. *A Dream of Islands*. New York and London: W. W. Norton & Co.

Diamond, J. 1995. "The Last Days of Easter Island." *Discover*, August, 63–69.

———. 1997 *Guns, Germs and Steel*. New York and London: W. W. Norton & Co.

Douglas, A. J. A., and P. H. Johnson 1926. *The South Seas Today: Being an Account of the Cruise of the Yacht St. George to the South Pacific*. London and New York: Cassell & Co., Ltd.

Dundas, C. 1870. "Notice of Easter Island, Its Inhabitants, Antiquities and Colossal Statues." *Proceedings of the Society of Antiquaries of Scotland* 8: 312–20.

Dunlap, G. D., and H. H. Shufeldt, eds. 1972. *Dutton's Navigation and Piloting*. Annapolis, Md.: Naval Institute Press.

Edge-Partington, J. 1901. "On the Origin of the Stone Figures or Incised Tablets from Easter Island." *Man: Journal of the Royal Anthropological Society of Great Britain and Ireland* 46: 9–10.

———. 1904. "A 'Domestic Idol' from Easter Island." *Man: Journal of the Royal Anthropological Society of Great Britain and Ireland* 46: 73–74.

Edmunds, H. P. 1994 "Germans." In Jesús Conte Oliveros, ed., *Isla de Pascua Horizontes Sombríos y Luminosos (Historia Documentada)*. 336–38. Santiago de Chile: Centro de Investigación de la Imagen. Documento no. 31.

Emory, K. P. 1939. *Archaeology of Mangareva and Neighboring Atolls*. Honolulu: Bernice P. Bishop Museum Bulletin 163.

Englert, Père S. 1964. *Primer Siglo Cristiano de la Isla de Pascua*. Imprenta Salesiana.

———. 1974. *La Tierra de Hotu Matu'a: Historia, Etnología, y Lengua de la Isla de Pascua*. Santiago: Padre de Casas.

———. 1978. *Idioma Rapanui*. Santiago: Universidad de Chile.

Ferdon, E. N., Jr. 1957. "Notes on the Present-Day Easter Islanders." *Southwestern Journal of Anthropology* 13 (3): 223–38.

———. 1958. "Easter Island Exchange Systems." *Southwestern Journal of Anthropology* 14 (2): 136–51.

———. 1961. "The Ceremonial Site of Orongo." In T. Heyerdahl and E. N. Ferdon Jr., eds., *Reports of the Norwegian Archaeological Expedition to Easter Island and the East Pacific*, Vol. 1, *Archaeology of Easter Island*, 221–56. Santa Fe: Monographs of the School of American Research and the Museum of New Mexico (24).

Fillippi, R. A. (Philippi). 1873. "Memorias cientificas y literarias: La Isla de Pascua y sus habitantes." *Annales de la Universidad de Chile* 43: 365–434.

Finney, B. (with others). 1994. *Voyage of Rediscovery*. Berkeley and Los Angeles: University of California Press.

Finney, J. C., and J. D. Alexander. 1998. "The Rapanui Language of Easter Island: Where Does It Fit in the Polynesian Family Tree?" In C. M. Stevenson et al., eds., *Easter Island in Pacific Context South Sea Symposium*, 20–32. Easter Island Foundation Occasional Paper 4. Los Osos: Bearsville and Cloud Mountain Presses.

Fischer, S. R. 1993a. "A Provisional Inventory of the Inscribed Artifacts in the Three Rapanui Scripts." In S. R. Fischer, ed., *Easter Island Studies: Contributions to the History of Rapanui in Memory of William T. Mulloy*, 177–81. Oxford: Oxbow Books Monograph 32.

———, ed. 1993b. *Easter Island Studies: Contributions to the History of Rapanui in Memory of William T. Mulloy*. Oxford: Oxbow Books Monograph 32.

———. 1998. "Reading Rapanui's *Rongorongo*." In C. M. Stevenson et al., eds., *Easter Island in Pacific Context South Seas Symposium*, 3–7. Easter Island Foundation Monograph 4. Los Osos: Bearsville and Cloud Mountain Presses.

Fisher, R. L., ed. 1958. *Preliminary Report on Expedition Downwind*. University of California, Scripps Institute of Oceanography IGY Cruise to the South Pacific. Washington, D.C.: IGY General Report Series 2.

Flenley, J. R. 1979. "Stratigraphic Evidence of Environmental Change on Easter Island." *Asian Perspectives* 22, 33–40.

Flenley, J. R., and S. M. King. 1984. "Late Quaternary Pollen Records from Easter Island." *Nature* 307 (5946): 47–50.

Flenley, J. R., S. M. King, J. T. Teller, M. E. Prentice, J. Jackson, and C. Chew. 1991. "The Late Quaternary Vegetational and Climatic History of Easter Island." *Journal of Quaternary Science* 6: 85–115.

Forbes, H. O. 1917. "Easter Island: Discussion." *The Geographic Journal* 49 (5): 346–47.

Force, R. W., and M. Force. 1971. *The Fuller Collection of Pacific Artifacts*. New York and Washington, D.C.: Praeger Publishers.

Forment, F. 1983. "Pou Hakanononga, God van de Tonijnvissers?" *Liber Memorialis Prof. Dr. P. J. Vandenhoute*. Brussels: Rijksuniversiteit te Gent.

Forster, G. 1777. *Voyage Around the World in His Britannic Majesty's Sloop, Resolution, Commanded by Captain James Cook, during the Years 1772–1775*. London: B. White.

Francis, Capt. n.d. (1853). PMB Microfilm 734, frames 253–344.

Frank, V. S. 1906. "A trip to Easter Island (A speck on the ocean)." *Journal* (Franklin Institute), September, 179–99.

Fuentes, F. 1913. "Reseña botánica sobre la Isla de Pascua." Boletín del Museo Nacional de Chile 5: 320–37.

Gaceta de Lima. 1771. Untitled article. 27 enero–30 mayo, p. 44.

Gana, I. L. 1870. "Descripción científica de la Isla de Pascua." In *Memoria, Que el Ministro de Estado en el Departamento de Marina Presenta al Congreso Nacional de 1870*. Santiago: Departamento de Marina, 90–109.

Gassner, J. S., trans. 1969. *Voyages and Adventures of La Pérouse*. From the 14th ed. of the F. Valentin abridgment, Tours, 1875. Honolulu: University of Hawai'i Press.

Gatty, C. T. 1880. *Catalogue of the Loan Exhibition . . . Held at the Walker Art Gallery, Liverpool, May 1880*. London.

Geiseler, Kapitä. 1883. "Die Oster-Insel: Eine Stätte prähistorischer Kultur in der Südsee. Bericht des Kommandanten S.M. Kbt. 'Hyäne', Kapitänleutnant Geiseler, über die ethnologische Untersuchung der Oster-Insel (Rapanui)." Berlin: *Beiheft zum Marine-Verordnungsblatt* 44: 1–54.

Godwin, G., ed. 1869. Untitled article in *The Builder* (London), 20 November, 930–31.

González (de Haedo), F. 1908. In B. G. Corney, ed., *The Voyage of Captain Don Felipe González in the Ship of the Line San Lorenzo, with the Frigate Santa Rosalia in Company, to Easter Island in 1770–1: Preceded by an Extract from Mynheer Jacob Roggeveen's Official Log of His Discovery of and Visit to Easter Island in 1722*. The Hakluyt Society, ser. II, no. 13, Kraus Reprint Ltd., 1967.

González-Ferrán, O. 1987. "Evolución geológica de las Islas Chilenas en el Océano Pacifíco. In J. C. Castilla, ed. *Islas Oceánicas Chilenas: Conocimiento Científico y Necesidades de Investigaciónes*, 37–54. Santiago: Ediciónes Universidad Católica de Chile.

Gough, G. M., ed. 1973. *To the Pacific and Arctic with Beechey: The Journal of Lieutenant George Peard of H.M.S. Blossom, 1825–1828*. Cambridge: Cambridge University Press for the Hakluyt Society.

Grau, J. 1987. *Aspectos Ecológicos de la Isla de Pascua*. Primeras Jornadas Territoriales Sobre Isla de Pascua. Santiago de Chile: Colección Terra Nostra 10, 83–90.

———. 1996. "Habitat Actuel du Jubaea le Palmier Chilien." *Les Palmiers* 13: 18–20.

Graves, M. W. 1993. "Preface." In M. W. Graves and R. C. Green, eds., *The Evolution and Organisation of Prehistoric Society in Polynesia*, 5. New Zealand Archaeological Association Monograph 19.

Green, R. C. 1988. "Subgrouping of the Rapanui language of Easter Island in Polynesia and its implications for East Polynesia prehistory." In C. Cristino F. et al., eds., *First International Congress, Easter Island and East Polynesia, 1984*, Vol. 1, *Archaeology*, 37–57. Santiago de Chile: Universidad de Chile, Facultad de Arquitectura y Urbanismo Instituto de Estudios Isla de Pascua.

———. 2001. "Commentary on the Sailing Raft, the Sweet Potato and the South American Connection." *Rapa Nui Journal* 15 (2): 69–77.

Green, R. C., and M. I. Weisler. 2000. *Mangarevan Archaeology: Interpretations using new data and 40-year-old excavations to establish a sequence from 1200 to 1900 A.D.* Dunedin: University of Otago Studies in Prehistoric Anthropology 19.

Haddon, A. C. n.d. "Problems of the Pacific." Review of *The Mystery of Easter Island: The Story of an Expedition*. News cutting on file, RGS WKR 7 4/1.

———. 1937. "Canoes of Oceania: The Canoes of Melanesia, Queensland, and New Guinea." V. 1. Honolulu: Bernice P. Museum Special Publication 28. Combined with v. 2 and reprinted, 1975.

Haddon, A. C., and J. Hornell. 1975. *Canoes of Oceania*. Three volumes combined into one. Honolulu: Bernice P. Bishop Museum Special Publications 27, 28, and 29.

Hagelberg, E. 1998. "Genetic Perspectives on the Settlement of the Pacific." In C. M. Stevenson et al., eds., *Easter Island in Pacific Context South Seas Symposium*, 214–17.

Easter Island Foundation Occasional Paper 4. Los Osos: Bearsville and Cloud Mountain Presses.

Handy, E. S. C. 1927. *Polynesian Religion.* Honolulu: Bernice P. Bishop Museum Bulletin 34. Kraus Reprint Co., 1971.

Harrison, Lt. James. 1866–69. Journal and Remark Book from HMS *Topaze.* Documents on file, Department of Ethnography, British Museum.

Hedgpeth, J. W. 1945. "The United States Fish Commission Steamer Albatross." *American Neptune* (Salem, Mass.) 5 (1).

Heyerdahl, T., and E. N. Ferdon Jr., eds. 1961. *Reports of the Norwegian Archaeological Expedition to Easter Island and the East Pacific,* Vol. 1, *Archaeology of Easter Island.* Santa Fe: Monographs of the School of American Research and the Museum of New Mexico (24).

Heyerdahl, T., A. Skjölsvold, and P. Pavel. 1989. "The 'Walking' moai of Easter Island." In A. Skjölsvold, ed., *Kon-Tiki Museum Occasional Papers,* 7–35. Oslo: Kon-Tiki Museum (1).

Hoffman, A. J., and C. Marticorena. 1987. "La Vegetación de Las Islas Oceánicas Chilenas." In J. C. Castilla, ed., *Islas Oceánicas Chilenas: Conocimiento Científico y Necesidades de Investigaciónes,* 127–65. Santiago: Ediciónes Universidad Católica de Chile.

Holmes, C., ed. 1984. *Captain Cook's Second Voyage: John Elliot & Richard Pickersgill.* London: Caliban Books.

Hotus y Otros, A. (Juan Chavez Haoa, Juan Haoa Hereveri, El Consejo de Jejes de Rapa Nui), 1988. *Te Mau Hatu'o Rapa Núi.* Editorial Emisión y el Centro de Estudios Políticos Latinoamericanos Simón Bolívar.

Illustrated London News. 1869. 20 March, 297. Untitled.

Irwin, G. 1992. *The Prehistoric Exploration and Colonisation of the Pacific.* Cambridge: Cambridge University Press.

Johnson, Major A. J. A., and P. H. Johnson. 1926. *The South Seas Today: Being an account of the cruise of the yacht St. George to the Pacific.* London and New York: Cassell and Co., Ltd.

Joppien, R., and B. Smith. 1985. *The Art of Captain Cook's Voyages,* Vol. 2, *The Voyage of the Resolution & Adventure.* New Haven and London: Yale University Press in association with the Australian Academy of the Humanities.

Kaeppler, A. L. 1978. *"Artificial Curiosities": being an Exposition of Native Manufactures Collected on the Three Pacific Voyages of Captain James Cook, R.N.* Honolulu: Bernice P. Bishop Museum Special Publication 66.

———. 2001. "Rapa Nui Art and Aesthetics." In E. Kjellgren, ed., *Splendid Isolation: Art of Easter Island,* 32–41. New York: The Metropolitan Museum of Art and Yale University Press.

Kirch, P. V. 1990. "Regional variation and local style: A neglected dimension in Hawaiian prehistory." *Pacific Studies* 13 (2), 41–54.

———. 2000. *On the Road of the Winds: An Archaeological History of the Pacific Islands before European Contact.* Berkeley: University of California Press.

Kjellgren, E., ed. 2001. *Splendid Isolation: Art of Easter Island.* New York: The Metropolitan Museum of Art and Yale University Press.

Klein S., O. 1988. *Iconografía de la Isla de Pascua.* Valparaíso: Universidad Técnica Federico Santa Maria.

Krupa, V. 1982. *The Polynesian Languages.* London: Routledge and Kegan Paul.

La Pérouse, J. F., Comte de. 1797. *A Voyage Round the World Performed in the Years 1785–1788.* London: Johnson.

Lee, G. 1992. *The Rock Art of Easter Island: Symbols of Power, Prayers to the Gods.* Los Angeles: University of California, Los Angeles Institute of Archaeology Monumenta Archaeologica 17.

Lisjanskij, U. 1814. *Voyage Round the World, 1803–1806, in the Ship Neva.* London: Longmans.

Love, C. M. 1984. *The Katherine Routledge Lantern Slide Collection of Easter Island and the South Pacific* (in the Museum of Mankind, British Museum). Western Wyoming College.

Magoffin, R. V. D. 1916. "Mysterious Easter Island." *Art and Archaeology* 4 (2): 125.

Malinowsky, B. 1916. "Baloma: The Spirits of the Dead in the Trobriand Islands." *Journal of the Royal Anthropological Institute* 46: 353–430. Reprinted in *Magic, Science and Religion* (Boston: Beacon Press, 1954).

Martinsson-Wallin, H. 1994. *Ahu—The Ceremonial Stone Structures of Easter Island.* Uppsala: Societas Archaeological Upsaliensis Aun 19.

Martinsson-Wallin, H., and P. Wallin. 1998. "Excavations at 'Anakena: The Easter Island Settlement Sequence and Change of Subsistence?" In P. Vargas C., ed., *Easter Island and East Polynesia Prehistory,* 179–86. Santiago: Universidad de Chile Facultad de Arquitectura y Urbanismo, Instituto de Estudios Isla de Pascua.

———. 2000. "Ahu and Settlement: Archaeological Excavations at 'Anakena and La Pérouse." In C. M. Stevenson and W. S. Ayres, eds., *Easter Island Archaeology Research on Early Rapanui Culture,* 27–44. Easter Island Foundation. Los Osos: Bearsville Press.

McCall, G. n.d. "The past in the present on Rapa Nui (Easter Island)." Unpublished manuscript on file with the author.

———. n.d. (1986). *Las Fundaciónes de Rapanui.* Trans. Lilian González Nualart and Gaston Vera. Isla de Pascua, Chile: Museo R. P. Sebastián Englert.

———. 1976. "Reaction to disaster: Continuity and change in Rapanui social organization." Ph.D. diss., Australian National University.

———. 1980. *Rapanui: Tradition and Survival on Easter Island.* Honolulu: University Press of Hawai'i (2nd rev. ed. 1994).

———. 1998. "Rapanui Wanderings: Diasporas from Easter Island." In C. Stevenson et al., eds., *Easter Island in Pacific Context South Seas Symposium,* 370–78. Easter Island Foundation Occasional Paper 4. Los Osos: Bearsville and Cloud Mountain Presses.

McCoy, P. C. 1976. *Easter Island Settlement Patterns in the Late Prehistoric and Protohistoric Periods.* New York: International Fund for Monuments, Inc., Bulletin 5, Easter Island Committee.

———. 1978. "The Off Near-Shore Islets in Easter Island Prehistory." *Journal of the Polynesian Society* 83 (3): 193–214.

Mellén Blanco, F. 1986. *Manuscritos y documentos españoles para la historia de la Isla de Pascua.* Madrid: Centro de Estudios Históricos de Obras Publicas y Urbanismo (CEHOPU).

Métraux, A. 1937. "The Kings of Easter Island." *Journal of the Polynesian Society* Auckland 46: 41–62.

———. 1940. *Ethnology of Easter Island.* Honolulu: Bernice P. Bishop Museum Bulletin 160.

Moorehead, A. 1969. *Darwin and the Beagle.* London and New York: Penguin Books.

Mulloy, E. R. 1961 "The Wrath of the Gods of Rapa Nui." *Science of Man* (Mentone, Calif.) 1 (3): 102–4.

Mulloy, W. S. 1961. "The Ceremonial Center of Vinapu. In T. Heyerdahl and E. N. Ferdon Jr., eds., *Reports of the Norwegian Archaeological Expedition to Easter Island and the East Pacific, Vol. 1, Archaeology of Easter Island,* 93–180. Santa Fe: Monographs of the School of American Research and the Museum of New Mexico (24).

———. 1968. *Preliminary Report of Archaeological Field Work, February–July, 1968, Easter Island.* New York: International Fund for Monuments, Inc., Bulletin 1, Easter Island Committee.

———. 1970. *Preliminary Report of the Restoration of Ahu Vai Uri, Easter Island.* New York: International Fund for Monuments, Inc., Bulletin 2, Easter Island Committee.

———. 1973. *Preliminary Report of the Restoration of Ahu Huri A Urenga and Two Unnamed Ahu at Hanga Kio'E, Easter Island.* New York: International Fund for Monuments, Inc., Easter Island Committee.

———. 1975. *Investigation and Restoration of the Ceremonial Center of Orongo, Easter Island.* New York: International Fund for Monuments, Inc., Bulletin 4, Easter Island Committee.

Mulloy, W. S., and G. Figueroa. 1978. "The A Kivi-Vai Teka Complex and Its Relationship to Easter Island Architectural Prehistory." *Asian and Pacific Archaeology,* ser. 1. University of Hawai'i at Manoa.

Nicoll, M. J. 1908. *Three Voyages of a Naturalist.* London: Witherby & Co.

Oliveros, Jesús Conte. 1994. *Isla de Pascua Horizontes Sombrios y Luminosos (Historia Documentada).* Santiago de Chile: Centro de Investigación de la Imagen.

Orliac, C. 2000. "The Woody Vegetation of Easter Island Between the Early 14th and the Mid–17th Centuries A.D." In C. M. Stevenson and W. S. Ayres, eds., *Easter Island Archaeology Research on Early Rapanui Culture,* 211–20. Los Osos: Bearsville Press.

Owsley, D. W., G. W. Gill, and S. D. Owsley. 1994. "Biological Effects of European Contact on Easter Island." In C. S. Larsen and G. R. Milner, eds., *In the Wake of Contact: Biological Responses to Conquest*. New York: Wiley-Liss, Inc.

Paté, T. M. *(tangata nu'u papa'i)*. 1986. *Relatos de la Isla de Pascua ('A 'Amu o Rapa Nui)*. Santiago de Chile: Editorial Andrés Bello.

Philbrick, N. 2000. *In the Heart of the Sea: The Tragedy of the Whaleship Essex*. New York: Viking.

Pinchot, G. 1930. *To the South Seas*. Chicago, Philadelphia, Toronto: The John C. Winston Company.

Porteous, J. D. 1981. *The Modernization of Easter Island*. Western Geographical Series, v. 19. British Columbia: University of Victoria.

Poulton, Sir E. B. 1917. "The Tragic History of a Butterfly." *Journal of the Entomological Society* (London).

Quinn, W. H., and V. T. Neal. 1987. "El Niño Occurrences Over the Past Four and a Half Centuries." *Journal of Geophysical Research* 92 (C13): 14,449–61.

Roe, M., ed. 1967. *The Journal and Letters of Captain Charles Bishop*. Cambridge: Cambridge University Press for the Hakluyt Society.

Roussel, Père R. 1908. "Vocabulaire de la Langue de l'Île-de-Pâques ou Rapa-nui." *Le Muséon* (Louvain: Congrégation des Sacrés-Coeurs de Picpus).

R.S. (Richard Sainthill), 1870. "Rapa Nui or Easter Island." *Macmillan's Magazine*, 21.

Sahlins, M. 1985. *Islands of History*. Chicago and London: University of Chicago Press.

Santelices, B. 1987. "Flora Marina Botánica de Las Islas Oceánicas Chilenas." In J. C. Castilla, ed., *Islas Oceánicas Chilenas: Conocimiento Científico y Necesidades de Investigaciones*, 101–26. Santiago: Ediciónes Universidad Católica de Chile.

Santelices, B., and I. A. Abbott. 1988. "Geographic and Marine Isolation: An Assessment of the Marine Algae of Easter Island." *Pacific Science* 41: 1–20.

Skjølsvold, A. 1961a. "The Stone Statues and Quarries of Rano Raraku." In T. Heyerdahl and E. N. Ferdon Jr., eds., *Reports of the Norwegian Archaeological Expedition to Easter Island and the East Pacific, Vol. 1, Archaeology of Easter Island*, 339–80. Santa Fe: Monographs of the School of American Research and the Museum of New Mexico (24).

———. 1961b. "Dwellings of Hotu Matu'a." In T. Heyerdahl and E. N. Ferdon Jr., eds., *Reports of the Norwegian Archaeological Expedition to Easter Island and the East Pacific, Vol. 1, Archaeology of Easter Island*, 273–76. Santa Fe: Monographs of the School of American Research and the Museum of New Mexico (24).

Steadman, D. W. 1989. "Extinction of birds in Eastern Polynesia: A Review of the Record, and Comparisons with Other Pacific Island Groups." *Journal of Archaeological Science* 16: 177–205.

Stevenson, C. M. 1986. "The Socio-political Structure of the Southern Coastal Area of Easter Island." In P. V. Kirch, ed., *Island Societies: Archaeological Approaches to Evolution and Transformation*. Cambridge: Cambridge University Press.

———. 1997. *Archaeological Investigations on Easter Island: Maunga Tari: An Upland Agricultural Complex*. Easter Island Foundation Occasional Paper 3. Los Osos: Bearsville and Cloud Mountain Presses.

Stevenson, C. M., and S. Haoa. 1998. "Prehistoric Gardening Systems and Agricultural Intensification in the La Pérouse Area of Easter Island." In C. M. Stevenson et al., eds., *Easter Island in Pacific Context South Seas Symposium*, 205–13. Los Osos: Bearsville and Cloud Mountain Presses.

Stevenson, C. M., and W. S. Ayres, eds. 2000. *Easter Island Archaeology Research on Early Rapanui Culture*. Easter Island Foundation. Los Osos: Bearsville Press.

Stokes, J. F. G. 1991. *Heiau of the island of Hawai'i*. T. Dye, ed. Bernice P. Bishop Museum Bulletin 103. Honolulu: Bishop Museum Press.

Stolpe, H. 1899. "Über die Tatowirung der Oster-Insulaner." In *Abhandlungen und Berichete des Königlisches, oologische und Antropologisch-Ethnolographisches Museum zu Dresden* 6: 1–13.

St. George Gray, H. 1904. "Another Type of 'Domestic Idol' from Easter Island." *Man: Journal of the Royal Anthropological Society of Great Britain and Ireland* (London) 96: 148.

Thomson, W. J. 1891. "Te Pito te Henua, or Easter Island." In *Report of the U.S. National Museum for the Year Ending 30 June 1889*. Washington, D.C.: Smithsonian Institution.

Topaze 1868 *Log*. PRO, London, ADM 53–9414.

Ubilla Toledo, N. n.d. "Juan Tepano Primer Militar Pascuense." Unpublished poem on file, Esperanza Pakarati.

Van Tilburg, J. 1986a. "Power and symbol: The stylistic analysis of Easter Island monolithic sculpture." Ph.D. diss., The Institute of Archaeology, UCLA.

———. 1986b. "Red Scoria on Easter Island: Sculpture, Artifacts and Architecture." *Journal of New World Archaeology* 7 (1): 1–28.

———. 1987. "Larger than life: The form and function of Easter Island monolithic sculpture." *Musées Royaux d'Art et d'Histoire Bulletin* 58 (2): 111–30.

———. 1988. "Stylistic variation of dorsal design on Easter Island statues." In J. M. Ramírez, ed., *Clava*, 95–108. Viña del Mar: Museo Sociedad Fonck (4).

———. 1988b. "Double Canoes on Easter Island? Reassessing the Orongo Petroglyph Evidence." In P. Vargas C., ed., *Easter Island and East Polynesia Prehistory*, 131–46. Santiago: Universidad de Chile, Facultad de Arquitectura y Urbanismo, Instituto de Estudios de Isla de Pascua.

———. 1990. "Respect for Rapa Nui: Exhibition and conservation of Easter Island stone statues." *Antiquity* 64: 249–58.

———. 1992. "HMS Topaze on Easter Island: Hoa Hakananai'a and Five Other Museum Statues in Archaeological Context." London: British Museum Press Occasional Paper 73.

———. 1993. "The use of photogrammetry, laser scan and computer-assisted drafting to define relationships between Easter Island statue morphology, transport technology and social organisation." In M. W. Graves and R. C. Green, eds., New Zealand Archaeological Association Monograph 19, 87–102.

———. 1994. *Easter Island Archaeology, Ecology and Culture*. London and Washington, D.C.: British Museum Press and Smithsonian Institution Press.

———. 1995. "Easter Island (Rapa Nui) Archaeology Since 1955: Some Thoughts on Progress, Problems and Potential." In J. M. Davidson et al., eds., *Oceanic Culture History: Essays in Honour of Roger Green*, 555–77. New Zealand Journal of Archaeology Special Publication.

———. 2001a. "Easter Island." In P. N. Peregrine and M. Ember, eds., *Encyclopedia of Prehistory, Vol. 3. East Asia and Oceania*, 45–59. New York, Boston, Dordrecht, London, Moscow: Kluwer Academic/Plenum Publishers in conjunction with the Human Relations Area Files (HRAF) at Yale University.

———. 2001b. "Changing Faces: Rapa Nui Statues in the Social Landscape." In E. Kjellgren, ed., *Splendid Isolation: Art of Easter Island*, 24–31. New York: The Metropolitan Museum of Art and Yale University Press.

———. 2002a. "O. G. S. Crawford and the Mana Expedition to Easter Island (Rapa Nui), 1914–1915." *Journal of the Polynesian Society* 3 (1): 65–78.

———. 2002b. "Thor Heyerdahl" (obituary). *The Guardian*. 19 April.

Van Tilburg, J., and C. Arévalo Pakarati. 2002. "The Rapanui Carvers' Perspective: Notes and Observations on the Experimental Replication of Monolithic Sculpture *(moai)*." In A. Herle et al., eds., *Pacific Art: Persistence, Change and Meaning*. Bathurst, NSW: Crawford House.

Van Tilburg, J., and T. Ralston. 1999. "Engineers of Easter Island." *Archaeology*, November–December, 40–45.

———. 2002 (in press). "Megaliths and Mariners: Experimental Archaeology on Easter Island (Rapa Nui)." In K. L. Johnson, ed., *Onward and Upward! Papers in Honor of Clement W. Meighan*. University Press of America, Inc.

Van Tilburg, J., and P. Vargas C., 1998. "Easter Island Statue Inventory and Documentation: A Status Report." In P. Vargas Casanova, ed., *Easter Island and East Polynesia Prehistory*, 187–94. Santiago: Universidad de Chile, Facultad de Arquitectura y Urbanismo, Instituto de Estudios Isla de Pascua.

Vargas C., P. 1993. "The Easter Island Prehistoric Sequence and Developments in its Settlement Patterns." In M. W. Graves and R. C. Green, eds., *The Evolution and Organisation of Prehistoric Society in Polynesia*, 103–5. Auckland: New Zealand Archaeological Monograph 19.

———, ed. 1998. *Easter Island and East Polynesia Prehistory*. Santiago: Universidad de Chile Facultad de Arquitectura y Urbanismo, Instituto de Estudios Isla de Pascua.

Vargas C., P., L. González N., R. Budd P., and R. Izaurieta S. 1990. *Estudios del Asientamiento en Isla de Pascua: Prospección Arqueológica en la Península del Poike y Sector de Mahatua*. Santiago: Universidad de Chile Facultad de Arquitectura y Urbanismo, Instituto de Estudios Isla de Pascua.

Weisler, M., and R. C. Green. 2001. "Holistic Approaches to Interaction Studies: A Polynesian Example." In M. Jones and P. Sheppard, eds., *Austronesian Connections and New Directions: Research in Anthropology and Linguistics* 5. Auckland, New Zealand.

Wheeler, Sir M. n.d. "South Sea Vikings" (review of A. Métraux volume, 1940). *Daily Telegraph*. News cutting on file, Katherine and Scoresby Routledge Papers, RGS WKR 7.

Withey, L. 1989. *Voyages of Discovery*. Berkeley and Los Angeles: University of California Press.

Wozniak, J. A. 1998. "Settlement Patterns and Subsistence on the Northwest Coast of Rapa Nui." In C. M. Stevenson et al., eds., *Easter Island in Pacific Context South Seas Symposium*, 185–92. Easter Island Foundation Occasional Paper 4. Los Osos: Bearsville and Cloud Mountain Presses.

Wycherley, G. 1928. *Buccaneers of the Pacific*. Indianapolis: The Bobbs-Merrill Company.

Zuhmbohm, R. P. G. 1868. "Lettre du R. P. Gaspard Zuhmbohm au TRP Rouchouze, Rapa Nui, 10 April 1868." Rome: Archives of the Fathers of the Sacred Heart (Picpus), 213.

———. 1879. "Lettres du R. P. Gaspard Zuhmbohm au directeur des annales sur la mission de L'Île de Pâques." *Annales de la congregation des Sacrés-Coeurs de Jésus et de Marie*. V. 5. Paris.

———. 1880. "Lettres du R. P. Gaspard Zuhmbohm au directeur des annales sur la mission de L'Île de Pâques." *Annales de la congregation des Sacrés-Coeurs de Jésus et de Marie*. V. 6. Paris.

MANA AND THE MANA EXPEDITION TO EASTER ISLAND (SELECTED)

Anon. 1912a. "Easter Island Mystery: Expedition to the Southern Seas." *Daily News*, 1 June. RGS WKR 7.

———. 1912b. "Aims of the Expedition." *The* (London) *Times*, 25 December. RGS WKR 7.

———. 1912c. "The Scientific Expedition to Easter Island." S.S.A. *Report*, October. RGS WKR 7.

———. 1913. "The Riddle of the Pacific." *Buenos Aires Herald*. 3 September. RGS WKR 7.

———. 1915a. "Three Years of Adventuring in War Sown Seas." Honolulu *Advertiser*, 15 November. RGS WKR 7.

———. 1915b. "Socialism Rules Pitcairn Island." Honolulu *Advertiser*, 16 November.

———. 1915–16. "Easter Island Stone Statues." *The Christian Science Monitor*. RGS WKR 7.

———. 1916a "Mana Arrives." *The* (London) *Times*, 30 June, 7F. RGS WKR 7.

———. 1916b. "Mrs Scoresby Routledge has returned." *The* (London) *Times*, Court Circular, 16 May. RGS WKR 7.

———. 1916c. "Wrong Stories Sent Out About Hawaii." *The Christian Science Monitor*, 24 July. RGS WKR 7.

———. 1919a. "Easter Island." *Pall Mall Gazette*, 5 December. RGS WKR 7.

———. 1919b. "The World of Books." *The Nation*. (London) 23 November. RGS WKR 7.

———. 1920. "The Mana." *The Yachting Monthly*, June, p. 5. RGS WKR 7.

———. 1921. "The Mystery of Easter Island." *The Geographical Review*. (American Geographical Society), July. RGS WKR 7.

———. 1923a. "Mangareva: Link with Easter Island." *The Sydney Morning Herald*, 23 March. RGS WKR 7.

———. 1923b. "Lost Among Unknown Islands: Pacific Expedition." *Yorkshire Observer*, 28 May. RGS WKR 7.

———. 1939. "Lone Britons in Tribe Revolt: Warship Went to Rescue." London *Daily Mail*, August. RGS WKR 7.

Fallaize, E. N. 1916. "The Routledge Expedition to Easter Island." *Nature* 97: 261–62.

Nickols, J. 1995. "Easter Island Expedition." *The Boatman*, November, p. 18.

PEASE, KATHERINE M. (KATHERINE [MRS. SCORESBY] ROUTLEDGE)

Pease, K. (Katherine Maria Pease Routledge). 1903. "Some Experiences of South Africa." In E. F. Valentine, ed., *Darlington Training College Magazine*, 97–102. Darlington: W. Dresser and Sons.

A Silent Member (Katherine M. Routledge [born Pease]). 1916. *The Ministry in Wartime: An Open Letter* (pamphlet on file, with attached correspondence). London: The Library, Friends House, box 219.

PEASE FAMILY AND QUAKER HISTORY

Anderson, V. 1980. *Friends and Relations: Three Centuries of Quaker Families*. London: Hodder and Stoughton.

Anon. (Kate Pease). 1896. "Emma G. Pease." *Annual Monitor* (London), 137–44.

———. 1862. "Marriage at the Friends' Meeting House, Darlington." *Darlington and Stockton Times*, 16 August.

———. 1924. "Gilbert Gilkes." *The Friend* (London), 751–52.

———. 1989. "Recalling the Names of Early Friends." *Darlington and Stockton Times*, 19 August.

Benson, M.E., and J. S. Benson. 1949. *Descendants of Isaac and Rachel Wilson Photographic Pedigree*. V. 1, rev. Middlesbrough: William Appleyard and Sons, Ltd.

———. 1962. *Descendants of Isaac and Rachel Wilson, Supplement to the 1949 Edition*. V. 1, additions and corrections. Gloucester: L. A. Smart and Son, Ltd.

Benson, R. S. 1912, 1920. *Descendants of Isaac and Rachel Wilson Photographic Pedigree*. V. 1. Middlesbrough: William Appleyard and Sons, Ltd.

Besse, J. 1753. *Sufferings of the People Called Quakers*. London: L. Hinde.

Braithwaite, J. B. 1857. *Memoirs of Joseph John Gurney*. Philadelphia: J. B. Lippincott & Co.

———. 1905. *Memoirs of Anna Braithwaite*. London: Headley Bros.

Brayshaw, A. N. 1982. *The Quakers, Their Story and Message*. York: William Sessions, Ltd.

The British Workman. 1873. "Tribute to the Memory of the Late Mr. Joseph Pease." January Special Number.

Brock, P. 1990. *The Quaker Peace Testimony, 1660–1914*. York: Sessions Book Trust.

Brodie, A. 1993. "The Spiritual Ferment—Lucy Violet Hodgkin in Havelock North, New Zealand." *Journal of the Friends Historical Society* 56 (4): 296–310.

Dean, D., and S. 1984. *Darlington in the 1930s & '40s*. Lancashire: Hendon Publishing Co., Ltd.

"Dictionary of Quaker Biography" (typescripts filed under personal names of subjects). London: The Friends House Library.

Durham Quarterly Meeting. 1896. *Yearly Meeting Proceedings*. London: The Friends House Library.

Emden, P. H. 1939. *Quakers in Commerce: A Record of Business Achievement*. London: Sampson Low, Marston & Co., Ltd.

Evening Dispatch. 1972a. "Is Darlington being destroyed?" (preserving Southend). 10 August.

———. 1972b. "Ring Road 'vital' to control of traffic" (preserving Southend). 21 November.

Fenwick, F. n.d. (early 1900s). "Weardale Memorials." A thirty-page, privately circulated booklet. Durham County Library.

Foster, J. 1891. *Pease of Darlington*. Printed for private circulation. London: Friends Library.

Foster, S. B. 1890. *The Pedigree of Wilson of High Wray & Kendal, and the Families Connected with Them*. Printed for private circulation.

Fothergill, G. n.d. *An Old Raby Hunt Club, 1786–1899*. Printed for private circulation.

Fox, G. 1984. "The Journal of George Fox." In D. Steere, ed., *Quaker Spirituality: Selected Writings*, 59–136. New York, Ramsey, Toronto: Paulist Press.

Glover, M. R. 1984. *The Retreat, York: An Early Experiment in the Treatment of Mental Illness*. York: William Sessions, Ltd.

Gorman, G. 1973. *The Amazing Fact of Quaker Worship*. London: Quaker Home Service.

Hazlehurst, C., and C. Woodland, eds. 1994. *A Liberal Chronicle: Journals and Papers of J. A. Pease, First Lord Gainford, 1908–1910*. London: Historic Press.

Henry, F. 1989. *The New Zealand Journeys of Lucy Violet Hodgkin*. Ed. J. Brodie and A. Brodie. Wellington: The Beechtree Press for the New Zealand Yearly Meeting of the Society of Friends.

Hewison, H. H. 1989. *Hedge of Wild Almonds: South Africa, the Pro-Boers and the Quaker Conscience, 1890–1910*. Portsmouth, N.H.: Heinemann; Cape Town: D. Philip; London: J. Currey.

Hodgkin, T. 1911. *Human Progress and the Inward Light*. London: Published for the Woodbrooke Extension Committee by Hendlye.

Illustrated London News. 1854. "Peace Deputation to the Czar." 11 March.

Kelly, T. R. 1984. "The Gathered Meeting." In D. Steere, ed., *Quaker Spirituality: Selected Writings*, 312–15. New York, Ramsey, Toronto: Paulist Press.

Kirby, M. 1984. *Men of Business and Politics: The Rise and Fall of the Quaker Pease Dynasty of North-East England, 1700–1943*. London: George Allen & Unwin.

Lidbetter, H. 1995. *The Friends Meeting House*. York: William Sessions Ltd.

Lloyd, C. n.d. "Mansions fit for Friends." Darlington *Echo Memories*.

———. 1989. "A far cry from quelling fires with milk or beer!" (Pease fire engine donated). *Echo Extra*, 20 July.

———. 1990a. "A Quaker who broke the mould of politics" (Joseph Pease, MP). Darlington *Echo Extra*, 20 June.

———. 1990b. "Father of the House" (Sir Joseph Whitwell Pease, MP). Darlington *Echo Extra*, 27 June.

———. 1990c. "Rooms with a marvelous view" (Hummersknott). Darlington *Echo Extra*, 11 July.

———. 1990d. "Portrait of an upright citizen, M.P. and mayor" (Sir Theodore Fry). Darlington *Echo Extra*, 1 August.

Meadows, P., and E. Waterson. 1993. *Lost Houses of County Durham*. York: Jill Raines.

Northern Echo. 1933. "The First Quaker M.P.: How Joseph Pease took his seat." 7 February.

Pease, Sir Alfred Edward. 1907. *The Diaries of Edward Pease, the Father of English Railways*. London: Headley Brothers.

———. 1917. "Random Notes." Manuscript on file, Joseph Gurney Pease.

———. 1919. *My Son Christopher*. Middlesbrough: William Appleyard and Sons, Ltd.

———. 1928. *A Dictionary of the Dialect of North Riding of York*. Whitby: Horne & Son, Ltd.

———. 1932. *Elections and Recollections*. London: John Murray.

———. 1912, ed. *15 Books of Old Recipes as used in the Pease and Gurney Households in the XVIIIth Century*. Newcastle-on-Tyne: Andrew Reid & Company, Ltd.

Pease, J. A., Baron Gainsford. 1895. "How We Countenance Slavery in East African British Protectorates." London: British and Foreign Anti-Slavery Society.

Pease, J. G., ed., 1992. *A Wealth of Happiness and Many Bitter Trials: The Journals of Sir Alfred Edward Pease, a Restless Man*. York: William Sessions Ltd., The Ebor Press.

Pease, J. G., and J. Van Tilburg. n.d. (1996). "Chronology of Recorded Extracts from Diaries of Wilson Pease, Sir. J. W. Pease, Sir Alfred E. Pease and Ethel Buxton (née Pease) Diary when Aged 17." Manuscript on file with the authors.

Pease, J. H. 1930. "An Old Darlington Friend Now in Need." *Darlington and Stockton Times*. Darlington Library Local History Room PB15 U4189, no. 1

Raistrick, A. 1950. *Quakers in Science and Industry*. London: Bannisdale Press.

Richardson, J. N. 1899. *The Quakers at Lungan and Grange*. UCLA Special Collections, microfilm.

Rose, J. 1980. *Elizabeth Fry, a Biography*. London: Macmillan and Co.

Sansome, C. 1963. *Heart and Mind Prepared*. London: Friends House, Quaker Home Service. Reprint, 1992.

Simmons, J., ed. 1975. *RAIL 150: The Stockton & Darlington Railway and What Followed*. London: Eyre Methuen.

Somervell, J. 1924. *Isaac and Rachel Wilson, Quakers, of Kendal, 1714–1785*. London: The Swarthmore Press Ltd.

Steere, D. V. 1984. *Quaker Spirituality: Selected Writings*. New York, Ramsey, Toronto: Paulist Press.

Sturge, J. 1854. "Address of the Society of Friends to Nicholas I, Emperor of Russia; with His Remarks Thereon." Darlington: Harrison Penney, Printer.

Swift, D. E. 1962. *Joseph John Gurney: Banker, Reformer, and Quaker*. Middletown, Conn.: Wesleyan University Press.

Taylor, E. E. 1947. *The Valiant Sixty*. London: Bannisdale Press.

Wedgewood, M. n.d.a. "New chapter for the town: Pease dream came true." *Darlington Library Supplement* 2.

———. n.d.b. "The heiress who wrecked the Pease family fortunes." *Darlington Library Supplement* 3.

ROUTLEDGE, KATHERINE (PEASE) (AUTHOR)

1914. "The Riddle of Easter Island: First Impressions." *The Spectator* 113 (8 August) 196–97. RGS WKR 7.

1916a. "Recent Culture on Easter Island and Its Relation to Past History." Abstract of a paper read at British Association for the Advancement of Science Annual Meeting, Newcastle-on-Tyne. *Man: Journal of the Royal Anthropological Society of Great Britain and Ireland* (London) 85 (140).

1916b. "Easter Island Expedition: German Squadron's Visit." *The* (Bermuda) *Times*, 13 May. RGS WKR 7.

1917a. "The bird cult of Easter Island." *Folk-Lore* 28 (4): 338–55.

1917b. "Easter Island." *Royal Geographical Society Journal* (London) 49 (5): 321–40.

1919. *The Mystery of Easter Island: The Story of an Expedition*. London: Sifton, Praed & Co., Ltd. AMS reprint of 1919 edition, including preface to the second edition, 1920.

1920. "Survey of the village and carved rocks of Orongo, Easter Island, by the Mana Expedition." *Man: Journal of the Royal Anthropological Institute of Great Britain and Ireland* (London) 50: 425–51.

1921a. "The Mystery of Easter Island." *National Geographic Magazine* 60 (6): 628–48.

1921b. "The Frenchman Abroad." *The Spectator*, 26 November RGS WKR 7.

1923. "Mangarevan Folk-lore." Paper read at the British Association for the Advancement of Science 91st Annual Meeting, Liverpool.

1924. "The Mysterious Images of Easter Island." In J. A. Hammerton, ed., *Wonders of the Past: The Romance of Antiquity and Its Splendours*. New York and London: G. P. Putnam's Sons.

1925a. "Domestic Servants and the 'Dole.'" Letter to the Editor. *The Spectator*, 9 May. RGS WKR 7.

1925b. "Lord Milner." Letter to the Editor. *The* (London) *Times*, 19 May. RGS WKR 7.

1963. *The Mystery of Easter Island*. Excerpt reprinted as "The Routledge Expedition to Easter Island." In J. Hawkes, ed., *The World of the Past*, 268–311. New York: Alfred A. Knopf.

ROUTLEDGE, W. S. (AUTHOR)

1906. "An Akikuyu Image." *Man: Journal of the Royal Anthropological Society of Great Britain and Ireland* (London) 1: 1–3.

1916. "Megalithic Remains on Easter Island." Abstract of a paper read at the British Association for the Advancement of Science Annual Meeting, Newcastle-on-Tyne. *Man: Journal of the Royal Anthropological Society of Britain and Ireland* (London) 85: 141.

1917. "Physiography, etc., of Easter Island." Abstract of a paper read before the Geological Society on January 24. *Quarterly Journal of the Geological Society of London* 73: ix–x.

1919. "Part IV: The Homeward Voyage—Continued. San Francisco to Southampton." In

Mrs. Scoresby Routledge, *The Mystery of Easter Island: The Story of an Expedition,* 335–88. London: Sifton, Praed & Co.

ROUTLEDGE AND ROUTLEDGE

n.d. Routledge Papers. Royal Geographical Society, London, Archives. Copies held at Auckland Public Library, New Zealand; Instituto de Estudios, Universidad de Chile, Santiago; Pacific Manuscripts Bureau, Canberra, Australia; Rock Art Archive, The Cotsen Institute of Archaeology at UCLA.

1910. *With a Prehistoric People: The Akikuyu of British East Africa.* London: Frank Cass & Co., Ltd. Reprint, 1968.

1921. "Notes on Some Archaeological Remains in the Society and Austral Islands." *Man: Journal of the Royal Anthropological Society of Great Britain and Ireland* (London) 51: 438–55.

ROUTLEDGE FAMILY

Blair, R. E. 1987. "Routledge" and "Twycross." Unpublished manuscripts with bibliography on file, Pauleen West Family Papers.

Davies, R. A., ed. 1988. *The Letters of Thomas Chandler Haliburton.* Toronto and Buffalo: University of Toronto Press.

Haliburton, T. C. 1829. *An Historical and Statistical Account of Nova-Scotia.* 2 vols. Halifax: J. Howe.

———. 1838. *Judge Haliburton's Yankee Stories.* Philadelphia: T. B. Peterson.

Milne, J. 1898. *Seismology.* London: K. Paul, Trench, Trubner & Co., Ltd.

———. 1911. *A Catalogue of Destructive Earthquakes,* A.D. *7 to 1899.* London: British Association for the Advancement of Science, Seismological Committee.

Twycross-Raines, J. B., ed. n.d. "Some Souvenirs of Professor John Milne Collected by his Cousin the Late Christian Smith." Unpublished manuscript and videotape on file, C. Lopez. The Twycross Burrell Collection of Photographs and Family Papers.

MISCELLANEOUS SELECTED ARTICLES

n.d.a. "Easter Island Mystery." *Evening Standard.* RGS WKR 7.

n.d.b. "General News." Canadian Pacific Wireless *News.* RGS WKR 7.

1922. "Island Disappears." *Daily Mirror,* 17 November. RGS WKR 7.

1923a. "Easter Island: Explorers Do Not Believe Report That It Has Disappeared." *Daily Graphic,* 28 May. RGS WKR 7.

1923b. "Mr. Wilson Pease: Death at His London Residence." *The North Star,* 20 June. RGS WKR 7.

1923c. "The Easter Island Statues." *Nature,* September. RGS WKR 7.

1924. "Coral Strands Preferred." *Daily Graphic,* 11 December. RGS WKR 7.

1928a. "Woman in Locked Mansion." *The* (London) *Times,* 2 June. PB Family Papers.

1928b. "Locked House Woman." *The* (London) *Times,* June. PB Family Papers.

1928c. "Hyde Park 'Siege.'" London *Daily Mail,* June. PB Family Papers.

1928d. "Bailiff at Mrs. Routledge's." London *Daily Mail,* June. PB Family Papers.

1928e. "Mrs. Routledge Leaves." London *Daily Mail,* July. PB Family Papers.

1928f. "Mrs. Routledge Taken to Nursing Home." London *Daily Mail,* July. PB Family Papers.

1935a. "Mrs. K. Routledge's Estate." *The* (London) *Times.* PB Family Papers.

1939b. "Obituary: Mr. Scoresby Routledge." London *Daily Telegraph.* PB Family Papers.

1939c. "Obituary: Mr. Scoresby Routledge: The Mystery of Easter Island." *The* (London) *Times.* PB Family Papers.

1972. "Obituario: Santiago Pakarati Langitani, Murió Patriarca de la Isa de Pascua." *El* (Santiago de Chile) *Mercurio,* 15 December.

ACKNOWLEDGMENTS

✦

FROM OUR FIRST CONTACT ON AUGUST 7, 1995 KATHER-ine Routledge's second cousin Joseph Gurney Pease has been a fountain of information and a source of wisdom. He has graciously spent countless hours combing through family diaries, journals, and letters for mention of her as Katie Pease and has read this book in draft. His considerable skills as biographer to his late father, Sir Alfred Edward Pease, and his rigorous atten-tion to detail are revealed in enlightening letters that I have preserved as valuable research documents. Peter Bucknall, Katherine's great-nephew, gave me exclusive access to papers, photographs, and letters from the painful period of Katherine's last illness and final commitment to Ticehurst. It is impossible to thank him enough for his frankness and trust. Peter traveled to Bursledon and photographed Ewers, and he and his wife, Didi, introduced me to Katherine's great-niece Diana Ford (née Cole-Hamilton) and her daughter.

Two uncommon British women, Margaret Jacques and Dr. Darien Lott, gave this project unwavering support and me steadfast friendship. They cheerfully ran my "London office," and Leonie Jones facilitated e-mail com-munication. Many archive files and public records available on the Internet today were not on-line when I began this research. Margaret hunted down birth certificates, marriage certificates, medical records, university files, pho-tographic files, and other official documents the hard, pre-electronic-data-base way. Margaret and Darien sought Scoresby's family in Eastbourne, then visited and photographed Ticehurst. Darien and her late husband, Laurie, hospitably hosted me in their beautiful home on several research trips to England.

Reggie Barnes deserves full credit for tracking *Mana* through multiple owners and for combing insurance records, construction plans, and details of the vessel's sad demise. It was Reggie who first went to Bursledon and checked out Wilson Pease's description of how and where *Mana* was moored just prior to her departure for Easter Island. Later, Reggie and I went down to Bursledon and, through a really remarkable coincidence, met Mr. Michael Richardson, a distant relative of the Pease family and current owner of Ewers. Mr. Richardson kindly showed us the house and garden.

Reggie and Peter Bucknall helped me sort out design details of *Mana* that conflicted with misidentified photos in the Mana Expedition collection of the British Museum. Thanks for additional help with *Mana* and crew queries are due Lord Cochrane, Earl of Dundonald; J. Price, MBE, and Martin Walford of the Royal Cruising Club; Jane Howe of the Royal Yacht Squadron; R. Cornwall, Departmental Record Officer, Ministry of Defense; Barbara Jones, librarian at Lloyd's Register of Shipping Offices, and N. J. Mills, Historical Search Room of the Scottish Record Office; the staffs at Portsmouth Museums and Records Service, Southampton City Council, and the vicar of St. James' Church, Emsworth; Theodore Gillam and Mike and Carol Jeffery.

Dorota Starzecka, former assistant keeper of ethnology at the Museum of Mankind, British Museum, helped me to copy precious Pease family documents and, as always, took a supportive interest in my research. Special thanks to Brian Durrans, Lissant Bolton, Alison Deeprose, James Hamill, and Harry Persaud. In 1990–91 British Museum Tours (now British Museum Traveller) launched its operation with a tour to Easter Island, which I was pleased to lead. Nearly every year since then I have shared my love of Easter Island with tour participants, all of whom have taught me something about how the English regard the world. I am grateful especially to Edan Harvey and Ann Harper, who have a special place in their hearts for Easter Island; Brenda Cockshott; Joan Percy Davis; David and Gay Edwards; Dick and Peg Foster; Alex Lowry; John Lipscomb; Keith and Cynthia Oldale, who introduced me to the writings of Elizabeth Gaskell; Valerie Scrieven; Charles Shine; Robert Simmons; Katie Tompkins, Tessa Wilson and Dorothy Wilson.

Linda Feinstone and her staff at Archaeological Tours have assembled remarkable bands of dedicated American travelers for our many trips to Easter Island. All of them have been thoroughly supportive and unfailingly interested in my Routledge and Easter Island research—and some of them had enough confidence to order copies of this book from me years before it was even finished!

The Royal Geographical Society (with the Institute of British Geographers) holds the unpublished Routledge fieldnotes and other papers and has been fully cooperative in furthering my research. I appreciate the early assistance of past director John Hemming and past archivists Christine Kelly and Paula Lucas. Special thanks to Keeper Dr. Andrew Tatham, who read and commented on the book in draft; Assistant Archivist Huw Thomas; Curator of Maps Francis Herbert and the staff of the Map Room;

Joanna Wright and Justin Hobson of the Picture Library and Rachel Rowe of the Library.

At the Geological Society, Wendy Cawthorne sought Routledge correspondence at my request through Ian Meighan, Queen's University, Belfast. Jenny Hurst of the British Geological Survey searched for geological specimens deposited by Scoresby, as did Graham McKenna, chief librarian and archivist, British Geological Survey. Thanks to Charles Shine and Samantha Crossley at the Royal Botanic Gardens, Kew, and to Susan Snell, archivist at the Natural History Museum. Staff of the Oriental and India Office Collection, British Library, assisted me with the Cornelia Sorabji papers. Thanks to the Reverend Canon Roger Grey at the office of the bishop of Gloucester. Pauline Adams, librarian and archivist, and Susan Purver, assistant librarian, Somerville College, Oxford, researched college records. Ms. Adams read and commented on the first draft of the Oxford chapter. Richard Aspin, The Wellcome Institute for the History of Medicine, shed light on the final years of Katherine's life.

Quaker archives were extremely useful in my research, and all those who bear the responsibility of managing them were consistently generous. At Friends House, London, Assistant Archivist Rosamund Cummings, Librarian Malcolm Thomas, and Assistant Librarian Peter Daniels were patient and thorough. At Friends Meeting House, Skinnergate, Darlington, Warden Janet Wadey, Dorothy H. Mounsey, and historian Thomas Eden were extremely helpful. In the United States, I am grateful to Betsy Brown and Ann Upton of the Quaker Collection, Haverford College; the staffs of Swarthmore College Library, Whittier College Library, and the First Friends Church of Whittier.

Marieka Van Tilburg Kline dug up answers to questions posed on many obscure issues and researched public records in Darlington and the genealogical files of the Family History Center, Church of Jesus Christ of Latter-day Saints. Her husband, Matthew, read and commented on the final draft. Gina Minervini sought news accounts, film documentation, and genealogical references. Jimmy Smull shared with me her doctoral research on the subject of women and organized religion. Journalist Leonard Gross firmly pointed me in good stylistic directions. John McNally located Toys Hill House in Tunbridge Wells, photographed it, and interviewed the house's current owners, Julia and Phillip Grey. Antoinette Padgett researched the life of Vicente "Varta" Pont. Stan Louis unearthed valuable correspondence between Katherine Routledge and American anthropologists A. L. Kroeber and H. E. Gregory on file, Bancroft Library, University of California, Berkeley. Thanks also to Gary Fong, *San Francisco Chronicle*; Irene A. Stachura, reference librarian, San Francisco Maritime National Historical Park; Emily Wilson, California Historical Society, and the staffs of the San Francisco History Center, the San Francisco Public Library; the Phoebe Hearst Museum of Anthropology; the L. Hanson Little History Room, Mill Valley Public Library; and Ron Schaeffer, archivist, Bernice P. Bishop Museum. Patricia Gebhard gave me a copy of *The Mystery of Easter Island* from her late husband's personal library that had been inscribed by Katherine and helped to pinpoint her movements in 1920–21.

In New Zealand the late Audrey Burke, biographer of Lucy Violet Hodgkin, unearthed diary entries describing Katherine's visit with her family, and Joy Axford, curator of archives, Hawke's Bay Museum, researched local records. At McGill University in Canada, Archivist Phebe Chartrand sought information on Katherine's friendship with Ethel Hurlblatt. Thanks are due to Jack Davis and Anne Escott, The Mitchell Library, Glasgow; J. R. Maddicott, librarian and archivist, and Mrs. Lorise C. Topliffe, sublibrarian, Exeter College, Oxford; Len Pole, curator of ethnography, Royal Albert Memorial Museum and Art Gallery; the staff of the Fawcett Society, London; Wendy Hebbitt, Writtle Archives; the Eskridge Family Association and Neal Hatayama, librarian of the Hawai'i and Pacific Section, Hawai'i State Library.

Many people researched family records for mention of Katherine, including especially Kari Blackburn, Robin Hodgkin, Esmé Johnston, Stephen J. Whitwell, Suzanne Marett-Crosby, and Lord Wardington. Peter Inchbald, great-nephew of Katherine's best friend Lyle McAllum, provided insight into that friendship. Connie Freeman graciously showed me the garden and interior of her home, remodeled from 4 Hyde Park Gardens. Thanks to the many kind people of Darlington, especially Maureen Jackson at Southend; Darlington Public Library and Local Studies Centre staff K. Bennett, C. Copeland, Katherine Williamson, Niki Burke, and G. Wilson. Jennifer Gill, County Durham archivist, provided access to Gurney Pease's diaries, Katherine Pease's journals, Gwendolen Margaret Pease's papers, and the diaries of Katherine's brother Wilson Pease and their transcriptions by Humphrey Allen Bucknall. Some pages and, perhaps, whole volumes of Wilson Pease's diaries are missing, destroyed, or never given to the Durham Record Office by Wilson's brother John Henry Pease or nephew John Charles Gurney Pease. Wilson had intended that his journals would one day be published. Although their chief value today is due to his sister's accomplishments, I grew to like Wilson a lot and to appreciate the deep and forgiving love he felt for Katherine. I hope he finds a kind of immortality in these pages.

Information about Scoresby was more difficult to track. A major breakthrough came when Margaret Jacques located Miss C. Parker, who passed on my letter to Rosemary Elizabeth Blair, Scoresby's niece, to Rosemary's daughter Pauleen West. Pauleen and Brian West kindly shared notes made by

Rosemary Elizabeth Blair in preparation for drafting a biographical sketch of her family. Pauleen read and commented on the manuscript. Chris Lopez generously cooperated in my research into Twycross family history, and John and Mary Twycross shared their family tree and photographs. Nicholas Stanley-Price unearthed valuable details of Scoresby's movements on Cyprus, and Roger Green's fine sleuthing put me in touch with David Frankel and Jenny Webb, who located Eve Dray Stewart. Eve, whose eyesight is failing, nevertheless wrote long letters to me that included invaluable recollections of her father's friendship with Scoresby. Linda Clougherty at UCLA and her colleagues Pamela Gaber, A. H. S. Megaw, Dimitri Michaelides, and Robert S. Merrillees assisted with further questions about Cyprus archaeology.

Thanks to Victoria Dunlop and to Sir Nicholas Harington (whose grandfather was a lifelong friend of Scoresby's and whose father, J. C. D. Harington, rescued the Mana Expedition photographic negatives). When a research trip to Bodleian Library, University of Oxford, was abruptly canceled by the international crisis of September 11, 2001, J. G. Pusey, admissions officer; O. House, senior library assistant, Modern Papers Reading Room; and Steven Tomlinson, assistant librarian, Department of Special Collections and Western Manuscripts—all came to my aid and helped me to arrange with Samuel Hyde, senior library assistant, Department of Special Collections and Western Manuscripts, to consult the recently derestricted O. G. S. Crawford papers in my stead. His assistance was absolutely invaluable. Thanks also to Bob Wilkins, O. G. S. Crawford Photographic Archive, University of Oxford; Kate Manners, assistant archivist, The Library, University College London; R. M. W. Naylor of Mayo & Perkins, Solicitors; Denis Walker, formerly of Stapley and Hurst, Solicitors; the staffs of St. Catherine's House and Somerset House and Kay O. Walters, assistant librarian, Athenaeum Club. In Santiago de Chile my friend Danielle von Muhlen arranged for Catherine Kenrick Lyon and Alison Wiegand to research the Routledges in Viña del Mar.

While I was on safari with my family in Kenya, the celebrated game warden and guide Brian Nicholson suggested Colonel R. Meinertzhagen's *Kenya Diary, 1902–1906* to me and patiently answered endless questions about turn-of-the-century life in a tented camp, even as we crashed headlong in his truck through the brush of the Maasai Mara. Anthony and Maria Dodds (and Anthony's mother) ran down elusive details of local history; John Hatt of Eland Books clarified the question of Meinertzhagen's unreliability as a source. Margaret Jacques contacted Coleen Gray and Kitsy Mitchell, who sought the Routledges' African photos in Autotype International Ltd. archives. In Nairobi, rock art colleague David Coulsen kindly opened the Muthaiga Club library to me. Journalist Malcolm Coad shared a magazine article on the Silberrad Affair and lent encouragement.

On Easter Island I am most indebted, as always, to Cristián Arévalo Pakarati. Nikko Haoa Cardinali helped me explore Katherine's campsite at Mataveri and researched his family history. Jorge Edmunds Rapahango shared childhood memories of his father, Percy Edmunds, and toured the ruins of their Mataveri house (since demolished) with me; René Edmunds shed light on Percy's impact on the next generation, as did Petero Edmunds, current mayor of Hanga Roa. René's daughter Elizabeth Edmunds researched family records. Graciela Hucke Atan hunted down historic photographs and told me stories of her own ancestors and the Fati, Pont, Haoa, and Tepano families. Esperanza Pakarati and the late Felipe Teao A. told me about Juan Tepano, as did the last resident of the island's leper colony and his family, who request that their name not be used.

Lilian González N., who married into the Pakarati family, described her chats about Katherine Routledge with the late Amelia Tepano Ika and outlined bewildering family divisions within Hanga Roa, Moeroa, and Mataveri. Edmundo Edwards told me stories of the visionary Angata, as did Father Francisco Nahoe. Archaeologist E. N. Ferdon Jr. shared his insight into the Tepano family, and Grant McCall kindly clarified many details of labyrinthine Rapa Nui genealogies. Thomas Lavachery, biographer of his grandfather Henri Lavachery; Edgar Krebs, biographer of anthropologist Alfred Métraux; and archaeologist Sonia Haoa searched Franco-Belgian Expedition records for mention of Katherine. The late Thor Heyerdahl shared his memories of Métraux. Adrienne L. Kaeppler, valued colleague and friend, read and commented on the draft manuscript during the two weeks we spent together on Rapa Nui in 2001. Gavan Daws very helpfully commented on the book at the galley stage.

Editor Lisa Drew, agent Alan Nevins, and Paul Rubenstein, Esq., provided highly professional guidance; Kathryn Sylvester Bowers edited and formatted the manuscript in its early stages, and my nephew William E. Becker Jr. solved heart-stopping computer glitches. Gordon Hull and Alice Hom, and all of my colleagues at the UCLA Rock Art Archive, were unstinting in their support. Above all, I am indebted to my husband, Johannes (Jan) Van Tilburg, who sought Katherine's story with me in Darlington, London, Scotland, and Kenya and read and commented on draft chapters of this manuscript. Jan gives order to our family world and, through his constant and inspiring support, makes my work possible. This book is a small and grateful tribute to his patience, forgiveness, loyalty, and gallantry.

INDEX

✦